THE *unofficial* GUIDE

TO Las Vegas

2015

BOB SEHLINGER

with CAM USHER, AL MANCINI,
MAX JACOBSON, XANIA V. WOODMAN,
LEN TESTA, *and* SETH KUBERSKY

keen
communications

Please note that prices fluctuate in the course of time and that travel information changes under the impact of many factors that influence the travel industry. We therefore suggest that you write or call ahead for confirmation when making your travel plans. Every effort has been made to ensure the accuracy of information throughout this book, and the contents of this publication are believed to be correct at the time of printing. Nevertheless, the publishers cannot accept responsibility for errors or omissions, for changes in details given in this guide, or for the consequences of any reliance on the information provided by the same. Assessments of attractions and so forth are based upon the authors' own experiences; therefore, descriptions given in this guide necessarily contain an element of subjective opinion, which may not reflect the publisher's opinion or dictate a reader's own experience on another occasion. Readers are invited to write the publisher with ideas, comments, and suggestions for future editions.

Published by:
Keen Communications, LLC
P.O. Box 43673
Birmingham. AL 35243

Cover design by Scott McGrew

Cover photo © Yaacov Dagan / Alamy

Text design by Vertigo Design and Annie Long

For information on our other products and services or to obtain technical support, please contact us from within the United States at 888-604-4537 or by fax at 205-326-1012.

Keen Communications, LLC, also publishes its books in a variety of electronic formats. Some content that appears in print may not be available in electronic formats.

ISBN: 978-1-62809-022-2; eISBN: 978-162809-023-9

Distributed by Publishers Group West

Manufactured in the United States of America

5 4 3 2 1

CONTENTS

MAPS *and* ILLUSTRATIONS

ACKNOWLEDGMENTS

THE PEOPLE OF LAS VEGAS love their city and spare no effort to assist a writer trying to dig beneath the facade of flashing neon. It is important to them to communicate that Las Vegas is a city with depth, diversity, and substance. "Don't just write about our casinos," they demand; "take the time to get to know us."

We made every effort to do just that, enabled each step of the way by some of the most sincere and energetic folks a writer could hope to encounter. Thanks to gambling pro **Anthony Curtis** for his tips on the best places to play, and to **Cam Usher** for her work capturing the essence of Las Vegas hotels. **Xania V. Woodman,** nightlife editor at *seven* magazine, handled the nightlife scene.

Restaurant critic **Al Mancini** ate his way through dozens of new restaurants to update more than 70 restaurant reviews, while **Grace Bascos** covered buffets and tasting menus and **Heidi Rinella** gave us the lowdown on dining Downtown and in Chinatown.

Jim McDonald of the Las Vegas Police Department shared his experiences and offered valuable suggestions for staying out of trouble. **Larry Olmsted** evaluated Las Vegas golf courses, **Chris McBeath** created our spa chapter, and forest ranger **Debbie Savage** assisted us in developing material on wilderness recreation. Thanks also to **Fred Hazleton** and **Seth Kubersky,** who reviewed shows and attractions.

Much gratitude to Steve Jones, Annie Long, Molly Merkle, Holly Cross, Darcie Vance, Ritchey Halphen, and Ann Cassar, the pros who turned all this effort into a book.

INTRODUCTION

ON *a* PLANE *to* LAS VEGAS

I NEVER WANTED TO GO TO LAS VEGAS. I'm not much of a gambler and have always thought of Las Vegas as a city dedicated to separating folks from their money. As it happens, however, I have some involvement with industries that hold conventions and trade shows there. For some years I was able to persuade others to go in my place. Eventually, of course, it came my turn to go, and I found myself aboard a Delta jumbo jet on my first trip to Las Vegas.

Listening to the banter of those around me, I became aware that my fellow passengers were divided into two distinct camps. Some obviously thought themselves on a nonstop flight to paradise and could not have been happier. Too excited to remain seated, they cavorted up and down the aisles, clapping one another on the back. The other passengers, by contrast, groused and grumbled. These people, as despondent as sailors en route to a VD clinic, lamented their bad luck and cursed those who had made a trip to such a place necessary.

To my surprise, I thoroughly enjoyed Las Vegas. I had a great time without gambling and have been back many times with never a bad experience. The people are friendly, the food is good, the hotels are among the nicest in the country, it's an easy town to find your way around, and there is plenty to do (24 hours a day, if you are so inclined).

It's hard to say why so many folks have such strong feelings about Las Vegas (even those who have never been there). Among our research team, we had people willing to put their kids in boarding school for a chance to go, while others begged off to have root-canal surgery or prune their begonias. A third group wanted to go very badly but maintained the pretense of total indifference, reminding me of people who own five TVs yet profess never to watch television. They clearly had not mustered the courage to come out of the closet.

What I discovered during my first and subsequent visits is that the nongambling public doesn't know very much about Las Vegas. Many people cannot see beyond the gambling, cannot see that there could possibly be anything of value in Las Vegas for nongamblers or those only marginally interested in gambling.

When you ask these people to describe their ideal vacation, they wax eloquent about lazy days relaxing in the sun, playing golf, enjoying the luxury of resort hotels, eating in fine restaurants, sightseeing, shopping, and going to the theater. Outdoor types speak no less enthusiastically about fishing, boating, hiking, and, in winter, skiing. As it happens, Las Vegas offers all of this. Gambling is just the tip of the iceberg in Las Vegas, but it's all many people can see.

Las Vegas is, of course, about gambling, but there's so much more. Vegas has sunny, mild weather two-thirds of the year, some of the finest hotels and restaurants in the world, the most diversified celebrity and production-show entertainment to be found, unique shopping, internationally renowned golf courses, and numerous attractions. For the outdoor enthusiast, Red Rock Canyon National Conservation Area, Lake Mead National Recreation Area, and Toiyabe National Forest offer some of the most exotic and beautiful wilderness resources in North America.

This guide is designed for those who *want* to go to Las Vegas but also for those who *have* to go to Las Vegas. If you are a recreational gambler and/or an enthusiastic vacationer, we will show you ways to have more fun, make the most of your time, and spend less money. If you are one of the skeptics, unwilling companions of gamblers, business travelers, or people who think they would rather be someplace else, we will help you discover the seven-eighths of the Las Vegas iceberg that is hidden.

—*Bob Sehlinger*

LOOKING BACK, LOOKING AHEAD

IN 1946, BUGSY SIEGEL OPENED the Flamingo Hotel, kicking off the metamorphosis that changed three miles of mostly barren desert into what is now the Las Vegas Strip. The original Flamingo was an eye-popper in its day and established a baseline that all subsequent casinos had to at least match, if not improve upon.

As new hotels appeared in the neon Valhalla, each contributed something different, and occasionally something better, raising the bar incrementally. Two properties, the Desert Inn and Caesars Palace, advanced the standard significantly, but because they catered to an exclusive clientele, their competitors chose not to follow suit.

Then, in 1989, came the Mirage, a large hotel-casino offering the spectacle of Caesars and the refinement of the Desert Inn (almost) but, more importantly, targeting not the carriage trade but rather the average tourist. The Mirage was equal parts tourist attraction, hotel, and casino, and each part was executed with imagination and flair. Not many Vegas tourists could afford the Mirage's expensive guest rooms, but the place was nonetheless a must-see for every visitor.

The IMPACT of the MIRAGE

THE MIRAGE'S SUCCESS demonstrated that gamblers, contrary to prevailing opinion, actually paid attention to their gaming environment and, if given a choice, preferred an interesting, dynamic, and attractive setting to the cramped, noisy, monochromatic boiler room that was then the casino norm. Beyond a doubt, the Mirage was in a class by itself. Observers waited impatiently to see if any competitor would challenge the Mirage, but most believed the standard was impossibly high.

The answer was not long in coming. A veritable explosion of new developments was rushed from the drawing board to the construction zone. First was the Excalibur in 1990. It was big, plastic, gaudy, and certainly no direct competitor to the Mirage, but its Knights of the Round Table theme played incredibly well with the blue-collar and family markets. Next came the Class of 1993, which included the pyramid-shaped Luxor, Treasure Island (then a sister property to the Mirage), and the MGM Grand Hotel and Theme Park. Though the MGM Grand Theme Park was a bust, the hotel and casino were immediately successful. Likewise, the Luxor and Treasure Island (TI), with their knockout themes, rocketed up the pop chart.

In the three years before the next wave of new hotels opened in 1996, the vital signs of both the newer and older properties were monitored closely. The MGM Grand was the largest hotel-casino in the world, Excalibur was a close second, and the other new hotels offered more than 2,500 rooms each. As with the bull stock market in the late 1990s, there was endless speculation and debate about how long the building boom could last. But the preliminary data seemed to indicate that the new properties were responsible for increasing the aggregate market. Room occupancy rates remained high.

SURVIVAL of the OLDER CASINOS

THOUGH MORE VISITORS WERE COMING to Las Vegas, the lion's share of the business was going to the newer, high-profile hotels. Older properties, including some of the Strip's most established casinos, found themselves increasingly at the margins. So too, Downtown Las Vegas was in a tailspin, with gaming revenues down, or flat, year after year. The new marching orders, avoided or ignored for so long, were crystal clear: if you want to play in the big league, you have to upgrade. And upgrading meant approximating the Mirage standard.

The response from Downtown Las Vegas was to combine the Fremont Street casinos into a mega–gaming venue, a new Glitter Gulch, tied together by a pedestrian plaza under the canopy of the Fremont Street Experience, an electric light show. Back on the Strip, older properties, including Bally's, the Flamingo, the Tropicana, the Sahara, the Boardwalk, Circus Circus, and the Riviera, scrambled to upgrade. The venerable Caesars Palace alone managed to stay ahead of the game, making improvements each year to maintain its position at or near the top of the Strip food chain.

HONEY, I BLEW UP *the* CASINO!

IN 1991, BOB STUPAK'S quirky Vegas World was demolished to make way in 1996 for the Stratosphere Hotel and Casino, which has the tallest observation tower in the United States. The fireworks had just begun. Farther south on the Strip, the Monte Carlo hit the scene. In 1997, New York–New York opened its doors. With more than 100,000 visitors a day during its first weeks of operation, New York–New York quickly dispelled the notion that the Strip was overbuilt. In typical Las Vegas go-for-broke style, the Dunes, the Sands, El Rancho, the Boardwalk, the Hacienda, the old Aladdin, the New Frontier, and the Stardust were blown up to make room for a new wave of gargantuan gambling palaces.

The boom proceeded at warp speed, with a construction frenzy that through 2001 added a whopping 28,000 new rooms to Las Vegas's inventory (now totaling roughly 150,000). Bellagio (opened in 1998) draws its inspiration from Italy's Lake Como, adding 4,000 rooms to the MGM Resorts International (MRI) galaxy and catering to the upscale market. Across the street is 2,900-room Paris Las Vegas with its own 50-story Eiffel Tower. Just south is Planet Hollywood (formerly the Aladdin), a 2,600-room complex with a Hollywood theme. On the site of the old Sands is The Venetian. An all-suite property with 3,000 suites in its first building phase and 1,013 in its second, The Venetian features a shopping complex in a Venice-canal setting complete with gondola rides. A sister hotel, The Palazzo, with 3,000-plus suites, joined The Venetian complex in 2008. At the southern end of the Strip on the old Hacienda property, the 3,300-room Mandalay Bay opened in 1999. Steve Wynn opened Wynn Las Vegas in 2005 with 2,700 rooms and doubled down with a second hotel, Wynn Encore, in 2008, both on the site of the fabled Desert Inn.

More and more new casinos were built around town in an effort to cater to the local population and visitors who don't want to battle the traffic of the Strip. In 2006, the Red Rock Resort opened with 400 rooms overlooking Red Rock Canyon. Also to the west of the Strip is JW Marriott, a 550-room spa and golf resort in the Las Vegas suburb of Summerlin.

The locals' response to Red Rock Resort demonstrated that the then-growing population of Las Vegas appreciated upscale casinos, too. M Resort, on the Strip about 12 miles south of Mandalay Bay, opened in 2009 to serve the affluent residents of the south Las Vegas valley. Similarly, Aliante Station opened in the same year to serve the suburbs of north Las Vegas.

The GREAT MERGERS and ACQUISITIONS

THEN THERE ARE THE MERGERS and acquisitions. In 2000, Steve Wynn, the visionary behind the Mirage (and the Las Vegas transformation it started), sold the Mirage, Bellagio, TI, Golden Nugget, and half of Monte Carlo to MGM Grand for $6.4 billion. Wynn, meanwhile, purchased the Desert Inn, where he built a 2,700-room nonthemed resort called Wynn Las Vegas, stating ironically that "themes are a thing of the past." Wynn always seems to be a step ahead of the pack and might be correct about themes. Still, it's like Dr. Spock saying that children are a thing of the past.

The Mandalay Resort Group, which owned Luxor, Mandalay Bay, Excalibur, Circus Circus, and half of the Monte Carlo, was acquired in June of 2004 by MGM Grand for a whopping $6 billion, forming MGM Mirage (now MGM Resorts International) with control of 36,000 Strip hotel rooms. Only months earlier, Hilton's casino subsidiary, Park Place Entertainment, bought Caesars Palace and O'Shea's, adding them to a lineup that already included Bally's, Paris, and the Flamingo. In 2004, Park Place changed its name to Caesars Entertainment to reflect the prestige of its flagship property. In an even bigger (not to mention surprising) deal, Harrah's bought Caesars Entertainment in a $9.4 billion deal, thus becoming the largest casino-gambling company in the world. Subsequently, Harrah's also acquired the Rio, Imperial Palace (now The LINQ Hotel & Casino), Planet Hollywood, and the Barbary Coast (now The Cromwell). In 2010, Harrah's changed its corporate name back to Caesars Entertainment.

GLUTTONS ARE MORE LIKELY to CHOKE to DEATH

THIS FOLKSY SAYING DESCRIBES the unbridled development of the Las Vegas Strip built precariously (some would say recklessly) on a rapidly deteriorating street-and-highway infrastructure. And it's only going to get worse.

For many years there have been sizable undeveloped parcels of land along the Strip, most conspicuously between Circus Circus and the Stratosphere. In the middle of the Strip, small retailers and second-string hotels squatted on some of the planet's most valuable real estate.

No more. In a development frenzy that makes the 1990s hotel crop look like home gardening, the land has been gobbled up and giant construction cranes have redefined the Strip's skyline. High-rise mania hit Las Vegas with a vengeance. Believe it or not, this city is running out of room to develop horizontally, so it's turning vertical. Nearly 80 high-rise condominium, time-share, and condo-hotel towers have been announced or built, encompassing more than 30,000 units.

The projects are not just huge hotels as in the past, but veritable self-contained cities rising above every existing resort and containing hotels (yes, plural), residential condos, restaurants, entertainment, shopping, parks, and even their own road networks. CityCenter, an MRI $9.2-billion development, was the largest construction project in the United States.

Plans for all of the combined resort and residential developments call for on-site supermarkets, pharmacies, and other services that the residents and guests will need. This is fortunate indeed because almost nothing is being done to the infrastructure to accommodate the many thousands of additional people who will live, work, and play along the Strip. We've seen units of the condos for sale in these developments and can report that they're quite lovely, which is good, because their denizens are likely to be held hostage by surrounding traffic arteries that are already completely overwhelmed.

Sooner or later, the Strip is going to choke to death. Already the Strip is the most sclerotic traffic artery imaginable, making 45-minute slogs of a half-mile trip. Some hope of relief came in 2004 in the form of a monorail, which runs along the east side of the Strip and loops over to the Las Vegas Convention Center, then on to the SLS. Problem is, the stations are so far removed from the Strip that only a fraction of the riders necessary to break even are using the monorail.

OZ STUMBLES ...
and RECOVERS

FROM 2008 TO 2013, HOTELS DEALT WITH decreased visitation and depressed room rates, experienced significant losses in gaming revenue, halted or postponed construction, or shut down entirely. For example, Binion's Horseshoe on Fremont Street moth-balled the hotel's 365-room tower, but the casino remains open. However, the light at the end of the tunnel became brighter in 2013 and 2014—39,668,221 visitors came to Las Vegas in 2013, making the city the second most popular destination in the world after Orlando. Gaming revenue recovered, with the Strip hitting the $6.5 billion mark, a 4.8% increase, but the meeting and convention sector really stepped up. Las Vegas hosted a whopping 22,027 conventions with 5,107,416 attendees in 2013 and was on pace to shatter that record in 2014. Hotels all over town added new convention space in 2014, and the Las Vegas Convention Center is in the process of a 500,000-square-foot expansion. Room occupancy held steady at 84.3% (91% on weekends), 22 percentage points higher than the national average.

Several Strip hotels took advantage of the recent downtime to refurbish existing inventory and have spent major bucks to upgrade their accommodations. From 2008 to 2014, about 18,000 guest rooms underwent a remodel. The trend was away from the ornate, and a more masculine look prevailed. Properties offering rooms with a new look include the Bellagio, Bally's, Boulder Station, Circus Circus, Flamingo, MGM Grand, Rio, Excalibur, Tropicana, Wynn Las Vegas, Four Seasons, Monte Carlo, Palms, Paris, and Silver Sevens (formerly Terrible's). Eight Downtown hotels also remodeled, reopened, or reinvented themselves.

Wishing to exude hipness, hotels are changing their identity and abandoning picturesque monikers and themes. The Imperial Palace is now The LINQ Hotel & Casino, and Fitzgerald's is The D. Continuing this trend toward the bland along with new ownership of existing properties and their transformation into upscale boutique experiences, Bill's Gamblin' Hall has emerged as The Cromwell, Mandalay Bay's THEhotel was renamed The Delano, and the Sahara became the SLS. Remodeled sections creating sub-branding within hotel complexes are Nobu at Caesars Palace, Monte Carlo's Hotel 32, Paris's Red Rooms, the Sky Lofts and Stay Well rooms at MGM Grand, and The Delano and forerunner Four Seasons within Mandalay Bay.

Caesars Entertainment has completed construction of The LINQ, a retail, restaurant, and entertainment district located along a shortcut between the Flamingo and The LINQ Hotel & Casino. The LINQ's focal point is a giant observation wheel called the High Roller. Not to be outdone, MRI has created yet another entertainment district, called The Park, in the 63-acre canyon of open space between the Monte Carlo and New York–New York.

McCarran recently introduced Terminal 3 for international flights and larger aircraft covering long-haul routes. The price of gasoline heavily impacts the drive-in market and regional visitation. Five dollars per gallon seems to be the breaking point for many drivers, although the difference in cost from Los Angeles would be about $18 each way. The higher cost of airline fuel will increase the price of airline tickets, primarily affecting the leisure traveler. Locally, the Las Vegas Monorail is still in trouble with static ridership, and the projected airport leg is on hold. Entire buildings of Strip-vicinity high-rise luxury condos have been revamped as apartments or hotel rooms. Although one über-resort, Genting's Resorts World, is on the horizon for 2016, for now, small boutique nongaming hotels are the wave of the future.

When MRI's glamorous CityCenter urban complex with 6,000 rooms was introduced with a flourish in 2009, along with The Cosmopolitan's 2,995 suites a year later, 8,995 more accommodations were added in a down market and Las Vegas's citywide room inventory reached a jaw-dropping 148,935 units. However, bottom-line profits for several Las Vegas hotel corporations come not from local properties but from their Asian casinos and the establishment of their brands as both gaming and nongaming retreats in Dubai, China, Abu Dhabi, and Singapore. To stem the flood of currency away from Nevada, the state has legalized certain types of Internet gaming.

While the convention market has rebounded, the business has changed with the new popularity of regional meetings overcoming corporate and nonprofit associations' previous ardor for annual megaconventions. Even with the increased prices and hassles of air travel and the reluctance of organizations to provide more funding for business trips, this market segment is intensifying. While conventioneers will spend more on hotel rooms, they demonstrate a lower propensity to gamble and have curbed their enthusiastic splurging for entertainment, cocktails, and luxury dining.

A few major resorts have become pet-friendly, adding a per-night surcharge for canines. Seeking additional earnings, most hotels now levy unpopular resort fees, ranging from $5 to $40 per night, for items such as local phone calls, Wi-Fi and Internet access, and fitness center access, which previously had been complimentary. Another source of income is personalized guest reservations to guarantee a view, kings or double-doubles, early check-in, or extended check-out. Hotels with showrooms have identified entertainment sales as a growing revenue stream, offering more afternoon acts, show passes (admission to multiple shows within a limited time frame), backstage tours, and meet-and-greets with performers, in addition to dinner-show-nightclub packages. Often rivaling the casino as a profit center, nightclubs have become highly visible, sometimes earning more per square foot than gaming. The largest lounges cover more than 55,000 square feet, and limited operating hours mean lower operating expenses. March through October, entry-fee beach clubs (some top-tional) and pool parties with concerts abound, and nightclubs have expanded poolside, adding water diversions to their inventory of pleasures. Many young visitors scrimp on rooms and meals and spend on pricey entry fees and cocktails. Food courts have proliferated, while gourmet restaurants come and go. Another trend is the small plate—less food for slightly less money.

WHAT IT MEANS *to* YOU

INTERESTINGLY, IF YOU CRUISE the Strip or Downtown, everything looks pretty normal. The better shows still play to packed audiences, long queues at hotel registration desks continue to frustrate, and the casinos seem to be bustling. All of the above, however, is attributable as much to hotels and casinos discounting, especially when it comes to rooms, as to a rebounding economy. Condo developers trying to generate cash flow compound the discounting by dumping empty and unsold units into the city's hotel room inventory. A quick gallop around a hotel search engine will turn up dozens of lodging options in properties that were supposed to be residences. Even so, both Las Vegas occupancy rates and room rates were on an uptick as we went to press. We expect room discounting to continue, though perhaps not so aggressively, through 2015. A number of hotels not only discount rooms but also throw in free show tickets and other sweeteners. The Mirage promoted $85-per-night rooms packaged with a $40 dining credit and admission for four to its Secret Garden attraction. To find deals coupled with sweeteners check your favorite search engine for "name of hotel and promotions"—for example, "Caesars Palace and promotions" or "Luxor and promotions." You get the idea. Also check **lvahotels.com.**

Because the larger and newer hotels have more appeal and drawing power, they can always put people in beds by discounting. Older hotels, such as the Riviera and Circus Circus, among others, are forced to both upgrade *and* discount to fill their rooms. This is especially true of properties such as the Riviera, which counts heavily on meeting attendees. Likewise, more isolated hotels are forced to offer deeper discounts. Silverton and Southpoint, both located south of Las Vegas off Interstate 15, usually represent exceptional value.

The Las Vegas entertainment scene was the last to succumb to the storms of recession. Remarkably, in 2009, the average price of undiscounted tickets for long-running shows topped $80 for the first time. 2014, on the other hand, was another story, with a succession of two-fers, dollars-off coupons in visitor mags and on the Internet, and the bundling of shows with hotel stays at bargain rates. A lot of discounting results from initially overpricing shows. This notwithstanding, the average undiscounted price of a show ticket hit an all-time high of $83 in 2014. There are still two dozen or so shows where admission tops $100, but for the first time some of these shows have become available at the local half-price ticket discounters. If you've ever wanted to see a Cirque du Soleil show on the

unofficial **TIP**
A few high-quality afternoon productions offer a bargain alternative to the mortgage-the-farm-priced shows playing the major showrooms.

cheap, now's the time. Nothing's guaranteed, however, and half-price tickets to premium productions may be scarce on weekends. Tickets must be purchased in person at one of the discounter locations on the same day as the performance. Higher-price VIP seating, once relegated to topless revues and celebrity headliner shows, is now ubiquitous but rarely worth the steep tariff. You'll usually get a good seat buying general admission. Leave the VIP seats to myopic old coots who can't tell a nipple from a fried egg absent a telescope. If shows are too expensive, discounts notwithstanding, live music in casino lounges abounds, continuing a six-decade tradition as Las Vegas's best entertainment value.

The recession forced many restaurants, both in and out of casinos, to close, though a bumper crop of chefs and eateries rushed to fill the void in 2013 and 2014. For the most part, restaurant prices haven't come down, although some of the better restaurants now offer fixed-price "tasting" menus at reasonable prices to lure you in. It can be a good deal and perhaps a time-limited opportunity to try a restaurant you couldn't ordinarily afford. Just be mindful of what you order in addition to the fixed-price meal—that's where you can lose. Most of the signs of stress we're observing on the dining scene come in the form of a proliferation of two-for-one deals, discount coupons, free appetizers, and the like. As with hotels and casinos, restaurants know that the first step is to get you through the door, so that's where they're putting their energy.

The QUIET CONTENDER

A FEW YEARS BACK, the big buzz was Las Vegas as a family destination. Insiders understood, however, that all the talk was just that. At most, the family thing was a public relations exercise to make Las Vegas appear more wholesome. It was tacitly understood that the big dogs would never allow theme parks and other family-oriented attractions to actually compete with the casinos for a visitor's time. Lost in the backwash of this hollow debate, however, was the exponential burgeoning of theme shopping. Shopping is something that reached critical mass almost unnoticed and that keeps visitors out of the casinos. At present, the case can be made that shopping is almost as potent an attraction in Las Vegas as gambling. On the Strip are four huge themed shopping venues (Forum Shops, Grand Canal Shoppes, Crystals, and Miracle Mile Shops) and a comparatively white-bread mall, but one that's buttressed with every big-name department store in North America. Hotels where emphasis on shopping has been lagging are frantically creating new Strip-side venues. By mid-2015 new shopping complexes will open at New York–New York, Monte Carlo, Tropicana, and Bally's. And we're not talking about small shops in subterranean corridors on the way to the parking garage. All the new complexes will feature premium brands in sparkling modern settings. Not to be left in the wake, Downtown offers the Las Vegas Premium Outlets complex, which features 150 stores, all flogging upmarket brands. For the first time, there is something powerful enough to suck the players right out of the casinos, and it arrived on the scene as stealthily as a Trojan horse.

Irrespective of venue, from the tony Forum Shops to hotel sundry stores, sale signs are everywhere. Sales, mind you, are relative, and even at half off, the $1,500 sport coat at Bellagio is going to cost a not-inconsiderable $750.

A TALE *of* TWO CITIES

FOR AT LEAST 40 YEARS Las Vegas has been referred to as "Disneyland for Adults." At the time this tongue-in-cheek appellation was gaining currency Las Vegas was anything but. Disneyland was systematically planned, highly polished, absolutely regimented, and totally plastic. Las Vegas, by contrast, grew like a weed, was raw, unrefined, and freewheeling, and was as real as a one-way ticket home on Greyhound with an empty wallet. Disneyland was a sanitized version of fantasy and history, Las Vegas the last vestige of the western frontier.

When we began covering Las Vegas some years ago, the casinos were predominantly independent. Each had a distinct identity free of the corporate veneer that blankets Las Vegas today. Personality, or the lack thereof, was defining. As with cakes at a church fund-raiser, what was on the inside was what mattered. Now it's the icing that counts, or, expressed differently, the icon (Statue of Liberty, Sphinx, pirate ship, Eiffel Tower . . . you choose) that sits in the casino's front yard. Inside, the product is largely the same. Four casino megacorporations now run most of Las Vegas. On the Strip it's worse. Two companies—Caesars Entertainment and MGM Resorts International—own every casino except the Tropicana, Riviera, Venetian, Stratosphere, The Cosmopolitan, TI, SLS, and Wynn Resorts. Standards for restaurants, hotel rooms, entertainment, theme, and just about everything else offer all the predictability of a nice chain hotel. The maverick casinos and their rough-and-tumble owners are all but gone, and with them the gritty, boom-or-bust soul of this gambling town. Making a clichéd joke a fulfilled prophecy—Las Vegas has in fact become Disneyland.

If you'd like a taste of the old Las Vegas, now's the time. Tomorrow, or soon after, it will largely be gone. While you can, walk Glitter Gulch; enjoy a shrimp cocktail at the Golden Gate; or see *Jubilee!*, the quintessential Las Vegas Parisian revue. Linger over the porterhouse special at the Redwood Bar and Grill at the California, or the duck flambé anise at Hugo's Cellar at the Four Queens. Make no mistake, this is not slumming; each example represents the best of Las Vegas in both a current and historical sense. And if you wait too long? Well, enjoy the new Las Vegas: systematically planned, highly polished, absolutely regimented, and totally plastic.

As most of you know, we also publish guides to Disneyland and Walt Disney World and have never for a moment doubted the overall quality of the Disney product. Comparing the new Las Vegas with Disneyland is a long way from a condemnation. Though we liked the sultry, wide-open, sinful feel of the old Vegas, we can't argue that corporate Las Vegas has built an Oz that no maverick dreamer could have envisioned. Whether the old Las Vegas or the new Las Vegas is better, we'll leave you to judge.

LETTERS, COMMENTS, AND QUESTIONS FROM READERS

WE EXPECT TO LEARN FROM OUR MISTAKES, as well as from the input of our readers, and to improve with each edition. Many of those who use the *Unofficial Guides* write to us to ask questions, make comments, or share their own discoveries and lessons learned in Las Vegas. We appreciate all such input, both positive and critical, and encourage our readers to continue writing. Readers' comments and observations will be frequently incorporated in revised editions of the *Unofficial Guide* and will contribute immeasurably to its improvement.

How to Write the Author

Bob Sehlinger
The Unofficial Guide to Las Vegas
P.O. Box 43673
Birmingham, AL 35243
unofficialguides@menasharidge.com

If you write us, rest assured that we won't release your name and address to any mailing-list companies, direct-mail advertisers, or other third parties. Unless you tell us otherwise, we'll assume that you're OK with being quoted in the *Unofficial Guide*. Be sure to put your return address on both your letter and the envelope—sometimes envelopes and letters get separated. If you e-mail us (preferred), tell us where you're from and the gender and ages of those in your party. And please remember, our work often takes us out of the office for long periods of time, so forgive us if our response is delayed.

Reader Survey

At the back of this guide, you will find a short questionnaire that you can use to express opinions concerning your Las Vegas visit. Clip the questionnaire along the dotted line and mail it to the above address.

HOW INFORMATION IS ORGANIZED: BY SUBJECT AND BY GEOGRAPHIC AREAS

TO GIVE YOU FAST ACCESS to information about the *best* of Las Vegas, we've organized material in several formats.

HOTELS Because most people visiting Las Vegas stay in one hotel for the duration of their vacation or business trip, we have summarized our coverage of hotels in charts, maps, ratings, and rankings that allow you to quickly focus your decision-making process. We do not ramble on for page after page describing lobbies and rooms which, in the final analysis, sound (and look) much the same. Instead, we concentrate our coverage on the specific variables that differentiate one hotel from another: location, size, room quality, services, amenities, and cost. The accommodations are compared by rankings on pages 167–169, and the hotels' vital information is provided in the chart on pages 170–186.

RESTAURANTS We give you a lot of detail when it comes to restaurants. Because you will probably eat a dozen or more restaurant meals during your stay, and because not even you can predict what kind of fare you might be in the mood for on, say, Saturday night, we provide detailed profiles of the very best restaurants Las Vegas has to offer.

ENTERTAINMENT AND NIGHTLIFE Visitors frequently try several different shows or clubs during their stay. Because shows and nightspots, like restaurants, are usually selected spontaneously after arriving in Las Vegas, we believe detailed descriptions are warranted. All continuously running stage shows, as well as celebrity showrooms, are profiled and reviewed in the entertainment section of this guide. The best nightspots and lounges in Las Vegas are profiled alphabetically under nightlife in the same section.

GEOGRAPHIC AREAS   Though it's easy to find your way around in Las Vegas, you may not have a car or the inclination to venture far from your hotel. To help you locate the best restaurants, shows, nightspots, and attractions convenient to where you are staying, we have divided the city into geographic areas:

• South Strip and Environs	• West of Strip	• East of Strip
• Mid-Strip and Environs	• Downtown Las Vegas	
• North Strip and Environs	• Southeast Las Vegas–Henderson	

All profiles of hotels, restaurants, and nightspots include area names. For example, if you are staying at the Flamingo and are interested in Italian restaurants within walking distance, scanning the restaurant profiles for restaurants in the Mid-Strip area will provide you with the most convenient choices.

COMFORT ZONES   For each hotel-casino we have created a profile that describes the casino's patrons and gives you some sense of how it might feel to spend time there. The purpose of the comfort-zone section is to help you find the hotel-casino at which you will feel most welcome and at home. These comfort-zone descriptions begin on page 85 in Part 1, Accommodations and Casinos.

LAS VEGAS: *An Overview*

GATHERING INFORMATION

LAS VEGAS HAS THE BEST selection of complimentary visitor guides of any American tourist destination we know. Available at the front desk or concierge table at almost every hotel, the guides provide a wealth of useful information on gaming, gambling lessons, shows, lounge entertainment, sports, buffets, meal deals, tours and sightseeing, transportation, shopping, and special events. Additionally, most of the guides contain coupons for discounts on dining, shows, attractions, and tours.

Recommended publications include *Vegas Seven* (**vegasseven.com**), a great source of information and news for both locals and visitors; *Las Vegas Magazine* (**lasvegasmagazine.com**), affiliated with the *Las Vegas Sun* newspaper; *Vegas2Go*; and *Where Magazine of Las Vegas* (**wheremagazine.com**). All three have much of the same information discussed above, plus feature articles. The best magazine for keeping abreast of nightlife, concerts, and happenings is *Las Vegas Weekly* (**las vegasweekly.com**). Although all of the freebie Las Vegas visitor magazines contain valuable information, they are rah-rah rags, and their primary objective is to promote. So don't expect any critical reviews of shows, restaurants, attractions, or anything else for that matter.

The *Las Vegas Advisor* is a 12-page monthly newsletter containing some of the most useful consumer information available on gaming, dining, and entertainment, as well as deals on rooms, drinks, shows, and meals. With no advertising or promotional content, the newsletter serves its readers with objective, prescriptive, no-nonsense advice, presented with a sense of humor. The *Advisor* also operates a dynamite website at **lvahotels.com.** At a subscription rate of $50 a year (or $37 a year for an online membership), the *Las Vegas Advisor* is the best investment you can make if you plan to spend four or more days in Las Vegas each year. If you are a one-time visitor but wish to avail yourself of all this wisdom, single copies of the *Las Vegas Advisor* can be purchased for $5 at the *Las Vegas Advisor* website with the other subscription options or at the Gamblers Book Club inside the Gambler's General Store at 800 South Main St. downtown. (☎ 702-382-7555 or 800-522-1777) or visit **gamblersbookclub.com.** For additional information:

Las Vegas Advisor/Huntington Press
3665 S. Procyon Ave.
Las Vegas, NV 89103
☎ 702-252-0655 or 800-244-2224
lvahotels.com

Las Vegas and the Internet

The explosive growth of Las Vegas is not only physical but also virtual. The following are the best places to go on the web to launch yourself into Las Vegas cyberspace:

The site of the *Las Vegas Advisor,* **lvahotels.com,** is a great source of information on recent and future developments, hotels, dining, entertainment, and gambling. The site features everything you need to plan your trip, as well as informative blogs and podcasts. It also has a function for finding hotel deals called "Book a Room" (located in the center of the home page under "Features"). You can sort the results by price. A forum with user questions, maps, and other visitor information is also available.

The official website of the Las Vegas Convention and Visitors Authority is **lasvegas.com.** This site has hundreds of links to hotels, casinos, the airport, and area transportation, plus information on the convention center, sightseeing, and dining.

Another big Las Vegas travel website, with an excellent listing of hotels and their dining and entertainment options, is **vegas.com.** Try *What's On* magazine's **whats-on.com** for shows and *Las Vegas Weekly*'s **lasvegas weekly.com** for nightlife. Another good site for entertainment information is *Las Vegas Magazine*'s **lasvegasmagazine.com.**

Our favorite websites for news, rumors, and the pulse of the city are **vegaschatter.com** and **vegasseven.com.** *Vegas Seven* is also available in a printed version.

The most active Las Vegas message board/forum is **lasvegasadvisor .com/forum.** Divided into two forums, one for members/subscribers

Las Vegas Strip Area

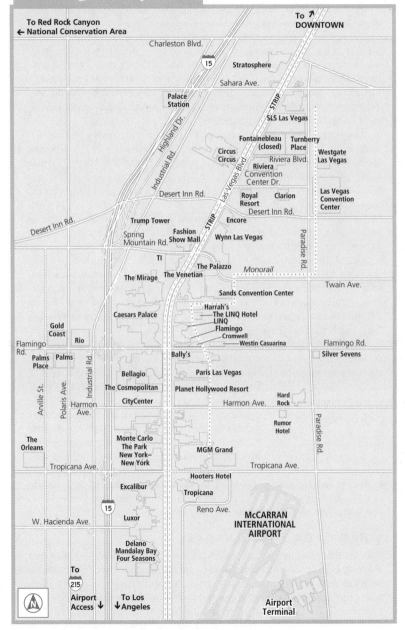

To Red Rock Canyon
← National Conservation Area

To ↗
DOWNTOWN

Charleston Blvd.

15

Stratosphere

Sahara Ave.

STRIP

Palace
Station

SLS Las Vegas

Highland Dr.

Fontainebleau   Turnberry
(closed)   Place

Circus   Westgate
Circus   Riviera Blvd.   Las Vegas

Industrial Rd.

Riviera
Convention
Center Dr.

Las Vegas Blvd.

Desert Inn Rd.   Las Vegas
                                              Convention
                    Royal   Clarion   Center
                    Resort
                           Desert Inn Rd.

Desert Inn Rd.

STRIP

Trump Tower   Encore

Spring   Fashion
Mountain Rd. Show Mall   Wynn Las Vegas   Paradise Rd.

TI

The Palazzo   Monorail

The Mirage   The Venetian

                                                Twain Ave.

Sands Convention Center

Caesars Palace   Harrah's
                            The LINQ Hotel
                            LINQ
Gold   Flamingo
Coast   Rio   Cromwell
                            Westin Casuarina
Flamingo   Flamingo Rd.
Rd.
Palms   Palms   Bally's   Silver Sevens
Palms Place

Arville St.
        Polaris Ave. Bellagio   Paris Las Vegas
        Industrial Rd.

The Cosmopolitan   Planet Hollywood Resort

CityCenter   Hard
Harmon   Harmon Ave.   Rock
Ave.

                                        Rumor
The   Hotel
Orleans   Monte Carlo
          The Park
          New York–
          New York   MGM Grand

Tropicana Ave.   Tropicana Ave.

                        Hooters Hotel

Excalibur   Tropicana

                        Reno Ave.

15

W. Hacienda Ave.   Luxor   McCARRAN
                                        INTERNATIONAL
                                        AIRPORT

          Delano
          Mandalay Bay
          Four Seasons

To
215

N

Airport   To Los
Access ↓   ↓ Angeles   Airport
                                        Terminal

Paradise Rd.

and one that anyone can access, the *Las Vegas Advisor* forums offer posts on a vast array of Vegas and gambling topics. The forum open to nonmembers has an aptly named Vegas Free-For-All category. Just about anything you'd want to know is in the Vegas Free-For-All forum . . . somewhere. At last count there were almost 18,000 topics in the forum, so finding the nugget of information you need is, well, challenging. The members-only forum, conversely, is nicely organized, allowing a direct route to the topic of your choice. Another message board/forum that we like is Vegas Message Board (**vegasmessageboard.com**). This forum is free, but you must register to post. It's nicely organized, with 25 self-explanatory categories.

The best sites for finding discounts on hotels are **lvahotels.com,** the most reliable source for the best rates (see pages 69–71), and **kayak .com,** which allows you to compare room rates offered by a wide range of discounters.

Hotels make deals available to select markets and populations through the use of discount codes. For example, a deal targeted to San Diego, California, will be publicized in that area and a special code will be provided to obtain the discount when booking a reservation. However, for most codes, anyone who has the code can use it, even if they are not in the area or market being targeted. A good resource for finding these codes is Smarter Vegas at **smartervegas.com,** where promotional codes for the city's best hotels are routinely available. Similar sites are Vegas View at **vegasview.com,** Las Vegas Hotel Promotions at **vegas-hotels-online.com,** and Early Vegas at **earlyvegas .com.** Also see Broadway Box described below.

Find promotional tickets for Las Vegas shows, including celebrity headliners, at **vegas.com/shows.** Note that not all tickets offered on the site are discounted. Both hotel and show discounts are available at Broadway Box at **broadwaybox.com.** Broadway Box is a web community that shares discount codes. There are no membership fees or other costs, and no tickets are sold on the site.

*un*official **TIP**
The winter months in Las Vegas provide an unbeatable combination of good value and choice of activities.

Look for coupons for restaurant discounts at **citycoups.com.** Simply print the coupons for restaurants you're considering. Discount codes for rental cars are available at **mousesavers.com.** Though the site is dedicated to saving money at Walt Disney World and Disneyland, the rental car codes listed can be used anywhere.

WHEN TO GO TO LAS VEGAS

THE BEST TIME TO GO TO LAS VEGAS is in the spring or fall, when the weather is pleasant. If you plan to spend most of your time indoors, it doesn't matter what time of year you choose. If you intend to golf, play tennis, run, hike, bike, or boat, try to go in March, April, early May, October, November, or early December. Spring and winter can be exceedingly windy. Once, on an April kayak trip down the Black Canyon of the Colorado, 22-mph winds actually blew us upstream!

Las Vegas Weather and Dress Chart

MONTH	POOLS O = OPEN
JANUARY Average daytime temp. 57° F | Average evening temp. 32° F *Recommended attire:* Coats and jackets are a must.	-
FEBRUARY Average daytime temp. 50° F | Average evening temp. 37° F *Recommended attire:* Dress warmly—jackets and sweaters.	-
MARCH Average daytime temp. 69° F | Average evening temp. 42° F *Recommended attire:* Sweaters for days but a jacket at night.	O
APRIL Average daytime temp. 78° F | Average evening temp. 50° F *Recommended attire:* Still cool at night—bring a jacket.	O
MAY Average daytime temp. 88° F | Average evening temp. 50° F *Recommended attire:* Sweater for evening, but days are warm.	O
JUNE Average daytime temp. 99° F | Average evening temp. 68° F *Recommended attire:* Days are hot; evenings are moderate.	O
JULY Average daytime temp. 105° F | Average evening temp. 75° F *Recommended attire:* Bathing suits.	O
AUGUST Average daytime temp. 102° F | Average evening temp. 73° F *Recommended attire:* Dress for the heat—spend time at a pool!	O
SEPTEMBER Average daytime temp. 95° F | Average evening temp. 65° F *Recommended attire:* Days warm, sweater for evening.	O
OCTOBER Average daytime temp. 81° F | Average evening temp. 53° F *Recommended attire:* Bring a jacket or sweater for evening.	O
NOVEMBER Average daytime temp. 67° F | Average evening temp. 40° F *Recommended attire:* Sweaters and jackets for days, but coats at night.	-
DECEMBER Average daytime temp. 58° F | Average evening temp. 34° F *Recommended attire:* Coats and jackets are a must—dress warmly.	-

Because spring and fall are the nicest times of year, they are also the most popular. The best time for special deals is December (after the National Finals Rodeo in early December and excluding the week between Christmas and New Year's), January, and during the scorching summer months.

Weather in December, January, and February can vary incredibly. While high winds, cold, rain, and snow are not unheard of, chances are that temperatures will be mild and the sun will shine. Though the weather is less dependable than in spring or fall, winter months are generally well suited to outdoor activities. We talked to people who in late February water-skied on Lake Mead in the morning and snow-skied in the afternoon at Lee Canyon. From mid-May through mid-September, however, the heat is blistering. During these months, it's best to follow the example of the gambler or the lizard—stay indoors or under a rock.

unofficial **TIP**
For a stress-free arrival at the airport, good availability of rental cars, and a quick hotel check-in, try to arrive Monday afternoon through Thursday morning (Tuesday and Wednesday are best).

Crowd Avoidance

In general, weekends are busy and weekdays are slower. The exceptions are holiday periods and when large conventions or special events are held. Most Las Vegas hotels have a lower guest-room rate for weekdays than for weekends. Las Vegas hosts huge conventions and special events (rodeos, prize fights) that tie up hotels, restaurants, transportation, showrooms, and traffic for a week at a time. Likewise, major sporting events such as the Super Bowl, the NCAA football bowl games, the men's NCAA basketball tournament, Triple Crown horse races, the World Series, and the NBA championship fill every hotel in town on weekends. If you prefer to schedule your visit at a time when things are a little less frantic, we provide a calendar that lists the larger citywide conventions and regularly scheduled events to help you avoid the crowds. Note that two or three medium-sized conventions meeting at the same time can affect Las Vegas as much as one big citywide event.

Because conventions of more than 12,000 attendees can cause problems for the lone vacationer, the list of conventions and special events on pages 20–22 will help you plan your vacation dates. Included are the convention date, the number of people expected to attend, and the convention location (with hotel headquarters, if known at the time of publication). For a complete list of conventions scheduled during your visit, go to **vegasmeansbusiness.com** and click on "Convention Calendar." You can enter dates and get a full list or narrow it with different keywords or search terms. Although there are usually 6–12 conventions being staged in Las Vegas at any given time, the effect of any convention or trade show on hotels, shows, and restaurants is negligible citywide for conventions of 10,000 or fewer, except at the host hotel or convention venue. Note that four or five concurrent conventions averaging 4,000 attendees each can impact tourism to the same extent as one large convention.

A larger Las Vegas hotel can handle small conventions without a hiccup, and the meeting or trade show might actually be an inducement to stay there . . . or not. Staying at the Rio during the International Lingerie Show certainly could be interesting. The annual Star Trek Convention also at the Rio is a hoot, the National Industrial Fastener Show at the Sands Expo and Convention Center less so. The BedBug University North America Summit, formerly at Red Rock Casino, departed Vegas in 2013 and hopefully took their little red friends with them. On the other hand, The International Perfume Bottle Convention at the Tropicana came off smelling like a rose. You get the idea. If you stay somewhere that's hosting a convention, avoid arriving or departing on the same day as the attendees.

ARRIVING *and* GETTING ORIENTED

IF YOU DRIVE, YOU WILL HAVE TO TRAVEL through the desert to reach Las Vegas. Make sure your car is in good shape. Check your spare tire and toss a couple of gallons of water in the trunk, just in case. Once en route, pay attention to your fuel and temperature gauges. Virtually all commercial air traffic into Las Vegas uses McCarran International

Airport. At McCarran, a well-designed facility with good, clear signs, you will have no problem finding your way from the gate to the baggage-claim area, though it is often a long walk. Fast baggage handling is not the airport's strongest suit, so don't be surprised if you have to wait a long time on your checked luggage.

If you do not intend to rent a car, getting from the airport to your hotel is no problem. Shuttle services are available at a cost of $7–$11 one-way and $13–$17 round-trip. Sedans and "stretch" limousines cost about $40–$100 one-way. For taxis, the fare is the same no matter how many passengers are traveling (maximum five). Cabs charge a $3.30 trip fee with $2.60 per mile thereafter. If a taxi ride originates at McCarran International Airport, an additional airport surcharge of $2 per trip is added. Cab fare to Las Vegas Strip locations is $13–$20 one-way, plus tip. One-way taxi fares to Downtown run about $30. For more accurate point-to-point cab fare estimates see **taxifarefinder.com/main.php?city=lv**. Fares are regulated and should not vary from company to company. Note that most cabs in southern Nevada do not accept credit cards. If you're going to take a taxi from the airport, it's a good idea to check out the best route on **mapquest.com** or **googlemaps.com**. Cab driver revenues have not quite recovered from the recession, and some drivers will take a circuitous route to bump up fares. Be mindful, however, that traffic in Las Vegas is horrendous and that a route that seems circuitous may take less time than a more direct route. The most common "long-haul" route used to pad fares is traveling to Strip hotels or Downtown via the airport tunnel to I-215 and I-15.

The limo service counters are in the hall just outside the baggage-claim area. Cabs are at the curb. Additional information concerning ground transportation is available at the McCarran International Airport website (**mccarran.com**) and at the Nevada Taxi Cab Authority's website (**taxi.nv.gov**).

unofficial **TIP**
Any use of cell phones while driving is now against the law in Las Vegas. Keep your phone in your pocket and avoid big fines.

TAXI OPERATORS	
• Ace Cab Co. ☎ 702-736-8383	• Nellis Cab Co. ☎ 702-248-1111
• ANLV ☎ 702-643-1041	• Union ☎ 702-736-8444
• Henderson Taxi ☎ 702-384-2322	• Western Cab ☎ 702-736-8000
• Yellow Checker and Star Transportation ☎ 702-873-2000	

If you rent a car, you will need to catch the courtesy shuttle to the new consolidated McCarran Rent-A-Car Center located about two miles from the airport. The shuttle boards at the middle curb of the authorized vehicle lanes just outside terminal doors 10 and 11 on the ground level. The individual car-rental companies no longer operate shuttles of any kind, so all car-rental customers use the same shuttle.

Continued on page 22

Conventions and Special Events Calendar

DATES	CONVENTION/EVENT	ATTENDANCE	LOCATION
2014			
Sep 2-5	Photoshop World Conference & Expo	3,000	Mandalay Bay
Sep 7-10	ABC Kids Expo	14,000	LVCC
Sep 9-11	Super Mobile Show	40,000	Sands Expo Ctr.
Sep 9-11	Glassbuild America	7,000	LVCC
Sep 10-12	Interbike Expo	25,000	Mandalay Bay
Sep 10-11	Int'l Health, Racquet, & Sportsclub Assoc. Convention & Trade Show	3,000	Mandalay Bay
Sep 15-19	DevConnections	1,750	Aria
Sep 16-18	Electronic Retailing Assoc. Convention	3,000	Wynn LV
Sep 17-20	Las Vegas Souvenir & Resort Show	4,000	LVCC
Sep 18-20	Int'l Vision Expo West	14,000	Sands Expo Ctr.
Sep 19-21	Mr. Olympia	30,000	LVCC
Sep 23-28	5LINX	8,000	Orleans
Sep 23-25	Int'l Mining Show	5,000	LVCC
Sep 30-Oct 2	G2E: Global Gaming Expo	17,000	Sands Expo Ctr.
Oct 4-19	Chevrolet Dealer Business Meeting	2,500	Mandalay Bay
Oct 6-8	Nat'l Assoc. of Convenience Stores, Inc. Annual Meeting & Expo	25,000	LVCC
Oct 7-9	PubCon	2,000	LVCC
Oct 8-10	LRP Publications HR Technology Conference	8,000	Mandalay Bay
Oct 14-16	IMEX America	8,300	Sands Expo Ctr.
Oct 21-23	Solar Energy Trade Show	15,000	LVCC
Oct 22-24	Specialty Graphics Annual Nat'l Convention	23,000	LVCC
Oct 22-24	Nat'l Industrial Fastener & Mill Supply Expo	5,500	Sands Expo Ctr.
Oct 25	Seventh-Day Adventist Church Nevada/Utah Conference Las Vegas Convocation	5,000	Cashman Ctr.
Oct 26-28	Medical Group Management Assoc. Conf.	6,000	LVCC
Oct 30-Nov 2	Automatic Transmission Rebuilders Assoc. Annual Powertrain Expo	2,500	Rio
Nov 1-3	Automotive Parts Remanufacturers Big R ReMaTecUSA	1,500	Rio
Nov 4-7	Automotive Aftermarket Industry Week	140,000	Sands Expo/LVCC
Nov 10-13	TEAMS Conference & Expo	2,000	LVCC
Nov 18-21	LRP Publications Nat'l Workers Comp & Disability Conference	4,500	Mandalay Bay
Nov 19-22	Diving Equipment & Marketing Assoc. Show	10,000	LVCC
Nov 19-22	Traders Expo Las Vegas	5,000	Caesars Palace
Nov 19	Project Homeless Connect	2,000	Cashman Ctr.
Nov 21-23	Live Design Int'l	15,000	LVCC
Dec 9-11	VFX Mega Show Americas Import & Export Trade Show	30,000	Mandalay Bay
Dec 10-11	National Groundwater Expo & Annual Meeting	5,000	LVCC
Dec 11-13	American Academy of Anti-Aging Annual World Congress on Anti-Aging, Regenerative, and Aesthetic Medicine	3,000	Venetian
Dec 12-14	Las Vegas Numismatic Society Show	3,000	Riviera

Conventions and Special Events Calendar

DATES	CONVENTION/EVENT	ATTENDANCE	LOCATION
2015			
Jan 6-9	International CES	155,000	LVCC
Jan 13-15	Promotional Products Assoc. Int'l Expo	18,500	Mandalay Bay
Jan 14-16	Sports Licensing & Tailgate Show	9,000	LVCC
Jan 18-22	Las Vegas Market—Winter 2015	50,000	World Market Ctr.
Jan 20-22	Kitchen and Bath Industry Show	30,000	LVCC
Jan 20-22	International Builders Show	62,000	LVCC
Jan 20-23	Shooting, Hunting, & Outdoor Trade Show	61,000	Sands Expo Ctr.
Jan 21-23	Surfaces 2015	25,000	Mandalay Bay
Jan 21-24	Adult Entertainment Expo/AVN Adult Expo	25,000	Hard Rock
Jan 24	AVN Awards	3,000	Hard Rock
Jan 25-27	Redken Labs Int'l Symposium	10,000	Mandalay Bay
Jan 28-29	Tobacco Plus Expo	4,000	LVCC
Feb 3-6	World of Concrete	50,000	LVCC
Feb 5-10	Vacuum Dealers Trade Assoc.	4,000	LVCC
Feb 8-11	Structured Finance Industry Group/IMN/ABS	2,100	Aria
Feb 15-19	Western Veterinary Conference	14,000	Mandalay Bay
Feb 24-26	Strategies in Light—Pennwell	5,000	Sands Expo Ctr.
Feb 24-26	American Wholesale Marketers Assoc. Show	2,000	Paris Las Vegas
Mar 1-5	Exhibitor 2015	5,200	Mandalay Bay
Mar 10-11	CaterSource Event Solutions Annual Conference & Trade Show	9,500	LVCC
Mar 10-12	Travel Goods Show	4,200	LVCC
Mar 11-12	Digital Signage Expo	4,500	LVCC
Mar 18-19	Int'l Wireless Communications Expo	10,000	LVCC
Mar 22--29	Orthopaedic Research Society Annual Meeting	2,000	MGM Grand
Mar 23-28	American Academy of Orthopaedic Surgeons Annual Meeting	33,000	Sands Expo Ctr.
Mar 24-26	Annual Int'l Pizza Expo	12,000	LVCC
Mar 24-26	Globalshop	10,000	Mandalay Bay
Mar 29-Apr 1	American Academy of Professional Coders Nat'l Conference	2,000	Rio
Mar 31-Apr 1	Nightclub & Bar Show	37,000	LVCC
Apr 13-16	National Assoc. of Broadcasters	96,000	LVCC
Apr 15-17	Int'l Security Conference West	17,000	Sands Expo Ctr.
Apr 22-24	NAMA OneShow	4,500	LVCC
Apr 23-25	The Car Wash Show	6,000	LVCC
Apr 28-May 3	Western Psychological Assoc.	1,600	Red Rock Resort
May 5-7	National Hardware Show	32,000	LVCC
May 17-20	RECon	30,000	LVCC
June 2-4	Waste Expo	16,000	LVCC
June 11-19	Western States Roofing Contractors Assoc. Annual Convention and Trade Show	4,000	Paris Las Vegas
June 20-22	Int'l Esthetics Cosmetic and Spa Conference	25,000	LVCC

Conventions and Special Events Calendar

DATES	CONVENTION/EVENT	ATTENDANCE	LOCATION
2015 *(continued)*			
June 20–26	Int'l Bowl Expo	7,000	LVCC
June 25–27	Nat'l Apt. Assoc. Education Conference & Expo	6,000	Mandalay Bay
July 13–16	LRP Publications FDR Conference	3,000	Paris Las Vegas
July 21–23	SuperZoo West	12,000	Mandalay Bay
July 22–25	Assoc. of Woodworking & Furnishing Suppliers Fair	12,500	LVCC
Aug 2–6	Las Vegas Market—Summer 2015	50,000	World Market Ctr.
Aug 2–4	Imprinted Sportswear Show	2,500	LVCC
Aug 5–8	Int'l Billiard & Home Recreation Expo	2,100	South Point
Sep 2–4	Photoshop World Conference & Expo	3,000	Mandalay Bay
Sep 15–17	Nat'l Recreation & Park Assoc. Congress & Expo	8,000	Mandalay Bay
Sep 16–18	EMS World Expo	7,500	LVCC
Sep 21–23	Building Industry Consulting Service Int'l Fall Conference	5,000	Mandalay Bay
Sep 26–Oct 2	Las Vegas Souvenir & Resort Show	4,000	LVCC
Sep 27–Oct 6	Nat'l Academic Advising Assoc. Conference	3,000	Caesars Palace
Sep 29–Oct 1	G2E: Global Gaming Expo	17,000	Sands Expo Ctr.
Oct 4–12	Society of Diagnostic Medical Sonography Annual Meeting	1,700	The Cosmopolitan
Oct 6–8	Electronic Retailing Assoc. Convention	3,000	Wynn LV
Oct 12–14	Nat'l Assoc. of Convenience Stores, Inc. Annual Meeting & Expo	30,000	LVCC
Oct 13–15	IMEX America	8,300	Sands Expo Ctr.
Oct 19–21	LRP Publications HR Technology Conference	4,300	Mandalay Bay
Oct 19–21	ISPA Conference & Expo	3,000	
Oct 21–23	Nat'l Industrial Fastener & Mill Supply Expo	5,500	Sands Expo Ctr.
Oct 21–23	ISSA/INTERCLEAN North America	15,000	LVCC
Nov 14–17	American Academy of Opthalmology Meeting	25,000	Sands Expo Ctr.
Nov 16–23	Nat'l Communication Assoc. Meeting	2,000	Rio
Nov 17–20	LRP Publications Nat'l Workers Comp & Disability Conference	3,800	Mandalay Bay
Nov 17–19	Nat'l Business Aviation Assoc. Convention	32,000	LVCC
Dec 2–10	American Assoc. of Equine Practitioners Conf.	3,800	Mandalay Bay
Dec 8–10	Power-Gen Int'l Conference	27,000	LVCC
Dec 13–18	Nat'l Groundwater Expo & Meeting	5,000	LVCC

Continued from page 19

If someone is picking you up, go to ground level on the opposite side of the baggage-claim building (away from the main terminal) to the baggage-claim and arrivals curb. If your ride wants to park and meet you, hook up on the ground level of the baggage-claim building where the escalators descend from the main terminal.

There are two ways to exit the airport by car. You can depart via the old route, Swenson Street, which runs north–south roughly paralleling the Strip, or you can hop on the new spur of I-215. Dipping south from the airport, I-215 connects with I-15. The tunnel and I-215 will often deliver you to a point of huge congestion and delays where I-215 intersects I-15. As a general rule, exiting the airport on Swenson and then turning left (west) on the closest east–west street to your destination is the best bet for all Strip hotels. Swenson Street is also a better route if you're going to the Las Vegas Convention Center, to the University of Nevada, Las Vegas (UNLV), or to hotels on or east of the Strip.

CONVENIENCE CHART To give you an idea of your hotel's convenience to popular local destinations such as the Strip, Downtown, the Las Vegas Convention Center, UNLV, and the airport, we have provided a section on getting around. Included in the next chapter is a "convenience chart" that lists estimated times by foot or cab from each hotel to the destinations outlined on pages 52–54. In the same section are tips for avoiding traffic congestion and for commuting between the Strip and Downtown.

RENTAL CARS

ALL OF THE RENTAL-CAR COMPANIES previously located at the airport terminal, plus a few off-site companies, have moved to the huge McCarran Rent-A-Car Center situated two miles south of the airport. The airport provides large buses departing approximately every 5 minutes for the 7-to-12-minute commute to the facility. On arriving at the Rent-A-Car Center, you'll find all of the rental-car companies listed in the chart below on the ground floor.

RENTAL-CAR AGENCIES AT THE McCARRAN RENT-A-CAR CENTER		
ADVANTAGE/US RENT A CAR	800-777-9377	us-rentacar.com
ALAMO	800-462-5266	alamo.com
AVIS	800-331-1212	avis.com
BUDGET	800-922-2899	budget.com
DOLLAR	800-800-4000	dollar.com
ENTERPRISE	800-736-8222	enterprise.com
HERTZ	800-654-3131	hertz.com
NATIONAL CAR RENTAL	800-227-7368	nationalcar.com
PAYLESS CAR RENTAL	800-729-5377	paylesscarrental.com
SAVMOR CAR RENTAL	800-634-6779	(no website)
THRIFTY	800-367-2277	thrifty.com

When the rental-car companies were located at the airport, rental customers arrived at the rental counters in a relatively steady stream. At the new off-airport location, however, rental customers arrive by the busload, inundating the rental counters. Now, the only way to avoid a substantial wait to be processed is to join the special-customer clubs of the respective rental-car companies. These clubs (or programs)

Rental-Car Return and Pickup

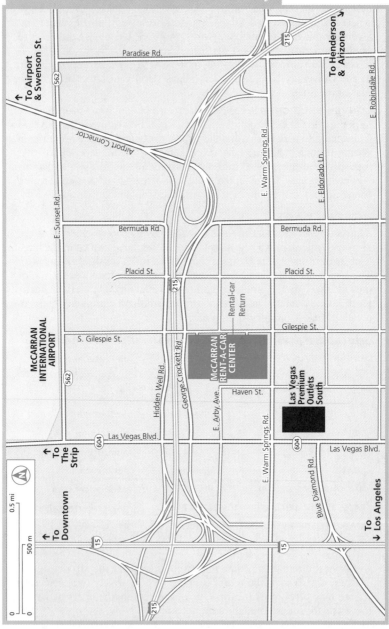

allow you to bypass the regular queue and to receive preferential processing. Just visit the website of the company of your choice and you'll see instructions for signing up. You don't have to rent cars often to join. Sign up about four weeks before you make a rental reservation so you'll have your membership number when you're ready to reserve.

Because the Rent-A-Car Center shuttles run more often than buses provided by the rental-car companies under the old system, it doesn't take any longer than before to commute to the center or to get back to the airport once you've returned your car. En route to the Rent-A-Car Center, sit near a door so that you can be one of the first to disembark. If you're traveling with others, let them attend to the luggage while you sprint to the rental counter. This will ensure that you'll be ahead of your fellow bus passengers. To avoid a free-for-all of passengers trying to retrieve their bags from the onboard storage racks, most bus drivers prefer to handle luggage loading and unloading. It's about order and safety, not tips, so just go with it. Generally, after all riders have disembarked, the driver will unload the luggage via the rear doors.

All of the rental cars are under one roof. Upon completion of your paperwork you'll be directed to a specified area of the garage to pick up your car. Having picked up your car, chances are about 95% that you'll find yourself disoriented in a part of Las Vegas you've never laid eyes on. Follow the instructions below to reach your final destination.

After you pick up your rental car, you'll exit the Rent-A-Car Center onto Gilespie Street, where you'll find signs directing you to the Strip as well as to I-15 and I-215. Unfortunately, if you follow the signs, you'll end up in a traffic jam of the first order (welcome to Las Vegas!), owing to an inadequate number of right-turn lanes and a multitude of traffic signals. The exit from the Rent-A-Car Center onto Gilespie Street forces you to turn right (south), but to avoid the traffic jams you really want to be heading in the opposite direction (north) on Gilespie. From the Rent-A-Car Center exit, this can be accomplished by working your way immediately across the southbound lanes on Gilespie to a left-turn lane and then making a U-turn. Alternatively, you can go a block or so south and then get turned around less hurriedly. Once you're headed northbound on Gilespie do the following:

TO REACH THE LAS VEGAS CONVENTION CENTER, UNLV, AND HOTELS ON THE EAST SIDE OF THE STRIP, head north on Gilespie Street and turn right onto George Crockett Road. Follow signs to the airport via the Airport Connector. You'll pass through a tunnel under the runways and pop out on Swenson Street just before the intersection with Tropicana. Use the maps in this guide to reach your final destination from there.

TO REACH DOWNTOWN AND HOTELS ON THE WEST SIDE OF THE STRIP VIA I-15, head north from the Rent-A-Car Center on Gilespie, cross the bridge over I-215, and turn left on Hidden Well Road. Follow Hidden Well Road to I-15 (northbound only). Use the maps in this guide to navigate to your final destination from there.

TO ACCESS I-215 NORTHWEST TOWARD RED ROCK CANYON AND SUMMERLIN, go north on Gilespie, cross the bridge over I-215, and turn left on Hidden Well Road. Follow Hidden Well Road to the I-215 west-bound ramp.

The following directions do not require going north on Gilespie:

TO ACCESS I-215 SOUTHEAST TOWARD HENDERSON, GREEN VALLEY, AND LAKE LAS VEGAS, turn right on Gilespie from the Rent-A-Car Center and turn left at the first traffic signal onto Warm Springs Road. Follow Warm Springs Road west to the intersection of I-215.

TO ACCESS LAS VEGAS BOULEVARD SOUTH OF THE I-15/I-215 INTER-CHANGE, stay in the far-right lane on exiting the Rent-A-Car Center and turn right on Warm Springs Road. Warm Springs Road intersects Las Vegas Boulevard South.

TO ACCESS I-15 SOUTHBOUND TOWARD LAUGHLIN AND LOS ANGELES, turn right on Gilespie from the Rent-A-Car Center and then right on Warm Springs Road. After two blocks, turn south on Las Vegas Boulevard South, turning right on Blue Diamond Road. Follow the signs to I-15.

Fortunately, returning your rental car is much easier and there is little opportunity to become embroiled in a serious traffic jam in the environs of the Rent-A-Car Center. The same cannot be said, however, of I-15 and I-215, especially during rush hours. If you are coming from the east side of the Strip, take Paradise Road to the airport and follow the well-marked signs to the rental-car return. Likewise, as you come toward the airport on I-15 and I-215, follow the rental-car-return signs.

Although rental cars are comparatively cheap in Las Vegas, taxes and fees are not. If you rent a car at the airport (which includes both terminal and off-terminal locations on airport property), here's what you can expect to pay:

State Sales Tax 8.1%	
Nevada Rental Service Fee 10.0%	
Clark County Rental Fee 2.0%	
Airport Concession Recovery Fee 10.0%	
Reimbursement of Registration and License Fee Varies*	
Total 30.1+%	

*This fee varies among retailers and is explained further at **tax.state.nv .us.** All fees must be fully disclosed in the lease agreement.*

Had enough? Powers at the airport don't think so. In addition to the above you are charged a $3 per day Consumer Facility Charge. You can avoid the 10% fee and the $3 per day by renting the car at some non-airport locations, like your hotel. Be advised, however, that it's not un-usual for agencies to bump up the rental price at such locations.

In the dollar-and-cents department, prices fluctuate so much from week to week that it's anyone's guess who will offer the best deal dur-ing your visit. Usually the best deals are on the company's website, but expedia.com, carrentals.com, and kayak.com are often worth checking, especially if you're visiting during a particularly busy time, such as during a citywide convention. On rental company websites, counter-intuitively, you can often get a better deal if you don't indicate that you're a member of AAA, AARP, and the like. After you get your quote, see if you can improve the deal by trying again, entering your organizational or age information.

Be aware that Las Vegas is a feast-or-famine city when it comes to rental-car availability. On many weekends, or when a citywide convention is in town, it may be impossible to get a rental car unless you reserved way in advance. If, on the other hand, you come to town when business is slow, the rental agencies will practically give you a car. We have been able to rent from the most expensive companies for as little as $22 a day under these circumstances. If you are visiting during a slow time, reserve a car in advance to cover yourself, and then, on arrival, ask each rental company to quote you its best price. If you can beat the price on your reserved car, go for it.

unofficial TIP
Before you leave the lot, inspect your rental car with care, examining every inch, and have the rental agency record anything you find.

Improbably, one of the best places for rental-car deals is **mouse savers.com,** a site dedicated to finding deals at Disneyland and Walt Disney World. The site lists rental-car codes that you can use to get great discounts. Some of the codes are for Orlando and Southern California only, but many others apply anywhere in the United States. The site also offers some great tips on how to compare different codes and deals.

Another way to score a deal on a rental car is to bid on **priceline .com.** We've used Priceline to get cars at less than $20 per day. Understand, however, that if your bid is accepted, the entire rental cost will be nonrefundably charged to your credit card. In other words, no backing out for any reason. Before placing your bid, check our conventions and special events calendar on pages 20–22. If there's a big convention in town, demand will be high and a lowball bid might not work.

When you (or your travel agent) call to reserve a rental car, ask for the smallest, least expensive car in the company's inventory, even if you ultimately intend to rent a larger vehicle. It's possible that you will be upgraded without charge when you arrive. If not, rental agencies frequently offer on-site upgrade incentives that beat any deals you can make in advance. Always compare daily and weekly rates.

If you decline insurance coverage on the rental car because of protection provided by your credit card, be aware that the coverage provided by the credit card is secondary to your regular auto insurance policy. In most situations the credit-card coverage only reimburses you the deductible on your regular policy. Happily, most car insurance covers rental cars as well as your personal vehicle. If you're not sure about your coverage, contact your insurance agent. Also be aware that some car-rental contracts require that you drive the car only in Nevada. If you, like many tourists, visit Hoover Dam or trek out to the Grand Canyon, you will cross into Arizona. Another item to check in advance, if applicable, is whether your rental agency charges for additional drivers.

When you rent your car, make sure you understand the implications of bringing it back empty of fuel. Some companies will charge as much as $9 per gallon if they have to fill the tank on return. At one agency, we returned a car with between a third and a half-tank of gas remaining and were charged the same as if we had coasted in with a completely empty tank. Also, beware of signs at the car-rental counters reading "Gas today—$4 per gallon" or some such. That usually applies to the price of the gas already in the car when you rent it, not the price per gallon of a fill-up should you return the car empty. The price per gallon for a fill-up on return will be somewhere in the fine print of your rental contract.

Another rental-car problem we encountered involved a pinhead-sized chip on the windshield. Understanding the fine print of rental car contracts, and because we always decline the insurance offered by the agencies, we inspect our cars thoroughly for any damage before accepting the car and leaving the lot. In this instance, as always, we inspected the car thoroughly and did not notice any windshield flaws. When we returned the car after three days, we were requested to remain at the counter to complete an "accident report." Insisting that we were unaware of any damage, we requested that the car be retrieved for our inspection. Still unable to find the alleged damage, we asked the counter agent to identify it for us. The agent who was responsible for the accident report then had to scrutinize the windshield before she could find the mark, even though she knew its exact location from the employee who checked the car in. The conclusion to be drawn here is that if you decline coverage, the rental agency may hold you responsible for even the tiniest damage, damage so slight that you may never notice it. Check your car out well before you leave. This will not inhibit them from charging you for damage sustained while the car is in your possession, but at least you will have the peace of mind of knowing that they are not putting one over on you.

Some rental companies will charge you for "loss of use" if you have an accident that takes the car out of use. Because some car insurance policies do not pay loss-of-use charges, check your coverage with your insurance agent before you rent.

MEGABUS, GREYHOUND, AND X TRAIN

IF YOU'RE COMING FROM SOUTHERN CALIFORNIA, consider Megabus. A round-trip on the Wi-Fi–equipped modern buses runs about $25, less than most round-trip cab rides to and from the airport. There are four buses a day departing from Union Station's Patsaouras Transit Plaza Bay and terminating at the RTC South Strip Transfer Terminal. The trip takes 5–6 hours. Visit **us.megabus.com** for schedules and additional information.

Greyhound runs both express buses and puddle jumpers from southern California to Las Vegas. Five or six express buses run each day, making a pit stop in either Barstow or San Bernardino. Travel time is about 5–6 hours, including the stop. Round-trip prices range from $52 to $268 (for a fully refundable ticket).

Las Vegas Railway Express is on schedule to operate a luxury express train from the Fullerton Station in southern California to Downtown Las Vegas. The 5-hour trip runs eastbound Thursday and Friday and westbound on Sunday. For additional information, see **vegasxtrain.com.**

LAS VEGAS CUSTOMS AND PROTOCOL

IN A TOWN WHERE THE MOST BIZARRE behavior imaginable is routinely tolerated, it is ironic that so many visitors obsess over what constitutes proper protocol. This mentality stems mainly from the myriad customs peculiar to gaming and the *perceived* glamour of the city itself. First-timers attach a great deal of importance to "fitting in." What makes this task difficult, at least in part, is that half of the people with whom they are trying to fit in are first-timers too.

The only hard rules for being accepted Downtown or on the Strip are to have a shirt on your back, shoes on your feet, some manner of clothing below the waist, and a little money in your pocket. Concerning the latter, there is no maximum. The operational minimum is bus fare back to wherever you came from.

This notwithstanding, there are three basic areas in which Las Vegas first-timers tend to feel especially insecure:

GAMBLING The various oddities of gaming protocol are described in this book under the casino games in Part 3, Gambling (page 313). Despite appearances, however, gambling is very informal. While it is intelligent not to play a game when/if you do not know how, it is unwarranted to abstain because you are uncertain of the protocol. What little protocol exists (things like holding your cards above the table and keeping your hands away from your bet once play has begun) has evolved to protect the house and honest players from cheats. Dealers (a generic term for those who conduct table games) are not under orders to be unfriendly, silent, or rigid. Observe a game that interests you before you sit down. Assure yourself that the dealer is personable and polite. Never play in a casino where the staff is surly or cold; life's too short.

EATING IN FANCY RESTAURANTS Many are meat-and-potatoes places with fancy names, so there is no real reason to be intimidated. Others are designer, pay-big-bucks restaurants with famous chefs. In either case, service is friendly. Men will feel more comfortable in sport coats, but ties are rarely worn. Women turn up in everything from slacks and blouses to evening wear. When you sit down, a whole platoon of waiters will attend you. Do not remove your napkin from the table; only the waiters are allowed to place napkins in the laps of patrons. After the ceremonial placement of the napkin, the senior waiter will speak. When he concludes, you may order cocktails, consider the menu, sip your water, or engage in conversation. If there are women in your party, their menus will not have prices listed. If your party includes only women, a menu with prices listed will be given to the woman who looks the oldest. When you are ready to order, even if you only want a steak and fries, do not speak until the waiter has had an opportunity to recite in French from the menu. To really please your waiters, order something that can be prepared tableside with dramatic flames and explosions. If your waiters seem stuffy or aloof, ask them to grind peppercorns or grate Parmesan cheese on something. This will usually loosen them up.

There will be enough utensils on the table to perform a triple bypass. These items are considered expendable; use a different utensil for each dish and surrender it to the waiter along with the empty plate at the end of each course.

TIPPING Because about a third of the resident population of Las Vegas are service providers in the tourist industry, there is no scarcity of people to tip. From the day you arrive until the day you depart, you will be interacting with porters, cabbies, valet-parking attendants, bellhops, waiters, maître d's, dealers, bartenders, keno runners, housekeeping personnel, room service, and others.

Tipping is an issue that makes some travelers very uncomfortable. How much? When? To whom? Not leaving a tip when one is customary makes you feel inexperienced. Not knowing how much to tip makes you feel vulnerable and out of control. Is the tip you normally leave at home appropriate in Las Vegas?

The most important thing to bear in mind is that a tip is not automatic, nor is it an obligation. A tip is a reward for good service. The suggestions in the "Tipping Guidelines" chart on page 32 are based on traditional practices in Las Vegas.

LAS VEGAS PHONE NUMBERS

BECAUSE THE 702 AREA CODE for Las Vegas was running out of numbers to assign, the Public Utilities Commission of Nevada approved a second area code in the same geographic region to ensure a continuing supply of telephone numbers. The new area code, 725, is assigned to all new phone numbers. Area code 702 remains the same for numbers assigned prior to June 3rd, 2014.

To complete local calls, the new dialing procedure requires callers to dial the **area code + telephone number.** This means that all calls in the 702 area code that are currently dialed with seven digits will need to be dialed using the 10-digit **area code + telephone number.** Local calls, which include Las Vegas, Boulder City, Henderson, Laughlin, Mesquite, Moapa Valley, and North Las Vegas, do not require prefacing your call by dialing "1." You will continue to dial 1 + area code + telephone number for all long-distance calls. You can still dial just three digits to reach 911 and 411.

Seven-digit numbers will need to be reprogrammed to use the new dialing procedures. Some examples are life-safety systems, fax machines, Internet dial-up numbers, alarm and security systems, gates, speed dialers, call-forwarding settings, and voicemail services.

BEWARE OF WATER VENDORS

WE ADVISE YOU *not* to buy bottled water from street vendors either on the Strip or Downtown. The bottles are not sealed, and it's open to speculation where the water came from. If you want to beat minibar or hotel shop prices, go to a convenience store.

FENDER BENDERS

AS OF APRIL 2013, in order to reallocate Las Vegas Metro Police resources, police no longer respond to non-injury traffic accidents. The wisdom of this policy is debatable, but for certain it deprives the involved drivers of an impartial officer to assess the scene, with the probable outcome of conflict, deceit, and litigation. If you have such an accident, you may be on your own in terms of collecting information for your insurance company. We advise you to take photographs, exchange insurance information, obtain contact info from witnesses, and, if the other driver is agreeable, write a short summary of what happened that both of you sign. If the other driver demurs, write a summary anyway while the facts are fresh in your mind.

Rental-car companies almost always require a police report. A Las Vegas Hertz representative strongly suggests that you call the police irrespective of the new policy and tell them that a rental car was involved. If the police decline to come, make note of the name of the person declining. Then call the rental-car company and advise them of the situation. Sometimes the company will send someone out to inspect the scene.

For the record, Nevada is not a no-fault state, thus liability has to be assigned. Also, auto insurance is mandated in Nevada, but because there are so many out-of-state drivers, you should confirm that your policy has uninsured and under-insured motorist coverage. Finally, the Nevada Division of Insurance has posted tips on its website at **doi.nv.gov.** Click on "News & Notices" at the top, then click "Press Releases," and scroll down to find the release titled "Nevada Division of Insurance Offers Auto Accident Tips to Las Vegas Drivers."

STAYING TUNED IN

SURPRISINGLY, one of the most frequently posed questions to rental-car agents and hotel concierges is "How do I tune in NPR (National Public Radio)?" NPR station KNPR can be found at 88.9 FM.

BRINGING YOUR PET TO LAS VEGAS

FOR THE MOST PART "pet" in Las Vegas means a dog. Various restrictions apply, including weight limitations. Major hotels that welcome pets include Trump International, Westin Casuarina, Four Seasons at Mandalay Bay, and Alexis Park Hotel. The best pet programs can be found at the Caesars Entertainment properties: Bally's, Caesars Palace, Flamingo, The Cromwell, Harrah's, The LINQ Hotel & Casino, Paris, Planet Hollywood, and Rio. Incorporating PetStay Las Vegas (**petstaylas vegas.com**), these hotels have set aside specific floors and public areas

Tipping Guidelines

PORTERS A dollar a bag

CAB DRIVERS A lot depends on service and courtesy. For good service tip $5 or 15–20% of the total fare. If you are asking the cabbie to take you only a block or two, the fare will be small, but your tip should be large ($5) to make up for his wait in line and to partially compensate him for missing a better-paying fare. Add an extra dollar for a lot of luggage handling.

VALET PARKING Two dollars is correct if the valet is courteous and demonstrates some hustle. A dollar will do if the service is just OK. Only pay when you take your car out, not when you leave it. Because valet attendants pool their tips, both of the individuals who assist you (coming and going) will be taken care of. If the valet service is jammed, hand over a $10 or $20 to the person who takes your claim ticket and tell him you'd like the car brought up right away. You'll be moved to the head of the

BELLMEN When a bellhop greets you at your car with a rolling cart and handles all of your bags, $5 is about right. The more luggage you carry yourself, of course, the less you should tip. Sometimes bellhops who handle only a small bag or two will put on a real performance when showing you your room. We had a bellhop in one hotel walk into our room, crank up the air-conditioner, turn on the TV, open the blinds, flick on the lights, flush the commode, and test the water pressure in the tub. Give us a break. We tipped the same as if he had simply opened the door and put our luggage in the room.

WAITERS Whether in a coffee shop, a gourmet room, or ordering from room service, the standard gratuity for acceptable service is 15–20% of the total tab, before sales tax. At a self-serve buffet or brunch, it is customary to leave $3–$5 for the folks who bring your drinks and bus your dishes.

COCKTAIL WAITERS AND BARTENDERS Tip by the round. For two people, $1 a round; for more than two people, $2 a round. For a large group, use your judgment: Is everyone drinking beer or is the order long and complicated? In casinos where drinks are sometimes on the house, it is considered good form to tip the server $1 per round.

DEALERS AND SLOT ATTENDANTS If you are winning, it is a nice gesture to tip the dealer or place a small bet for him. How much depends on your winnings and on your level of play. With slot attendants, tip when they perform a specific service or you hit a jackpot. In general, unless other services are also rendered, it is not customary to tip change makers or cashiers.

KENO RUNNERS Tip if you have a winner or if the runner provides exceptional service. How much to tip will vary with your winnings and level of play.

SHOWROOM MAÎTRE D'S, CAPTAINS, AND SERVERS There is more to this than you might expect. If you are planning to take in a show, see our suggestions for tipping in Part 2, Entertainment and Nightlife (see pages 206–207).

HOTEL MAIDS On checking out, leave $3–$5 for each day you stayed (more if you're really messy), providing the service was good.

that are designated as pet-friendly sections. There are on-property pathways and relief areas as well as grooming, pet sitters and pet walkers, and a directory of on-call veterinarians. Leashed canine guests must check in with their owners and weigh less than 50 pounds. A maximum of two dogs are permitted per room. An amenity package for pooches includes special dishes for food and water, doggie snacks, and comfy sleeping mats. Depending on the hotel, the rate is $25–$40 plus tax per night. Pet stays can be booked at **caesars.com** or (800) 427-7247.

A list of Las Vegas chain and proprietary hotels that welcome pets can be found at **officialpethotels.com** and **dogfriendly.com** (click on Dog Travel Guides—Nevada).

If puppies visit, can cats be far behind?

LAS VEGAS *as a* FAMILY DESTINATION

OCCASIONALLY THE PUBLISHER sends us around to promote the *Unofficial Guide* on radio and television, and every year we are asked the same question: Is Las Vegas a good place for a family vacation?

Las Vegas is definitely not a family-friendly destination. Casinos are very particular about who's occupying their beds, and the least preferred customers of all are families with children. Children can't gamble, they annoy adults who come to Las Vegas to avoid kids, and they reduce or make impossible the time their parents spend in the casino. For many years, there were only two casinos that targeted the family trade: Circus Circus and Excalibur. Almost 20 years later, guess what: Circus Circus is the only one. Excalibur is making a concerted effort to ditch the family market.

However, if you don't object to being persona non grata, Las Vegas is a great place for a family vacation. Food and lodging are a good value for the dollar, and there are an extraordinary number of things, from swimming to rafting through the Black Canyon on the Colorado River, that the entire family can enjoy together. If you take your kids to Las Vegas *and forget gambling,* Las Vegas compares favorably with every family tourist destination in the United States. The rub, of course, is that gambling in Las Vegas is pretty hard to ignore.

TAKING YOUR CHILDREN TO LAS VEGAS TODAY

LAS VEGAS IS PREDOMINANTLY an adult tourist destination. As a city (including the surrounding area), however, it has a lot to offer children. What this essentially means is that the Strip and Downtown have not been developed with children in mind, but if you are willing to make the effort to venture away from the gambling areas, there are a lot of fun and wholesome things for families to do. As a rule, however, people do not go to Las Vegas to be continually absent from the casinos.

Persons under age 21 are not allowed to gamble, nor are they allowed to hang around while *you* gamble. If you are gambling, your children have to be somewhere else. On the Strip and Downtown, the choices are limited. True, most hotels have nice swimming pools, but summer days are much too hot to stay out for long. While golf and tennis are possibilities, court or greens fees are routinely charged, and you still must contend with limitations imposed by the desert climate.

After a short time, you will discover that the current options for your children's recreation and amusement are as follows:

1. You can simply allow your children to hang out. Given this alternative, the kids will swim a little, watch some TV, eat as much as their (or your) funds allow, throw water balloons out of any hotel window that has not been hermetically sealed, and cruise up and down the Strip (or Fremont Street) on foot, ducking in and out of souvenir stores and casino lobbies.

2. If your children are a mature age 10 or older, you can turn them loose at the Adventuredome at Circus Circus. The kids, however, will probably cut bait and go cruising after about an hour or two.

3. You can hire a babysitter to come to your hotel room and tend your children. This works out pretty much like option 1, without the water balloons and the cruising.

4. You can abandon the casino (or whatever else you had in mind) and "do things" with your kids. Swimming and eating (as always) will figure prominently into the plan, as will excursions to places that have engaged the children's curiosity. You can bet that your kids will want to go to the Adventuredome at Circus Circus. The white tigers, dolphins, and exploding volcano at the Mirage; The Forum Shops; and the Stratosphere Tower are big hits with kids. New York–New York features a roller coaster. If you have two children and do a fraction of all this stuff in one day, you will spend $80–$250 for the four of you, not counting meals and transportation.

   If you have a car, however, there are lots of great, inexpensive places to go—enough to keep you busy for days. We recommend Red Rock Canyon and Hoover Dam, for sure. On the way to Hoover Dam, you can stop for a tour of the Ethel M. Chocolate Factory.

   A great day excursion (during the spring and fall) is a guided raft trip through the Black Canyon on the Colorado River. This can easily be combined with a visit to Hoover Dam. Trips to the Valley of Fire State Park (driving, biking, hiking) are also recommended during the more temperate months.

   Around Las Vegas there are a number of real museums and museums-tourist attractions. The Discovery Children's Museum (adjacent to the Smith Center Downtown) is worthwhile, affordable, and a big favorite with kids age 14 and younger. While you are in the neighborhood, try the Natural History Museum almost directly across the street.

5. You can pay someone else to take your kids on excursions. Some in-room sitters (bonded and from reputable agencies) will take your kids around as long as you foot the bill. For recommendations, check with the concierge or front desk of your hotel. If your kids are over age 12, you can pack them off on one of the guided tours advertised by the handful in the various local visitor magazines.

Hotels that Solicit Family Business

As Excalibur gets out of the family trade, Circus Circus stands alone as the only casino that welcomes children. Circus Circus actively seeks the family market with carnival game midways where children and adults can try to win stuffed animals, foam-rubber dice, and other totally dispensable objects. A great setup for the casinos, the midways turn a nice profit while innocuously introducing the youngsters to games of chance.

In addition, Circus Circus operates the Adventuredome theme park and offers free circus acts each evening, starring top-notch talent, including aerialists (flying trapeze artists).

Parents traveling with children are grudgingly accepted at all of the larger hotels, though certain hotels are better equipped to deal with children than others. If your children are water puppies and enjoy being in a swimming pool all day, Mandalay Bay, Venetian, M Resort, Planet Hollywood, Flamingo, Monte Carlo, MGM Grand, Mirage, Aria, Rio, Tropicana, Caesars Palace, Wynn Las Vegas, Wynn Encore, Bellagio, Red Rock Resort, Green Valley Ranch, and TI have the best pools in town. Westgate Las Vegas, SLS, and Hard Rock Hotel, among others, also have excellent swimming facilities.

If your kids are older and into sports, the MGM Grand, Caesars Palace, Westgate Las Vegas, and Bally's offer the most variety.

For child care and special programs, The Orleans, Red Rock Resort, Boulder Station, Palms, Texas Station, Sunset Station, and Santa Fe Station provide child-care facilities.

Our favorite hotel for a family vacation is Green Valley Ranch Resort, a Station casino and resort about 15 minutes southeast of the Strip. Its location is convenient to Lake Mead, Hoover Dam, the Black Canyon of the Colorado, and Red Rock Canyon, for starters. It has great swimming areas, good restaurants, and lovely guest rooms. And when you want to sneak into the casino or have an adults-only meal, the concierge will arrange child care for you. Best of all, Green Valley Ranch is isolated. There's no place nearby where your kids can get into trouble (right!).

Babysitting

An organization called **Nannies & Housekeepers U.S.A.** (☎ 702-451-0021; **nahusa.com**) offers 24/7 in-room babysitting. Nannies & Housekeepers, which puts their sitters through a lengthy and rigorous screening, is the exclusive babysitting agency for many Las Vegas hotels, including Wynn Las Vegas, Wynn Encore, and MGM Grand.

PART ONE

ACCOMMODATIONS *and* CASINOS

WHERE *to* **STAY:** *Basic Choices*

LAS VEGAS HAS AN ASTOUNDING INVENTORY of about 150,000 hotel rooms. Washington, D.C., by way of contrast, has 31,000. Occupancy rates are over 91% on weekends and average 84% for the whole week, compared to a national average of 62%. Even during the slow recession recovery, occupancy rates for Strip hotels remained high. However, with the glut of new rooms that came online in 2009 and 2010, including unsold condo and timeshare units, expect great deals on rooms until at least late summer of 2014.

THE LAS VEGAS STRIP AND DOWNTOWN

FROM A VISITOR'S PERSPECTIVE, Las Vegas is more or less a small town that's fairly easy to navigate. Most of the major hotels and casinos are in two areas: Downtown and on Las Vegas Boulevard, known as the Strip.

The Downtown hotels and casinos are often characterized as older and smaller than those on the Strip. While this is true in a general sense, there are both large and elegant hotels Downtown. What really differentiates Downtown is the incredible concentration of casinos and hotels in a relatively small area. Along Fremont Street, Downtown's main thoroughfare, the casinos present a continuous, dazzling galaxy of neon and twinkling lights for more than four city blocks. Known as Glitter Gulch, these dozen-plus gambling emporiums are sandwiched together in colorful profusion in an area barely larger than a parking lot at a good-sized shopping mall.

Contrast in the size, style, elegance, and presentation of the Downtown casinos provides a varied mix, combining extravagant luxury and cosmopolitan sophistication with an Old West–boomtown decadence. Though not directly comparable, Downtown Las Vegas has the feel of New Orleans's Bourbon Street: alluring, exotic, wicked, sultry, foreign, and, above all, diverse. It is a place where cowboy, businessperson, showgirl, and retiree mix easily. And, like Bourbon Street, it is all accessible on foot.

If Downtown is the French Quarter of Las Vegas, then the Strip is Plantation Row. Here, huge resort hotels–casinos sprawl like estates along a 4-mile section of Las Vegas Boulevard South. Each hotel is a vacation destination unto itself, with casino, hotel, restaurants, pools, spas, landscaped grounds, and even golf courses. While the Downtown casinos are fused into a vibrant, integrated whole, the huge hotels on the Strip demand individual recognition.

Although the Strip is literally a specific length of Las Vegas Boulevard South, the large surrounding area is usually included when discussing hotels, casinos, restaurants, and attractions. East and parallel to the Strip is Paradise Road, where the Las Vegas Convention Center and several hotels are located. Also included in the Strip area are hotels and casinos on streets intersecting Las Vegas Boulevard, as well as properties to the immediate west of the Strip (on the far side of Interstate 15).

CHOOSING A HOTEL

THE VARIABLES THAT FIGURE MOST prominently in choosing a hotel are price, location, your itinerary, and your quality requirements. There is a wide selection of lodging with myriad combinations of price and value. Given this, your main criteria for selecting a hotel should be its location and your itinerary.

The Strip versus Downtown for Leisure Travelers

Though there are some excellent hotels on the Boulder Highway and elsewhere around town, the choice for most vacation travelers is whether to stay Downtown or on (or near) the Strip. Downtown offers a good choice of hotels, restaurants, and gambling, but only a limited choice of entertainment and fewer amenities such as swimming pools and spas. There are no golf courses and only four tennis courts Downtown. If you have a car, the Strip is an 8- to 15-minute commute from Downtown via I-15. If you do not have a car, public transportation from Downtown to the Strip is as efficient as Las Vegas traffic allows and quite affordable.

If you stay on the Strip, you are more likely to need a car or require some sort of transportation. There are more hotels to choose from on the Strip, but they are spread over a much wider area and are often (but not always) pricier than Downtown. On the Strip, one has a sense of space, as many of the hotels are constructed on a grand scale. The selection of entertainment is both varied and extensive, and the Strip's recreational facilities rival those of the world's leading resorts.

Downtown is a multicultural, multilingual melting pot with an adventurous, raw, robust feel. Everything in this part of town seems intense and concentrated, an endless blur of action, movement, and light. Diversity and history combine in lending vitality and excitement to this older part of Las Vegas, an essence more tangible and real than the monumental, plastic themes and fantasies of many large Strip establishments.

Though Downtown caters to every class of clientele, it is less formal and, with exceptions, more of a working man's gambling town. Here, the truck driver and welder gamble alongside the secretary and the rancher. The Strip, likewise, runs the gamut but tends to attract more high rollers, middle-class suburbanites, and business travelers going to conventions.

Downtown: Phoenix Rising

For years, Downtown casinos watched from the sidelines as Strip hotels turned into veritable tourist attractions. There was nothing Downtown to rival the exploding volcano at the Mirage, the theme park at Circus Circus, the pirate battle at Treasure Island (TI), or the view from the Stratosphere Tower. As gambling revenue dwindled and more customers defected to the Strip, Downtown casino owners finally got serious about mounting a counterattack.

The counterattack, known as the Fremont Street Experience, was launched at the end of 1995. Its basic purpose was to transform Downtown into an ongoing event, a continuous party. Fremont Street through the heart of Glitter Gulch was forever closed to vehicular traffic and turned into a park, with terraces, outdoor stage concerts, and landscaping. By creating an aesthetically pleasing environment, Las Vegas–style, the project united all of the casinos in a sort of diverse gambling mall.

The surge and nucleus of much of Las Vegas's economic and tourism growth is now centered on Fremont Street. While the town's politicos have forged ahead with various redevelopment projects throughout the Las Vegas Valley, the most dynamic development is the collective renaissance of hotels in the vicinity of the Fremont Street Experience. Confident of the positive direction in which the area is heading, several aging properties in Downtown's casino corridor have completed extensive revitalization: the Plaza was thoroughly renovated; the Golden Nugget added the Rush Tower with 500 rooms; Fitzgeralds was renamed The D Las Vegas and received an exterior facelift and interior makeover; the El Cortez has been updated and added a wing of 64 Cabana Suites; the Golden Gate constructed a five-story tower with 100 rooms; and the Lady Luck became the Downtown Grand Hotel & Casino. Total number of guest rooms completed is approximately 2,800 in eight properties. Much of these interior-exterior remodels maintain a nostalgic Vegas vibe: it continues to glitter, but Fremont Street is no longer a gulch.

The Downtown 3rd Development Group is privatizing 3rd Street and creating a mixed-use urban mall. Future plans for the neighborhood at 3rd and Stewart Streets include a farmers' market in the former Transportation Center and retail shops nearby. The National Museum of Organized Crime and Law Enforcement expropriated the historic post office on Stewart Avenue. Attracting locals and visitors alike, directly east of Fremont Street Experience, is Fremont Street East, a thriving club and restaurant redevelopment district expanding with a cross section of idiosyncratic bars, funky shops, galleries, lounges, and ethnic eateries, with the El Cortez as the cornerstone and overseen by vintage neon signs.

Also on Fremont Street East, the multilevel Neonopolis arcade is adding shops and restaurants, while the unconventional Container Park development has added zing. Nearby, historic businesses have reopened or have been repurposed. Atomic Liquors is back: the oldest noncasino bar in Las Vegas was built in 1952 and so named because of customers' penchant for sitting on the roof while viewing nearby nuclear testing blasts. The Fremont Medical Center building is now Emergency Arts (a gallery); the former Sears is Backstage Bar & Billiards. More transformations are underway.

Downtown has gone hi-tech as well. Two hotels, The D and the Golden Gate, accept Bitcoins, and free Wi-Fi, provided by **LV.net**, can be accessed from laptops and smart phones within a 3-mile radius. In temperate October, the annual three-day "Life Is Beautiful" urban festival (**lifeisbeautiful.com**) provides food, art, and music in a cordoned 11-block area lined with food trucks, vendors, artists, and bandstands.

Much of the renaissance of the Downtown quadrant is attributed to Tony Hsieh, CEO of the Zappos online shoe company, who moved his corporate offices to the area. He has also created the Downtown Project, which is funding many community growth ventures in the neighborhoods surrounding Fremont Street.

The arts have blossomed as well. South of the hotel center but still considered Downtown is the First Friday Art Experience, which is encroaching toward the Fremont Street Experience as more art galleries, memorabilia stores, and other hip businesses move into the area. The free, family-friendly event runs 5–11 p.m. and features local artists, food trucks, music on three stages, and an interactive KidZone.

Adding new life to the neighborhood at the west boundary of Downtown is 61-acre Symphony Park. In what used to be the Union Pacific rail yards, the acreage has been transformed into a sophisticated three-theater performing arts center, outdoor concert venue, and public art gallery. Peripheral neighbors are the massive World Market Center and the Frank Gehry–designed Cleveland Clinic Lou Ruvo Center for Brain Health. Boutique hotels will join the assemblage in two years, as will several restaurants.

Transformative events on the ground aside, however, the main draw of the Fremont Street Experience is up in the air. Four blocks of Fremont Street are covered by a 1,400-foot-long, 90-foot-high "space frame"—an enormous, vaulted geodesic matrix. This futuristic structure totally canopies Fremont Street. In addition to providing nominal shade, the space frame serves as the stage for a nighttime attraction that has definitely improved Downtown's fortune. Set into the inner surface of the space frame are 12.5 million LEDs, which come to life in a computer-driven, multisensory show. The LEDs are augmented by 40 speakers on each block, booming symphonic sound in syncopation with the lights.

We at the *Unofficial Guide* enjoy and appreciate Downtown Las Vegas, and all of us hope that the Fremont Street Experience will continue to have a beneficial effect. We are amazed and appalled, however, by the city's general lack of commitment to improving its infrastructure, particularly the traffic situation. The market, in terms of aggregate number of gamblers, is undeniably located out on the Strip. To create an attraction sufficiently compelling to lure this market Downtown is to fight only half the battle. The other half of the battle is to make it easy for all those folks on the Strip to get Downtown.

A Caveat Concerning Noise

Both Downtown and on the Strip, street entertainment of various ilk can pose problems for people trying to sleep. On the Strip it's frantic traffic and erupting volcanoes, while Downtown it's a couple of outdoor concert stages plus the soundtrack of the Fremont Street Experience. The noise situation is more problematic Downtown because the hotels are not as tall and many guest room windows lack adequate soundproofing. The stage at the western end of Fremont Street in particular hosts rock bands that literally rattle the windows of the Plaza, Golden Gate, Las Vegas Club, and to a lesser extent the Golden Nugget. If you stay at any of these hotels and plan to be in the sack before 1 a.m., forgo the Fremont Street view and request a room in the back of the house.

If You Visit Las Vegas on Business

If you are going to Las Vegas for a trade show or convention, you will want to lodge as close as possible to the meeting site (ideally within easy walking distance) or, alternatively, near a monorail station. Many Strip hotel-casinos—including the Riviera, Flamingo, The Venetian, Wynn Las Vegas, Paris, Bellagio, Mandalay Bay, Planet Hollywood, Westgate Las Vegas (formerly the LVH), Aria, Encore, MGM Grand, TI, Tropicana, Mirage, Caesars Palace, Harrah's, and Bally's—host meetings from 100 to upward of 5,000 attendees, offer lodging for citywide shows and conventions held at the Las Vegas Convention Center and the Sands Expo and Convention Center, and have good track records with business travelers. Our maps should provide some assistance in determining which properties are situated near your meeting site.

Because most large meetings and trade shows are headquartered at the convention center or on the Strip, lodging on the Strip is more convenient than staying Downtown. Citywide conventions often provide shuttle service from the major hotels to the Las Vegas Convention Center, and, of course, cabs and the monorail are available too. Las Vegas traffic is a mess, however, particularly in the late afternoon, and there is a finite number of cabs.

LARGE HOTEL-CASINOS VERSUS SMALL HOTELS AND MOTELS

LODGING PROPERTIES IN LAS VEGAS range from tiny motels with a dozen rooms to colossal hotel-casino complexes of 5,000 rooms. As you might expect, there are advantages and drawbacks to staying in either a large or small hotel. Determining which size is better for you depends on how you plan to spend your time in Las Vegas.

If your leisure or business itinerary calls for a car and a lot of coming and going, the big hotels can be a real pain. At The Venetian, Excalibur, and MGM Grand, to name a few, it can take as long as 15 minutes to get from your room to your car if you use the self-parking lot. A young couple staying at the Westgate Las Vegas left their hotel room 40 minutes prior to their show reservations at the Mirage. After trooping to their van in the Westgate's distant self-parking lot, the couple discovered they had forgotten their show tickets. By the time the husband ran back to their room to retrieve the tickets and returned to the van, only 5 minutes remained to drive to the Mirage, park, and find the showroom. As it turned out, they missed the first 15 minutes of the performance.

If the hike to the self-park garage is onerous, you can always valet park. It's cheap ($2 tip when you pick up your car) and convenient, with most valet services located just a short walk from the guest elevators. But whether it saves you any time depends on when you retrieve your car. We've waited over 40 minutes to get our car during the morning when many guests are checking out and leaving the hotel. Valets are also inundated after performances in major showrooms conclude.

Many large hotels have multistory, self-parking garages that require lengthy and dizzying drives up and down ramps. If you plan to use the car frequently and do not want to deal with the hassle of remote parking lots, big garages, or the tipping associated with valet parking, we recommend staying in a smaller hotel or motel that provides quick and convenient access to your car.

Quiet and tranquility can also be reasons for choosing a smaller hotel. Many Las Vegas visitors object to passing through a casino whenever they go to or leave their room. Staying in a smaller property without a casino or a large nongaming property like the Trump Hotel Las Vegas permits an escape from the flashing lights, the never-ending noise of slot machines, and the unremitting, frenetic pace of an around-the-clock gambling town. While they may not be as exciting, smaller hotels tend to be more restful and homelike.

The ease and simplicity of checking in and out of smaller properties has its own appeal. To be able to check in or pay your bill without standing in a line, or to unload and load the car directly and conveniently, significantly diminishes the stress of arriving and departing. When we visited the registration lobby of one of the larger hotels on a Friday afternoon, for example, it reminded us of Kennedy International Airport shut down by a winter storm. Guests were stacked dozens deep in the check-in lines. Others, having abandoned any hope of registering in the near future, slept curled up around their luggage or sat reading on the floor. The whole lobby was awash in suitcases, hanging bags, and people milling about. Though hotel size and check-in efficiency are not always inversely related, the sight of a registration lobby fitted out like the queuing area of Disneyland's Jungle Cruise should be enough to make a sane person think twice. Along similar lines, a large hotel does not ensure more comfortable or more luxurious accommodations. In Las Vegas there are exceptionally posh and well-designed rooms in both large and small hotels, just as there are threadbare and poorly designed rooms in properties of every size. A large establishment does, however, usually ensure a superior range of amenities, including on-site entertainment, room service, spas or exercise rooms, concierge services, valet parking, meeting rooms, babysitting, shoe shining, dry cleaning, shopping, 24-hour restaurants, copy and fax services, check cashing, and, of course, gambling.

If you spill a cosmopolitan on your khakis, however, you may want to think twice before ponying up for the hotel-casino in-house laundry service. You'll pay by the piece, and you'll pay dearly. After a couple of days' laundry pile up on the bed, do like we do and take advantage of an area wash-and-fold service. Our favorite is

unofficial **TIP**
Try a local wash-and-fold service as an affordable alternative to expensive hotel-casino laundry services.

Wizard of Suds (4275 Arville St.), where the courteous staff will wash and fold your dirties for cheap. At $1.49 per pound (10-pound minimum), and with quick turnaround if you drop off before noon, you can't beat the Wizard; ☎ 702-873-1453.

If you plan to do most of your touring on foot or are attending a convention, a large hotel in a good location has advantages. There will be a variety of restaurants, entertainment, shopping, and recreation close at hand. If you are a night owl, you will be able to eat or drink at any hour, and there will always be lots going on. Many showrooms offer 11 p.m. or midnight shows, and quite a few hotels (Sam's Town, Suncoast, Gold Coast, The Orleans, South Point, Red Rock, Texas Station, Sunset Station, and Santa Fe Station) have 24-hour bowling. Almost as good, **Brooklyn Bowl** at the LINQ, the only bowling complex on the Strip, is open 11 a.m. to 2 a.m. Sunday through Thursday and 11 a.m. to 4 a.m. Friday and Saturday.

For visitors who wish to immerse themselves in the atmosphere of Las Vegas, to live in the fast lane, and to be where the action is, a large hotel is recommended. These people feel they are missing something unless they stay in a big hotel-casino. For them, it is important to know that the excitement is only an elevator ride away.

WHAT'S *in an* ADDRESS?

DOWNTOWN

THE HEART OF THE DOWNTOWN casino area is Fremont Street between 4th Street (on the east) and Main Street (on the west). Hotel-casinos situated along this quarter-mile four-block stretch known as Glitter Gulch include the Plaza Hotel, Golden Gate, Las Vegas Club, Binion's Gambling Hall, Golden Nugget, Fremont, Four Queens, and The

D Las Vegas. Parallel to Fremont and one block north is Ogden Avenue, where the California and Downtown Grand are located. Main Street Station is situated on Main Street at the intersection of Ogden Avenue.

All of the Downtown hotel-casinos are centrally positioned and convenient to the action, with the exception of the El Cortez, which sits three blocks to the east. While there is a tremendous difference in quality and price among the Downtown properties, the locations of all the hotels are excellent. When you stay Downtown, everything is within a 5-minute walk. By comparison, on the Strip it takes longer to walk from the entrance of Caesars Palace to the entrance of the Mirage, next door, than to cover the whole four blocks of the casino center Downtown.

THE STRIP

WHILE LOCATION IS NOT A MAJOR CONCERN when choosing from among the Downtown hotels, it is of paramount importance when selecting a hotel on the Strip.

unofficial **TIP**
If you stay on the Strip, you want to be somewhere in the Mandalay Bay–Stratosphere stretch. Even there, though, some sections are more desirable than others.

We once received a flier from a Las Vegas casino proclaiming that it was located "right on the Strip." It supported the claim with a photo showing its marquee and those of several other casinos in a neat row with their neon ablaze. What recipients of this advertisement (except those familiar with Las Vegas) never would have guessed was that the photo had been taken with a lens that eliminated all sense of distance. While the advertised casino appeared to be next door to the other casinos in the picture, it was in reality almost a mile away.

A common variation on the same pitch is "Stay Right on the Las Vegas Strip at Half the Price." Once again, the promoter is attempting to deceive by taking advantage of the recipient's ignorance of Strip geography. As it happens, the Las Vegas Strip (Las Vegas Boulevard South) starts southwest of the airport and runs all the way Downtown, a distance of about seven miles. Aside from the South Point Hotel some miles south of the airport, only the 4-mile section between Mandalay Bay and the Stratosphere contains the large casinos and other attractions of interest to visitors. South of Mandalay Bay "on the Strip" are the airport boundary, some small motels, discount shopping, and nice desert. North of the Stratosphere en route to Downtown, the Strip runs through a commercial area sprinkled with wedding chapels, fast-food joints, and small motels.

The Best Locations on the Strip

Beware of hotels and motels claiming to be on the Strip but not located between Mandalay Bay and the Stratosphere. Mandalay Bay basically anchors the south end of the Strip, about a quarter mile from the Luxor, its closest neighbor. Likewise, at the other end, the Stratosphere is somewhat isolated. In between are distinct clusters of hotels and casinos.

STRIP CLUSTER 1: THE CLUSTER OF THE GIANTS At the intersection of the Strip (Las Vegas Boulevard South) and Tropicana Avenue are five of the world's largest hotels. The MGM Grand Hotel is the second-largest hotel in the world. Diagonally across the intersection from the MGM Grand is the Excalibur, the ninth-largest hotel in the world. The other two corners of the intersection are occupied by New York–New York and the Tropicana. Nearby to the south are the Luxor (fifth largest) and Mandalay Bay, the Four Seasons, and the Delano (collectively sixth largest). To the north is the Monte Carlo on the Strip. Hooters is situated on Tropicana Avenue across from the MGM Grand. From the intersection of the Strip and Tropicana Avenue, it is a half-mile walk south to Mandalay Bay. The next cluster of major hotels and casinos is at the intersection of the Strip and Harmon Avenue less than a half mile north. Including all the hotels from Mandalay Bay to Monte Carlo, Strip Cluster 1 challenges the status, at least in terms of appeal and diversity, of Strip Cluster 3 at the heart of the Strip. Progress always has its dark side, however; here it is the phenomenal increase of traffic and congestion on East Tropicana Avenue as it nears the Strip.

STRIP CLUSTER 2 At Harmon Avenue and the Strip is MRI's CityCenter, a mammoth three-hotel lodging, dining, shopping, entertainment, and gaming complex with approximately 6,000 rooms and suites—it's truly a city within a city. Positioned at the northeast corner of CityCenter is the indie Cosmopolitan—a bi-towered, 2,995-suite glittering high-rise with full casino, 14 restaurants, three pools, a showroom, and much more. The Cosmo is the latest addition to Las Vegas's inventory of mid-to-high-end uber-resorts. Situated across the Strip from CityCenter and The Cosmo is Planet Hollywood, a hip hotel that targets younger Las Vegas visitors with its shows, nightlife, and restaurants. Elara, a Hilton Grand Vacation Club property, rubs shoulders with Planet Hollywood. Planet Hollywood is also attached to the Miracle Mile Shops, one of the major shopping venues on the Strip. Collectively, CityCenter, The Cosmopolitan, Elara, and Planet Hollywood compose the most exciting and avant-garde combination on the Strip.

STRIP CLUSTER 3: THE GRAND CLUSTER From Flamingo Road to Spring Mountain Road (also called Sands Avenue, and farther east, Twain Avenue) is the greatest numerical concentration of major hotels and casinos on the Strip. If you wish to stay on the Strip and prefer to walk wherever you go, this is the best location. At Flamingo Road and Las Vegas Boulevard are Bally's, Caesars Palace, The Cromwell, Paris, and Bellagio. Heading east on Flamingo Road is the Westin Casuarina. Toward town on the Strip are the Flamingo, O'Shea's, LINQ Hotel & Casino, Mirage, Harrah's, Casino Royale, The Venetian/Palazzo, and TI. Also in this cluster are the Forum Shops and the Grand Canal Shoppes, Las Vegas's most distinctive shopping venues. A leisure traveler could stay a week in this section (without ever getting in a car or cab) and not run out of interesting sights, restaurants, or entertainment. On the negative side, for those with cars, traffic congestion on the Strip and at the intersection of the Strip and Flamingo Road is the worst in the city.

Hotel Clusters

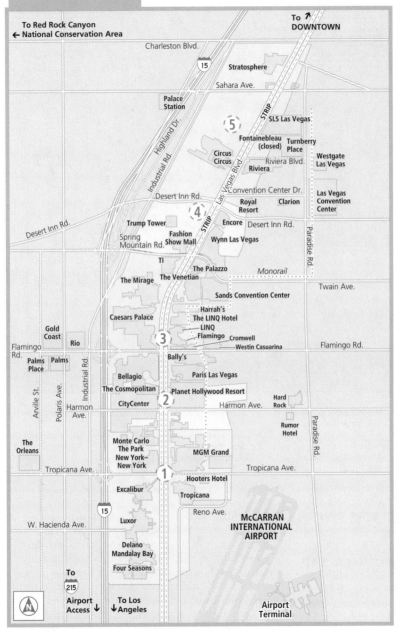

Downtown Accommodations

■ **ACCOMMODATIONS**

1. Binion's Gambling Hall*
2. California
3. The D
4. Downtown Grand
5. El Cortez
   * Only casino open

6. El Cortez Cabana Suites
7. Four Queens
8. Fremont
9. Golden Gate
10. Golden Nugget
11. Las Vegas Club*

12. Main Street Station
13. Plaza

STRIP CLUSTER 4 Another nice section of the Strip is from Spring Mountain Road up to Wynn Encore and Wynn Las Vegas. This cluster, pretty much in the center of the Strip, is distinguished by its easy access. Visitors who prefer a major hotel on the Strip but want to avoid daily traffic snarls could not ask for a more convenient location. Though Wynn Encore and Wynn Las Vegas are about a quarter mile from the nearest casino cluster in either direction, they are situated within a 10-minute walk of Fashion Show Mall, one of the most diversified upscale

unofficial **TIP**
Try Strip Cluster 4 for convenience and to escape traffic congestion.

South Strip Accommodations

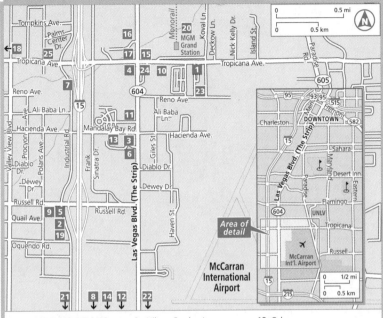

■ **ACCOMMODATIONS**

1. America's Best Value Inn
2. Courtyard by Marriott
Las Vegas South
3. Delano at Mandalay Bay
4. Excalibur
5. Fairfield Inn & Suites
Las Vegas South
6. Four Seasons at
Mandalay Bay
7. Hampton Inn Tropicana

8. Hilton Garden Inn
Las Vegas Strip South
9. Holiday Inn Express
10. Hooters Casino Hotel
11. Luxor
12. M Resort
13. Mandalay Bay
14. Manor Suites
15. MGM Grand
16. Monte Carlo
17. New York–New York

18. Orleans
19. Residence Inn by
Marriott Las Vegas
South
20. Signature at MGM Grand
21. Silverton
22. South Point
23. Travelodge Las Vegas
Airport North
24. Tropicana
25. Wild Wild West

shopping centers in the United States. There are also some very good restaurants here, both in the hotels and in the mall. Finally, this cluster is a 4-minute cab ride (or a 16-minute walk) from the Las Vegas Convention Center.

STRIP CLUSTER 5 The next cluster up the Strip is between Convention Center Drive and Riviera Boulevard. Arrayed along a stretch slightly more than a half mile long are the Riviera and Circus Circus with its Adventuredome theme park. Casinos and hotels in this cluster are considerably less upscale than those in the other clusters but offer acceptable selections for dining and entertainment, as well as proximity to the Las Vegas Convention Center. Finally, about a third of a mile toward

Mid-Strip Accommodations

■ **ACCOMMODATIONS**
1. Bally's
2. Bellagio
3. Caesars Palace
4. Casino Royale
5. CityCenter
6. The Cosmopolitan
7. The Cromwell

8. Elara
9. Flamingo
10. Gold Coast
11. Harrah's
12. LINQ Hotel & Casino
13. Mirage
14. The Palazzo
15. Palms

16. Paris
17. Planet Hollywood
18. Rio
19. TI
20. The Venetian
21. Westin Casuarina
22. Wynn Las Vegas and
     Wynn Encore

town from the intersection of Las Vegas Boulevard and Sahara Avenue are the Stratosphere and the SLS, on the site of the old Sahara. Though fairly isolated if you intend to walk, for visitors with cars or monorail riders the Stratosphere and SLS provide convenient access to the Strip, the convention center, and Downtown.

JUST OFF THE STRIP

IF YOU HAVE A CAR, and if being right on the Strip is not a big deal to you, there are some excellent hotel-casinos on Paradise Road and to the east and west of the Strip on intersecting roads. The Rio, Palms, and Gold Coast on Flamingo Road; Palace Station on Sahara Avenue; and The Orleans on Tropicana Avenue offer exceptional value. They are less than a half mile west of the Strip and are situated at access ramps to I-15, 5–10 minutes from Downtown. To the east of the Strip are the Hard Rock, Rumor, and Alexis Park on Harmon Avenue; the Tuscany, Silver Sevens, and the Platinum on Flamingo Road; and the Westgate Las Vegas on Paradise Road, among others.

North Strip Accommodations

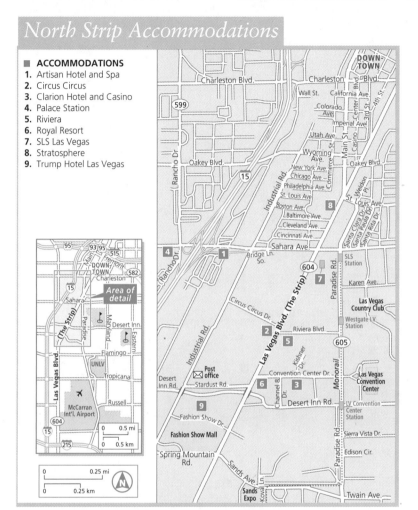

■ ACCOMMODATIONS
1. Artisan Hotel and Spa
2. Circus Circus
3. Clarion Hotel and Casino
4. Palace Station
5. Riviera
6. Royal Resort
7. SLS Las Vegas
8. Stratosphere
9. Trump Hotel Las Vegas

BOULDER HIGHWAY, GREEN VALLEY, SUMMERLIN, AND NORTH LAS VEGAS

TWENTY MINUTES FROM THE STRIP in North Las Vegas are Texas Station, Fiesta Rancho, the Cannery, Aliante Casino + Hotel, and, on the edge of civilization, Santa Fe Station. All have good restaurants, comfortable guest rooms, and lively, upbeat themes. Hotel-casinos on Boulder Highway southeast of town include Boulder Station, Sam's Town, Eastside Cannery, and Arizona Charlie's Boulder. Also to the southeast are Sunset Station, Fiesta Henderson, and Green Valley Ranch Resort and Spa. Like the North Las Vegas hotels, the Boulder Highway properties cater primarily to locals. West of town is the posh JW Marriott Las Vegas, with two

East of Strip Accommodations

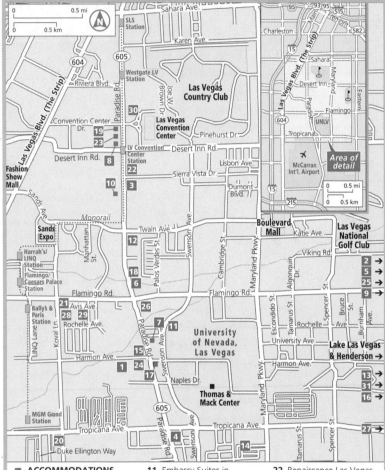

■ ACCOMMODATIONS

1. Alexis Park Resort and Villas
2. Arizona Charlie's Boulder
3. Best Western
   Mardi Gras Hotel
   and Casino
4. Best Western McCarran Inn
5. Boulder Station
6. Candlewood Suites
7. Comfort Inn Paradise Road
8. Courtyard by Marriott
9. Eastside Cannery
10. Embassy Suites Convention
    Center

11. Embassy Suites in
    Las Vegas
12. Fairfield Inn Las Vegas
    Airport
13. Fiesta Henderson
14. Green Valley Ranch
15. Hard Rock Hotel
16. Hilton at Lake Las Vegas
17. Hyatt Place
18. La Quinta Las Vegas
    Airport North
19. Las Vegas Marriott
20. Motel 6 Tropicana
21. Platinum Hotel

22. Renaissance Las Vegas
23. Residence Inn
24.   by Marriott LVCC
25. Rumor
    Sam's Town
26. Silver Sevens
27. Sunset Station
28. Super 8
29. Tuscany
30. Westgate Las Vegas
31. Westin Lake Las Vegas

upscale hotels and the Tournament Player's Club (TPC) at the Canyons Golf Course. Nearby are the Suncoast and the unique Red Rock Resort. Also northwest of the Strip is Arizona Charlie's Decatur.

GETTING AROUND:
Location and Convenience

LAS VEGAS LODGING CONVENIENCE CHART

THE CHART ON PAGES 52–54 will give you a feel for how convenient specific hotels and motels are to common Las Vegas destinations. Both walking and cab-commuting times are figured on the conservative side. You should be able to do a little better than the times indicated, particularly by cab, unless you are traveling during rush hour or attempting to navigate the Strip on a weekend evening.

Regarding the monorail, times listed include loading and unloading as well as the actual commuting time. The Strip monorail stations are located at the far rear of the host casinos, so, for example, the walk from the Strip entrance of the MGM Grand to the station is about 7–10 minutes. The MGM Grand station is the closest station to the Excalibur on the west side of the Strip. From your guest room at the Excalibur it will take about 20–25 minutes to walk to the MGM Grand station. In our experience, because of the walking required to reach the nearest monorail station from casinos on the Strip's west side, you might want to consider a cab if you're in a hurry. Always check traffic conditions before you hop in a cab. If the Strip is grid-locked (very common), head for the monorail.

Commuting to Downtown from the Strip

Commuting to Downtown from the Strip is a snap on I-15 during non–rush hours. From the Strip you can get on or off I-15 at Tropicana Avenue, Flamingo Road, Spring Mountain Road, or Sahara Avenue. Once on I-15 heading north, stay in the right lane and follow the signs for Downtown and US 95 South. Exiting onto Casino Center Boulevard, you will be in the middle of Downtown with several large parking garages conveniently at hand. Driving time to Downtown Las Vegas varies from about 16 minutes from the south end of the Strip (I-15 via Tropicana Avenue) to about 6 minutes from the north end (I-15 via Sahara Avenue). I-15, however, is totally overwhelmed during rush hour from 7 to 9 a.m. and 3:30 to 7 p.m. During these hours you're probably better off using surface streets.

Commuting to the Strip from Downtown

If you are heading to the Strip from Downtown, you can pick up US 95 North (and then I-15 South) by going north on either 4th Street

Continued on page 54

Commuting Times in Minutes

FROM	TO LAS VEGAS STRIP	TO CONVEN-TION CENTER	TO DOWNTOWN	TO McCARRAN AIRPORT	TO UNLV THOMAS & MACK CENTER
Alexis Park Resort and Villas	5/cab	8/cab	15/cab	5/cab	6/cab
Aliante Station	35/cab	40/cab	25/cab	47/cab	49/cab
Ambassador Strip Travelodge	3/cab	9/cab	15/cab	4/cab	6/cab
Arizona Charlie's Boulder	12/cab	18/cab	12/cab	20/cab	22/cab
Arizona Charlie's Decatur	19/cab	18/cab	12/cab	21/cab	20/cab
Artisan Hotel and Spa	5/walk	5/cab	14/cab	14/cab	14/cab
Atrium Suites	4/cab	6/cab	15/cab	6/cab	6/cab
Bally's	on Strip	8/mono	15/cab	7/cab	7/cab
Bellagio	on Strip	11/mono	15/cab	11/cab	12/cab
Best Western Mardi Gras Hotel and Casino	6/cab	10/walk	15/cab	9/cab	7/cab
Best Western McCarran Inn	6/cab	9/cab	15/cab	4/cab	7/cab
Binion's Gambling Hall	14/cab	15/cab	Downtown	19/cab	19/cab
Boulder Station	19/cab	18/cab	12/cab	21/cab	20/cab
Caesars Palace	on Strip	7/mono	12/cab	10/cab	10/cab
California	13/cab	15/cab	Downtown	19/cab	19/cab
Candlewood Suites	5/cab	6/cab	15/cab	6/cab	6/cab
Cannery	23/cab	26/cab	20/cab	30/cab	30/cab
Casino Royale	on Strip	7/mono	14/cab	10/cab	10/cab
Circus Circus	on Strip	5/cab	13/cab	14/cab	13/cab
CityCenter Hotels	on Strip	12/cab	14/cab	15/cab	11/cab
Clarion Hotel and Casino	7/walk	5/walk	14/cab	9/cab	11/cab
Comfort Inn Paradise Road	4/cab	5/cab	15/cab	10/cab	9/cab
The Cosmopolitan	on Strip	12/cab	14/cab	15/cab	11/cab
Courtyard Las Vegas South	4/cab	14/cab	15/cab	8/cab	12/cab
Courtyard Paradise Road	4/cab	5/walk	15/cab	9/cab	8/cab
The Cromwell	on Strip	7/mono	15/cab	8/cab	9/cab
The D Las Vegas	14/cab	15/cab	Downtown	17/cab	17/cab
Days Inn at Wild Wild West	3/cab	13/cab	14/cab	8/cab	11/cab
Delano Las Vegas	on Strip	14/cab	15/cab	7/cab	13/cab
Downtown Grand	14/cab	15/cab	4/walk	18/cab	17/cab
Eastside Cannery	20/cab	25/cab	30/cab	19/cab	18/cab
El Cortez	11/cab	15/cab	6/walk	16/cab	17/cab
El Cortez Cabana Suites	11/cab	15/cab	7/walk	16/cab	17/cab
Elara	on Strip	8/cab	15/cab	7/cab	8/cab
Ellis Island	4/cab	6/cab	14/cab	8/cab	8/cab
Embassy Suites Convention Ctr.	6/cab	10/walk	15/cab	9/cab	7/cab
Embassy Suites in Las Vegas	4/cab	6/cab	15/cab	6/cab	6/cab
Excalibur	on Strip	13/cab	14/cab	7/cab	8/cab
Fairfield Inn Las Vegas Airport	5/cab	5/cab	15/cab	9/cab	8/cab
Fairfield Inn and Suites Las Vegas South	4/cab	14/walk	15/cab	8/cab	12/cab
Fiesta Henderson	18/cab	17/cab	19/cab	17/cab	15/cab

Commuting Times in Minutes

FROM	TO LAS VEGAS STRIP	TO CONVENTION CENTER	TO DOWNTOWN	TO McCARRAN AIRPORT	TO UNLV THOMAS & MACK CENTER
Fiesta Rancho	18/cab	18/cab	10/cab	22/cab	22/cab
Flamingo	on Strip	7/mono	13/cab	8/cab	8/cab
Four Queens	15/cab	15/cab	Downtown	19/cab	17/cab
Four Seasons	on Strip	14/cab	15/cab	7/cab	13/cab
Fremont	15/cab	15/cab	Downtown	19/cab	17/cab
Gold Coast	4/cab	13/cab	14/cab	10/cab	10/cab
Golden Nugget	14/cab	15/cab	Downtown	18/cab	19/cab
Green Valley Ranch Resort and Spa	15/cab	18/cab	16/cab	15/cab	14/cab
Hampton Inn Tropicana	10/walk	6/cab	9/cab	10/cab	6/cab
Hard Rock Hotel	4/cab	6/cab	15/cab	6/cab	6/cab
Harrah's	on Strip	5/mono	15/cab	10/cab	10/cab
Hilton Garden Inn	13/cab	23/cab	26/cab	14/cab	21/cab
Hilton Lake Las Vegas	45/cab	49/cab	43/cab	37/cab	46/cab
Holiday Inn Express	4/cab	14/cab	15/cab	8/cab	12/cab
Hooters	5/walk	11/mono	15/cab	6/cab	8/cab
Hyatt Place	4/cab	7/walk	15/cab	10/cab	9/cab
JW Marriott Las Vegas	18/cab	21/cab	15/cab	23/cab	24/cab
La Quinta Las Vegas Airport	5/cab	6/cab	15/cab	6/cab	6/cab
Las Vegas Club	14/cab	15/cab	Downtown	19/cab	18/cab
Las Vegas Marriott Suites	14/cab	5/walk	15/cab	10/cab	9/cab
LINQ Hotel & Casino	on Strip	5/mono	15/cab	10/cab	10/cab
Luxor	on Strip	13/cab	15/cab	8/cab	10/cab
M Resort	20/cab	27/cab	30/cab	22/cab	27/cab
Main Street Station	14/cab	15/cab	Downtown	19/cab	19/cab
Mandalay Bay	on Strip	14/cab	16/cab	7/cab	13/cab
Manor Suites	10/cab	17/cab	20/cab	12/cab	17/cab
MGM Grand	on Strip	11/mono	15/cab	9/cab	9/cab
Mirage	on Strip	6/mono	15/cab	11/cab	10/cab
Monte Carlo	on Strip	11/mono	15/cab	11/cab	12/cab
Motel 6 Tropicana	3/cab	12/cab	15/cab	6/cab	8/cab
New York–New York	on Strip	11/mono	15/cab	11/cab	12/cab
The Orleans	4/cab	15/cab	14/cab	11/cab	11/cab
Palace Station	5/cab	10/cab	10/cab	14/cab	15/cab
The Palazzo	on Strip	6/mono	14/cab	8/cab	8/cab
Palms	5/cab	13/cab	14/cab	10/cab	10/cab
Paris	on Strip	9/mono	15/cab	8/cab	8/cab
Planet Hollywood	on Strip	8/cab	15/cab	7/cab	8/cab
Platinum Hotel	8/walk	5/cab	17/cab	7/cab	7/cab
Plaza Hotel	14/cab	15/cab	Downtown	19/cab	18/cab
Quality Inn Las Vegas	5/cab	13/cab	14/cab	10/cab	10/cab
Ramada Las Vegas	5/cab	5/cab	14/cab	8/cab	10/cab
Red Rock Resort	18/cab	21/cab	15/cab	23/cab	24/cab

Commuting Times in Minutes

FROM	TO LAS VEGAS STRIP	TO CONVEN- TION CENTER	TO DOWNTOWN	TO McCARRAN AIRPORT	TO UNLV THOMAS & MACK CENTER
Renaissance Las Vegas	5/cab	10/walk	14/cab	9/cab	8/cab
Residence Inn Convention Ctr.	4/cab	6/cab	15/cab	12/cab	12/cab
Residence Inn Las Vegas South	4/cab	14/cab	15/cab	8/cab	12/cab
Rio	5/cab	14/cab	13/cab	10/cab	10/cab
Riviera	on Strip	4/cab	14/cab	11/cab	10/cab
Royal House Resort	3/walk	5/cab	14/cab	13/cab	11/cab
Rumor	4/cab	6/cab	15/cab	6/cab	6/cab
Sam's Town	20/cab	25/cab	20/cab	18/cab	17/cab
Santa Fe Station	27/cab	30/cab	23/cab	33/cab	36/cab
Silver Sevens	5/cab	6/cab	15/cab	6/cab	6/cab
Silverton	10/cab	17/cab	20/cab	12/cab	17/cab
SLS Las Vegas	on Strip	6/mono	13/cab	13/cab	11/cab
South Point	16/cab	23/cab	26/cab	18/cab	23/cab
Stratosphere	3/cab	7/cab	9/cab	14/cab	14/cab
Suncoast	18/cab	21/cab	15/cab	23/cab	24/cab
Sunset Station	18/cab	17/cab	18/cab	16/cab	15/cab
Texas Station	17/cab	16/cab	13/cab	22/cab	22/cab
TI	on Strip	6/mono	14/cab	11/cab	10/cab
Tropicana	on Strip	11/mono	15/cab	6/cab	9/cab
Trump Hotel Las Vegas	10/walk	10/cab	11/cab	13/cab	11/cab
Tuscany	5/cab	5/cab	14/cab	8/cab	10/cab
The Venetian	on Strip	6/mono	14/cab	8/cab	8/cab
Westgate Las Vegas	5/mono	5/walk	13/cab	10/cab	8/cab
Westin Casuarina	4/walk	11/mono	15/cab	7/cab	7/cab
Westin Lake Las Vegas	45/cab	49/cab	43/cab	37/cab	46/cab
Wynn Encore	on Strip	8/cab	13/cab	10/cab	9/cab
Wynn Las Vegas	on Strip	8/cab	13/cab	10/cab	9/cab

Continued from page 51

or Las Vegas Boulevard. Driving time from Downtown to the Strip takes 10–20 minutes, depending on your destination.

Free Connections

Traffic on the Strip is so awful that the hotels, both individually and in groups, are creating new alternatives for getting around.

1. On the west side, a shuttle tram serves the Excalibur, Luxor, Mandalay Bay, Four Seasons, and the Delano.

2. Coast Casinos operates a shuttle connecting the Gold Coast, The Orleans, and Bally's.

3. M Resort provides shuttle service to and from the airport and Fashion Show Mall.

4. A tram connects the Spa Tower of the Bellagio to the Monte Carlo with an intermediate stop at Crystals shopping complex at CityCenter.

5. A tram connects TI and the Mirage, though the hike to the tram takes more time than to commute back and forth on the Strip.

6. The Palms has a shuttle that loops to the Forum Shops and Fashion Show Mall and then back to the Palms from 10 a.m. to 5 p.m.

7. Rampart Casino runs a shuttle to and from Fashion Show Mall.

8. Red Rock Resort provides shuttles to and from the airport and to Fashion Show Mall.

9. Sam's Town provides shuttles to the Strip and Downtown.

10. The Silverton provides shuttles to the airport and the Forum Shops.

11. There is a shuttle service between Harrah's and the Rio, and a similar service between Bally's and the Rio. Both run from 10 a.m. until 1 a.m. No luggage is allowed.

LAS VEGAS MONORAIL

THE LONG-AWAITED $650-MILLION Las Vegas Monorail began service in 2004 with nine trains running the 4-mile route between the MGM Grand and the SLS Las Vegas (formerly the Sahara). The route parallels the Strip between Tropicana and Sands Avenues and then cuts east

unofficial **TIP**
Because monorail stations are located at the extreme rear of the casinos served, you're better off walking to your destination if you are going less than a mile.

to the Las Vegas Convention Center and the Westgate Las Vegas (formerly LVH) before continuing to the last stop at the SLS. Trains run approximately every 10 minutes between 7 a.m. and midnight on Monday, until 2 a.m. Tuesday–Thursday, and until 3 a.m. on weekends. From one end of the line to the other takes about 15 minutes and includes seven stops. The fare for a single one-way ride is $5. A better deal is a one-day fare (24 hours from first use) at $14 or three-day unlimited travel fare for $30. Check the website for special rates; **lvmonorail.com.** The monorail is a godsend to convention and trade-show attendees commuting from Strip hotels to the Las Vegas Convention Center and the Sands Exposition Center; ☎ 702-699-8200.

BUSES

LAS VEGAS'S CITIZEN'S AREA TRANSIT (CAT) provides reliable bus service at reasonable rates. Although one-way fares along the Strip are $6 for the double-decker Deuce, one-way fares in residential areas are only $2. You can also purchase an all-day pass for the Strip for $8 and an all-day pass for residential areas for $5. The pass is good for 24 hours from the time of purchase. Children age 5 and under ride all routes free. All public transportation requires exact fare. All CAT buses are equipped with wheelchair lifts and bicycle racks, both of which are provided at no extra charge. Disabled persons who are certified in their home state for door-to-door service should call ☎ 702-676-1834 or 702-228-4800 for reservations. People who are not certified in their home state cannot get door-to-door service in Las Vegas. For general route and fare information or to request a schedule through the mail, call ☎ 702-228-7433 or visit **rtcsnv.com/transit.**

COMMONLY USED PUBLIC TRANSPORTATION ROUTES				
	ROUND-TRIP FROM/TO	HOURS OF OPERATION	FREQUENCY OF SERVICE	FARE
MONORAIL	MGM Grand/ SLS	Mon. 7 a.m.–midnight; Tues.–Th. 7 a.m.–2 a.m.; [3 a.m. weekends]	Every 5 minutes	$5
CITIZEN'S AREA TRANSIT DEUCE LINE	South Strip Transfer Terminals/ Downtown Transportation Center	24 hours	Every 12 minutes	$3

THE LIGHTS OF LAS VEGAS: TRAFFIC ON THE STRIP

DURING THE PAST DECADE, Las Vegas has experienced exponential growth—growth that unfortunately has not been matched with the development of necessary infrastructure. If you imagine a town designed for about 300,000 people being inundated by a million or so refugees (all with cars), you will have a sense of what's happening here.

The Strip, where a huge percentage of the local population works and where more than 80% of tourists and business travelers stay, has become a clogged artery in the heart of the city. The heaviest traffic on the Strip is between Tropicana Avenue and Spring Mountain Road, in the heart of the Strip. Throughout the day and night, local traffic combines with gawking tourists, shoppers, and cruising teenagers to create a 3-mile-long, bumper-to-bumper bottleneck.

When folks discuss the "lights of Las Vegas," it used to be that they were talking about the marquees of the casinos. Today, however, the reference is to the long, multifunctional traffic lights found at most every intersection on the Strip. These lights, which flash a different signal for every possible turn and direction, combine with an ever-increasing number of vehicles to ensure that nobody goes anywhere. The worst snarls occur at the intersection of the Strip and Flamingo Road. Trying to cross the Strip on perpendicular east-to-west-running roads is also exceedingly difficult. Desert Inn Road, which tunnels under the Strip, is the fastest way to get from one side to the other. Unfortunately, if you're heading west, Desert Inn Road is hard to access on the east side of the Strip, especially from Paradise Road. To use the tunnel from the east side, turn west on Desert Inn Road from Swenson Street.

Strip traffic is the Achilles heel of Las Vegas development and growth. It is sheer lunacy to believe you can plop a litter of megahotels on the Strip without compounding an already horrific traffic situation. While city government and the hospitality industry dance around the issue, traffic gets worse and worse. Approximately 48,000 hotel rooms were added along the Strip during the 1990s, about 30,000 more came online since the millennium, and another 10,000 or more are under construction or planned. The monorail along the east side of the Strip represents a great alternative to driving, but it has not noticeably mitigated gridlock. Also, stations are positioned so far to the rear of the casinos that walking is faster than taking the train for distances up to one mile. In another effort, I-15 between Downtown and the I-215 junction to the south has been widened and the interchanges improved. While welcome, the project has done little to alleviate traffic. Interestingly, the only initiative that has worked is the construction of elevated pedestrian bridges over the major Strip intersections. In addition to improving safety, the bridges remove pedestrians from the street, leaving the battlefield to vehicles.

Coping with Las Vegas Traffic

Even more challenging than beating the casinos in Las Vegas is beating the traffic. Las Vegas traffic is like health insurance costs in the United States. You just wonder how bad it has to get before anyone does anything about it. As it stands, there are not many good alternatives for getting around and lots of places you'll want to avoid.

We at the *Unofficial Guide* feel the impact directly when we conduct our research in Las Vegas. Where once we required about 5–20 minutes to go from one Strip hotel to another by car, we now allocate over an hour. If our destination is a mile or less away, we just walk.

When you plan your Las Vegas visit it's essential to get a handle on how much moving around will be necessary. The most stress-free trip is one where you can walk anywhere you need to go. Choose a hotel near the restaurants, shows, and attractions you wish to experience, or the venue for your business meeting or trade show. If you're attending a convention or trade show at the Las Vegas Convention Center, stay at a hotel within easy walking distance of the convention center, at one of the hotels on the east side of the Strip connected to the Las Vegas Monorail, or at a hotel such as Wynn Las Vegas or Wynn Encore that provides a free shuttle service. If you're thinking you can lodge on the west side of the Strip and walk across the street to catch the monorail, think again. The average time to walk from the main elevator bank of a west-side Strip hotel to an east-side monorail station is 30 minutes or more. It takes a comparable amount of time to walk from an east-side hotel that doesn't have a monorail station to one that does.

If you're like us and need to use a car, you're probably better off at one of the hotels on the west side of the Strip or alternatively one of the off-Strip properties. Either way, you'll need to study a map of Las Vegas and familiarize yourself with the road network surrounding the Strip. As we'll discuss, there are some roads to avoid and others that will make getting around easier. If your visit centers around the Strip, here are the ones that are most important:

LAS VEGAS BOULEVARD SOUTH—THE STRIP The worst part of the Strip is from Tropicana Avenue north to Spring Mountain Road (Twain Avenue). Avoid this section whenever possible. North of Spring Mountain Road traffic on Las Vegas Boulevard South flows pretty

North–South Roads to Know

Las Vegas Boulevard South—the Strip Connects the Strip to Downtown Las Vegas. Avoid between Tropicana Avenue and Spring Mountain Road.

I-15 Avoid between the I-15/I-215 interchange and Downtown.

Swenson Street (Joe W. Brown Drive) Best north–south alternative on the east side of the Strip. Runs from the airport to East Sahara Avenue.

Paradise Road Tends to clog between the Las Vegas Convention Center and Twain Avenue. Good north–south alternative south of Twain. Leads directly to the airport.

Koval Lane Avoid between Twain and Tropicana from 3–8:30 p.m.

Dean Martin Drive Best north–south alternative on the west side of the Strip.

Frank Sinatra Drive Parallels I-15 and the Strip and offers easy access to some hotels on the west side of the Strip.

South Main Street Low-traffic alternative for commuting Downtown from the Strip. Intersects Las Vegas Boulevard South at East St. Louis Avenue near the Stratosphere.

smoothly all the way to Downtown Las Vegas except for where it crosses Sahara Avenue.

I-15 The main north–south freeway, I-15 stays jammed from the I-215 interchange south of Las Vegas to the US 95 interchange near Downtown. Avoid this section between 7 and 10 a.m. and from 2:45 until 7:15 p.m. Even during non-rush periods, traffic moves at a crawl, but at least it moves. Between 8:30 p.m. and 6:30 a.m. is the least-congested period of the day. If you use I-15 during daylight hours, your best bet is to stay in the right lanes so you can bail at the next exit if necessary.

SOUTH DEAN MARTIN DRIVE AND FRANK SINATRA DRIVE The best alternate north–south route on the west side of the strip is South Dean Martin Drive, which becomes Industrial Road after it passes under the interstate highway to the east side of I-15 at West Twain Avenue. Dean Martin Drive/Industrial Road closely parallels the Strip and I-15 and is the best choice for accessing Circus Circus, Adventuredome, Trump Las Vegas, Fashion Show Mall, CityCenter and The Cosmopolitan (via Jerry Lewis Road and West Harmon Avenue), and Excalibur, Luxor, and Mandalay Bay (including Four Seasons and the Delano) via Aldebaran Avenue and West Hacienda Avenue. You can likewise easily access TI and the Mirage by taking Mel Torme Way east from Industrial Road, and Caesars Palace and the Forum Shops by taking Frank Sinatra Drive off Industrial Road to Jay Sarno Way. Dean Martin Drive/Industrial Road is also the best way to access east–west streets, including Sahara Avenue, Spring Mountain Road, Flamingo Road, and Tropicana Avenue. An easy route Downtown is Industrial Road north turning east (right) on Wyoming Road and then north again on South Main Street or Las Vegas Boulevard South. Frank Sinatra Drive can be accessed from I-15 northbound, West Russell Road, and Industrial Road. Running north–south directly behind hotels situated on the west side of the Strip, it provides easy access to self-parking at

East–West Roads to Know

Sahara Avenue Usually congested at the intersection with the Strip. Otherwise fine.

Desert Inn Road Tunnels under the Strip. Best road for commuting to the west side from the east side and vice versa.

Twain Avenue (Spring Mountain Road) Crosses the Strip at one of the more efficient intersections.

Harmon Avenue Currently T-intersects the Strip and doglegs into CityCenter and then crosses over I-15 to the west side.

Flamingo Road Extreme congestion westbound at the intersection with the Strip. Avoid.

Tropicana Avenue Flows well except westbound at the intersection with the Strip.

I-215 Westbound, avoid the I-15 North exit.

Mandalay Bay/Delano Las Vegas, Luxor, Excalibur, Monte Carlo, Caesars, and Fashion Show Mall. It does not provide public access to New York–New York, CityCenter, Crystals (mall), The Cosmopolitan, or Bellagio. Frank Sinatra Drive is a main thoroughfare for Strip hotel employees to access employee parking lots and becomes very congested between 7:30–9:30 a.m. and 2:30–5:30 p.m., when hotel shift changes occur.

SWENSON STREET On the east side of the Strip the traffic situation is more complex. Although a half mile or more from the Strip, Swenson Street is the most free-flowing north–south traffic artery east of the Strip. Swenson runs from I-215 and the airport all the way north to East Sahara Avenue (the name changes to Joe W. Brown Drive after crossing Desert Inn Road). If you're driving north you can take Swenson for its full length. Going south you'll be diverted to Paradise Road, a block to the west, as Swenson becomes one-way northbound between the airport and Harmon Avenue and Paradise Road becomes one-way southbound from Harmon to the airport.

KOVAL LANE Slightly to the west and running parallel to Swenson Street and Paradise Road is Koval Lane, once a favorite for dodging Strip traffic. Now Koval is gridlocked except during non-rush periods. This is unfortunate given that Koval Lane links roads providing rear access to the parking garages of the MGM Grand, Flamingo, LINQ Hotel & Casino, Harrah's, and the Venetian. Smaller streets joining Koval to the garages remain largely free of congestion, but on Koval you're likely to become gridlocked on the section from Tropicana Avenue north to Twain Avenue. Afternoons from 3 to about 8:30 p.m., Koval is especially bad. During this period, your best bet for reaching the valet or self-parking area of the hotels mentioned above is to access Harmon Avenue westbound from Swenson or Paradise, cross Koval, and then turn right on LINQ Lane. Coming out of the garages onto LINQ will frequently land you in some congestion at the LINQ–Harmon intersection, but suffering three cycles of the traffic signal is about as bad as it gets. Finally, adding to the

Self-Parking

HOTELS ON THE EAST SIDE OF THE STRIP *(from north to south)*

RIVIERA Use self-parking garage off Paradise Road.

WYNN ENCORE Use self-parking garage off the Strip. You can access the hotel elevators, casino, and showrooms from self-parking faster than by using the valet service.

WYNN LAS VEGAS Use self-parking garage off the Strip. Once again, you can access the hotel elevators, casino, and showrooms from self-parking faster than by using the valet service.

THE VENETIAN/PALAZZO Very confusing self-parking garage. There is rear access from Koval Lane or front access from the Strip. Both are subject to considerable congestion. Park at Wynn Las Vegas or Fashion Show Mall and walk to The Venetian or use valet parking.

HARRAH'S Straightforward garage. To access it drive west on Harmon Avenue, then right on LINQ Lane and left on Winnick Avenue.

THE LINQ Somewhat confusing but linear. To access it drive west on Harmon Avenue, then right on LINQ Lane and left on Winnick Avenue.

FLAMINGO Confusing garage layout. Park at Harrah's and walk to the Flamingo.

THE CROMWELL Self-parking garage off Flamingo Road. Hard to access because traffic waiting for the light at Flamingo and the Strip blocks the entrance.

BALLY'S Drive east on Harmon Avenue and then left on LINQ Lane to the garage.

PARIS Drive east on Harmon Avenue and then left on LINQ Lane to the garage.

PLANET HOLLYWOOD Very confusing garage accessible from Harmon Avenue. After parking you must walk through the Miracle Mile Shops to reach the hotel.

MGM GRAND Parking is accessible via Tropicana Avenue westbound or off Koval Lane. Very difficult to exit onto Koval Lane. To exit go north on LINQ Lane out of the garage and take the first left (west) to the Strip.

TROPICANA Go west on Tropicana Avenue, then left on Koval Lane and right on Reno Avenue. Large outdoor parking lot plus parking garage. Easy access by foot to Excalibur, MGM Grand, and New York–New York.

congestion, the LINQ entertainment and shopping complex has its own parking lot accessible from Koval between Flamingo and Twain.

THE TUNNEL An extension of Paradise Road tunnels under the airport runways and connects to I-215 and beyond to the rental-car return center. The approach to the tunnel gets really jammed between 2:45 and 6:30 p.m., so if you're returning a rental car during those hours give yourself extra time. An alternative, particularly if you're coming from west of the Strip, is to take Dean Martin Drive to Warm Springs Road. Turn east (left) on Warm Springs, cross I-15, and proceed four big blocks to Gilespie Street. Go left at Gilespie to the rental car center. If you're coming west from Green Valley or Henderson on I-215, transiting the tunnel northbound to Swenson Street is a better way to reach Strip destinations than continuing to I-15 northbound.

Parking

VALET PARKING All Strip hotels offer both valet and self-parking. There is no charge to use valet parking beyond a $2 or so tip when you retrieve your car. Many hotels, including Mandalay Bay, The Cosmopolitan, and Caesars Palace, provide valet service at both the front and rear entrances. As a general rule, the hotel's main entrance will be busier than the rear

Self-Parking

HOTELS ON THE WEST SIDE OF THE STRIP *(from north to south)*

CIRCUS CIRCUS Large outdoor lot and garages accessible from Industrial Road.

FASHION SHOW MALL Garage near the Strip is an excellent place to park if you're going to Wynn Las Vegas, The Palazzo, The Venetian, or TI. Enter from Spring Mountain Road or West Fashion Show Drive. Work your way to the southeast corner of the garage near the Neiman Marcus valet entrance. Along the wall that borders the Strip, look for a green, grassy area and stairs leading up to the Strip.

TI Very straightforward garage—among the most convenient on the Strip. Best access is via Spring Mountain Road.

MIRAGE Access also off Spring Mountain Road. It's a little convoluted, but just follow the signs.

FORUM SHOPS From Industrial Road go south on Frank Sinatra Drive and then turn left on Jay Sarno Way.

CAESARS PALACE From Industrial Road go south on Frank Sinatra Drive and then turn left on Jay Sarno Way.

BELLAGIO The only way to access the Bellagio is via the Strip. Valet service is good here, though. Just don't get caught when half the audience from Cirque du Soleil's "O" suddenly appears at the valet claim desk.

CITYCENTER AND THE COSMOPOLITAN From Dean Martin Drive turn west on Jerry Lewis Way, then left on West Harmon. Don't be surprised if they rename this section of West Harmon CityCenter Drive or some such.

MONTE CARLO Take Frank Sinatra Drive to Rue de Monte Carlo.

EXCALIBUR Excalibur has some of the most distant, far-flung parking of any hotel in Las Vegas. The closest parking is off East Reno Avenue or in the south end of the parking garage at Luxor Drive and East Reno. Luxor Drive is accessible via Dean Martin Drive, then west on Aldebaran Avenue, then right (east) on West Hacienda Avenue (West Mandalay Bay Drive), and finally left on Luxor Drive.

LUXOR This is one of our favorite parking garages. Park on the top level. Take Dean Martin Drive, then go west on Aldebaran Avenue, then right (east) on West Hacienda Avenue (West Mandalay Bay Drive), and finally left on Luxor Drive.

MANDALAY BAY Take Dean Martin Drive, then go west on Aldebaran Avenue, then right (east) on West Hacienda Avenue (West Mandalay Bay Drive), and finally right on Luxor Drive.

entrance. The problem with main-entrance valet service is that you will probably exit onto the traffic of the Strip. With rear-entrance valet you usually have the option to exit onto a side street. Though most valet services are pretty efficient, they do get swamped from time to time, such as when a show or concert has just concluded.

SELF-PARKING With the exception of the Bellagio and New York–New York, self-parking is easier at the hotels on the west side of the Strip. At any parking garage, don't park until you have located the garage entrance to the casino or the elevators leading to it. This can be tricky because some elevators deliver you to a walkway or sidewalk on the ground level quite removed from the casino. Staying oriented in such large garages is challenging, but what you want to do is park as close as possible to the most direct entrance to the hotel or casino. There are always elevators, so it doesn't really matter on which level you park as long as you're near the casino entrance or the elevators that descend to it. Our experience is that close-in parking spots are most readily available on the second to highest level. If a garage has five levels, for example, you're more likely to find available close-in spots on level four than on the other levels. Some of the garages are huge, so always jot down the level and row where you've parked. We should note that all of the hotels listed in the self-parking chart on pages 60–61 have Strip parking and valet entrances except Monte Carlo, New York–New York, MGM Grand, Bally's, and The Cromwell. The objective of this chart is to help you avoid Strip traffic by accessing the hotels (where possible) from other streets.

SELF-PARKING DOWNTOWN In Downtown Las Vegas we always park at Binion's garage on Casino Center Drive between Stewart and Ogden Avenues. It's centrally located and rarely crowded. It's also free if you have your ticket punched at the cashier's cage in Binion's.

ROOM RESERVATIONS:
Getting a Good Room, Getting a Good Deal

FOR DECADES LAS VEGAS had the highest room-occupancy rates in the United States, averaging 98% on weekends and 92% during the week. However, the downturn in the economy and the addition of a glut of new rooms to the city's room inventory have conspired to create a buyer's market. Some of the newly available rooms come from condo projects that were originally designed to be residences. With supply up and demand down, even the most prestigious properties continue to discount. Upscale hotels are faring better than moderate and value hotels because their clientele is more well-heeled and less price sensitive. But make no mistake, the recovery may be too slow for a number of properties.

As 2014 wore on, occupancy rates improved, but much of the increase was largely attributable to bargain room rates, though rates overall were the highest they've been since 2007. People were in beds, but they were not spending as much on dining or gambling. The city, however, can go from empty to full overnight as a consequence of a large convention or major sporting event. In general, we expect the deals to be around for a while, but you still need to scope out your specific dates.

THE WACKY WORLD OF LAS VEGAS HOTEL RESERVATIONS

THOUGH THERE ARE ALMOST 150,000 hotel rooms in Las Vegas, getting one is not always a simple proposition. In the large hotel-casinos, there are often five or more separate departments that have responsibility for room allocation and sales. Of the total number of rooms in any given hotel, a number are at the disposal of the casino; some are administered by central reservations or the front desk; some are allocated to independent wholesalers for group and individual travel packages; others are blocked for special events (fights, Super Bowl weekend, and the like); and still others are at the disposal of the sales and marketing department for meetings, conventions, wedding parties, and other special groups. Hotels that are part of a large chain (Holiday Inn and such) have some additional rooms administered by their national reservations systems.

At most hotels, department heads meet regularly to review all the room allocations. If rooms blocked for a special event, say a golf tournament, are not selling, some of those rooms will be redistributed to other departments. Since special events and large conventions are scheduled far in advance, the decision-makers have significant lead time. In most hotels, a major reallocation of rooms takes place 40–50 days before the dates for which the rooms are blocked, with minor reallocations made right up to the event in question.

If you call the reservations number at the hotel of your choice and are informed that no rooms are available for the dates that you've requested, it does not mean the hotel is sold out. What it does mean is that central reservations has no more rooms remaining in their allocation. It is a fairly safe assumption that all the rooms in a hotel have not been reserved by guests. The casino will usually hold back some rooms for high rollers, the sales department may have some rooms reserved for participants in deals they are negotiating, and some rooms will be in the hands of tour wholesalers or blocked for a citywide convention. If any of these remaining rooms are not committed by a certain date, they will be reallocated. So a second call to central reservations may get you the room that was unavailable when you called two weeks earlier.

THE INTERNET REVOLUTION

PURCHASING TRAVEL ON THE INTERNET has revolutionized the way both consumers and hotels do business. For you it makes shopping for a hotel and finding good deals much easier. For the hotel it makes possible a system of room inventory management often referred to as dynamic pricing or "nudging." Here's how it works. Many months in advance, hotels establish rates for each day of the coming year. In developing their rate calendar, they take into consideration all of the variables that affect occupancy in their hotel as well as in Las Vegas in general. They consider weekend versus weekday demand; additional demand stimulated by holidays, major conventions, trade shows, and sporting events; and the effect of the four seasons of the year on occupancy.

After rates for each date are determined, the rates are entered into the hotel's reservation system. Then hotel management sits back to see what happens. If the bookings for a particular date are in accord with management's expectations, no rate change is necessary. If demand is greater than management's forecast for a given date, they might raise the rate to take advantage of higher than expected bookings. If demand eases off, the hotel can revert back to the original rate.

If demand is less than expected, the hotel will begin nudging, that is, incrementally decreasing the rate for the day or days in question until booking volume increases to the desired level. Though this sort of rate manipulation has been an integral part of room inventory management for decades, the Internet has made it possible to rethink and alter room rates almost at will. A hotel can theoretically adjust rates hourly on its own website. Major Internet travel sellers (also called Online Travel Agencies or OTAs), such as Travelocity, Hotels.com, and Expedia, among others, are fast and agile and quite capable of getting a special deal (that is, a lower rate) in front of travel purchasers almost instantaneously. For the hotel, this means they can manage their inventory on almost a weekly or daily basis, nudging toward full occupancy by adjusting their rates according to demand. Of course, the hotels don't depend entirely on the Internet. Lower rates and various special deals are also communicated by e-mail to preferred travel agents, and sometimes directly to consumers (especially players-club members) via e-mail, print advertisements, or direct-mail promotions.

GETTING THE BEST DEAL ON A ROOM

COMPARED TO HOTEL RATES in other destinations, lodging in Las Vegas is so relatively inexpensive that the following cost-cutting strategies may seem gratuitous. Yes, there are $500-per-night rooms, but if you are accustomed to paying $130 a night for a hotel room, you can afford 80% or more of the hotels in town. You may not be inclined to wade through all the options listed below to save $20 or $30 a night. If, on the other hand, you would like to obtain top value for your dollar, read on.

	ROOM RATES AND PACKAGES	SOLD OR ADMINISTERED BY
1.	Gambler's rate	Casino or hotel
2.	December, January, and summer specials	Hotel room reservations or marketing department
3.	Internet discounts	Internet travel vendors
4.	Wholesaler packages	Independent wholesalers
5.	Tour-operator packages	Tour operators
6.	Reservation-service discounts	Independent wholesalers and consolidators
7.	Corporate rate	Hotel room reservations
8.	Hotel standard-room rate	Hotel room reservations
9.	Convention rate	Convention sponsor

Sorting Out the Sellers and the Options

To book a room in a particular hotel for any given date, there are so many different in-house departments as well as outside tour operators and wholesalers selling rooms, that it is almost impossible to find out who is offering the best deal. This is not because the various deals are so hard to compare but because it is so difficult to identify all the sellers.

Though it is only a rough approximation, see the chart above for a list of the types of rates and packages available, ranked from the best to the worst value.

The room-rate ranking is subject to some interpretation. A gambler's rate may, at first glance, seem to be the least expensive lodging option available, next to a complimentary room. If, however, the amount of money a guest is obligated to wager (and potentially lose) is factored in, the gambler's rate might be by far the most expensive.

Complimentary and Discounted Rooms for Gamblers

Most Las Vegas visitors are at least peripherally aware that casinos provide complimentary or greatly discounted rooms to gamblers. It is not unusual, therefore, for a business traveler, a low-stakes gambler, or a non-gambling tourist to attempt to take advantage of these deals. What they quickly discover is that the casino has very definite expectations of any guest whose stay is wholly or partially subsidized by the house. If you want a gambler's discount on a room, they will ask what game(s) you intend to play, the amount of your average bet, how many hours a day you usually gamble, where (at which casinos) you have played before, and how much gambling money you will have available on this trip. They may also request that you make an application for credit or provide personal information about your occupation, income, and bank account.

If you manage to bluff your way into a comp or discounted room, you can bet that your gambling (or lack thereof) will be closely monitored after you arrive. If you fail to give the casino an acceptable amount of action, you will probably be charged the nondiscounted room rate when you check out.

Even for those who expect to do a fair amount of gambling, a comp or discounted room can be a mixed blessing. By accepting the casino's hospitality, you incur a certain obligation (the more they give you, the bigger the obligation). You will be expected to do most (if not all) of your gambling in the casino where you are staying, and you will also be expected to play a certain number of hours each day. If this was your intention all along, great. On the other hand, if you thought you would like to try several casinos or take a day and run over to Hoover Dam, you may be painting yourself into a corner.

Taking Advantage of Special Deals

When you call, always ask the reservationist if the hotel has any package deals or specials. If you plan to gamble, be sure to ask about gaming specials. If you do not anticipate gambling enough to qualify for a gambling package, ask about other types of deals. On the Internet, always check the hotel's website. It's also helpful to Google the name of the hotel and the word "promotion." This sometimes turns up deals on dining and entertainment as well as room rates.

Hotels generally offer their best deals to gamblers, so the smart thing is to get yourself categorized as a gambler on their snail-mail and email lists by enrolling in the casinos' players clubs. In the past you had to sign up in person at the casino. Now, you can join the clubs of the casinos listed on the next page online. Unfortunately, for those not listed, you still have to join in person. You're absolutely under no obligation to bet a nickel, but you'll rack in all the good deal notifications nonetheless.

PLAYERS CLUBS THAT ACCEPT ONLINE REGISTRATION
• Aria• Bally's • Bellagio • Caesars Palace • California
• The Cosmopolitan • The Cromwell • Downtown Grand • El Cortez
• Excalibur • Flamingo • Fremont • Gold Coast • Golden Gate
• Golden Nugget • Hard Rock • Harrah's • Hooters
• LINQ Hotel & Casino • Luxor • Main Street Station • Mandalay Bay
• MGM Grand • Mirage • New York–New York • The Orleans • Palazzo
• Palms • Paris • Planet Hollywood • Plaza • Rampart • Rio • Riviera
• Sam's Town • SLS • South Point • Suncoast • TI
• Tropicana • Venetian • Westgate LV • Wynn • Wynn Encore

Being a member of a hotel's players club can also come in handy when rooms are scarce. Once, trying to book a room, we were told the hotel was sold out. When we mentioned that we had a players card, the reservationist miraculously found us a room. If you are a players-club member, it is often better to phone the club-member services desk instead of the hotel-reservations desk.

If you don't see a hotel listed above that you're interested in, check its website for a "Sign our guestbook" feature or some equivalent. This, at a minimum, will get you on the hotel's email list to receive news and offers of various kinds.

As far as rooms go, it's rare in our experience to find a deal on the hotel's website that's better than the ones they quote you on the phone. A reservationist on the phone knows she has a good prospect on the line and will work with you within the limits of her authority. On the web there's no give or negotiation: it's a take-it-or-leave-it deal. Finally, many hotels, including many of the new super-properties, really haven't learned how to merchandise rooms through their website.

Having shopped the hotel for deals, start checking out Las Vegas vacation or weekend packages advertised in your local newspaper, and compare what you find with packages offered in the Sunday edition of the *Los Angeles Times*.

Timing Is Everything

Timing is everything when booking a guest room in Las Vegas. If a particular hotel has only a few rooms to sell for a specific date, it will often, as we discussed earlier, bounce up the rate for those rooms as high as it thinks the market will bear. Conversely, if the hotel has many rooms available for a certain date, it will lower the rate accordingly. The practice remains operative all year, although the likelihood of hotels having a lot of rooms available is obviously greater during off-peak periods. As an example, we checked rates at an upscale nongaming hotel during two weeks in October. Depending on the specific dates, the rate for the suite in question ranged from $75 (an incredible bargain) to $240 (significantly overpriced) per night.

Which day of the week you check in can also save or cost you some money. At some hotels a standard room runs 20% less if you check in on a Monday through Thursday (even though you may stay through the weekend). If you check into the same room on a weekend, your rate will be higher and may not change if you keep your room into the following week. A more common practice is for the hotel to charge a lower rate during the week and a higher rate on the weekend.

NO ROOM AT THE INN (FOR REAL)   More frequently than you would imagine, Las Vegas hotels overbook their rooms. This happens when guests do not check out on time, when important casino customers arrive on short notice, and when the various departments handling room allocations get their signals crossed. When this occurs, guests who arrive holding reservations are told that their reservations have been canceled.

To protect yourself, always guarantee your first night with a major credit card (even if you do not plan to arrive late) and insist on a written confirmation of your reservation. When you arrive and check in, have your written confirmation handy.

Precautions notwithstanding, the hotel still might have canceled your reservation. When a hotel is overbooked, it will take care of its serious gambling customers first, its prospective gambling customers (leisure travelers) second, and business travelers last. If you are told that you have no room, demand that the hotel honor your reservation by finding you a room or by securing you a room at another hotel of comparable or better quality at the same rate. Should the desk clerk balk at doing this, demand to see the reservations manager. If the reservations manager stonewalls, go to the hotel's general manager. Whatever you do, don't leave until the issue has been resolved to your satisfaction.

Hotels understand their obligation to honor a confirmed reservation, but they often fail to take responsibility unless you hold their feet to the fire. We have seen convention-goers, stunned by the news that they have no room, simply turn around and walk out. Wrong. The hotel owns the problem, not you. You should not have to shop for another room.

HOW TO GET THE BEST DEAL ON THE INTERNET

THE INTERNET, UNMATCHED IN TERMS OF efficient and timely distribution of information, has become the primary resource for travelers seeking to shop for and book their own air, hotels, rental cars, entertainment, and travel packages. It's by far the best direct-to-consumer distribution channel in history.

The evolution of selling travel on the web has radically altered the way travel product producers such as airlines, hotels, cruise lines, and rental-car companies do business. Before the Internet, companies depended on travel agents or direct contact with customers via telephone. Transaction costs were high because the producers were obligated to pay commissions and fund labor-intensive in-house reservations departments.

With the advent of the Internet, inexpensive e-commerce transactions became possible. Airlines and rental-car companies were able to effectively cut travel agents out of the sales process and off-load the bulk of their booking activity to their own websites. Hotels followed suit with their own websites but also continued to sell to wholesalers and through travel agents.

It didn't take long before independent websites appeared that sold travel products from a wide assortment of travel suppliers, often at deep discounts. These sites, called Online Travel Agents or OTAs, include such familiar names as **Travelocity, Orbitz, Priceline, Expedia, Hotels.com,** and **Hotwire.** Those mentioned and others like them attract huge numbers of customers shopping for hotels.

In the beginning hotels paid the OTAs about the same commission as they paid travel agents, but then the OTAs began applying the thumbscrews, transitioning hotels from a simple commission model to what's called a merchant model. Under this model hotels provide an OTA with a deeply discounted room rate, which the OTA then marks up and sells. The difference between the marked-up price and the discounted rate provided by the hotel is the OTA's gross profit.

The merchant model, originally devised for wholesalers and tour operators, has been around since long before the Internet. Wholesalers and tour operators, then and now, must commit to a certain volume of business, commit to guaranteed room allotments, pay deposits, and bundle the discounted rates with other travel services so that the actual hotel rate remains hidden within the bundle. The merchant model costs the hotel 2–2.5 times the normal travel agent commission, considered justifiable because the wholesalers and tour operators also promote the hotel though brochures, trade shows, print ads, and events.

OTAs, in contrast, demand the equivalent of a wholesale commission and higher but are not subject to any of the requirements imposed on wholesalers and tour operators. The OTAs don't have to commit to a specified volume of sales or keep discounted rates opaque. Hotels give up 20–50% of gross profit and are rewarded by having their rock-bottom rates plastered all over the Internet with corresponding damage to their image and brand. The cost of a direct multiday booking on the hotel's own website is $10–$12, including website hosting, marketing costs, website analytics, and management fees. This is several times cheaper than the same booking through an OTA.

By way of example, an OTA might demand a 30% discount off the hotel's best available published rate. So if the hotel is offering rooms at $100, the rate to the OTA would be $70 ($100 less 30% = $70). The OTA then marks up the rate and posts it on its site. The OTA might sell the room for $100, the same rate advertised on the hotel's site, or it might undercut the hotel by offering the room for $95 or less. When the OTA sells the room it pays the hotel $70 and pockets whatever the mark-up is. As you can see, the hotel makes $100 if it sells the room itself but only $70 for the same room if it's sold by an OTA. For the hotel, doing business with OTAs is very expensive.

In the hotel industry, occupancy rates are important, but simply getting people in beds doesn't guarantee a profitable operation. A more critical metric is revenue per available room, or RevPAR. For a hotel full of guests who booked through an OTA, RevPAR will be 20%–50% lower than a full house of guests who booked the hotel directly (either via the hotel's website or by phone).

It's no wonder then that hotels and OTAs have a love-hate relationship. Likewise, it's perfectly understandable that it's a priority for hotels to increase direct bookings through their website and minimize OTA bookings. Current economic conditions occasioned by the recent recession, coupled in Las Vegas with a glut of rooms exceeding demand, makes this strategy difficult.

The problem is that the better-known OTAs draw a lot more website traffic than the hotel's (or even the hotel chain's) website. So the challenge for the hotel becomes how to shift room shoppers away from the OTAs and channel them to the hotel's website.

The Silver Bullet

For years we've been looking for a fast, easy way to help you find the best hotel rates in Las Vegas. Search engines such as **kayak.com** are helpful. They search large numbers of OTAs to determine which OTA has the best price for a particular hotel on a given night. Problem is, the rates that come up might not approximate the lowest obtainable, and in any event are subject to vagaries in demand the shopper might not be aware of such as conventions and sporting events.

Enter the *Las Vegas Advisor,* the newsletter and gambling book publisher that has been providing subscribers with no-nonsense consumer information and tips on Las Vegas for years. Their publications are candid, straightforward, and pull no punches. Simply put, they can be trusted to put their readers first (also a primary objective of the *Unofficial Guides*).

Like the *Las Vegas Advisor* newsletter, its **lvahotels.com** website is the most objective source of information on Las Vegas available on the Internet and is the preferred site for frequent Las Vegas visitors and especially gamblers. Assessing the needs of its readership and the needs of hotels, the *Advisor* developed an elegant win-win solution that would secure its readers the best room rates and at the same time provide hoteliers a powerful incentive to offer the best possible rates.

Here's how it works. Participating hotels provide the *Advisor* with truly exceptional deals on rooms and other services, which the *Advisor* lists on its website. Each deal has a code number. When you click on a specific deal you're routed to the hotel's website for additional information and booking. The hotel pays the *Advisor* a small commission for sending the booking its way, but only a fraction of what it would sacrifice in gross profit if the room were sold through an OTA.

The hotel's incentive for giving the *Advisor* the best deals available are as follows:

1. Bookings are made directly with the hotel, thus increasing both occupancy and RevPAR.

2. The *Advisor* website is a high-traffic site, visited exclusively (unlike OTA sites) by persons specifically interested in Las Vegas.

3. The *Advisor* has a longstanding record of objective consumer reporting and analysis, so the hotel knows its deals will be regarded as legitimate and trustworthy.

4. A large percentage of the *Advisor*'s visitors and readers are gamblers, the most desirable customer for any hotel with a casino.

5. The *Advisor* program is what's called a "disintermediary" model, a fancy name for cutting out the middlemen (intermediaries) in the channels of distribution.

To check out the deals go to **lvahotels.com.** On the home page click "LVA Hotel Deals" on the left side of the page. All of the hotels offering special rates will appear. You'll notice that a number of the deals listed include extras like resort credit, meals, entertainment, or other sweeteners in addition to the room. If you find a special that sounds good, an additional click will link to the hotel's website for additional information and booking.

At the insistence of the hotels, some of the best discounts are not listed on the website but can be accessed by signing up for the LVA Gold Membership. This costs nothing and can be accomplished quickly online without divulging any sensitive personal information. Special deals not available on the website are e-mailed to LVA Gold Members weekly. What's going on here is some legal and semantic hair-splitting. If a deal is listed on the *Advisor* site, it's regarded as "published" or public. Hotels have some restrictions concerning published deals. On the other hand, if deals are offered to a certain population that has requested information, in this case LVA Gold Member subscribers, then the hotel has more latitude in regard to what it can offer.

Tests

In multiday tests of the LVA program, we found that it does indeed offer incredible deals on hotel rates but that the participating hotels control the availability of those deals (and change them at their discretion, sometimes without notifying the *Advisor*). Such control is to be expected given that the hotels are trying to boost RevPAR for days or periods of low occupancy. Consequently, being flexible concerning your proposed dates and especially being willing to plan your stay to incorporate some weeknights (i.e., Sunday through Thursday) vastly improve your chances of getting the best deal. Searching for available dates will require some work on your part—work that you may judge well worth the effort to save $40 or $50 per night, but perhaps not so much to save only $10 or $15 a night over the best OTA rates. Sometimes also, if you don't find the quoted promotional rate for the days you want, there are frequently other deals for the same hotel on the LVA site, perhaps $10 to $20 more than the deal you wanted but still much better than OTA rates.

Many participating hotels offer availability calendars when you click through to their site, so you can determine pretty quickly when the deal you're interested in is available. Four or five months can be viewed in just a couple of seconds. Hotel sites that don't have availability calendars, however, are a pain in the patootie. On these you have to keep entering different dates in hopes of finding the rate listed on the *Advisor*'s site. For a dozen hotels we had to search weekday rates three to four months out before finding the quoted rate listed on the *Advisor*'s site. If a visitor plugs away entering date after date (like we did) and finally gets to the middle of summer before he finds the advertised rate, he'll think big deal, everybody knows there are great deals in the dead of summer. There's nothing deceptive or dishonest here, but it makes you put in a lot of effort only to come away unsuccessful in the end.

Since LVA launched the hotel deals program it has made a lot of refinements, and recent tests have garnered better rates with less effort. As the program matures, it's hoped that hotel sites that don't have availability calendars will develop them, if for no other reason than to stay competitive.

There's evidently demand for a number of hotels with which the *Advisor* has no direct business relationship. These include Downtown hotels and some Strip and near-Strip hotels such as TI, Riviera, Hard Rock, Westgate Las Vegas, and The Orleans. The *Advisor* is currently engaged in bringing these properties into its hotel direct program, but in the meantime it makes them available through **i4vegas.com.** Because i4vegas.com is itself an OTA, you probably won't score as deep a discount for the hotels booked through i4vegas.com. If you want to book one of these hotels, check the i4vegas.com rate and then phone the hotel directly and ask them for their lowest rate. Or, if you want to be more direct, quote the i4vegas.com rate and ask if they can beat it or offer room upgrades or other goodies to sweeten the deal.

For deals where the *Advisor* has a direct relationship with the hotel there will be a code. If there's no code shown, it usually means there's another middleman (like i4vegas.com) involved.

If you use the LVA site, be sure to jot down the code of the deal you want before clicking through to the hotel's site for availability and booking. Sometimes the link to the hotel site will bring up a screen for the deal you're interested in. Other times, however, there's some ambiguity as to whether the site is responding to the discount code on lvahotels.com or whether you've ended up on the hotel's general central reservations screen. If the latter, you'll need to enter the discount code to bring up the deal. The LVA site works best for four- and five-star properties, though sometimes three-star hotels throw dining, shows, and room upgrades into the mix to create a really great value. As is often asked, "how much time do you spend in your room anyway?"

*un*official **TIP**
Regarding hotel specials, hotel reservationists do not usually inform you of existing specials or offer them to you. In other words, you have to ask.

HOTEL-SPONSORED PACKAGES

IN ADDITION TO SELLING rooms through Internet retailers, tour operators, consolidators, and wholesalers, most hotels periodically offer exceptional deals of their own. Sometimes the packages are specialized, as with golf packages, or are offered only at certain times of the year, for instance December and January. Promotion of hotel specials tends to be limited to the hotel's primary markets, which for most properties is Southern California, Arizona, Utah, Colorado, Hawaii, Texas, and the Midwest. If you live in other parts of the country, you can take advantage of the packages but probably will not see them advertised in your local newspaper.

Some hotel packages are unbelievable deals. Once, for instance, a hotel offered three nights' free lodging, no strings attached, to any adult from Texas. On certain dates in November, December, and January, the Flamingo offered a deal that included a room for two or more nights at $35 per night (tax inclusive), with two drinks and a show thrown in for good measure. In July of 2014, 41 hotels offered rates less than $40. Look for the hotel specials in Southern California newspapers, check the promotion code sites previously listed, or call the hotel and ask.

HOW TO EVALUATE A TRAVEL PACKAGE

HUNDREDS OF LAS VEGAS PACKAGE TRIPS and vacations are offered to the public each year. Almost all include round-trip transportation to Las Vegas and lodging. Sometimes a package will include room tax, transportation from the airport, a rental car, shows, meals, welcome parties, and/or souvenirs.

In general, because the Las Vegas market is so competitive, packages to Las Vegas are among the best travel values available. Las Vegas competes head-to-head with Atlantic City for eastern travelers and with Reno, Lake Tahoe, Laughlin, and other Nevada destinations for western visitors. Within Las Vegas, Downtown competes with the Strip, and individual hotels go one-on-one to improve their share of the market. In addition to the fierce competition for the destination traveler, the extraordinary profitability of gambling also works on the consumer's behalf to keep Las Vegas travel economical. For a large number of hotels, amazing values in dining and lodging are used to lure visitors to the casino.

Packages should be a win–win proposition for both the buyer and the seller. The buyer (or travel agent) has to make only one phone call and deal with a single salesperson to set up the whole trip: transportation, lodging, rental car, show admissions, and even golf, tennis, and sightseeing. The seller, likewise, has to deal with the buyer only one time, eliminating the need for separate sales, confirmations, and billings. In addition to streamlining selling, processing, and administration, some packagers also buy airfares in bulk on contract like a broker playing the commodities market. Buying or guaranteeing a large number of airfares in advance allows the packager to buy them at a significant savings from posted fares. The same practice also applies to hotel rooms. Because selling packaged trips is an efficient way of doing business, and the packager can often buy individual components (airfare, lodging) in bulk at a discount, savings in operating expenses realized by the seller are sometimes passed on to the buyer. So the package is not only convenient but an exceptional value. In any event, that is the way it is supposed to work.

In practice, the seller occasionally realizes all of the economies and passes none of the savings along to the buyer. In some instances, packages are loaded with extras that cost the packager next to nothing but run the retail price sky-high. While this is not as common with Las Vegas packages as those to other destinations, it occurs frequently enough to warrant some comparison shopping.

When considering a package, choose one that includes features you are sure to use. Whether you use all the features or not, you will most certainly pay for them. Second, if cost is of greater concern than convenience, call or check the Internet to see what the package would cost if you booked its individual components (airfare, lodging, rental car) on your own. If the package price is less than the à la carte cost, the package is a good deal. If the costs are about the same, the package is probably worth it for the convenience.

AN EXAMPLE Bob's niece and a friend were looking at a package they found with Delta Vacations. The package included round-trip airfare (on Delta) from Atlanta, four nights' lodging (Wednesday through Saturday) at the Luxor, and about 10 "bonus features," including:

- Airport parking discounts
- Discounted Lake Mead boat cruises
- $25 food and beverage credit
- Planet Hollywood $10 certificate

The price, tax included, was $777 per person, or $1,554 for both. Checking the Luxor and a number of airlines, they found the following:

Same room at the Luxor, 2 people to a room, for 4 nights with room tax included	$520
Transportation to and from the airport	$23
SUBTOTAL	**$543**

Subtracting the $543 (lodging and airport transfers) from the cost of Delta's package total of $1,555, they determined that the air and "bonus features" portion of the package was worth $1,012 ($1,555 – $543 = $1,012). If they were not interested in using any of the bonus features, and they could fly to Las Vegas for less than $1,012, they would be better off turning down the package.

Scouting around, the lowest fare they could find was $469 per person on AirTran with an advance-purchase ticket. This piece of information completed their analysis as follows:

OPTION A: Delta Vacation package for 2	$1,555
OPTION B: Booking their own air and lodging	
Lodging, including tax	$520
Airfare on AirTran for 2	$938
Transportation to and from hotel	$23
TOTAL	**$1,481**

In this example, the package costs more. Most of the two-fers and other deals bundled into the package are available through freebie Las Vegas visitor magazines if you take time to discover them. Be aware that it doesn't always work out this way. We analyze dozens of packages each year, and there are as many bad deals as good deals. The point is, always do your homework.

HOTEL RESORT FEES

FREQUENT TRAVELERS are all too well acquainted with added fees and surcharges, some hidden and some stated up front. Many such fees were initiated during the depth of the recent recession to make up for lost volume. Sales are back up, however, and the original rationale for the ancillary charges is hardly defensible, but once the hand is in the cookie jar it is loathe to withdraw.

Airline à la carte fees are despised but tolerated because they are industry wide (read inescapable) with one or two exceptions, most notably Southwest Airlines. Though Southwest doesn't charge for the first two bags of checked luggage, it continues to expand fees for a variety of boarding and seating options. At least with Southwest, however, you can always opt out. (For a comparative chart of airline fees, see **travelnerd.com** and **airfarewatchdog.com.**)

Like airlines, hotel development is capital intensive in the extreme, and the major players are willing to risk antagonizing guests to boost the bottom line. As Ted Mandigo, a hotel consultant, put it, "There's a lot of institutional ownership of properties, and they're very aggressive about the return on their investment. They've watched the airlines nickel and dime people for features and extra services, and the hotel industry has adopted that as an approach."

In the hotel business this "approach" consists of adding so-called resort fees to room rates. If you're searching for a Las Vegas hotel on the Internet and you're using one or more of the various search engines, the alternatives that come up will often not include or mention resort fees. Thus, a room that seems like a good deal at $100 a night is conspicuously less so if you tack on a $25 per day resort fee. Worse, the resort fee is often the tip of the iceberg, meaning that you're likely to incur other charges for other services, most of which have historically been included in the price of the room.

Resort fees usually run $5–$25 per day plus tax, with $25 being the norm at upscale hotels and $15–$22 the norm for midrange properties. The features and services included in resort fees are all over the map. A common package consists of in-room Internet, local and toll-free phone calls, fitness center access, and complimentary printing of boarding passes. Depending on the hotel, other possible perks and services might include a daily newspaper, valet parking, tennis court access, in-room safes, in-room coffeemakers, two bottles of water daily, incoming and sometimes outgoing faxes (usually with page-count limitations), Internet in the public areas, notary public services, shuttle services, and various discounts and deals for on-site restaurants, shows, shops, and attractions. Sometimes, to the consternation of guests, even pool access is listed as a feature. The resort fee covers a set package, so there's no cherry picking the features and services you want. Because most guests don't use all the features, and because many features cost the hotel little or nothing, most of the fee flows to the hotel's bottom line.

Fortunately, hotels don't march in lockstep like the airlines, and many differentiate their product by charging nominal resort fees or not charging resort fees at all. Resort fees are less prevalent at Downtown hotels. By contrast, all MGM Resorts International hotels levy resort fees (Aria, Vdara, Mandarin Oriental, Mirage, MGM Grand, Bellagio, New York–New York, Monte Carlo, Excalibur, Luxor, Mandalay Bay, and Circus Circus), as do all Caesars Entertainment properties (Caesars Palace, Bally's, LINQ Hotel & Casino, Harrah's, Flamingo, Paris, The Cromwell, Rio, and Planet Hollywood). A frequently updated list of resort fees and what they include can be found at **vegaschatter.com,** but these, as of press time, are the remaining hotels that do *not* charge resort fees: California, Cannery, Casino Royale Best Western Plus, Eastside Cannery, Elara (at Planet Hollywood), Four Queens, Fremont, Hilton Grand Vacations on the Las Vegas Strip (north of Circus Circus), Hilton Grand Vacations Las Vegas Convention Center, Hilton Grand Vacations at the Flamingo, M Resort, Main Street Station, and the Platinum.

If you find a hotel with a low or no resort fee, you may not be quite out of the woods. Take Internet service, for example. Bandwidth available almost always supports basic office tasks and checking e-mail but will prove inadequate if you want to Skype or stream movies. Some hotels that are wired to do all of the above are implementing a tiered-service plan, where basic service, slower but adequate for web surfing and e-mail, is included in the room rate or resort fee package. On the other hand, if you have multiple bandwidth-hogging devices or want to Skype or stream movies over a high-speed connection, an additional fee is charged. Note that older hotels are less likely to provide stellar Internet service because they are extremely expensive to retrofit. When it's done the hotel often charges premium prices for sub-par access. Finally, the majority of midrange and budget hotels do not charge for Internet access, or alternatively roll it into the room rate—it's one of the ways they differentiate their product.

If there's no resort fee, things usually in the resort fee package, such as fitness center access, printing boarding passes, and receiving faxes, will be billed separately on an à la carte basis. Even so, at least you're using what you pay for.

There are several fees that you'll be seeing more often. Many hotels are beginning to charge for baggage storage, as when you check out but store your luggage with the bell desk until you're ready to go to the airport. Another trend, which will make you reconsider using the minibar, is a restocking fee for items consumed. In addition to the $5 Diet Coke, already expensive enough, you'll be charged an extra $2.95–$5 per item for restocking. Also look for early-departure penalties and more draconian cancellation policies. Concerning the latter, it's happening. If you're not in the habit of reading the cancellation policy of your reservation, now's a good time to start.

HOTEL CREDIT CARD SCAM

IN A VERY CONVINCING SCAM that's metastasizing all over the country, a guest receives a phone call in his room. The caller addresses him by name and may know the names of others in the same room. Usually, apologetically, the caller purports to be calling from the front desk and tells you there has been a system failure and that she needs the credit card number of the card that was used at check-in in order to expedite your check-out. In some versions the scam is very elaborate, with the caller offering her employee number, putting her "manager" on the line, offering a discount on your bill for the inconvenience, offering to hang up so you can dial zero to verify the legitimacy of the call, or, in lieu of providing her your card info, inviting you to come to the front desk and handle the matter in person. All bluff. The calls are often made in the middle of the night when you're sleepy and don't have your thinking cap on, and when you're naturally reluctant to get dressed and hoof down to the front desk.

Here's what you need to know: (1) A hotel won't ask you to provide sensitive information on the phone; and (2) a hotel won't call you in the middle of the night. At this juncture, the authorities don't know how the scammers are matching guest room phone numbers with the names of the occupants. If any version of this happens to you, terminate the call and phone hotel security.

For BUSINESS TRAVELERS

CONVENTION RATES: HOW THE SYSTEM WORKS

BUSINESS TRAVELERS, particularly those attending trade shows or conventions, are almost always charged more for their rooms than leisure travelers. For big meetings, called citywide conventions, huge numbers of rooms are blocked in hotels all over town. These rooms are reserved for visitors attending the meeting in question and are usually requested and coordinated by the meeting's sponsoring organization in cooperation with the Las Vegas Convention and Visitors Authority.

Individual hotels negotiate a nightly rate with the convention sponsor, who then frequently sells the rooms through a central reservations system of its own. Because the hotels would rather have gamblers or leisure travelers than people attending conventions (who usually have limited time to gamble), the negotiated price tends to be high, often $10 to $50 per night above the going rate.

Meeting sponsors, of course, blame convention rates on the hotels. Meanwhile the hotels maintain a stoic silence, not wishing to alienate meeting organizers.

To be fair, convention sponsors should be given some credit simply for having their meeting in Las Vegas. Even considering the inflated convention rates, meeting attendees will pay 15–40% less in Las Vegas for comparable lodging than in other major convention cities. As for the rest, well, let's take a look.

Sam Walton taught the average American that someone purchasing a large quantity of a particular item should be able to obtain a better price (per item) than a person buying only one or two. If anyone just walking in off the street can buy a single hotel room for $50, why then must a convention sponsor, negotiating for 900 rooms for five nights in the same hotel (4,500 room nights in hotel jargon), settle for a rate of $60 per night?

Many Las Vegas hotels take a hard-line negotiating position with meeting sponsors because (1) every room occupied by a convention-goer is one less room available for gamblers, and (2) they figure that most business travelers are on expense accounts. In addition, timing is a critical factor in negotiating room rates. The hotels do not want business travelers occupying rooms on weekends or during the more popular times of the year. Convention sponsors who want to schedule a meeting during high season (when hotels fill their rooms no matter what) can expect to pay premium rates. In addition, and regardless of the time of year, many hotels routinely charge stiff prices to convention-goers as a sort of insurance against lost opportunity. "What if we block our rooms for a trade show one year in advance," a sales manager asked, "and then a championship prizefight is scheduled for that week? We would lose big-time."

A spokesman for the Las Vegas Convention and Visitors Authority indicated that the higher room rates for conventioneers are not unreasonable given a hotel's commitment to the sponsor to hold rooms in reserve. But reserved rooms, or room blocks as they are called, fragment a hotel's inventory of available rooms, and often make it harder, not easier, to get a room in a particular hotel. The bottom line is that convention-goers pay a premium price for the benefit of having rooms reserved for their meeting—rooms that would be cheaper, and often easier to reserve, if the sponsor had not reserved them in the first place. For a major citywide convention, it is not unusual for attendees to collectively pay in excess of $1 million for the peace of mind of having rooms reserved.

Whether room-blocking is really necessary is an interesting question. The Las Vegas Convention and Visitors Authority works with convention sponsors to ensure that there is never more than one citywide meeting in town at a time and to make sure that sponsors do not schedule their conventions at a time when Las Vegas hotels are otherwise normally sold out (National Finals Rodeo week, Super Bowl weekend, New Year's, and so on). Unfortunately for meeting planners, some major events (prizefights, tennis matches) are occasionally scheduled in Las Vegas on short notice. If a meeting planner does not block rooms and a big fight is announced for the week the meeting is in town, the attendees may be unable to find a room. This is such a nightmare to convention sponsors that they cave in to high convention rates rather than risk not having rooms. The actual likelihood of a major event being scheduled at the same time as a large convention is small, though the specter of this worst-case scenario is a powerful weapon in the bargaining arsenal of the hotels.

Working through the Maze

If you attempt to bypass the sponsoring organization and go directly through the hotel, the hotel will either refer you to the convention's central reservations number or quote you the same high price. Even if you do not identify yourself as a convention-goer, the hotel will figure it out by the dates you request. In most instances, even if you lie and insist that you are not attending the convention in question, the hotel will make you pay the higher rate or claim to be sold out.

By way of example, we tried to get reservations at the Riviera for a major trade show in the spring, a citywide convention that draws about 30,000 attendees. The show runs six days plus one day for setting up, or seven days total, Saturday through Friday. Though this example involves the Riviera, we encountered the same scenario at every hotel we called.

When we phoned reservations at the Riviera and gave them our dates, they immediately asked if we would be attending a convention or trade show. When we answered in the affirmative, they gave us the official sponsor's central reservations phone number in New York. We called the sponsor and learned that a single room at the Riviera (one person in one room) booked through them would cost $130 per night, including room tax. The same room (we found from other sources) booked directly through the Riviera would cost $98 with tax included.

We called the Riviera back and asked for the same dates, this time disavowing any association with the trade show, and were rebuffed. Obviously skeptical of our story, the hotel informed us that they were sold out for the days we requested. Unconvinced that the hotel was fully booked, we had two different members of our research team call. One attempted to make reservations from Wednesday of the preceding week through Tuesday of the trade show week, while our second caller requested a room from Wednesday of the trade show week through the following Tuesday. These respective sets of dates, we reasoned, would differ sufficiently from the show dates to convince the Riviera that we were not conventioneers. In each case we were able to make reservations for the dates desired at the $98-per-night rate.

It should be stressed that a hotel treats the convention's sponsoring organization much like a wholesaler who reserves rooms in a block for a negotiated price. What the convention, in turn, charges its attendees is out of the hotel's control. Once a hotel and convention sponsor come to terms, the hotel either refers all inquiries about reservations to the sponsor or accepts bookings at whatever nightly rate the sponsor determines. Since hotels do not want to get in the way of their convention sponsors (who are very powerful customers) or, alternatively, have convention attendees buying up rooms intended for other, nonconvention customers, the hotel reservations department carefully screens any request for a room during a convention period.

Strategies for Beating Convention Rates

1. CHECK THE INTERNET Unlike packagers and wholesalers, Internet sellers serve as a communications nexus and can often point you to a hotel you had not considered that still has rooms available, or to a property that has some last-minute rooms because of cancellations. Try the aforementioned **lvahotels.com, kayak.com,** or one of the promotion-code sites. If you link to the hotel's website through a deal on **lvahotels .com,** you'll most likely be classified as a gambler.

2. BUY A PACKAGE FROM A TOUR OPERATOR OR A WHOLESALER This tactic makes it unnecessary to deal with the convention's central reservations office or with an individual hotel's reservations department. Many packages allow you to buy extra days at a special discounted room rate if the package dates do not coincide perfectly with your meeting dates.

If you are able to beat the convention rate by booking a package or through the Internet, don't blow your cover when you check in. If you walk up to the registration desk in a business suit and a convention ID badge, the hotel will void your package and charge you the full convention rate. If you are supposed to be a tourist, act like one, particularly when you check in and check out.

3. FIND A HOTEL THAT DOES NOT PARTICIPATE IN THE CONVENTION ROOM BLOCKS Many of the Downtown, North Las Vegas, and Boulder Highway hotels, as well as a few of the Strip hotels, do not make rooms available in blocks for conventions. If you wish to avoid convention rates, obtain a list of your convention's "official" hotels from the sponsoring organization and match it against the hotels listed in this guide. Any hotel listed in this book that does not appear on the list supplied by the meeting sponsors is not participating in blocking rooms for your convention. This means you can deal with the nonparticipating hotels directly and should be able to get their regular rate.

STRIP-AREA HOTELS THAT RARELY PARTICIPATE IN ROOM BLOCKS		
Four Seasons	Artisan (west of Strip)	The Cromwell
DOWNTOWN HOTELS THAT SELDOM PARTICIPATE IN ROOM BLOCKS		
California	El Cortez	The D Las Vegas
Four Queens	Fremont	Golden Gate

Most citywide trade shows and conventions are held at the Las Vegas Convention Center. If you stay at any of the nonparticipating hotels, you will have to commute to the convention center by shuttle, cab, or car.

4. RESERVE LATE Thirty to sixty days prior to the opening of a citywide convention or show, the front-desk room-reservations staff in a given hotel will take over the management of rooms reserved for the meeting from the hotel's sales and marketing department. "Room Res," in conjunction with the general manager, is responsible for making sure that the hotel is running at peak capacity for the dates of the show. The general manager has the authority to lower the room rate from the price negotiated with the sponsor. If rooms are not being booked for the convention in accordance with the hotel's expectations, the general manager will often return a number of reserved rooms to general inventory for sale to the public. A convention-goer who books a room at the last minute might obtain a lower rate than an attendee who booked early through the sponsor's central-housing service. Practically speaking, however, do not expect to find rooms available at the convention headquarters hotel or at most of the hotels within easy walking distance. As a rule of thumb, the farther from the convention center or headquarters a hotel is, the better the chances of finding a discounted room at the last minute.

Room Blocks from a Different Perspective

Room blocks are high-volume business for hotels. Convention sponsors leveraging this volume can often obtain deal sweeteners such as catered events, hospitality suites, entertainment, and a whole range of other services and extras that make the convention experience richer and more enjoyable for attendees. If you book your room outside the room block, it could compromise the sponsoring organization's negotiating position for subsequent conventions. Also, organizations that cannot fill a sufficient percentage of its contracted room block often must pay attrition damages. This is especially true for conventions that contract a room block only in the convention headquarters hotel. The take-away here is that you can help the sponsoring organization enhance the quality of the meeting by supporting the room block.

THE LAS VEGAS CONVENTION CENTER

THE LAS VEGAS CONVENTION CENTER (LVCC) is the largest single-level convention and trade show facility in the United States and recently acquired the coveted World Trade Center site designation. Last year Las Vegas hosted 55 of the largest trade shows and conventions, more than the next two destinations combined. Annually, the city hosts more than 19,000 meetings, generating $6.3 billion to the local economy and supporting 58,000 jobs.

This 3.2-million-square-foot LVCC with more than 2 million square feet of exhibit space is divided into two main buildings: the South Hall and the older North Hall. A pedestrian bridge over Desert Inn Road connects the halls. Trade shows that crowd facilities in Washington,

San Francisco, and New York fit with ease in this immense Las Vegas complex. In addition to the exhibit areas, the center has a new lobby and public areas, a kitchen that can cater a banquet for 12,000 people, and 144 meeting rooms seating 20–7,500 delegates. Serving as headquarters for shows and conventions drawing as many as 150,000 delegates, the convention center is on Paradise Road, one very long block off the Las Vegas Strip and three miles from the airport.

For both exhibitors and attendees, the Las Vegas Convention Center is an excellent site for a meeting or trade show. Large and small exhibitors can locate and access their exhibit sites with a minimum of effort. Numerous loading docks and huge bay doors make loading and unloading quick and simple for large displays arriving by truck. Smaller displays transported in vans and cars are unloaded on the north side of the main hall and can be carried or wheeled directly to the exhibit area without climbing stairs or using elevators. The exhibit areas and meeting rooms are well marked and easy to find.

The two major restaurants in the Convention Center are **Banners** in the North Hall and the **International Food Court** in the South Hall. Throughout the complex are 18 permanent concessions with fast-food choices in sidewalk settings: a deli; two Starbucks cafes; fresh soups, sandwiches, and salads; Mexican; Asian; pasta and pizza; and burgers, hot dogs, and barbecue. Free wireless Internet access is available in all lobbies and in the two large restaurants. The center no longer provides banks of pay phones, although a few phones are scattered throughout each building. Especially helpful to business travelers is **Speed Check Advance,** the on-site baggage handler that checks luggage for five airlines from 3 to 12 hours before departure and delivers to McCarran Airport prior to flight time. Ideally, you and your gear will arrive together. Two on-site business centers provide a menu of services, including cable TV and voice and data services. The large Visitor Information Center sits next to the escalators at the base of the north pedestrian bridge across Paradise Road. A concierge desk handles show tickets and tours inside the main entrance. State-of-the-art Internet, data, and telephone products are available throughout the complex. The LVCC is easily navigable with a profusion of locator maps and data screens.

The Las Vegas Convention and Visitors Authority also operates Cashman Field Center, home of Las Vegas's AAA baseball team. In addition to a baseball stadium, the center contains a 1,922-seat theater and 98,100 square feet of meeting and exhibit space. For more information, call ☎ 702-892-0711 or browse **lvcva.com.**

Lodging within Walking Distance of the Las Vegas Convention Center

Although participants in citywide conventions lodge all over town, a few hotels are within easy walking distance of the LVCC. Next door, and closest, is the huge Westgate Las Vegas, formerly the LVH. Westgate routinely serves as headquarters for meetings and shows in the convention center and provides, if needed, an additional 220,000 square feet of exhibit, ballroom, banquet, special event, and meeting-room space. Many smaller conventions conduct all their meetings, including exhibits, at the Westgate. The walk from the lobby of the Westgate to the LVCC is about 5 minutes for most people.

HOTELS WITHIN A 20-MINUTE WALK OF THE CONVENTION CENTER		
BEST WESTERN MARDI GRAS HOTEL	314 suites	12-minute walk
CIRCUS CIRCUS	3,770 rooms	18-minute walk
COURTYARD (MARRIOTT)	149 rooms	6-minute walk
HILTON GRAND VACATIONS LVCC	419 suites	17-minute walk
HYATT PLACE	202 suites	7-minute walk
WESTGATE LAS VEGAS	2,956 rooms	5-minute walk
LAS VEGAS MARRIOTT CONVENTION CENTER	278 suites	9-minute walk
RENAISSANCE LAS VEGAS (MARRIOTT)	548 rooms	4-minute walk
RESIDENCE INN (MARRIOTT)	192 suites	10-minute walk
RIVIERA HOTEL	2,072 rooms	10-minute walk

A long half-block away is the rear entrance of the Riviera Hotel. Like the Westgate, the Riviera is often the headquarters for large shows and meetings at the convention center. With 150,000 square feet of meeting and banquet space, the Riviera also hosts entire meetings and provides supplemental facilities for events at the convention center. The walk from the rear (eastern) entrance of the Riviera to the convention center takes about 10 minutes.

Marriott International offers 1,466 rooms with a range of price points among five properties in proximity to the LVCC. Across the street on Paradise Road is SpringHill Suites, which backs up to the Riviera. A half-block west on Convention Center Drive is the Las Vegas Marriott with 278 guest rooms. Adjacent to the convention center on the south is the upscale Marriott Renaissance with 548 rooms, and directly across from the center on Paradise Road are two economy properties, the Marriott Residence Inn and Courtyard by Marriott.

The Royal Resort and Clarion Hotel and Casino are inexpensive properties a long block west on Convention Center Drive. Embassy Suites is three blocks south on Paradise Road but closer to restaurants. For large conventions, the Wynn Resorts provide a shuttle bus to carry hotel guests along the resort's tree-lined golf course to the southwest corner of Paradise Road and Desert Inn Road. From there, it's just across the street to the convention center and monorail station.

Cabs and Shuttles to the Convention Center

Large citywide conventions often provide complimentary bus service from major hotels to the convention center. If you are staying at a smaller hotel and wish to use the shuttle bus, walk to the nearest large hotel on the shuttle route. Though cabs are plentiful and efficient in Las

Distance from the Convention Center

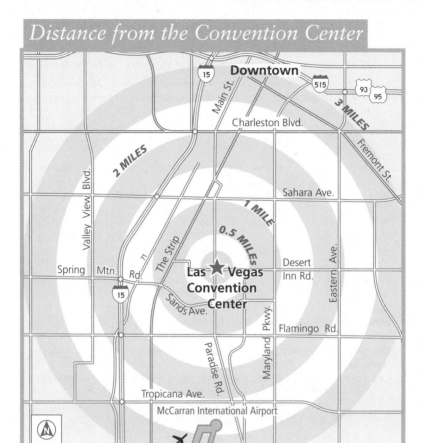

Vegas, they are sometimes in short supply at convention or trade show opening and closing times. Public transportation—CAT buses ($3)—is also available from the larger hotels. Exact fare is required. Your best bet is to stay within walking distance of the convention center. If you end up staying too far away to walk, a car is often less trouble than depending on cabs and shuttle buses.

Monorail to the Convention Center

If you are staying at a hotel in the section of the Strip between Tropicana and Sands (Spring Mountain Road) Avenues, or at SLS or the Stratosphere, the best way to commute to the convention center is via the monorail. It's a no-brainer for guests in hotels on the east side of the Strip. For convention-goers who are lodging on the west side of the Strip, it's often a long walk to the nearest station. If traffic on the Strip isn't snarled, west-siders may want to take a cab. Note also that most hotels on the west side of the strip have rear or side entrances. These allow cabbies to choose an alternate route if the Strip is gridlocked.

Lunch Alternatives for Convention and Trade-Show Attendees

The convention center's food service provides a better-than-average lunch and snack selection. As at most convention centers, however, prices are high. Outside of the convention center, but within walking distance, are the buffet and coffee shop at the Westgate and restaurants at the Marriott Renaissance. The better restaurants at the Westgate are not open for lunch.

The restaurants mentioned above provide decent food and fast service but are bustling eateries not particularly conducive to a quiet business lunch. At 3900 Paradise Rd., however, **Park Center** (only 3 minutes from the convention center by cab and a little less than a mile by foot) offers several quiet, high-quality ethnic restaurants, including Moroccan, Brazilian, and Asian cuisines. Also located in the shopping center is a sub shop and an American steakhouse.

Café 325 in the Las Vegas Marriott on Convention Center Drive is open 6:30 a.m.–10:30 p.m. for casual dining, as is **ENVY Steakhouse** in the Renaissance next door to the center's South Hall. Tucked away in the Clarion Hotel and Casino on Convention Center Drive is the **Bistro,** where steaks, pasta, and Continental cuisine are available for lunch. **The Barrymore** in the Royal Resort is also a good choice. Across the street, **Meskerem** restaurant in the Somerset Shopping Center offers Ethiopian cuisine daily, 11 a.m.–3 a.m. At the intersection of Las Vegas Boulevard South and Convention Center Drive are **Denny's, Kimchi Korean BBQ,** and the **Peppermill,** long a locals' favorite.

Parking at the Las Vegas Convention Center

In all, there are 5,200 parking spaces for cars in nine color-coded parking lots at the LVCC. The most convenient parking is in the Silver Lots right in front of the main entrance. The largest and third-most convenient parking is in the Gold Lots across Paradise Road north of Convention Center Drive. On the east side of the convention center are the Blue, Orange, Red, and Green lots. The Blue Lot, tucked into the northeast corner of the property, is second only to the Silver Lots in convenience, but is used exclusively by convention-center employees. The Orange Lot on the southeast side is likewise convenient, but it is largely reserved for tractor-trailer parking during large trade shows. The Red Lot is adjacent to the new South Hall and is a good choice if the South Hall is where you'll spend most of your time. Finally, the Green Lot is the most remote of all, though more acceptable if your primary business is in the South Hall.

Though access to the exhibit floor varies from meeting to meeting, attendees are often required to enter through the convention center's main entrance off Paradise Road. If not parked in the Gold or Silver lots, convention-goers must hike around the complex to reach the front door (a 7- to 12-minute walk). For other meetings, attendees with proper credentials (those with registration badges) are permitted to enter the exhibit halls by one of several doors along the sides of the convention center halls. As a rule, getting out is not as hard as getting in, and attendees are usually permitted to exit through the side doors.

COMFORT ZONES:
Matching Guests with Hotels

WE REMEMBER A GOOD FRIEND, a 32-year-old single woman, who, in search of a little romance, decided to take a Caribbean cruise. Thinking that one cruise was pretty much like any other, she signed up for a cruise without doing much shopping around. She ended up on a boat full of retired married folks who played bingo or bridge every evening and were usually in the sack by 10:30 p.m. Our friend mistakenly assumed, as have many others, that cruises are homogeneous products. In fact, nothing could be further from the truth. Each cruise provides a tailored experience to a specific and narrowly defined market. If our friend had done her homework, she could have booked passage on a boat full of young single people and danced and romanced into the night.

In Las Vegas, it is likewise easy to assume that all the hotels and casinos are fairly similar. True, they all have guest rooms, restaurants, and the same mix of games in the casino, but each property molds its offerings to appeal to a well-defined audience. This concerted effort to please a specific population of guests creates what we call a "comfort zone." If you are among the group a hotel strives to please, you will feel comfortable and at home and will have much in common with the other guests. However, if you fail to determine the comfort zone before you go, you may end up like our friend—on the wrong boat.

Visitors come to Las Vegas to vacation and play or to attend a meeting or convention. While these reasons for coming to Las Vegas are not mutually exclusive, there is a marked difference between a recreational visitor and a business traveler. The vacationer is likely to be older (45 years and up), retired, and from the Midwest, Southern California, Arizona, Colorado, Texas, or Hawaii. The business traveler is younger on average and comes from just about anywhere. Individual hotels and casinos pay close attention to these differences and customize their atmosphere, dining, and entertainment to satisfy a specific type of traveler.

The California Hotel, Downtown, for example, targets Hawaiians and maintains a food store and restaurants that supply their clientele with snacks and dishes from the islands. On the Boulder Highway, Sam's Town is geared toward cowboys and retired travelers. Entertainment at Sam's Town consists of bowling and country-western dancing. Circus Circus on the Strip attracts the RV crowd (with its own RV park) but also offers large, low-priced rooms, buffets, free circus acts, and an amusement park to lure families. Cosmopolitan, Palms, Planet

Hollywood, and the Hard Rock Hotel target a hip, younger audience, while the Westgate and The Venetian, both next door to the convention centers, go the extra mile to make business travelers feel at home.

Some hotels are posh and exclusive, while others are more spartan and intended to appeal to younger or more frugal visitors. Each property, however, from its lounge entertainment to its guest-room decor or the dishes served in its restaurants, is packaged with a certain type of guest in mind.

Because Las Vegas is basically a very informal town, you will not feel as out of place as our friend did on her cruise if you happen to end up in the wrong hotel. At any given property, there is a fairly broad range of clientele. There always will be hotels where you experience a greater comfort level than at others, however. In a place as different as Las Vegas, that added comfort can sometimes mean a lot.

DEMOCRACY IN THE CASINOS

WHILE LAS VEGAS HOTELS AND CASINOS continue to be characterized as appealing to "high rollers" or "grinds," the distinction has become increasingly blurred. High rollers (or whales), of course, are wealthy visitors who come to gamble in earnest, while grinds are less affluent folks who grudgingly bet their money a nickel or quarter at a time. For many years, the slot machine was symbolic of the grinds. Unable to join the action of the high-stakes table games, these gamblers would sit for hours pumping the arms of the slots. More recently, however, the slots are the symbol of casino profitability, contributing anywhere from 40% to 100% to a given casino's bottom line.

The popularity of the slot machine among gamblers of all types has democratized the casino. The casinos recognize that the silver-haired lady at the quarter slots is an extremely valuable customer and that it is good business to forgo the impression of exclusivity in order to make her comfortable. In Las Vegas there are casinos that maintain the illusion of catering to an upper-crust clientele while quietly practicing an egalitarianism that belies any such pretense. By virtue of its economic clout, the slot machine has broadened the comfort zone of the stuffiest casinos and made Las Vegas a friendlier, more pleasant (albeit noisier) place.

THE FEEL OF THE PLACE

LAS VEGAS'S HOTEL-CASINOS have distinctly individual personalities. While all casinos contain slot machines, craps tables, and roulette wheels, the feel of each particular place is unique, a product of the combined characteristics of management, patrons, and design. This feel, or personality, determines a hotel-casino's comfort zone, the peculiar ambience that makes one guest feel totally at home while another runs for the exit.

HOTELS *with* CASINOS

HOW TO AVOID READING THE HOTEL-CASINO DESCRIPTIONS If you don't care how a place "feels" but just want to know whether it has room service and tennis courts, or when checkout time is, you can skip to the alphabetical Hotel Information Chart at the end of this chapter.

Aliante Casino + Hotel (aliantegaming.com)

THE CLASSY ALIANTE CASINO + HOTEL in North Las Vegas is the only high-rise within a 9-mile radius. The tower stands boldly against the nearby Sheep Mountain range in the northwest Las Vegas Valley. This desert chic metro-resort borders the master-planned development of Aliante (meaning "to soar"), about 20 minutes north of Downtown Las Vegas via I-15, and is adjacent to the intersection of the North 215 Expressway and Aliante Parkway. Given the suburban location and distance from tourist attractions and facilities, a car is a must. The customer base is predominantly vacationers visiting family and friends, motor-sports enthusiasts, business travelers, and locals.

Designed to merge with the stark beauty of the surrounding desert, Aliante Casino + Hotel blends the region's neutral color palette and natural materials. The 40-acre complex includes a 202-room hotel; casino with smoke-free poker area, 170-seat sports book with individual screens, 40 table games, and more than 2,000 slot and video-poker machines; three restaurants and a food court; showroom; fitness center and spa; 16-screen Regal IMAX Theater; and 14,000-square-foot conference center.

E.T.A., a trendy nightclub, features DJ entertainment and dancing. On weekends, eclectic headliner concerts at moderate prices invigorate the Access Showroom.

Food seekers can choose from several brand names at the eateries that ring the casino. The hotel's flagship dining experience, complete with a lovely outdoor patio, is MRKT (pronounced Market) Sea & Land. Try The Salted Lime for margaritas and Mexican fare, or check out Bistro 57 for European-inspired dishes. The Medley Buffet offers Tex-Mex, American, barbecue, Asian, and Italian cooking stations, a salad board, and freshly made hand-packed ice cream at the dessert bar.

The nine-story tower houses tasteful rooms of approximately 400 square feet. Sustaining the rich beige-and-chocolate color scheme throughout the guest rooms are creamy marble, tan granite, and dark woods, again emphasizing organic textures. About 60% percent of the accommodations are configured with showers only, so if you prefer a tub, be sure to request one. All rooms include flat-panel TVs, minibars, and iPod docking stations and are wired for high-speed Internet. Eastward-facing rooms have a sweeping view of the Sheep Mountains and the southeast Las Vegas skyline. To the west, rooms look toward Mount Charleston and the Spring Mountains. Despite the expansive panoramas, the views are somewhat bleak—definitely not the desert at its best. The expressway's proximity notwithstanding, the tower is silent and tranquil.

Situated off the lobby, the spacious first-floor pool oasis is shaded by tall palms. A fitness center overlooks the pool. Just across the street is Aliante Golf Club. Joggers can enjoy a run in nearby Aliante Discovery Nature Park.

Although Aliante is somewhat remote, it is not isolated by any means and is a good-choice getaway for guests seeking style, value, and sophistication in a contemporary urban desert retreat.

Arizona Charlie's Boulder and Decatur
(arizonacharlies.com)

PATRONIZED MAINLY BY LOCALS, Arizona Charlie's are working-persons' casinos with a southwestern ranch flavor. Everything is informal, a sort of shirt-sleeves place. And it's busy. There is an energy, a three-ring circus feel—lots of slots, some table games, a sports book, several restaurant options, and a lounge. The hotel rooms are passable, but the real reason to patronize Arizona Charlie's is the video poker—they're among the best machines in town, and considering what town you're in, this means they're among the best machines anywhere. The original Arizona Charlie's is on Decatur, west of the Strip. The newer Arizona Charlie's Boulder is on the Boulder Highway.

Bally's (ballyslasvegas.com)

BALLY'S BILLS ITSELF AS "the classic Las Vegas experience." Targeted to the gamer of any age, the emphasis is clear when you step inside the main entrance from under the broad, sky-lit porte cochere. On your right, a football-field-long casino stretches beyond you. The casino is immense, open, and elegantly modern—sophisticated in a formal, understated way, like a tuxedo. Active without being claustrophobic, and classy without being stiff, Bally's captures the style of modern European casinos without sacrificing American informality. On the left of the same great room is the registration desk, and a coffee bar and newsstand are conveniently located directly in the lobby area.

Originally themed for Hollywood, now Bally's doesn't bear much of a specific visual motif. This is not a shortcoming. Bally's simply carries itself with a certain forthrightness, with a kind of class that says "We are confident to be who we are—timeless Las Vegas." After all, Bally's has the enduring, quintessential topless show *Jubilee!,* with which it celebrates its 35th anniversary in 2015. Million-dollar sets and Bob Mackie and Pete Menefee costumes, skimpy though they may be, hark back to the days of Sinatra and gang.

Formerly the South Tower, the renamed and fully renovated Jubilee Tower rooms are more spacious than the norm at 450 square feet. Named after the hotel's famed Parisian review, the Jubilee accommodations are holdovers from the 70s, when properties were not concerned with decreasing room size and increasing inventory to billet more gamers. These rooms dazzle with signature shades of chile red, white, and brown, creating an upbeat and contemporary look. All rooms have plenty of lighting, plus window sheers and black-out drapes, and views north or south. All rooms feature 36-inch flat-panel TVs and Wi-Fi, and many have wet bars and refrigerators. Updated marble bathrooms feature walk-in showers (but no tubs), with a make-up counter beside the bathroom. The Indigo (North) Tower will undergo the identical makeover this year. Indigo rooms are the same size as the new Jubilee rooms, but until the renovations are complete, the decor may be dated. One-bedroom grand suites have king-size beds and a whirlpool spa. To enjoy this layout you should be very comfortable with your traveling partner, as most of the bathroom is exposed to the sleeping area.

Bally's is blessed with exceptional restaurants and one of the better buffets in Las Vegas. Options for imbibing and ingesting are BLT Steak, SEA: The Thai Experience, Tequila Bar and Grill, Nosh, Nathan's, and Java Coast. Redefined nightlife venues are Evening Call, Indigo Lounge (fashionable attire required), and Liaison, the leading-edge LGBT nightclub created by Victor Drai and taking over Drai's After Hours space. That club has returned to its original home at The Cromwell across the street.

Although quite spread out, Bally's is easy to navigate. Amenities include a 13,000-square-foot health club and spa. Bally's was one of the first hotels to create an extensive retail arcade, located in the basement level but easily accessible from the casino and conference center. There's also a small parking lot nearby and a bank of entry doors so shoppers can easily access the shops and bypass the casino. Among the 20 Bally's Avenue vendors are home decor, clothing and bling, memorabilia and collectibles, tech supplies, and a food court.

For those who drive, the guest parking is all valet out front. There is limited self-parking in the back, but it is mainly for oversized vehicles. The hot tip is to park at Bally's sister property, Paris Las Vegas (the hotels are internally connected). Demonstrating legitimate concern about the traffic congestion on the Strip, Bally's joined with the MGM Grand in constructing a monorail that was the first link in the Las Vegas Monorail line. Subsequently, the monorail was extended north along the Strip, with a loop over to the Las Vegas Convention Center. Bally's also offers airport check-in shuttle service and another free shuttle every 30 minutes to take you to Caesars, Paris, Rio, and Harrah's (all Caesars Entertainment properties).

Bally's caters to meetings and conventions and is one of the few hotels where you will not feel out of place in a business suit. Guests are frequently under age 40 here and come from all over, but particularly Southern California, Chicago, and elsewhere in the Midwest. Bally's also has a loyal Spanish-speaking clientele.

Bellagio (bellagio.com)

WITH ITS MAIN ENTRANCE OFF THE STRIP just south of Flamingo Road, the Bellagio is inspired by an Italian village overlooking Lake Como in the sub-Alpine north of Italy. The facade of the Bellagio will remind you somewhat of the themed architecture Steve Wynn employed at TI, only this time it's provincial Italian instead of Caribbean. The Bellagio village is arrayed along the west and north sides of a man-made lake, where dancing fountains provide allure and spectacle, albeit more dignified than the Mirage's exploding volcano.

Rising behind the village facade in a gentle curve is the 3,933-room hotel, complete with casino, restaurants, shopping complex, spa, and pool. Added in late 2004 was a 33-story Spa Tower with 819 hotel rooms and 109 suites. Bundled with the tower are a restaurant, four shops, and additional convention space. Imported marble is featured throughout, even in the guest rooms and suites, as are original art, traditionally styled furnishings, and European antiques. Guest rooms and meeting rooms also feature large picture windows affording views of lushly landscaped grounds and formal gardens.

The Bellagio recently remodeled 2,568 guest rooms in its original Bellagio Tower. Jewel-toned color palettes are derived from the property's extensive gardens, floral pageants, and fountains. Inspired by the hotel's renowned horticultural exhibits, botanical photographs line the walls, and there is enough lighting to illuminate a Cirque du Soleil performance. Most welcome is the laptop-sized safe and iHome docking station in the nightstand. Each room features a minibar and high-speed Internet. Rest assured these newly renovated accommodations readily deliver the abundant charm and class anticipated at the AAA Five Diamond property.

Surprisingly, the Italian village theme of Bellagio's lakefront facade is largely abandoned in the hotel's interior. Though a masterpiece of integrated colors, textures, and sight lines, the interior design reflects no strong sense of theme. In two steps, passing indoors, you go from a provincial village on a very human scale to a monumentally grand interior with proportions reminiscent of national libraries. The vast spaces are exceedingly tasteful and unquestionably sophisticated, yet they fail to evoke the fun, whimsy, and curiosity so intrinsic to the Mirage and TI

Perhaps because Las Vegas has conditioned us to a plastic, carnival sort of stimulation, entering the Bellagio is like stepping from the midway into the basilica. The surroundings impress but do not engage our emotions—except, of course, for the art, and that is exactly the point. Seen as a rich, neutral backdrop for the extraordinary works of art displayed throughout Bellagio, the lapse of thematic continuity is understandable. No theme could compete, and none should.

The art is everywhere, even on the ceiling of the registration lobby, where a vibrant, colorful blown-glass piece by Dale Chihuly hangs. Wonderful works are showcased in the Bellagio's restaurants. Original Picassos, for example, are on exhibit in the restaurant of the same name. The Bellagio Gallery of Fine Art is touted as Las Vegas's premier art gallery.

Architecturally, Bellagio's most creative and interesting spaces are found in its signature conservatory and botanical gardens and in its restaurants. As you walk into the main entrance the primary garden is straight ahead. The opulent and oversized displays change seasonally according to the theatrical floral whimsies of the supremely accomplished botanical staff.

If you spend time at the Bellagio, visit each of the restaurants for a moment, if only to take in their stunning design. Many of Bellagio's restaurants, including a Las Vegas branch of Le Cirque, feature panoramic views. Some offer both indoor and outdoor dining experiences. In addition to the restaurants, Bellagio serves one of Las Vegas's best—and not unexpectedly one of the city's most expensive—buffets. With the exception of the buffet and coffee shop, Bellagio's restaurants require reservations, preferably made a month to six weeks before you leave home.

The Bellagio's showroom hosts a production of the justly acclaimed Cirque du Soleil. Though terribly expensive, the show is one of Cirque's most challenging productions yet, featuring a one-of-a-kind set that transforms seamlessly from hard surface to water. Like Bellagio itself, the Cirque production *"O"* (from the pronunciation of the French word *eau,* meaning "water") lacks the essential humor and humanness of Cirque's *Mystère* at TI but is nonetheless one of the hottest Cirque tickets in town.

Retailers in the shopping venue include Chanel, Tiffany, Prada, and Giorgio Armani. Bellagio's purported target market includes high rollers and discriminating business travelers who often eschew gaming properties.

If you stay at Bellagio, you will find the same basic informality typical of the rest of the Strip, and, surprisingly, you will encounter in the hotel more people like you than super-rich. Expressed more directly, Bellagio is a friendly place to stay and gamble and not at all pretentious.

Binion's (binions.com)

BINION'S IS ONE OF THE ANCHORS OF GLITTER GULCH. The casino is large and active, with row upon row of slots clanking noisily under a suffocatingly low ceiling. The table games are less congested, occupying an extended vertical space canopied by mirrors. With an Old West theme executed in the obligatory reds and lavenders, Binion's is dark, but not dark enough to slow the enthusiasm of the locals and "real gamblers" who hang out there. One of the city's top spots for poker and craps, Binion's is famous for not having any maximum bet limitations. You can bet $1 million on a single roll of the dice if you wish.

On the lower (basement) level is the coffee shop and what may be one of the most pleasant bars in the city; it, too, is dark but for once is paneled in rich woods. Twenty or so stories up from the cellar is the Top of Binion's Steakhouse restaurant and lounge, offering a great view of the city. The recession hit Downtown Las Vegas harder than the Strip. One of the casualties was the hotel at Binion's, which closed and was mothballed in 2010. Prospects for its reopening appear slim.

Boulder Station (boulderstation.com)

SITUATED ON BOULDER HIGHWAY an easy 10 minutes from Downtown Las Vegas and 10 miles from McCarran Airport, Boulder Station is one of the smaller of the 10 Station Casinos properties but boasts the largest gaming area. It is the fraternal twin of Station Casinos' matriarch Palace Station, with its train theme, concert schedule, and appetizing affordable menus in multiple restaurants and bars.

All 300 guest rooms in the 15-floor tower have been recently renovated to emit a fresh, contemporary appeal with a bolder color scheme of scarlet, coffee, and black. Safes are available at the front desk. Room service is available 6 a.m.–9 p.m.

The low-ceilinged casino zigzags through several wings and boasts the newest animated slots with 2,900 machines, 34 table games, E-Z baccarat, Texas Hold 'Em, three-card poker, a bewildering variety of Asian card games, keno, bingo, a poker room, and a superior 33-screen race and sports book. Meal options abound with a diversity of fast-food choices (Burger King, Subway, Winchell's, Metro Pizza, Starbucks), along with The Broiler Steakhouse, the stylish Pasta Cucina, Cabo Restaurant y Tequila Bar, Slices Pizzeria, 24-hour Grand Café, Viva Salsa, and the multitudinous Feast Buffet. Generous portions are the hallmark of Boulder Station's food service. A variegated show series leans toward 1970s and '80s rock and blues, country-western acts, and current jazz artists in the 600-seat Railhead Lounge.

The rear of the property houses a video arcade and an 11-screen movie theater alongside an indoor kids' playground. The pool and fitness center are adequate but miniscule. Along with valet parking and a rear garage, there are acres of free parking on all sides, a testament to the casino's popularity with locals. Boulder Station is convenient for guests who prefer the east side of Las Vegas or who wish to be near the Lake Mead National Recreation Area.

Caesars Palace (caesarspalace.com)

FORTY-EIGHT YEARS OLD IN 2014, Caesars Palace was the first of the themed hotels and casinos to fully realize its potential, and it is among the foremost at staying fresh through constant updating and remodeling. The perennial classic that reinvents itself, Caesars is a must-see even if you don't stay there.

An exercise in whimsical fantasy and excess, Caesars' Roman theme has been executed with astounding artistry and attention to detail. Everywhere fine mosaics, handsome statuary, mythological references, and famous sculptures delight the eye and mind. Creating an atmosphere of informality in surroundings too pretentious to believe is hard to pull off, but that is exactly what Caesars Palace has done.

If Caesars was on a small scale it would be exquisite kitsch, but it's on a grand scale that elevates you into some kind of time machine where the bustling commerce of ancient Rome lives again. Gambling at Caesars does feel a little like pitching horseshoes in the Supreme Court, but, incredibly, it works. Everywhere the vaulted ceilings, classic statuary, and graceful arches easily accommodate the legions (pun intended) of slots, activity of the pits, shopping, dining, and lolling about in opulent pools surrounded by towering gardens.

Caesars Palace provides three spacious and luxurious casinos, including a poker room with celebrity events, many excellent restaurants and cafes, beautiful landscaping, and top celebrity entertainment. For all of the guests who inhabit its 3,348 superb rooms, Caesars has all of the services and amenities of a world-class resort.

The pool area is arguably the most stately in Las Vegas. Framed by hotel towers, the complex offers six different pools, all in the Roman motif, including the 10,000-square-foot pool of the Temple, which is capped by a rotunda and decorated with marble and mosaics. For lusty sinews there's the Neptune pool with 5,000 square feet for lap swimmers; and for European-style (aka topless) bathers, the Venus pool is neatly tucked away within an evergreen enclave. All pools have cabanas available for rent.

Caesars is constantly renovating and reinventing its hotel towers. Guests can choose from an amazing array of rooms and suites in six towers: Roman, Forum, Palace, Octavius, Augustus, and the new Nobu Hotel (formerly Caesars' Centurion Tower; see details below).

Note that the Octavius Tower adjoins the Augustus Tower to form the southernmost section of the property. The towers have their own entrance off Flamingo with valet but no self-parking. The entrance leads to a small registration lobby that allows Octavius and Augustus guests to bypass Caesars' busy main front desk. Speaking of the namesake Octavius and Augustus, guess what? It's the same guy. Octavius was born Gaius Octavius Thurinus. Posthumously adopted by his great-uncle Julius Caesar according to his will, Octavius was officially renamed Gaius Julius Caesar. In 27 BC the Senate awarded him the honorific Augustus, and he was thenceforth known as Caesar Augustus. If he had changed his name again, Caesars would have built yet another tower.

Some say the spa is Caesars' best-kept secret. With the Roman penchant for water joys, it's logical that Caesars would have a full line of luxurious treatments and settings for men and women. Situated on the second floor of the Augustus

Tower, the spa has 51 therapy rooms, signature Roman baths with hot, cold, and tepid pools, and sculpted stone chaise longues submerged in heated pools and designed as pre-massage relaxers.

Caesars is on a roll with its nightlife scene, offering four hot nightspots. FIZZ is a lavish champagne lounge located between the Forum Shops and the Colosseum. At Shadow, silhouetted dancers contort to DJ-spun hip-hop. Cleopatra's Barge, a decades-old dance club on a free-floating boat, continues to rock on. Nearby is the Seahorse Lounge, where you can watch the endangered species variety drift by in the aquarium.

For the less nocturnal, there are two shopping venues. At the Appian Way (look for the *David*) you can purchase apparel, gifts, art, and jewelry, including Caesars logo items. The extensive Forum Shops is an entirely different kind of experience. The astonishing adjoining Forum Shops give Caesars Palace the distinction of offering one of the most unusual themed shopping complexes in the United States, with 160 mercantile venues and 13 restaurants and specialty food shops. Ambling through its gently cobblestoned "streets," replete with slightly sloping gutters, the sightseer and shopper alike can be delighted and charmed by full-scale fountains featuring Neptune and Bacchus and building facades topped by second-story "residences," all set against the background of a sweeping Italian sky at sunset. At every turn, you find the perfect blend of old-world commerce and cutting-edge merchandise, including, of course, the famous Italians Versace and Armani.

Dining at Caesars has been totally revamped with the addition of Rao's, a clone of Frank Pelligrino's fabled Italian eatery in New York; Beijing Noodle No. 9; Atlantic City legend Old Homestead Steakhouse; Mesa Grill; Nobu by chef Nobu Matsuhisa; and Payard Patisserie & Bistro. The star in the lineup is Restaurant Guy Savoy, overlooking the Roman Plaza. Headed by Parisian restaurateur Guy Savoy, recently named Chef of the Year in France, the restaurant offers one of the most singular dining experiences in town. For casual dining, there's Gordon Ramsay Pub & Grill; Central by Michel Richard, an American bistro; Munchbar; Cypress Street Marketplace, an all-hours gourmet deli and food court; and Serendipity 3, another New York import specializing in burgers, dogs, stuffed sandwiches, and its signature frozen hot chocolate (don't drink too many of these before bedtime). The Bacchanal Buffet features many made-to-order specialties and is located in a large sun-drenched room overlooking the Garden of the Gods pool complex; it's a welcome balm in counterpoint to the constant clamor of the gaming floor.

Originally designed for high rollers, from the beginning Caesars opened its arms to the world, marketing far and wide. Enjoyed by a broad range of clientele from the East, the Midwest, and Southern California, it's also popular with Asian and Hispanic visitors. Of course, it also hosts meetings and caters to business travelers in its conference center. No matter what the motivation for a visit, each guest—supported by a staff of 6,000—no doubt feels like Caesar.

NOBU HOTEL AT CAESARS PALACE (nobucaesarspalace.com) Ever the vanguard, Caesars has remodeled its Centurion Tower into a luxury Japanese hotel that melds with the resort's Roman Empire theme. The interior of the tower has been transformed into a stylish boutique hotel managed by high-end international brand Nobu Hospitality and is designated Nobu Hotel Las Vegas.

Tapping into the global vision of Chef Nobu Matsuhisa, the 181 tranquil guest rooms feature natural materials, a low L-shaped leather sofa, fine white linens, a refrigerator stocked with Asian snacks and spirits, silk robes and slippers, and other amenities reflecting time-honored Japanese hospitality and service. Enhancing the muted cream, black, and gray rooms are expressionist and classic ethnic art and calligraphy created specifically for each unit. Bathrooms refine the design of a traditional Japanese bathhouse. Standard rooms have small closets and no desks nor bathtubs. Completing the tradition is a red DO NOT DISTURB tassel.

Situated off the Appian Way retail mall, the minimalist Nobu lobby is managed by Japanese-speaking staff and concierges. A ritual tea service welcomes guests, who are then escorted through a Zen garden and up in the artistic wood-paneled elevator to their accommodations for personalized in-room iPad registration. At the tower's base is the large yet intimate 327-seat Nobu Restaurant and Lounge, featuring private booths, a sushi bar, and teppanyaki tables. On-site Nobu chefs also provide 24-hour room service with both Western and distinctly Asian selections. Expect a truly all-Nipponese experience.

California (thecal.com)

A FRIENDLY ALOHA SPIRIT REIGNS at Downtown's California Hotel. Despite its West Coast name, the property provides a taste of Hawaii, Las Vegas style. From the floral-shirted staff, tropical decor, and Island cuisine to the steel guitar music in the background, except for the casino, The Cal could be beachfront in Honolulu. With the sports book upstairs, the full casino covers two levels and includes a variety of Asian games of chance. Bordering both floors of the gaming area are four bars and moderately priced restaurants: Pasta Pirate, Redwood Room with steak and seafood, Market Street, and the Cal Club 24-hour coffee shop. All offer Hawaiian and Asian favorites but no buffet.

The 500 guest rooms are not overtly tropical but do suggest a Polynesian tone, with light blue and green wallpapers, plantation shutters, prints of native flowers and plants, and white linens. All rooms are furnished with a flat-panel TV and a refrigerator. In room Wi-Fi is available for a minimal daily charge, and there is no resort fee. A no-frills 40-by-20-foot pool sits rooftop.

The mezzanine Bridge Arcade off the sports book features Hawaiian-flavored retail shops and eateries: Vegas 808 gift shop, Lappert' s Ice Cream, a liquor store, Ethel M. chocolates, a logo emporium, and the Aloha Specialties Coffee Shop. Along the crossover to sister property Main Street Station is the Golden Arm Wall of Fame, honoring players who successfully held the dice and rolled craps for longer than an hour. Two blocks north of the Fremont Street Experience, this Boyd Gaming property is practically the Las Vegas headquarters for the sizeable Hawaiian and Filipino market.

Cannery and Eastside Cannery (cannerycasinos.com)

FOUR MILES NORTH OF DOWNTOWN on Craig Road, the Cannery opened in January 2003 and expanded in 2004 with the usual locals' formula: big casino, small hotel. The theme has nothing to do with Steinbeck or fish, though the industrial, 1940s-style structure of corrugated metal and steel beams would be right at home on Cannery Row. Instead, produce, specifically vegetables and fruit, take center stage with murals and paintings of colossal berries, apples, and veggies.

The roomy, uncluttered casino is roughly circular, surrounding an elevated lounge. Restaurants, including a good Mexican eatery, a steakhouse, fast-food court, and a respectable buffet, are arrayed around the periphery. For entertainment, there's a 16-screen movie theater and The Club for concerts. A recent expansion added 15,000 square feet to the casino, including a poker room and a race and sports book. Also new are a parking garage and an Italian restaurant.

Guest rooms are smallish, with oak-finish furniture and brightly colored soft goods. Views from guest-room windows are about as uninspiring as it gets.

Eastside Cannery opened in 2009 on Boulder Highway near Sam's Town. A copy of the original Cannery in many ways, Eastside offers clearly superior guest rooms with floor-to-ceiling windows in its sleek hotel tower. The restaurant lineup is led by Waverly's Steak House. Like the original, Eastside rounds out the dining options with a Casa Cocina Mexican restaurant, a 24-hour cafe, a buffet, and Vino's Pizzeria. In addition to the usual table games and the locals' favorite slots, Eastside offers bingo and an active poker room. The Eastside Events Center is a venue large enough for concerts and boxing matches, while the more intimate Marilyn's Lounge showcases top Las Vegas lounge acts. Like the Cannery, Eastside targets locals, but the upscale rooms, club scene, restaurants, poker room, and lounge entertainment make it a good play for visitors as well.

Casino Royale (casinoroyalehotel.com)

ANY SIMILARITY BETWEEN THIS CASINO ROYALE and the James Bond playground of the same name is strictly coincidental. The Las Vegas version is a lively place ready to show you a good time with low-limit games, penny slots, reasonable room rates, and inexpensive dining options within and nearby. The low-rise Casino Royale inhabits a zillion-dollar location nestled between The Venetian and Harrah's hotel towers and directly across Las Vegas Boulevard from the Mirage and TI. The casino is chaotic, noisy, and congested, with seven double doorways spaced along 170 feet of Strip frontage. The unpretentious main entrance is obscured by limitless pedestrians, and if you're rolling luggage, it's an effort to reach the tiny front desk, which is situated behind racks of sale clothing, giving the impression that you're entering a bargain basement.

All 152 rooms on four floors have been newly remodeled and include a refrigerator. Entry into each hallway is by key-card access only. On-site dining options include an Outback Steakhouse, a 24/7 Denny's, and a food court at the rear of the gaming area. Next door are a Chipotle, Panda Express, and McDonald's.

The small kidney-shaped pool is surrounded on three sides by monumental buildings, so tanning is relegated to mornings, but the area is marginally cooler in the shade during summer afternoons. Fortunately, libations are available. Parking is located at the rear of the hotel. If you can't find center-Strip lodging at the mega-hotels, this property is a convenient and value-priced substitute.

Circus Circus (circuscircus.com)

CIRCUS CIRCUS IS VERY LIKELY the only hotel on the Strip that has an escalator from within the casino to a McDonald's, and that tells you pretty much what you need to know. Although most hotels do not cater to families with young children, Circus Circus is a notable exception. For parents who must bring their children, it's a good alternative and a bargain to boot.

With so many swarming, milling, and mewing short people, the lobby can sometimes remind you of a day-care center. The main casino has a second level called the Midway with good reason, as it features the simple kinds of games found at a state fair venue (wham a spring-loaded chicken into a moving pot and win a prize sort of thing). At the core of the Midway is a small grandstand that features very competent regular circus acts, also primarily for children. A new roster of circus acts has been added to the daily show schedule of aerialists and acrobatic artists above the casino floor, with a new show every 45 minutes between 11 a.m. and 10 p.m. weekdays and until midnight on weekends. These are Cirque du Soleil–quality performers who prefer day jobs and the flexibility of rotating schedules. The entire casino affair is obviously designed as an easy hand-off platform for such directives as, "Here, honey, you take the kids for 45 minutes while I go play the quarter slots."

In 1993, Circus Circus launched what is now the Adventuredome, formerly Grand Slam Canyon, a desert canyon–themed amusement park totally enclosed in a giant pink dome. Here guests can enjoy two roller coasters, spinner rides, and more. A detailed description of Adventuredome can be found in Part Five on pages 428–429. Maps and signs throughout the facility indicate the "Green Zone," where children are allowed (because the law against children lingering in the gaming areas is very strictly enforced in Las Vegas). Children can walk through the casino if they must, but the general atmosphere does not encourage this practice.

Perhaps because of price, in addition to families, Circus Circus also attracts some seniors and novice gamblers who don't mind dodging strollers and jacked-up kids in this ADD paradise. The labyrinthine casino has low ceilings and is frenetic, loud, and always busy, but sometimes in contrast to the main public spaces it can seem like an oasis of sanity. Nickel slots abound, as do table games, including dollar blackjack. The circus theme, both colorful and wholesome, is extended to every conceivable detail of the hotel's physical space and operation. However, most of the garish circus theme decor that once defined guest rooms at Circus Circus has happily given way to more restful, mature colors and appointments.

About 3,000 guest rooms are distributed among three towers: the original Casino Tower with 15 floors over the gaming area, the Skyrise Tower with 29 floors and its own parking garage along the north edge, and the West Tower of 35 levels above the lobby and closest to valet parking and the two immense southside parking garages. The ample rooms in each tower have been remodeled and happily have lost their flashy pink carnival flair. The neon colors have been diffused to mellow beige and ochre tones against muted gold walls with swatches of avocado, claret, or blue; the new color palette provides a sensation of sanity and a getaway from the frenzy in the public areas below. New flat-panel TVs and black-topped cherry furniture lend a contemporary feel, and all rooms have Wi-Fi and Internet access. Connecting rooms are available in all towers.

Offset from the central hotel complex and across Circus Circus Drive is the five-wing, low-rise Manor Motor Lodge. The 700-plus rooms here have also been refreshed. The complex includes two pools with a snack bar, kids' playground, and a separate garage, as well as parking lots beside the individual lodges. Access to the motor lodge from hotel central is via the Promenade Level overpass, which connects with an enclosed moving sidewalk along Circus Circus Drive. The Promenade houses the Adventuredome, several restaurants, and multiple shops selling bling and rhinestone-studded everything.

Adjacent the Manor is a KOA Campground with 399 spaces, a private pool, a hot tub and sauna, a playground, a launderette, pet runs, and a convenience store. RV-less visitors wishing to rent an RV can do so on-site. Drivers should avoid the difficult west exit on busy Industrial Drive, the Strip alternative for locals during rush hours.

Circus Circus has a very good steakhouse (one of the only escapes from the circus theme); a huge, inexpensive buffet; and a monorail shuttle that connects the property's two main buildings. And, to give credit for great innovation, Circus Circus was the first casino to set aside a nonsmoking gaming area. A hotel tower, as well as a shopping and restaurant arcade, adjoin Adventuredome. The arcade restaurants provide Circus Circus with much-needed alternatives to the steakhouse and the buffet. For parents with children, Circus Circus is a great alternative, but for happily child-free others, it might feel more like a zoo.

CITYCENTER (citycenter.com)

LAS VEGAS'S NEWEST DESTINATION within a destination, MRI's innovative CityCenter is truly dazzling. From glass towers reflecting sunlight by day to a skyline of crystalline pillars aglow at night, the 67-acre hotel, residence, shopping complex, and permanent public art exhibition between the Monte Carlo and Bellagio Resorts transcends anything in Las Vegas or elsewhere. Designed to offer a new dimension in urban living, the complex radiates energy.

The largest privately funded commercial development in the United States, this zillion-dollar metroplex is comprised of Aria, a 61-story, 4,004-room casino resort; Vdara and Mandarin Oriental, two nongaming hotels and residences; Veer, the dual-tower residential condominium; Crystals entertainment and retail district; plus interior and exterior space featuring a $40-million curated public fine-art program. Prominently fronting a quarter mile on the Las Vegas Strip, the first impression of CityCenter is visually vertical and geometric. Reminiscent of Dorothy's awestruck reaction to the Emerald City, you will be overwhelmed by yards and acres and miles of glass on the facades of the hotel spires and the roof of Crystals. Each is distinguished by a signature hue. Facing the complex and looking left to right, the towers are the silver-blue Mandarin Oriental, white-hot Aria, lemon-tinted Veer, and slate-black Vdara. In front is the multiangled clear roof of Crystals.

For this city within a city, the elevated promenade begins at the Strip and draws visitors into the innovative development. The campus is configured with pedestrian passageways through an informal outdoor-indoor contemporary art museum. More than 15 extraordinary paintings, sculptures, and large-scale works in a variety of postmodern styles created by world-class artists are displayed. Maya Lin, Claes Oldenburg and Coosje van Bruggen, Henry Moore, Richard Long, Jenny Holzer, and Nancy Rubins are represented. Set aside at least 90 minutes for a self-conducted tour. Brochures describing the bold and eclectic collection are available on site, and small plaques detail each work. It's a must-see for art lovers!

There are only two auto entrances into the development from the Strip and one from Dean Martin Drive via Jerry Lewis Road and West Harmon Avenue. The north entrance into CityCenter is a west turn onto Harmon Avenue from the stoplight on Las Vegas Boulevard South or straight on Harmon crossing Las Vegas Boulevard. It traverses the entire north side and exits 1.5 miles to the west after crossing over the busy I-15 freeway. Midway through CityCenter on Harmon Avenue is an elevated circular drive with signage directing vehicles to Vdara and the north entrance of Aria. A second street south of Harmon Avenue is named CityCenter Place, which also has a stoplight on the Strip. That west turn will put you onto CityCenter Place, which is short and becomes a semicircle passing Veer Towers, Crystals, the Aria's main entrance and returning to the Strip. The Mandarin Oriental Hotel is accessed by a left turn immediately after turning onto CityCenter Place.

Valet parking and pickup is available at both entrances to Aria, the Vdara, and at Mandarin Oriental. Valet parking for Veer and Crystals is located in the subterranean parking garage. The self-parking garage is convenient to the Mandarin Oriental and Aria by foot and to Crystals and Vdara via the tram. The garage itself is less confusing than most, with elevators to the hotels and tram station situated at the northeast corner of each level. On each level about 20% of available spaces are marked "no parking," presumably to accommodate modest pillars that intrude into the parking space. Practically speaking, however, most cars sedan size and smaller could fit very nicely in the verboten spaces.

CityCenter has its own tram gliding between the Bellagio and Monte Carlo resorts with an intermediate stop at Crystals. The Bellagio station serves Vdara; the Crystals station serves Aria, Veer, and Crystals; and the Monte Carlo station serves the Mandarin Oriental and Aria.

For pedestrians, the Strip sidewalk is elevated from CityCenter Place to Harmon Avenue. There is also an elevated sidewalk on the latter into the complex, but only along the north side. On CityCenter Place, the walkway gradually inclines 20 feet until it reaches Aria. There is no exterior walkway diagonally across the complex, but the tram will ferry walkers. Otherwise, to reach Vdara or Nancy Rubins' colorful *Big Easy* boat sculpture from CityCenter Place, one must walk through Aria Resort and exit the north entrance, then walk along the circular section of Harmon Avenue. So immense is the complex, there is an on-site fire station and power plant.

Not to be confused with a themed destination, CityCenter is its own unique and original concept.

Aria Resort and Casino at CityCenter (aria.com)

THE SHOWPIECE OF CITYCENTER is the ultramodern Aria Resort and Casino, midpoint in the 67-acre complex. Just as Aria ascends to placement in the Las Vegas skyline, the name derives from an elaborate melody for a single voice rising musically. The 61-story imposing and graceful curved-glass hotel includes 4,004 rooms, an 1,800-seat showroom, nine bars and lounges, a nightclub, 16 restaurants, a spa and salon, shopping arcade, pool deck, sizeable conference center, subterranean parking, and the only casino within the CityCenter development. The structure is comprised of two high, sweeping curvilinear glass towers, two perpendicular wings, and anchored by a low-rise curved base.

The 150,000-square-foot casino is well configured with natural light streaming through walls of angled windows. Along the edge, private salons house high-end table games and slots, while various zones divide the extensive casino floor into more intimate sections.

Guest rooms and suites are richly appointed with customized furniture. Accents of mocha, taupe, and sienna predominate. Average room size is 520 square feet. These guest rooms are a techie's delight with keyless locks and one user-friendly remote controlling the temperature, drapes, lights, music, TV, wake-up calls, and other guest services. Work stations can accommodate wired, high-speed, and wireless equipment. Laptops, cameras, MP3 players, and game consoles can be connected to the 42-inch LCD high-def TV. This TV can also be programmed to wake guests through controlled lights, drapes, and music. Safes are large enough to secure a laptop and other valuables. All rooms come with stocked minibars, robes, double closets, and a dresser in the foyer dressing area. As a result of the hotel's unusual squares-on-curves architectural design, every room has front and corner views through floor-to-ceiling windows. Twice-daily housekeeping and turndown service complete the room amenities.

At the far end of the casino, escalators draw showgoers up to the elevated multilevel showroom. Cirque du Soleil's popular *Viva Elvis* has recently left the building for a life on tour. The hotel now hosts the Cirque extravaganza *Zarkana*, a surreal rock opera with original music played out in a spellbinding scenario with a magician as the protagonist. The world of magic permeates the story with technical wizardry that exceeds state of the art.

International cuisines satisfying every palate abound with restaurants from casual cafes and bistros to steakhouses and gourmet dining. Asian cuisine includes Blossom for classic Chinese, Lemongrass for modern Thai, barMASA for nouvelle Japanese, and Tetsu, featuring teppan dining within barMASA. Presenting European cuisine are Sirio Ristorante for Italian, Spain's Julian Serrano tapas lounge, Jean-Georges Steakhouse for steak and seafood, and Jean-Philippe Maury's Patisserie Chocolate. Not to be outdone, American cuisine is well represented by Shawn McLain's Sage and Five50 Pizza Bar, Aria Café, Roasted Bean, and The Buffet. Try Javier's for authentic Mexican cuisine. Several themed bars and lounges keep the venues buzzing, while the gigantic HAZE Nightclub throbs with electricity.

At Liquid, the vast 215,000-square-foot elevated pool complex that can accommodate up to 1,500 guests, there are three oval pools, the secluded adult (topless) pool, fountains, and several hot tubs set in a tropical forest of palm, acacia, and pine trees. Fifty cabanas are interspersed among the water features and abundant foliage. Breeze Café provides all-day refreshments.

In addition to a complete menu of international beauty treatments, the 80,000-square-foot, two-level Spa at Aria, the largest in Las Vegas, includes a full-service beauty salon and barbershop, redwood saunas, eucalyptus steam rooms, a salt room, heated stone beds, fitness and group exercise studios, a co-ed balcony pool, meditation rooms, and a tanning area. Spa treatments are available poolside at Liquid.

Aria is a benchmark of sustainable environmental programs. Through contemporary design, water-and-energy conservation measures, use of natural and recycled materials, indoor air filtering, on-site generated power, and extensive use of natural light, CityCenter has earned six coveted Leadership in Energy and Environmental Design (LEED) Gold certifications.

Four artists in CityCenter's $40-million public art program are displayed at Aria. At the lower north valet exit on Harmon Circle, Jenny Holzer has created *Vegas,* an elongated LED sign stretching 266 feet and incorporating scrolling text to entertain guests. Three elegant stainless steel columns by sculptor Tony Cragg welcome visitors into the self-parking lobby atrium. At the mezzanine level, suspended over the Promenade, floats Antony Gormley's *Feeling Material XXVIII,* an 8-foot spiral steel bar conveying the human body and visually suggesting stillness centered in a field of energy. The reception area houses celebrated artist Maya Lin's signature work, *Silver River.* Suspended above the front desk is the 84-foot shimmering interpretation of the Colorado River cast entirely in reclaimed silver.

Aria Resort and Casino offers an unbeatable blend of visionary architecture, cutting-edge technology, impressive dining, distinguished personalized service, high-adrenalin entertainment, lush surroundings, and environmentally conscious design.

Mandarin Oriental Las Vegas at CityCenter
(mandarinoriental.com/lasvegas)

TRULY A GLOBAL BRAND with hotels in 25 countries, the Mandarin Oriental Las Vegas is the newest venture of the 41-property international hospitality group. With a prime Strip-front placement, the 47-story glass pillar is the first hotel on the left when entering CityCenter via CityCenter Place. Exuding a refined Asian flavor reminiscent of its corporate origins, the 392-room non-gaming boutique hotel provides Eastern hospitality in a Western setting. Half hotel and half condominium, the lower floors are transient accommodations, and the upper half are residences. In the tower's center is the spectacular 23rd-level sky lobby.

After entering the streetside porte cochere, the elevator whisks guests up to check-in on the 23rd floor. This midtower placement of lobby, bars, and restaurants is distinctive, and the skyline view from the Mandarin Bar is one of the best in Las Vegas. Oriental sculptures, pottery, baskets, prints, oil paintings, and occasional pieces are showcased in the understated public areas. Twist features classic haute cuisine with a French twist accompanied by the gorgeous cityscape. The intimate Tea Lounge serves traditional high tea along with a mix of exotic and herbal beverages. MOzen Bistro offers international and pan-Asian fare alongside a theater kitchen near the third-floor, glass-walled conference center.

Merging Asian decor and Western design, the 850-square-foot deluxe rooms have a contemporary look and Eastern zest with dark woods, vibrant red accents, and stylized oriental patterns. All rooms have walk-in closets and valet privacy closets for room deliveries. Catering to business travelers, accommodations include spacious desks, wireless Internet access, and plug-and-play capabilities with room-control technologies managing the entertainment center, drapes, and lights from one component. Bathrooms highlight the skyline view through an exterior window. Another window with a retractable curtain separates the bathroom from the bedroom. Freestanding tubs are an appealing departure from the usual hotel wall-affixed bathtub configuration, and there is a separate glass shower. Flat-panel TVs are embedded in the mirrors with double sinks underneath.

Swimmers will be keen on the two narrow lap pools, an uncommon feature of the eighth-level pool deck. Between them is a small center island shaped like a fan—the hotel's logo. White lounges and 20 private cabanas line the perimeter surrounding the pools, two hot tubs, and a plunge. The outdoor Poolside Cafe serves light meals and snacks. A wind wall shields guests from gusts. The soothing bi-level 27,000-square-foot Spa at Mandarin Oriental is located near the pool on the seventh and eighth floors. A business center and small conference facility assist business travelers. Cell-phone and laptop rentals are available, as well as secretarial services.

The works of two Japanese artists are prominently displayed within the hotel. The entrance showcases Masatoshi Izumi's *CACTUS Life—living with Earth,* a minutely carved 16-foot basalt lava sculpture honoring balance in nature. The lobby features three glazed ceramic monoliths by Jun Kaneko. These three rotund pieces of the *Untitled Dango Series* typify their Japanese name "dumpling." Inside the Tea Lounge, Jack Goldstein's fiery 8-by-8-foot acrylic *Untitled (Volcano)* brings vigor to the quiet setting. In the courtyard near the hotel's entrance is poised *Typewriter Eraser, Scale X.* This celebrated work by Dutch pop artists Claes Oldenburg and Coosje van Bruggen is a 4-ton, 19-foot fiberglass and stainless-steel rendering of a huge red-and-blue typewriter eraser. The connecting walkway area is also a great spot to view two murals by Richard Long, which are visible through the lobby windows of Veer Towers across the street.

Parking and valet service are available at the porte cochere and also beneath the hotel. When entering from the Strip onto CityCenter Place, the left turn to the Mandarin Oriental is in the center of the road and a very short distance in. Be aware that it appears very soon. Some parking is also available in the garage south of the hotel with entry from the Monte Carlo access road. Directly in front of the Mandarin Oriental on the Las Vegas Strip is a pharmacy and souvenir gift shop.

The hotel appeals to globetrotters familiar with the extensive Mandarin Oriental name, business travelers, and tourists wishing to experience the Mandarin's well-deserved reputation for refined Eastern hospitality. With the exception of the occasionally busy sky lobby, the Mandarin Oriental Las Vegas is serene and Zen-like.

Vdara Hotel at CityCenter (vdara.com)

VDARA WAS THE FIRST of the three hotels at CityCenter to debut. Rising 57 floors into rarified air, the stylish all-suite nonsmoking, nongaming hotel and spa is situated in the northwest quadrant of CityCenter between Aria and Bellagio. Vdara is connected to its sister property, the Bellagio Spa Tower, by an enclosed elevated walkway. Bordering the hotel on the west side is a small park with benches. Just east of the entrance is Karim Rashid's *Seven Continents of the World* sculpture with connecting silver spheres representing the fusion of cultures among land masses. The name *Vdara* was conceived to convey a sense of international sophistication.

An art-infused property, Vdara's main entrance at Harmon Circle is dominated by *Big Edge,* Nancy Rubins' cantilevered 50-by-80-foot work of art incorporating more than 200 colorful aluminum canoes, rowboats, and other small aquatic vessels fused together to create a bouquet of boats in a desert harborage. The abstract Expressionist *Damascus Gate Variation I,* an 8-by-32-foot fluorescent resin work of linked semicircles by Frank Stella, overlooks the reception desk. Two vertical stacked die-cut paper tapestries cascade on the east and west walls of the concierge lobby near the elevator bank. Titled *Day for Night, Night for Day* by Peter Wegner, together they parallel sunrise and sunset with appropriate solar and lunar colors reflecting the transition. To reflect the space, Wegner has added an original celestial light fixture suspended between the two pieces. On loan from the Bellagio, *Lucky Dream,* an 8.5-by-14-foot collage of found objects by Robert Rauschenberg, is in the lobby.

The three overlapping, crescent-shaped jet black and silver towers afford wondrous views of Las Vegas and the encompassing mountains. Corner rooms present the most panoramic sight lines. All guest rooms have heat-reflective horizontal windows. Imparting a residential feel, the expansive and tony 575-plus-square-foot suites feature king or double-queen bedrooms and a pull-out queen sofa in the living room. Large bathrooms, some with windows, continue the hotel's spa theme with large soaking tubs and separate showers. Many accommodations provide a washer-dryer unit. For guests choosing to dine in, all suites are furnished with a refrigerator, stocked minibar, microwave, cook-top stove, and dishwasher. There is 24-hour room service, a food-stocking service, and an on-site mini-mart for provisions. About 1,150 of the hotel's 1,495 suites are for nightly rental; the balance are residential condominiums.

A focal point is Vdara Health and Beauty at levels two and three. This peaceful wood-paneled, 16,000-square-foot spa offers men's and women's salons; three relaxation lounges; eucalyptus steam, sauna, and heated plunge; holistic health treatments; a work-out room; a spa retail store; and a Champagne-and-smoothie bar with vegan and vegetarian snacks. Personal trainers and fitness classes are available to guests willing to temporarily suspend relaxation. Bar Vdara, the 24-hour lobby bar and coffee lounge with swings and a curved reflecting pool connecting to an outdoor garden is Vdarling.

On the second level above the porte cochere is the landscaped Sky Pool with swimming and dipping options of varying sizes and depths. Among the cabanas is a semisecluded plunge. Sky Lounge on the pool deck serves specialty cocktails, tapas, and appetizers. Loungers gazing skyward have a stunning view of the surrounding urban cityscape.

Parking is valet only at the main entrance. The business center and 10,000-square-foot conference area are near the front desk.

Vdara is a smallish hotel by Las Vegas standards, yet the level of service is high. The staff has an uncanny ability to remember the names of all guests. Vdara has an air of quiet seclusion, a hideaway in the midst of a busy urban center. The resort is ideal for those who favor a more restful and exclusive Las Vegas experience yet desire proximity to CityCenter and access to its nearby action and energy.

Clarion Hotel and Casino (clarionhotel.com)

THE CLARION IS LOCATED ON Convention Center Drive within 5–7 minutes of the Las Vegas Convention Center by foot. Originally the Paddlewheel, the property was purchased by Debbie Reynolds and completely renovated. So extensive were Debbie's improvements that she couldn't pay the mortgage and sold the place to, get this, the World Wrestling Federation (now known as World Wrestling Entertainment). WWE turned out to be (big surprise) clueless about running a hotel and sold it to the folks who turned it into the Greek Isles. In summer 2010, Choice Hotels took over the property. Operating with a small, slots-only casino, the Bistro, a pool, and a designed-by-Debbie showroom with bizarrely eclectic entertainment, the property offers nice guest rooms at great rates to convention and trade-show attendees. The Clarion is pet-friendly and a good choice if Fido is vacationing too.

The Cosmopolitan of Las Vegas
(cosmopolitanlasvegas.com)

GLITTERING IS THE WORD best ascribed to this unthemed, design-driven mid-to-high-end super-resort. The property exudes energy and an offbeat hipness, making it truly an indie hotel. Positioned at the northeast corner of the CityCenter complex, the dual-tower hotel is a 2,995-suite high-rise with a full casino, 14 restaurants, three pools, a showroom, day and night clubs, a spa, a retail arcade, two fitness centers, tennis courts, three floors of meeting space, and subterranean parking. Situated on 8.7 acres, this footprint makes the layout overwhelmingly vertical with plenty of escalators and elevators: ride more, walk less. Pedestrian overpasses along CityCenter lead into the second level, three entrances provide access from the Strip, and there are large foyers at the East and West Towers from the West Harmon Avenue approach.

The literal and figurative centerpiece of the property, and its premier attraction, is the soaring 65-foot showcase chandelier of opulent transparent crystal drapes suspended from the fourth floor. Comprised of two million octagon-shaped crystal beads, these translucent panels enclose three cocktail lounges on three levels. Enjoy a beverage as walls of sparkling curtains shimmer around you.

Epitomizing an affluent lifestyle, the distinctive Terrace Studios, configured as 620-square-foot suites, are spacious and handsomely appointed. Each includes a den with sofa, easy chairs, and a desk separated by a low divider and a small kitchen. The latest technology allows guests to book reservations for spa, restaurants, and shows and preset music, lights, heat, and air-conditioning. For a few dollars more, the slightly larger City Rooms are similarly configured and decorated. Most rooms have sliding glass doors opening onto private open-air terraces with wicker loveseats and footstools, allowing guests to enjoy views of the Bellagio's lake and gardens, the towers of CityCenter, the Strip's skyline, or the Las Vegas cityscape. Smoking is allowed on the terraces.

Countless glistening reflective surfaces of clear and colored glass, metal, marble, tile, crystals, bulbs, and mirrors invigorate the curved 110,000-square-foot casino. Overhead is a rampage of visually voluptuous designer lighting that delineates the slot, table games, roulette, and high-limit sections. Sheer fabrics divide gaming sectors but do not minimize the size of the casino. Along the periphery are the 1950s vintage Vesper lounge adjacent the lobby, Book & Stage live entertainment venue with sports wagering, the Queue Bar (so-named for its line-up foyer for the upstairs Marquee nightclub), Henry's Scottish-themed restaurant and bar at the north entrance, and the street-level Bond Bar. Because of horizontal space constraints, the Race and Sports book is not adjacent the casino but located on the second floor. The Chelsea Showroom, booking top-flight, nontraditional rock, R&B, and rap acts, is in the fourth-floor convention area.

Three distinct rooftop pools grace the property. Largest is the fourth-floor Boulevard Pool on the east side, which overlooks the Strip and is configured with an infinity pool, heated pool, and Jacuzzis. The play area offers complimentary ping pong, volleyball, croquet, a pool table, Play Station, and more. The Overlook is a six-level sunning and shading terrace with lounges, daybeds, and tables with umbrellas. A stage provides entertainment, including summer concerts, and movies can be watched on the marquee. The Overlook Bar and Grill serves alfresco small plates and blue-plate specials. The Marquee Club Day Pool on the south side has four levels of lounges, tables, and umbrellas along with three-story cabana lofts. In the evening it is an extension of the nightclub. The 14th floor's permanently sunlit southern exposure houses the curving Bamboo Pool, with stationary in-pool mattresses and cabanas dotting the perimeter. A bar with flat-panel TVs allows additional visual distractions.

The posh four-level Marquee nightclub is divided into three sections: the small Boom Box with high-tech audio and visual; the quiet (really!) Library looks like an English club with dark woods, deep leather chairs and divans, pool tables, and a library of books about Las Vegas; and the three-stage main club opens onto the private area of the Boulevard Pool.

All restaurants make their Las Vegas debut at the Cosmo, and many are clustered on the third floor: José Andrés's Jaleo tapas bar; D.O.C.G. wine bar, serving Italian comfort food; Scarpetta, offering seasonal Italian cuisine; high-end STK chop house with on-site DJ; Comme Ça, an atypical French brasserie; Estiatorio Milos, with fresh Mediterranean fish and crustaceans flown in daily; Rose. Rabbit. Lie., combining upscale dining and creative cocktails; and Blue Ribbon Bar and Grill, for Japanese fusion. Framed menus are mounted at all host counters.

The high-end, second-floor cavalcade of shops features retailers who have no brick-and-mortar stores elsewhere in Las Vegas. Dining options on this floor include Va Bene café, Holstein's burgers and franks, and China Poblano with noodles and tacos to take out or eat in. Tucked away in the convention area is the Wicked Spoon buffet. For a great photo opportunity, check out the giant spike heels along the corridor.

The serene Sahra ("desert") Spa & Hammam offers holistic treatments in a 30,000-square-foot Turkish- and Moroccan-themed facility designed with native desert materials. The Violet Salon provides hair, nail, and other beauty services. There are 30 treatment rooms for Thai, Turkish, Swedish, Champi, or Shiatsu massages; scrubs, baths, and soaks; hot stones; and reflexology. Calming Berber music plays throughout.

Each tower has its own fitness center. The larger 5,250-square-foot, 14th-floor gym in the West Tower overlooks the tennis courts and at the far end features a boxing studio with regulation ring for sparring. Both facilities provide every conceivable model of exercise machine on the market. Outdoor Pilates and yoga classes or individual instruction can be scheduled. The smaller 14th-floor 2,087-square-foot East Tower gym is open 24 hours.

In the lobby, too few counters and only four kiosks for automated check-in mean significant waits. To compensate, a staff of floaters with iPads monitors the area to assist guests. Concierges are stationed throughout the main floor, including the casino, to provide more accessibility and service to guests.

In keeping with CityCenter's commitment to public art, The Cosmopolitan takes it to a new level: the entire property is a gallery of non-traditional art forms. At P3 art studio visitors can observe on-site artists creating art. Cutting-edge creativity prevails in new mediums: from the commissioned garage graffiti to abstract wall murals, LED displays, the four-sided electronic rooftop marquee with revolving artwork, and faux cigarette machines dispensing diminutive original pieces of jewelry, prints, ceramics, and paintings.

Vehicle entry into the hotel's expansive porte cochere is on West Harmon Avenue, the north entrance into CityCenter. Drivers need to pay attention because at the entry several lanes quickly converge into separate driveways for valet, guest registration, and ramps leading down to the underground garage's five floors. Glass elevators at both ends whisk guests to the casino and restaurant-retail levels. Avoid the north exit, which leads to a small alley with right turn only, crossing the busy sidewalk on the Strip. Day and night, the wait to turn is interminable as pedestrians stroll by.

The target guest market for the Cosmo is sophisticated urban dwellers and travelers with a taste for the offbeat. The Cosmopolitan is fun and mildly unconventional. While the resort is a serious contender for the Las Vegas visitor, the refreshing impression imparted by the hotel is that it does not take itself too seriously and exudes a sense of fun.

The Cromwell (thecromwell.com)

PREVIOUSLY, OUR READERS BECAME AWARE of the new Gansevoort Las Vegas, and one name change later, the hotel has been re-christened the classy Cromwell. The beige and purple cornerstone property at the lively Flamingo Center-Strip intersection is an upscale gentrification by Caesars Entertainment of the workaday Bill's Gamblin' Hall & Saloon (née the Barbary Coast). The aristocratic new name implies noblesse and style; the glamorous space is the manifestation of all things vibrant and upbeat.

Standard rooms in the 188-room high-end boutique hotel are Parisian-infused, with hardwood floors, dark wood, and vintage leather furnishings. Custom photographs adorn the walls, and one panel is lined with ornate violet Regency wallpaper. Rooms are equipped with flat-panel TVs, Wi-Fi, and Internet hookups. All units have two minibars: one with traditional drinks and snacks, and another "beauty" bar provisioned with cosmetics and toiletries. The black-and-white mosaic tiled showers (no tubs) recall a turn-of-the-century salle de bain complete with whimsical French-English idioms scrawled inside. Windows, uncommon in Las Vegas hotel bathrooms, are part of the scenario here. A complimentary morning coffee cart and late-afternoon iced teas, lemonades, and flavored waters are placed along the hallways on each floor. Many rooms on the north side face the Flamingo hotel tower just a few feet away and have limited light and sight lines. Other rooms on the north side look across a covered gap in the Cromwell at a wall. Worse, the covered top of the gap leaves these rooms in perpetual depressing shade with the overall effect of looking into a tunnel. Ask for a room on the south side of the resort. Lower floors could be noisy since the south side fronts hectic Flamingo Road, a major east-west artery crossing the city. High up on the west (Strip) or south sides should provide a quieter experience.

Most of the property's second floor is dedicated to Food Network chef Giada De Laurentiis's new GIADA restaurant. An exhibition kitchen, antipasto bar, and al fresco dining with a panoramic view are attractive features of the eatery, which specializes in fresh pastas and California-style Italian cuisine. Lobby bars include the Interlude Lounge and the clubby library-inspired Bound, which also serves barrista-style early-riser coffee and pastries. The property's zenith is the three-level, 65,000-square-foot rooftop Drai's Beach Club • Nightclub and outdoor pool complex overlooking the Strip and encompassed by the nocturnal blaze of thousands of lights from surrounding hotel towers. To describe this rarified setting as gorgeous is an understatement. The two palm-lined day pools are surrounded with bungalows, cabanas, and daybeds that easily transition into the post-sunset nightlife DJ experience. Downstairs, the celebrated Drai's After Hours club (open 3–11 a.m.) has returned to the original black-and-gold basement site where it all began back in 1997.

Given the intimate nature of the property, the casino is cozy as well; 440 slots join 66 table games and a secluded high-limit gaming salon on the entry level. Notice the absence of a poker room or noisy sports book. Guest-centric touches include a complimentary General Manager's Reception happy hour on weekends 5–6 p.m.

Parking has always been a problem at this location with access and egress possible only from Flamingo Road in the block before its intersection with the Strip. This block is notorious for bumper-to-bumper traffic backing up from the intersection. The Cromwell, therefore, is not a great choice if you plan a lot of coming and going in your car. Taxis, of course, face the same problem. If you need a cab, your best bet is to catch one at the Flamingo Resort next door. If you must drive to the Cromwell, heed the following information.

The hotel's porte cochere is on the north side of Flamingo Road and reachable from the westbound lanes only. Two adjacent covered driveways lead taxis and private automobiles from Flamingo Road onto the property. Signage indicates both taxi and valet lanes. A third sign points to the far right lane directing drivers to the nearby self-parking garage that is shared with the Flamingo. In addition to the two Flamingo Road entries, vehicles heading to the hotel from northbound Las Vegas Boulevard can take a quick right turn after the stoplight at Flamingo Road onto a pedestrian-packed access street that bisects the real estate belonging to the Cromwell and Flamingo hotels. Directional signs indicate the main entrance and valet parking areas of each property—the Flamingo is to the left and the Cromwell to the right.

There is one exit to Flamingo Road from the Cromwell porte cochere, but that egress is a challenge because traffic is dense and relentless at all hours. It is possible to head in just one direction—west to the intersection at the Strip. No U-turns! The previously mentioned access street between the two hotels is an easier exit heading east (right) under the elevated monorail tracks to LINQ Lane. A right turn at the stoplight at LINQ Lane takes drivers one short block to Flamingo Road, where a traffic signal permits turns of choice. Allow extra time to navigate these maneuvers.

To be clear, there is no on-site self-parking at the Cromwell; the complimentary garage is shared with the neighboring Flamingo hotel. To reach self-parking, take the designated right lane exiting the covered driveways, turn right on the access street, and make a third right turn into the multilevel parking garage. When departing the garage, make a right turn to reach LINQ Lane. The walk from the shared garage back to the lobby is an obstacle course, although the garage does provide stairways on the Cromwell (west) side. The services of Lewis and Clark plus a compass would be helpful here.

The D Las Vegas (thed.com)

THE D LAS VEGAS HOTEL-CASINO is the second metamorphosis of the original Sundance Hotel built in 1979, which at 34 floors was once the tallest building in Nevada. The property was reincarnated as Fitzgeralds Casino & Hotel, and after two decades has just been rebranded as the dynamic D Las Vegas. Shedding its Irish theme and leaving shamrocks in the dust of renovation, the hotel is moving forward with a fresh look and lively demeanor paralleling the resurgence of Fremont Street. It is no coincidence that the new "D" moniker symbolizes Downtown.

The most obvious cosmetic changes occur on the facade and inside the two-level casino. The first floor is lined with cutting-edge slots and video games, a sports book, and table games hosted by high-energy dancing dealers. Longbar, Las Vegas's most lengthy bar at 100 feet, hugs the west wall, displaying 15 giant flat-panel TVs and 36 video games atop the extended counter. Rotating acts provide live music day and night. The second level houses the keno lounge and an authentic 1950s-era gaming experience, including vintage coin-fed one-armed bandits, a green-felt jungle, and other retro gambling devices. Even the background music, highlighting the fabled Rat Pack members, enhances the time capsule. On Fremont Street, the outdoor D Bar concocts specialty and frozen cocktails created by agile bartenders who juggle careening bottles as part of the show. A one-way escalator shuttles guests to the casino's second floor.

The hotel's 638 value-priced rooms have been updated with contemporary taupe and persimmon hues. Restaurants on the second floor include Andiamo Steakhouse, D Grill, and a murder mystery dinner show. An afternoon comedy club shares space later in the corner showroom with Frankie Scinta nightly and *Purple Reign,* a Prince tribute show, Thursday–Sunday nights. The upstairs Vue Bar balcony is a great spot to watch zipliners zoom past. The registration area, valet parking, and the parking garage are on the south side of the hotel with the entrance on Carson Street.

Borrowing a phrase from composer Cole Porter, the new look is D-lightful . . . it's D-limit . . . it's D-lovely.

Days Inn at Wild Wild West (daysinn.com/lasvegas)

LOCATED JUST WEST OF THE STRIP, at Exit 37 off I-15 at Tropicana Avenue, Wild Wild West is a small, 260-room hotel and casino that is convenient to the Strip, Downtown, and the airport. Its guest rooms, renovated in 2009, are cheerful and comfortable. For east-facing rooms, however, there is a lot of road noise from I-15. The casino offers mostly slots and video poker, with a few table games and a sports book thrown in to keep up appearances. There is a lounge, a pool and Jacuzzi, and in case you're packing a pig, a barbecue pit. The adjacent Wild Wild West Truck Plaza offers more than 15 acres of paved and lighted parking, security patrol, and easy access from I-15. Also available are diesel and unleaded fuel, a truck wash, convenience store, and weigh station. Wild Wild West markets to locals and truckers.

Delano (delanolasvegas.com)

A RE-BRAND WITHIN THE MANDALAY BAY resort complex, Delano Las Vegas is a stand-alone, 46-floor tower that was originally known as THEHotel. Now a sister property to Morgans Hotel Group's Delano in Miami's South Beach, the Las Vegas concept debuts a cool white aseptic vogue. The new look begins in the redesigned Garden Lobby, a luxurious and serene interior landscape with boulders stacked front and center, translucent drapery columns, an aerial rock sculpture, and warm woods and beige flooring bringing Nevada's Mojave Desert indoors. An expansive mosaic of the Grand Canyon is inlaid on the marble floor and surrounded by patterned tiles resembling drifting sands. Serving sandwiches, pastries, artisanal teas, and more, 3940 Coffee and Tea features comfy seating and a fireplace and does double duty serving cocktails later in the day. It's a quiet place to gear up or wind down. Across the foyer, the Franklin lounge offers contemporary sounds and small plates throughout the evening.

The understated room decor is now a crisp *blanc de blanc*. The 1,100 all-suite accommodations are 725–750 square feet each and elicit a mid-century modern look with white bedding, tufted white headboards, and sheer drapes. A white love seat, white desk with chair, media center with flat-panel TV, refrigerator, and wet bar complete the accoutrements. The only accents in the all-ivory surroundings are the beige carpet and a chocolate leather side chair. A conversation piece is the ice bucket modeled after 32nd President Franklin Delano Roosevelt's hat box. Along with a large spa-style bath, each unit includes a powder room just inside the tiled entry.

On-site restaurants are chef Alain Ducasse's spectacular Rivea on the 46th floor, serving French and Italian cuisine, and a streamlined farm-to–urban kitchen concept near registration on the main level. The BATHHOUSE Spa is open daily 6 a.m.–8:30 p.m. and includes a smallish gym, salon, saunas, and steam rooms. The target market at the Delano is Gen Xers and upscale travelers familiar with the Morgans brand.

Downtown Grand (downtowngrand.com)

IN LAS VEGAS, the past has a way of colliding with the future. This is particularly true Downtown. The original 1946 structure that housed the vintage Lady Luck hotel-casino for 35 years has morphed into the Downtown Grand hotel-casino and is the first new inner-city hotel in three decades. This bold industrial-chic property sits at the center of the Downtown 3rd redevelopment complex at 3rd Street and Ogden Avenue, one block north of the Fremont Street Experience. A combination of rustic and urban rawness novel in local casino design, the entirely rebuilt property resembles an early-20th-century factory, using the shell of the Lady Luck and its original catwalks, exposed trusses, ducts, and old brick walls, which can be seen in the public areas. These elements provide a hip yet nostalgic look.

The hotel's five-lane main entrance and porte cochere encompass the entire block of 4th Street between Ogden and Stewart Avenues, while the lobby is mid-casino and spills out onto 3rd Street. The property includes the 17-floor East and the 25-floor West Towers bisected by 3rd Street and connected by an elevated transparent pedestrian walkway. An escalator zips up three levels to where elevators then transport hotel guests to accommodations in either tower. The 650-room inventory features an eclectic combination of modern furniture and clean retro design. The handsome guest rooms are predominantly beige and brown with splashes of chartreuse or cobalt. About 20% of the rooms have a subtle Chinese motif and color scheme and feature electric teapots and an assortment of Chinese teas.

On-site dining options include Stewart + Ogden for American cusisine and Red Mansion for Chinese; both are located off the casino floor. The Art Bar, adjacent to the lobby, features cocktails, small bites, and works by local artists. The casino offers 700 slots, baccarat, an assortment of 30 tables, including a pit of Asian games, a race and sports book, and a poker room.

Picnic, the 40,000-square-foot, south-facing, third-level pool deck, can accommodate up to 1,200 people for sun worship and soirees and features a restaurant (open for lunch daily 11 a.m.–7 p.m.), a fire pit, cabanas, chaises, umbrella tables, and an al fresco gaming area. Adjacent to the pool complex is the fitness center and spa. Valet parking is available, and free self-parking is in the hotel's garage on Ogden Avenue.

Downtown 3rd, the privatized 3rd Street area between Ogden and Stewart Avenues, is a cutting-edge hub of indoor-outdoor bars and restaurants managed by the Downtown Grand. Among the food and beverage establishments on the street are Hogs & Heifers Saloon, Pizza Rock, Triple George Grill, The Mob Bar, the Speakeasy Supper Club, and Richard Sandoval's The Commissary, featuring three food venues. The north end is anchored by the National Museum of Organized Crime and Law Enforcement and flanked by a new farmers' market that entices with fresh produce and homemade specialty food products every Friday, 9 a.m.–2 p.m.

It must be said that in its first year, the Downtown Grand was pretty boring, with little entertainment or much of anything going on in the evening. It depends instead on the preexisting bars and restaurants arrayed along 3rd Street and the action on Fremont Street, two blocks away.

El Cortez (elcortezhotelcasino.com)

THE STORIED EL CORTEZ IS THE NEXUS of the funky Fremont East entertainment district in the rejuvenated Downtown quadrant. Immediately east of the five-block Fremont Experience, the 72-plus-year-old El Cortez at Sixth and Fremont has undergone a transformation and added an annex of 64 glitzy cabana suites to the existing tower, bringing total room inventory to 364. The hotel-casino, one of the most historic in Las Vegas, was owned by the infamous Bugsy Siegel for a quick turnaround in the mid-1940s. The property retains the original façade, a wing of sleeping rooms, and a section of the casino built in 1941 and is listed on the National Register of Historic

Places. The casino also operates under Las Vegas's oldest gaming license, issued in 1941.

In the hotel's main tower, guest rooms are decorated in a tropical Tommy Bahama fashion and feature dark woods, rattan, and pineapple images. Located directly above the casino and reached by a stairway are the hotel's original accommodations, now with queen beds and decorated in a modified island motif. The El Cortez recently hosted a competition inviting local designers to redecorate the tower's luxury suite inventory. With reasonable rates, the sleek individualistic results reflect an edgy modern take on the surrounding desert and historic Las Vegas.

In a freestanding building across Ogden Avenue are the stylish black-and-white Art Deco Cabana Suites. Newly upgraded, the all-king rooms shimmer with reflective surfaces: glass furniture on black carpet, metal lamps, mirrors, shiny patterned wallpaper. A black bench, white faux leather headboard, white linens, and lime green walls complete the look. All accommodations are equipped with a flat-panel TV, Wi-Fi, and iPod dock. The Cabana Suites maintain a separate check-in with a small lobby. A business center and gym are also located in this wing.

Tucked away in the rambling and comfortable casino are several cozy slot nooks; included in the slot inventory are 245 coin machines, long gone from most casinos. Along with its famous poker room, blackjack, roulette, craps, keno, and a sports book are also available. The friendly, 24-hour Siegel's 1941 coffee shop and a Subway are the hotel's dining options. A holdover from the old days is meal service alongside the gaming tables for uninterrupted casino play. A lobby bar and lounge are opposite check-in, and two more bars are interspersed along the slot floor. A gift shop and vintage barber shop are also nearby. Once a month, on the first Friday, the El Cortez hosts Sessions, a concert series presenting indie artists.

The handsome brick porte-cochere and valet entrance are on South 6th Street. Free parking in the low-ceilinged garage is accessed from South 7th Street—lower antennas and watch luggage racks! With the front desk at the west entrance, the valet side is far more convenient.

Long a haven for locals, El Cortez is friendly, and the chatty employees treat customers as family. A visit to the El Cortez is like going back home and visiting with the neighbors.

Ellis Island Casino and Brewery (ellisislandcasino.com)

ELLIS ISLAND, ON KOVAL LANE NEAR HARMON AVENUE just minutes from the Strip, is the most modest casino imaginable, but a treasure for those in the know. Its $8 complete New York Strip–steak dinner has been among the best meal deals in town for years. Wash it down with a crafted beer from the on-site microbrewery. The casino is joined at the hip to an equally modest Super 8 hotel.

Excalibur (excalibur.com)

THE EXCALIBUR IS A HOTEL IN TRANSITION, attempting to chunk its family business for a more adult, middle-income market. Although it's difficult to transform a medieval-themed casino the size of an airplane hanger,

Excalibur has succeeded to a remarkable degree. The new hotel lobby, as well as the casino, are tasteful, with dark woods and stylish lighting fixtures. Gone are the cheap plastic look rendered in a Walmart color palette and the ridiculous faux Knights of the Round Table artifacts. There are still vestiges of Ozzie and Harriet's decorating touch, but the Excalibur no longer assaults the senses like it did in the good olde days.

The guest rooms likewise have received a makeover—the medieval theme has been mercilessly exorcised and replaced by surprisingly luxurious rooms replete with plush bedding, dark-wood furnishings, and contemporary baths. Though the windows are not huge, the views are great.

Excalibur's restaurants and shops are on the top floor of three levels. On the lower floor is a midway-type games arcade (with a zippy SpongeBob SquarePants 4-D ride) and the showroom, where jousting tournaments are featured. Other entertainment offerings include a male strip show and a Bee Gees tribute show. The cavernous middle level contains the casino.

The Excalibur is (for the moment) the ninth-largest hotel in the world and the sixth largest in Las Vegas, and it certainly features the world's largest hotel parking lot (so far removed from the entrance that trams are dispatched to haul in patrons). If you can get past the parking-lot commute and the fact that most guest rooms have showers only (no tubs), and you do not object to joining the masses, there is good value at the Excalibur. The food is good and economically priced, as is the entertainment. The staff is friendly and accommodating, and you won't go deaf or blind, or become claustrophobic, in the casino. A high-energy nightclub, several pools, a spa, and a workout facility round out Excalibur's product mix. If you need a change of pace, a covered walkway connects the Excalibur with the Luxor next door, pedestrian bridges provide direct access to New York–New York and the Tropicana, and an overhead train runs to Luxor and Mandalay Bay.

Fiesta Henderson
(fiestahendersonlasvegas.com)

FIESTA HENDERSON'S PARENT COMPANY, Station Casinos, has stripped this property of its stuffed monkeys and lions (it was formerly The Reserve) and made it southwestern/Mexican in flavor. Located southeast of Las Vegas at the intersection of I-515 and West Lake Mead Drive, Fiesta Henderson offers a 37,000-square-foot casino, a 12-screen movie theater, three restaurants, a buffet, a food court, and three bars. As is the case with all Station casinos, the Fiesta Henderson caters primarily to locals.

Fiesta Rancho (fiestarancholasvegas.com)

THE FIESTA RANCHO WAS THE FIRST of two casinos to be situated at the intersection of Rancho Drive and Lake Mead Boulevard in North Las Vegas (the other is Texas Station). With 100 guest rooms and a video-poker-packed, 40,000-square-foot casino (including the Spin City annex), the Fiesta features an Old Mexico theme. Entertainment includes a lounge, a nightclub, and a $40-million ice arena. Restaurants specializing in southwestern food are the Fiesta's major draw. An excellent buffet features a mesquite grill. A food court and a Denny's round out the dining options. There is a very basic outdoor swimming pool and, perhaps equally enticing on a hot day, a tequila bar (20 different margaritas—*olé*!). The Fiesta depends primarily on local clientele.

Flamingo (flamingolasvegas.com)

ONE OF THE EARLIEST RESORTS on the Las Vegas Strip, the Flamingo opened in 1946 at the south end of old Highway 91, the empty dirt road heading out of town to Los Angeles. Named after gangster Bugsy Siegel's leggy girlfriend's long limbs, which he likened to those of the slinky bird, the Flamingo is downplaying its hot pink signature shade and upgrading most of its 3,550 guest rooms while rebranding the four-tower complex. A new masculine look forgoes the tropical theme and reinvigorates the 67-year-old property, but not to worry—the pink isn't going away, it's just less pervasive so the decor is less flashy.

Most noticeable upon entry into the guest rooms is the wood laminate floor accented with area rugs. Macho colors of ebony, brown, and crimson are juxtaposed with gray walls. Pink is understated with a small faux fur coverlet, a humorous touch atop the chalk white bed linens. In homage to its historic past, the Flamingo has added a photo of the original hotel in each room, along with abstract prints. Small dogs are welcome.

The main casino's race and sports book, keno lounge, and high-limit area have been remodeled as well. The Promenade Food Court includes Mrs. Fields, TCBY, and Java Detour, while the larger food court houses Johnny Rockets, Pan Asian, Bonnano's NY Pizza, and LA Subs. The Paradise Garden Buffet, Tropical Breeze Café, Pink Bean, Hamada of Japan, and Sin City Brewing are just off the casino. Adding to the restaurant repertoire are Center Cut Steakhouse and Carlos 'n Charlie's Mexican cantina and pool-view patio.

Along the north side of the property, joining Jimmy Buffett's energetic Margaritaville restaurant, is the new Strip-side Margaritaville-branded casino and deck equipped with 220 themed slots, 22 table games, and youthful dealers in tropical attire high-fiving players when they hit 21. This perch for Parrotheads and fun-seekers sports chandeliers shaped like lime slices, beachlike flooring, a 20-foot model of the world's largest margarita, and a retail outlet anchored by the 5 O'Clock Somewhere bar.

The gated Beach Club pool and waterslide playground is small for the size of the property; however, the adjacent 15 acres of lush gardens and palms incorporate a wildlife sanctuary that is a habitat for a flock of flamingos, a passel of penguins, and an exotic bird aviary. Turtles, koi, ducks, and swans paddle this Xanadu's ponds and streams. The dense landscape, waterfall, and gazebo provide a rain forest backdrop for photos and weddings.

Mainstays of the hotel's entertainment line-up are *X Burlesque* and singing siblings Donny and Marie Osmond, with Flamingo newcomer Olivia Newton-John rounding out the group. The property lacks a nightclub, but with the non-stop party at Margaritaville, it is not missed.

Amenities include a spa and fitness center and golf privileges at two Caesars Entertainment courses. The Flamingo is the southern gateway to the LINQ entertainment district, which opened in 2014.

Four Queens (fourqueens.com)

THE FOUR QUEENS, situated in the heart of Downtown, offers good food, respectable hotel rooms, and a positively cheery casino. Joining its neighbor, the Golden Nugget, as a member of the "All Right to Be Bright Club," the Four Queens casino was among the first to abandon the standard brothel red in favor of a glistening, light decor offset by a tropical-print carpet. The result, as at the Golden Nugget, is a gaming area that feels fun, upbeat, and clean. Loyal Four Queens hotel guests tend to be middle-aged or older and come from Southern California, Texas, Hawaii, and the Midwest. The Four Queens also caters to the motor-coach-tour market. In the casino there is a mix of all ages and backgrounds. Locals love Hugo's Cellar restaurant, a Las Vegas landmark.

Four Seasons (fourseasons.com/lasvegas)

THE AAA FIVE-DIAMOND FOUR SEASONS was the first hotel-within-a-hotel in Las Vegas. The concept of a high-end boutique hotel within a larger gaming property took flight at the millennium's turn back in 1999. The successful result has influenced other fusions, but it happened here first. The sophisticated Four Seasons inventory of 424 guest rooms is allocated to the 35th–39th levels of Mandalay Bay Resort's towers. With the restyling of all units completed in 2013, the new look reflects an Art Deco influence with a cool black, white, and silver color scheme. The airy rooms combine glass, metal, and wood appointments, resulting in a profusion of glossy surfaces and patterns. Floor-to-ceiling windows afford abundant views of the Strip, McCarran Airport's three runways, or the extensive Vegas Valley.

The Verandah restaurant (open 6:30 a.m.–10 p.m.) specializes in seasonal regional Italian cuisine. Guests can savor alfresco dining day or night, and a formal tea service is presented weekdays 3–4 p.m. Open nightly is the esteemed Charlie Parker Steak. PRESS, the new indoor-outdoor lobby bar, offers a barista experience, libations, and small plates. A 24-hour business center serves a diverse clientele of international visitors.

The palm-lined pool features a pool bar, hot tub, kids' pool, and playground. Access is from the elevator lobby by the Desert Oasis Spa and fitness center. The Four Seasons' private pool area is separate from Mandalay Bay's Beach; however, Four Seasons guests are welcome at the multihydrous complex.

The Four Seasons' porte cochere is to the left of Mandalay Bay's entrance on Las Vegas Boulevard South, but guests can access the hotel from Mandalay Bay's casino through a designated door and an elegant marble-floored hallway leading into the Four Seasons lobby. We recommend using valet parking; self-parking is inconvenient and a long trek from the distant Mandalay Bay parking garage or convention area. This tranquil nongaming hotel caters to the luxury market and guests seeking anonymity.

Fremont (fremontcasino.com)

THE FREMONT IS ONE OF THE LANDMARKS of Downtown Las Vegas. Acquired by the Boyd family in 1985, the Fremont offers good food, budget lodging, and a robust casino. Several years ago they redecorated and considerably brightened the casino, which is noisy and crowded. The table games are roomily accommodated beneath a high ceiling ringed in neon, while the slots are crammed together along narrow aisles like turkeys on their way to market. Locals love the Fremont, as do Asians, Hawaiians, and the inevitable Southern Californians. The Fremont, like all Boyd properties, is friendly, informal, and comfortable.

Gold Coast (goldcoastcasino.com)

SITUATED A HALF MILE WEST of the strip on Flamingo Boulevard, the lively Gold Coast feels right in the middle of the Strip's bustling action. The property recently remodeled all 711 sleeping rooms with a soothing cream, taupe, and gray color scheme, creating a serene environment away from the casino's buzz. Wi-Fi and Internet access are available for a low fee.

The genial and rambling T-shaped casino, scheduled for a fresh rework next year, offers generous gaming odds, along with afternoon and evening lounge acts. Saturday is Latin Dance Night, with salsa music pulsing into the early hours. Restaurants include T.G.I. Friday's, the Cortez Room steakhouse, Ping Pang Pong for Chinese, the Noodle Exchange, Ports of Call buffet, Red Zone sports bar, Java Vegas, and Subway. Bowlers will love the 24-hour, 70-lane, cutting-edge bowling complex above the casino; the complex also houses a video arcade and Nevada's largest bingo hall, seating 720 players. There's a low-rise covered parking garage in front of the hotel, but for easier check in, the larger east garage and valet service have better access to the reception area.

The Gold Coast is a popular gathering spot for locals and a member of the respected Boyd Gaming Group, long known for great deals and low rates. The hotel specializes in competitively priced NASCAR and National Finals Rodeo packages.

Golden Gate (goldengatecasino.net)

THE OLDEST HOTEL IN LAS VEGAS, the Golden Gate is a vintage property with an even more vintage casino. Retaining its historical flavor while undergoing an update, the casino has been enlarged and a five-story wing has been added at the south end. While the main pedestrian entrance remains on the Fremont Street Experience, the south side sports a new porte cochere facing Carson Street. The remodeled registration area with period furniture and memorabilia adjoins that entry lobby. Most of the interior is little changed since the hotel opened in 1906 as the Hotel Nevada at 1 Fremont St., across from the train depot. New-fashioned patterned ceiling tile, freshly painted red and brown walls, and natural stonework are evocative of the way it was. Pillars, dark woods, chandeliers, carved glass, and mirrors in the low-ceilinged gaming area create the illusion that you're gambling during the Roaring Twenties. The flapper-costumed Dancing Dealers add nightly fun to this ambience.

The aura at today's Golden Gate is old is new again. The original guest rooms in the older building are beyond compact, and none of the 106 rooms are similar in size and configuration, reminiscent of a time before building codes and uniformity. Rooms are decorated in black, white, and rose red. Queens and double-doubles are available. Bathrooms are tiny with stall showers, and the floors retain their centenary black-and-white tile. The new 500-square-foot tower rooms repeat the signature tobacco and brick shades in the casino. All rooms have been upgraded and offer Wi-Fi and iHome docking stations. Bathrooms are larger but again feature showers only.

As the Hotel Nevada, the Golden Gate was assigned Las Vegas's first telephone number, "1," and proudly displays the town's first telephone, along with old ledgers, registers, and other historical documents from the era. In the 1930s, the hotel was inanely called the "Sal Sagev" ("Las Vegas" in reverse), but it was rechristened the Golden Gate in 1951, when new owners from San Francisco took over. The same family has owned and managed the property ever since.

Home to the original and still-famous shrimp cocktail, the casino's rear deli is dedicated to serving this honorable $2.99 snack to hundreds of customers weekly. Also on site is DuPar's, with old-fashioned counter service and booths from the hotel's original restaurant. One of the casino's two permanent outside bars on Fremont Street features bar-top dancers, frozen drinks, and beer, while the other refreshment stand spotlights Flair bartenders whose cocktail-creation skills are showstoppers. A bandstand provides live music nightly. The hotel appeals to the budget-minded, Gen X–ers interested in a historic property, and old-timers reliving Las Vegas's very early days.

Golden Nugget (goldennugget.com/lasvegas)

THE UNDISPUTED FLAGSHIP OF THE DOWNTOWN hotels and one of the most meticulously maintained and managed properties in Las Vegas, the Golden Nugget is smack in the middle of Glitter Gulch. The hotel offers newly renovated bright, cheery rooms, a showroom, plus lounge entertainment, excellent restaurants, a large pool, a first-rate spa, a shopping arcade, a workout room, two on-site Starbucks, and a chapel and wedding planner. The casino is clean and breezy, with white enameled walls and white lights. The feel here is definitely upscale, though comfortable and informal. There is breathing room at the Golden Nugget, and an atmosphere that suggests a happy, more fun-filled approach to gambling.

The Golden Nugget recently underwent a $200-million renovation and expansion, the first since 1973 for the perpetual AAA Four-Diamond Award winner. At the heart of the new, improved Golden Nugget are a 500-room hotel tower and the renovated 600-seat showroom. Other elements of the makeover include a new covered porte cochere, a new VIP lounge, Vic and Anthony's steakhouse, and Lillie's Asian Cuisine specializing in Cantonese and Szechuan fare. Plus, the spa and fitness center has been modernized and expanded. The most intriguing touch is the reconfiguration of the swimming complex to surround a 30-foot-deep shark aquarium. (More on that below.) Overlooking the aquarium is a revamped buffet, and integrated into the shark tank and pool is Grotto, a trattoria-style Italian restaurant.

The Golden Nugget's 25-floor smoke-free [Gold] Rush Tower brings Strip-scene energy to Downtown's premium property. Located on the west side of the hotel's footprint, where 1st Street right-angles Carson Avenue, the new tower has a separate porte cochere with valet parking. The 500 Rush rooms are 20% larger than the rest of the hotel's inventory, with a marginally higher rate. Boasting a brown, orange, and gold palette with cream down comforters and linens and a dark leather sectional and ottoman, the rooms resemble an upscale condo and impart a southwestern Zen flavor. Original oil paintings created by the hotel's artists soften the bronze walls. Each unit includes an iPod docking station, Internet access, and flat-panel TV. The sizable bathrooms feature parquet floors, oversize tub–glass shower combos, double raised sinks, and stylish brushed chrome fixtures. King rooms make up 95% of the tower's inventory.

Snaking through the Rush lobby is a dazzling white, umber, and yellow crystal chandelier, which coils above the registration counter. The area includes two new restaurants: Red Sushi and Chart House, housing a 75-gallon coral-reef fish tank surrounded by turquoise walls and floors. Upstairs is Gold Diggers nightclub with an above-bar stage where guests can strut their above-average stuff. There's also a splendid outdoor patio overlooking the Fremont Street Experience. Popular impressionist and comedian Gordie Brown impresses in the showroom.

The updated three-level Tank aquatorium was voted among the "Top Ten Extreme Pools" by the Travel Channel. The focal point is a 30-foot-deep 200,000-gallon carnivorous fish aquarium, which sharks call home. A three-story yellow tube shoots thrill seekers down an elongated chute that becomes clear acrylic straight through the shark habitat . . . all the better to see you with, my dear. H2O offers drinks and snacks amid a fire pit with multipillowed seating. Blackjack is available at shaded gaming tables. The circular second level includes seven private cabanas; the third level features the Hideout, with a bar and lounge, warm-water infinity pool, and six more cabanas.

In the lobby near the hotel's display of authentic golden nuggets, you can purchase gold from an untraditional ATM Machine. GOLD-to-go dispenses 24-karat-gold bars in seven weight choices from 1 gram to 250 grams. With spot pricing, the price can fluctuate every 10 minutes depending on the gold market. Gold coins and Golden Nugget souvenir pieces are also available. Each is presented in a gift box. Cash only!

Though the Golden Nugget has always been Downtown's prestige address, the new hotel tower and top-to-bottom makeover has catapulted it into the rarified atmosphere of the premiere Strip resorts. More, the Golden Nugget's renovation and expansion have helped trigger the metamorphosis of all of Downtown Las Vegas. The casino is popular with Hawaiians and Pacific Islanders and also appeals to Texans and the Southern California drive-in market. Younger travelers (ages 28–39) like the Golden Nugget, as do older tourists and retirees, many of whom arrive on motor-coach tours.

Green Valley Ranch Resort, Spa, and Casino
(greenvalleyranchresort.com)

IF YOU LIKE PAMPERING AND FRESH AIR with your gambling and dining, you'll love Green Valley Ranch. This Mediterranean-Mission–style, indulgent retreat, perched on a hill overlooking the distant Strip and the mountains, is in an upscale residential area about 15 minutes southeast of the Strip at the intersection of Green Valley Parkway and the I-215 Beltway. The property offers a 490-room hotel, a casino with 55 table games and more than 2,650 slot and video-poker machines, eight restaurants (including a buffet), a spa, and a 10-screen cinema complex. Like all Station casinos, Green Valley Ranch provides locals with high-pay slots, good dining value, an excellent players club, and high-quality lounge entertainment.

Unlike most Station casinos, however, Green Valley Ranch is very upscale. The restaurants are trendy, featuring some of Las Vegas's best-known chefs. Watering holes include the elegant Drop Bar, the Lobby Bar, and Quinn's Irish Pub. The hotel and its enfolding guest rooms are truly luxurious. Many of the guest rooms feature great views of the pool and spa areas and/or the desert and Strip beyond.

The eight-acre pool complex is lovely, more resembling a country-club setting than that of a Las Vegas hotel. Features include vanishing-edge pools near the spa and a large, centrally located swimming pool with a sandy beach at one end, perfect for the kids. There is also a small grassy playground.

Dining options abound. Hank's is a plush, masculine chophouse and martini bar. Other fine-dining options include Terra Verde and the ultra-hip Sushi + Sake. The Feast Buffet is one of Las Vegas's best. An informal Chinese bistro, an oyster bar, cafe, and a food court complete the culinary collage.

The 30,000-square-foot spa is a real star. The curving path from the hotel proper to the relaxation center is lined by a small vineyard offset by red roses. In addition to a wonderful array of treatments, the soothing architectural aesthetics at Green Valley do their part in providing a higher-quality experience. For example, on the treadmills you can meditate on the Zen sculpture arising from the three-lane lap pool or contemplate the Spring Mountains. The steam room has an outdoor view. Pilates and yoga classes are held in a perfect wood, glass, and mirrored high-ceilinged studio.

Located within easy striking distance of Lake Mead, Hoover Dam, the Black Canyon of the Colorado, and Red Rock Canyon, Green Valley Ranch offers a super option for families, the outdoor-oriented traveler, and for those who believe in the healing powers of being pampered.

Hard Rock Hotel (hardrockhotel.com)

HARD ROCK HOTEL AND CASINO, living up to its name, honestly rocks around the clock. The hotel is fun, comfortable, and informal. Powerful music elevates the energy level with a constant percussive din.

After a $750-million expansion, the Hard Rock tops out at 1,506 rooms. The addition of a 40,000-square-foot casino, three restaurants, an upgraded spa, Harmon Avenue porte cochere and parking garage, and two new towers of power repositions the small property to medium size and provides more pampering and amenities. HRH has become a major player in the quest for tourists and casino guests.

The 18-floor Paradise Tower, the larger of the two towers, presents 490 tribal tattoo rock-and-roll decadent rooms with all the high-tech bells and whistles. Bathrooms are spacious but offer showers only. This tower is convenient to the conference area. Request a poolside room for a voyeur's view overlooking the tropical gardens.

The all-suite HRH Tower, with a higher level of service, appeals to an older, more affluent demographic. The tower's subdued lobby provides guests with a private registration area. A KISS photo-montage tapestry, a gigantic hologram of Jimi Hendrix, and Michael Jackson's $50,000 sequined white glove grace the lobby's black walls.

The guest rooms have a clean, contemporary look in muted beige, white, and black with parquet floors at the entry. A glass wall divides the bedroom and bath, with an optional curtain. Every room features a wet bar and photos and lithographs of iconic rock stars. A detached wall with back-to-back wide-screen TVs divides the sitting area and bedroom. Guests will want to rock out to the in-room Sound Matters Sound Bar jukebox with 2,000 songs available at a touch. Choose a genre, artist, or decade and download songs to your own iPod.

The Hard Rock's expansion includes a 40,000-square-foot casino extension where The Joint (Las Vegas's first rock venue) used to be. This ancillary casino is more spacious and features an international pit offering Asian-preferred games: pai gow, baccarat, mini- and midi-baccarat, slots, and a high-limit room. Both casinos exhibit museum-quality rock memorabilia. The upsized Joint showroom seats 4,000 and features top rock artists. While the sound system is state-of-the-art, the floor-seating configuration is not inclined, so sight lines are poor from the middle and rear of the showroom.

The 25,000-square-foot Reliquary Water Sanctuary & Spa creates a luxurious experience in spartan surroundings. Although there are detached areas for men and women, the high-decibel bathhouse and lounge are co-ed, so fraternizing is encouraged. Twenty-one treatment rooms include an area for couples massage with a tub and four-person party rooms with treatment beds and TVs for bachelor and bachelorette groups. Atypical is the pole-dance studio with group lessons for bachelorette parties. The small fitness center has 26 machines and an adjoining hair salon. With the opening of Reliquary, the downstairs Rock Spa is now a well-equipped fitness center with a 53-machine gym, steam room, and Jacuzzi.

The extensive Beach Club pool complex is notorious for its televised anything-goes Rehab parties. Five pools are divided into two sections, with the walled Rehab zone imposing a cover charge on afternoons when a TV crew is filming. An elevated infinity pool adjoins the Skybar and Restaurant and overlooks the shallow dish pool. The complex features island-themed evening concerts. Avoid the Rehab side on summertime Sundays if you're seeking solitude and the sounds of silence.

The 14,000-square-foot Vanity Nightclub is adorned with antique mirrors, crystals, pearl light fixtures, diamond patterns, and shiny copper walls pierced with metallic gold threads. Above the dance floor is the centerpiece $1-million cyclone chandelier, composed of 20,000 LED lights that can produce a Technicolor image, text, or movies. Unlike other clubs, Vanity boasts open seating. A fire pit dominates the casual outdoor patio overlooking the Beach Club.

Along the casino perimeter and in the shopping arcade are restaurants Nobu, Pink Taco, 35 Steaks + Martinis, Mr. Lucky's cafe, and Starbucks. The Espumoso coffee and smoothie bar in the Paradise Tower lobby offers light Latin snacks. Boutiques include Rocks (jewelry), Love Jones (lingerie), Affliction (trendwear), Fuel (sundries), Hart & Huntington Tattoo Co., and John Varvatos (men's clothing with a bandstand and musical-instrument array where shoppers can jam or be jammed). Adjacent to the hotel in front of the property is the legendary Hard Rock Cafe; although it's separately owned and operated, the two Hard Rock enterprises maintain a cordial relationship.

Situated three-quarters of a mile east of the Strip, the Hard Rock's Paradise Road at Harmon Avenue location eliminates many of the traffic hassles confronting Strip visitors and gives guests excellent access to the airport, Las Vegas

Convention Center, and major freeways I-15, I-215, and I-95. HRH caters to all ages but targets the hip and wannabes primarily from Southern California, the Midwest, Canada, and Asia. Lots of satisfaction here, but it's not for the faint of heart or hard of hearing. If you're a rock fan from any era, this is rock and roll heaven if you don't mind the constant ear-numbing wall of sound.

Harrah's (harrahslasvegas.com)

A LAS VEGAS STAPLE, jazzy Harrah's occupies the middle of the Strip's most prestigious block and is within easy walking distance of Bally's, the Flamingo, the Mirage, Caesars Palace, Paris, Bellagio, The Venetian, and TI. Unpretentious and upbeat, Harrah's offers 2,652 guest rooms as well as a beautiful showroom, a comedy club, above-average restaurants, a buffet alongside the casino, a dance club, a pool, an exercise room, and a spa.

Harrah's theme celebrating carnival and Mardi Gras is evident in the two giant gold-leaf court jesters hefting a 10-ton, 22-foot-diameter globe that first welcome you on either side of the main hotel entrance, and a gold-swirled ceiling above the registration area continues the theme. The casino is decorated with brightly colored confetti-patterned carpet, ceiling murals, and fiber-optic lighting. Although the theme treatment is bright, it sports a somewhat tired feeling, rather like a Mardi Gras dawn.

The L-shaped casino of 87,000 square feet is loud beyond average. It can be entered directly from the Strip alongside an open-air lounge with very talented "show" bartenders and a stage that hosts mostly rock music. This covered amphitheater adds to the raucous, let-loose feeling of Harrah's, but might interrupt the sleep of some guests.

Though it is hard to imagine anyone not feeling comfortable at Harrah's, its clientele tends to be older visitors from the Midwest and Southern California, as well as business and convention travelers.

Other enticements include a large but otherwise unremarkable swimming area where you get sound bleed from the outdoor stage, a cozy upscale steakhouse with a view of the Strip, and an outdoor plaza with fountains. With its "Let the good times roll" spirit, Harrah's is blend of modern and vintage Las Vegas.

Hilton Lake Las Vegas (hilton.com)

ORIGINALLY A RITZ-CARLTON, then the Ravella for a short stint, this nongaming, 349-room Lake Las Vegas resort is now owned by Hilton. Within tranquil surroundings, the 15-acre lakefront property is approximately 22 miles from McCarran Airport and 25 miles from the Las Vegas Strip.

The rectangular lobby is furnished in gleaming dark woods and rich area rugs over tile and wood floors and divided into three sections: a business networking lounge with handsome library tables and complimentary Wi-Fi hookups, a center social lounge, and the Firenze Bar serving cocktails and light dinners. Cocktails are served on the outdoor terrace overlooking the formal Florentine garden and fire pit, the marina, and the lake. Downstairs, Café Medici is open for breakfast 7 a.m.–2 p.m.

Situated on eight floors, the 486-square-foot guest rooms are serenely decorated in a pale Mediterranean palate. Marble bathrooms are oversized with a two-sink vanity, weight scale (ouch!), and separate tub and shower.

Stretching across the west lip of the lake is the three-story 375-foot Ponte Vecchio Bridge over untroubled waters. Sailboats and kayaks glide underneath the bridge. This wing of the hotel houses guest rooms facing east toward the lake or west toward the stark desert hillsides. An additional parking lot lies at the north end of the span.

The peaceful 30,000-square-foot two-story Ravella Spa is a separate building across from the hotel's circular drive and sits atop a sandy beach and waterfall with handsome heated pool adjacent at water's edge. A fitness center, salon services, a variety of European massages, and 24 holistic treatment rooms are available. The facility includes a private garden proffering outdoor yoga classes, exercise sessions, and a meditation area. A restful terrace overlooks the pool, gardens, and the lagoon. For guests relishing the outdoors, hiking and biking trails hug the lake, and paddle boats, canoes, and kayaks are available for rental.

Valet parking is accessible and convenient. The parking garage near the southside meeting rooms is a distant stroll from the hotel lobby and elevators. A wedding chapel, wedding planner, and florist are also on site. The business center is in the conference area.

Nearby Casino MonteLago offers 275 slot machines and electronic table games. Golf is available at the nearby Southshore Golf Club, the first Jack Nicklaus Signature Course in Nevada. The hotel can arrange airport transfers, but most guests prefer to rent a car for flexibility. Pets are accepted.

Hooters Casino Hotel (hooterscasinohotel.com)

LET'S GET ONE THING SETTLED at the beginning. If you like Hooters—the chain of restaurants featuring hot wings and other pub grub served by waitresses in tight T-shirts and hot pants—then you will love the Hooters Casino Hotel. If you don't like Hooters restaurants, you won't much care for this place either, as the Hooters "mystique" is omnipresent from the casino floor to the hotel rooms (the latter even replaces typical hotel chairs with Hooters-style barstools). However, if you're not constitutionally averse to the brand, you might be surprised at how well the restaurateurs transformed the darkly dank San Remo into this bright, happening, and admittedly fun place. The casino floor looks remarkably like a Hooters restaurant, with the same light blonde wood, cheerful lighting, and simple orange accents. A large Hooters-like square bar greets you at the front door. At the gaming tables, rotating shifts of dealers are often attired in full Hooters uniform, right down to the orange hot pants. In addition to a pleasant lounge and coffee shop, there's an actual Hooters restaurant inside as well, and it draws huge lines of eager diners at peak times. A decent-sized pool dominates the back of the hotel, complete with waterfall, pool bar, and stage for live music. The reasonable room rates, utter lack of pretension or attitude, and party-hearty atmosphere draw a mix of middle-aged patrons and college kids, with a few families thrown in for good measure. Rooms have a vaguely Florida-tropical decor and are trimmed in Hooters orange, with moderate-budget amenities (bathrooms are a little on the cheap side). Although Hooters has been a breakout hit, the company tried to sell it to Hedwigs, a California investment group. Plans fell through, however, and Hooters is now looking for a new suitor.

JW Marriott Las Vegas/Rampart Casino
(jwlasvegasresort.com; rampartcasino.com)

THE JW MARRIOTT LAS VEGAS was the first of several upscale properties to offer a Scottsdale–Palm Beach resort experience as an alternative to
the madness of the Strip. Situated west of town near Red Rock Canyon, the
JW Marriott Las Vegas consists of two southwestern-style hotels built around
the Tournament Players Club (TPC) golf course. The JW Marriott officially
opened as The Resort at Summerlin in 1999, and a year or so later changed its
name to The Regent Las Vegas. Marriott acquired the property in late 2001,
and the name changed again. As an added twist, the classy, circular casino
has yet another name, Rampart Casino (after the road on which the casino is
located). The JW Marriott operates primarily as a meeting venue with a secondary emphasis on golf and the resort's exceptional spa. The casino, operated by an independent contractor, targets the local market.

Standard hotel rooms are huge at 560 square feet. In many rooms, French
doors open onto a balustrade overlooking the pools and gardens (11 acres of
palms and pines tower over the winding pools, waterfalls, and walkways), or
better yet, the mountains to the west, a stirring alternative to the usual neon.
Baths feature a whirlpool tub, separate shower, bathrobes, and telephone.

Restaurants serve Italian, Continental, Japanese, Irish, and American fare. The
buffet here is one of the better spreads in town. Although the lounges, including
the Irish pub, offer live entertainment, there is no showroom. The JW Marriott is
pricey but perfect for those who come to enjoy the beauty and recreational
resources of the mountains and valleys west of Las Vegas. Only minutes away
are world-class hiking, rock climbing, mountain biking, and road biking.

Las Vegas Club (lasvegasclubcasino.com)

THE LAS VEGAS CLUB is a trip back in time and a nostalgic look at classic Las Vegas. This longstanding Downtown landmark is now owned and managed by Play LV, which also operates the neighboring Plaza Hotel. Las Vegas
Club is well positioned at the corner of Main Street and the Fremont Street
Experience and takes up the entire block between First and Main. While the
casino is open 24/7 of course, the hotel portion of the property is currently
closed while the place gets a remodel. Guests can be accommodated at the
Plaza, its sister property across the street.

Housing one of the oldest race and sports books in Las Vegas, the friendly
casino is mirrored with high ceilings and offers mostly slots and video games
along with blackjack, roulette, three-card and pai gow poker, craps, and Frisky's
sports betting bar. A busy beef-jerky shop stocks Pacific Island snacks.

Given its sports memorabilia theme with museum-quality displays of baseball,
boxing, and basketball greats, this icon of Downtown caters to long-time players,
the Hawaiian market, and Gen Y–ers seeking a taste of the hotel's colorful past.

The LINQ Hotel & Casino (caesars.com/thelinq)

CAESARS WORLD HAS HEADS SPINNING—and we're not talking
about its new HIgh Roller observation wheel. It is yet again rebranding and
re-energizing the former Imperial Palace. This incarnation is the LINQ Hotel
& Casino, capitalizing on the nearby LINQ entertainment district.

During the property's brief stint as The Quad, interior renovations were completed that eliminated the tired Asian motif and introduced a contemporary look to the public spaces, including the front desk and lobby, retail arcade, and fifth-floor restaurant area. The expanded casino is now awash in designer shades of red, taupe, and black.

On tap to be completed by winter 2014 are a major renovation of all 2,256 guest rooms and suites and a much-needed exterior update. If the press materials are any indication, we expect the new guest rooms to be urban-chic with modern furnishings and subdued color schemes. All rooms will have floor-to-ceiling windows, high-tech gadgets, and Wi-Fi. We'll see if the Luv Tubs from the old IP make the cut. And let's hope they do something about those tortoise-speed elevators. *Note:* Our current room rating for the LINQ is based on the old guest rooms, but we expect the rating to increase significantly once renovations are complete. A new spa and pool deck are scheduled to debut in early 2015.

The front entrance has been relocated to the north side of the complex and can be accessed by driving through the parking garage via Koval Road on the east side of the property, or through the Harrah's tunnel off Las Vegas Boulevard South. A covered pedestrian walkway to The LINQ entertainment district commences at Harrah's Carnival Food Court and passes through The LINQ Hotel. There are also two reconfigured entries from the Strip.

Current entertainment offerings include Frank Marino's *Divas;* juggling, stunts, and more by family-friendly Jeff Civillico; and the boisterous *Recycled Percussion.*

Guy Fieri, UNLV hometown grad and Emmy award–winning chef, has launched his first local restaurant, Guy Fieri's Vegas Kitchen & Bar, at the LINQ Hotel. Also included in the dining inventory are Chayo Mexican Kitchen and Hash House A Go Go. TAG Sports Bar features an array of beers from around the world and televised sports 24/7. Many more dining, drinking, and entertainment choices are adjacent at The LINQ entertainment district.

Luxor (luxor.com)

THE LUXOR IS ON THE STRIP south of Tropicana Avenue next to the Excalibur. Representing Mandalay Resort Group's (now MRI) first serious effort to attract a more upscale, less family-oriented clientele, the Luxor is among the more tasteful of Las Vegas's themed hotels. Though originally not believed to be on a par with TI and the MGM Grand, the Luxor may be the most distinguished graduate of the much-publicized hotel class of 1993. While the MGM Grand is larger and TI originally more ostentatious, the Luxor demonstrates an unmatched creativity and architectural appeal.

Rising 30 stories, the Luxor is a huge pyramid with guest rooms situated around the outside perimeter from base to apex. Guest-room hallways circumscribe a hollow core containing the world's largest atrium. Inside the atrium, inclinators rise at a 39-degree angle from the pyramid's corners to access the guest floors. While the perspective from inside the pyramid is stunning, it is easy to get disoriented. Stories about hotel guests wandering around in search of their rooms are legend. After reviewing many complaints from readers, we seriously recommend carrying a small pocket compass.

The Luxor's main entrance is from the Strip via a massive sphinx. From the sphinx, guests are diverted into small entryways designed to resemble the interior passages of an actual pyramid. From these tunnels, guests emerge into the dramatic openness of the Luxor's towering atrium. Rising imposingly within the atrium is an exotic cityscape. The Luxor has succumbed to the let's-nuke-our-theme contagion and is merrily spending $300 million to drive the Egyptians back to Egypt.

Proceeding straight ahead at ground level from the main entrance brings you into the open and attractive 120,000-square-foot casino. One level below the casino and the main entrance is the Luxor's main showroom. Entertainment includes *JABBAWOCKEEZ,* a dance production; *Fantasy,* a topless revue; Cirque's *CRISS ANGEL Believe,* a magic-themed production show; comedy headliner, Carrot Top; and *Menopause: The Musical,* an off-Broadway musical. One floor above entry level, on a mezzanine of sorts, is an array of structures that reach high into the atrium. These dramatic buildings and facades transform the atrium. The atrium is home to three exhibits. Score is an interactive sports museum. *Bodies . . . The Exhibition* is an extraordinary and riveting introduction to human anatomy through authentic, preserved human bodies. It takes you stepwise through every part of the human body explaining its many systems. The last exhibit is *Titanic: The Artifact Exhibition,* which takes guests on a chronological odyssey from the design and building of the ocean liner to life on board to its sinking. Luxor's 26,000-square-foot LAX nightclub is one of the hottest late-night venues in the city.

Flanking the pyramid are two hotel towers that were part of an expansion, which also included a health spa and fitness center and additional meeting and conference space. Soft goods play off the mixed wood tones of the furniture to create some of the warmest and most visually appealing guest rooms in Las Vegas. In all, the Luxor offers 4,450 guest rooms.

The Luxor's large, attractive pool complex, surrounded by private cabanas, desperately needs some additional plants and trees. Self-parking is not as much a problem at the Luxor as at most large properties. Valet parking is quick and efficient, however, and well worth the tip. The Luxor is within a 5- to 12-minute walk of the Excalibur, the Tropicana, and the MGM Grand. A moving walkway connects the Luxor to the Excalibur and an overhead "cable liner" (a monorail propelled by a cable à la San Francisco cable cars) connects it with Mandalay Bay.

M Resort (themresort.com)

REPLACING SOUTH POINT as the most upscale resort south of the Strip, M Resort opened in March 2009 at Las Vegas Boulevard South and Saint Rose Parkway, about 10 miles from Mandalay Bay. The *M* of M Resort could easily stand for "mirage," given how it rises all by itself, shimmering in the desert. That letter, however, is actually from the family name Marnell, in honor of founder and CEO Anthony Marnell III. Active in Las Vegas hospitality and gaming for decades, the Marnells previously built and operated the Rio, establishing a reputation for style and innovation. The Marnells have always produced a high-quality product geared to the local population. With a refreshing lack of spectacle and abundance of modern elegance, M Resort is specifically located to serve the affluent residential developments in the south Las Vegas Valley.

The well-configured casino with spacious aisles groups similar slots together with ample playing room. Blackjack, pai gow, mini-baccarat, roulette, and craps are arranged in small groups of eight tables. Dealers are assigned to the same table for an entire month, so players partial to a lucky dealer can return to his table. The race and sports book is intimate, seating just 50 people, but absolutely cutting edge.

The 110,000-square-foot Villagio Del Sole and Entertainment Piazza is expansive. Bamboo and palm trees line the left side of the marble entry staircase where running water tumbles over large marble cubes along the steps. Private cabanas line the perimeter of the grounds, and two hot tubs are positioned at each rear corner along with a fire pit and tall metal torches. Tucked away on the west side is the Daydream pool for adults. The infinity pool is divided along the center by a walkway scattered with orange daybeds. An outdoor stage at the north end of the pool features concerts regularly. You can score the best seats in the house by dining on the terrace of the Hash House A Go Go, which directly overlooks the concert stage. During normal operations, with just 390 rooms at the M, the 2.3-acre pool area is seldom congested.

Dining options include the Studio B buffet, which includes unlimited beer and wine for dinner and adds special seafood dishes to the usual lineup on weekends. With the exception of the Studio B buffet and Vig Deli, the restaurants have terraces and outdoor dining to take advantage of the breathtaking view of Las Vegas, enhanced by the hotel's elevation (400 feet higher than the Strip). To better control the quality and price point of meat offerings, the resort maintains a butcher shop on the premises with fresh beef, pork, and lamb flown in from its own Montana ranch. Fine-dining options include Anthony's, specializing in prime steak, seafood, and an oyster bar, and Marinelli's for regional Italian cuisine and homemade pastas.

Lounges are stylish and feature some of the best free entertainment anywhere. Check out the Ravello lounge for high-energy music that includes all the classics of rock, pop, and jazz as well as modern favorites. If you crave a taste of the grape or the fruit of the barley, M has you covered. 32º Draft offers 96 different beers on tap, while at Hostile Grape, a chic and cozy wine cellar, you can sample 160 different wines by the glass. Vintages from all the great wine-producing areas of the world are represented. Oh yeah, cola and soft-drink fans have their oasis too with a free soft-drink dispenser just off the casino, a first in any casino.

Guest rooms feature floor-to-ceiling windows with electric drapes, Bose radios, high-speed Internet, iPod docking stations, and 42-inch flat-panel TVs as well as bathroom TVs embedded in the mirrors. Standard rooms are large at 420 square feet, and views can be either of the Nevada desert landscape to the south or the Strip to the north, overlooking the pool. The luxury bath has a glass wall that faces the center of the room and the window.

Though it feels remote, M Resort is only a 10- to 12-minute drive on I-15 from the heart of the Strip. One caution, however: do not miss the Saint Rose Parkway exit when you're driving southbound. It's 23 miles to the next exit.

Main Street Station (mainstreetcasino.com)

SITUATED ON MAIN STREET between Ogden and Stewart Avenues in Downtown Las Vegas, Main Street Station originally opened in 1992 as a paid-admission nighttime entertainment complex with a casino on the side. Owned and managed by an Orlando, Florida, entrepreneur with no casino experience, it took Main Street Station less than a year to go belly-up. The property was acquired several years later by Boyd Gaming, which used Main Street Station's hotel to accommodate overflow guests from the California across the street. In 1997, the Boyds reopened the casino, restaurants, and shops, adding a brewpub in the process.

The casino is one of the most unusual in town (thanks largely to the concept of the original owner). With the feel of a turn-of-the-20th-century gentlemen's club and enough antiques, original art, and oddities to furnish a museum, Main Street Station is a must-see. With its refurbished guest rooms, brewpub, excellent buffet, and unusual casino, it is both interesting and fun, adding some welcome diversity to the Downtown hospitality mix.

Mandalay Bay (mandalaybay.com)

MANDALAY BAY OPENED on March 2, 1999, on the site of the old Hacienda, imploded on New Year's Day 1998. It completes the Mandalay Bay "Miracle Mile," which stretches along the Strip south from the Bellagio and includes CityCenter, the Monte Carlo, New York–New York, the Excalibur, Luxor, and finally Mandalay Bay. A cable liner connects Excalibur, Luxor, and Mandalay Bay every 15 minutes, 24 hours a day (it stops at Luxor on the northbound leg only).

Mandalay Bay, with 4,756 rooms (including the on-site Four Seasons Hotel and the Delano), is a megaresort in the true sense of the overworked word. Within the sprawling complex are the 43-story, three-wing tower; a 12,000-seat arena; a 1,600-seat theater; an 1,800-seat House of Blues concert venue; two dozen restaurants; an 11-acre water park; three large lounges; and the third-largest convention facility in Las Vegas. Mandalay Bay had Las Vegas's first hotel-within-a-hotel on the property: the 424-room Four Seasons. The whole schmear cost a cool billion plus. Adjoining the main casino is a second on-site hotel, the Delano, with 1,120 suites. Both the Four Seasons and the Delano are profiled in this section under their own names.

But that's not the half of it, because Mandalay Bay isn't your standard megaresort. It's clear that the planners and designers set out to take a few risks and appeal to a young, hip, fun-seeking market—as opposed to Bellagio, which targets a more refined, sophisticated, older clientele. If Bellagio is the crowning culmination of 20th-century Las Vegas, Mandalay Bay might be Las Vegas's first foray into the 21st. All the different ideas jammed into Mandalay Bay might not always add up to a cohesive whole, but so many parts of the sum are unique that you can't help being intrigued.

The signature spectacle is the four-story wine tower at Manhattan celebrity chef Charlie Palmer's restaurant, Aureole. This nearly 50-foot-tall glass-and-stainless-steel structure stores about 10,000 bottles of wine. Lovely, athletic women dressed all in black—spandex tights, racing gloves, hard hats—manipulate the motorized cable, one on each of the four sides, that raises them up to retrieve a selected bottle and lowers them back down to deliver it.

Red Square Russian restaurant has a one-of-a-kind refrigerated walk-in showcase, open to the public, which stores 200 different varieties of vodka at 15°F. Drinks are served on a long bar top that has a thick strip of ice running its length. The House of Blues restaurant and entertainment complex serves food (Southern-style and Creole-Cajun) and has the world's largest collection of Deep South folk art, as well as a strange dark bar with a crucifix theme. House of Blues also puts on a Sunday gospel brunch and holds rock and pop concerts in its 1,800-seat theater. Beef eaters are well served with two upscale chop houses, Michael Mina's STRIPSTEAK and Charlie Palmer Steak. Other restaurants include Wolfgang Puck's Lupo (serving Italian fare), Fleur by Hubert Keller (serving globally inspired small plates), Rick Moonen's RM Seafood, Mix (an Alain Ducasse French eatery with midcentury-modern furniture and knockout views of the Strip), Border Grill (serving Mexican cuisine), Mizuya (a sushi spot), a noodle room, a coffee shop, a somewhat disappointing buffet, and ice-cream and coffee counters.

A main attraction at Mandalay Bay is Shark Reef, a 90,000-square-foot aquarium exhibit with a walk-through acrylic tunnel. The aquarium is home to about 2,000 marine species, including Nile crocodiles, moray eels, stingrays, and, of course, sharks.

In the nightlife department, Mix offers innovative cocktails and a stunning view, while Eyecandy Sound Lounge & Bar, a sprawling DJ dance venue, makes clubbing hassle-free. The newly resurrected Light nightclub lures guests with its stable of resident DJs.

Speaking of acreage, the casino is typically monumental, with plenty of elbowroom between machines and tables. The race and sports book boasts the largest screen in town, which is only right, since the book is so big the screen must be seen from long distances. The 80-seat (each one an oversized, velour-covered easy chair) lounge and the large poker room are connected.

The pool area is also imaginative. The 11-acre Mandalay Bay Beach has a lazy river, a placid pool, a beachfront cafe and bar, and a wedding chapel. The centerpiece, however, is a huge wave pool. The surf can be cranked up from one to six feet.

The Shoppes at Mandalay Place, in the pedestrian passage that connects Mandalay Bay with the Luxor, features about 35 boutiques and restaurants.

All in all, Mandalay Bay accomplishes what every mega–casino-hotel sets out to do—deliver an inventive and hip experience that sets a standard for all the megajoints that follow.

MGM Grand (mgmgrand.com)

MGM GRAND CLAIMS THE DISTINCTION of having Vegas's largest casino. Within the 112-acre complex, there is a 16,800-seat special-events arena, 380,000 square feet of convention space, 171,500 square feet of casino space, and a multilevel parking facility. There's also a small casino outside the lobby of the Mansion, MGM's ultra-upscale whale digs. Finally, a 6.6-acre pool-and-spa complex took over a chunk of the now-defunct amusement park along with the dedicated convention center.

The MGM Grand is on the northeast corner of Tropicana Avenue and the Strip. The Strip entrance passes beneath a 45-foot-tall MGM Lion atop a 25-foot pedestal, all surrounded by three immense digital displays. The lion entrance leads to a domed rotunda with table games and a Rainforest Cafe, and from there to the MGM Grand's four larger casinos. All of the casinos are roomy and plush, with high ceilings and a comfortable feeling of openness.

A second entrance, with a porte cochere 15 lanes wide, serves vehicular traffic from Tropicana Avenue. For all practical purposes, this is the main entrance to the MGM Grand, permitting you to go directly to the hotel lobby and its 53 check-in windows without lugging your belongings through the casinos. Just beyond the registration area is the elevator core, with 35 elevators servicing 30 guest floors.

Beyond the elevator core, a wide passageway leads toward five of the MGM Grand's many restaurants. The MGM Grand's supernova restaurant is Joël Robuchon, which serves a French culinary feast of the highest quality and greatest exclusivity. Other fine-dining stars in the hotel's galaxy include L'Atelier de Joël Robuchon, serving more fine French cuisine via counter service (dishes are prepared in front of you); Tom Colicchio's Craftsteak, offering beef and seafood; Hecho en Vegas, a Mexican restaurant; Fiamma, an Italian trattoria; Shibuya, a Japanese restaurant; Emeril's New Orleans Fish House, offering Creole-Cajun dishes; Hakkasan, specializing in modern Cantonese; Pearl, serving traditional Chinese; and Wolfgang Puck Bar & Grill and Crush for fancy American cuisine. Less formal are The Grand Wok and Sushi Bar, featuring Asian specialties from a half dozen countries; the Rainforest Cafe; Michael Mina Pub 1842; Tap Sports Bar; and the Avenue Café. MGM Grand's buffet adjoins the casinos between the porte cochere and lion entrances. For fast food there is a food court.

There are two showrooms at the MGM Grand. The 740-seat Hollywood Theater features headliners, and the larger *KÀ* Theatre is home to Cirque du Soleil's *KÀ*. The new Brad Garrett comedy club has moved downstairs between the parking garage and an underground retail passageway. Nightclubs include Beecher's Madhouse, with quirky, edgy stage acts, and Hakkasan, which replaced Studio 54 in 2014 as MGM Grand's premiere nightspot. It features celebrity DJs, high-tech lighting, and three levels of activity with a variety of areas and atmospheres. Entertainment is also offered in the casino's four lounges. In addition, the MGM Grand's special-events arena can accommodate boxing, tournament tennis, rodeo, and basketball, as well as major exhibitions.

Amenities at the MGM Grand, not unexpectedly, are among the best in Las Vegas. The swimming complex is huge—23,000 square feet of pool area, with five interconnected pools graced with bridges, fountains, and waterfalls. Other highlights of the complex include an artificial stream to float in, a poolside bar, and luxury cabanas. Adjoining the swimming area is a complete health club and spa. For those to whom recreation means pumping quarters into a machine, there is an electronic games arcade supplemented by a "games-of-skill" midway. In the transportation department, the MGM Grand is the southern terminus of the Las Vegas Monorail.

In 2012, 3,570 of the hotel's 5,044 guest rooms were given a facelift with grand results. The lion logo remains, but the Hollywood theme predicated by the hotel's name is gone with the wind, and in its place are a sleek 21st-century vogue and the latest in-room technology. Remodeled rooms are located in four wings of the east tower. Remember that the MGM Grand is the second-largest hotel in the world, so be prepared for a hike from the elevator banks to your accommodations. Request a higher floor where the views are spectacular.

A rare enclave of peace and privacy, MGM Grand's Signature condo-hotel towers are a 5- to 7-minute walk east of the main casino. Conspicuous by its absence is on-site gambling. For more details on the Signature, see page 159.

Drawing from a wide cross section of the leisure market, the MGM Grand gets the majority of its business from individual travelers and tour and travel groups, but with a rising percentage coming from trade-show and convention attendees. Midrange room rates make the MGM Grand accessible to a broad population. Geographically, the MGM Grand targets Southern California, Phoenix, Denver, Dallas, Houston, Chicago, and the Midwest.

Mirage (mirage.com)

THE MIRAGE HAS HAD AN IMPACT on the Las Vegas tourist industry that will be felt for years to come. By challenging all the old rules and setting new standards for design, ambience, and entertainment, the Mirage precipitated the development of a class of super-hotels in Las Vegas, redefining the thematic appeal and hospitality standard of hotel-casinos.

Exciting and compelling without being whimsical or silly, the Mirage has demonstrated that the public will respond enthusiastically to a well-executed concept. Blending the stateliness of marble with the exotic luxury of tropical greenery and the straightforward lines of polished bamboo, the Mirage has created a spectacular environment that artfully integrates casino, showroom, shopping, restaurants, and lounges. Both lavish and colorful, inviting and awe-inspiring, the Mirage has avoided cliché. Not designed to replicate a famous palace or be the hotel version of "Goofy Golf," the Mirage makes an original statement.

An atrium rain forest serves as a central hub from which guests can proceed to all areas of the hotel and casino. Behind the hotel's front desk, a 60-foot-long aquarium contains small and colorful tropical fish. Outside, instead of blinking neon, the Mirage has a 55-foot-tall erupting volcano that disrupts traffic on the Strip every hour on the hour (6–11 p.m.). There is also a live dolphin exhibit and a modern showroom that is among the most well designed and technologically advanced in Las Vegas.

The Mirage boasts several fine-dining opportunities, including Japonais, a concept restaurant featuring Japanese and "old-style" European cuisine; Fin, serving contemporary Chinese; Tom Colicchio's Heritage Steak, a chop, seafood, and lobster house; STACK, an American grill; Samba, a Brazilian *churrascaria;* Portofino by Michael LaPlaca, one of the city's better Italian restaurants; and Morimoto Las Vegas for Japanese cuisine and signature sushi. For more casual fare, try acclaimed Chef Laurent Tourondel's BLT Burger or the California Pizza Kitchen. For bulk eaters, there is an excellent and affordable buffet. *LOVE,* a Cirque du Soleil production based on the music of the Beatles, plays in one of two showrooms. Amenities include a swimming and sunning complex with waterfalls, inlets, and an interconnected series of lagoons; a shopping arcade; and a spa with exercise equipment. The casino is huge and magnificently appointed, yet informal, with its tropical motif and piped-in Jimmy Buffett music. Guest rooms at the Mirage are among the nicest in town.

With its indoor jungle and traffic-snarling volcano, the Mirage remains one of Clark County's top tourist attractions. Whether by foot, bus, cab, or bicycle, every Las Vegas visitor makes at least one pilgrimage. The Mirage has become the Strip's melting pot and hosts the most incredible variety of humanity imaginable.

Monte Carlo (montecarlo.com)

APPEARING ON THE SCENE IN 1996 with 3,006 guest rooms, the Monte Carlo ranks as one of the larger hotels in Las Vegas. The megaresort is modeled after the Place du Casino in Monte Carlo, Monaco, with ornate arches and fountains, marble floors, and a Gothic, glass registration area. If the Monte Carlo fails as a resort, the building will be a perfect place to relocate the Nevada State Capitol.

In an effort to pep things up, however, the resort hatched an idea that turned the dull Monte Carlo theme on its head. Astonishingly, they tacked a Diablo's Cantina restaurant onto the south corner of the resort, with a wildly colorful Strip-side exterior complete with an eye-popping, scantily clad she-devil statue straddling the roof. The cantina effectively drains the stuffiness of the namesake theme and achieves a contrast (or dissonance) that could only be matched by grazing yaks in the casino.

On the surface, it's yet another huge hotel in the Las Vegas Age of the Megaresort. But scratch the surface just a little and you glimpse the future of Monopoly-board Las Vegas and the gambling business in general.

The guest rooms, furnished with marble entryways and French-period wall art, are mid- to upper-priced. In 2009, the Monte Carlo opened Hotel 32 on the 32nd and highest floor of the hotel. The idea (they say) is to provide a high-roller, VIP experience at an affordable price. Five different configurations of studios and suites are available. Extras include a "suite assistant" (butler?) and a private lounge.

There is an elaborate swimming complex with slides, a wave pool, and a man-made stream. There is also an exceptional health and fitness center, an interesting shopping arcade, and a brewpub with a DJ on Friday and Saturday nights. The casino, about a football field long and similarly shaped, is capped with simulated skylights and domes. The showroom features the Blue Man Group. Restaurants cover the usual bases, offering steak, Italian, and Asian specialties, with the brewpub thrown in for good measure. The signature restaurant is Andre's (after chef André Rochat), serving traditional French cuisine and offering a wine list with 1,500 selections.

Compared to the powerful themes of New York–New York and the Luxor, the Monte Carlo's turn-of-the-century Monegasque theme fails to stimulate much excitement or anticipation. Besides being beyond the average tourist's frame of reference, the theme lacks any real visceral dimension. The word *grand* comes to mind, but more in the context of a federal courthouse or the New York Public Library.

New York–New York (newyorknewyork.com)

WHEN IT OPENED IN JANUARY 1997, this architecturally imaginative hotel-casino set a new standard for the realization of Las Vegas megaresort themes. It's a small joint by megaresort standards ("only" around 2,000 rooms), but the triumph is in the details. The guest rooms are in a series of distinct towers reminiscent of a mini–Big Apple skyline, including the Empire State, Chrysler, and Seagram Buildings. Though the buildings are connected, each offers a somewhat different decor and ambience.

A half-size Statue of Liberty and a replica of Grand Central Station lead visitors to one entrance, while the Brooklyn Bridge leads to another. The interior of the property is broken into themed areas such as Greenwich Village, Wall Street, and Times Square. The casino, one of the most visually interesting in Las Vegas, looks like an elaborate movie set. Table games and slots are sandwiched between shops, restaurants, and a jumble of street facades.

The street scenes are well executed, conveying both a sense of urban style and tough grittiness. New York–New York sacrificed much of its visual impact, however, by not putting in an imitation sky. At Sunset Station, by way of contrast, the Spanish architecture is augmented significantly by vaulted ceilings, realistically lighted and painted with clouds. This sort of finishing touch could have done wonders for New York–New York.

Like its namesake, New York–New York is congested to the extreme, awash day and night with curious sightseers. There are so many people just wandering around gawking that there's little room left for hotel guests and folks who actually came to gamble. Because aisles and indoor paths are far too narrow to accommodate the crowds, New York–New York succumbs periodically to a sort of pedestrian gridlock.

Manhattan rules, however, do not apply at New York–New York: it's OK here to make eye contact and decidedly rude to shove people out of the way to get where you want to go. If you find yourself longing for the thrill of a New York cab ride, go hop on the roller coaster. New York–New York's coaster isn't the only one on the Strip, but it's the only one where you can stand on the street and hear the riders scream.

The showroom features Cirque du Soleil's *Zumanity*. Lounges include a dueling-pianos bar, a high-energy dance club, and a Coyote Ugly bar. Based on the movie of the same name, the bar features a platoon of dancing female bartenders with enough attitude to stop a real New Yorker dead in his tracks.

Guest rooms at New York–New York have been renovated and upgraded. However, the swimming area and health and fitness center are just average. Full-service restaurants are a little better than average, though Gallagher's Steakhouse, a real Big Apple import, can hold its own with any beef place, in or out of Las Vegas. Nine Fine Irishmen is a pub serving up live Irish music nightly, along with excellent pub fare that proves the Irish cuisine has come a long way. There is no buffet. Counter-service fast food is quite interesting, if not altogether authentic New York.

The Orleans (orleanscasino.com)

ORLEANS IS JUST WEST OF I-15 on Tropicana Avenue. Marketed primarily to locals, The Orleans has a New Orleans–bayou theme executed in a hulking cavern of a building. The casino is festive with bright carpets, high ceilings, a two-story replication of a French Quarter street flanking the table games, and a couple of nifty bars. The Orleans has a celebrity showroom that attracts great talent. For fine dining there's Canal Street, specializing in seafood and steaks, and the Prime Rib Loft. The buffet, which serves Creole-Cajun dishes, is good but can't quite match Louisiana standards. Upstairs, over the slots and buffet area, is a 70-lane bowling complex. The Orleans Arena is a 9,000-seat facility and home to the Las Vegas Wranglers pro hockey team. Two hotel towers with a total of 1,886 large guest rooms, an 18-screen movie complex, a games arcade, and a child-care center complete the package.

Palace Station (palacestation.com)

LOCATED 4 MINUTES OFF THE STRIP on West Sahara Avenue, Palace Station is a local favorite that also attracts tourists. With great lounge acts, a first-rate buffet, dependable restaurants that continuously offer amazing specials, a tower of Holiday Inn–caliber guest rooms, good prices, and a location that permits access to both Downtown and the Strip in less than 10 minutes, Palace Station is a standard setter for locals' casinos. Decorated in a railroad theme, the casino is large and busy with a heavy emphasis on slots (which are supposedly loose—that is, having a high rate of payoff).

Palms (palms.com)

THERE IS A NEW VIBE AT THE PALMS, which has been re-energized with contemporary nightlife spaces and culinary spots, an expanded pool complex, a reconfigured casino, and upgraded guest rooms. The resort where trendy and affluent Gen X and Y guests partied 12 years ago has matured, and so have the guests, with all transitioning to a more upscale experience.

Guest rooms in the Ivory and Fantasy Towers are cutting-edge with très chic purple and cream velvet and splashes of bright turquoise or red. White linens are topped by violet bolsters, and above the headboards are arresting murals that combine palm leaves and pairs of eyes that follow you around the room. Wide windows offer Strip or mountain views.

Though the casino is roomy, at 95,000 square feet, it's the Palms' nightlife mix that sets the hotel apart. Atop the 55-story Fantasy Tower is The View, a lounge with panoramic views of the entire Las Vegas Valley. On the ground level of the same tower is Rain, a high-energy dance club with pulsing fountains and high-tech special effects. Atop the Ivory Tower is Ghostbar, a sophisticated boutique nightclub with still more knockout views. Social, the casino's center bar, offers whiskey-based cocktails. Also on the casino floor are Tonic, The Mint, and Scarlet—all fine places to grab a drink. Off the lobby you'll find the Rojo Lounge. A show lounge, a 14-screen cinema, and Pearl—a very cool concert venue—complete the entertainment mix.

The restaurant lineup, equally impressive, leads off with Alizé, serving gourmet French cuisine and stunning views from the top story; N9NE, a steakhouse imported from Chicago; and Nove Italiano, an elegant room graced by topiaries in the form of classic nudes. Rounding out the dining mix are Back Room Burger, 24 Seven Café, Fortunes (located within 24 Seven Café) for Chinese cuisine, Kerry Simon's Simon for modern American, the Bistro Buffet, and The Eatery food court.

Palms is too far from the Strip for most guests to feel comfortable walking. For those with a car, however, the coming and going is easy, and the hotel location on West Flamingo Road facilitates accessing Strip casinos via alternate routes rather than joining the gridlock on Las Vegas Boulevard. Shuttle service is provided to the Forum Shops on the Strip next to Caesars Palace.

Paris (parislasvegas.com)

ON THE STRIP NEXT TO BALLY'S and across from Bellagio, Paris trots out a French-Parisian theme in much the same way New York–New York caricatures the Big Apple. Paris has its own 50-story Eiffel Tower (with a restaurant halfway up) and an Arc de Triomphe. Thrown in for good measure are the Champs-Elysées, Parc Monceau, and the Palais Garnier.

Like New York–New York, Paris presents its iconography in a whimsical way. The casino sits in a parklike setting roughly arrayed around the base of the Eiffel Tower, three legs of which protrude through the roof of the casino. The video-poker schedules are lackluster, but the casino offers all of the usual table games.

Flanking the tower and branching off from the casino are dining and shopping venues designed to re-create Parisian and rural *petit village* street scenes. Though spacious, the casino and other public areas at Paris are exceedingly busy, bombarding the senses with color, sound, and activity. While at The Venetian you have the sense of entering a grand space, at Paris the feeling is more of envelopment.

The hotel towers, with almost 3,000 guest rooms, rise in an L shape framing the Eiffel Tower. The rooms are quite stunning and rank along with the dining as one of Paris's most outstanding features.

Paris recently updated the 400 *chambres* on floors 26–30 and designated them "Red Rooms," although they aren't overly red or even very Parisian. Nevertheless, the new decor has reinvigorated the rooms so they appear more spacious and less froufrou bucolic. There's a photo of the Eiffel Tower in each room, plus the rooms on the Strip side are endowed with a view of the octagon-shaped pool and the giant reproduced tower itself.

The pool complex is on the roof. The facility is spacious but rather plain and underdeveloped in comparison with the rest of the property. A spa and health club connect both to the pool area and the hotel.

The flagship Eiffel Tower Restaurant is situated 11 stories above the Strip in the, of course, Eiffel Tower. Several other restaurants, closer to the ground, and including the buffet, also feature French cuisine. Options include the Italian-French Le Provençal; Gordon Ramsay Steak; Mon Ami Gabi, serving French bistro fare on an outdoor terrace overlooking the Strip; Le Café Île St. Louis, a sidewalk cafe serving classic French and American cuisine 24/7; and Sugar Factory American Brasserie, serving a wide array of sweet treats as well as salads, sandwiches, and more.

In the entertainment department, Paris features *Jersey Boys,* the Tony Award–winning Broadway musical, and hypnotist Anthony Cools.

You'll find two shopping venues. The Paris-Bally's Promenade offers French jewelry, women's accessories, an art gallery of French and French-inspired work, and more. Le Boulevard houses boutiques, a home-and-garden store, a gourmet food shop, and a newsstand, among other shops. And, of course, if you don't mind a little waiting, you can take an elevator to the top of the Eiffel Tower for a knockout view of the Strip.

Paris and its next-door neighbor, Bally's, share a monorail station, making both hotels a very convenient choice if you're attending a convention at the Las Vegas Convention Center.

Planet Hollywood (planethollywoodresort.com)

PLANET HOLLYWOOD IS THE LATEST AND BEST incarnation of the Aladdin. The Aladdin opened in 1963 as the Tally Ho but was renamed the King's Crown in 1964. In 1966, the King's Crown was purchased by Milton Prell, who gave the property a $3-million facelift with an Arabian Nights theme and dubbed it the Aladdin. For the next 30 years, the Aladdin changed ownership many times, which resulted in an eclectic, constantly changing identity. Each new owner of the Aladdin tacked on a wing, changed the carpeting, or removed the wall art inherited from the previous owner.

While the Aladdin was choking on its own mixed metaphors, the real estate it occupied became increasingly valuable. In the late 1990s, the Aladdin was once more acquired and promptly blown up to make way for a brand-new Aladdin, where the exotic Arabian Nights theme could realize its full potential and where there was room for a Middle Eastern bazaar–themed mall to compete with Caesars' Forum Shops and The Venetian's Grand Canal Shoppes. Though the vision of the new Aladdin was executed with flair and imagination, it failed to attract enough patrons to offset the considerable debt. After passing into receivership, the Aladdin was sold in 2003 to Planet Hollywood and Starwood Hotels, and then again in 2010 to Caesars Entertainment.

From the beginning, Planet Hollywood, or PH as it bills itself now, was committed to throwing the exhausted Arabian Nights under the bus in favor of a youthful, upscale, Hollywood look. PH, however, took its own sweet time in making the change.

The new look, clubby and masculine with dark woods and rich textiles, is drop-dead gorgeous. Carpet patterns and stone works capture the feel and beauty of a desert canyon and integrate them into a whole that is both sophisticated and relaxing. Face it, there are dozens of casinos that awe and overwhelm the senses, but only a handful that are artful and soothing.

Placement of the hotel lobby separates quite distinctly the bustle of guests and baggage from the casino, eliminating the flow of almost all transitory traffic in the casino. The casino floor, at almost three acres, offers the usual slots and table games but feels more exclusive. In fact, the whole casino has the ambience of sequestered high-roller gaming areas in other hotels. As for theme, there are some strictly Hollywood touches, but in the public areas it's quite understated.

The guest rooms are created around a focal object of Hollywood memorabilia and a room-long combination wardrobe and entertainment center with a flat-panel TV. The furniture is a little large and plentiful for the size of the room, but the distinctly masculine overall effect is one of luxury and great attention to ergonomic detail.

Additional accommodations are available in Elara, a nongaming, all-suite timeshare property positioned over the Miracle Mile shopping mall. For additional information on Elara, see pages 157–158.

Planet Hollywood has three showrooms, including the 7,000-seat Theatre for the Performing Arts. Two additional showrooms in the adjoining Miracle Mile Shops (formerly Desert Passage) make PH one of the most happening entertainment venues in Las Vegas. The shopping venue has undergone a multimillion-dollar makeover, which converted the original Middle Eastern Bazaar design to a more contemporary look. PH also has a rooftop pool and a Spa by Mandara.

Retained from the Aladdin is the highly acclaimed Spice Market Buffet. Fine-dining options include Gordon Ramsay BURGR; KOI, serving Japanese-California fusion fare; and a clone of New York City's Strip House restaurant. A host of more casual restaurants, including Yolö's for Mexican and P.F. Chang's, round out the options.

Paris Las Vegas is only an 8-minute walk to the north, but the closest hotel to the south is the MGM Grand about a third of a mile away. The new CityCenter resort, however, is right across the street. Self-parking at Planet Hollywood is very confusing, and you must troop through the Miracle Mile Shops to reach the hotel or casino. If you are a hotel guest, definitely plan on using valet parking. If you're going to hit the shops, self-parking is fine.

PH targets an under-50 market from the southwestern United States and is also active in the European, Asian, and Latin American markets.

Plaza (plazahotelcasino.com)

THE VALUE-PRICED PLAZA has the distinction of being the only hotel in Las Vegas with its own railroad station, though passenger trains no longer run on this stretch of track. Occupying the historic site of the 16.5-acre Union Pacific train depot, the iconic Plaza Hotel and Casino at 1 Main St. presides at the west entrance to the Fremont Street Experience. The property was completely renovated and its two towers with 22 floors, casino, and public space resumed providing Downtown hospitality in the fall of 2011. With tower elevators nearby, the front desk and lobby are just steps from the 10,000-light porte cochere. The lively adjacent lounge beckons with happy-hour drink specials, nightly dueling pianos, karaoke, and comedy shows.

The sleek remodeled rooms, some of the largest Downtown, boast a sitting area and portable refrigerators. Every room is adorned with an imposing 1970s black-and-white photo of the original Union Plaza. Views from both towers sweep above Downtown and suburban Las Vegas.

The casino features 820 of the latest and greatest video poker machines and slots, a full pit of popular casino games, Lucky's Race and Sports Book, as well as a private pit where groups can gamble and party together. Bingo, now a rarity in most Downtown casinos, is also available. Throughout the casino, even the original chandeliers were refurbished.

Casual restaurants are the Hash House A Go-Go diner, Island Sushi Hawaiian Grill, and Pop Up Pizza. Adjoining the lobby are Caffelatte, a video arcade, a sundries shop, and a food court. On the third floor, and named after Las Vegas's popular former mob lawyer and mayor Oscar Goodman, the signature Oscar's Steakhouse is well positioned under the glass dome with an unparalleled sight line down Glitter Gulch and its neon canopy. Entertainment includes rotating afternoon lounge acts; Emmy award–winning comedian Louie Anderson playing Wednesday–Saturday nights at 7 p.m.; and Bonkerz Comedy Club.

The expansive fifth-floor Sports Deck features Downtown's only tennis and basketball courts, a small pool with chaises and cabanas, plus a snack and cocktail bar. A summer concert series is planned. A 24-hour fitness center, hair salon, and a wedding chapel round out the Plaza's amenities. The parking garage at the property's south entrance is free to hotel guests. Customers are drive-ins from surrounding states, the Mid-west, and Texas.

Red Rock Casino Resort Spa (redrock.sclv.com)

CONTINUING THE UPSCALE EVOLUTION begun with Green Valley Ranch Resort and Spa, Station Casinos created a very similar and even tonier property in the Red Rock Casino Resort Spa. Set about 10 miles west of the

Strip on Charleston Boulevard and isolated from any other property of similar stature, Red Rock attempts to make itself a destination worth the trip. It's an impressive place, with a low, curving, monolithic roofline meant to echo the desert landscape and slopes of nearby Red Rock Canyon. Inside, stone, wood, and glass predominate; again, forms and colors are often meant to echo the surrounding geography. The overall impression is reminiscent of an accessible, upscale desert spa hotel, as opposed to the more glitzy palaces on the Strip. The casino's arrangement is similar to that of Green Valley Ranch—wide alleys between banks of slots and rings of table games—and the two casinos even share some of the same restaurants. Several of the restaurants open onto the pool area, which, while not staggeringly huge, is quite elegant. Tiers of outdoor lounges and patios overlook smaller wading pools and rentable cabanas, plus the inevitable pool bar. As you proceed farther through the casino, the feel gets more and more "local"; the entrance on the far end is in fact specifically geared to locals, with close parking on the outside and local-friendly assortments of games right inside the door. This is also where you find the attached movie theater and Kids Quest children's complex, making it convenient to drop off the offspring en route to the casino.

Red Rock Resort takes advantage of its location by offering a number of outdoor adventure programs, including guided rock climbing, hiking, and mountain-biking outings, among others. The spa at Red Rock Resort can hold its own with any on the Strip in variety of treatments and amenities offered.

Rooms and suites are extremely mod in appearance and in amenities, mixing chocolate browns and other earth tones with high-tech gadgetry and high-end appointments. Best of all, however, are the guest-room views. West-facing rooms look out onto Red Rock Canyon, while east-facing rooms peer down the valley to the Las Vegas Strip.

Dining at Red Rock Resort is predominantly casual, except for T-Bones Chophouse. Other options include Rossa for Italian cuisine, Mercadito for Mexican fare, Yard House, Lucille's Bar-B-Que, a top-notch buffet, a cafe, and quick eats. In the entertainment department, Rocks Lounge is the place for wee-hour dancing, while Onyx Bar and Lucky Bar provide stunning settings for a drink. For the sedentary there's a 16-screen cinema, and for the more active a 72-lane bowling complex.

Finally, a navigation note. Although Red Rock Resort is located at the West Charleston Boulevard exit off I-215, it's faster to commute to the Strip and Downtown on West Charleston. It's usually about a 25-minute trip.

Resorts World Las Vegas (resortsworld.com)

WEST WILL MEET EAST at the rejuvenated North Strip when a new Asian-themed, 6,500-room megaresort opens in 2016 on the vacated site of the historic Stardust Hotel. The 87-acre metropolis will resemble a contemporary Forbidden City, featuring a red pagoda village promenade of shops, a panda zoo, and an indoor water park framed by two of the property's six high-rise towers. Proposed amenities include restaurants offering an array of Far East cuisines, a convention complex, an extensive multilevel casino with areas for Malaysian-style stadium gaming, a 28-lane bowling alley, a 4,000-seat theater, two showrooms, an eight-screen cinema complex, a retail zone, and exhibits presenting reproductions of the Great Wall and the terra cotta warriors of

Xi'an. The multinational Kuala Lumpur–based Genting Group, one of the world's largest gaming and hospitality companies, is the developer. Target market is middle-income Asians worldwide.

Rio (riolasvegas.com)

THE RIO IS ONE OF LAS VEGAS'S great treasures. Vibrantly decorated in a Latin American carnival theme, the Rio offers resort luxury at local prices. The guest rooms (all plush one-room suites) offer exceptional views and can be had for the price of a regular room at many other Las Vegas hotels. The combination of view, luxury, and price makes the Rio a great choice for couples on romantic getaways or honeymoons. On Flamingo Road, 3 minutes west of the Strip, the Rio also allows easy access to Downtown via I-15.

The Rio's dining scene is headed by Búzio's Seafood Restaurant; Martorano's, an Italian eatery under the direction of Fort Lauderdale legend Steve Martorano; and the Royal India Bistro. VooDoo Steak & Lounge and the more casual All-American Bar Grille are the Rio's chophouses. Rounding out the Rio's restaurant line-up are KJ Dim Sum & Seafood, the Wine Cellar & Tasting Room, and BK Whopper Bar, a slower take on the fast-food king. The Rio has two buffets that are perennially at the top of everyone's hit parade. Carnival World Buffet offers 300 dishes from a dozen cuisines prepared fresh daily, while Village Seafood Buffet is one of the best seafood buffets in Las Vegas.

With five showrooms and a high-energy stage show in the casino, the Rio's entertainment mix is one of the most varied and extensive in Las Vegas. Long-running shows include the *Penn & Teller* comedy-magic show and the *Chippendales* beefcake revue. Nightspots include the rooftop VooDoo Lounge, one of the city's most dynamic and enduring clubs, and Flirt Lounge, where guys can flirt with women warmed up by a just-concluded *Chippendales* show. Factoring in the extensive Masquerade Village shopping arcade, a workout room, and an elaborate swimming area, the Rio offers exceptional quality in every respect. Festive and bright without being tacky or overdone, the casino is so large that it's easy to get disoriented.

If it's thrills you're seeking, check out the Rio's high-intensity thrill ride, VooDoo ZipLine. This 70-second zip ride packs a big adrenaline punch. For details, see Part 5, page 434.

Joining the current trend of extensive refurbishment, the Rio has completed a rework of its 2,520 all-suite inventory. The carnival decor no longer encroaches on the guest rooms, which have introduced the current fewer-frills look, but there is still plenty of space to samba and drink caipirinhas. Each standard suite is an airy 600 square feet with a defined parlor. Flashes of pomegranate on pillows and other vivid touches accent the ivory and cocoa duvet and dark furniture. For additional sleeping space in the king rooms, the couch expands into a double bed. The Pet Stay program welcomes small dogs for a per-night charge.

The Rio staff ranks very high in terms of hospitality, warmth, and an eagerness to please. The Rio is one of the few casinos to successfully target both locals and out-of-towners, particularly Southern Californians.

If you want to spend time on the Strip, the Rio offers a complimentary shuttle service with departures every 30 minutes to Harrah's and Bally's.

Riviera (rivierahotel.com)

EXTENDING FROM THE STRIP halfway to Paradise Road (and the Las Vegas Convention Center), the Riviera is well positioned to accommodate both leisure and business travelers. The Riviera provides a complete package of gambling, entertainment, and amenities and has more long-running shows (seven) than any other hotel in Las Vegas. These include a comedy club, a topless revue, a production show, a hypnotist, and celebrity entertainers and lounge acts.

Guests on the move can choose from a number of fast-food restaurants in the food court. R Steak and Seafood is the Riviera's signature restaurant. As for amenities, the Riviera provides a spacious pool and sunbathing area, a shopping arcade, and a wedding chapel. Guest rooms, particularly in the towers, are more comfortable than the public areas suggest. If you book, insist on a renovated room.

The casino is large (big enough you can get lost on the way to the restroom) and somewhat of a maze. There is always a lot of noise and light, and a busy, unremitting flurry of activity. Walk-in traffic mixes with convention-goers, retirees on "gambling sprees," and tourists on wholesaler packages. Asians, Asian Americans, and Southern Californians also patronize the Riviera.

Royal Resort (royalhotelvegas.com)

A REVIVAL OF THE FORMER AND VERY TIRED Royal Las Vegas, the newly refashioned Royal Resort is a boutique inn with 191 rooms. At 99 Convention Center Dr. and literally in the shadow of Wynn Encore, the Royal is well positioned on the corridor between the Strip and the Las Vegas Convention Center.

The lobby, with its original white marble floors, now resembles an art gallery and exhibits a gilt pool table, Haight-Ashbury washed piano, Foosball and shuffle board games, a chess board, photographs and mixed media, and a collection of shoe art Imelda Marcos would appreciate. The somber lobby bar borders on Gothic, with its dark counters, tables, and stools of varying heights. Adjoining is the carpeted dance floor and DJ station. As yet casino-less, a slot parlor is proposed. Future plans include an expanded comedy club and a hair and tanning salon. Guest rooms are modest but comfortable.

The upscale Barrymore is the property's only restaurant and offers an updated take on vintage 1960s menu selections. Nearby are a heated outdoor patio and comfortable inside bar with a welcoming ambience.

The pool area features four bright cabanas and an elevated spa with three waterfalls. The business center hides two computer stations and displays an IBM Selectric typewriter in keeping with the hotel's quirky look. Acres of free parking at the rear of the property provide easy drive-in access. Occasionally the lot becomes an outdoor art and music festival. This niche hotel speaks to trendy indies, millenniums, and those wanting to get their mojo back. It's a kick to visit this off-beat property that has generated lots of buzz.

Sam's Town (samstownlv.com)

ABOUT 20 MINUTES EAST of the strip on Boulder Highway, Sam's Town is a long, rambling set of connected buildings with an Old West mining-town motif. In addition to the hotel and casino, there is a bowling complex, a very good buffet, one of Las Vegas's better Mexican eateries, a steakhouse, a T.G.I. Friday's, a café, and two RV parks. Roxy's lounge is popular with both locals and visitors and features an eclectic mix of live music and dancing. Sam's Town Live is the Boulder Strip's first real concert venue.

Other pluses include a free-form pool, a sand volleyball court, and a spa. Joining the "let's be an attraction" movement, Sam's Town offers an atrium featuring plants, trees, footpaths, waterfalls, and even a "mountain." A waterfall in the atrium is the site of a free but very well-done fountains-and-light show (keep your eye on the robotic wolf). Frequent customers, besides the locals, include seniors and cowboys.

Santa Fe Station (santafestationlasvegas.com)

SANTA FE STATION is about 20 minutes northwest of Las Vegas, just off US 95. Like Sam's Town, the Rio, and the Suncoast, Santa Fe Station targets both locals and tourists. Bright and airy, with a warm southwestern decor, Santa Fe Station is one of the more livable hotel-casinos in Las Vegas.

Santa Fe Station offers a spacious casino with a poker room and sports book. Restaurants include the upscale Charcoal Room steakhouse, as well as a Mexican restaurant and Station Casino's signature Feast buffet. The Chrome showroom features an eclectic mix of country and rock headliners, and there is also entertainment in the lounge. In addition to a pool, there is a bowling complex and a movie theater. Guest rooms, also decorated in a southwestern style, are nice and a good value.

Silver Sevens (silversevenscasino.com)

AFFINITY GAMING, WHICH ACQUIRED TERRIBLE'S from the locally prominent Herbst Family, initiated a new name for the property to capitalize on gaming's lucky number 7 along with Nevada's reputation as the Silver State. The result is the Silver Sevens Hotel & Casino, still a no-frills property offering exceptional rates and value for the budget-minded traveler. A renovation of the 327 low-rise and tower rooms has imparted a cool aura and created a tranquil space away from the hotel's busy public areas. Wi-Fi is available for a fee.

The iconic Terrible's cowboy mascot has been donated to Downtown's expanding Neon Museum, and the hotel's new look is classy vintage Vegas. The casino has been reconfigured, and players can choose from 21, craps, roulette, slots, video games, and a sports book. On the upper level a buffet, 24-hour café, and expanded bingo parlor can be accessed by an escalator. Doubling as hotel check-in and cashier's cage, the guest services desk sits at the far end of the casino. Unless the ventilation system was on the blink the days we visited, Silver Sevens is the smokiest casino in Las Vegas. The well-trimmed grounds and pool area are a quiet oasis. Just outside the casino and convenient to the tower rooms is the rear parking garage, and there's easy access to acres of parking in front of the hotel. Silver Sevens, located at the intersection of East Flamingo and Paradise Roads, is less than a mile from the Strip and 2 miles from the airport. Complimentary shuttle service to McCarran Airport runs 8 a.m.–midnight. Guests are an equal mix of Canadian and Asian tourists and locals.

Silverton (silvertoncasino.com)

SOUTHWEST OF LAS VEGAS at the Blue Diamond Road exit off I-15, Silverton opened in 1994 as Boomtown, with a nicely executed Old West mining-town theme. The casino has since removed or replaced much of the mining paraphernalia, however. The Silverton just might be the best-kept secret in Las Vegas. Its luxurious guest rooms feature dark hardwood furniture, leather couches, pillow-top mattresses, and tile bathrooms. Thick drapes and good soundproofing insulate the rooms from highway noise. At rack rates of about $100, Silverton hotel rooms are among the best values.

As concerns dining, the Twin Creeks Steakhouse can hold its own with any chophouse in town, and the 24-hour Sundance Grill, aside from serving excellent food, is a gorgeous room, reminiscent in decor of the celebrity chef restaurants on the Strip. On the quirky side is the Shady Grove Lounge, with a 1967 Airstream trailer and a couple of bowling lanes worked into the theme. There's also a Mexican restaurant and an excellent buffet. And good lounge entertainment is a Silverton's tradition.

The large casino is designed around $5-million worth of freshwater and saltwater aquariums. And speaking of fish, an adjacent retail development includes a 165,000-square-foot Bass Pro Shops Outdoor World megastore with indoor archery, a putting range, a driving range, and a stuffed specimen of every mammal on Earth. There's probably more dead stuff in the Bass Pro Shops than in many cemeteries. Even if you're not outdoorsy, this veritable natural history museum is worth a visit.

Just 10 minutes from the Strip, Silverton is in a great position to snag Southern Californians. It also targets the RV crowd with a large, full-service RV park across the street.

SLS Las Vegas (slslasvegas.com)

SOMETHING LOVELY STARTING? Sexy Little Secrets? Previously the legendary Sahara Hotel and once the bastion of the Rat Pack, Louis Prima, and Keely Smith and friends, the property has been transformed into the sleek SLS Las Vegas, generating new vitality and a So-Cal beat to the dormant North Strip neighborhood. Of the original hotel's DNA, three towers have been completely renovated, while the layout of the 50s-era low-rise core buildings has been brought up to a 2015 standard. Perimeter palm trees suggest a West Coast skyline, while the crisp white and glass façades exude a sophisticated Sunset Strip motif and house a maze of 20 restaurants, lounges, bars, and nightclubs—one with concert capabilities. Clubbers will want to immediately don their drinking shoes. Adding to the mix are the redesigned reception area, casino, conference center, and an after-six sector, including clubs and a satellite casino open only in the evenings. The original pool complex has been modernized, and a second rooftop pool has been installed above the casino.

The inventory of 1,622 streamlined guest rooms is spread throughout three historic towers: the World Tower comprises high-tech-driven standard hotel rooms aimed toward business travelers; the LUX Tower is entirely suites; and the Story Tower, with in-room bar/vanity combos, is the party tower adjacent to the main pool. The stylish, minimalist rooms, many with balconies, are predominantly white with splashes of muted rose or bright saffron on black plaid or brown swirl-patterned carpet. A white sofa is strategically placed at the end of the king beds. Desks, side tables, and lamps are chrome. Reminiscent of the days when Strip hotel rooms were sizeable, these accommodations are airier than expected, but the bathrooms are snug. The ornate LUX World Tower suites provide an upgraded residential lifestyle with concierge services.

The restaurants also have an LA vibe and include Bazaar Meat by chef José Andrés, Katsuya by master sushi chef Katsuya Uechi, and Cleo for Mediterranean cuisine. More casual dining options include Ku Noodle, 800 Degrees Neapolitan Pizzeria, Perq coffee, a buffet, and a 24/7 Vegas version of LA's beloved Griddle Cafe. Positioned along the hotel's Strip frontage is an indoor/outdoor patio housing Umami Burger, Monkey Bar, an alfresco beer garden, and the sports book. The nightclub trio is celeb-centric Sayers Club, LIFE, and Foxtail, plus the SHOT Bar; all serve the celebratory new cocktail SaharaToSLS with a rosemary twist. High-end LA brand Fred Segal is the exclusive retailer, with seven boutiques offering men's and women's fashions, jewelry, art and books, beachwear, beauty products, and a jeans bar. The Ciel Spa and Fitness Center offers herbal wraps, massages, beauty treatments, and other rehab services.

Depending on how you look at it, the SLS is the first or last stop on the monorail line. Now closer to the hotel's Paradise Road entrance, the boarding station has been moved from its original position across the vast eastside parking lot. The abundant 2,500-space parking garage is best entered from Paradise Road. Despite its glitz, the resort offers affordable rates. Its target market is young and trendy Southern Californians. The property has joined the Preferred Hotels and Hilton HHonors guest loyalty programs. The flagship of SBE Entertainment, SLS's goal is to be the avatar of **S**tyle, **L**uxury, and **S**ervice.

South Point (southpointcasino.com)

ACQUIRED BY MICHAEL GAUGHAN, the South Point sits almost alone in a huge desert plot off the south end of Las Vegas Boulevard, well away from the Strip. Rising up with nothing of comparable size anywhere nearby, South Point looks gigantic. This isn't just a trick of perspective, as South Point contains 2,163 large guest rooms, an 80,000-square-foot casino, two lounges, an enormous bingo auditorium, and a unique equestrian center. The latter, already being touted as one of the better indoor horse facilities in the country, includes a 4,600-seat arena and 1,200 climate-controlled horse stalls. The equestrian center hosts a number of prestigious equestrian events each year. For those without a horse, there's a 64-lane bowling complex, a 500-seat showroom that doubles as a dance club, a spa and fitness center, and a manicured swimming pool complex. Restaurants include Michael's Gourmet Room, a longtime Las Vegas culinary standard setter; the Silverado Steakhouse; an Italian bistro; an oyster bar; Primarily Prime Rib; Baja Miguel's Mexican; and a better-than-average buffet.

The decor of public spaces is ostensibly inspired by design accents from Southern California and the Pacific Coast, but the overriding visual theme is lots and lots and lots of yellow—deep golds to light wheats to every other shade in the crayon box. It's attractive and soothing, though not particularly memorable or interesting. Locals and regional guests are much beloved, and the roomy casino floor is a vast, open rectangle designed for their enjoyment. You only need walk along the walls to find the restaurants and lounges; the bowling lanes and bingo hall are up an escalator. The guest rooms are quite large and have nicer-than-average beds.

Stratosphere (stratospherehotel.com)

KNOWN PRIMARILY FOR its high-altitude thrill rides at the top of the "tallest (1,149 feet) free-standing observation tower in the United States," the Stratosphere has decanted money into its guest rooms and casino and emerges crisp, bright, and a more significant player in the mid-priced competition for tourists. The main entrance has been moved directly on the Strip, xeriscape landscaping added, and an impressive porte cochere replaces the original side-street entry. The hotel has created 909 "Stratosphere Select"–grade accommodations, which cost $10–$20 more than a standard room. And the standard rooms are worthy, with a comfortable color scheme of cream and taupe bedding accented with dark furniture. The upgrade to the "Select" level is the standard room with more attention to decor. These rooms also include a safe and MP3 alarm clock.

The 80,000-square-foot casino meanders, the result of consecutive additions to the property over the last 15 years. New spectral cove lighting along the ceiling changes hues throughout the hours and is engaging to watch. You'll find the standard mix of table games and slots, but the Double-Down Pit Girls add glamour and fun. The property has aligned itself with NASCAR and the Dale Earnhardt brand and displays Earnhardt memorabilia, collectibles, and slots. Along the perimeter are Starbucks, the C (circular) Bar, and Images Lounge. The sports book telecasts daily sports events and horse racing on nine screens in the second-floor showroom.

The huge eighth-floor pool deck faces south and west for plenty of sun. Blue lounges and chartreuse umbrellas provide color and cover alongside two free-form pools and several white cabanas. There's a store for pool necessities, and bikini-clad Blackjack dealers provide eye candy during the summer months. For great food, a well-kept secret is the pool's Café Bar at Level 8, offering unique sandwiches at attractive prices. The multiple-choice mojito and margarita menu entices as well. A 24-hour fitness center is outfitted with weights and exercise machines and is free to hotel guests. The Roni Josef Salon and Spa provides beauty treatments and massages. Both amenities are in the second-floor Tower Shops arcade. Restaurants include the Top of the World, Plate Buffet, 24-hour Roxy's 50s Diner, Tower Pizzeria, and Fellini's Italian cuisine.

The property's crown jewel is the four-floor Observation Deck at levels 106 through 109 offering unsurpassed *National Geographic*–quality views of Las Vegas, the surrounding desert, mountains, and beyond. Level 106 boasts the rotating haute cuisine Top of the World restaurant, open for lunch and dinner. The Level 107 Lounge, Las Vegas's highest bar, is the focal point of the 107th floor. Level 108 features the indoor observation deck and Air Bar nightclub. The outdoor observation deck and entrance to three thrill rides are on Level 109. X-Scream is a roller coaster hurtling riders on a track over the top side of the tower. It stops and goes abruptly and dangles interminably. Insanity is a merry-go-round-like apparatus that swings riders in metal baskets over the edge at speeds of three g's. Most popular is the Big Shot, a gravity thrill experience that rockets riders up and down the tower's needle with a force of four g's. Day passes can be purchased for unlimited rides on these three attractions. The most recent addition is the Sky Jump, a controlled free fall from the 108th floor. Riders are suited up in special coveralls with cables attached to a high-speed Descender and then plunge 855 feet at 40 mph down the side of the tower. Those in the three top-floor restaurants, bars, and decks can watch these over-the-edge exploits.

The vast parking garage is on the west side of the property. At the bottom of the garage, escalators whisk guests into the casino, where the friendly information staff is spot-on providing assistance. Clients are primarily auto sports fans, regional drive- and fly-ins, and adrenaline junkies seeking an airborne rush.

Suncoast (suncoastcasino.com)

LIKE MOST OF THE COAST CASINOS, Suncoast is designed to attract locals. Located west of Las Vegas in Summerlin near some of the area's best golf courses, Suncoast offers high-return slots and video poker, a surprisingly good (for a locals joint) fitness center, 64 lanes of bowling, and a 16-screen movie complex. In the food department, the clubby SC Prime Steakhouse tops the roster. There's also a decent buffet, as well as a T.G.I. Friday's and restaurants serving Italian and Mexican. The casino is open and uncrowded, rendered in a southwestern-Mission style. A 500-seat showroom featuring name bands and a pool round out the offerings. For its size (427 rooms and an 80,000-square-foot casino), Suncoast offers a pretty amazing array of attractions and amenities. Perhaps Suncoast's most extraordinary yet unheralded feature is the breathtaking view of the mountains to the west as seen through floor-to-ceiling windows in every guest room. And, speaking of mountains, the Suncoast is a perfect location for anyone interested in hiking, rock climbing, mountain biking, or road biking in the nearby canyons and valleys.

Sunset Station (sunsetstation.com)

SUNSET STATION OPENED IN JUNE 1997, the fourth Station Casino (after Palace, Boulder, and Texas), just off I-215 in far southeast Las Vegas Valley about a 20-minute drive from the Strip. Known as the "Henderson highrise," the 21-story tower presides over a fast-growing residential neighborhood; with 457 rooms, Sunset is large for a locals' casino. It's also one of the classiest, most highly themed, and architecturally realized of the Station Casinos, decorated to replicate a Spanish village. The casino's centerpiece is the Gaudí Bar; with its tiled floors and stained-glass ceilings, it reflects the eccentric vision of Barcelona architect Antoni Gaudí.

Station's formula of good food, lounge entertainment and movies, child care, and extra touches prevails. It boasts a steakhouse, Italian and Mexican restaurants, the Feast Buffet, a 24-hour coffee shop, and fast food galore. There's also a Kids Quest child-care center, the 500-seat Club Madrid lounge, a 13-screen movie theater, and a $26-million bowling center—the largest in Las Vegas. Extras include a pool and plaza area featuring two sand volleyball courts, a badminton court, and a 5,000-seat amphitheater.

All in all, it's worth staying in the slightly oversized and moderately priced rooms at Sunset Station if you're visiting friends and relatives in Henderson or want to be close to Hoover Dam, Lake Mead, or Valley of Fire.

Texas Station (texasstation.com)

ALSO OWNED BY STATION CASINOS, Texas Station has a single-story full-service casino with 91,000 square feet of gaming space, decorated with black carpet sporting cowboy designs such as gold, boots, ropes, revolvers, covered wagons, and such. The atmosphere is contemporary Western, a subtle blend of Texas ranch culture and Spanish architecture. This property offers full-service restaurants serving steak and Mexican cuisine, a good buffet, plenty of fast-food options, three bars, a dance hall, a 60-lane bowling center, child-care facilities, and an 18-screen movie theater. Texas Station caters to locals and cowboys and is at the intersection of Rancho Drive and Lake Mead Boulevard in North Las Vegas.

TI (Treasure Island) (treasureisland.com)

ONE OF THREE MEGACASINO RESORTS that opened during the fall of 1993, Treasure Island is now the hipper TI. On the southwest corner of the Strip at Spring Mountain Road next door to the Mirage, TI is Caribbean in style. Management thought the original buccaneer theme was juvenile and Disneyesque, and further believed that it was responsible for luring thousands of unwanted families with children to the resort. So down came all the pirate hats, sabers, skulls, crossbones, and all the other grisly skeletal parts that were the, shall we say, backbone of the joint's decor. The new adult version is fine but a little dull by comparison.

TI scrapped its most iconic attraction, the pirates versus sirens battle. Replacing the ship, moat, and most everything else is a three-level shopping complex scheduled to open in early 2015. Anchoring the "retail-tainment" center is a CVS pharmacy on the main floor, and restaurants, shops, and bars will occupy the upper two levels.

The casino continues the neutered Caribbean theme, with carved panels and whitewashed, beamed ceilings over a black carpet, punctuated with fuchsia, sapphire blue, and emerald green. The overall impression is one of tropical comfort: exciting, but easy on the eye and spirit. In addition to the usual slots and table games, a comfortable sports book is provided.

The main interior passageway leads to a shopping arcade, restaurants, and the buffet. Dining selections include Pho, serving Vietnamese fare; Pizzeria Francesco's; Phil's Italian Steak House; Gilley's BBQ; and Kahunaville, a sort of Parrothead joint serving Bahamian and Caribbean dishes. TI amenities include a beautifully landscaped swimming area and a luxurious, well-equipped health club and spa.

TI is home to Cirque du Soleil's extraordinary *Mystère,* which is performed in a custom-designed 1,629-seat theater. Nightlife options include Kahunaville, a Jimmy Buffet Margaritaville clone, and a Gilley's Saloon.

Guest rooms at TI are situated in a Y-shaped, coral-colored tower that rises directly behind the pirate village. Decorated in soft, earth-toned colors, the rooms provide a restful retreat from the bustling casino. Additionally, the rooms feature large windows affording a good view of the Strip or (on the east side) of the mountains and sunset. The balconies that are visible in photos of TI are strictly decorative and cannot be accessed from the guest rooms. Self-parking is easier at TI than at most Strip hotels. Valet parking is fast and efficient. An elevated tram connects TI to the Mirage next door.

Tropicana (troplv.com)

THE SOUTHERNMOST HOTEL on the east side of Las Vegas Boulevard South, the reestablished New Tropicana is well located at the busy intersection of Tropicana Avenue and the Strip across from the MGM Grand, New York–New York, and the Excalibur. Once the "Tiffany of the Strip," the completely renovated Tropicana has been reinvented with a South Beach theme. Vibrant tropical colors and music, natural light, and equatorial fibers and florals percolate throughout the property. The upgrades have created a fun-in-the-sun laid-back lifestyle in the mid-price market. With the deconstruction of an entire wing and a phalanx of rooms enlarged as lofts, inventory has decreased to a cozy 1,658 rooms, almost placing the Trop in Las Vegas's boutique class of properties.

The guest rooms feel like an expansive oasis in a rain forest, with light hardwood, bamboo, and rattan trim throughout. Oversized standard rooms feature jungle red-and-white spreads, a desk console, and a russet-cushioned daybed. Instead of drapes, plantation shutters cover the windows, and even more unusual—the windows open! All rooms include Wi-Fi. Coffeemakers and refrigerators are available on request for a small fee. For an additional $75 per night, larger triangular corner rooms with a sitting area and a dramatic view of one of the Strip's major intersections are available.

The reconfigured oblong casino offers 21 tables, midi and mini-baccarat, roulette, and craps. A poker room, slots, video poker, and the high-limit area dominate the casino's sidelines. The large Sports Book and Pub near the front desk has been updated and conveniently has an outside entrance. The Rotunda has become a party pit gaming area next to the Ambhar Lounge.

The Tropicana Beach Club provides luxuriant pool gardens, some of the most famous in Las Vegas, with 4.2 acres of mature palms and lawn embracing two pools, waterfalls, a lagoon cave, and two heated Jacuzzis—all surrounded by white chaises. An outdoor café and bar features swim-up blackjack, sand volleyball, Champagne beds, lounges, cabanas, misters, bottle service with hors d'oeuvres, outdoor concerts, and a private island at pool center.

The three-level Mandara Spa overlooks the lush pool from the south side, with each floor specializing in a specific fitness and spa component: exercise room, an esthetician salon and barber shop, and massage treatment rooms.

All restaurants have been remodeled with new menus and themes. On the main floor is the airy 24-hour Beach Café, a bar and buffet that overlook the pool. Close by is the South Beach food court. On the second floor are the spare and elegant Biscayne Steak Sea & Wine with pool view, adjacent wine bar, and Carla Pellegrino's Bacio, a delightful upscale trattoria.

In the Convention Pavilion are the wedding chapel, business center, and a second Starbucks. Entertainment options include the Laugh Factory comedy club; the Tropicana Lounge with free (for now) live music; Xposed, an LGTBQ Saturday beach party; and an afternoon magic show. For adrenaline junkies, a new thrill ride, the Polercoaster, promises to raise the bar (see Part 5, page 436).

Recognizing an opportunity to snare the thousands of visitors strolling daily across the quadrangle of bridges at Tropicana Avenue and the Strip, the Tropicana Resort is adding a two-level enclosed mall at the celebrated intersection. Retailers, bars, restaurants, and a food court will share space in the South Beach–flavored complex. Part of the development is situated above the casino, with an entrance on the second level, so the graceful Tiffany stained glass ceiling is being repurposed elsewhere. With more than 20,000 hotel rooms encompassed in the four street corners, the potential market of shoppers is enormous.

Tuscany (tuscanylv.com)

THE TUSCANY'S LODGING footprint is 15 three-story buildings spread over several acres with an abundance of drive-up parking. Mature landscaping of tall shade trees and extensive grass is vigilantly maintained, and the complex feels like a large residential compound. Off the lobby near the fireplace are Tuscany Garden Italian restaurant and the Piazza lounge, which features nightly live music or a DJ and dancing. Beachfront Coffee displays luscious pastries, sandwiches, and drinks for poolside snacks. Although connected by a passageway, the lobby and the casino are separate wings. The Cantina and Marilyn's Café with take-out counter are in the casino, along with the games typical of a full casino—but all are downsized.

An all-suite property, the Tuscany's midsize studio suites have been remodeled but still have a neutral look with a brown-and-cream color scheme. Walls display stereotypical watercolor prints of Italian villages. The 25-inch TV is dated (no flat-panels here) and sits on a bureau against the window, creating a glare if you're watching daytime TV. Tiny kitchens include a round table with two chairs, a wet bar, a small refrigerator, and a coffeemaker; microwaves can be requested. Bathrooms are serviceable with a separate tub and glass-door shower and one sink.

Amenities include two fenced pools (one is a lap pool) and a fitness center with Laundromat. Internet is free in the public areas, but there is a charge for in-room connections.

THE VENETIAN AND THE PALAZZO
The Venetian (venetian.com)

THE VENETIAN AND PALAZZO HOTELS, two separate and distinct sister properties owned by Las Vegas Sands Inc., rise side by side on the Strip at Sands Boulevard and together sustain an inventory of 7,100 rooms.

The Venetian draws its theme from the plazas, architecture, and canals of Venice, Italy, and follows the example of New York–New York, Mandalay Bay, Luxor, and Paris Las Vegas in bringing the icons of world travel to Las Vegas. Visiting The Venetian is like taking a trip back to the artistic, architectural, and commercial center of the world in the 16th century. You cross a 585,000-gallon canal on the steep-pitched Rialto Bridge, shadowed by the Campanile Bell Tower, to enter the Doge's Palace. Inside, reproductions of famous frescoes, framed by 24-karat-gold molding, adorn the 65-foot domed ceiling at the casino entrance. The geometric design of the flat-marble lobby floor provides an M. C. Escher–like optical illusion that gives the sensation of climbing stairs—a unique touch. Behind the front desk is a large illustrated map of the island city, complete with buildings, landmarks, gondolas, and ships. Characters in period costumes from the 12th to 17th centuries roam the public areas, singing opera, performing mime, and jesting.

Although The Venetian claims that its bread-and-butter customers are business travelers and shoppers, it hasn't neglected to include a casino in its product mix. In fact, the Venetian casino, at 116,000 square feet, is larger than that of most Strip competitors. When the Lido Casino came online, the overall resort topped out at more than 200,000 square feet of casino. The Venetian casino is styled to resemble a Venetian palace with architecture and decor representative of the city's Renaissance era. Period frescoes on recessed ceilings over the table games depict Italian villas and palaces. The huge and stupefyingly ornate casino offers 139 table games and 1,700 slot and video-poker machines. The perimeter of the casino houses a fast-food court, along with French, Italian, and southwestern restaurants, and one of the fanciest coffee shops in town.

Upstairs are the Grand Canal Shoppes, with more than 60 stores, mostly small boutiques. The Escher-like floor design continues throughout the shopping venue, with different colors and shapes providing variations on the theme. The centerpiece of the mall is the quarter-mile Grand Canal itself, enclosed by brick walls and wrought-iron fencing and cobbled with small change. Gondolas ply the waterway, steered and powered by gondoliers who serenade their passengers. Passing beneath arched bridges, the canal ends at a colossal reproduction of St. Marks Square. Like The Forum Shops, the Grand Canal Shoppes are arranged beneath a vaulted ceiling painted and lighted to simulate the sky. The Venetian adjoins its sister property, The Palazzo, via a shopping mall that connects the Grand Canal Shoppes to The Shoppes at The Palazzo, which offer an additional 49 stores and six restaurants.

The Venetian's restaurants, most designed by well-known chefs, provide a wide range of dining environments and culinary choice. Wolfgang Puck's Postrio, Emeril Lagasse's Delmonico Steakhouse, Thomas Keller's Bouchon, Tom Moloney's AquaKnox, Zefferino Belloni's Zefferino, and Mario Batali's B&B Ristorante are some of the culinary power-hitters represented.

An all-suite hotel, The Venetian offers guest accommodations averaging 700 square feet and divided into sleeping and adjoining sunken living areas. The living-room areas provide adequate space for meetings or entertaining. Every suite has been recently upgraded to meet the Palazzo criteria and shares its similar subdued earth tone palette, with pops of colorful peach creating a classy urban Apennine look. The property is LEED Gold Certified.

The five-acre swimming complex and spa area are situated on the roof-top over the shopping venue and are well insulated from the bustle of the Strip. You'll find two standard pools, one lounge pool, and a hot tub. One of the largest of its kind in the country, the ultra-upscale bi-level Canyon Ranch Spa offers fitness equipment and classes, therapies, and sauna and steam rooms, as well as a 40-foot indoor rock-climbing wall, medical center, beauty salon, and cafe.

The Venetian targets the convention market with its mix of high-end business lodging, power restaurants, unique shopping, and proximity to Sands Expo and Convention Center (second in size only to the Las Vegas Convention

Center). The Venetian certainly welcomes tourists and gamblers, who come mostly on the weekend, but the other five days are largely monopolized by the trade-show crowds.

The Palazzo (palazzo.com)

IT'S A TESTAMENT to The Palazzo's designers to see tourists who've already walked past replica pyramids, New York City skyscrapers, and million-dollar fountain displays still whip out their cell-phone cameras the first time they see The Palazzo's lobby. Much more pedestrian-friendly than the neighboring (and similarly ultraluxe) Wynn or the down-the-Strip Bellagio, The Palazzo is arguably the best combination of shopping, dining, and lodging in Las Vegas.

Opened in December 2007, The Palazzo is connected to The Venetian by walkways and the Grand Canal waterway. Like The Venetian, The Palazzo employs in its public spaces such architectural touches as arched passageways, Doric columns, fountains, and painted ceilings in neutral beige, yellow, and brown hues. Even with a three-story lobby, however, The Palazzo's decor is more subtle than that of The Venetian. That subtlety extends to The Palazzo's 105,000-square-foot casino, where the tables and slots seem to have slightly more walking room between them than at, say, the Bellagio. The net effect is a quieter, more relaxed feel. Depending on your preference (and your luck), you might consider this either a welcome relief or boring beyond words.

The Palazzo's restaurants cover everything from Italian to Peruvian, including three steakhouses associated with celebrity chefs: Mario Batali's Carnevino, Wolfgang Puck's CUT, and Eric Bauer's Morel's French Steakhouse and Bistro. Asian cuisine is also well represented with Zine Noodles Dim Sum and Sushisamba. If you're in the mood for Italian, Lavo is the fancy place, and Espressamente Illy is the cafe. Emeril Lagasse's Table 10 holds down the fine-dining category for American cuisine. In-room dining has an equally wide variety of choices and isn't as expensive as one might think, given the setting.

Shopping options abound at The Shoppes at The Palazzo, with 49 upscale stores, including Barneys New York and Michael Kors. Shoe aficionados can debate the merits of Jimmy Choo and Christian Louboutin at their namesake stores, and there's no lack of jewelry and other designer-clothing options, especially for women. Slightly more affordable options are available at The Venetian's Grand Canal Shoppes, which connect to The Palazzo's stores and together provide hours of window-shopping opportunities.

A Canyon Ranch Spa provides everything from massages, facials, and a full health club to simple haircuts. While reservations for all-day treatments are recommended, we didn't have any trouble getting a walk-in hair appointment on 15 minutes' notice during one of the busier times of the year.

The Palazzo's 3,066 rooms are all suites. Rooms come in 720-, 940-, or 1,280-square-foot configurations. All have sunken living rooms and two flat-panel TVs; most have a single king bed, but some 940-square-foot rooms also have two queen beds. Bathrooms are spacious, and showers boasts multiple massage heads with enough water pressure to work out the knots in your spine after a long day hunched over the slots; it's one of the best showers we've had in any hotel in the United States.

Similar to concierge floors is the Prestige lounge and business center section of the Palazzo tower. For $100 more per night, guests receive a daily newspaper, Internet connectivity, access to the Azure luxury pool complex and Canyon Ranch Spa, complimentary continental breakfast, all-day teas and coffees, desserts and fruit, and a nightly cocktail and hors d'oeuvres reception. The 23rd-floor lounge (open 7 a.m.–9 p.m.) also provides Champagne check-in, a DVD library, meeting space and work counters, and other business services.

Service at The Palazzo is excellent: the staff is prompt and easy to find, without giving the impression that you're being watched. When we asked for directions, more often than not an employee walked us to our destination rather than describe how to get there.

Westgate Las Vegas (westgateresorts.com)

AS WE WENT TO PRESS, Westgate Resorts took over the hotel-casino that was briefly the LVH—Las Vegas Hotel & Casino—and for many years the fabled Las Vegas Hilton. The self-contained 64-acre resort is a decidedly by-the-book classic 1970s property. Room inventory is unchanged at 2,956 rooms; it is still one of the largest convention facilities in town; and it maintains its spacious 30,000-square-foot sports book and 74,000-square-foot casino, along with 10 restaurants, 4 lounges and bars, and headline entertainment.

Westgate Las Vegas has the advantage of being adjacent to the Las Vegas Convention Center. What it lacks in convenient access to the Strip (a 10- to 12-minute walk or 5-minute monorail ride away), it makes up for in one-stop partying for the conventioneer who can go to sessions via a hall connecting the hotel and convention center. Consequently, this hotel does more meeting, trade-show, and convention business than any other hotel in town. Operating under the valid assumption that many of its guests may never leave the hotel during their Las Vegas stay (except to go to the convention center), Westgate is an oasis of self-sufficiency. It boasts a huge pool, an exercise room, a shopping arcade, a buffet, and a coffee shop. It is also next door to a golf course.

Architecture is vintage high-rise—bland, smooth, and unmemorable, but not unpleasant. Rooms are more than adequate—accommodating but not glitzy, with a comfortable, neutral environment for the business clientele.

Westgate has a decent buffet and some excellent fine-dining options with enough ethnic and culinary variety to keep most guests happy. The main showroom hosts big-name headliners, while the intimate Shimmer Cabaret hosts musical acts and small production shows.

Westgate is the most convenient place to stay in town if you are attending a trade show or convention at the Las Vegas Convention Center. If, however, you are in Las Vegas for pleasure, staying there is like being in exile. Anywhere you go you will need a cab, a car, or the monorail with a station right at the hotel. If you park in one of the property's far-flung, self-parking lots, it will take you as long as 15 minutes to reach your car from your room.

Westin Casuarina (starwoodhotels.com/westin)

TALK ABOUT PHOENIX RISING. Westin acquired the old Maxim hotel, a place where business travelers reluctantly stayed when they couldn't get into Bally's, and transformed it into a high-end boutique hotel. Both the casino and showroom are modest by Las Vegas standards, but the guest rooms, though small, are exceptionally nice. The Westin caters to business travelers, so each room is equipped with dual-line telephones and a cordless phone, but you'll have to pay for high-speed Internet access. There is ample meeting space for small meetings and conventions. If you travel with Fido, he's welcome at the Westin (they even supply a special dog bed), though you will have to pay a $35 cleaning fee and a $150 pet deposit. Travelers with some downtime can enjoy the pool, full-service spa, and fitness center. As for dining, the Westin offers Suede, which serves an excellent breakfast buffet. Situated about a block from the heart of the Strip, the Westin is within easy walking distance of dozens of shows and hundreds of restaurants. If you have a car, the Westin has ample parking and is easy to enter and exit. Finally, in case you're interested, a casuarina is a type of tree that is native to the Cayman Islands. If you want to see one, the Cayman Islands is where you'll have to go: there are no casuarina trees at the Casuarina.

Westin Lake Las Vegas (westinlakelasvegas.com)

FANCY AN ESCAPE to the celluloid realm of *Casablanca?* Themed after the mythic 1942 film set in the vast sands bordering the northwest rim of Africa, the 493-room Westin resort is perfect for an exotic desert getaway. The former Loews, newly acquired by Westin, provides a spectacular backdrop at the east end of Lake Las Vegas, with a view of Lake Mead in the near distance. The property envelops you with its sultry Moroccan vibe, invoking images of minarets, magic carpets, caravans, and camels from the moment you enter the lobby. A quick glimpse at the expanse of two lakes through floor-to-ceiling windows verifies that you have reached a 21st-century oasis.

The main entry, beyond the tree-lined circular drive and fountain guarded by sculptured desert tortoises, is positioned at the fourth level of the property. Guest rooms extend along Levels 1–7 in two wings. The large and comfortable Berber-influenced accommodations reaffirm the desert-inspired decor with dark wood furniture, an unusual red bureau, hammered metal–framed mirrors, leather chair and ottoman, white linens, and wall art depicting Arabic cityscapes. Room service is available 24/7. Accommodations offer a view of Lake Las Vegas or the resort grounds and surrounding mountains—the lakeside rooms are definitely worth the slightly higher rate.

The heart of the property is the tri-level Arabesque indoor lounge connected to the outdoor patio. Inside, the seating and appointments reflect the Saharan motif with studded leather furniture, wooden side tables and screens, leather and ceramic amphoras, extensive mosaic tile wall designs, and terra-cotta floors all accented by indigenous desert foliage. Sam's piano bar ("Play it again") is tucked inside.

The palm-shaded lower patio includes an infinity pool, waterfall, two fireplaces, and several conversation areas overlooking a lagoon and sandy beach where kayaks and paddle boats are available for aquatic excursions. Jogging and biking trails are also nearby. A dock in the Andalucian Gardens tethers small watercraft.

Dining choices include Rick's Café, Marrakesh Express deli, Marssa gourmet and sushi bar, the Arabesque Lounge, and a poolside bar and grill.

A business center and gift and resort wear shops adjoin the conference area, while the fitness center and Spa Moulay are situated downstairs from the patio. A wedding planner and chapel are also on site. Although there was gaming in the film's Rick's Café, this restyled version of Casablanca is without a casino. Anchoring the far end of the complex is a basketball court.

Four times daily, a shuttle runs guests to the Strip, with drop-off at the Casuarina, the Westin's sister property. The hotel can arrange airport pick-up, but given the sequestered location, a car would ease transportation.

WYNN RESORTS
Wynn Las Vegas (wynnlasvegas.com)

WITH EACH PROPERTY HE DEVELOPS on the Las Vegas Strip, Wynn's vision for the ultimate megaresort-casino becomes more sophisticated. Wynn Las Vegas opened in May 2005 and did so without whumping volcanoes, jets of water undulating to Frank Sinatra tunes, or pirate-versus-siren skirmishes. The handsome swoosh of the sunlit-copper glass facade stands in stark contrast to the immediate, raucous fun of traditional Las Vegas hotel-casinos. Up close, the building positively looms, and there's no attraction, no show, no kitsch visible to the passerby from any vantage point. That is the point. This mega–hotel-casino wasn't designed to lure visitors in from the sidewalk. Instead, it is internally focused, stylish, and mysterious. It's grown-up, and it's for grown-ups in the best sense of the word.

Wynn Las Vegas is all about exclusivity. The resort was ostensibly designed to bring to mind the exclusive boutique hotels of New York City, but with 2,716 rooms, 200,000 square feet of meeting space, a 111,000-square-foot casino, 76,000 square feet of shopping, an 18-hole golf course, an art gallery, and 22 places to have a meal or whet your whistle, that's one hell of a boutique. The trick, and it's done well, is to create intimate spaces within the larger whole.

But don't think that the exclusivity means that tourists and visitors aren't welcome at Wynn Las Vegas. Just the opposite. We found the staff to be one of the most courteous and helpful of any major resort on the Strip. The cocktail servers make frequent passes on the casino floor, the front desk and concierge are pleased to answer questions, and the security staff monitoring who goes where is kind and not in the least condescending.

One of the most remarkable aspects of this resort is that entering visitors aren't immediately shunted through a brain-rattling casino cavern, as is typical in most hotel-casinos. This adds to the impression that WLV is a resort first and a casino second. From both the main entrance, off the Strip, and the south entrance, off Sands Avenue, visitors are welcomed with a spacious, verdant atrium lobby. The ceiling is a high, domed skylight above an elaborate indoor garden where balls of flowers dangle like oversize Christmas ornaments from the branches of trees overhead. In addition to these two main entrances, the South Tower entrance, reserved for guests staying in the Tower, shares a drive with the south entrance.

In the casino proper, just to the left of the lobby, ceilings are raised over aisles and walkways and lowered over the gaming tables, instead of the other way around, as is common in many casino designs. We at the *Unofficial Guide* have lamented for years the suffocating atmosphere in most casinos and are pleased as punch to find a casino that provides gamblers with natural light and room to breathe. Another gaming amenity at WLV is a poolside casino (guests only), where you can work on your tan while you empty your wallet. Of course, there is the usual run of slots and gaming tables in the casino area, a 26-table poker room, sports book, keno, baccarat, and so on. The poker area is just across from the Ferrari–Maserati dealership, should you win really, really big.

The resort is loaded with exclusive brands like Ferrari and nowhere-else-in-Vegas shopping, most positioned along the shopping Esplanade, which begins across the main entrance lobby from the casino. Boutiques include couturier Chanel, Manolo Blahnik for the serious shoe diva, and the requisite Louis Vuitton, Cartier, and many others. Then there are the shops exclusive to WLV: Wynn & Company Jewelry; Wynn & Company Watches; and the Wynn Signature Shop. By all means check out the shopping on the Esplanade, but be aware that there aren't any retailers here you're likely to find in the mall at home. If you're prepared to drop $500 (and up) for a pair of fabulous heels, this is your place. If you need an extra pair of khakis or flip-flops, head across the street to the Fashion Show Mall.

There are many upscale options for a drink or a meal at WLV, all under the guidance of executive chef David Snyder. Both Wynn Las Vegas and sister resort Wynn Encore have their share of celebrity chefs. At Wynn, however, the chefs do more than lend their name to the restaurant—they actually prepare your meal. Steve Wynn insists that his chefs take full responsibility, and that includes being present. Standouts include Tableau for American fare, Bartolotta for Mediterranean seafood and shellfish (AAA Four-Diamond winner), SW Steakhouse, Wing Lei for French-influenced Shanghai specialties, La Cave for small plates, and Lakeside for nouvelle American cuisine (and a spectacular view overlooking the Lake of Dreams).

"Water features" are an integral part of creating intimate spaces at Wynn Las Vegas. The five different water features are keyed to various viewing areas such as registration, nightclubs, and restaurants. Probably the ultimate WLV water feature is *Le Rêve*. Under the creative direction of Franco Dragone, creator of Cirque du Soleil's watery *"O," Le Rêve* is an aquatic Cirque-style show performed in the round. The claim is that no seat is more than 40 feet from the performance, which may be true. On the Wynn Las Vegas website, this warning is issued: "You will get wet in rows A through C of every section. In row A you may get soaked."

If *Le Rêve* inspires you to get wet, wade into the dog bone–shaped swimming pool, the long stretch of which will give lap swimmers just about 100 yards for stroking. The water is kept at a constant 82°F, and the landscaping surrounding you will delight and soothe when you come up for air. There is a complete spa, and the gym has Cybex equipment with plenty of amenities, such as one of the best free-weight training areas we've seen.

Aim high, if you can, in your choice of rooms, for the elevators are speedy, gentle, and quiet. Your reward will be an exhilarating view of the Strip, the golf course, or the mountains through your room's floor-to-ceiling window wall. All guest rooms were remodeled in 2012, and the result is a sunny and soothing residential aura. Deluxe tower accommodations are 640 square feet, and the warm schematic includes colors near the top of the rainbow—lemon and tawny yellows, butterscotch, and cream with rust accents. Great attention to detail, a

Wynn given, is prevalent in each room. The Signature Dream Beds were specially designed for the hotel.

Pluses include the self-parking garage that is closer to the guest elevators than valet parking. There's not a large hotel in Las Vegas that matches it for convenience. An unexpected minus was the signature nightclub Tryst, where we found it impossible to get in without proffering a serious bribe to the gatekeepers.

Steve Wynn has again definitely raised the bar with WLV. Overall, despite its critics, WLV delivers, as promised, the innovative touches the city has come to expect from Steve Wynn. It's a resort for the 21st century, and its neighbors are going to have to get busy if they intend to keep up with the Wynns.

Wynn Encore (wynnlasvegas.com)

WYNN LAUNCHED CONSTRUCTION on a second hotel on the first anniversary of Wynn Las Vegas. This 2,034-suite hotel, called Wynn Encore, is similar in size and design to the original hotel. More than an expansion of Wynn Las Vegas, Encore is a full-scale resort with a 74,000-square-foot casino, an elaborate pool complex, five fine-dining venues, a half-dozen lounges and bars (including a hot and très-chic nightclub), a showroom, an upscale shopping venue, and, of course, a spa and fitness center. Standard accommodations at Encore are 700-square-foot suites with separate sleeping and sitting areas. According to Steve Wynn, the casino is modeled on Wynn's Macau casino (**wynnmacau.com**).

The signature components of Encore's environment are the color red, flowers, natural sunlight, and butterflies. Each is featured throughout the hotel with subtle and obvious flair. The rich, vibrant reds signify luck—appropriate for a gaming establishment—and the whimsical, beautiful, and colorful butterflies denote evolution and change. The flowers, predominantly red roses and red chrysanthemums, are effusive throughout.

The Oriental influence at Encore is apparent from the moment you arrive at the hotel's dual porte cocheres, where two bronze sculptures greet arrivals. The Foo Dogs are replicas of large canines that historically guarded Asian palaces and temples by thwarting evil spirits. One dog sitting over a ball representing earth symbolizes power, and the other straddling a baby is the symbol of good fortune. Guests are invited to rub the paws of each dog.

The entire hotel feels open and airy. A deluge of sunlight flows though vaulted translucent ceilings and vertical windows at the main entrance atrium, as well as in the casino, conference center, shopping area, and nooks overlooking the pool. Those same windows transmit radiant moonlight as well. Affecting the light are lustrous white-and-beige marble floors and walls, which reflect the glow.

Encore restaurants include Sinatra, serving classical Italian cuisine; Botero, a chophouse; Society Café Encore, serving American cuisine; Wazuzu, featuring pan-Asian preparations; Andrea's, for Asian fusion; and the Lobby Bar and Café, a more casual venue. All Encore restaurants offer a sophisticated and visually exciting environment.

The largest water features are the two oval plunges immediately outside the casino. The pools impart a St. Tropez vibe with white cabanas, lily pods (reclining cushions surrounding umbrellas), and in-pool daybeds. The Resort pool is bordered by a formal garden of slender amphora vases, flowering plants, palms, and evergreen magnolia trees. The European pool's island bar encourages guests to dip their feet while enjoying cocktails. Several blackjack tables are positioned poolside. Adjacent to XS nightclub, this lounge area merges with the nightclub's festive and sultry environment after dark.

Unlike many casinos that are an enormous spread of tables and slots, the Encore gaming floor is sectioned by columns and drapery to suggest intimacy and privacy. In addition to the standard casino games, Encore offers both pai gow and pai gow tiles. Roulette slots are included among the 1,600 slot and video-poker machines. For gaming comfort, there are low- and high-rise blackjack tables.

The second floor of the 61,000-square-foot Spa and Salon at Encore combines marble, flowing water, sunlight, and huge windows to provide an opulent indoor-outdoor feeling while you are beautified and pampered. The wow factor occurs at the entry to the 51 treatment rooms housed along two dimly lit extended passages featuring water silently sliding down cylindrical urns. At the far end is an inscrutable Buddha. A well-equipped fitness center adjoins the spa.

The Esplanade shopping arcade is well placed and leads to not only the Encore Theater but also completes a seamless transition from Encore into the Wynn Las Vegas casino. At the southwest end of the Esplanade is the Le Rêve Theater at Wynn Las Vegas. At the northeast end of the Esplanade are Botero restaurant and XS nightclub. Between these entertainment, dining, and nightlife venues are 27,000 square feet of shopping bliss.

Encore nightlife centers around XS (as in "excess"), a plush lounge arranged around lighted pools in a design that emulates the curves of the female body. Because XS is contiguous with Encore's outdoor pool, there is limited complimentary seating at the pool's lounge tables. If you're fortunate enough to score a complimentary seat, maybe you can make up for it by ordering an Ono—a Champagne-Cognac mix that sells for $10,000 and is served with XS-logo silver cufflinks for men or a black-pearl pendant necklace for women (I promise I'm not making this up).

Guest rooms at Encore offer lovely views of the Strip or Downtown through floor-to-ceiling, wall-to-wall windows with electric-powered drapes and sheers. The sleeping area is separated from the living area by a three-foot partition crowned by a high-definition TV on a swivel base. Seating in the living room is oriented to enjoying the vistas, with no furniture of any kind blocking the windows. Baths offer a separate tub and shower, as well as a private toilet with a locking door. Room lighting is high-tech with multiple control panels. With a lot of head-scratching you can figure it out on your own, but we recommend having someone from the bell staff or housekeeping give you a lesson. Signature suites are located at the west end of the hotel tower and have their own private reception area and elevators. Views are superior there (though not by much), and the suites are a bit wider than the standard suites.

Wynn Encore and Wynn Las Vegas each have a self-parking garage. The Wynn LV parking garage, placed between the Encore and Wynn LV resorts and entered from the Strip, is more convenient for those heading toward the Encore casino, Esplanade arcade, XS nightclub, and the Encore and Wynn LV showrooms. A subtle door in the northeast corner on the garage's second level provides an almost-covert entry into the Esplanade. The larger Encore parking garage is on the property's east side and is accessed from the Strip and an extended drive on the north side of the property. That entry is handier to the front desk, conference area, spa, and hotel elevators. Like the Wynn LV garage, an LED sign at each level indicates the number of spots still available.

Coming and going is easy at Encore. The main entrance is on the Strip, but in a section that's rarely congested. You can exit Encore onto the Strip in either direction or onto eastbound Desert Inn Road. Both Wynn LV and Encore provide complimentary shuttle service to the Las Vegas Convention Center and the Convention Center monorail station.

The client base at Encore is Wynn Resort customers eager to experience the newest famed Wynn hospitality and Asian visitors familiar with the Wynn casino in Macau. International visitors are plentiful since the Wynn brand is synonymous worldwide with classic grace, style, and service.

In addition, plans are afoot to develop the land occupied by the Wynn Golf Club. On tap are a 1.5-million-square-foot convention center flanked by two additional hotels with a total of 5,200 guest rooms. The new hotels and convention center would be situated closer to Paradise Road and be separated from Wynn Las Vegas and Wynn Encore by a 20-acre lake similar to that of Bellagio. At last word, construction was delayed by economic conditions in Las Vegas.

NAVIGATING *the*
LAND *of the* GIANTS

GRAND HOTELS OF LAS VEGAS are celebrated on television, in film, and, of course, in countless advertisements. These are the prestige properties in a town that counts more hotel rooms than any other city in the world. Located along the center and southern end of the Strip, these mammoths beckon with their glamour and luxury. Specifically we're talking about:

Aria	Bellagio	Caesars Palace	Cosmopolitan
Luxor	Mandalay Bay/Four Seasons/Delano		MGM Grand
Mirage	Monte Carlo	New York–New York	Paris Las Vegas
Planet Hollywood	TI	Venetian/Palazzo	Wynn Resorts

But can so many hotels actually mean less choice? From a certain perspective, the answer is yes. The Strip, you see, is suffering a paroxysm of homogeneity. After you've chosen your preferred icon (Statue of Liberty, Eiffel Tower, pyramid, gondolas, volcano, and so on), you've done the heavy lifting. Aside from theme, or lack thereof, the big new hotels are pretty much the same. First, they're all so large that walking to the self-park garage is like taking a hike. Second, there are high-quality guest rooms in all of the properties. This is a far cry from previous decades, say, when only a handful of hotels offered rooms comparable to what you'd find at a garden-variety Hyatt or Marriott. Third, all of the megahotels are distinguished by designer restaurants, each with its big-name chef, that are too expensive for the average guest to afford. Ditto for most of the showrooms.

So let's say you're a person of average means and you want to stay in one of the new, glitzy super-hotels. Location is not important to you as long as it's on the Strip. How do you choose? If you have a clear preference for gondolas over trapeze acts, or sphinx over lions, simply select the hotel with the theme that fires your fantasies. If, however, you're pretty much indifferent when it comes to the various themes, make your selection on the basis of price. Using the Internet, your travel agent, and the resources provided in this guide, find the colossus that offers the best deal. Stay there and venture out on foot to check out all the other hotels. Believe us, once you're ensconced, having the Empire State Building outside your window instead of a statue of Caesar won't make any difference.

As it happens, there are also a number of livable but more moderately priced hotels mixed in among the giants, specifically:

| Bally's | Casino Royale | Excalibur | Flamingo |
| Harrah's | LINQ Hotel & Casino | Tropicana | SLS |

Some of these hotels were the prestige addresses of the Strip before the building boom of the past two decades. They are still great places, however, and properties where you can afford to eat in the restaurants and enjoy a show. Best of all, they are located right in the heart of the action. It's cool, of course, to come home and say that you stayed at Wynn Las Vegas, but you could camp at the Excalibur for a week for what a Wynn Las Vegas weekend would cost.

BUSINESS HOTELS

MOST BUSINESS TRAVELERS stay in hotels with casinos or in all-suite hotels. There is one nongaming hotel, however, that merits special mention by virtue of its proximity to the Las Vegas Convention Center.

Renaissance Las Vegas Hotel (renaissancelasvegas.com)

NEIGHBORING THE LAS VEGAS CONVENTION CENTER sits the Renaissance Las Vegas, a haven of tranquility amid the buzz and traffic surrounding the vast meeting complex next door. This 15-floor property on Paradise Road is a 548-room, nonsmoking, nongaming sanctuary. The oversized guest rooms have restful sage, apricot, and beige accents with light cherry furniture. Well suited for business travelers, accommodations include a lounge chair with ottoman, an ergonomic chair and rectangular work desk, a coffeemaker, dual-line phone, Internet access, and complimentary newspaper. Bathrooms feature glass showers, separate tubs, marble floors, and granite counters. Guests with platinum and gold membership status can access the Club Lounge (located on the 15th floor), which provides complimentary breakfast and evening cocktails and appetizers, a boarding-pass station, and concierge service.

Through the main lobby, the large center courtyard has windows on three sides. A cozy outdoor area includes black-and-red tables, lounges, daybeds, and circle beds. Patio heaters warm the space on cool evenings. Food and beverage service is available. A small heated swimming pool and detached whirlpool are at the opposite end of the courtyard. The area is protected on all sides by the hotel's high walls—a welcome feature on Las Vegas's perennially windy days.

Award-winning ENVY Steakhouse, with a unique red marble floor, is open daily. There is also a glass-enclosed Wine Room, with more than 400 vintages and seating for 20. An abbreviated menu is available in the adjoining bar, and a popular Jazz Brunch is offered on Sundays.

Services include a business center, 24-hour in-room dining, a health club, an activities concierge, valet parking, a coffee cafe, and a sundries shop. The property is close to the monorail stop at the convention center but is four lengthy blocks to the Strip—better to cab it.

SUITE HOTELS

SUITES

THE TERM SUITE IN LAS VEGAS covers a broad range of accommodations. The vast majority of suites are studio suites consisting of a larger-than-average room with a conversation area (couch, chair, and coffee table) and a refrigerator added to the usual inventory of basic furnishings. In a one-bedroom suite, the conversation area is normally in a second room separate from the sleeping area. One-bedroom suites are not necessarily larger than studio suites in terms of square footage but are more versatile. Studio and one-bedroom suites are often available in Las Vegas for about the same rate as a standard hotel room.

Larger hotels, with or without casinos, usually offer roomier, more luxurious multiroom suites. Floor plans and rates for these premium suites can usually be obtained on the hotel's website.

There are some suite hotels that do not have casinos. Patronized primarily by business travelers and nongamblers, these properties offer a quiet alternative to the glitz and frenetic pace of the hotel-casinos. Because there is no gambling to subsidize operations, however, suites at properties without casinos are usually (but not always) more expensive than suites at hotels with casinos.

While most hotels with casinos offer suites, only the Rio, The Cosmopolitan, Tuscany, Signature at MGM Grand, Vdara at CityCenter, Delano Las Vegas, Wynn Encore, and The Venetian/Palazzo are all-suite properties. The basic studio suite is a plush, one-room affair with a wet bar and a sitting area but no kitchen facilities. The Rio sometimes makes its suites available at $49 per night and is one of the best lodging values in town. In addition, Signature and Tuscany are by far the easiest to get in and out of if you have a car.

Many thousands of condos and time-shares, some stand-alone nongaming properties and others associated with established casinos, were being developed when the bottom fell out of the economy.

The majority of these condos were pre-sold and under contract but for obvious reasons never closed. Now developers are trying to stay afloat by making these units available to the general public. If you check the travel search engine **kayak.com** or **lvahotels.com,** a number of these properties will pop up, usually at extremely attractive rates. As a corollary, developers dumping condos and timeshares into the city's room inventory has put downward pressure on hotel rates across the board.

SUITE HOTELS *without* CASINOS

Alexis Park Resort Hotel (alexispark.com)

THIS 496-SUITE NONGAMING PROPERTY was one of the first in Las Vegas to create this concept in the 1980s. Situated on 16 acres, the 19 buildings house a variety of suites ranging in size from bedroom-parlor combos to large two-level lofts. Front to back, all are being renovated. The standard junior suite is one room with king or double-double sharing space with a hide-a-bed love seat, two side chairs, and a desk. A corner wet bar with granite counters encloses a refrigerator, coffeemaker, and storage cabinets. Microwaves are available on request. In the larger one-bedroom suites, a Jacuzzi tub and glass-enclosed shower are alongside the king-size bed. There is a separate large living room with easy chairs and a sofa, more kitchen space, and a small powder room. Architectural prints line the walls. Ice machines are nearby.

The property features three medium-sized fenced pools and mature lawns and landscaping. Buildings are freshly painted, but the passageways underneath stairwells are underlit and all walkways are in need of resurfacing. The exterior of the complex appears fatigued. Along with a comedy club, the lobby includes an Internet station, poolside Alexis Gardens restaurant, and Pegasus lounge. Other amenities include a men's and women's hair salon, business center, and a downsized fitness center with limited equipment. Room service is available, and pets are accepted.

Best Western Mardi Gras Hotel and Casino (mardigrasinn.com)

THE MARDI GRAS OFFERS SPARTAN SUITES at good rates. Quiet, with a well-manicured courtyard and a pool, the Mardi Gras is only a short walk from the Las Vegas Convention Center. There is a coffee shop on the property, and a number of good restaurants are less than half a mile away. Though a sign in front of the property advertises a casino, there is only a small collection of slot machines.

Elara (hilton.com)

IF YOUR IDEA OF NIRVANA IS A LUXURY HOTEL atop a cosmopolitan shopping center, the Elara is a good choice. The hotel is positioned over the 170-boutique Miracle Mile shopping arcade and is an upscale satellite of the Planet Hollywood Resort & Casino. Accessible from East Harmon Avenue, the 52-story all-suite red-and-blue tower offers several suite combinations to a maximum of four bedrooms with a parlor. The top five floors are residential condos, and the lower 47 are vacation-ownership hotel suites. All units feature high-tech components along with fully equipped granite and stainless-steel kitchens. Next to the king bed in the spacious sleeping room is a zebra-striped chaise and mirrored whirlpool tub. There are four flat-panel TVs throughout. Photos of Marilyn Monroe, the hotel's muse, can be found in all suites. A spectacular rectangular pool, framed by tall palms, faces south for all-day rays and no sun blockage by vertical buildings. Other amenities include room service, a business center, a gift shop, a gym, Starbucks, and 24-hour concierge service. Elara is about a five-minute stroll through the mall's south wing to reach the hotel's nucleus. This is a plus and a minus for guests: The plus is nongaming serenity with immediate access to eclectic shopping, and the minus is the significant distance to all Planet Hollywood venues. Guests preferring to stay towerside can sample the 15 culinary offerings within the Miracle Mile. The property offers front-door valet parking, but self-parking is only available in the Miracle Mile garage.

Hyatt Place Las Vegas (lasvegas.place.hyatt.com)

AT PARADISE ROAD AND HARMON AVENUE, Hyatt Place Las Vegas offers contemporary one-room suites at good prices. In addition to a small fitness center, an outdoor pool, and a few small meeting rooms, Hyatt Place serves a complimentary Continental breakfast. By taxi, Hyatt Place is about 4 minutes from the Strip and 5 minutes from the Las Vegas Convention Center. The hotel offers a complimentary airport shuttle.

Platinum Hotel (theplatinumhotel.com)

THIS TRICOLOR, 17-STORY METROTOWER is one mega block from the famed Four Corners intersection of the Strip. An intimate all-suite, casino-less retreat, it's a non-Vegas hotel in the middle of Las Vegas. This property is a sleeper. The lobby looks and feels like a high-end high-rise. The Platinum's standard one-bedroom, the 910-square-foot Solitaire Suite, is huge in comparison to similar accommodations elsewhere. At the entry is a good-sized fully equipped kitchen. All bathrooms boast large Jacuzzi tubs, double sinks, and a separate glass shower. The celadon-and-tan bedrooms easily handle two double-queens or one king plus an easy chair or loveseat. In the parlor are a queen sofa sleeper, side chair, coffee table, desk, and Bose radio. High-speed wireless Internet access and overnight laundry are available. Both the bedroom and parlor are furnished with 42-inch flat-panel TVs. The even larger 1,150-square-foot Princess Suite contains the aforementioned accoutrements plus a washer and dryer and show fireplace in the bedroom and living room. All units feature balconies. West-facing rooms oversee the center Strip area, while east-facing rooms reveal suburban Las Vegas and Sunrise Mountain. Extended stays are welcome. Amenities include a year-round, heated indoor-outdoor pool; KIL@watt restaurant (open for breakfast and lunch); the ground-floor STIR lounge; WELL Spa; and a fitness center.

Residence Inn (residenceinn.com)

ACROSS FROM THE LAS VEGAS CONVENTION CENTER, the Residence Inn by Marriott offers comfortable one- and two-bedroom suites with full kitchens. Patronized primarily by business travelers on extended stays, the Residence Inn provides a more homelike atmosphere than most other suite properties. While there is no restaurant at the hotel, there is an excellent selection within a half-mile radius. Amenities include a pool, hot tubs, and a coin laundry. A second Residence Inn is about a mile away at the Hughes Center.

Rumor (rumorvegas.com)

THIS ALL-SUITE BOUTIQUE HOTEL sits directly across from the Hard Rock Hotel and Casino. Formerly the St. Tropez, the recently remodeled property is swathed in black, silver, and white with plum and metal accents creating a crisp mid-century techno look and feel. Like its boisterous neighbor, the hotel is geared toward a youthful market. Tucked into a corner of the lobby is the airy Addiction restaurant open daily. Alongside a small bar, the restaurant spills outside into the firepit lounge furnished with white leather couches shaded by mature palms and a white canopy.

The 150 suites, like the public areas, are a juxtaposition of dark and light. Charcoal walls and dark gray carpet play off cream-colored bedding and plum accents. Most accommodations feature an elevated triangular hot tub alongside the bed. The living room includes a love seat, coffee table, and a side chair. All rooms have garden-view patios or balconies.

The three-pool "Gossip" complex offers cabanas and daybeds and a plush lawn for hammocks and chaises. With the property's circular configuration, self-parking is limited, but free valet parking is available. Since the property has no gym, Rumors has a reciprocal agreement with the Hard Rock, so guests are invited to use the fitness facilities across the street.

The Signature at MGM Grand
(signaturemgmgrand.com)

LOCATED A 5- TO 7-MINUTE WALK east of MGM's main casino, the Signature condo-hotel towers provide a welcome respite from the frantic action of Las Vegas, yet still offer proximity to the bustle and endless amenities and entertainment options at MGM Grand. Suite accommodations feature floor-to-ceiling windows, full kitchens, flat-panel TVs, Jacuzzi tubs, and high-speed Internet connections. Signature's suites are not especially large but are beautifully appointed, and many units have private balconies. Each tower has its own pool, 24-hour concierge service, lounge, deli, fitness center, business center, and a private entrance with valet parking. The private entrance on Harmon Avenue makes for easy coming and going if you have a car. And it's only a 5-minute walk to the MGM Grand monorail station.

SpringHill Suites
Las Vegas Convention Center (marriott.com)

WITH AN OUTDOOR POOL AND HOT TUB, a fitness center, a full-service restaurant, and room service, SpringHill Suites offers the amenities you would expect from a Marriott. And the small building and easy access to parking make the property easy to navigate. Suites are tastefully decorated, though not as plush as some Marriott properties. SpringHill Suites is directly across from the convention center, with a monorail station adjacent, and two blocks from the Strip.

Trump Hotel Las Vegas
(trumplasvegashotel.com)

OPENED IN 2008, TRUMP LAS VEGAS is a nongaming all-suite hotel located on Fashion Show Drive about 600 yards west of the Strip. It's a hotel, not a tourist attraction, offering studios and one-, two-, and three-bedroom suites. Its 64-story tower is situated to provide good views in every direction through floor-to-ceiling windows. While there is no showroom or nightclub, there is gourmet dining at the DJT (Donald J. Trump) restaurant, libations at the H2(eau) lounge, an adequate pool, and an excellent spa and fitness center. When we inspected Trump Las Vegas we were immediately struck by the quiet of the place. From the lobby to the restaurants to the guest suites, it was restful and relaxing. The suites provide all the connectivity a business traveler could want, as well as full kitchens in the one- to three-bedroom units. Furnishings are Scandinavian contemporary, mixing dark and blond wood tones and restful pastel soft goods. Though it's a 10-minute walk to the Strip, Trump is directly across Fashion Show Drive from the Fashion Show Mall, Las Vegas's largest shopping venue. The Las Vegas Convention Center is about 10 minutes away by cab, and the Sands Convention Center is about 10 minutes distant by foot.

HOTELS *with* BALCONIES

LAS VEGAS IS A GREAT PLACE TO HAVE FUN, and for some, a great place to get married. Evidently, it's also a favorite place for splashy suicides. Consequently, very few Las Vegas hotels have balconies. Likewise, bugs are a problem—those tiny critters can fly a lot higher than you might think. Following is a list of the hotels with at least some balconies. At Hooters, Royal Resort, and the Trop, you have to request a balcony room:

Cosmopolitan	Hooters	Platinum	Royal Resort
Signature at MGM Grand	Staybridge Suites	Tropicana Garden Rooms	

LAS VEGAS MOTELS

BECAUSE THEY MUST COMPETE with the huge hotel-casinos, many Las Vegas motels offer great rates or provide special amenities, such as a complimentary breakfast. Like the resorts, motels often have a very specific clientele. La Quinta Inn, for instance, caters to government employees, while the Best Western on Craig Road primarily serves folks visiting Nellis Air Force Base.

For the most part, national motel chains are well represented in Las Vegas. We have included enough chain and independent motels in the following ratings-and-rankings section to give you a sense of how these properties compare with hotel-casinos and all-suite hotels. Because chain hotels are known entities to most travelers, no descriptions are provided beyond the room-quality ratings. After all, a Comfort Inn in Las Vegas is pretty much like a Comfort Inn in Louisville, and we are all aware by now that Motel 6 leaves the light on for you.

RV CAMPING *in* LAS VEGAS

MANY CASINOS, including Main Street Station, Circus Circus, Sam's Town, and Arizona Charlie's (Boulder), operate RV campgrounds with full facilities. There are also quite a few KOA or independent campgrounds. Of these, we prefer the **Las Vegas RV Resort** (**lasvegasrvresort .com, ☎** 866-846-5432), one of the largest in town with 400 sites. Limited to adults, this palm tree–lined RV complex is located two blocks north of Sam's Town on Boulder Highway at 3890 S. Nellis Blvd. The 18-acre resort offers full hook-ups for pull-thrus and multiple slide-outs. Standard, deluxe, and premium sites are available. Each site includes a picnic table. Amenities include a heated pool and hot tub, a clubhouse with lounge seating and big-screen TV, two Laundromats, multiple shower and restroom facilities, free wireless Internet, and two pet runs. A small fitness facility is open daily, 8 a.m.–11 p.m. Propane deliveries can be preordered. Daily, weekly, or monthly rentals are available.

ACCOMMODATIONS:
Rated and Ranked

WHAT'S IN A ROOM?

EXCEPT FOR CLEANLINESS, state of repair, and decor, most travelers do not pay much attention to hotel rooms. There is, of course, a discernible standard of quality and luxury that differentiates Motel 6 from Holiday Inn, Holiday Inn from Marriott, and so on. In general, however, most hotel guests fail to appreciate that some rooms are better engineered than other rooms.

Contrary to what you might suppose, designing a hotel room is (or should be) a lot more complex than picking a bedspread to match the carpet and drapes. Making the room usable to its occupants is an art, a planning discipline that combines both form and function.

Decor and taste are important, certainly. No one wants to spend several days in a room where the furnishings are dated, garish, or even ugly. But beyond the decor, there are variables that determine how "livable" a hotel room is. In Las Vegas, for example, we have seen some beautifully appointed rooms that are simply not well designed for human habitation. The next time you stay in a hotel, pay attention to the details and design elements of your room. Even more than decor, these are the things that will make you feel comfortable and at home.

ROOM RATINGS

TO SEPARATE PROPERTIES according to the relative quality, tasteful-ness, state of repair, cleanliness, and size of their standard rooms, we have grouped them into classifications denoted by stars. Star ratings in this guide apply to Las Vegas properties only and do not necessarily corre-spond to ratings awarded by Forbes, AAA, or other travel critics. Because stars have little relevance when awarded in the absence of commonly recognized standards of comparison, we have tied our ratings to expected levels of quality established by specific American hotel corporations.

Star ratings apply to *room quality only* and describe the property's standard accommodations. For almost all hotels and motels, a "stan-dard accommodation" is a hotel room with either one king bed or two queen beds. In an all-suite property, the standard accommodation is either a studio or one-bedroom suite. Also, in addition to standard accommodations, many hotels offer luxury rooms and special suites, which are not rated in this guide. Star ratings for rooms are assigned without regard to whether a property has a casino, restaurant(s), rec-reational facilities, entertainment, or other extras.

In addition to stars, we also employ a numerical rating system. Our rating scale is 0–100, with 100 as the best possible rating and zero (0) as the worst. Numerical ratings are presented to show the difference we perceive between one property and another. Rooms at the Riviera, Monte Carlo, and The Orleans, for instance, are all rated as ★★★½ (three-and-a-half stars). In the supplemental numerical ratings, the Riviera and the Monte Carlo are rated 79 and 82, respectively, while The Orleans is rated 75. This means that within the three-and-a-half-star category, the Riviera and the Monte Carlo are comparable, and both have somewhat nicer rooms than The Orleans.

HOW THE HOTELS COMPARE

ON PAGES 167–169 is a comparison of hotel rooms in town. We've focused on room quality only and excluded any consideration of location, services, recreation, or amenities. In some instances, a one- or two-room suite can be had for the same price or less than that of a hotel room.

If you used an earlier edition of this guide, you will notice that many of the ratings and rankings have changed. These changes are occasioned by such positive developments as guest-room renova-tion, improved maintenance, and improved housekeeping. Failure to properly maintain guest rooms and poor housekeeping affect the rat-ings negatively. Finally, some ratings change as a result of enlarging our sample size. Because we cannot check every room in a hotel, we inspect a number of randomly chosen rooms. The more rooms we inspect in a particular hotel, the more representative our sample is of the property as a whole. Some of the ratings in this edition have changed as a result of extended sampling.

The guest rooms in many Las Vegas hotels can vary widely in quality. In most hotels the better rooms are situated in high-rise structures known locally as "towers." More modest accommodations, called "garden rooms," are routinely found in one- and two-story outbuildings. It is important to understand that not all rooms in a particular hotel are the same. When you make inquiries or reservations, always define the type of room you are talking about.

Finally, before you begin to shop for a hotel, take a hard look at this letter we received from a couple in Hot Springs, Arkansas:

> We canceled our room reservations to follow the advice in your book [and reserved a hotel room highly ranked by the Unofficial Guide]. We wanted inexpensive, but clean and cheerful. We got inexpensive, but [also] dirty, grim, and depressing. I really felt disappointed in your advice and the room. It was the pits. That was the one real piece of information I needed from your book! The room spoiled the holiday for me aside from our touring.

Needless to say, this letter was as unsettling to us as the bad room was to our reader. Our integrity as travel journalists, after all, is based on the quality of the information we provide to our readers. Even with the best of intentions and the most conscientious research, however, we cannot inspect every room in every hotel. What we do, in statistical terms, is take a sample: we check out several rooms selected at random in each hotel and base our ratings and rankings on those rooms. The inspections are conducted anonymously and without the knowledge of the management. Although it would be unusual, it is certainly possible that the rooms we randomly inspect are not representative of the majority of rooms at a particular hotel. Another possibility is that the rooms we inspect in a given hotel are representative but that by bad luck a reader is assigned a room that is inferior. When we rechecked the hotel our reader disliked, we discovered that our rating was correctly representative, but that he and his wife had unfortunately been assigned to one of a small number of threadbare rooms scheduled for renovation.

The key to avoiding disappointment is to snoop around in advance. We recommend that you check out the hotel's website before you book. Be forewarned, however, that some hotel chains use the same guest room photo for all hotels in the chain; a specific guest room may not resemble the brochure photo. When you or your travel agent call, ask how old the property is and when your guest room was last renovated. If you arrive and are assigned a room inferior to that which you had been led to expect, demand to be moved to another room deserving of your expectations.

Cost estimates are based on the hotel's published rack rates for standard rooms, averaged between weekday and weekend prices. Rack rates during the recession, as you can imagine, are in a continual state of flux, so with a little effort you should be able to significantly beat the rates listed. Each "$" represents $50. Thus a cost symbol of "$$$" means a room (or suite) at that hotel will cost about $150 a night.

THE TOP 30 BEST DEALS IN LAS VEGAS

IN ADDITION TO LISTING the nicest rooms in town, we also reorder the list to rank the best combinations of quality and value in a room. Again, rankings are made without consideration of location or the availability of restaurants, recreation, entertainment, and/or amenities.

A reader recently complained to us that he had booked one of our top-ranked rooms in terms of value and had been very disappointed in the room. We noticed that the room the reader occupied had a quality rating of ★★½. We would remind you that the value ratings are intended to give you some sense of value received for dollars spent. A ★★½ room at $30 may have the same value rating as a ★★★★ room at $85, but that does not mean the rooms will be of comparable quality. Regardless of whether it's a good deal or not, a ★★½ room is still a ★★½ room.

Listed on the facing page are the best room buys for the money, regardless of location or star classification, based on averaged rack rates. Note that sometimes a suite can cost less than a hotel room.

WHEN ONLY THE BEST WILL DO

THE TROUBLE WITH PROFILES is that details and distinctions are sacrificed in the interest of brevity and information accessibility. For example, while dozens of properties are listed as having swimming pools, we've made no qualitative discriminations. In the alphabetized profiles, a pool is a pool.

In actuality, of course, though most pools are quite basic and ordinary, some (Wynn Las Vegas, Wynn Encore, Mirage, Tropicana, Flamingo, Monte Carlo, MGM Grand, Planet Hollywood, Mandalay Bay, Bellagio, Caesars Palace, M Resort, The Venetian, JW Marriott Las Vegas, Aria at CityCenter, and the Rio) are pretty spectacular. To distinguish the exceptional from the average in a number of categories, we provide a best-of list below.

BEST OF . . .

MOST VISUALLY INTERESTING HOTELS	
1. The Venetian	**9.** Red Rock Resort
2. Caesars Palace	**10.** Mirage
3. Wynn Las Vegas/Wynn Encore	**11.** New York–New York
4. Bellagio	**12.** Paris Las Vegas
5. Main Street Station	**13.** M Resort
6. Aria at CityCenter	**14.** Rio
7. Mandalay Bay	**15.** The Cosmopolitan
8. Luxor	**16.** Planet Hollywood

Top 30 Best Deals

	HOTEL	STAR RATING	ROOM RATING	COST $ = $50	LOCATION
1.	Silverton	★★★★	88	$+	South of Las Vegas
2.	Best Western Mardi Gras Hotel and Casino	★★★	73	$	East of Strip
3.	Silver Sevens	★★★½	78	$+	East of Strip
4.	Riviera	★★★½	79	$+	North Strip
5.	Clarion Hotel and Casino	★★★	65	$	North Strip
6.	South Point	★★★½	81	$+	South of Las Vegas
7.	Boulder Station	★★★½	76	$+	Boulder Highway
8.	Westgate Las Vegas	★★★½	80	$$-	East of Strip
9.	Eastside Cannery	★★★★	83	$$-	Boulder Highway
10.	Palace Station (tower rooms)	★★★½	81	$$-	North Strip
11.	Aliante Station	★★★★	88	$$	North Las Vegas
12.	Days Inn at Wild Wild West	★★★	68	$+	South Strip
13.	Palms	★★★★½	95	$$$-	West of Strip
14.	Main Street Station	★★★½	75	$$-	Downtown
15.	Arizona Charlie's Boulder	★★★	74	$+	Boulder Highway
16.	Embassy Suites in Las Vegas	★★★★	86	$$+	East of Strip
17.	Signature at MGM Grand (all suites)	★★★★★	96	$$$	East of Strip
18.	Embassy Suites Convention Center	★★★★	87	$$+	East of Strip
19.	Royal Resort	★★★	73	$+	North Strip
20.	Arizona Charlie's Decatur	★★★	66	$+	West Las Vegas
21.	El Cortez	★★★	72	$+	Downtown
22.	Golden Gate	★★★½	75	$$-	Downtown
23.	Fiesta Henderson	★★★	72	$+	Henderson
24.	Sam's Town	★★★½	79	$$-	Boulder Highway
25.	Alexis Park Resort and Villas	★★★½	78	$$-	East of Strip
26.	Bally's	★★★★	85	$$+	Mid Strip
27.	Fremont	★★★	70	$+	Downtown
28.	Flamingo	★★★★	87	$$+	Mid Strip
29.	Hooters Casino Hotel	★★★	73	$+	South Strip
30.	Comfort Inn Paradise Road	★★★	68	$+	East of Strip

BEST FOR SHOPPING ON-SITE OR WITHIN AN 8-MINUTE WALK

1. Caesars Palace
2. The Venetian
3. Mirage
4. Wynn Las Vegas/Wynn Encore
5. TI
6. Planet Hollywood
7. CityCenter
8. Trump Hotel Las Vegas
9. The Cosmopolitan

BEST BUFFETS

1. Caesars Bacchanal Buffet
2. The Cosmopolitan Wicked Spoon Buffet
3. Aria Buffet
4. Bellagio Buffet
5. Wynn Buffet
6. PH's Spice Market Buffet
7. Mirage Cravings/Buffet at TI
8. M Resort Studio B Buffet
9. Feast GVR/Feast Texas Station
10. Main Street Station Garden Court

BEST DINING (Expense No Issue)

1. The Cosmopolitan
2. Wynn Las Vegas/Wynn Encore
3. The Venetian/Palazzo
4. CityCenter
5. Bellagio
6. Caesars Palace
7. MGM Grand
8. Mandalay Bay
9. Mirage

BEST DINING (For Great Value)

1. The Orleans
2. Suncoast
3. California
4. Main Street Station
5. Gold Coast
6. Palace Station
7. South Point
8. Fiesta Rancho
9. Boulder Station
10. Sam's Town

BEST SUNDAY BRUNCHES

- **Bally's:** Sterling Brunch • **Bellagio:** Jasmine
- **House of Blues at Mandalay Bay:** Gospel Brunch • **Palms Place:** Simon Brunch
- **Wynn Las Vegas:** Cookin' with Jazz Brunch

BEST FOR BOWLING

- Gold Coast • The Orleans • Red Rock Resort • Sam's Town
- Sante Fe Station • South Point • Sunset Station • Texas Station

BEST SPAS

- Bellagio • Caesars Palace • CityCenter: Aria, Mandarin Oriental, Vdara
- The Cosmopolitan • Green Valley Ranch Resort and Spa
- Mandalay Bay/Delano/Four Seasons • MGM Grand • Mirage • Monte Carlo
- The Palazzo • Paris Las Vegas • Red Rock Resort • TI • Trump Hotel Las Vegas
- The Venetian • Wynn Encore • Wynn Las Vegas

BEST FOR GOLF

- Aliante Station • Hilton Lake Las Vegas • JW Marriott Las Vegas
- Westgate Las Vegas • Suncoast • Wynn Las Vegas

BEST FOR TENNIS

- Bally's • Flamingo • Paris Las Vegas • Riviera • Westgate LV

How the Hotels Compare in Las Vegas

HOTEL	STAR RATING	ROOM RATING	COST $ = $50	LOCATION
Delano (all suites)	★★★★★	96	$$$$+	South Strip
Mandarin Oriental at CityCenter	★★★★★	96	$x6-	Mid Strip
Signature at MGM Grand (all suites)	★★★★★	96	$$$	East of Strip
Wynn Encore	★★★★★	96	$x7	Mid Strip
Wynn Las Vegas	★★★★★	96	$x8-	Mid Strip
Aria at CityCenter	★★★★½	95	$$$$+	Mid Strip
Bellagio	★★★★½	95	$x5+	Mid Strip
Caesars Palace	★★★★½	95	$x5-	Mid Strip
Four Seasons at Mandalay Bay	★★★★½	95	$x7	South Strip
Hard Rock Hotel	★★★★½	95	$$$$+	East of Strip
The Palazzo (all suites)	★★★★½	95	$x5	Mid Strip
Palms	★★★★½	95	$$$-	West of Strip
Trump Hotel Las Vegas (all suites)	★★★★½	95	$$$	North Strip
Vdara at CityCenter	★★★★½	95	$$$$-	Mid Strip
The Cosmopolitan	★★★★½	94	$x5	Mid Strip
Nobu Hotel	★★★★½	94	$x6-	Mid Strip
The Venetian	★★★★½	94	$x5-	Mid Strip
Elara	★★★★½	93	$$$$-	Mid Strip
JW Marriott Las Vegas	★★★★½	93	$$$+	Summerlin
Mandalay Bay	★★★★½	92	$$$+	South Strip
Paris	★★★★½	91	$$$+	Mid Strip
Red Rock Resort	★★★★½	91	$$$$+	Summerlin
Golden Nugget (Rush Tower)	★★★★½	90	$$$$-	Downtown
M Resort	★★★★½	90	$$$+	South of Las Vegas
MGM Grand	★★★★½	90	$$$-	South Strip
Mirage	★★★★½	90	$$$$-	Mid Strip
Renaissance Las Vegas	★★★★½	90	$$$-	East of Strip
SLS Las Vegas	★★★★	89	$$$-	North Strip
Tropicana	★★★★	89	$$$-	South Strip
Aliante Station	★★★★	88	$$	North Las Vegas
Hilton Lake Las Vegas	★★★★	88	$$$-	Henderson
Platinum Hotel	★★★★	88	$$$-	East of Strip
Silverton	★★★★	88	$+	South of Las Vegas
Westin Lake Las Vegas	★★★★	88	$$$	Henderson
Embassy Suites Convention Center	★★★★	87	$$+	East of Strip
Flamingo	★★★★	87	$$+	Mid Strip
Green Valley Ranch Resort and Spa	★★★★	87	$x5-	Henderson
Luxor	★★★★	87	$$$	South Strip

How the Hotels Compare in Las Vegas

HOTEL	STAR RATING	ROOM RATING	COST $ = $50	LOCATION
Planet Hollywood	★★★★	87	$$$$	Mid Strip
Sunset Station	★★★★	87	$$$-	Henderson
Embassy Suites in Las Vegas	★★★★	86	$$+	East of Strip
Residence Inn by Marriott Las Vegas South	★★★★	86	$$$-	South Strip
Rio	★★★★	86	$x5	West of Strip
Bally's	★★★★	85	$$+	Mid Strip
The Cromwell	★★★★	85	$x5-	Mid Strip
New York–New York	★★★★	85	$$$-	South Strip
Las Vegas Marriott	★★★★	84	$$$+	East of Strip
TI (Treasure Island)	★★★★	84	$$$	Mid Strip
Eastside Cannery	★★★★	83	$$-	Boulder Hwy.
Residence Inn by Marriott Las Vegas Convention Center	★★★★	83	$$$	East of Strip
Westin Casuarina	★★★★	83	$$$+	East of Strip
Monte Carlo	★★★½	82	$$	Mid Strip
Plaza	★★★½	82	$$	Downtown
Suncoast	★★★½	82	$$$-	Summerlin
Circus Circus (tower rooms)	★★★½	81	$$+	North Strip
Downtown Grand	★★★½	81	$$	Downtown
Harrah's	★★★½	81	$$	Mid Strip
Palace Station (tower rooms)	★★★½	81	$$-	North Strip
South Point	★★★½	81	$+	South of Las Vegas
Westgate Las Vegas	★★★½	80	$$-	East of Strip
Candlewood Suites	★★★½	79	$$	East of Strip
Courtyard by Marriott LV Convention Center	★★★½	79	$$$-	East of Strip
The D Las Vegas	★★★½	79	$$$-	Downtown
El Cortez Cabana Suites	★★★½	79	$$-	Downtown
Riviera	★★★½	79	$+	North Strip
Sam's Town	★★★½	79	$$-	Boulder Hwy.
Stratosphere	★★★½	79	$$	North Strip
Alexis Park Resort and Villas	★★★½	78	$$-	East of Strip
Artisan Hotel and Spa	★★★½	78	$$$+	North Strip
Golden Nugget	★★★½	78	$$$-	Downtown
Rumor	★★★½	78	$$$-	East of Strip
Silver Sevens	★★★½	78	$+	East of Strip
Boulder Station	★★★½	76	$+	Boulder Hwy.
Excalibur	★★★½	76	$$+	South Strip
Courtyard by Marriott Las Vegas South	★★★½	75	$$$-	South Strip
Fairfield Inn & Suites Las Vegas South	★★★½	75	$$+	South Strip

How the Hotels Compare in Las Vegas

HOTEL	STAR RATING	ROOM RATING	COST $ = $50	LOCATION
Golden Gate	★★★½	75	$$-	Downtown
Holiday Inn Express	★★★½	75	$$+	South Strip
Main Street Station	★★★½	75	$$-	Downtown
The Orleans	★★★½	75	$$$-	South Strip
Arizona Charlie's Boulder	★★★	74	$+	Boulder Hwy.
Palace Station (courtyard)	★★★	74	$$-	North Strip
Best Western Mardi Gras Hotel and Casino	★★★	73	$	East of Strip
Hooters Casino Hotel	★★★	73	$+	South Strip
Royal Resort	★★★	73	$+	North Strip
Santa Fe Station	★★★	73	$$	Rancho Drive
El Cortez	★★★	72	$+	Downtown
Fairfield Inn Las Vegas Airport	★★★	72	$$+	East of Strip
Fiesta Henderson	★★★	72	$+	Henderson
Hampton Inn Tropicana	★★★	72	$$	South Strip
Hilton Garden Inn Las Vegas Strip South	★★★	72	$$+	South of Las Vegas
Hyatt Place	★★★	72	$$$	East of Strip
Best Western McCarran Inn	★★★	71	$$-	East of Strip
Four Queens	★★★	70	$$-	Downtown
Fremont	★★★	70	$+	Downtown
Texas Station	★★★	70	$$-	Rancho Drive Area
Tuscany	★★★	70	$$	East of Strip
La Quinta Las Vegas Airport	★★★	69	$$	East of Strip
Comfort Inn Paradise Road	★★★	68	$+	East of Strip
Days Inn at Wild Wild West	★★★	68	$+	South Strip
LINQ Hotel & Casino*	★★★	68	$$	Mid Strip
California	★★★	67	$$-	Downtown
Manor Suites	★★★	67	$$-	South of Las Vegas
Arizona Charlie's Decatur	★★★	66	$+	West Las Vegas
Clarion Hotel and Casino	★★★	65	$	North Strip
Cannery	★★½	64	$$+	North Las Vegas
Casino Royale	★★½	64	$$$-	Mid Strip
Circus Circus (manor rooms)	★★½	62	$$-	North Strip
Fiesta Rancho	★★½	62	$$-	Rancho Drive
Gold Coast	★★½	58	$$-	West of Strip
Motel 6 Tropicana	★★	53	$	East of Strip
Super 8	★★	52	$+	East of Strip
Travelodge Las Vegas Airport North	★½	43	$$+	South Strip
America's Best Value Inn	★	33	$	South Strip

* Rating based on unremodeled guest rooms

Hotel Information Chart

Alexis Park Resort and Villas
★★★½
375 E. Harmon Ave.
Las Vegas, NV 89169
☎ 702-796-3300
FAX 702-796-4334
TOLL-FREE 800-453-8000
alexispark.com

RACK RATE	$$-
ROOM QUALITY	78
LOCATION	East of Strip
NO. OF ROOMS	495
CHECKOUT TIME	11
NONSMOKING	•
CONCIERGE	•
CONVENTION FACIL.	•
MEETING ROOMS	•
VALET PARKING	•
RV PARK	Limited
ROOM SERVICE	•
FREE BREAKFAST	—
FINE DINING/TYPES	Continental
COFFEE SHOP	•
24-HOUR CAFE	—
BUFFET	Breakfast
CASINO	—
LOUNGE	—
SHOWROOM	—
GIFTS/DRUGS/NEWS	—
POOL	•
EXERCISE ROOM	•

Aliante Station ★★★★
7300 Aliante Pkwy.
North Las Vegas, NV 89084
☎ 702-692-7777
TOLL-FREE 877-477-7627
aliantecasinohotel.com

RACK RATE	$$
ROOM QUALITY	88
LOCATION	North Las Vegas
NO. OF ROOMS	202
CHECKOUT TIME	11
NONSMOKING	•
CONCIERGE	•
CONVENTION FACIL.	•
MEETING ROOMS	•
VALET PARKING	•
RV PARK	•
ROOM SERVICE	•
FREE BREAKFAST	—
FINE DINING/TYPES	Steak, seafood, Italian, Mexican
COFFEE SHOP	•
24-HOUR CAFE	•
BUFFET	•
CASINO	•
LOUNGE	•
SHOWROOM	•
GIFTS/DRUGS/NEWS	•
POOL	•
EXERCISE ROOM	•

Aria at CityCenter ★★★★½
3730 Las Vegas Blvd. S.
Las Vegas, NV 89109
☎ 702-590-7111
FAX 702-590-7112
TOLL-FREE 866-359-7757
arialasvegas.com

RACK RATE	$$$$+
ROOM QUALITY	95
LOCATION	Mid-Strip
NO. OF ROOMS	4,004
CHECKOUT TIME	Noon
NONSMOKING	•
CONCIERGE	•
CONVENTION FACIL.	•
MEETING ROOMS	•
VALET PARKING	•
RV PARK	•
ROOM SERVICE	•
FREE BREAKFAST	—
FINE DINING/TYPES	Steak, Italian, Asian, Thai, American
COFFEE SHOP	•
24-HOUR CAFE	•
BUFFET	•
CASINO	•
LOUNGE	•
SHOWROOM	•
GIFTS/DRUGS/NEWS	•
POOL	•
EXERCISE ROOM	Health spa

Bally's ★★★★
3645 Las Vegas Blvd. S.
Las Vegas, NV 89109
☎ 702-739-4111
FAX 702-967-4405
TOLL-FREE 800-634-3434
ballyslasvegas.com

RACK RATE	$$+
ROOM QUALITY	85
LOCATION	Mid-Strip
NO. OF ROOMS	2,814
CHECKOUT TIME	11
NONSMOKING	Floors
CONCIERGE	•
CONVENTION FACIL.	•
MEETING ROOMS	•
VALET PARKING	•
RV PARK	•
ROOM SERVICE	•
FREE BREAKFAST	—
FINE DINING/TYPES	Continental, steak, sushi, Italian
COFFEE SHOP	•
24-HOUR CAFE	•
BUFFET	•
CASINO	•
LOUNGE	•
SHOWROOM	Production show, headliners
GIFTS/DRUGS/NEWS	•
POOL	•
EXERCISE ROOM	Health spa/tennis

Bellagio ★★★★½
3600 Las Vegas Blvd. S.
Las Vegas, NV 89109
☎ 702-693-7444
FAX 702-693-8585
TOLL-FREE 888-987-6667
bellagio.com

RACK RATE	$$$$$+
ROOM QUALITY	95
LOCATION	Mid-Strip
NO. OF ROOMS	3,933
CHECKOUT TIME	Noon
NONSMOKING	•
CONCIERGE	•
CONVENTION FACIL.	•
MEETING ROOMS	•
VALET PARKING	•
RV PARK	•
ROOM SERVICE	•
FREE BREAKFAST	—
FINE DINING/TYPES	Continental
COFFEE SHOP	•
24-HOUR CAFE	•
BUFFET	•
CASINO	•
LOUNGE	•
SHOWROOM	Production show
GIFTS/DRUGS/NEWS	•
POOL	•
EXERCISE ROOM	Health spa

Best Western Mardi Gras Hotel and Casino ★★★
3500 Paradise Rd.
Las Vegas, NV 89169
☎ 702-731-2020
FAX 702-731-4005
TOLL-FREE 800-634-6501
mardigrasinn.com

RACK RATE	$
ROOM QUALITY	73
LOCATION	East of Strip
NO. OF ROOMS	314
CHECKOUT TIME	11
NONSMOKING	•
CONCIERGE	—
CONVENTION FACIL.	•
MEETING ROOMS	•
VALET PARKING	—
RV PARK	—
ROOM SERVICE	—
FREE BREAKFAST	—
FINE DINING/TYPES	American
COFFEE SHOP	—
24-HOUR CAFE	—
BUFFET	—
CASINO	Slots
LOUNGE	•
SHOWROOM	—
GIFTS/DRUGS/NEWS	—
POOL	—
EXERCISE ROOM	—

Arizona Charlie's Boulder
★★★
4575 Boulder Hwy.
Las Vegas, NV 89121
☎ 702-951-9000
FAX 702-951-1046
TOLL-FREE 888-236-9066
arizonacharliesboulder.com

RACK RATE	$+
ROOM QUALITY	74
LOCATION	Boulder Hwy.
NO. OF ROOMS	301
CHECKOUT TIME	11
NONSMOKING	•
CONCIERGE	—
CONVENTION FACIL.	•
MEETING ROOMS	•
VALET PARKING	—
RV PARK	•
ROOM SERVICE	—
FREE BREAKFAST	—
FINE DINING/TYPES	American, steak
COFFEE SHOP	•
24-HOUR CAFE	•
BUFFET	•
CASINO	•
LOUNGE	•
SHOWROOM	Live music
GIFTS/DRUGS/NEWS	•
POOL	•
EXERCISE ROOM	—

Arizona Charlie's Decatur ★★★
740 S. Decatur Blvd.
Las Vegas, NV 89107
☎ 702-258-5111
FAX 702-258-5192
TOLL-FREE 888-236-8645
arizonacharliesdecatur.com

RACK RATE	$+
ROOM QUALITY	66
LOCATION	West Las Vegas
NO. OF ROOMS	258
CHECKOUT TIME	11
NONSMOKING	•
CONCIERGE	—
CONVENTION FACIL.	•
MEETING ROOMS	—
VALET PARKING	—
RV PARK	—
ROOM SERVICE	—
FREE BREAKFAST	—
FINE DINING/TYPES	American, steak
COFFEE SHOP	•
24-HOUR CAFE	•
BUFFET	•
CASINO	•
LOUNGE	•
SHOWROOM	Local bands
GIFTS/DRUGS/NEWS	•
POOL	•
EXERCISE ROOM	—

Artisan Hotel and Spa ★★★½
1501 W. Sahara Ave.
Las Vegas, NV 89102
☎ 702-214-4000
FAX 702-733-1571
TOLL-FREE 800-554-4092
theartisanhotel.com

RACK RATE	$$$+
ROOM QUALITY	78
LOCATION	North Strip
NO. OF ROOMS	64
CHECKOUT TIME	11
NONSMOKING	•
CONCIERGE	•
CONVENTION FACIL.	—
MEETING ROOMS	•
VALET PARKING	•
RV PARK	—
ROOM SERVICE	•
FREE BREAKFAST	—
FINE DINING/TYPES	Italian
COFFEE SHOP	—
24-HOUR CAFE	—
BUFFET	—
CASINO	—
LOUNGE	•
SHOWROOM	—
GIFTS/DRUGS/NEWS	—
POOL	•
EXERCISE ROOM	•

Best Western McCarran Inn ★★★
4970 Paradise Rd.
Las Vegas, NV 89119
☎ 702-798-5530
FAX 702-798-7627
TOLL-FREE 800-528-1234
bestwestern.com

RACK RATE	$$−
ROOM QUALITY	71
LOCATION	East of Strip
NO. OF ROOMS	100
CHECKOUT TIME	Noon
NONSMOKING	•
CONCIERGE	—
CONVENTION FACIL.	—
MEETING ROOMS	•
VALET PARKING	—
RV PARK	•
ROOM SERVICE	—
FREE BREAKFAST	•
FINE DINING/TYPES	—
COFFEE SHOP	—
24-HOUR CAFE	—
BUFFET	—
CASINO	—
LOUNGE	—
SHOWROOM	—
GIFTS/DRUGS/NEWS	—
POOL	•
EXERCISE ROOM	—

Boulder Station ★★★½
4111 Boulder Hwy.
Las Vegas, NV 89121
☎ 702-432-7777
FAX 702-432-7730
TOLL-FREE 800-683-7777
boulderstation.com

RACK RATE	$+
ROOM QUALITY	76
LOCATION	Boulder Hwy.
NO. OF ROOMS	300
CHECKOUT TIME	Noon
NONSMOKING	•
CONCIERGE	•
CONVENTION FACIL.	•
MEETING ROOMS	•
VALET PARKING	•
RV PARK	•
ROOM SERVICE	•
FREE BREAKFAST	—
FINE DINING/TYPES	Steak, seafood, Italian, Mexican
COFFEE SHOP	•
24-HOUR CAFE	•
BUFFET	•
CASINO	•
LOUNGE	•
SHOWROOM	Live music
GIFTS/DRUGS/NEWS	•
POOL	•
EXERCISE ROOM	•

Caesars Palace ★★★★½
3570 Las Vegas Blvd. S.
Las Vegas, NV 89109
☎ 702-731-7110
FAX 702-866-1700
TOLL-FREE 800-634-6661
caesarspalace.com

RACK RATE	$$$$$−
ROOM QUALITY	95
LOCATION	Mid-Strip
NO. OF ROOMS	3,348
CHECKOUT TIME	11
NONSMOKING	Floors
CONCIERGE	•
CONVENTION FACIL.	•
MEETING ROOMS	•
VALET PARKING	•
RV PARK	—
ROOM SERVICE	•
FREE BREAKFAST	—
FINE DINING/TYPES	Asian, French, Japanese, Italian, steak
COFFEE SHOP	•
24-HOUR CAFE	•
BUFFET	•
CASINO	•
LOUNGE	•
SHOWROOM	Celebrity headliners
GIFTS/DRUGS/NEWS	•
POOL	•
EXERCISE ROOM	Health spa

Hotel Information Chart *(continued)*

California ★★★
12 E. Ogden Ave.
Las Vegas, NV 89101
☎ 702-385-1222
FAX 702-388-2670
TOLL-FREE 800-634-6255
thecal.com

RACK RATE	$$–
ROOM QUALITY	67
LOCATION	Downtown
NO. OF ROOMS	781
CHECKOUT TIME	Noon
NONSMOKING	•
CONCIERGE	—
CONVENTION FACIL.	•
MEETING ROOMS	•
VALET PARKING	•
RV PARK	•
ROOM SERVICE	•
FREE BREAKFAST	
FINE DINING/TYPES	Pasta, seafood, steak, Hawaiian
COFFEE SHOP	•
24-HOUR CAFE	•
BUFFET	•
CASINO	•
LOUNGE	•
SHOWROOM	—
GIFTS/DRUGS/NEWS	•
POOL	•
EXERCISE ROOM	•

Candlewood Suites ★★★½
4034 S. Paradise Rd.
Las Vegas, NV 89109
☎ 702-836-3660
FAX 702-836-3661
TOLL-FREE 877-226-3539
candlewoodsuites.com

RACK RATE	$$
ROOM QUALITY	79
LOCATION	East of Strip
NO. OF ROOMS	276
CHECKOUT TIME	Noon
NONSMOKING	•
CONCIERGE	—
CONVENTION FACIL.	—
MEETING ROOMS	•
VALET PARKING	—
RV PARK	—
ROOM SERVICE	—
FREE BREAKFAST	
FINE DINING/TYPES	—
COFFEE SHOP	—
24-HOUR CAFE	•
BUFFET	—
CASINO	—
LOUNGE	—
SHOWROOM	—
GIFTS/DRUGS/NEWS	—
POOL	•
EXERCISE ROOM	•

Cannery ★★½
2121 E. Craig Rd.
Las Vegas, NV 89030
☎ 702-507-5700
FAX 702-507-5750
TOLL-FREE 866-999-4899
cannerycasinos.com

RACK RATE	$$+
ROOM QUALITY	64
LOCATION	North Las Vegas
NO. OF ROOMS	201
CHECKOUT TIME	Noon
NONSMOKING	•
CONCIERGE	•
CONVENTION FACIL.	•
MEETING ROOMS	•
VALET PARKING	•
RV PARK	•
ROOM SERVICE	•
FREE BREAKFAST	
FINE DINING/TYPES	American, Italian Mexican, steak
COFFEE SHOP	•
24-HOUR CAFE	•
BUFFET	•
CASINO	•
LOUNGE	•
SHOWROOM	Live music
GIFTS/DRUGS/NEWS	•
POOL	•
EXERCISE ROOM	—

The Cosmopolitan ★★★★½
3708 Las Vegas Blvd. S.
Las Vegas NV 89109
☎ 702-698-7000
FAX 702-698-7007
TOLL-FREE 877-551-7778
cosmopolitanlasvegas.com

RACK RATE	$$$$$
ROOM QUALITY	94
LOCATION	Mid-Strip
NO. OF ROOMS	2,995
CHECKOUT TIME	11
NONSMOKING	•
CONCIERGE	•
CONVENTION FACIL.	•
MEETING ROOMS	•
VALET PARKING	•
RV PARK	—
ROOM SERVICE	•
FREE BREAKFAST	
FINE DINING/TYPES	American, Italian, Mediterranean, French, Asian
COFFEE SHOP	•
24-HOUR CAFE	•
BUFFET	•
CASINO	•
LOUNGE	•
SHOWROOM	•
GIFTS/DRUGS/NEWS	•
POOL	•
EXERCISE ROOM	Health spa/tennis

Courtyard by Marriott Las Vegas Convention Center ★★★½
3275 Paradise Rd.
Las Vegas, NV 89109
☎ 702-791-3600
FAX 702-796-7981
TOLL-FREE 800-321-2211
marriott.com

RACK RATE	$$$–
ROOM QUALITY	79
LOCATION	East of Strip
NO. OF ROOMS	149
CHECKOUT TIME	Noon
NONSMOKING	•
CONCIERGE	•
CONVENTION FACIL.	—
MEETING ROOMS	•
VALET PARKING	•
RV PARK	•
ROOM SERVICE	—
FREE BREAKFAST	—
FINE DINING/TYPES	American
COFFEE SHOP	—
24-HOUR CAFE	—
BUFFET	• (Breakfast only)
CASINO	—
LOUNGE	•
SHOWROOM	—
GIFTS/DRUGS/NEWS	—
POOL	•
EXERCISE ROOM	•

Courtyard by Marriott Las Vegas South ★★★½
5845 Dean Martin Dr.
Las Vegas, NV 89118
☎ 702-895-7519
FAX 702-895-7568
TOLL-FREE 800-321-2211
marriott.com

RACK RATE	$$$–
ROOM QUALITY	75
LOCATION	South Strip
NO. OF ROOMS	146
CHECKOUT TIME	Noon
NONSMOKING	•
CONCIERGE	—
CONVENTION FACIL.	—
MEETING ROOMS	—
VALET PARKING	•
RV PARK	•
ROOM SERVICE	•
FREE BREAKFAST	—
FINE DINING/TYPES	American
COFFEE SHOP	—
24-HOUR CAFE	—
BUFFET	• (Breakfast only)
CASINO	—
LOUNGE	—
SHOWROOM	—
GIFTS/DRUGS/NEWS	—
POOL	•
EXERCISE ROOM	•

Casino Royale ★★½
3411 Las Vegas Blvd. S.
Las Vegas, NV 89109
☎ 702-737-3500
FAX 702-650-4743
TOLL-FREE 800-854-7666
casinoroyalehotel.com

RACK RATE	$$$-
ROOM QUALITY	64
LOCATION	Mid-Strip
NO. OF ROOMS	152
CHECKOUT TIME	Noon
NONSMOKING	•
CONCIERGE	—
CONVENTION FACIL.	—
MEETING ROOMS	—
VALET PARKING	—
RV PARK	•
ROOM SERVICE	—
FREE BREAKFAST	—
FINE DINING/TYPES	American, Italian
COFFEE SHOP	•
24-HOUR CAFE	•
BUFFET	—
CASINO	•
LOUNGE	•
SHOWROOM	—
GIFTS/DRUGS/NEWS	•
POOL	•
EXERCISE ROOM	—

Circus Circus ★★★½—★★½*
2880 Las Vegas Blvd. S.
Las Vegas, NV 89109
☎ 702-734-0410
FAX 702-794-3896
TOLL-FREE 800-634-3450
circuscircus.com

RACK RATE	$$+/$$-
ROOM QUALITY	81/62*
LOCATION	North Strip
NO. OF ROOMS	3,773
CHECKOUT TIME	11
NONSMOKING	Floors
CONCIERGE	•
CONVENTION FACIL.	•
MEETING ROOMS	•
VALET PARKING	•
RV PARK	•
ROOM SERVICE	•
FREE BREAKFAST	—
FINE DINING/TYPES	Steak, Italian, Mexican
COFFEE SHOP	•
24-HOUR CAFE	•
BUFFET	•
CASINO	•
LOUNGE	•
SHOWROOM	Circus acts, theme park
GIFTS/DRUGS/NEWS	•
POOL	•
EXERCISE ROOM	•

tower rooms/manor rooms

Clarion Hotel and Casino ★★★
305 Convention Center Dr.
Las Vegas, NV 89109
☎ 702-952-8000
FAX 702-952-8100
TOLL-FREE 800-633-1777
clarionhotel.com

RACK RATE	$
ROOM QUALITY	65
LOCATION	North Strip
NO. OF ROOMS	202
CHECKOUT TIME	11
NONSMOKING	•
CONCIERGE	•
CONVENTION FACIL.	—
MEETING ROOMS	•
VALET PARKING	—
RV PARK	—
ROOM SERVICE	•
FREE BREAKFAST	•
FINE DINING/TYPES	•
COFFEE SHOP	•
24-HOUR CAFE	•
BUFFET	—
CASINO	•
LOUNGE	•
SHOWROOM	•
GIFTS/DRUGS/NEWS	•
POOL	•
EXERCISE ROOM	•

The Cromwell ★★★★
3595 Las Vegas Blvd. S.
Las Vegas, NV 89109
☎ 702-777-3777
TOLL-FREE 844-426-2766
thecromwell.com

RACK RATE	$$$$$-
ROOM QUALITY	85
LOCATION	Mid-Strip
NO. OF ROOMS	188
CHECKOUT TIME	11
NONSMOKING	•
CONCIERGE	•
CONVENTION FACIL.	—
MEETING ROOMS	•
VALET PARKING	•
RV PARK	•
ROOM SERVICE	•
FREE BREAKFAST	—
FINE DINING/TYPES	Italian
COFFEE SHOP	—
24-HOUR CAFE	—
BUFFET	—
CASINO	•
LOUNGE	•
SHOWROOM	•
GIFTS/DRUGS/NEWS	•
POOL	•
EXERCISE ROOM	Health spa

The D Las Vegas ★★★½
301 Fremont St.
Las Vegas, NV 89101
☎ 702-388-2400
FAX 702-388-2181
TOLL-FREE 800-274-5825
thed.com

RACK RATE	$$$-
ROOM QUALITY	81
LOCATION	Downtown
NO. OF ROOMS	638
CHECKOUT TIME	Noon
NONSMOKING	Floors
CONCIERGE	•
CONVENTION FACIL.	—
MEETING ROOMS	•
VALET PARKING	•
RV PARK	—
ROOM SERVICE	•
FREE BREAKFAST	—
FINE DINING/TYPES	Steak, American
COFFEE SHOP	•
24-HOUR CAFE	•
BUFFET	•
CASINO	•
LOUNGE	•
SHOWROOM	•
GIFTS/DRUGS/NEWS	•
POOL	•
EXERCISE ROOM	—

Days Inn at Wild Wild West ★★★
3330 W. Tropicana Ave.
Las Vegas, NV 89103
☎ 702-739-5003
FAX 702-736-7106
TOLL-FREE 800-777-1514
daysinn.com/lasvegas

RACK RATE	$+
ROOM QUALITY	68
LOCATION	South Strip
NO. OF ROOMS	260
CHECKOUT TIME	Noon
NONSMOKING	•
CONCIERGE	—
CONVENTION FACIL.	—
MEETING ROOMS	—
VALET PARKING	—
RV PARK	—
ROOM SERVICE	—
FREE BREAKFAST	—
FINE DINING/TYPES	American
COFFEE SHOP	—
24-HOUR CAFE	—
BUFFET	—
CASINO	—
LOUNGE	—
SHOWROOM	—
GIFTS/DRUGS/NEWS	—
POOL	•
EXERCISE ROOM	—

Hotel Information Chart (continued)

Delano ★★★★★
3950 Las Vegas Blvd. S.
Las Vegas, NV 89119
☎ 702-632-7777
FAX 702-632-7228
TOLL-FREE 877-632-7800
delanolasvegas.com

RACK RATE	$$$$+
ROOM QUALITY	96
LOCATION	South Strip
NO. OF ROOMS	1,110
CHECKOUT TIME	11
NONSMOKING	•
CONCIERGE	•
CONVENTION FACIL.	•
MEETING ROOMS	•
VALET PARKING	•
RV PARK	—
ROOM SERVICE	•
FREE BREAKFAST	—
FINE DINING/TYPES	American, French, Italian
COFFEE SHOP	•
24-HOUR CAFE	Nearby
BUFFET	Nearby
CASINO	Nearby
LOUNGE	•
SHOWROOM	Production show, live music
GIFTS/DRUGS/NEWS	•
POOL	•
EXERCISE ROOM	Health spa

Downtown Grand ★★★½
206 N. 3rd St.
Las Vegas, NV 89101
☎ 702-719-5100
TOLL-FREE 855-384-7263
downtowngrand.com

RACK RATE	$$
ROOM QUALITY	81
LOCATION	Downtown
NO. OF ROOMS	650
CHECKOUT TIME	11
NONSMOKING	•
CONCIERGE	•
CONVENTION FACIL.	•
MEETING ROOMS	•
VALET PARKING	•
RV PARK	—
ROOM SERVICE	•
FREE BREAKFAST	—
FINE DINING/TYPES	American, Chinese
COFFEE SHOP	•
24-HOUR CAFE	•
BUFFET	—
CASINO	•
LOUNGE	•
SHOWROOM	—
GIFTS/DRUGS/NEWS	•
POOL	•
EXERCISE ROOM	•

Eastside Cannery ★★★★
5255 Boulder Hwy.
Las Vegas, NV 89122
☎ 702-856-5300
eastsidecannery.com

RACK RATE	$$-
ROOM QUALITY	83
LOCATION	Boulder Hwy.
NO. OF ROOMS	300
CHECKOUT TIME	Noon
NONSMOKING	•
CONCIERGE	—
CONVENTION FACIL.	—
MEETING ROOMS	•
VALET PARKING	•
RV PARK	—
ROOM SERVICE	—
FREE BREAKFAST	—
FINE DINING/TYPES	Steak, European
COFFEE SHOP	•
24-HOUR CAFE	•
BUFFET	•
CASINO	•
LOUNGE	•
SHOWROOM	•
GIFTS/DRUGS/NEWS	•
POOL	•
EXERCISE ROOM	—

Embassy Suites Convention Center ★★★★
3600 S. Paradise Rd.
Las Vegas, NV 89169
☎ 702-893-8000
FAX 702-893-0378
TOLL-FREE 800-EMBASSY
hilton.com

RACK RATE	$$+
ROOM QUALITY	87
LOCATION	East of Strip
NO. OF ROOMS	286
CHECKOUT TIME	Noon
NONSMOKING	•
CONCIERGE	—
CONVENTION FACIL.	•
MEETING ROOMS	•
VALET PARKING	•
RV PARK	•
ROOM SERVICE	•
FREE BREAKFAST	•
FINE DINING/TYPES	American
COFFEE SHOP	—
24-HOUR CAFE	—
BUFFET	—
CASINO	—
LOUNGE	—
SHOWROOM	—
GIFTS/DRUGS/NEWS	•
POOL	•
EXERCISE ROOM	•

Embassy Suites in Las Vegas ★★★★
4315 Swenson St.
Las Vegas, NV 89119
☎ 702-795-2800
FAX 702-795-1520
TOLL-FREE 800-EMBASSY
hilton.com

RACK RATE	$$+
ROOM QUALITY	86
LOCATION	East of Strip
NO. OF ROOMS	220
CHECKOUT TIME	Noon
NONSMOKING	•
CONCIERGE	•
CONVENTION FACIL.	—
MEETING ROOMS	•
VALET PARKING	—
RV PARK	—
ROOM SERVICE	—
FREE BREAKFAST	•
FINE DINING/TYPES	American
COFFEE SHOP	—
24-HOUR CAFE	—
BUFFET	—
CASINO	—
LOUNGE	—
SHOWROOM	—
GIFTS/DRUGS/NEWS	•
POOL	•
EXERCISE ROOM	•

Excalibur ★★★½
3850 Las Vegas Blvd. S.
Las Vegas, NV 89109
☎ 702-597-7777
FAX 702-597-7163
TOLL-FREE 800-937-7777
excalibur.com

RACK RATE	$$+
ROOM QUALITY	76
LOCATION	South Strip
NO. OF ROOMS	3,991
CHECKOUT TIME	11
NONSMOKING	Floors
CONCIERGE	•
CONVENTION FACIL.	•
MEETING ROOMS	•
VALET PARKING	•
RV PARK	•
ROOM SERVICE	•
FREE BREAKFAST	•
FINE DINING/TYPES	Mexican, steak, Italian, American
COFFEE SHOP	•
24-HOUR CAFE	•
BUFFET	•
CASINO	•
LOUNGE	•
SHOWROOM	Production show, Tournament of Kings
GIFTS/DRUGS/NEWS	•
POOL	•
EXERCISE ROOM	•

Elara ★★★★½
80 E. Harmon Ave.
Las Vegas, NV 89109
☎ 702-669-6700
FAX 702-669-6948
TOLL-FREE 800-445-8667
hilton.com

RACK RATE	$$$$–
ROOM QUALITY	93
LOCATION	Mid-Strip
NO. OF ROOMS	1,201
CHECKOUT TIME	10
NONSMOKING	•
CONCIERGE	•
CONVENTION FACIL.	–
MEETING ROOMS	–
VALET PARKING	•
RV PARK	–
ROOM SERVICE	•
FREE BREAKFAST	–
FINE DINING/TYPES	–
COFFEE SHOP	•
24-HOUR CAFE	–
BUFFET	–
CASINO	–
LOUNGE	–
SHOWROOM	–
GIFTS/DRUGS/NEWS	•
POOL	•
EXERCISE ROOM	•

El Cortez ★★★
600 E. Fremont St.
Las Vegas, NV 89101
☎ 702-385-5200
FAX 702-474-3726
TOLL-FREE 800-634-6703
elcortezhotelcasino.com

RACK RATE	$+
ROOM QUALITY	72
LOCATION	Downtown
NO. OF ROOMS	363
CHECKOUT TIME	Noon
NONSMOKING	•
CONCIERGE	–
CONVENTION FACIL.	•
MEETING ROOMS	•
VALET PARKING	•
RV PARK	–
ROOM SERVICE	•
FREE BREAKFAST	–
FINE DINING/TYPES	Steak, Chinese
COFFEE SHOP	–
24-HOUR CAFE	•
BUFFET	•
CASINO	•
LOUNGE	•
SHOWROOM	–
GIFTS/DRUGS/NEWS	•
POOL	–
EXERCISE ROOM	–

El Cortez Cabana Suites ★★★½
651 E. Ogden Ave.
Las Vegas, NV 89101
☎ 702-385-5200
FAX 702-474-3726
TOLL-FREE 800-634-6703
elcortezhotelcasino.com

RACK RATE	$$–
ROOM QUALITY	79
LOCATION	Downtown
NO. OF ROOMS	64
CHECKOUT TIME	Noon
NONSMOKING	•
CONCIERGE	–
CONVENTION FACIL.	–
MEETING ROOMS	–
VALET PARKING	• (at El Cortez)
RV PARK	• (at El Cortez)
ROOM SERVICE	•
FREE BREAKFAST	•
FINE DINING/TYPES	•
COFFEE SHOP	–
24-HOUR CAFE	–
BUFFET	–
CASINO	–
LOUNGE	•
SHOWROOM	–
GIFTS/DRUGS/NEWS	–
POOL	–
EXERCISE ROOM	•

Fiesta Henderson ★★★
777 W. Lake Mead Pkwy.
Henderson, NV 89015
☎ 702-558-7000
FAX 702-567-7373
TOLL-FREE 888-899-7770
fiestahendersonlasvegas.com

RACK RATE	$+
ROOM QUALITY	72
LOCATION	Henderson
NO. OF ROOMS	224
CHECKOUT TIME	Noon
NONSMOKING	Floors
CONCIERGE	•
CONVENTION FACIL.	–
MEETING ROOMS	•
VALET PARKING	•
RV PARK	–
ROOM SERVICE	• (Breakfast only)
FREE BREAKFAST	–
FINE DINING/TYPES	Steak, Mexican
COFFEE SHOP	•
24-HOUR CAFE	•
BUFFET	•
CASINO	•
LOUNGE	•
SHOWROOM	Live music
GIFTS/DRUGS/NEWS	•
POOL	•
EXERCISE ROOM	–

Fiesta Rancho ★★½
2400 N. Rancho Dr.
Las Vegas, NV 89130
☎ 702-631-7000
FAX 702-638-3605
TOLL-FREE 888-899-7770
fiestarancho.sclv.com

RACK RATE	$$–
ROOM QUALITY	62
LOCATION	Rancho Drive
NO. OF ROOMS	100
CHECKOUT TIME	Noon
NONSMOKING	•
CONCIERGE	–
CONVENTION FACIL.	–
MEETING ROOMS	•
VALET PARKING	•
RV PARK	–
ROOM SERVICE	–
FREE BREAKFAST	–
FINE DINING/TYPES	Mexican, Italian, steak, Chinese
COFFEE SHOP	•
24-HOUR CAFE	•
BUFFET	•
CASINO	•
LOUNGE	•
SHOWROOM	–
GIFTS/DRUGS/NEWS	•
POOL	•
EXERCISE ROOM	–

Flamingo ★★★★
3555 Las Vegas Blvd. S.
Las Vegas, NV 89109
☎ 702-733-3111
FAX 702-733-3285
TOLL-FREE 888-902-9929
flamingolasvegas.com

RACK RATE	$$+
ROOM QUALITY	87
LOCATION	Mid-Strip
NO. OF ROOMS	3,352
CHECKOUT TIME	Noon
NONSMOKING	Floors
CONCIERGE	–
CONVENTION FACIL.	•
MEETING ROOMS	•
VALET PARKING	•
RV PARK	•
ROOM SERVICE	•
FREE BREAKFAST	–
FINE DINING/TYPES	Steak, Mexican, Japanese
COFFEE SHOP	•
24-HOUR CAFE	•
BUFFET	•
CASINO	•
LOUNGE	•
SHOWROOM	Production show, comedy, headliners
GIFTS/DRUGS/NEWS	•
POOL	•
EXERCISE ROOM	Health spa/tennis

Hotel Information Chart *(continued)*

Four Queens ★★★
202 Fremont St.
Las Vegas, NV 89101
☎ 702-385-4011
FAX 702-387-5160
TOLL-FREE 800-634-6045
fourqueens.com

RACK RATE	$$-
ROOM QUALITY	70
LOCATION	Downtown
NO. OF ROOMS	690
CHECKOUT TIME	Noon
NONSMOKING	Floors
CONCIERGE	—
CONVENTION FACIL.	—
MEETING ROOMS	•
VALET PARKING	•
RV PARK	—
ROOM SERVICE	•
FREE BREAKFAST	—
FINE DINING/TYPES	American
COFFEE SHOP	•
24-HOUR CAFE	•
BUFFET	—
CASINO	•
LOUNGE	•
SHOWROOM	•
GIFTS/DRUGS/NEWS	•
POOL	•
EXERCISE ROOM	—

Four Seasons at Mandalay Bay ★★★★½
3960 Las Vegas Blvd. S.
Las Vegas, NV 89119
☎ 702-632-5000
FAX 702-632-5195
TOLL-FREE 877-632-5000
fourseasons.com/lasvegas

RACK RATE	$$$$$$$
ROOM QUALITY	95
LOCATION	South Strip
NO. OF ROOMS	424
CHECKOUT TIME	Noon
NONSMOKING	•
CONCIERGE	•
CONVENTION FACIL.	•
MEETING ROOMS	•
VALET PARKING	•
RV PARK	—
ROOM SERVICE	•
FREE BREAKFAST	—
FINE DINING/TYPES	American, Continental
COFFEE SHOP	—
24-HOUR CAFE	—
BUFFET	—
CASINO	—
LOUNGE	•
SHOWROOM	—
GIFTS/DRUGS/NEWS	•
POOL	•
EXERCISE ROOM	Health spa

Fremont ★★★
200 E. Fremont St.
Las Vegas, NV 89101
☎ 702-385-3232
FAX 702-385-6270
TOLL-FREE 800-634-6182
fremontcasino.com

RACK RATE	$+
ROOM QUALITY	70
LOCATION	Downtown
NO. OF ROOMS	447
CHECKOUT TIME	Noon
NONSMOKING	—
CONCIERGE	—
CONVENTION FACIL.	—
MEETING ROOMS	•
VALET PARKING	•
RV PARK	—
ROOM SERVICE	—
FREE BREAKFAST	—
FINE DINING/TYPES	Ribs, Chinese, American
COFFEE SHOP	•
24-HOUR CAFE	•
BUFFET	•
CASINO	•
LOUNGE	•
SHOWROOM	—
GIFTS/DRUGS/NEWS	•
POOL	—
EXERCISE ROOM	—

Green Valley Ranch Resort and Spa ★★★★
2300 Paseo Verde Pkwy.
Henderson, NV 89052
☎ 702-617-7777
FAX 702-617-7778
TOLL-FREE 866-782-9487
greenvalleyranchresort.com

RACK RATE	$$$$$-
ROOM QUALITY	87
LOCATION	Henderson
NO. OF ROOMS	490
CHECKOUT TIME	Noon
NONSMOKING	•
CONCIERGE	•
CONVENTION FACIL.	•
MEETING ROOMS	•
VALET PARKING	•
RV PARK	—
ROOM SERVICE	•
FREE BREAKFAST	—
FINE DINING/TYPES	Italian, steak, seafood, Asian
COFFEE SHOP	•
24-HOUR CAFE	•
BUFFET	•
CASINO	•
LOUNGE	•
SHOWROOM	Headliners
GIFTS/DRUGS/NEWS	•
POOL	•
EXERCISE ROOM	•

Hard Rock Hotel ★★★★½
4455 Paradise Rd.
Las Vegas, NV 89109
☎ 702-693-5000
FAX 702-693-5021
TOLL-FREE 800-473-7625
hardrockhotel.com

RACK RATE	$$$$+
ROOM QUALITY	95
LOCATION	East of Strip
NO. OF ROOMS	1,506
CHECKOUT TIME	11
NONSMOKING	Floors
CONCIERGE	•
CONVENTION FACIL.	•
MEETING ROOMS	•
VALET PARKING	•
RV PARK	—
ROOM SERVICE	•
FREE BREAKFAST	—
FINE DINING/TYPES	Steak, Asian, Mexican, pub
COFFEE SHOP	•
24-HOUR CAFE	•
BUFFET	—
CASINO	•
LOUNGE	•
SHOWROOM	Live music
GIFTS/DRUGS/NEWS	•
POOL	•
EXERCISE ROOM	Health spa

Harrah's ★★★½
3475 Las Vegas Blvd. S.
Las Vegas, NV 89109
☎ 702-369-5000
FAX 702-369-6014
TOLL-FREE 800-214-9110
harrahslasvegas.com

RACK RATE	$$
ROOM QUALITY	81
LOCATION	Mid-Strip
NO. OF ROOMS	2,652
CHECKOUT TIME	11
NONSMOKING	•
CONCIERGE	•
CONVENTION FACIL.	•
MEETING ROOMS	•
VALET PARKING	•
RV PARK	—
ROOM SERVICE	•
FREE BREAKFAST	—
FINE DINING/TYPES	Steak, seafood, Italian, Asian
COFFEE SHOP	•
24-HOUR CAFE	•
BUFFET	•
CASINO	•
LOUNGE	•
SHOWROOM	Production show, comedy show, magic show
GIFTS/DRUGS/NEWS	•
POOL	•
EXERCISE ROOM	Health spa

Gold Coast ★★½
4000 W. Flamingo Rd.
Las Vegas, NV 89103
☎ 702-367-7111
FAX 702-367-8575
TOLL-FREE 800-331-5334
goldcoastcasino.com

RACK RATE	$$-
ROOM QUALITY	58
LOCATION	Mid-Strip
NO. OF ROOMS	711
CHECKOUT TIME	Noon
NONSMOKING	Floors
CONCIERGE	—
CONVENTION FACIL.	•
MEETING ROOMS	•
VALET PARKING	•
RV PARK	•
ROOM SERVICE	•
FREE BREAKFAST	—
FINE DINING/TYPES	Steak, Chinese, American
COFFEE SHOP	•
24-HOUR CAFE	—
BUFFET	•
CASINO	•
LOUNGE	•
SHOWROOM	Dancing
GIFTS/DRUGS/NEWS	•
POOL	•
EXERCISE ROOM	•

Golden Gate ★★★½
1 Fremont St.
Las Vegas, NV 89101
☎ 702-385-1906
TOLL-FREE 800-426-1906
goldengatecasino.com

RACK RATE	$$-
ROOM QUALITY	75
LOCATION	Downtown
NO. OF ROOMS	106
CHECKOUT TIME	11
NONSMOKING	•
CONCIERGE	•
CONVENTION FACIL.	—
MEETING ROOMS	—
VALET PARKING	—
RV PARK	—
ROOM SERVICE	—
FREE BREAKFAST	—
FINE DINING/TYPES	—
COFFEE SHOP	•
24-HOUR CAFE	•
BUFFET	—
CASINO	•
LOUNGE	•
SHOWROOM	—
GIFTS/DRUGS/NEWS	•
POOL	—
EXERCISE ROOM	—

Golden Nugget
★★★★½—★★★½
129 E. Fremont St.
Las Vegas, NV 89101
☎ 702-385-7111
FAX 702-387-4422
TOLL-FREE 800-634-3454
goldennugget.com

RACK RATE	$$$$-/$$$-
ROOM QUALITY	90/78
LOCATION	Downtown
NO. OF ROOMS	1,900
CHECKOUT TIME	Noon
NONSMOKING	Floors
CONCIERGE	•
CONVENTION FACIL.	•
MEETING ROOMS	•
VALET PARKING	•
RV PARK	—
ROOM SERVICE	•
FREE BREAKFAST	—
FINE DINING/TYPES	Italian, Asian, steak, seafood
COFFEE SHOP	•
24-HOUR CAFE	•
BUFFET	•
CASINO	•
LOUNGE	•
SHOWROOM	Headliners
GIFTS/DRUGS/NEWS	•
POOL	•
EXERCISE ROOM	•

Hilton Garden Inn Las Vegas Strip South ★★★
7830 Las Vegas Blvd. S.
Las Vegas, NV 89123
☎ 702-453-7830
FAX 702-453-7850
TOLL-FREE 877-782-9444
hiltongardeninn.com

RACK RATE	$$+
ROOM QUALITY	72
LOCATION	South of Las Vegas
NO. OF ROOMS	155
CHECKOUT TIME	Noon
NONSMOKING	•
CONCIERGE	—
CONVENTION FACIL.	—
MEETING ROOMS	—
VALET PARKING	—
RV PARK	—
ROOM SERVICE	• (Evening only)
FREE BREAKFAST	—
FINE DINING/TYPES	American
COFFEE SHOP	—
24-HOUR CAFE	—
BUFFET	• (Breakfast only)
CASINO	—
LOUNGE	•
SHOWROOM	—
GIFTS/DRUGS/NEWS	•
POOL	•
EXERCISE ROOM	•

Hilton Lake Las Vegas ★★★★
1610 Lake Las Vegas Pkwy.
Henderson, NV 89011
☎ 702-567-4700
FAX 702-567-4777
TOLL-FREE 888-810-0440
hilton.com

RACK RATE	$$$-
ROOM QUALITY	88
LOCATION	Henderson
NO. OF ROOMS	349
CHECKOUT TIME	Noon
NONSMOKING	•
CONCIERGE	•
CONVENTION FACIL.	•
MEETING ROOMS	•
VALET PARKING	•
RV PARK	—
ROOM SERVICE	•
FREE BREAKFAST	—
FINE DINING/TYPES	American, Italian
COFFEE SHOP	•
24-HOUR CAFE	—
BUFFET	—
CASINO	•
LOUNGE	•
SHOWROOM	—
GIFTS/DRUGS/NEWS	•
POOL	•
EXERCISE ROOM	Health spa/tennis

Hooters Casino Hotel ★★★
115 E. Tropicana Ave.
Las Vegas, NV 89109
☎ 702-739-9000
FAX 702-736-1120
TOLL-FREE 866-584-6687
hooterscasinohotel.com

RACK RATE	$+
ROOM QUALITY	73
LOCATION	South Strip
NO. OF ROOMS	689
CHECKOUT TIME	Noon
NONSMOKING	Floors
CONCIERGE	•
CONVENTION FACIL.	•
MEETING ROOMS	•
VALET PARKING	•
RV PARK	—
ROOM SERVICE	•
FREE BREAKFAST	—
FINE DINING/TYPES	American, steak, seafood, wings
COFFEE SHOP	•
24-HOUR CAFE	•
BUFFET	•
CASINO	•
LOUNGE	•
SHOWROOM	•
GIFTS/DRUGS/NEWS	•
POOL	•
EXERCISE ROOM	•

Hotel Information Chart (continued)

Hyatt Place ★★★
4520 Paradise Rd.
Las Vegas, NV 89169
☎ 702-369-3366
FAX 702-369-0009
TOLL-FREE 888-492-8847
lasvegas.place.hyatt.com

RACK RATE	$$$
ROOM QUALITY	72
LOCATION	East of Strip
NO. OF ROOMS	202
CHECKOUT TIME	Noon
NONSMOKING	•
CONCIERGE	—
CONVENTION FACIL.	•
MEETING ROOMS	•
VALET PARKING	—
RV PARK	•
ROOM SERVICE	•
FREE BREAKFAST	•
FINE DINING/TYPES	—
COFFEE SHOP	—
24-HOUR CAFE	—
BUFFET	—
CASINO	—
LOUNGE	—
SHOWROOM	—
GIFTS/DRUGS/NEWS	—
POOL	•
EXERCISE ROOM	•

JW Marriott Las Vegas ★★★★½
221 N. Rampart Blvd.
Las Vegas, NV 89145
☎ 702-869-7777
FAX 702-869-7339
TOLL-FREE 877-869-8777
marriott.com

RACK RATE	$$$+
ROOM QUALITY	93
LOCATION	Summerlin
NO. OF ROOMS	548
CHECKOUT TIME	Noon
NONSMOKING	•
CONCIERGE	•
CONVENTION FACIL.	•
MEETING ROOMS	•
VALET PARKING	•
RV PARK	•
ROOM SERVICE	•
FREE BREAKFAST	—
FINE DINING/TYPES	Health food, Irish, Italian, Japanese
COFFEE SHOP	•
24-HOUR CAFE	•
BUFFET	•
CASINO	•
LOUNGE	•
SHOWROOM	•
GIFTS/DRUGS/NEWS	•
POOL	•
EXERCISE ROOM	Health spa

Las Vegas Marriott ★★★★
325 Convention Center Dr.
Las Vegas, NV 89109
☎ 702-650-2000
FAX 702-650-9466
TOLL-FREE 800-228-9290
marriott.com

RACK RATE	$$$+
ROOM QUALITY	84
LOCATION	East of Strip
NO. OF ROOMS	277
CHECKOUT TIME	Noon
NONSMOKING	•
CONCIERGE	—
CONVENTION FACIL.	•
MEETING ROOMS	•
VALET PARKING	—
RV PARK	—
ROOM SERVICE	•
FREE BREAKFAST	—
FINE DINING/TYPES	American
COFFEE SHOP	—
24-HOUR CAFE	—
BUFFET	—
CASINO	—
LOUNGE	—
SHOWROOM	—
GIFTS/DRUGS/NEWS	•
POOL	•
EXERCISE ROOM	•

Main Street Station ★★★½
200 N. Main St.
Las Vegas, NV 89101
☎ 702-387-1896
FAX 702-386-4421
TOLL-FREE 800-713-8933
mainstreetcasino.com

RACK RATE	$$-
ROOM QUALITY	75
LOCATION	Downtown
NO. OF ROOMS	406
CHECKOUT TIME	Noon
NONSMOKING	•
CONCIERGE	•
CONVENTION FACIL.	—
MEETING ROOMS	•
VALET PARKING	•
RV PARK	•
ROOM SERVICE	—
FREE BREAKFAST	—
FINE DINING/TYPES	Brewery
COFFEE SHOP	•
24-HOUR CAFE	•
BUFFET	•
CASINO	•
LOUNGE	—
SHOWROOM	•
GIFTS/DRUGS/NEWS	•
POOL	•
EXERCISE ROOM	—

Mandalay Bay ★★★★½
3950 Las Vegas Blvd. S.
Las Vegas, NV 89119
☎ 702-632-7777
FAX 702-632-7234
TOLL-FREE 877-632-7800
mandalaybay.com

RACK RATE	$$$+
ROOM QUALITY	92
LOCATION	South Strip
NO. OF ROOMS	4,756
CHECKOUT TIME	11
NONSMOKING	Floors
CONCIERGE	•
CONVENTION FACIL.	•
MEETING ROOMS	•
VALET PARKING	•
RV PARK	—
ROOM SERVICE	•
FREE BREAKFAST	—
FINE DINING/TYPES	Russian, French, Italian, Mexican
COFFEE SHOP	•
24-HOUR CAFE	•
BUFFET	•
CASINO	•
LOUNGE	•
SHOWROOM	Headliners, live music, sports
GIFTS/DRUGS/NEWS	•
POOL	•
EXERCISE ROOM	Health spa

Mandarin Oriental at CityCenter ★★★★★
3752 Las Vegas Blvd. S.
Las Vegas, NV 89109
☎ 702-590-8888
FAX 702-590-8880
TOLL-FREE 888-881-9578
mandarinoriental.com/lasvegas

RACK RATE	$$$$$$-
ROOM QUALITY	96
LOCATION	Mid-Strip
NO. OF ROOMS	392
CHECKOUT TIME	Noon
NONSMOKING	•
CONCIERGE	•
CONVENTION FACIL.	•
MEETING ROOMS	•
VALET PARKING	•
RV PARK	—
ROOM SERVICE	•
FREE BREAKFAST	—
FINE DINING/TYPES	Asian, French
COFFEE SHOP	—
24-HOUR CAFE	—
BUFFET	—
CASINO	Adjacent
LOUNGE	•
SHOWROOM	—
GIFTS/DRUGS/NEWS	Adjacent
POOL	•
EXERCISE ROOM	Health spa

The LINQ Hotel & Casino ★★★
3535 Las Vegas Blvd. S.
Las Vegas, NV 89109
☎ 702-731-3311
FAX 702-731-3063
TOLL-FREE 800-351-7400
caesars.com/thelinq

RACK RATE	$$
ROOM QUALITY	68
LOCATION	Mid-Strip
NO. OF ROOMS	2,256
CHECKOUT TIME	11
NONSMOKING	•
CONCIERGE	•
CONVENTION FACIL.	•
MEETING ROOMS	•
VALET PARKING	•
RV PARK	—
ROOM SERVICE	•
FREE BREAKFAST	—
FINE DINING/TYPES	American, Mexican
COFFEE SHOP	•
24-HOUR CAFE	•
BUFFET	•
CASINO	•
LOUNGE	•
SHOWROOM	
GIFTS/DRUGS/NEWS	•
POOL	•
EXERCISE ROOM	Health spa

Luxor ★★★★
3900 Las Vegas Blvd. S.
Las Vegas, NV 89119
☎ 702-262-4444
FAX 702-262-4137
TOLL-FREE 877-386-4658
luxor.com

RACK RATE	$$$
ROOM QUALITY	87
LOCATION	South Strip
NO. OF ROOMS	4,450
CHECKOUT TIME	11
NONSMOKING	•
CONCIERGE	—
CONVENTION FACIL.	•
MEETING ROOMS	•
VALET PARKING	•
RV PARK	—
ROOM SERVICE	•
FREE BREAKFAST	—
FINE DINING/TYPES	American, seafood, steak, Asian, Mexican
COFFEE SHOP	•
24-HOUR CAFE	•
BUFFET	•
CASINO	•
LOUNGE	•
SHOWROOM	Production show
GIFTS/DRUGS/NEWS	•
POOL	•
EXERCISE ROOM	Health spa

M Resort ★★★★½
12300 Las Vegas Blvd. S.
Henderson, NV 89044
☎ 702-797-1000
TOLL-FREE 877-673-7678
themresort.com

RACK RATE	$$$+
ROOM QUALITY	90
LOCATION	Henderson
NO. OF ROOMS	390
CHECKOUT TIME	11
NONSMOKING	•
CONCIERGE	•
CONVENTION FACIL.	•
MEETING ROOMS	•
VALET PARKING	•
RV PARK	—
ROOM SERVICE	•
FREE BREAKFAST	—
FINE DINING/TYPES	Steak, Italian, American
COFFEE SHOP	•
24-HOUR CAFE	•
BUFFET	•
CASINO	•
LOUNGE	•
SHOWROOM	•
GIFTS/DRUGS/NEWS	•
POOL	•
EXERCISE ROOM	Health spa

MGM Grand ★★★★½
3799 Las Vegas Blvd. S.
Las Vegas, NV 89109
☎ 702-891-1111
FAX 702-891-3036
TOLL-FREE 877-880-0880
mgmgrand.com

RACK RATE	$$$–
ROOM QUALITY	90
LOCATION	South Strip
NO. OF ROOMS	5,044
CHECKOUT TIME	11
NONSMOKING	Floors
CONCIERGE	•
CONVENTION FACIL.	•
MEETING ROOMS	•
VALET PARKING	•
RV PARK	—
ROOM SERVICE	•
FREE BREAKFAST	—
FINE DINING/TYPES	Steak, seafood, Cajun, Italian, Chinese, French
COFFEE SHOP	•
24-HOUR CAFE	•
BUFFET	•
CASINO	•
LOUNGE	•
SHOWROOM	Production show, visiting headliners
GIFTS/DRUGS/NEWS	•
POOL	•
EXERCISE ROOM	Health spa/tennis

Mirage ★★★★½
3400 Las Vegas Blvd. S.
Las Vegas, NV 89109
☎ 702-791-7111
FAX 702-792-7632
TOLL-FREE 800-627-6667
mirage.com

RACK RATE	$$$$–
ROOM QUALITY	90
LOCATION	Mid-Strip
NO. OF ROOMS	3,044
CHECKOUT TIME	Noon
NONSMOKING	Floors
CONCIERGE	•
CONVENTION FACIL.	•
MEETING ROOMS	•
VALET PARKING	•
RV PARK	—
ROOM SERVICE	•
FREE BREAKFAST	—
FINE DINING/TYPES	Asian, seafood, Italian, Brazilian
COFFEE SHOP	•
24-HOUR CAFE	•
BUFFET	•
CASINO	•
LOUNGE	•
SHOWROOM	Production show, headliner
GIFTS/DRUGS/NEWS	•
POOL	•
EXERCISE ROOM	Health spa

Monte Carlo ★★★½
3770 Las Vegas Blvd. S.
Las Vegas, NV 89109
☎ 702-730-7777
FAX 702-730-7250
TOLL-FREE 800-311-8999
montecarlo.com

RACK RATE	$$
ROOM QUALITY	82
LOCATION	South Strip
NO. OF ROOMS	3,006
CHECKOUT TIME	11
NONSMOKING	Floors
CONCIERGE	—
CONVENTION FACIL.	•
MEETING ROOMS	•
VALET PARKING	•
RV PARK	—
ROOM SERVICE	•
FREE BREAKFAST	—
FINE DINING/TYPES	Steak, Asian, Italian, French, seafood, Mexican
COFFEE SHOP	•
24-HOUR CAFE	•
BUFFET	•
CASINO	•
LOUNGE	•
SHOWROOM	Magic show, comedy
GIFTS/DRUGS/NEWS	•
POOL	•
EXERCISE ROOM	Health spa

Hotel Information Chart (continued)

New York–New York ★ ★ ★ ★
3790 Las Vegas Blvd. S.
Las Vegas, NV 89109
☎ 702-740-6969
FAX 702-740-6700
TOLL-FREE 866-815-4365
newyorknewyork.com

RACK RATE	$$$–
ROOM QUALITY	85
LOCATION	South Strip
NO. OF ROOMS	2,024
CHECKOUT TIME	11
NONSMOKING	Floors
CONCIERGE	•
CONVENTION FACIL.	•
MEETING ROOMS	•
VALET PARKING	•
RV PARK	—
ROOM SERVICE	•
FREE BREAKFAST	—
FINE DINING/TYPES	Steak, Chinese, Italian, Mexican, Irish, deli
COFFEE SHOP	•
24-HOUR CAFE	•
BUFFET	• (Breakfast only)
CASINO	•
LOUNGE	•
SHOWROOM	Production show, comedy
GIFTS/DRUGS/NEWS	•
POOL	•
EXERCISE ROOM	Health spa

The Nobu Hotel ★ ★ ★ ★ ½
3570 Las Vegas Blvd. S.
Las Vegas, NV 89109
☎ 702-785-6677
TOLL-FREE 800-634-6661
nobucaesarspalace.com

RACK RATE	$$$$$$–
ROOM QUALITY	94
LOCATION	Mid-Strip
NO. OF ROOMS	181
CHECKOUT TIME	11
NONSMOKING	•
CONCIERGE	•
CONVENTION FACIL.	At Caesars
MEETING ROOMS	At Caesars
VALET PARKING	•
RV PARK	—
ROOM SERVICE	•
FREE BREAKFAST	—
FINE DINING/TYPES	Japanese
COFFEE SHOP	At Caesars
24-HOUR CAFE	At Caesars
BUFFET	At Caesars
CASINO	At Caesars
LOUNGE	•
SHOWROOM	At Caesars
GIFTS/DRUGS/NEWS	•
POOL	•
EXERCISE ROOM	Health spa

The Orleans ★ ★ ★ ½
4500 W. Tropicana Ave.
Las Vegas, NV 89103
☎ 702-365-7111
FAX 702-365-7500
TOLL-FREE 800-675-3267
orleanscasino.com

RACK RATE	$$$–
ROOM QUALITY	75
LOCATION	South Strip
NO. OF ROOMS	1,886
CHECKOUT TIME	Noon
NONSMOKING	•
CONCIERGE	•
CONVENTION FACIL.	•
MEETING ROOMS	•
VALET PARKING	•
RV PARK	—
ROOM SERVICE	•
FREE BREAKFAST	—
FINE DINING/TYPES	Steak, Cajun, Asian, Mexican
COFFEE SHOP	•
24-HOUR CAFE	•
BUFFET	•
CASINO	•
LOUNGE	Pub
SHOWROOM	Headliners, sports events
GIFTS/DRUGS/NEWS	•
POOL	•
EXERCISE ROOM	Health spa

Paris ★ ★ ★ ★ ½
3655 Las Vegas Blvd. S.
Las Vegas, NV 89109
☎ 702-946-7000
FAX 702-946-4405
TOLL-FREE 888-266-5687
parislasvegas.com

RACK RATE	$$$+
ROOM QUALITY	91
LOCATION	Mid-Strip
NO. OF ROOMS	2,916
CHECKOUT TIME	11
NONSMOKING	Floors
CONCIERGE	•
CONVENTION FACIL.	•
MEETING ROOMS	•
VALET PARKING	•
RV PARK	—
ROOM SERVICE	•
FREE BREAKFAST	—
FINE DINING/TYPES	French, Italian, steak
COFFEE SHOP	•
24-HOUR CAFE	•
BUFFET	•
CASINO	•
LOUNGE	•
SHOWROOM	Dancing
GIFTS/DRUGS/NEWS	•
POOL	•
EXERCISE ROOM	Health spa/tennis

Planet Hollywood ★ ★ ★ ★
3667 Las Vegas Blvd. S.
Las Vegas, NV 89109
☎ 702-736-7114
FAX 702-785-5558
TOLL-FREE 877-333-9474
planethollywoodresort.com

RACK RATE	$$$$
ROOM QUALITY	87
LOCATION	Mid-Strip
NO. OF ROOMS	2,567
CHECKOUT TIME	11
NONSMOKING	•
CONCIERGE	•
CONVENTION FACIL.	•
MEETING ROOMS	•
VALET PARKING	•
RV PARK	—
ROOM SERVICE	•
FREE BREAKFAST	—
FINE DINING/TYPES	Asian, steak, Mexican, burgers
COFFEE SHOP	•
24-HOUR CAFE	•
BUFFET	•
CASINO	•
LOUNGE	•
SHOWROOM	Headliners
GIFTS/DRUGS/NEWS	•
POOL	•
EXERCISE ROOM	Health spa

Platinum Hotel ★ ★ ★ ★
211 E. Flamingo Rd.
Las Vegas, NV 89169
☎ 702-365-5000
FAX 702-636-2500
TOLL-FREE 877-211-9211
theplatinumhotel.com

RACK RATE	$$$–
ROOM QUALITY	88
LOCATION	East of Strip
NO. OF ROOMS	255
CHECKOUT TIME	11
NONSMOKING	•
CONCIERGE	•
CONVENTION FACIL.	•
MEETING ROOMS	•
VALET PARKING	•
RV PARK	—
ROOM SERVICE	•
FREE BREAKFAST	—
FINE DINING/TYPES	American
COFFEE SHOP	•
24-HOUR CAFE	•
BUFFET	—
CASINO	—
LOUNGE	•
SHOWROOM	—
GIFTS/DRUGS/NEWS	•
POOL	•
EXERCISE ROOM	•

Palace Station
★★★½–★★★★*
2411 W. Sahara Ave.
Las Vegas, NV 89102
☎ 702-367-2411
FAX 702-367-2478
TOLL-FREE 800-678-2846
palacestation.com

RACK RATE	$$–
ROOM QUALITY	81/74*
LOCATION	North Strip
NO. OF ROOMS	1,028
CHECKOUT TIME	Noon
NONSMOKING	Floors
CONCIERGE	•
CONVENTION FACIL.	•
MEETING ROOMS	•
VALET PARKING	•
RV PARK	—
ROOM SERVICE	•
FREE BREAKFAST	—
FINE DINING/TYPES	Seafood, Chinese, Mexican, Italian
COFFEE SHOP	•
24-HOUR CAFE	•
BUFFET	•
CASINO	•
LOUNGE	•
SHOWROOM	Comedy, music
GIFTS/DRUGS/NEWS	•
POOL	•
EXERCISE ROOM	•

tower rooms/courtyard rooms

The Palazzo ★★★★½
3325 Las Vegas Blvd. S.
Las Vegas, NV 89109
☎ 702-607-7777
FAX 702-414-1100
TOLL-FREE 866-263-3001
palazzo.com

RACK RATE	$$$$$
ROOM QUALITY	95
LOCATION	Mid-Strip
NO. OF ROOMS	3,066
CHECKOUT TIME	11
NONSMOKING	•
CONCIERGE	•
CONVENTION FACIL.	•
MEETING ROOMS	•
VALET PARKING	•
RV PARK	—
ROOM SERVICE	•
FREE BREAKFAST	—
FINE DINING/TYPES	Steak, Italian, Asian, French, Mexican
COFFEE SHOP	•
24-HOUR CAFE	•
BUFFET	—
CASINO	•
LOUNGE	•
SHOWROOM	Production show
GIFTS/DRUGS/NEWS	•
POOL	•
EXERCISE ROOM	Health spa

Palms ★★★★½
4321 W. Flamingo Rd.
Las Vegas, NV 89103
☎ 702-942-7777
FAX 702-942-6999
TOLL-FREE 866-942-7777
palms.com

RACK RATE	$$$–
ROOM QUALITY	95
LOCATION	Mid-Strip
NO. OF ROOMS	1,303
CHECKOUT TIME	11
NONSMOKING	Floors
CONCIERGE	•
CONVENTION FACIL.	•
MEETING ROOMS	•
VALET PARKING	•
RV PARK	—
ROOM SERVICE	•
FREE BREAKFAST	—
FINE DINING/TYPES	Asian, French, steak, Italian
COFFEE SHOP	•
24-HOUR CAFE	•
BUFFET	•
CASINO	•
LOUNGE	•
SHOWROOM	Headliners
GIFTS/DRUGS/NEWS	•
POOL	•
EXERCISE ROOM	Health spa

Plaza ★★★½
1 Main St.
Las Vegas, NV 89101
☎ 702-386-2110
FAX 702-382-8281
TOLL-FREE 800-634-6575
plazahotelcasino.com

RACK RATE	$$
ROOM QUALITY	82
LOCATION	Downtown
NO. OF ROOMS	1,052
CHECKOUT TIME	11
NONSMOKING	Floors
CONCIERGE	•
CONVENTION FACIL.	•
MEETING ROOMS	•
VALET PARKING	•
RV PARK	—
ROOM SERVICE	•
FREE BREAKFAST	—
FINE DINING/TYPES	American, Continental
COFFEE SHOP	•
24-HOUR CAFE	—
BUFFET	•
CASINO	•
LOUNGE	•
SHOWROOM	Production show, comedy
GIFTS/DRUGS/NEWS	•
POOL	• (Rooftop)
EXERCISE ROOM	•

Red Rock Resort ★★★★½
11011 W. Charleston Blvd.
Las Vegas, NV 89135
☎ 702-797-7777
FAX 702-797-7745
TOLL-FREE 866-767-7773
redrockcasinolasvegas.com

RACK RATE	$$$$+
ROOM QUALITY	91
LOCATION	Summerlin
NO. OF ROOMS	816
CHECKOUT TIME	Noon
NONSMOKING	Floors
CONCIERGE	•
CONVENTION FACIL.	•
MEETING ROOMS	•
VALET PARKING	•
RV PARK	—
ROOM SERVICE	•
FREE BREAKFAST	—
FINE DINING/TYPES	American, steak, BBQ, Italian
COFFEE SHOP	•
24-HOUR CAFE	•
BUFFET	•
CASINO	•
LOUNGE	•
SHOWROOM	Piano bar, live entertainment
GIFTS/DRUGS/NEWS	•
POOL	•
EXERCISE ROOM	Health spa

Renaissance Las Vegas
★★★★½
3400 Paradise Rd.
Las Vegas, NV 89169
☎ 702-784-5700
FAX 702-735-3130
TOLL-FREE 800-750-0980
renaissancelasvegas.com

RACK RATE	$$$–
ROOM QUALITY	90
LOCATION	East of Strip
NO. OF ROOMS	548
CHECKOUT TIME	Noon
NONSMOKING	Floors
CONCIERGE	•
CONVENTION FACIL.	•
MEETING ROOMS	•
VALET PARKING	•
RV PARK	•
ROOM SERVICE	•
FREE BREAKFAST	—
FINE DINING/TYPES	Steak, American
COFFEE SHOP	•
24-HOUR CAFE	•
BUFFET	—
CASINO	—
LOUNGE	•
SHOWROOM	—
GIFTS/DRUGS/NEWS	•
POOL	•
EXERCISE ROOM	•

Hotel Information Chart *(continued)*

Residence Inn by Marriott Las Vegas Convention Center ★★★★
3225 Paradise Rd.
Las Vegas, NV 89109
☎ 702-796-9300
FAX 702-796-9562
TOLL-FREE 800-677-8328
marriott.com

RACK RATE	$$$
ROOM QUALITY	83
LOCATION	East of Strip
NO. OF ROOMS	192
CHECKOUT TIME	Noon
NONSMOKING	Floors
CONCIERGE	—
CONVENTION FACIL.	—
MEETING ROOMS	•
VALET PARKING	—
RV PARK	—
ROOM SERVICE	—
FREE BREAKFAST	•
FINE DINING/TYPES	—
COFFEE SHOP	—
24-HOUR CAFE	—
BUFFET	—
CASINO	—
LOUNGE	—
SHOWROOM	—
GIFTS/DRUGS/NEWS	—
POOL	•
EXERCISE ROOM	• + tennis

Residence Inn by Marriott Las Vegas South ★★★★
5875 Dean Martin Dr.
Las Vegas, NV 89118
☎ 702-795-7378
FAX 702-795-3288
TOLL-FREE 800-677-8328
marriott.com

RACK RATE	$$$–
ROOM QUALITY	86
LOCATION	South Strip
NO. OF ROOMS	160
CHECKOUT TIME	Noon
NONSMOKING	•
CONCIERGE	—
CONVENTION FACIL.	—
MEETING ROOMS	•
VALET PARKING	—
RV PARK	—
ROOM SERVICE	—
FREE BREAKFAST	•
FINE DINING/TYPES	—
COFFEE SHOP	—
24-HOUR CAFE	—
BUFFET	—
CASINO	—
LOUNGE	—
SHOWROOM	—
GIFTS/DRUGS/NEWS	•
POOL	•
EXERCISE ROOM	• +tennis

Rio ★★★★
3700 W. Flamingo Rd.
Las Vegas, NV 89103
☎ 702-252-7777
FAX 702-967-3890
TOLL-FREE 800-752-9746
riolasvegas.com

RACK RATE	$$$$$
ROOM QUALITY	86
LOCATION	Mid-Strip
NO. OF ROOMS	2,520
CHECKOUT TIME	11
NONSMOKING	Floors
CONCIERGE	•
CONVENTION FACIL.	•
MEETING ROOMS	•
VALET PARKING	•
RV PARK	—
ROOM SERVICE	•
FREE BREAKFAST	—
FINE DINING/TYPES	Italian, Chinese, Indian, seafood, steak
COFFEE SHOP	•
24-HOUR CAFE	•
BUFFET	•
CASINO	•
LOUNGE	•
SHOWROOM	Live entertainment, headliners
GIFTS/DRUGS/NEWS	•
POOL	•
EXERCISE ROOM	Health spa

Sam's Town ★★★½
5111 Boulder Hwy.
Las Vegas, NV 89122
☎ 702-456-7777
FAX 702-454-8014
TOLL-FREE 800-897-8696
samstownlv.com

RACK RATE	$$–
ROOM QUALITY	79
LOCATION	Boulder Highway
NO. OF ROOMS	648
CHECKOUT TIME	Noon
NONSMOKING	•
CONCIERGE	•
CONVENTION FACIL.	—
MEETING ROOMS	•
VALET PARKING	•
RV PARK	•
ROOM SERVICE	—
FREE BREAKFAST	—
FINE DINING/TYPES	Steak, American, Mexican
COFFEE SHOP	•
24-HOUR CAFE	—
BUFFET	•
CASINO	•
LOUNGE	•
SHOWROOM	•
GIFTS/DRUGS/NEWS	•
POOL	•
EXERCISE ROOM	—

Santa Fe Station ★★★
4949 N. Rancho Dr.
Las Vegas, NV 89130
☎ 702-658-4900
FAX 702-658-4919
TOLL-FREE 866-767-7771
santafestationlasvegas.com

RACK RATE	$$
ROOM QUALITY	73
LOCATION	Rancho Drive
NO. OF ROOMS	200
CHECKOUT TIME	Noon
NONSMOKING	•
CONCIERGE	—
CONVENTION FACIL.	•
MEETING ROOMS	•
VALET PARKING	•
RV PARK	—
ROOM SERVICE	—
FREE BREAKFAST	—
FINE DINING/TYPES	Mexican, steak, seafood, American
COFFEE SHOP	•
24-HOUR CAFE	•
BUFFET	•
CASINO	•
LOUNGE	•
SHOWROOM	•
GIFTS/DRUGS/NEWS	•
POOL	•
EXERCISE ROOM	•

Signature at MGM Grand ★★★★★
145 E. Harmon Ave.
Las Vegas, NV 89109
☎ 702-797-6000
FAX 702-797-6150
TOLL-FREE 877-612-2121
signaturemgmgrand.com

RACK RATE	$$$
ROOM QUALITY	96
LOCATION	East of Strip
NO. OF ROOMS	1,734
CHECKOUT TIME	11
NONSMOKING	•
CONCIERGE	•
CONVENTION FACIL.	—
MEETING ROOMS	•
VALET PARKING	•
RV PARK	—
ROOM SERVICE	•
FREE BREAKFAST	—
FINE DINING/TYPES	Steak, seafood, Cajun, Italian, Chinese, French
COFFEE SHOP	•
24-HOUR CAFE	•
BUFFET	—
CASINO	—
LOUNGE	•
SHOWROOM	—
GIFTS/DRUGS/NEWS	•
POOL	•
EXERCISE ROOM	•

Riviera ★★★½
2901 Las Vegas Blvd. S.
Las Vegas, NV 89109
☎ 702-734-5110
FAX 702-794-9451
TOLL-FREE 800-634-3420
rivierahotel.com

RACK RATE	$+
ROOM QUALITY	79
LOCATION	North Strip
NO. OF ROOMS	2,076
CHECKOUT TIME	Noon
NONSMOKING	•
CONCIERGE	•
CONVENTION FACIL.	•
MEETING ROOMS	•
VALET PARKING	•
RV PARK	—
ROOM SERVICE	•
FREE BREAKFAST	—
FINE DINING/TYPES	Steak, seafood, brew pub
COFFEE SHOP	•
24-HOUR CAFE	•
BUFFET	•
CASINO	•
LOUNGE	•
SHOWROOM	•
GIFTS/DRUGS/NEWS	•
POOL	•
EXERCISE ROOM	• + tennis

Royal Resort ★★★
99 Convention Center Dr.
Las Vegas, NV 89109
☎ 702-735-6117
FAX 702-735-2546
TOLL-FREE 800-634-6118
royalhotelvegas.com

RACK RATE	$+
ROOM QUALITY	73
LOCATION	North Strip
NO. OF ROOMS	191
CHECKOUT TIME	11
NONSMOKING	Floors
CONCIERGE	•
CONVENTION FACIL.	—
MEETING ROOMS	•
VALET PARKING	—
RV PARK	—
ROOM SERVICE	•
FREE BREAKFAST	—
FINE DINING/TYPES	American
COFFEE SHOP	•
24-HOUR CAFE	—
BUFFET	—
CASINO	—
LOUNGE	—
SHOWROOM	•
GIFTS/DRUGS/NEWS	•
POOL	•
EXERCISE ROOM	—

Rumor ★★★½
455 East Harmon Ave.
Las Vegas, NV 89169
☎ 702-369-5400
TOLL-FREE 877-997-8667
rumorvegas.com

RACK RATE	$$$-
ROOM QUALITY	78
LOCATION	East of Strip
NO. OF ROOMS	150
CHECKOUT TIME	11
NONSMOKING	•
CONCIERGE	•
CONVENTION FACIL.	—
MEETING ROOMS	•
VALET PARKING	•
RV PARK	—
ROOM SERVICE	—
FREE BREAKFAST	—
FINE DINING/TYPES	Eclectic
COFFEE SHOP	—
24-HOUR CAFE	—
BUFFET	—
CASINO	—
LOUNGE	•
SHOWROOM	—
GIFTS/DRUGS/NEWS	•
POOL	•
EXERCISE ROOM	—

Silver Sevens ★★★½
4100 S. Paradise Rd.
Las Vegas, NV 89109
☎ 702-733-7000
FAX 702-791-2423
TOLL-FREE 800-640-9777
silversevenscasino.com

RACK RATE	$+
ROOM QUALITY	78
LOCATION	East of Strip
NO. OF ROOMS	330
CHECKOUT TIME	11
NONSMOKING	•
CONCIERGE	•
CONVENTION FACIL.	—
MEETING ROOMS	—
VALET PARKING	—
RV PARK	•
ROOM SERVICE	•
FREE BREAKFAST	—
FINE DINING/TYPES	American, Chinese, Mexican
COFFEE SHOP	•
24-HOUR CAFE	•
BUFFET	•
CASINO	•
LOUNGE	•
SHOWROOM	—
GIFTS/DRUGS/NEWS	•
POOL	•
EXERCISE ROOM	•

Silverton ★★★★
3333 Blue Diamond Rd.
Las Vegas, NV 89139
☎ 702-263-7777
FAX 702-893-7405
TOLL-FREE 800-588-7711
silvertoncasino.com

RACK RATE	$+
ROOM QUALITY	88
LOCATION	South of Las Vegas
NO. OF ROOMS	300
CHECKOUT TIME	Noon
NONSMOKING	Floors
CONCIERGE	•
CONVENTION FACIL.	—
MEETING ROOMS	•
VALET PARKING	•
RV PARK	—
ROOM SERVICE	•
FREE BREAKFAST	—
FINE DINING/TYPES	Seafood, steak
COFFEE SHOP	•
24-HOUR CAFE	•
BUFFET	•
CASINO	•
LOUNGE	•
SHOWROOM	—
GIFTS/DRUGS/NEWS	•
POOL	•
EXERCISE ROOM	•

SLS ★★★★
2535 Las Vegas Blvd. S.
Las Vegas, NV 89109
☎ 855-761-7757
slslasvegas.com

RACK RATE	$$$-
ROOM QUALITY	89
LOCATION	North Strip
NO. OF ROOMS	1,622
CHECKOUT TIME	Noon
NONSMOKING	•
CONCIERGE	•
CONVENTION FACIL.	—
MEETING ROOMS	•
VALET PARKING	•
RV PARK	—
ROOM SERVICE	•
FREE BREAKFAST	—
FINE DINING/TYPES	Eclectic, Asian, Mediterranean
COFFEE SHOP	•
24-HOUR CAFE	•
BUFFET	•
CASINO	•
LOUNGE	•
SHOWROOM	—
GIFTS/DRUGS/NEWS	•
POOL	•
EXERCISE ROOM	Health spa

Hotel Information Chart (continued)

South Point ★★★½	
9777 Las Vegas Blvd. S.	
Las Vegas, NV 89123	
☎ 702-796-7111	
FAX 702-797-8041	
TOLL-FREE 866-796-7111	
southpointcasino.com	
RACK RATE	$+
ROOM QUALITY	81
LOCATION	South of Las Vegas
NO. OF ROOMS	2,163
CHECKOUT TIME	Noon
NONSMOKING	•
CONCIERGE	—
CONVENTION FACIL.	•
MEETING ROOMS	•
VALET PARKING	•
RV PARK	•
ROOM SERVICE	•
FREE BREAKFAST	—
FINE DINING/TYPES	Italian, seafood, steak, Mexican
COFFEE SHOP	•
24-HOUR CAFE	•
BUFFET	•
CASINO	•
LOUNGE	•
SHOWROOM	Live music
GIFTS/DRUGS/NEWS	•
POOL	•
EXERCISE ROOM	•

Stratosphere ★★★½	
2000 Las Vegas Blvd. S.	
Las Vegas, NV 89104	
☎ 702-380-7777	
FAX 702-380-7732	
TOLL-FREE 800-998-6937	
stratospherehotel.com	
RACK RATE	$$
ROOM QUALITY	79
LOCATION	North Strip
NO. OF ROOMS	2,444
CHECKOUT TIME	11
NONSMOKING	Floors
CONCIERGE	•
CONVENTION FACIL.	•
MEETING ROOMS	•
VALET PARKING	•
RV PARK	•
ROOM SERVICE	•
FREE BREAKFAST	—
FINE DINING/TYPES	Seafood, steak, Italian, American
COFFEE SHOP	•
24-HOUR CAFE	•
BUFFET	•
CASINO	•
LOUNGE	•
SHOWROOM	Production show
GIFTS/DRUGS/NEWS	•
POOL	•
EXERCISE ROOM	Health spa

Suncoast ★★★½	
9090 Alta Dr.	
Las Vegas, NV 89145	
☎ 702-636-7111	
FAX 702-636-7288	
TOLL-FREE 877-677-7111	
suncoastcasino.com	
RACK RATE	$$$–
ROOM QUALITY	82
LOCATION	Summerlin
NO. OF ROOMS	427
CHECKOUT TIME	Noon
NONSMOKING	•
CONCIERGE	—
CONVENTION FACIL.	•
MEETING ROOMS	•
VALET PARKING	•
RV PARK	—
ROOM SERVICE	•
FREE BREAKFAST	—
FINE DINING/TYPES	Italian, Chinese, American, seafood, Mexican
COFFEE SHOP	•
24-HOUR CAFE	•
BUFFET	•
CASINO	•
LOUNGE	•
SHOWROOM	Headliners
GIFTS/DRUGS/NEWS	•
POOL	•
EXERCISE ROOM	•

Tropicana ★★★★	
3801 Las Vegas Blvd. S.	
Las Vegas, NV 89109	
☎ 702-739-2222	
FAX 702-739-3648	
TOLL-FREE 888-826-8767	
troplv.com	
RACK RATE	$$$–
ROOM QUALITY	89
LOCATION	South Strip
NO. OF ROOMS	1,658
CHECKOUT TIME	Noon
NONSMOKING	Floors
CONCIERGE	•
CONVENTION FACIL.	—
MEETING ROOMS	•
VALET PARKING	•
RV PARK	—
ROOM SERVICE	•
FREE BREAKFAST	—
FINE DINING/TYPES	Steak, Caribbean, Italian
COFFEE SHOP	•
24-HOUR CAFE	•
BUFFET	•
CASINO	•
LOUNGE	•
SHOWROOM	Production show, comedy club, magic
GIFTS/DRUGS/NEWS	•
POOL	•
EXERCISE ROOM	Health spa

Trump Int'l Hotel and Tower Las Vegas ★★★★½	
2000 Fashion Show Dr.	
Las Vegas, NV 89109	
☎ 702-982-0000	
FAX 702-476-8450	
TOLL-FREE 866-939-8786	
trumplasvegashotel.com	
RACK RATE	$$$
ROOM QUALITY	95
LOCATION	North Strip
NO. OF ROOMS	1,282
CHECKOUT TIME	11
NONSMOKING	•
CONCIERGE	•
CONVENTION FACIL.	—
MEETING ROOMS	•
VALET PARKING	•
RV PARK	—
ROOM SERVICE	•
FREE BREAKFAST	—
FINE DINING/TYPES	American, Mediterranean
COFFEE SHOP	•
24-HOUR CAFE	24-hour in-suite dining
BUFFET	—
CASINO	—
LOUNGE	•
SHOWROOM	—
GIFTS/DRUGS/NEWS	•
POOL	•
EXERCISE ROOM	Health spa

Tuscany ★★★	
255 E. Flamingo Rd.	
Las Vegas, NV 89169	
☎ 702-893-8933	
FAX 702-947-5994	
TOLL-FREE 877-887-2261	
tuscanylv.com	
RACK RATE	$$
ROOM QUALITY	70
LOCATION	East of Strip
NO. OF ROOMS	716
CHECKOUT TIME	11
NONSMOKING	Floors
CONCIERGE	•
CONVENTION FACIL.	•
MEETING ROOMS	•
VALET PARKING	•
RV PARK	—
ROOM SERVICE	•
FREE BREAKFAST	—
FINE DINING/TYPES	Italian, Mexican
COFFEE SHOP	•
24-HOUR CAFE	•
BUFFET	—
CASINO	•
LOUNGE	•
SHOWROOM	—
GIFTS/DRUGS/NEWS	•
POOL	•
EXERCISE ROOM	•

Sunset Station ★★★★
1301 Sunset Rd.
Henderson, NV 89014
☎ 702-547-7777
FAX 702-547-7744
TOLL-FREE 800-678-2846
sunsetstation.com

RACK RATE	$$$–
ROOM QUALITY	87
LOCATION	Henderson
NO. OF ROOMS	457
CHECKOUT TIME	Noon
NONSMOKING	Floors
CONCIERGE	—
CONVENTION FACIL.	•
MEETING ROOMS	•
VALET PARKING	•
RV PARK	—
ROOM SERVICE	•
FREE BREAKFAST	—
FINE DINING/TYPES	American, Italian, steak, seafood, Mexican
COFFEE SHOP	•
24-HOUR CAFE	•
BUFFET	•
CASINO	•
LOUNGE	•
SHOWROOM	Concerts
GIFTS/DRUGS/NEWS	•
POOL	•
EXERCISE ROOM	•

Texas Station ★★★
2101 Texas Star Ln.
Las Vegas, NV 89030
☎ 702-631-1000
FAX 702-631-8120
TOLL-FREE 800-654-8888
texasstation.com

RACK RATE	$$–
ROOM QUALITY	70
LOCATION	Rancho Drive Area
NO. OF ROOMS	200
CHECKOUT TIME	Noon
NONSMOKING	Floors
CONCIERGE	—
CONVENTION FACIL.	•
MEETING ROOMS	•
VALET PARKING	•
RV PARK	—
ROOM SERVICE	•
FREE BREAKFAST	—
FINE DINING/TYPES	Seafood, Italian, Mexican, steak
COFFEE SHOP	•
24-HOUR CAFE	•
BUFFET	•
CASINO	•
LOUNGE	•
SHOWROOM	•
GIFTS/DRUGS/NEWS	•
POOL	•
EXERCISE ROOM	—

TI (Treasure Island) ★★★★
3300 Las Vegas Blvd. S.
Las Vegas, NV 89109
☎ 702-894-7111
FAX 702-894-7414
TOLL-FREE 800-288-7206
treasureisland.com

RACK RATE	$$$
ROOM QUALITY	84
LOCATION	Mid-Strip
NO. OF ROOMS	2,885
CHECKOUT TIME	Noon
NONSMOKING	Floors
CONCIERGE	—
CONVENTION FACIL.	•
MEETING ROOMS	•
VALET PARKING	•
RV PARK	—
ROOM SERVICE	•
FREE BREAKFAST	—
FINE DINING/TYPES	Italian, seafood, American
COFFEE SHOP	•
24-HOUR CAFE	•
BUFFET	•
CASINO	•
LOUNGE	•
SHOWROOM	Production show
GIFTS/DRUGS/NEWS	•
POOL	•
EXERCISE ROOM	Health spa

Vdara at CityCenter ★★★★½
2600 W. Harmon Ave.
Las Vegas, NV 89109
☎ 702-590-2111
FAX 702-590-2112
TOLL-FREE 866-745-7767
vdara.com

RACK RATE	$$$$–
ROOM QUALITY	95
LOCATION	Mid-Strip
NO. OF ROOMS	1,495
CHECKOUT TIME	Noon
NONSMOKING	•
CONCIERGE	•
CONVENTION FACIL.	•
MEETING ROOMS	•
VALET PARKING	•
RV PARK	—
ROOM SERVICE	•
FREE BREAKFAST	—
FINE DINING/TYPES	—
COFFEE SHOP	•
24-HOUR CAFE	—
BUFFET	—
CASINO	Adjacent
LOUNGE	•
SHOWROOM	—
GIFTS/DRUGS/NEWS	—
POOL	•
EXERCISE ROOM	Health spa

The Venetian ★★★★½
3355 Las Vegas Blvd. S.
Las Vegas, NV 89109
☎ 702-414-1000
FAX 702-414-1100
TOLL-FREE 866-659-9643
venetian.com

RACK RATE	$$$$$–
ROOM QUALITY	94
LOCATION	Mid-Strip
NO. OF ROOMS	4,027
CHECKOUT TIME	11
NONSMOKING	Floors
CONCIERGE	•
CONVENTION FACIL.	•
MEETING ROOMS	•
VALET PARKING	•
RV PARK	—
ROOM SERVICE	•
FREE BREAKFAST	—
FINE DINING/TYPES	Italian, French, Asian, gourmet
COFFEE SHOP	•
24-HOUR CAFE	•
BUFFET	—
CASINO	•
LOUNGE	•
SHOWROOM	Headliners, live music, production show
GIFTS/DRUGS/NEWS	•
POOL	•
EXERCISE ROOM	Health spa

Westgate Las Vegas ★★★½
3000 Paradise Rd.
Las Vegas, NV 89109
☎ 702-732-5111
FAX 702-732-5805
TOLL-FREE 888-732-7117
westgateresorts.com

RACK RATE	$$–
ROOM QUALITY	80
LOCATION	East of Strip
NO. OF ROOMS	2,950
CHECKOUT TIME	Noon
NONSMOKING	•
CONCIERGE	•
CONVENTION FACIL.	•
MEETING ROOMS	•
VALET PARKING	•
RV PARK	—
ROOM SERVICE	•
FREE BREAKFAST	—
FINE DINING/TYPES	Steak, American, Mexican, Asian
COFFEE SHOP	•
24-HOUR CAFE	•
BUFFET	•
CASINO	•
LOUNGE	•
SHOWROOM	Production show
GIFTS/DRUGS/NEWS	•
POOL	•
EXERCISE ROOM	Health spa/tennis

Hotel Information Chart *(continued)*

Westin Casuarina ★★★★
160 E. Flamingo Rd.
Las Vegas, NV 89109
☎ 702-836-5900
FAX 702-836-9776
TOLL-FREE 866-716-8132
starwoodhotels.com/westin

RACK RATE	$$$+
ROOM QUALITY	83
LOCATION	Mid-Strip
NO. OF ROOMS	826
CHECKOUT TIME	11
NONSMOKING	•
CONCIERGE	•
CONVENTION FACIL.	•
MEETING ROOMS	•
VALET PARKING	•
RV PARK	—
ROOM SERVICE	•
FREE BREAKFAST	—
FINE DINING/TYPES	American
COFFEE SHOP	•
24-HOUR CAFE	•
BUFFET	• (Breakfast only)
CASINO	•
LOUNGE	•
SHOWROOM	—
GIFTS/DRUGS/NEWS	•
POOL	•
EXERCISE ROOM	Health spa

Westin Lake Las Vegas ★★★★
101 Montelago Blvd.
Henderson, NV 89011
☎ 702-567-6000
FAX 702-567-6067
starwoodhotels.com

RACK RATE	$$$
ROOM QUALITY	88
LOCATION	Henderson
NO. OF ROOMS	493
CHECKOUT TIME	Noon
NONSMOKING	•
CONCIERGE	•
CONVENTION FACIL.	—
MEETING ROOMS	•
VALET PARKING	•
RV PARK	•
ROOM SERVICE	•
FREE BREAKFAST	—
FINE DINING/TYPES	Continental, Japanese
COFFEE SHOP	•
24-HOUR CAFE	—
BUFFET	—
CASINO	•
LOUNGE	•
SHOWROOM	—
GIFTS/DRUGS/NEWS	•
POOL	•
EXERCISE ROOM	Health spa/tennis

Wynn Encore ★★★★★
3121 Las Vegas Blvd. S.
Las Vegas, NV 89109
☎ 702-770-7000
FAX 702-770-1500
TOLL-FREE 888-320-7123
wynnlasvegas.com

RACK RATE	$$$$$$$
ROOM QUALITY	96
LOCATION	Mid-Strip
NO. OF ROOMS	2,034
CHECKOUT TIME	Noon
NONSMOKING	•
CONCIERGE	•
CONVENTION FACIL.	•
MEETING ROOMS	•
VALET PARKING	•
RV PARK	—
ROOM SERVICE	•
FREE BREAKFAST	—
FINE DINING/TYPES	Italian, steak, seafood, Asian
COFFEE SHOP	•
24-HOUR CAFE	•
BUFFET	•
CASINO	•
LOUNGE	•
SHOWROOM	•
GIFTS/DRUGS/NEWS	•
POOL	•
EXERCISE ROOM	Health spa

Wynn Las Vegas ★★★★★
3131 Las Vegas Blvd. S.
Las Vegas, NV 89109
☎ 702-770-7000
FAX 702-770-1500
TOLL-FREE 888-320-7123
wynnlasvegas.com

RACK RATE	$$$$$$$$–
ROOM QUALITY	96
LOCATION	Mid-Strip
NO. OF ROOMS	2,716
CHECKOUT TIME	Noon
NONSMOKING	Floors
CONCIERGE	•
CONVENTION FACIL.	•
MEETING ROOMS	•
VALET PARKING	•
RV PARK	—
ROOM SERVICE	•
FREE BREAKFAST	—
FINE DINING/TYPES	French, Italian, seafood, Asian
COFFEE SHOP	•
24-HOUR CAFE	•
BUFFET	•
CASINO	•
LOUNGE	•
SHOWROOM	Production show
GIFTS/DRUGS/NEWS	•
POOL	•
EXERCISE ROOM	Health spa

PART TWO

ENTERTAINMENT *and* NIGHTLIFE

LAS VEGAS SHOWS *and* ENTERTAINMENT

LAS VEGAS CALLS ITSELF the "Entertainment Capital of the World." This is arguably true, particularly in terms of the sheer number of live-entertainment productions staged daily. On any given day in Las Vegas, a visitor can select from dozens of presentations, ranging from major production spectaculars to celebrity headliners, from comedy clubs to live music in lounges. The standard of professionalism and value for your entertainment dollar is very high. There is no other place where you can buy so much top-quality entertainment for so little money.

 Jubilee!, a full-blown Las Vegas production show, is one of the best buys in town, with tickets as low as $69.50 plus tax.

But here's the bad news: The average price of a ticket to one of the major production shows has topped $80. However, the standard of quality for shows has likewise soared. And variety, well, there's now literally something for everyone, from traditional Las Vegas feathers and butts to real Broadway musicals. And believe it or not, the value is still there—maybe not in the grand showrooms and incessantly hyped productions, but in the smaller showrooms and lounges and in the main theaters of off-Strip hotels. There's more of everything now, including both overpriced shows and bargains. Regarding the former, you'll be numbed and blinded by their billboards all over town. As concerns the latter, you'll have to scout around, but you'll be rewarded with some great shows at dynamite prices. And there are always discount coupons floating around.

CHOICES, CHOICES, CHOICES

MOST LAS VEGAS LIVE ENTERTAINMENT offerings can be lumped into one of the following categories:

• Celebrity headliners	• Elvis shows
• Long-term engagements	• Magic and illusion shows
• Broadway and off-Broadway shows	• Musical-tribute and nostalgia shows
• Production shows	• Impersonator shows
• Skin shows	• Comedy-headliner shows
• Hypnosis shows	• Comedy clubs
• Lounge entertainment	

Celebrity Headliners

As the name implies, these are concerts or shows featuring big-name entertainers on a limited-engagement basis, usually one to four weeks, but sometimes for a one-night stand. Performers such as David Copperfield and Jay Leno play Las Vegas regularly. Some even work on a rotation with other performers, returning to the same showroom for several engagements each year. Other stars, such as Barbra Streisand, Paul McCartney, and the Rolling Stones, play Las Vegas only rarely, transforming each appearance into a truly special event. While there are exceptions, the superstars are regularly found at the MGM Grand, the Mirage, Mandalay Bay, Caesars Palace, Planet Hollywood, Westgate Las Vegas (formerly the LVH), Bally's, Flamingo, Wynn Encore, and the Hard Rock. Big-name performers in the city's top showrooms command premium admission prices. Headliners of slightly lesser stature play at various other showrooms.

There's a new category of headliners who are said to be "in residence." This means they are contracted to a particular venue but perform usually 35 or fewer shows a year. For example, Celine Dion is the primary headliner for the Colosseum at Caesars Palace, but when she's on break, Elton John, Rod Stewart, or Shania Twain performs. Boyz II Men sub for Terry Fator at the Mirage, playing 78 shows, and Carlos Santana performs on 33 nights at Mandalay Bay. Joining the residency ranks recently are Tim McGraw and Faith Hill, and Britney Spears.

Long-Term Engagements

These are shows by the famous and once-famous who have come to Las Vegas to stay. Comic Rita Rudner is making a go of it at The Venetian, Celine Dion is back and better than ever at Caesars Palace, and Marie and Donny Osmond continue to hold sway with the PG-preferred crowd at the Flamingo.

Broadway and Off-Broadway Shows

Las Vegas showrooms have dallied with Broadway shows for a long time. Some caught on, but most didn't, and many were signed for limited engagements. The tide has turned, however, and there are now a goodly number of shows that originated on Broadway or in London playing long-term engagements in Las Vegas. As of this writing, these include *Blue Man Group, Jersey Boys, Defending the Caveman, Tony 'n' Tina's Wedding, Rock of Ages,* and *The Million Dollar Quartet.*

Production Shows

These are continuously running, Broadway-style theatrical and musical productions. Cast sizes run from a dozen performers to more than 100, with costumes, sets, and special effects spanning a comparable range. Costing hundreds of thousands, if not millions, to produce, the shows feature elaborate choreography and great spectacle. Sometimes playing twice a night, six or seven days a week, these shows often run for years.

Production shows generally have a central theme to which a more or less standard mix of choreography and variety acts (also called specialty acts) are added. Favorite central themes are magic and illusion, rock and roll retrospectives, and "best of Broadway." Defying categorization, Cirque du Soleil now offers eight shows.

Las Vegas puts its own distinctive imprint on all this entertainment, imparting a degree of homogeneity and redundancy to the mix of productions. The quality of Las Vegas entertainment is quite high, even excellent, but most production shows seem to operate according to a formula that fosters a numbing sameness. Particularly pronounced in the magic-illusion shows and the Broadway-style musical productions, this sameness discourages sampling more than one show from each genre. While it is not totally accurate to say that "if you've seen one Las Vegas production or magic show, you've seen them all," the statement comes closer to the truth than one would hope.

Sadly, only one show, *Jubilee!* at Bally's, carries on the tradition of the *Ziegfeld Follies*–inspired, Las Vegas grand production show. These immense productions once dominated Las Vegas showrooms, and even spawned a new genre of musical theater, the "Las Vegas–Style Musical Revue," that is alive and well in a much-scaled-down form on cruise ships and elsewhere throughout the Western world. The Parisian *Folies Bergère* went dark permanently in 2009 after a 49-year run at the Tropicana, leaving only *Jubilee!* to carry on the tradition. When *Jubilee!* ends its decades-long run, a fabled piece of Las Vegas history will die with it (though a newer presentation, *Vegas! The Show,* does an outstanding job of chronicling the evolution of production shows using the traditional ensemble number–specialty act formula).

While they share a common format, production shows, regardless of theme, can be differentiated by the size of the cast and by the elaborateness of the production. Other discriminating factors include the creativity of the choreography, the attractiveness of the performers, the pace and continuity of the presentation, and its ability to build to a crescendo. Strength in these last-mentioned areas sometimes allows a relatively simple, lower-budget show to provide a more satisfying evening of entertainment than a lavish, long-running spectacular.

Impersonator Shows

These are usually long-running production shows, complete with dancers, that feature the impersonation of celebrities, both living (Joan Rivers, Cher, Neil Diamond, Tina Turner, Madonna) and deceased (Marilyn

Monroe, Elvis Presley, Liberace, Blues Brother John Belushi). In shows such as *Legends in Concert,* the emphasis is on the detail and exactness of the impersonation. In general, men impersonate male stars and women impersonate female stars (as you might expect). There are productions, however, featuring males impersonating female celebrities. But no one—dead or alive, male or female—is impersonated as frequently as The King. The Las Vegas Convention and Visitors Authority says there are at least 260 Elvis impersonators locally. We'd love to see them all in the same show. Wouldn't that be "a hunk-a hunk-a burnin' love"!

Comedy-Headliner Shows

These are stand-up comedy presentations usually featuring a warm-up comic followed by a well-known, if not famous, comedian. Though Jerry Seinfeld, Jay Leno, Ray Romano, and David Spade regularly play Las Vegas, this discussion is limited to the several comics who perform year-round. They're all good, and happily, all different in style, tone, personality, and delivery. Here is a chart showing the long-engagement comics and what they are known for. Reviews can be found later in this chapter.

VINNIE FAVORITO | Flamingo Known for shock comedy. The bluest comic in town. X-rated and sharp tongued—audience beware.
RITA RUDNER | The Venetian Sweet and empathetic but savvy. Playful with audience. Very clean.
CARROT TOP | Luxor Furious pace makes us dizzy. Highly dependent on props and sight gags. PG-13.

Several top-name comics such as Louie Anderson and Brad Garrett have opened clubs of their own. These clubs charge a premium price on nights when the namesake comic is on the bill.

Comedy Clubs

Stand-up comedy has long been a tradition in Las Vegas entertainment. With the success of comedy clubs around the country and the comedy-club format on network and cable television, stand-up comedy in Las Vegas was elevated from lounges and production shows to its own specialized venue. Las Vegas comedy clubs are small- to medium-sized showrooms featuring anywhere from two to five comedians per show. As a rule, the shows change completely each week, with a new group of comics rotating in. Each showroom has its own source of talent, so there is no swapping of comics from club to club. Comedy clubs are one of the few Las Vegas entertainments that draw equally from both the tourist and local populations. While most production shows and many celebrity-headliner shows are packaged for the over-40 market, comedy clubs represent a concession to youth. Many of the comics are young, and the humor is often raw and scatological, and almost always irreverent.

Comedy Clubs pop up and disappear like dandelions, but there are usually six to eight clubs operating in any given year. Following were the choices when we went to press:

BRAD GARRETT'S COMEDY CLUB	MGM Grand	Nightly, 8 p.m.
IMPROV COMEDY CLUB	Harrah's	Tuesday–Sunday, 8:30 and 10:30 p.m.
KING'S COMEDY CLUB	Rio	Monday–Wednesday, 7 p.m.
LA COMEDY CLUB	Bally's	Tuesday–Sunday, 9:30 p.m.
LAS VEGAS LIVE COMEDY CLUB	Miracle Mile Shops	Nightly, 9 p.m.
LAUGH FACTORY	Tropicana	Nightly, 8:30 and 10:30 p.m.
LIPSHTICK	Venetian	Friday, 10 p.m.; Saturday, 7:30 p.m.
LOUIE ANDERSON LIVE	Plaza	Wednesday–Saturday, 7 p.m.
RIVIERA COMEDY CLUB	Riviera	Nightly, 8:30 p.m.

The comedy club format is simple and straightforward. Comedians perform sequentially, and what you get depends on who's performing. The range of humor runs from slapstick to obscene to ethnic to topical to just about anything. Some comics are better than others, but all the talent is solid and professional. There's no way to predict which club will have the best show in a given week. In fact, there may not be a "best" show since response to comedy is a matter of individual sense of humor.

Among Las Vegas comedy clubs there are exceptions to the standard template. Brad Garrett and Louie Anderson have their own clubs at which they perform regularly. When they're off, the usual rotation of comics holds sway. In what you might call comedy club writ large, the California-based, multiclub Laugh Factory is partnering with the Tropicana and Fun World Media to produce Laugh Factory Superstar Comedy Concerts for the 1,000-seat Tropicana Theater. It's a big venue for a comedy club format that traditionally thrives best in intimate showrooms. Ticket prices vary depending on who's playing.

Performances at all clubs last about 70–75 minutes. Admission prices range from about $37 at the Riviera Comedy Club to $84 at the King's Comedy Club when Eddie Griffin is performing. Average prices run in the $42–$52 range, but there are half-price tickets available most nights from Tix4Tonight and coupons for discounts in the local visitor mags. Finally, several shows around town, such as the Sin City Comedy Show at the Miracle Mile Shops, seem to be comedy clubs but are actually production shows with singers, dancers, and skits in addition to stand-up comedy.

Elvis Shows

Much to our disappointment, the *Viva Elvis* show by Cirque du Soleil was terminated in 2012. But fear not, Elvis lives on in Vegas. Although there are dozens, if not hundreds, of Elvis impersonators, the pick of the crop is Trent Carlini who stars in a full-fledged Elvis production at the Westgate Las Vegas. Performing at the same hotel-casino where Elvis actually performed, he's backed by a five-piece band and a trio of dancers who buzz around while Carlini changes costumes. This happens every 10–15 minutes, and Carlini isn't as fast as Cher, so you'll see a lot of the dancers (see **thelvh.com** or **westgateresorts.com** for info).

If you don't want a whole show centering on Elvis, *Legends in Concert* at the Flamingo caps every performance with an excellent Elvis impersonator finale. For a free Elvis, and a good one at that, our favorite is Big Elvis (Pete Vallee), who had a gig at Bill's Gamblin' Hall for ages and can now be seen Monday, Tuesday, Thursday, and Friday at The Piano Bar at Harrah's.

Off the stage, there are Elvises who can marry you and Elvises who are available to sing at your birthday party or other big event. For a guide to Elvis options in Las Vegas, see **vegas.com/traveltips /guide/elvis.html.** If you want to rent an Elvis, a good selection can be found at **gigmasters.com.** Rates range from $100 for an Elvis "that doesn't play guitar very well" to over $10,000 for impersonator superstars like Steve Connolly. Finally, if you don't like your Elvis to gyrate (prudish TV producers in the '60s would only show him from the waist up), your best bet is the Elvis at Madame Tussauds Wax Museum at The Venetian who doesn't move anything. You can touch and pose with him, but he won't give you a scarf.

Magic and Illusion Shows

There are usually five to eight Las Vegas production shows dedicated to magic and illusion. The rage in these shows is to put unlikely creatures or objects into boxes or behind curtains and make them disappear. Some featured magicians repeat this sort of tiresome illusion as often as a dozen times in a single performance, with nothing really changing except the size of the box and the object placed into it. Into these boxes go doves, ducks, parrots, dwarves, showgirls, lions, tigers, panthers, motorcycles (with riders), TV cameras (with cameramen), and even elephants. Sometimes the illusionist himself gets into a box and disappears, reappearing seconds later in the audience. Generally the elephants and other animals don't reappear until the next performance. These box illusions are amazing the first time or two, but become less compelling after that. After he had seen all of the illusion shows in Las Vegas, our reviewer commented that the only thing not seen vanishing from a box was his mortgage. Food for thought.

Most Las Vegas magic and illusion shows trot out variations of the same tricks. You'll see daring escapes (usually involving sharp objects or fire); the aforementioned box tricks; and an inexhaustible inventory of elaborate contraptions. All magicians have comely assistants, and large-stage productions throw in some dancers as well. Small stages can only accommodate small contraptions and thus are limited in the scale of the illusion. For example, the "Giant Screw of Death" on which Melinda, The First Lady of Magic, was impaled nightly for years wouldn't fit on the stage at O'Shea's or the Wolf Theater at the Clarion. So, if you want to see big stuff disappear, try a production in a larger showroom. Sleight of hand and close work are perfect for small, intimate showrooms, but you usually won't find competent practitioners such as Joseph Gabriel of *Vegas! The Show* and David Copperfield working there. For the foreseeable future, contraptions rule.

If you've never seen a Las Vegas magic and illusion show, you'll probably be very happy with whichever show you choose. Even in the small showrooms, the magician has to be a pro to play Las Vegas. If you have seen a Vegas magic show or two, you can expect more of the same, albeit with each performer adding a personal twist. Leaving aside magicians such as Joseph Gabriel, who performs a short magic specialty act in a multifaceted Vegas extravaganza, you have two genres of shows to choose from: traditional productions devoted to serious magic and illusion, and so-called "comedy magic shows." As concerns the latter, there's generally more comedy than magic, but what magic there is tends to be of high quality. The comedy magic shows are upbeat and lots of fun, but the comedic patter consumes most of the show.

The following chart lists the magicians and illusionists who regularly work Las Vegas showrooms with their own productions. Most of the shows are reviewed later in this chapter. If the past is any indicator, however, many of the featured magicians without a regular gig will turn up in other productions.

COMEDY MAGIC			
SHOW	HOTEL	ROOM SIZE	DESCRIPTION
PENN & TELLER	Rio	Large	Best (and bluest) big-room comedy magic act.
MAC KING	Harrah's	Small	Pioneer of the genre and best small-room act.
NATHAN BURTON	Saxe Theater	Large	Frenetic pace, sexy showgirls; more magic than comedy.
MIKE HAMMER	Fours Queens	Small	Quick-witted with sharp tongue and good sleight of hand.
MURRAY SAWCHUCK	Tropicana	Small	Wild hair and a mischievous persona; turns comic stage mishaps into clever illusions.
TRADITIONAL MAGIC AND ILLUSION			
SHOW	HOTEL	ROOM SIZE	DESCRIPTION
CRISS ANGEL	Luxor	Large	Talented and creative but self-aggrandizing; lowest rated Cirque du Soleil production.
DAVID COPPERFIELD	MGM Grand	Large	The gold standard. Best magic and illusion show in Vegas.
LANCE BURTON	N/A	N/A	Second only to Copperfield. Retired but young enough to come back.
STEVE WYRICK	N/A	N/A	Longtime Vegas veteran. Makes big things disappear (like airplanes!).
DIRK ARTHUR	N/A	N/A	Longtime Vegas veteran. Uses tigers and is given to big illusions when he plays larger showrooms.
RICK THOMAS	N/A	N/A	Longtime Vegas veteran. Another big-illusion, big-cat guy.
JAN ROUVEN	Riviera	Large	Talented newcomer known for daring escapes. Easy rapport with audience.
MICHAEL TURCO	N/A	N/A	Competent execution of classic illusions. Upstaged by dancers.
SETH GRABEL	N/A	N/A	Talented newcomer from *America's Got Talent.* Excellent close-up work and sleight of hand.
STEPHAN VANEL	N/A	N/A	2011 Magician of the Year known for his sleight-of-hand and manipulation skills.

Musical Tribute and Nostalgia Shows

Musical tribute shows can be defined as contemporary musicians and vocalists recreating the sound and appearance of a legendary singer or group. Some musical tribute shows, such as *Country Superstars* and *Legends in Concert,* present a whole lineup of performers, each impersonating a different musical superstar. Although several musical tribute shows, such as *Jersey Boys* (The Four Seasons) and *Million Dollar Quartet* (Harrah's), have transcended the genre to become fully realized production shows with story lines, elaborate sets, and eye-popping ensemble numbers, most tribute shows are very minimalist productions that simply try to capture the feel of hearing the famous singer or group in concert at a club or small theater. In other words, don't expect dancers, variety acts, and the like.

Though more than half of the musical tribute shows in Las Vegas honor a specific singer or group, others focus on a musical genre or period. *Human Nature* at The Venetian and *Hitzville* at the Miracle Mile Shops, for example, reprise the Motown hits of the 1960s and '70s. Here the performers nail the Motown sound but identify themselves by their real names and do not pretend to be specific Motown stars. A musical tribute variation is the nostalgia show, where performers seek to capture the impersonated stars in a particular time and place. *The Rat Pack Is Back* at the Rio takes the audience back to an early-'60s performance at the Copa Room in the Sands Hotel with Frank Sinatra, Dean Martin, Joey Bishop, and Sammy Davis Jr. Here the Copa Room setting is replicated and the impersonators stay in character throughout. The performers banter, smoke, and drink in a very effective recollection of the Rat Pack and the old Vegas club scene. In all shows the impersonators do their own singing and play their instruments. There are no recorded tracks or lip-syncing. Everything, in other words, is live.

Just about anyone will enjoy shows like *The Rat Pack Is Back* and *Jersey Boys.* It doesn't matter whether you're a Rat Pack or Four Seasons fan. For other tribute shows, your enjoyment will probably pivot on how much you like the impersonated singer/group or musical genre. Those who don't like country music are not good candidates for *Country Superstars.* Similarly, if you're not big on the Bee Gees or disco, it might be best to punt on *The Australian Bee Gees Show.* If you're a fan, however, you'll be as hyped up as a gnat in a glass of wine.

Several major shows have beefed up the genre. *Million Dollar Quartet* at Harrah's is about an impromptu jam session at the Sun Records studio when Elvis, Johnny Cash, Carl Perkins, and Jerry Lee Lewis all dropped in on the same evening. *Rock of Ages* at The Venetian is a full-blown, high-energy production featuring heavy rock tunes from the 1980s and dancing with attitude. *Raiding the Rock Vault* at Westgate Las Vegas is a retrospective of rock and roll performed by musicians from some of the groups that created the classics being played. Cirque du Soleil's newest spectacular, *Michael Jackson ONE,* at Mandalay Bay celebrates the mystique, dance, and music of the late superstar with the most riveting choreography ever seen in Las Vegas.

Following are musical tribute and nostalgia shows that are likely to still be around when you visit. Absent from the chart are impersonator shows where the performers sing along with recorded tracks. All of the shows listed are high-quality productions. We don't rank them because your personal taste in music will largely dictate, with the exception of *Jersey Boys* and *Michael Jackson ONE,* which show you'll like best. Our personal favorites include *Country Superstars* and *Purple Reign,* the Prince tribute show, for their energy; *The Rat Pack Is Back* for its retrospective of old Las Vegas; and *Human Nature* for its walk down Motown's memory lane. *Jersey Boys* and *Michael Jackson ONE* are in our top-10 list of Las Vegas shows irrespective of genre, and Trent Carlini is simply, well, The King if you're big into Elvis. Most of the shows are reviewed later in this chapter.

SHOW	HOTEL	TRIBUTE TO
Australian Bee Gees	**Excalibur**	Bee Gees
B-A Tribute to the Beatles	**Miracle Mile Shops**	Beatles
Country Superstars	**Bally's**	County music
Hitzville	**Miracle Mile Shops**	Motown
Human Nature	**The Venetian**	Motown
Jersey Boys	**Paris**	Four Seasons
Legends in Concert	**Flamingo**	Various music legends
Michael Jackson ONE	**Mandalay Bay**	Michael Jackson
Million Dollar Quartet	**Harrah's**	Elvis, Johnny Cash, Jerry Lee Lewis, Carl Perkins
Purple Reign	**The D Las Vegas**	Prince
Raiding the Rock Vault	**Westgate Las Vegas**	Rock anthems from 1950 to 1990
The Rat Pack Is Back	**Rio**	The Rat Pack and old Las Vegas
Rock of Ages	**The Venetian**	1980s rock (mostly hard)
Trent Carlini—The King	**Westgate Las Vegas**	Elvis Presley

Skin Shows

There are seven topless productions for male and mixed audiences, and three (occasionally four) beefcake shows for the ladies. Additionally, the Ziegfeld-style show *Jubilee!* at Bally's, Cirque du Soleil's *Zumanity* at New York–New York, and *Absinthe* at Caesars Palace feature topless acts as part of extravagant multidimensional production shows. Most of the T&A efforts play in smaller showrooms albeit in large hotels. The intimacy of small rooms is a boon for the myopic, though in most productions the showgirls are covered as much, if not more, of the time as they're topless. Several showrooms have flat floors, meaning that shorter patrons need to sit up front. Most shows are reviewed later in this chapter.

SHOW	HOTEL	DESCRIPTION
Crazy Girls	**Riviera**	Longest-running show by decades. The revamped edition features 6 out of 7 dancers with natural breasts. Flat-floored showroom.
Dream Angels Topless Review	**House ShowClub**	Major casino-quality show performed in a "gentlemen's club." Hot and athletic.

SHOW	HOTEL	DESCRIPTION
Fantasy	**Luxor**	Good choreography but not as steamy as *Zumanity*. Arguably the hottest showgirls. Very comfortable modern showroom.
Pin Up	**Stratosphere**	Lingerie and corset high-stepping backed by a live band. High energy but not too steamy.
Sidney After Dark	**Planet Hollywood**	New topless burlesque show with brassy Australian showgirls, aerial performances, and sultry vocalist Natalie Conway.
X-Burlesque	**Flamingo**	A teaser. Less erotic than athletic with excellent choreography. Flat-floored showroom.
X Rocks	**Rio**	The most sexual production next to *Zumanity*. Deserves a better showroom.

There are three long-running beefcake shows for women. These shows are a lot rowdier than the topless revues because (1) admission is restricted to women; (2) women attend in large groups of friends; and (3) there's a lot more interaction between the audience and the performers. You get a lot of "What Happens in Vegas Stays in Vegas" moments at these shows. All three shows are reviewed later in this chapter.

SHOW	HOTEL	DESCRIPTION
American Storm	**Currently on tour**	So-so choreography but really good at working up the audience. Gets off to a slow start.
Chippendales	**Rio**	Very sensual with simulated sex acts. Explores female fantasies. Tight dance routines.
Thunder From Down Under	**Excalibur**	Guy-next-door types. Much tamer than Chippendales. Athletic more than sensual. Flat-floored showroom.

Hypnosis Shows

In hypnosis shows, volunteers from the audience are invited onto the stage to be hypnotized. The volunteers really do get hypnotized. We have had medical clinicians who use hypnosis in their practice review the shows and verify the authenticity of the trance. Folks that fake being under hypnosis or for whom the hypnotic state is marginal are quickly identified by the hypnotist and returned to their seats. To the best of our knowledge, there are no plants or ringers.

Most, if not all, of the Las Vegas hypnosis shows are very blue. This means that volunteers may end up doing things which after the fact may embarrass them immensely. We've seen volunteers attempt to have sex with a folding chair, perform fellatio on imaginary objects, enjoy orgasms, and audition for a job as an exotic dancer. We should make it clear that the contestants do all of this fully clothed. Most showrooms record each performance and make a DVD available for sale after the show.

The quality(?) and relative outrageousness of any given performance depends on the number of volunteers and their susceptibility to hypnosis. So if you prefer to be a voyeur instead of a volunteer, your best chance for a really wild spectacle is to choose a show in a big hotel where the size of the audience is likely to be large. We profile only the Anthony Cools hypnosis show at Paris Las Vegas, but his review is pretty representative of the genre.

Afternoon Shows

Afternoon shows can be an affordable alternative to the high-priced productions playing in the major showrooms at night. Most cost under $50, and many can be enjoyed for even less by taking advantage of coupons and special offers found in local freebie visitor magazines. Because afternoon shows sprout and disappear like wildflowers (or weeds), it's not possible to review all of them in the *Unofficial Guide*. What we can do, however, is profile the ones that have demonstrated staying power.

Below is a chart listing the afternoon shows profiled later in this chapter. There has been a numbing proliferation of afternoon shows recently, and as you might expect, the shows vary immensely in terms of quality. Finding the good ones and avoiding the bad ones is not unlike threading your way through a minefield. The good ones are better than a lot of the high-ticket productions that hold down stages around town at night. But the bad ones . . . heaven help us.

REVIEWED AFTERNOON SHOWS (in alphabetical order)	
B-A Tribute to the Beatles	Miracle Mile Shops
Jeff Civillico—Comedy in Action	The LINQ Hotel & Casino
Mac King Comedy Magic Show	Harrah's
Menopause: The Musical	Luxor
Nathan Burton Comedy Magic	Miracle Mile Shops

Afternoon shows are often instrumental in giving new talent a chance to break into the Las Vegas entertainment scene. Leading the search for new talent is the Clarion Hotel and Casino (**clarionhotelvegas.com**), formerly the Greek Isles, and before that Debbie Reynolds Hotel, and before that—in the olden days—the Paddlewheel. Offering several afternoon presentations, the Clarion is an incubator showroom for new productions and up-and-coming entertainers. The showroom, the Star Theater, was built by Debbie Reynolds and is modeled after the legendary Crystal Room at the Desert Inn. In other words, it's not a curtained-off section of hallway. A second showroom, the Wolf Theater, is more like the hallway. As we went to press, the Clarion show roster included a Frank Sinatra tribute show, a magic and illusion show, and a comedy production. The Clarion shows come and go too fast for us to review, but if you want to take a chance, you might see a new Las Vegas icon in the making. Self-parking at the Clarion is probably the most convenient in town. Down Convention Center Drive from the Clarion is Royal Resort, also a talent incubator.

Lounge Entertainment

Many casinos offer exceptional entertainment at all hours of the day and night in their lounges. For the most part, lounges feature musical groups. On a given day almost any type of music, from oldies rock to country to jazz to folk, can be found in Las Vegas lounges. Unlike the production and headliner showrooms and comedy clubs, no reservations are required to take advantage of most lounge entertainment. If you like what you hear, just walk in. Sometimes there is a one- or two-drink minimum for sitting in the lounge during a show, but just as often there are no restrictions at all. You may or may not be familiar with the lounge entertainers by name, but you can trust that they will be highly talented and very enjoyable. Lounge entertainment is a great barometer of a particular casino's marketing program; bands are specifically chosen to attract a certain type of customer.

To find the type of music you prefer, consult one of the local visitor guides available free from the front desk or concierge at your hotel. There are a number of online sites that offer lounge entertainment information, but most stick to opening hours and nuts-and-bolts stuff such as address and phone number. Many are hopelessly out of date (one still lists the lounge at the long-ago imploded Stardust). The better sites are **insidervlv.com/entertainment/lounges.html** and **lasvegas weekly.com/clubs,** where there is some, but by no means comprehensive, information on scheduled performers. You can download a copy of *Las Vegas Lounge Entertainment Magazine* at **lvlem.com.** The magazine provides an almost-overwhelming list of bars and lounges around town, the vast majority of them local hangouts. It lists what type of entertainment (live music, DJ, karaoke, and so on) is available at each establishment but offers no details as to who's performing. The mag is big into karaoke and publishes a near-comprehensive roster of karaoke bars all over town. Karaoke aside, the best resource is blogger Evan Davis's **evandavisjazz.com.** Evan compiles a weekly list of who is playing where, mostly at venues that do not charge a cover.

unofficial **TIP**
In general, if you find a casino with lounge entertainment that suits your tastes, you will probably be comfortable lodging, dining, and gambling there also.

As an alternative to high ticket prices in Las Vegas showrooms (more than a dozen shows now cost upward of $100), several casinos have turned their nightclubs and lounges into alternative show venues with ticket prices in the $30–$60 range. We've seen a number of marginal or unsuccessful clubs turned into showrooms over the years, but this is the first time we've observed highly successful nightspots converted. In the main, we don't care for this trend. True, it offers some low-price shows, but at the cost of sacrificing some of the city's best lounges and nightclubs.

THEY COME AND THEY GO

LAS VEGAS SHOWS come and go all the time. Sometimes a particular production will close in one Las Vegas showroom and open weeks later in another. Some shows actually pack up and take their presentations to other cities, usually Reno/Lake Tahoe or Atlantic City. Other shows close permanently. The bottom line: It's hard to keep up with all this coming and going. Don't be surprised if some shows reviewed in this guide have bitten the dust before you arrive. Also do not be surprised if the enduring shows have changed or moved to another casino.

LEARN WHO IS PLAYING BEFORE YOU LEAVE HOME

ON THE INTERNET, check out **vegas.com/shows.** The site also provides information and reviews on long-run headliners and production shows. The *Las Vegas Advisor* (see page 14) offers a complete listing of shows on its website **lvahotels.com,** along with pretty good discounts on tickets. The Las Vegas Convention and Visitors Authority publishes a free Official Visitors Guide that lists shows alphabetically according to host hotel, tells who is playing, provides appearance dates, and lists information and reservation numbers. You can view this publication at **visitlasvegas.com.**

SHOW PRICES AND TAXES

ADMISSION PRICES for Las Vegas shows range from around $12 all the way up to $304 per person. Usually show prices are quoted exclusive of entertainment and sales taxes. Also not included are server gratuities.

Once, there was no such thing as a reserved seat at a Las Vegas show. If you wanted to see a show, you would make a reservation (usually by phone) and then arrive well in advance to be assigned a seat by the showroom maître d'. Slipping the maître d' a nice tip ensured a better seat. Typically, the price of the show included two drinks, or there would be waitstaff service and you would pay at your table after you were served. While this arrangement is still practiced in a few showrooms, the prevailing system is reserved seating. With reserved seating, you purchase your tickets at the casino box office (or by phone or online in advance with your credit card). As at a concert or a Broadway play, your seats are designated and preassigned at the time of purchase, and your section, aisle, and seat number will be printed on your ticket. When you arrive at the showroom, an usher will guide you to your assigned seat. Reserved seating, also known as "hard" or "box-office" seating, occasionally includes drinks but usually does not.

If there are two performances per night, the early show is often (but not always) more expensive than the late show. In addition, some shows add a surcharge on Saturdays and holidays. If you tip your server a couple of bucks and slip the maître d' or captain some currency for a good seat (in a showroom without reserved seating), you can easily end up paying $47 or more for a $40 list-price show and $63 or more for a $50 list-price show.

BUYING TICKETS

AS WITH MANY OTHER THINGS, the Internet has revolutionized how Las Vegas show tickets are sold. Now you can purchase all of your show tickets well in advance online before you leave home. Many sites have a seating chart of the theater to help choose where to sit. Sellers include the host casino's website; the Las Vegas Visitor and Convention Authority's **visitlasvegas.com;** sites offering discounts and special deals (seat upgrades, free drinks, etc.) such as **lvahotels.com** and **vegas.com/shows;** and national event and ticket-selling sites such as **ticketmaster.com.**

Buying in advance is definitely recommended if you want to see a popular show or celebrity headliner on a weekend. As an example, tickets went on sale for Celine Dion's show a year before it opened. Every show for the first several months sold out in just a couple of days.

Many of the online ticket vendors sell only at full retail, while others offer modest discounts on some but not all shows. Few of the online discounts come close to matching those of half-price ticket outlets in Las Vegas described below, but with the latter you have to buy your ticket in person on the day of the show.

You can also purchase tickets in advance at the host casino's box office, either in person or by phoning and using your credit card. The main advantage of phoning or going to the box office is that you're able to discuss seating options with a live person. The main disadvantage is that the box offices are usually understaffed. Because each buyer takes up a lot of agent time asking questions and going over seating charts, your chances of being stuck on hold or in a long line are about 80%. We were once in line at the MGM Grand box office behind a tour operator who purchased show tickets for a group of 60 people—can't begin to tell you how long that took.

unofficial **TIP**
Avoid buying show tickets from independent brokers. They tack on extra surcharges.

HOW TO SAVE BIG BUCKS ON SHOW TICKETS

THE EASIEST WAY TO SAVE is to see *Dr. Naughty X-Rated Hypnosis* instead of Celine Dion. OK, just kidding. Here are some practical tips:

1. Most of the high-price shows are in new, state-of-the art theaters, which often have several classifications of seats. You can see Celine Dion at Caesars Palace from a second-level mezzanine seat for far less than in a front orchestra seat at the same show.

2. Half-price ticket outlets. The preeminent half-price ticket seller in Las Vegas is **Tix4Tonight (tix4tonight.com),** with nine locations (see location chart below). Box offices open at 10 a.m., though show postings are available at 9:30 a.m. Each morning shows with unsold seats make some of those seats available to the half-price sellers. Sometimes it's a lot of seats, and other times it's just a handful, or none, depending on the show. The sellers post the available shows for customers to choose from. Before the recession, tickets to the most popular productions, such as the Cirque du Soleil shows and *Jersey Boys,* and most major celebrity headliners, were almost never available. Now, however, it's possible to find discounted tickets for just about any show in town, though the number of tickets for sale may be quite limited, or on weekends nonexistent.

   You have to go in person to one of the box offices the day of the show to purchase your tickets. If you're staying on the Strip, there's usually a discounter within a 15-minute walk. If you're driving, parking can be a hassle for the Strip locations but is usually not a problem for off-Strip box offices. Instead of an actual ticket, discounters will issue you a voucher that you can exchange for a ticket at the official box office of the show. If it's not terribly inconvenient, we recommend exchanging your voucher sometime during the day instead of waiting until just before showtime.

TIX4TONIGHT TICKET OUTLET LOCATIONS

- **CASINO ROYALE** (Mid-Strip) • **CIRCUS CIRCUS** (North Strip)
- **FASHION SHOW MALL** (North Strip; ground floor by Neiman Marcus)
- **FOUR QUEENS** (Downtown) • **GIANT COKE BOTTLE** (Mid-Strip)
- **HAWAIIAN MARKETPLACE** (Mid-Strip) • **SHOWCASE MALL** (South Strip)
- **SLOTS OF FUN** (Mid-Strip)
- **TOWN SQUARE SHOPPING CENTER** (South Strip)

You can blow a fair amount of time buying half-price tickets. Strip discounter locations are almost invariably understaffed. This, coupled with each purchaser asking untold questions, can combine for a long, slow-moving queue. At the Four Queens Tix4Tonight location Downtown, one couple monopolized the sole staffer for 35 minutes. Seriously. The average processing time for a person who knows exactly what they want is just over 10 minutes and requires showing photo ID and signing multiple documents. Most people have questions, so it takes longer. A lot of folks are afraid Tix4Tonight is a scam (it's not), forcing the ticket seller to waste time presenting his bona fides.

Parking is difficult for most locations. Out of the way but perhaps the easiest location to access if you're driving is the Tix4Tonight at Town Square Shopping Center. This is where we usually purchase our discounted tickets. Head south on Las Vegas Boulevard South and turn right into the shopping center on Town Square Parkway. Park in the South Garage. Tix4Tonight faces centrally located Town Square Park and the Children's Park.

It's helpful to have one of the local freebie visitor magazines with you when shopping. These publications always list the non-discounted price for show tickets. If you know the non-discounted price, you can calculate what a half-price ticket should cost. It's not uncommon in Las Vegas today for shows to offer VIP seating at a premium price. Often discounters will sell you a VIP seat without letting you know if there are less expensive seats available. For almost all shows, paying extra for a VIP seat is a waste of money. Tix4Tonight charges a service fee of $4 per ticket for processing your purchase. Coupons for $2 off this charge are available on the Tix4Tonight website and also in freebie magazines.

We found that after buying tickets, the discounters tell you to arrive at the show much earlier than necessary. True, you might encounter a logjam at the box office when you show up to exchange your vouchers, but arriving an hour in advance should be more than sufficient.

We're often asked whether the seats you're assigned when exchanging your voucher are inferior to those sold at full price. The answer is often, but not always, yes. As discussed above, you can improve your assigned seating somewhat by exchanging your voucher well in advance of showtime. If seats at a showroom are first-come, first-served, or assigned on the spot by a maître d', your chances of scoring a primo seat are as good as anyone else's.

3. At Las Vegas Advisor's **lvahotels.com,** you can buy discounted tickets in advance. Because the Las Vegas Advisor is the best-selling Vegas periodical for gamblers and frequent visitors, hotels and show producers offers **lvahotels .com** some of the better deals available. On the menu bar at the top of the page click shows and nightlife. When the Shows and Nightlife page comes up, click on production shows. At the end of the paragraph that precedes the listings, click Top LVA Show Deals.

4. Showrooms, like other Las Vegas hotel and casino operations, sometimes offer special deals. Sometimes free or discounted shows are offered with lodging packages. Likewise, coupons from complimentary local tourist magazines or casino "fun books" (see pages 13–14) provide discounts or two-for-one options. Since these specials come and go, your best bet is to inquire about currently operating deals and discounts when you call for show reservations. If you plan to lodge at a hotel-casino where there is a show you want to see, ask about room-show combo specials when you make your room reservations. When you arrive in Las Vegas, pick up copies of the many visitor magazines. Scour the show ads for discount coupons.

DINNER SHOWS

SOME DINNER SHOWS REPRESENT GOOD DEALS, others less so. Be aware that with all dinner shows, your drinks will be extra, and invariably expensive. Food quality at dinner shows varies. In general, it can be characterized as acceptable, but certainly not exceptional. What you are buying is limited-menu banquet service for 300–500 people. Whenever a hotel kitchen tries to feed that many people at once, it is at some cost in terms of the quality of the meal and the service.

At *Tournament of Kings,* all shows include a dinner of Cornish hen with soup, potatoes, vegetable, dessert, and choice of nonalcoholic beverage for about $59 per person, plus taxes and gratuities. *Tournament of Kings* is described in detail later in the chapter. *Tony 'n' Tina's Wedding* at Bally's integrates the meal into the unfolding story line of the show. At *Tony 'n' Tina's,* you're a wedding guest. You're sucked into the story and expected to role-play as the show demands. The same goes for the murder mystery production *Marriage Can Be Murder* at the D.

Several casinos offer show-and-dinner combos where you get dinner and a show for a special price, but dinner is served in one of the casinos' restaurants instead of in the showrooms. Many restaurants provide only coffee-shop ambience, but the food is palatable and a good deal for the money. At each casino, you can eat either before or after the early show.

Early versus Late Shows

If you attend a late show, you'll have time for a leisurely dinner before the performance. For those who prefer to eat late, the early show followed by dinner works best. Both shows are identical, except that for some topless revues the early show is covered and the late show is topless. On weekdays, late shows are usually more lightly attended. On weekends, particularly at the most popular shows, the opposite is often the case.

PRACTICAL MATTERS

What to Wear to the Show

While it is by no means required, guests tend to dress up a bit when they go to a show. For a performance in the main showrooms at Bellagio,

Caesars Palace, Mandalay Bay, Wynn Las Vegas, Wynn Encore, Aria, The Venetian, The Palazzo, or the Mirage, gentlemen will feel more comfortable in sport coats, with or without neckties. Women generally wear suits, dresses, skirt-and-blouse/sweater combinations, and even semiformal attire. That having been said, however, you'll find a third to a half of the audience at any of these casinos dressed more casually than described.

Showrooms at the Luxor, Stratosphere, Monte Carlo, New York–New York, Treasure Island (TI), the MGM Grand, Harrah's, Rio, Flamingo, Westgate Las Vegas, Paris Las Vegas, Tropicana, Planet Hollywood, and Riviera are a bit less dressy (sport coats are fine, but slacks and sweaters or sport shirts are equally acceptable for men), while showrooms at the Excalibur, The LINQ, The Orleans, Sam's Town, Suncoast, Sunset Station, Texas Station, House of Blues at Mandalay Bay, Golden Nugget, and Hard Rock are the least formal of all (come as you are). All of the comedy clubs are informal, though you would not feel out of place in a sport coat or, for women, a dress.

Getting to and from the Show

When you make your reservations, always ask what time you need to arrive for seating, and whether you should proceed directly to the showroom or stop first at the box office. You are normally asked to arrive 1 hour before the curtain rises, though ½ hour or even less will do if you already have your reserved-seat tickets (ticket will show a designated row and seat number). If you are driving to another hotel for a show and do not wish to avail yourself of valet parking, be forewarned that many casinos' self-parking lots are quite distant from the showroom. Give yourself an extra 20 minutes or more to park, walk to the casino, and find the showroom.

unofficial **TIP**
After shows, patrons flood the valets. To avoid delays, your best bet is to use self-parking and give yourself some extra time, or use valet parking and plan to stick around the casino for a while after the show.

A show with a large seating capacity in one of the major casinos can make for some no-win situations when it comes to parking. At all of the megahotels except Wynn Las Vegas and Wynn Encore, self-parking is either way off in the boonies or in a dizzying multistory garage, so your inclination may be to use valet parking. After the show, however, 1,000–1,650 patrons head for home, inundating the valets, particularly after a late show.

Invited Guests and Line Passes

Having arrived at the casino and found the showroom, you will normally join other show-goers waiting to be seated. If the showroom assigns reserved seats, the process is simple: just show your tickets to an usher and you will be directed to your seats. At many showrooms, generally those without reserved seating, you will encounter two lines. One line, usually quite long, is where you will queue up unless you are an "invited guest." There is a separate line for these privileged folks that allows them to be seated without waiting in line or coming an

unofficial **TIP**
If you are an invited guest under any circumstances, always arrive to be seated for a show at least 30 minutes early.

hour early. Most invited guests are gamblers who are staying at the host casino. Some have been provided with "comps" (complimentary admission) to the show. These are usually regular casino customers or high rollers. If you are giving the casino a lot of action, do not be shy about requesting a comp to the show.

Gamblers or casino-hotel guests of more modest means are frequently given line passes. These guests pay the same price as anyone else for the show but are admitted without waiting via the Invited-Guest line. To obtain a line pass, approach a floorman or pit boss (supervisory personnel are usually distinguished from dealers by their suits and ties) and explain that you have been doing a fair amount of gambling in their casino. Tell him or her that you have reservations for that evening's show and ask if you can have a line pass. Particularly if you ask on Sunday through Thursday, your chances of being accommodated are good.

Reservations, Tickets, and Maître d' Seating

If, like most guests, you do not have a line pass, you will have to go through the process of entering the showroom and being seated. A dwindling number of showrooms practice what is known as maître d' seating. This means that, except in the case of certain invited guests, no seats are reserved. If you called previously and made a reservation, that will have been duly noted and the showroom will have your party listed on the reservations roster, but you will not actually be assigned a seat until you appear before the maître d'.

At the comedy clubs and an increasing number of major showrooms, you will be directed to a booth variously labeled "Tickets," "Reservations," "Box Office," or "Guest Services." The attendant will verify your reservation and ask you to go ahead and pay. Once paid, you will receive a ticket to show the maître d' upon entering the showroom. The ticket does not reserve you any specific seat; you still need to see the maître d' about that. Also, the ticket does not include gratuities for your server in the showroom unless specifically stated.

As discussed earlier, most showrooms have discarded maître d' seating in favor of "box office" or "hard" seating. Specific reserved-seat assignments are printed on each ticket sold, as at a football game or on Broadway.

Where to Sit

When it comes to show seating, there are two primary considerations: visibility and comfort. The newer main showrooms at Caesars Palace, Mandalay Bay, Bellagio, Mirage, TI, MGM Grand, The Venetian, The Palazzo, Paris, Luxor, Wynn Las Vegas, Wynn Encore, Aria, Planet Hollywood, Monte Carlo, New York–New York, Stratosphere, and Westgate Las Vegas provide plush theater seats, many with drink holders in the arms. The best accommodations in older showrooms are roomy booths, which provide an unencumbered view of the show. The vast majority of seats in these showrooms, however, and all in some, will be at banquet tables—a euphemism for very long, narrow tables where a dozen or more guests are squeezed together so tightly they can hardly move much less eat. When the show starts, guests seated at the banquet tables must turn their chairs around in order to see. This requires no small degree of timing and cooperation, since every person on the same side of the table must move in unison.

Showrooms generally will have banquet-table seating right in front of the stage. Next, on a tier that rises a step or two, will be a row of plush booths. These booths are often reserved for the casino's best customers (and sometimes for big tippers). Many maître d's would rather see these booths go unoccupied than have high rollers come to the door at the last minute and not be able to give them good seats. Behind the booths and up a step will be more banquet tables. Moving away from the stage and up additional levels, the configuration of booths and banquet tables is repeated on each tier.

For a big production show on a wide stage *(Jubilee!,* Cirque du Soleil shows, Celine Dion, or *Jersey Boys)*, you want to sit in the middle and back a little. Being too close makes it difficult to see everything without wagging your head back and forth. Likewise, at a concert by a band or musical celebrity headliner, partway back and in the center is best. This positioning provides good visibility and removes you from the direct line of fire of amplifiers and lights. This advice, of course, does not apply to avid fans who want to fling their underwear or room keys at the star. For smaller production shows on medium-sized stages *(Penn & Teller, Legends in Concert,* and such), right up front is great. This is also true for headliners like Rita Rudner. For female impersonators the illusion is more effective if you are back a little bit.

 Be aware that comedians often single out unwary guests sitting down front for harassment, or worse, incorporate them into the act.

At comedy clubs and smaller shows, there are really no bad seats, provided the showroom has tiered seating (seating that is arranged in sloping tiers so that spectators in the back can see over the heads of those in front). In flat-floored showrooms you might not be able to see much at all if a taller person is seated in front of you. A high stage helps in flat-floored showrooms but doesn't completely resolve the problem.

Seat Switching

As mentioned earlier, VIP tickets are almost never a good deal. We buy general admission and then enter the showroom just a minute or two before showtime. Because shows rarely sell out their VIP tickets, we waltz to the front of the showroom and plop down in one of the invariably unoccupied VIP seats. This works best in small showrooms and for one or two people. Don't expect to score four VIP seats together. Here's another strategy we use for small showrooms where seats are assigned: Be seated where directed but scope out the better unoccupied seats. About 5 or so minutes into the show, when it's not likely someone will show up and occupy the better seats, we move into

them. One of our researchers who finds direct seat switching too bra-
zen exits the theater as if going to the restroom and then scores a better
seat when she reenters.

Getting a Good Seat at Showrooms with Maître d' Seating

1. ARRIVE EARLY No maître d' can assign you a seat that's already
taken. This is particularly important for Friday and Saturday shows. We
have seen comped invited guests (the casino's better customers) get lousy
seats because they waited until the last minute to show up.

2. TRY TO GO ON AN OFF NIGHT (that is, Sunday through Thursday)
Your chances of getting a good seat are always better on weeknights,
when there is less demand. If a citywide convention is in town, weekdays
also may be crowded.

**3. TRY TO KNOW WHERE (AS PRECISELY AS POSSIBLE) YOU WOULD LIKE
TO SIT.** In showrooms with maître d' seating, it is always to your advantage to specifically state your seating preferences.

4. UNDERSTAND YOUR TIPPING ALTERNATIVES Basically, you have
three options:

> **1.** Don't tip. **2.** Tip the maître d'. **3.** Tip the captain instead of the maître d'.

DON'T TIP Politely request a good seat instead of tipping. This option
actually works better than you would imagine in all but a few showrooms, particularly Sunday through Thursday. If the showroom is not
sold out and you arrive early, simply request a seat in a certain area. Tell
the maître d', "We would like something down front in the center." Then
allow the captain (the showroom staff person who actually takes you
to your seat) to show you the seats the maître d' has assigned. If the
assigned seat is not to your liking, ask to be seated somewhere else of
your choosing. The captain almost always has the authority to make the
seat-assignment change without consulting the maître d'.

TIP THE MAÎTRE D' When you tip the maître d', it is helpful to know
with whom you are dealing. First, the maître d' is the man or woman in
charge of the showroom. The showrooms are their domain, and they
rule as surely as battalion commanders. Maître d's in the better showrooms are powerful and wealthy people, with some maître d's taking in
as much as $1,650 a night. Even though these tips are pooled and shared
in some proportion with the captains, it's still a lot of money.

When you tip a maître d', especially in the better showrooms, you
can assume it will take a fairly hefty tip to impress him, especially on a
busy night. The bottom line, however, is that you are not out to impress
anyone; you just want a good seat. Somebody has to sit in the good
seats, and those who do not tip, or tip small, have to be seated regardless. So, if you arrive early and tip $15 to $20 (for a couple) in the major
showrooms, and $5 to $10 in the smaller rooms, you should get decent
seats. If it is a weekend or you know the show is extremely popular or
sold out, bump the tip up a little. If you arrive late on a busy night, ask
the maître d' if there are any good seats left before you proffer the tip.

Have your tip in hand when you reach the maître d'. Don't fool around with your wallet or purse as if you are buying hot dogs and beer at the ball park. Fold the money and hold it in the palm of your hand, arranged so that the maître d' can see exactly how big the tip is without unfolding and counting the bills. State your preference for seating at the same time you inconspicuously place the bills in the palm of his hand. If you think all this protocol is pretty ridiculous, we agree. But style counts, and observing the local customs may help get you a better seat.

A variation is to tip with some appropriate denomination of the casino's own chips. Chips are as good as currency to the maître d' and implicitly suggest that you have been gambling with that denomination of chips in his casino. This single gesture, which costs you nothing more than your cash tip, makes you an insider and a more valued customer in the eyes of the maître d'.

Many maître d's are warm and friendly and treat you in a way that shows they appreciate your business. These maître d's are approachable and reasonable, and they will go out of their way to make you comfortable. There are also a number of maître d's and captains, unfortunately, who are extremely cold, formal, and arrogant. Mostly older men dressed in tuxedos, they usually have gray hair and an imperious bearing and can seem rather imposing or hostile. Do not be awed or intimidated. Be forthright and, if necessary, assertive; you will usually be accommodated.

TIP THE CAPTAIN Using this strategy, tell the maître d' where you would like to sit, but do not offer a tip. Then follow the captain to your assigned seats. If your seats are good, you have not spent an extra nickel. If the assigned seats are less than satisfactory, slip the captain a tip and ask if there might be something better. If you see seats you would like to have that are unoccupied, point them out to the captain. Remember, however, that the first row of booths is usually held in reserve.

Before the Show Begins

Some showrooms serve drinks, while others offer self-service. A few of the variations you will encounter: A cash bar and no table service; if you want a drink before the show, you walk to the bar and buy it. Drinks are included, but there is no table service; you take a receipt stub to the bar and exchange it for drinks. In other showrooms there is table service where you can obtain drinks from a server.

In showrooms with table service, the servers run around like crazy trying to get everybody served before the show. Because all the people at a given table are not necessarily seated at the same time, the server responsible for that table may make five or more passes before everyone is taken care of. If your party is one of the last to be seated at a table, stay cool. You *will* be noticed and you *will* be served.

Bladder Matters

Be forewarned that in most showrooms there is no restroom, and that the nearest restroom is invariably a long way off, reachable only via a convoluted trail through the casino. Since the majority of show-goers arrive early and consume drinks, it is not uncommon to start feeling a little pressure on the bladder minutes before showtime. If you assume that you can slip out to the restroom and come right back, think again. If you are at the Westgate Las Vegas or the Tropicana, give yourself more than 10 minutes for the round-trip, and prepare for a quest. If you get to the can and back without getting lost, consider yourself lucky.

At most other showrooms, restrooms are somewhat closer but certainly not convenient. The Riviera, The LINQ, Luxor, Planet Hollywood, Harrah's, New York–New York, MGM Grand, Stratosphere, The Venetian/Palazzo, Wynn Las Vegas, Aria, and Mirage, however, seem to have considered that show guests may not wish to combine emptying their bladders with a 5-mile hike. Showrooms in these casinos are situated in close and much-appreciated proximity to the restrooms.

SELECTING *a* SHOW

SELECTING A LAS VEGAS SHOW is a matter of timing, budget, taste, and schedule. Celebrity headliners are booked long in advance but may play only for a couple of days or weeks. If seeing Elton John or Jerry Seinfeld is a big priority for your Las Vegas trip, you will have to schedule your visit to coincide with their appearances. If the timing of your visit is not flexible, as in the case of conventioneers, you will be relegated to picking from those stars playing when you are in town. To find out which shows and headliners are playing before you leave home, call the Las Vegas Convention and Visitors Authority at ☎ 702-892-7576 (**lvcva.com**). On the Internet, go to **visitlasvegas.com** or **lvahotels.com.**

Older visitors are often more affluent than younger visitors. It is no accident that most celebrity headliners are chosen, and most production shows created, to appeal to the 40-and-over crowd. If we say a Las Vegas production show is designed for a mature audience, we mean that the theme, music, variety acts, and humor appeal primarily to older guests. Most Las Vegas production shows target patrons 40–50 years old and up, while a few appeal to audiences 55 years of age and older.

As the post–World War II baby boomers have become older and more affluent, they have become a primary market for Las Vegas. Stars from the "golden days" of rock and roll, as well as folk singers from the 1960s, are turning up in the main showrooms all across town. On one occasion, Paul Revere and the Raiders, the Coasters, the Platters, the Temptations, the Four Tops, B. J. Thomas, and Arlo Guthrie were playing in different showrooms on the same night.

The hippest, avant-garde show in town is *Blue Man Group* (Monte Carlo), which targets younger audiences and is wild, loud, and conceptually very different from anything else in Las Vegas. A close runner-up is *PRISM*, a rap and hip-hop production popularly called JABBAWOCKEEZ after its featured dance crew. For in-your-face raunch with an acrobatic twist, try *Absinthe,* a hands-down favorite for under-40 Las Vegas locals. Another contender is *Recycled Precussion,* in which grooves are laid down with just about anything you can hit with a drumstick.

If you are younger than 35 years old you will also enjoy the Las Vegas production shows, though for you their cultural orientation (and usually their music) will seem a generation or two removed. Several production shows, however, have broken the mold, in the process achieving a more youthful presentation while maintaining the loyalty of older patrons. Cirque du Soleil's *Mystère* (TI) is an uproarious yet poignant odyssey in the European tradition, brimming over with unforgettable characters. Ditto for the other Cirque shows, especially *Michael Jackson ONE.* And, again, the comedy clubs have a more youthful orientation.

LAS VEGAS SHOWS FOR THE UNDER-21 CROWD

AN EVER-INCREASING NUMBER of showrooms offer productions appropriate for younger viewers. Circus Circus provides complimentary high-quality circus acts about once every half-hour, and *Tournament of Kings* at the Excalibur is a family dinner show featuring jousting and other benign medieval entertainments. Other family candidates include *Legends in Concert,* a celebrity-impersonation show at the Flamingo, and all Cirque du Soleil shows except *Zumanity.* Afternoon shows are also a good bet for families.

Many of the celebrity-headliner shows are fine for children, and a few of the production shows offer a covered early show to accommodate families. Of the topless production shows, some operate on the basis of parental discretion while others do not admit anyone under age 21. Comedy clubs and comedy theater usually will admit teenage children accompanied by an adult. All continuously running shows are profiled later in this section. The profile will tell you whether the show is topless or particularly racy. If you have questions about a given showroom's policy for those under age 21, call the showroom's reservation and information number listed in the profile.

▌ CELEBRITY-HEADLINER ROOMS

CHOOSING WHICH CELEBRITY HEADLINER to see is a matter of personal taste, though stars like Cher and David Copperfield seem to have the ability to rev up any audience. Our point is to suggest that the talent, presence, drive, and showmanship of many Las Vegas headliners often exceed all expectations, and that adhering to the limitations of your preferences may prevent you from seeing many truly extraordinary performers. Las Vegas is about gambling, after all. Do not be reluctant to take a chance on a headliner who is not familiar to you.

Most of the major headliners play at a relatively small number of showrooms. Profiles of the major celebrity showrooms and their regular headliners follow. The list is not all-inclusive, but it will give you an idea of where to call if you are interested in a certain headliner.

Long-running (that is, a year or more) celebrity-headliner shows, including Celine Dion, Rita Rudner, and so on, are reviewed in depth in our coverage of continuously running shows later in this chapter.

The Axis at Planet Hollywood

RESERVATIONS AND INFORMATION ☎ 855-234-7469 or 866-693-2425; planethollywoodresort.com

Frequent headliners Britney Spears, Justin Bieber, Jimmy Buffet, charity events, beauty pageants. Usual showtimes 8 p.m. Dark Varies. Approximate admission price $30–$400. Showroom size 4,500 seats.

DESCRIPTION AND COMMENTS Formerly The Aladdin Center for the Performing Arts, the Axis is a 4,500-seat concert venue with three tiered sections of seating arrayed in a fan-shaped configuration facing a broad stage. The venue hosts concerts, charity events, and beauty pageants, including Miss America, Miss Universe (no one from Klingon has ever won), and Miss USA. Acoustics are good, though the decibel level of rock concerts, such as Britney Spears's *Piece of Me* show, is overwhelming. Sight lines are universally good, though the rear third of the theater is quite distant from the stage. Nobody has opera glasses anymore, but the Axis might well be the place where they make a comeback.

CONSUMER TIPS The Axis is the land of big productions, so center seats a little less than one third back usually serve best. All seats are plush theater chairs. Restrooms are located near the showroom. If you drive, park in the Miracle Mile Shops garage rather than at Planet Hollywood.

Hard Rock Hotel—The Joint

RESERVATIONS AND INFORMATION ☎ 702-693-5000 or 800-693-7625; hardrockhotel.com

Frequent headliners Top current and oldies rock, pop, blues, folk, electronic, and world music stars. Usual showtimes 8 p.m. Dark Varies. Approximate admission price $25–$600. Showroom size 4,000 persons.

DESCRIPTION AND COMMENTS The Joint, once an intimate concert venue, has been redesigned and more than doubled in size with a new, larger stage and cutting-edge lighting and video effects. The main floor of the multi-level venue can be configured for theater-type seating, lounge seating (two to four chairs around a small cocktail table), or for standing only. So versatile is The Joint that it can set up for professional prize fights. Lines of sight are super, as is the sound system. For bands with a video dimension, there are 36 monitors, including a huge high-definition screen on each side of the stage. Paul McCartney, one of the first to perform in the expanded facility, said, "It's good in here, isn't it?" The upper levels of The Joint provide standing-room-only balcony viewing as well as seating and VIP accommodations. Acoustics are excellent with a feltlike material covering the walls to minimize echo and sound bleeds.

CONSUMER TIPS If you don't want to be put in balcony Siberia where you can hear well enough but see nothing, or pinned against the stage for the whole show by a crush of sweaty rowdies, don't buy standing-room tickets. Book early for reserved seating—or shrug and say, "Oh well."

The Hard Rock Hotel box office sells reserved seats to shows at The Joint. You can purchase tickets via phone using your credit card or in person at the box office. Shows at The Joint are hot tickets in Las Vegas and sell out quickly, so buy your tickets as far in advance as possible.

Mandalay Bay—House of Blues

RESERVATIONS AND INFORMATION ☎ 702-632-7600 or 877-632-7600; **hob.com**

Frequent headliners Santana, as well as current and former pop, rock, R&B, reggae, folk, and country stars. **Usual showtimes** Varies. **Dark** Varies. **Approximate admission price** $12–$100. **Showroom size** 1,800 seats.

DESCRIPTION AND COMMENTS House of Blues is a concert hall, very different from The Joint at the Hard Rock, with which it competes head-on for performers and concertgoers. The House of Blues is more like an opera house than the high school gym-like Joint: low-ceilinged, multi-tiered, and split-leveled, which gets the audience as close to the act as possible. To that end, the acoustics are much better than The Joint's, but the House of Blues can get claustrophobic. Also, the sight lines are highly variable, even bizarre, especially for a modern room—it's almost as if the designers were modifying an old theater. And it doesn't seem to have much to do with how much you pay for a seat: some bad seats (in the nosebleed section and on the sides of the stage) don't cost much less than the best seats or much more than the cheapest tickets.

Live music is presented almost every night of the year. Major headliners appear once or twice a week at 8 p.m.; for these shows you must be 21 years old to attend. Performers have included Ted Nugent, Rusted Root, Santana, Violent Femmes, Al Green, and Frank Zappa. Filling in the booking gaps are minor shows; check the hotline and website. You must be 18 years or older for most of them (the few others are designated "all ages").

CONSUMER TIPS The box office is open 9 a.m.–9 p.m. The headliner shows sell out extremely fast, though you can usually pick up standing-room-only tickets, where you'll be sardined in front of the stage (watch your wallet). If money is no object, try to get a VIP seat front and center in the balcony. If you can't, you might as well just opt for the cheap standing room, as the upper balcony and many of the loge seats aren't worth the extra money. Indeed, many people give up their bad reserved seats to move down to the floor where they can see the whole stage!

MGM Grand—Grand Garden Arena

RESERVATIONS AND INFORMATION ☎ 702-891-7777 or 800-929-1111; **mgmgrand.com**

Frequent headliners National acts, superstars, televised boxing, wrestling, and other sporting events. **Usual showtimes** Varies. **Dark** Varies. **Approximate admission price** $20–$1,250. **Showroom size** 16,800 seats.

DESCRIPTION AND COMMENTS This 275,000-square-foot special-events center is designed to accommodate everything from sporting events and concerts to major trade exhibitions. The venue also offers auxiliary meeting rooms and ballrooms adjacent to the entertainment center. Barbra Streisand christened this venue with her first concert in more than 20 years on New Year's Eve 1993. Championship boxing events are favorite attractions at the Grand Garden Arena, as are the many big-name musical concerts.

CONSUMER TIPS Reserved-seat tickets can be purchased one to two months in advance with your credit card online or by calling the MGM Grand main reservations number or Ticketmaster outlets (☎ 800-745-3000), for most but not all shows. If you are not staying at the MGM Grand, either arrive by cab or give yourself plenty of extra time to park and make your way to the arena.

MGM Grand—Hollywood Theatre

RESERVATIONS AND INFORMATION ☎ 702-891-7777 or 800-929-1111; **mgmgrand.com**

Frequent headliners David Copperfield, Howie Mandel, and Tom Jones. Usual showtimes Varies. Dark Varies. Approximate admission price $70–$100. Showroom size 740 seats.

DESCRIPTION AND COMMENTS A comfortable, modern showroom, with all front-facing seats, the Hollywood Theatre hosts a range of musical and celebrity-headliner productions for one- to three-week engagements.

CONSUMER TIPS Purchase reserved-seat tickets one to two months in advance with your credit card online or by calling the MGM Grand's main reservations number. Children are allowed at most presentations (check first). If you are not staying at the MGM Grand, either arrive by cab or give yourself of extra time to park and make your way to the showroom.

The Orleans—Orleans Showroom

RESERVATIONS AND INFORMATION ☎ 702-365-7111 or 800-675-3267; **orleanscasino.com**

Frequent headliners Clint Black, Michael Bolton, Air Supply, Four Tops, Kenny G, Bill Maher, Dennis Miller, and Don Rickles. Usual showtimes Varies. Dark Varies. Approximate admission price $35–$40. Showroom size 850 seats.

DESCRIPTION AND COMMENTS This small but comfortable showroom offers tiered theater seats arranged in a crescent around the stage. Designed for solo performers and bands, The Orleans Showroom is an intimate venue for concerts with good visibility from anywhere in the house. The star lineup runs the gamut with a concentration on country-and-western singer celebrities.

CONSUMER TIPS This showroom features some great talent at bargain prices. All seats are reserved. Tickets can be purchased at the box office to the left of the showroom, online, or over the phone.

Smith Center for the Performing Arts

RESERVATIONS AND INFORMATION ☎ 702-749-2000; 361 Symphony Park Ave., Las Vegas; **thesmithcenter.com**

Frequent headliners Touring Broadway musicals and dramas, classical and contemporary concerts, dance, and comedy. Usual Showtimes Varies. Dark Varies. Approximate admission price $24–$150. Showroom sizes 258–2,050 seats and an alfresco theater seating 2,500.

DESCRIPTION AND COMMENTS The zenith of Downtown's redevelopment is a world-class performance center in Symphony Park, presenting a mélange of entertainment primarily developed for locals and disproving the adage that Las Vegas is a cultural abyss. The new 61-acre campus includes three state-of-the-art theaters presenting major productions and artists: the Jazz Cabaret seating 258, the 300-seat Troesch Studio Theater, and the 2,050-seat Reynolds Hall. The fourth performance venue is an outdoor lawn seating up to 2,500 for starlight plays and concerts. The adjacent Boman Pavilion houses three resident companies: Nevada Ballet Theater, Las Vegas Contemporary Dance Theater, and The Las Vegas Philharmonic. The architectural design of the buildings pays homage to the 1935 Art Deco style of historic Hoover Dam, the genesis of Las Vegas's initial growth. The dam's towers are represented in the center's logo and replicated throughout the center, and the winged figures at the dam take flight in the Grand Lobby. The 170-foot tower's 47 carillon bells emit four-octave tonal canapes. Symphony Park itself is an open-air gallery of public art.

CONSUMER TIPS Moderately priced beverages and light snacks are served in the Jazz Cabaret and in the lobbies of Reynolds Hall. Each level features restrooms and concession stands, eliminating interminable lines at intermission. Wheelchair seating is easily accessible. Free parking is available in the North Lot on City Parkway. Valet parking is $8 and available in front of Reynolds Hall.

PRODUCTION SHOWS

LAS VEGAS PREMIER PRODUCTION SHOWS: COMPARING APPLES AND ORANGES

WHILE WE ACKNOWLEDGE THAT LAS VEGAS production shows are difficult to compare and that audiences of differing tastes and ages have different preferences, we have nevertheless ranked the continuously running shows to give you an idea of our favorites. This is definitely an apples-and-oranges comparison (how can you compare *Zumanity* to *Blue Man Group?*), but one based on each show's impact, vitality, originality, pace, continuity, crescendo, and ability to entertain.

We would hasten to add that even the continuously running shows change acts and revise their focus periodically. Expect our list, therefore, to change from year to year. Also, be comforted by the knowledge that while some shows are better than others, there are only one or two real dogs. The quality of entertainment among the continuously running production shows is exceptional. By way of analogy, we could rank baseball players according to their performance in a given All-Star game, but the entire list, from top to bottom, would still be All-Stars. You get the idea.

A Word about Small Showrooms

During the past couple of years, we have seen a number of casinos convert their lounge into a small showroom. Though the stage in these showrooms is routinely about the size of a beach towel, productions are mounted that include complex choreography, animal acts, and, in one notable demonstration, an illusionist catching bullets in his teeth. In the case of musical revues, as many as four very thin or three average-sized hula dancers can fit comfortably on the stage at one time.

A real problem with some smaller shows is that they often cost as much as productions in Las Vegas's major showrooms. Another problem is that small shows often play to even smaller crowds. We saw a performance of *That's Magic* at O'Shea's where the cast outnumbered the audience. Though the show featured talented illusionists, a good ventriloquist, and some dancers, the small facility made the production seem amateurish. It was heartrending to see professional entertainers work so hard for such a tiny audience. We felt self-conscious and uncomfortable ourselves, as well as embarrassed for the performers.

When it comes to smaller showrooms, simpler is better. That's why *Mac King* and *Purple Reign* work so well: both shows take a minimalist approach. Additionally, both shows play in casinos large enough to draw an audience. Little showrooms in smaller casinos that attempt to mount big productions create only parody and end up looking foolish. Better that they revert to offering lounge shows.

We've given up trying to cover the productions that play in these small showrooms, mostly because the shows are very short-lived. If a small-showroom production is exceptionally good and demonstrates staying power, however, we sometimes review it right along with the full-scale shows. In this edition, for example, we provide full reviews of seven small-room productions. (This discussion, by the way, does not apply to comedy clubs, which work best in small rooms.)

Gotta Keep on Movin'

If every player in major-league baseball were a free agent, the willy-nilly team-hopping would bear a close resemblance to the Las Vegas entertainment scene. If, after reading our show reviews, you discover that your preferred performer or production has disappeared from the listed showroom, don't despair. Chances are good that the show has moved to a different venue. Melinda, "The First Lady of Magic" (now retired), holds the all-time record, having played at almost a dozen different casinos during her career.

LAS VEGAS SHOW HIT PARADE

SIMPLY BASED ON EXCELLENCE, we rank the continuously running productions playing the showrooms of Las Vegas (see the facing page). We have apples, oranges, artichokes, and even pomegranates here, so we're not making any direct comparisons. For each show listed, all we're saying is that, in our opinion, that show is a better night's entertainment than those ranking below it.

Note: Excluded from the ranking but covered separately are celebrity headliners, long-engagement stand-up comics as well as comedy clubs, hypnosis shows, afternoon shows, and straight-up skin shows for both men and women. Preferences for the foregoing are primarily influenced by personal taste. The remaining shows can be appreciated by most anyone.

Las Vegas Show Hit Parade

RANK	SHOW	LOCATION
1.	Cirque du Soleil's *Mystère*	Treasure Island
2.	Cirque du Soleil's *LOVE*	Mirage
3.	*Jersey Boys*	Paris Las Vegas
4.	Cirque du Soleil's *KA*	MGM Grand
5.	Cirque du Soleil's *Michael Jackson ONE*	Mandalay Bay
6.	*Celine Dion*	Caesars Palace
7.	Cirque du Soleil's *Zarkana*	Aria
8.	Cirque du Soleil's *"O"*	Bellagio
9.	*Blue Man Group*	Monte Carlo
10.	*Terry Fator*	Mirage
11.	*Le Rêve*	Wynn Las Vegas
12.	Cirque du Soleil's *Zumanity*	New York–New York
13.	*Raiding the Rock Vault*	Westgate Las Vegas
14.	*David Copperfield*	MGM Grand
15.	*Vegas! The Show*	Miracle Mile Shops
16.	*Frankie Moreno*	Stratosphere
17.	*Jubilee!*	Bally's
18.	*Panda!*	The Palazzo
19.	*Penn & Teller*	Rio
20.	*Million Dollar Quartet*	Harrah's
21.	*Absinthe*	Caesars Palace
22.	*Gordie Brown*	Golden Nugget
23.	*Human Nature*	The Venetian
24.	*Rock of Ages*	The Venetian
25.	*Recycled Percussion*	LINQ Hotel
26.	*MO5AIC*	Westgate Las Vegas
27.	*The Rat Pack Is Back*	Rio
28.	*Donny & Marie*	Flamingo
29.	*JABBAWOCKEEZ PRISM*	Luxor
30.	*Illusions*	Riviera
31.	*Menopause: The Musical*	Luxor
32.	*Defending the Caveman*	Harrah's
33.	*Tournament of Kings*	Excalibur
34.	*Pin Up*	Stratosphere
35.	*Legends In Concert*	Flamingo
36.	*Hitzville The Show*	Miracle Mile Shops
37.	*Country Music Superstars*	Bally's
38.	Cirque du Soleil's *CRISS ANGEL Believe*	Luxor
39.	*Tony 'n' Tina's Wedding*	Bally's
40.	*V: The Ultimate Variety Show*	Miracle Mile Shops
41.	*Comedy Magic Show with Mike Hammer*	Four Queens
42.	*Australian Bee Gees Show*	Excalibur
43.	*Frank Marino's Divas Las Vegas*	LINQ Hotel
44.	*B-A Tribute to the Beatles*	Miracle Mile Shops
45.	*Marriage Can Be Murder*	The D

LAS VEGAS SHOW PROFILES

FOLLOWING IS A PROFILE OF EACH of the continuously running shows, listed alphabetically by the name of the show. If you are not sure of the name of a show, consult the previous section. Comedy clubs, afternoon shows, and limited-engagement celebrity-headliner showrooms are profiled in separate sections. Prices are approximate and fluctuate about as often as you brush your teeth.

Following the alphabetized profiles are comments regarding a number of productions that for various reasons we elected not to profile. Reasons range from too few performances to redundancy to mediocrity or worse.

Absinthe ★★★½

APPEAL BY AGE   **18-21** ★★★★   **21-37** ★★★★   **38-50** ★★★   **51+** ★★½

HOST CASINO AND SHOWROOM Caesars Palace—Spiegeltent on the Roman Plaza; ☎ 800-745-3000; **ticketmaster.com**

Type of show Low-tech, low-brow circus. **Admission** $99–$124. **Cast size** 23. **Night of lowest attendance** Wednesday. **Usual showtimes** Wednesday–Sunday, 8 and 10 p.m. **Dark** Monday and Tuesday. **Special comments** No one under 18 admitted. **Topless** Yes (male), almost (female). **Duration of presentation** 90 minutes.

DESCRIPTION AND COMMENTS It's a silly, sultry, risqué interactive and participatory experience. Equal parts cabaret, burlesque, circus, and midway sideshow, *Absinthe* incorporates an impudent cast of slick professionals. The aerial and acrobatic performances are separated by repartee, tomfoolery, and other shtick hosted by an in-your-face ringmaster and his ditzy female assistant. Among the rotating acts are a quartet of tubby aerialists, an acrobat balancing on a tower of chairs, a chanteuse who sings and strips while surrounded by four guys in drag, a limber lady on ropes, two musclemen with exceptional equilibrium, and a trio of highly focused low-wire tightrope walkers. While the performers are skilled and execute wonders on a tiny circular stage, without fail each act features the artists disrobing, which gives you an idea of the general tenor of the goings-on.

Occasionally, celebrity guests are featured. The show includes some audience participation. Expect raunch and lots of dirty jokes as the MC comments on the dress, physical attributes, proclivities, and vulnerabilities of the performers and audience members in the front rows and on the aisles. A libation or three will help you decide whether this is a clever lampoon of big-ticket gymnastic-infused performance art, a bawdy tour de farce, or a below-the-belt satire.

Outside of an Army barracks you'd be hard pressed to find language as raunchy as what you'll hear in *Absinthe*. And it doesn't stop there, visuals abound: consider a performer munching on a used Tampon. Yet this is perhaps the favorite show of Las Vegas locals under 40—the show they take out-of-town guests to see. There's definitely an age divide with *Absinthe*. Younger patrons more often than not love it, while those over 50 are frequently stunned to the point of being exceedingly uncomfortable. Unless you're going for shock value, this is probably not the show to see with your mom (or, for that matter, anyone who won't enjoy a lively discussion about vaginas, penises, breasts, and bowels).

CONSUMER TIPS The 600-seat venue is a round, circus tent–like pavilion with air-conditioning. Seating is in the round and very close to the stage, so close that a performer who screws up might literally fall in your lap. Be prepared to sit on a flat floor in folding chairs. Because the stage is elevated, however, there are good lines of sight from most seats. The pavilion is outside the casino on the southeast section of the Caesars property, near the pedestrian bridge over Flamingo Road.

There is no reserved seating except for those purchasing the VIP package. Box offices in the casino do not sell *Absinthe* tickets. The *Absinthe* box office is a small, stand-alone, tollbooth of a building situated in a beer garden adjacent to the show pavilion. There are not separate windows for ticket sales and will call, so everyone is forced to endure a lengthy queue. We arrived 40 minutes before showtime and still missed the beginning of the show (which started late incidentally). If it's possible, buy or pick up your tickets earlier in the day.

American Storm ★ ★ ★

APPEAL BY AGE	UNDER 21 ★★★★★	21-37 ★★★★	38-50 ★★★	51+ ★★★

HOST CASINO AND SHOWROOM Miracle Mile Shops; ☎ 702-701-7778; **miraclemileshopslv.com**

Type of show Stud-puppy strip show. **Admission** $50–$60 plus tax. **Cast size** 7. **Night of lowest attendance** Friday. **Usual showtimes** Friday and Saturday, 9 p.m. **Dark** Sunday–Thursday. **Topless** Buff pecs. **Duration of presentation** 75 minutes.

DESCRIPTION AND COMMENTS Judging by audience reaction, *American Storm* might well be called *The Mighty Clouds of Joy.* Although this oiled-up male-nudity show doesn't offer the "full Monty" (by law no Las Vegas establishment can show complete nudity and serve alcohol), that didn't seem to matter to the howling, whooping, screaming audience made up of almost entirely women. Anyone who is laboring under the notion that women are dainty creatures, foresworn of raucous sexuality, should be a fly on the wall for the 75 minutes of *American Storm,* where piercing chants of "Touch it!" can sometimes be heard over the fray.

The half-dozen men, roughly 25 years old, are gorgeous, with rippling physiques, and they're fair dancers, too. Their choreography in lightly themed numbers, featuring cowboys, gangsters, soldiers, and the like, however, definitely takes a back seat to general prancing, gyrating, grinding, and skipping about on stage and through the audience. Several women of various body types and ages were drafted to participate in transparently configured sex acts, which makes the evening sound lurid, but it seemed to be great fun for all involved. *American Storm's* men were approved in part by *Thunder from Down Under* creator Billy Cross, so the shows are relatively comparable.

CONSUMER TIPS Arrive early to get in line and sit in the front. Don't expect dazzling costumes. During the show, there is quite a bit of dancing and it actually takes these guys a while to get their clothes off. If the typical routine was anywhere from 7 to 10 minutes, you're looking at a good 5 minutes of dancing before the guys even start stripping. After the show, everyone is invited to pose for a free Polaroid with the cast.

Anthony Cools ★★★½

APPEAL BY AGE	UNDER 21 −	21-37 ★★★★	38-50 ★★	51+ ★

HOST CASINO AND SHOWROOM Paris—Anthony Cools Theater; ☎ 702-946-7000 or 877-374-7469; **parislasvegas.com** or **anthonycools.com**

Type of show Uncensored hypnosis comedy. **Admission** $56 and $78 plus tax. **Cast size** 3 (+12 volunteers). **Night of lowest attendance** Tuesday. **Usual showtimes** Thursday–Sunday and Tuesday, 9 p.m. **Dark** Monday and Wednesday. **Topless** No. **Special comments** Must be 18 or older to attend. **Duration of presentation** 90 minutes.

DESCRIPTION AND COMMENTS If you must see a hypnotist show—and you don't mind incessant cursing and dirty talking—then this is the show. Unlike his thematic predecessor, the late and unlamented "Dr. Naughty," Anthony Cools is a slick, adroit manipulator and a truly devious creator of setups for his hypnotized zombie minions. Medical professionals who use hypnosis in their practice confirm that the volunteers really are hypnotized and are unconsciously obeying the bizarre suggestions by Cools. Some audience members volunteer as a lark and feign being hypnotized. Cools spots them almost immediately and shoos them back to their seats. The remaining subjects are put through their, mostly blue, paces, including being afflicted with burning nether regions, dealing with uncontrollably vocal genitals, and making sweet love to a chair, among other torments.

CONSUMER TIPS Obviously, this is not a show for the easily offended or intimidated. Salacious humor is the order of the day, and it's one of the bawdiest productions in town. Get in early if you want a seat near the front, and feel free to volunteer (or volunteer your friends) if you'd like to get into the hypnosis thing. Taking photos during the show is encouraged; also, an instantly produced DVD of the show you just saw is available after it's over. Grade-A blackmail material. Hypnosis shows, including Anthony Cools, are only as good as the selection of volunteers. Try to catch a weekend show, when the audience is larger; this gives Cools more to work with and increases the chances for a better show.

The Australian Bee Gees Show ★★★

APPEAL BY AGE	UNDER 21 ★★½	21-37 ★★★	38-50 ★★★½	51+ ★★★

HOST CASINO AND SHOWROOM Excalibur—Thunder from Down Under Showroom; ☎ 702-597-7600; **excalibur.com**

Type of show Disco concert. **Admission** $45–$60. **Cast size** 5. **Night of lowest attendance** Tuesday. **Usual showtimes** Saturday–Thursday, 7 p.m. **Dark** Friday. **Topless** No. **Duration of presentation** 75 minutes.

DESCRIPTION AND COMMENTS I expected John Travolta to zip-line from the rafters Branson style. Such were the muddled synapses as old disco movies fused with Alvin and the Chipmunks falsettos in a 75-minute recollection of Bee Gees discography. The concert covers the Bee Gees' career, mixing lesser-known compositions from the group's early days with their legendary hits. While Travolta's absence was a disappointment, I warmed to the music and soon found myself pumping an imaginary bass drum. I was actually grooving on a sound that gave me hives back in the day.

The music didn't change, but evidently I did. Or perhaps I was won over by a compelling live presentation courtesy of three talented vocalists from Australia. Michael Clift is the long-haired Barry Gibb. David Scott, as the only member of the five-piece group who doesn't play an instrument, is the late Robin Gibb. Scott and Clift carry most of the lead vocals, while Wayne Hosking, as the late Maurice Gibb, harmonizes and plays keyboard. The trio is backed by electric bass and drums. The impersonators stay in role throughout and refer to each other by their Bee Gees names. I had to go online for a memory jog of how the Bee Gees actually looked and was surprised by how much the Aussies resemble them—not dead ringers, but close enough. The Aussies' sound, however, is right on.

CONSUMER TIPS If you're a Bee Gees fan, you'll eat this up. Ditto for disco fans. For others, primarily due to there being so little visual stimulation, not so much. The showroom has a flat floor with no rise, but the stage is high enough that sight lines from most seats are good. The totally PG performance coupled with the opportunity to dance makes the Aussie Bee Gees a good selection for kids. Atypically, there are restrooms inside the showroom, a convenience we'd like to see everywhere. Excalibur valet parking is frequently full, so if you drive give yourself enough time to use self-parking if necessary.

B-A Tribute to the Beatles ★★★

APPEAL BY AGE	UNDER 21 ★★	21-37 ★★★	38-50 ★★★	51+ ★★★½

HOST CASINO AND SHOWROOM Miracle Mile Shops—Saxe Theater;
☎ 866-932-1818; **beatleshowvegas.com**

Type of show Musical impressionist and tribute act. Admission $60–70. Cast size 8 (4 Beatles, 2 actors, 2 dancers). Night of lowest attendance Tuesday. Usual showtimes Nightly, 5:30 p.m. Dark None. Topless No. Duration of presentation 90 minutes.

DESCRIPTION AND COMMENTS It's immediately obvious that the performers in this Beatles tribute group have honed their craft. The four artists play their own instruments on stage—no backing tapes or synthesized tracks—and they briefly sing a cappella to prove their musical chops. Vocally they are dead-on, and the audience gets especially charged up and rowdy during sing-alongs like "Twist and Shout." The costumes and musical selections follow the Beatles' career, from the early 1960s through psychedelia and into the 1970s. Film clips from various eras (including BBC footage of Brits singing badly, and the chilling moment when Howard Cosell announced Lennon's assassination during Monday Night Football) add historical context. The Beatle-esque mannerisms and speech patterns are there, even if the physical resemblances are a bit loose; George is a dead ringer, and John and Paul look decent, but Ringo, who becomes the butt of most of the show's jokes, falls more into the "haircut impression" category. A pair of backup dancers put in intermittent appearances, and two impressionists (a good Ed Sullivan and an awful Austin Powers) help bridge the musical segments. Fans of the lads from Liverpool will get their money's worth.

CONSUMER TIPS The Saxe Theater is located in the Miracle Mile Shops at Planet Hollywood. Self-parking at Planet Hollywood funnels you directly into the Miracle Mile Shops not far from the theater. Arrive 40 minutes or more before show time if you are buying or picking up tickets or redeeming ticket vouchers. More expensive VIP tickets include assigned seating in the center of the modestly sized venue; cheaper general admission seats are on the sides, but the view is nearly as good.

Beacher's Madhouse ★★★

APPEAL BY AGE	UNDER 21 N/A	21-37 ★★★★	38-50 ★★★	51+ ★★½

HOST CASINO AND SHOWROOM MGM Grand—Beacher's Madhouse Theater; ☎ 702-891-3577; **beachersmadhouse.com**

Type of show Trendy nightclub meets carnival freakshow. **Admission** $75–125. **Cast size** Varies, about two dozen. **Night of lowest attendance** Tuesday. **Usual showtimes** Tuesday–Sunday, 8 p.m.; Thursday–Saturday, 10:30 p.m. **Dark** Monday. **Topless** Maybe. **Duration of presentation** 2 hours.

DESCRIPTION AND COMMENTS Like a later-day P.T. Barnum of anything-goes evenings, nightlife impresario Jeff Beacher has been ballyhooing his bizarro brand of neo-vaudeville for nearly 15 years, beginning in New York and branching out to Hollywood, with several Vegas stopovers in between. Now he's back in Sin City, having taken over an intimate theatre inside the MGM Grand and filled it with celebrity-attracting spectacle calculated to shock and pummel your politically correct instincts into submission. Upon entering, you could mistake the luxurious venue—with comfy high-backed booths, vintage clamshell footlights along the red-curtained stage, and half-dressed dancers half-heartedly gyrating on the tables—for a formerly upscale strip club gone to seed. Then you might notice the Times Square–style off-model Muppet mascots grinding on the girls . . . or a midget (no one uses the more polite term "little people" here) dressed in a bee costume hanging from a flying harness, delivering $600 bottles of Grey Goose to deep-pocketed patrons . . . or a Pee Wee Herman impersonator kibitzing with a guy pulling cigarettes out of thin air. And if you think that sounds odd, you ain't heard nothing yet; once the real show starts at midnight, the stage comes alive with an ever-changing parade of freaks, furries, and other nightmare fodder disguised as a variety show.

Some of the acts presented—a rolla-bolla balancing acrobat, a contortionist crawling into a washing machine, a magician making doves and cats appear, a 60-year-old jumping ropes—could have been at home on the Ed Sullivan Show. Others, such as an 11-year-old rapping DJ or a hip-hop violinist, are impressive yet inexplicable. And then there are the midgets: midget tag-team wrestlers, midget Psy galloping Gangnam-style, midget African cultural dancers, and even more midgets. The grand finale involved a midget Bon Jovi tribute band (with a bootleg Tigger on drums, natch) belting out "Livin' on a Prayer."

Beacher's bills itself as theatre, but it's really more of a next-generation nightclub with intermittent entertainment; during the late show, the 20-plus minute gaps between acts are filled with deafening dance music. With apologies to *Evita,* the best show in town is the crowd at Beacher's, who outshine the ironically apathetic employees in their enthusiastic embrace of the insanity. Beacher's Madhouse is certainly a trip (in the "don't take the brown acid" sense), recalling plasticized parody of The Limelight's mid-90s heyday as seen in the film *Party Monster.* But the late show at least needs a tighter pace between acts to become a coherent entertainment experience, and Jeff Beacher himself proves an indifferent host, barely introducing the opening act before vanishing for the remainder of the evening.

CONSUMER TIPS The early show runs 8–10 p.m., with doors opening for the late show at 10:30 p.m. However, the late show's stage doesn't get started for nearly 2 hours, during which time you'll be subjected to an endless slideshow of Beacher buddying up to celebrities. General admission tickets allow you standing room only; if you want a chair, you'll have to spring for reserved seating, and only VIP bottle service customers can claim a booth.

Blue Man Group ★★★★½

APPEAL BY AGE   UNDER 21 ★★★★½   21–37 ★★★★½   38–50 ★★★★   51+ ★★★

HOST CASINO AND SHOWROOM Monte Carlo—Monte Carlo Theatre;
☎ 877-459-0268; **blueman.com** or **montecarlo.com**

Type of show Performance-art production show. **Admission** $65–$140. **Cast size** 3 + a 15-piece band. **Nights of lowest attendance** Sunday and Monday. **Usual showtimes** Nightly, 7 p.m. and 9:30 p.m. **Dark** None. **Topless** No. **Special comments** Teenagers really like this show, but the blue guys, loud music, and dark colors could scare small children (we suggest 5 years as the minimum age). **Duration of presentation** 90 minutes.

DESCRIPTION AND COMMENTS *Blue Man Group* gives Las Vegas its first large-scale introduction to that nebulous genre called "performance art." If the designation "performance art" confuses you, relax—it won't hurt a bit. *Blue Man Group* serves up a stunning show that all kinds of folks ages 8–80 can appreciate. Younger children may be frightened by the silent, wide-eyed, blue men. When *Blue Man Group* moved from the Venetian to the Monte Carlo in 2013 the show was updated and refreshed.

The three blue men are just that—blue—and bald and mute. Wearing black clothing and skullcaps slathered with bright-blue greasepaint, their fast-paced show uses music (mostly percussion) and multimedia effects to make light of contemporary art and life in the information age. The Vegas act is just one expression of a franchise that started with three friends in New York's East Village. Now you can catch their zany, wacky, smart stuff in New York, Boston, Orlando, Chicago, Berlin, and Toronto.

Funny, sometimes poignant, and always compelling, *Blue Man Group* hooks the audience even before the show begins with digital messages that ultimately spin performers and audience alike into a mutual act of joyous complicity. The trio pounds out vital, visceral tribal rhythms on complex instruments (made of PVC pipes) and makes seemingly spontaneous eruptions of visual art rendered with marshmallows and a mysterious goo. Their weekly supplies include 25.5 pounds of Cap'n Crunch, 60 Twinkies, 75 gallons of Jell-O, 996 marshmallows, and 9.5 gallons of paint. If all this sounds silly, it is, but it's also strangely thought-provoking about such various topics as the role of modern art, DNA, the way rock music moves you, and how we are all connected. (*Hint:* It's not the Internet.)

Audience participation completes the Blue Man experience. The blue men often bring audience members on stage. And a lot of folks can't help standing up to dance—and laugh. Most fun of all is the finale, when the entire audience bats around illuminated exercise balls. Magicians for the creative spirit that resides in us all, *Blue Man Group* makes everyone a co-conspirator in a culminating joyous explosion.

CONSUMER TIPS This show is decidedly different and requires an open mind to be appreciated. It also helps to be a little loose, because everybody gets sucked into the production and leaves the theater a little bit lighter in spirit, judging by the rousing standing ovations. If you don't want to be pulled onstage to become a part of the improvisation, don't sit in the first half-dozen or so rows.

Britney Spears: *Piece of Me* ★★★½

APPEAL BY AGE	UNDER 21 ★★★★	21-37 ★★★★	38-50 ★★★	51+ ★★

HOST CASINO AND SHOWROOM Planet Hollywood—The Axis Theater;
☎ 855-234-7469; **planethollywoodresort.com**

Type of show High-decibel pop concert. **Admission** $59–$179. **Cast size** 19. **Night of lowest attendance** Wednesday. **Usual showtimes** Varies; usually Wednesday, Friday, and Saturday, 9 p.m. **Dark** Sunday–Tuesday, Thursday; only performed on select weeks. **Topless** No. **Duration of presentation** 100 minutes.

DESCRIPTION AND COMMENTS Britney's back, bitches! Britney Spears—maverick Mouseketeer turned turn-of-the-millennium pop princess and paparazzi poster-child—has bravely returned to the site of her headline-making quickie marriage, reclaiming Sin City with a greatest hits concert that emphasizes the role of spectacle in a rock show. Twenty-odd of her top tunes—from her late-1990s/early-2000s chart-busters ". . . Baby One More Time," "Crazy," and "Oops! . . . I Did It Again," through "Circus," "Toxic," and "Till The World Ends," to "Work Bitch" from her 2013 album *Britney Jean*—are presented in an eye-popping (and eardrum-puncturing) pageant of aerobatic stunts and special effects.

The songs, which are performed by a synthesizer-centric live band, are mashed up and re-orchestrated to be darker, harder, and grittier than the original recordings, providing a welcome element of surprise for those who know Spears's discography well. But the soundtrack is almost secondary to the spare-no-expense stage production, starting with the "world's largest" video projection wall, which creates dynamically evolving backdrops for Britney to strut in front of, as well as displays clips from her MTV heyday during her frequent wardrobe changes into a succession of Cher-worthy costumes. Signature visuals from her music videos are recreated using flaming hoops, flying harnesses, and walls of water, and all the while her athletic corps of backup dancers provide generous gyrating eye candy. The hardest working member of the production may be the subwoofer, which blasts bass beats so bombastic that you won't need a defibrillator if you happen to have a heart attack mid-show.

With such an undeniably impressive spectacle surrounding her, it is a shame that Britney's own showmanship at its center isn't stronger. Spears doesn't actually dance so much as pose and shimmy while her assistants do the heavy lifting; her attempts at being sexy fall embarrassingly flat; and if she is doing any actual live singing (rumors suggest otherwise), her vocals are so over-processed that it's impossible to tell. Most disappointingly, there's hardly any genuine interaction with the enraptured audience; unlike her former Mickey Mouse Club co-stars Justin Timberlake and Christina Aguilera, Spears doesn't seem to have matured much as a performer, and never reveals more than a glimpse of her personality. Just don't try telling any of that to her legions of fans—mostly females who were tweens during Britney's peak—who sell out every one of her shows, buy her merchandise from the boutique across from the theater, and down martinis at the themed bar next door.

CONSUMER TIPS The semicircular Axis Theater has been slimmed down from its 7,000-seat capacity to 4,600, but it still feels ginormous. Tickets up front are for a standing-room-only pit between the stage's runway, but even if you are farther back you won't get much use out of your seat, since the audience insists on standing throughout almost the entire show. Britney is contracted to play 50 dates in 2015, typically performing 3 shows a week in 4-week spurts, with a couple months off in between. If you are over the age of 30, bring a pair of ear plugs; the amplification employed here would put a jet engine to shame.

Carlos Santana ★★★★

APPEAL BY AGE UNDER 21 ★★★ 21-37 ★★★★ 38-50 ★★★★ 51+ ★★★★

HOST CASINO AND SHOWROOM Mandalay Bay—House of Blues; ☎ 702-632-7600 or 800-745-3000; **houseofblues/lasvegas.com, ticketmaster.com**

Type of show Guitar-centric rock concert. Admission $119–$154. Cast size 1 plus 10-piece band. Night of lowest attendance None. Usual showtimes Wednesday, Friday, and Sunday, 8 p.m.; Saturday, 10 p.m. Dark Varies. Topless No. Duration of Presentation 115 minutes.

DESCRIPTION AND COMMENTS *An Intimate Evening with Santana: Greatest Hits Live—Yesterday Today & Tomorrow.* The title just about sums up this show, which reaffirms why Santana richly deserves the #15 spot on *Rolling Stone*'s "Top 100 Greatest Guitarists of All Time" list, as well as membership in the Rock and Roll Hall of Fame. Fusing Latin beats, jazz, and blues, plus African rhythms and instruments, multiple Grammy winner and guitar virtuoso Carlos Santana rocks the 1,200-seat House of Blues. After three years at the Hard Rock's Joint showroom, this remodeled, more compact space at Mandalay Bay allows the six-stringer to interact more intimately with the audience while improvising his familiar classics. The show is purposely loose and unpredictable; there is no set list, and he frequently covers the music of personal favorites Bob Dylan, Marvin Gaye, or John Lennon. Occasionally a surprise vocal guest or jazz musician will join Santana on stage while his energetic band provides percussive back-up. Highlights are "Black Magic Woman," "Oye Como Va," and a vigorous extended take on "Smooth," with adrenaline running rampant. Throughout, the rear screen and monitors project vintage footage of his celebrated 1969 Woodstock performance, as well as highlights of a four-decade life in music.

CONSUMER TIPS Three seating choices are available. In addition to mosh-pit general admission and theater-style seats in the mezzanine, which is 150 feet from the stage, the venue has been reconfigured with VIP cabaret tables that place listeners alongside the band. Santana likes to jam with visiting musicians, so check who else is playing Las Vegas when you purchase tickets. There's a good chance you might see him mixing it up with performing pals at his gig. Santana's website or the hotel's will list performance dates. Must be 18 to attend the show.

Carrot Top ★★★

APPEAL BY AGE UNDER 21 ★★★★ 21-37 ★★★★ 38-50 ★★★ 51+ ★★

HOST CASINO AND SHOWROOM Luxor—Atrium Showroom; ☎ 702-262-4400 or 800-557-7428; **luxor.com**

Type of show Stand-up comedy. **Admission** $50–$66, $78–$89 with dinner buffet. **Cast size** 1. **Night of lowest attendance** Thursday. **Usual showtimes** Wednesday–Monday, 8:30 p.m. **Dark** Tuesday. **Topless** Only Carrot Top. **Special comments** Must be 18 or older to attend. **Duration of presentation** 1 hour 40 minutes.

DESCRIPTION AND COMMENTS Fans of comedian Carrot Top will love this fast-paced, high-energy, quick-spurting comedy orgy that strikes many mature themes. The redhead makes extensive use of the special effects, lighting, and sound capabilities of the room. These heighten the experience far beyond the boundaries of standard nightclub stand-up fare. Pulling from large crates and even a washing machine, Carrot Top relies heavily on "homemade" props. His basic routine runs to "look at this" as he pulls strange thing after strange thing from the containers.

His humor is highly topical: rednecks, rock musicians, NASCAR, etc. Many of his quips are tasteless and offensive to various groups and persuasions, but the delivery is so fast and so brief that it's hard to take offense. In fact, his full-tilt boogie onslaught makes it difficult to stay with him, and you find yourself tuning out just to give your brain a respite. The pacing may prompt recall of the comedic delirium of Robin Williams. But whereas Williams explores our common humanity, Carrot Top fires bullets past the head that never touch the heart. His routines could be described as quick-witted, but not brainy. The 100-minute show includes a 15-minute opening act with another comedian. Dedicated fans will be delighted, but the uninitiated may find that Carrot Top's comedy degenerates too quickly to the bottom drawer.

CONSUMER TIPS Alcohol is not served in the theater. The theater is tiered, and seats (all with good sight lines) are preassigned. Bring along a couple of aspirins—you'll need them for your headache after the show.

Celine Dion ★★★★★

| **APPEAL BY AGE** | **UNDER 21** ★★★ | **21–37** ★★★★★ | **38–50** ★★★★★ | **51+** ★★★★★ |

HOST CASINO AND SHOWROOM Caesars Palace—Colosseum; ☎ 702-731-7110 or 877-423-5463; **caesarspalace.com** or online reservations at **ticketmaster.com/celinedion**

Type of show Celebrity headliner. **Admission** $55–$250 plus tax. **Cast size** 1 plus 31-piece orchestra and 4 back-up singers. **Night of lowest attendance** Midweek. **Usual Showtimes** Friday–Wednesday, 7:30 p.m. **Dark** Thursday. **Topless** No. **Duration of presentation** 90 minutes.

DESCRIPTION AND COMMENTS It takes a big voice and a bigger personality to fill the 4,300-seat Colosseum at Caesars Palace. Celine Dion is blessed with both, which she amply demonstrates in her return to Las Vegas. She is emotional and energetic, graceful and glamorous, exquisitely gowned, and at the top of her very sophisticated game. Celine's show is dazzling, with an extravagance of spectacular visuals, lights, and music surrounding her versatile five-octave range.

She leads with "Open Arms" while a video clip updates the audience on her life during the three years since she left Caesars Palace. Like a vertical tsunami, a massive white drape billows then drops to the titanic 250-foot stage revealing the orchestra. After an abridged trip through her hits and a virtuoso pageant of power ballads, she heads for the path not taken: tributes to the music of James Bond, Michael Jackson, and subdued renderings of a lullaby by Billy Joel and a Carole King melody written for her.

Celine alone is more than enough, but she also duets with her on-screen self then duets again with a holographic Stevie Wonder or Andrea Bocelli. The powerful 31-piece orchestra and four back-up singers sit on five separate mobile stages that reconfigure contingent upon the requisite of the music. Sometimes it's just the horns, other times just the strings, a quartet, or a quintet as accompaniment.

Light panels beneath the orchestra change color depending on mood or theme. On the sides of the stage and extending over the audience are screens that depict family scenes or blaze with vibrant patterns of fire and fireworks, flowers, stardust, and hundreds of other 3-D images exploding toward the audience.

The set list is 20 songs followed by a wildly popular encore about an enduring heart, which she sings atop a fountain cascading water in stunning designs. Visually gorgeous and aurally breathtaking, this upbeat and refined event is a class act from initial downbeat to final note.

CONSUMER TIPS Celine's engagement runs for three years, and she is contracted for 70 shows per year. She performs for 3–4 weeks, goes on a short hiatus, then returns again. Check with Caesars Palace or **celinein vegas.com** for show dates. Tickets are available up to six months in advance. There are good sight lines from every seat. Plus, the enormity of the stage and scope of the production make sitting close to the stage less than desirable, unless you intend to chat up Celine on potato-pancake recipes or some such. If you drive to Caesars, use the valet parking at the adjoining Forum Shops rather than the hotel-casino valet service at Caesars' main entrance. There is also valet service, as well as self-parking, at the rear of the hotel, with an entrance convenient to the theater. Give yourself lots of extra time to process through the metal detectors and bag-purse search at the entrance to the theater.

Chippendales ★★★★

APPEAL BY AGE   18-20 ★★★★   21-37 ★★★★   38-50 ★★★★   51+ ★★★½

HOST CASINO AND SHOWROOM Rio—The Chippendales Theatre;
☎ 702-777-7776 or 888-746-7784; **riolasvegas.com**

Type of show Male revue. Admission $60–$90. Cast size 12. Night of lowest attendance Monday. Usual showtimes Nightly, 9 and 11 p.m. Topless Yes (male). Duration of presentation 75 minutes.

DESCRIPTION AND COMMENTS *Chippendales* strives to be the ultimate ladies' night out and succeeds. The show, which originated in Los Angeles and celebrates its 36th anniversary in 2014, is a mesmerizing erotic exploration of female fantasies. Performed by a cast of one dozen flawless model types, the men of *Chippendales* exude sex appeal while acting out a sequence of 11 vignettes. Most of the tightly synchronized dance routines are performed to contemporary R & B slow jams, creating a seductive and sensual atmosphere. Unlike the comparatively tame *Thunder from Down Under*, the *Chippendales* dancers feign sex acts and remove their G-strings entirely at several times during the show (albeit only when the guys have their backs turned to the audience). Large video screens surround the 600-or-more-person showroom, offering a close-up view of the dancers, who can be difficult to see at times from the general-admission seating. The dancers also venture into the audience at various points throughout the performance, although not as much as the *Thunder* cast. After the show, the men of *Chippendales* host a meet-and-greet session.

CONSUMER TIPS No smoking is allowed during the show. On weekends, tables are removed from the VIP/floor section to provide more seating, requiring guests to hold their drinks (which can be pricey, so be careful not to spill). The bathroom is located next to the Masquerade Bar, diagonally across the casino. Paying extra for floor seats is well worth it for ladies seeking the best view. A seating chart is available online.

CIRQUE DU SOLEIL SHOWS

CIRQUE DU SOLEIL has taken Las Vegas by frontal assault. As of 2015, there are eight Cirque du Soleil productions playing Las Vegas showrooms. First to open was *Mystère* at TI, followed some years later by *"O"* at the Bellagio. The third show to premier was *Zumanity* at New York–New York, with *KÀ* at the MGM Grand following close on its heels in 2005. *Cirque's* production *LOVE,* based on the music of the Beatles, opened in June of 2006; *CRISS ANGEL Believe* opened in September of 2008; *Zarkana,* an acrobatic tour de force, opened in November 2012; and Cirque's latest effort, *Michael Jackson ONE,* opened in 2013, celebrates the music and dance of Michael Jackson.

If you've never seen a Cirque du Soleil show, understand that Cirque productions completely redefine and elevate circus as a genre. They feature the best and most original circus acts you're ever likely to see, but those acts are woven into a whole that includes beloved characters, stunning costuming, deep symbolism, poignant drama, cutting-edge theatrical technology, and original musical scores. If you've seen a Cirque traveling production and were awed, you won't believe what Cirque is capable of in its Las Vegas custom-built theaters.

Zarkana, KÀ, Mystère, LOVE, and *"O"* are representative of Cirque shows everywhere, albeit on a grand scale, and are appropriate for all ages. Also appropriate for families is *Michael Jackson ONE,* an acrobatic and choreographic spectacular. *Zumanity,* an in-your-face celebration of everything sexual, is much different from the other productions. *CRISS ANGEL Believe* likewise breaks the mold and has only staging, lighting, and costumes in common with the other shows. All Cirque shows provide an awe-inspiring evening of entertainment, so you really can't go too wrong (assuming, in the case of *Zumanity,* that you're comfortable with the sexual content).

How to Choose a Cirque du Soleil Show

In choosing a Cirque show, I suggest you start with *Mystère.* That's where it all started, and it's still the best. From there, let your taste guide you. If you're really into the Beatles or Michael Jackson, see *LOVE* or *ONE* next. *"O"* and *KÀ* feature unique technological stagecraft that is totally captivating. *Zarkana* is most like *Mystère,* only darker. *Zumanity* celebrates all manner of sex. It's a great show, and steamier than any topless production in town, but don't see it with anyone you wouldn't feel comfortable watching soft porn with. Tickets for *Mystère* and *Zumanity* sell at $25–$45 less than for the other Cirque productions, making them by far the best value. For discounts on all eight shows, see **deals.lasvegasadvisor.com/shows.**

Below you will find reviews of all the Las Vegas Cirque du Soleil shows. This information will help you refine your choice of productions.

Cirque du Soleil's *CRISS ANGEL Believe* ★★★

APPEAL BY AGE	UNDER 21 ★★★½	21-37 ★★★	38-50 ★★★	51+ ★★★

HOST CASINO AND SHOWROOM Luxor—Luxor Showroom; ☎ 702-262-4400 or 800-557-7428; **luxor.com**

Type of show Magic and illusion. **Admission** $65–$143 plus tax. **Cast size** Not available. **Night of lowest attendance** Wednesday. **Usual showtimes** Tuesday–Saturday, 7 p.m.; Tuesday, Thursday, and Saturday, 9:30 p.m. **Dark** Sunday and Monday. **Topless** No. **Special comments** Not suitable for those under 12 years of age. **Duration of Presentation** 90 minutes.

DESCRIPTION AND COMMENTS Criss Angel is an illusionist who as an adolescent studied mysticism, music, martial arts, and dance and was inspired by Aldo Richiardi and especially Harry Houdini. In honor of Harry Houdini, Angel chose "Believe" as the title for his grand collaboration with Cirque du Soleil. On his death bed, reportedly, legendary magician and escape artist Harry Houdini told his wife: "After my death, many people will claim that they are still able to communicate with me. If their claims are valid, they will be able to tell you a code word—that word is 'Believe.'"

Angel made his television debut in the ABC special "Secrets." His surreal and critically acclaimed *Criss Angel Mindfreak* brought a new kind of entertainment to Broadway. He also created and starred in the A&E Network series *Criss Angel Mindfreak,* which ran from 2005 to 2010.

I had been mountain biking during the afternoon before I (Bob) reviewed *CRISS ANGEL.* Arriving at the showroom only minutes before the curtain rose, I hadn't had time to eat and was also parched and dehydrated. When I explained why I was running late to the Cirque publicist who met me, she immediately ran off and brought me back a Coke. I was both extremely embarrassed and eternally grateful. As it turned out, that coke was the best part of my evening with Criss Angel.

When *Believe* premiered in 2008, it was about a dream that took the form of a nice little morality play, the standard good-versus-evil thing except the bad guys were bunnies (I'm not making this up). Critics and the audience balked. Some wanted more Cirque du Soleil, while others wanted more Criss Angel. The producers straddled the fence for a long time, trying to please everyone. Ultimately, they decided to largely jettison the uniquely Cirque elements and zero in on Criss, his illusions, and his escape artistry. Problem is, the focus was always Criss. Then, and now even more so. Fine, if you're a big fan. Not so much if you just want a good show. Criss Angel is an excellent illusionist, but he's an even better cheerleader—for himself. He struts around the stage and down into the audience inviting adulation, and he's pretty much in your face about it: "What? I can't hear you! Louder!" There are enough bright spots to grasp the potential of a Cirque du Soleil production centering on magic and illusion, but loud, self-aggrandizing Criss Angel is the antithesis of Cirque's trademark subtlety and grace. It's almost an oil-and-water thing. Cirque and Criss Angel simply clash. You have to wonder how good this concept could have been if Cirque had teamed up with Lance Burton or David Copperfield.

Criss Angel has created some amazing illusions in his time, but they're not on display in *Believe*. In fact, a number of illusions in the show are very transparent. Angel specializes in levitation, floating, and wall-walking illusions, for example. After each such illusion you can see assistants moving behind him to unfasten his harness. I've always enjoyed seeing an illusion break new ground, but *Believe* does not deliver on this score either. As evidenced by his adroit sleight of hand, Angel is a talented magician, and *Believe* could have been a better show if the emphasis was magic and illusion. As it is, the show is about Criss, who demands the sort of hysteria and fan worship Justin Bieber elicits, but without delivering the goods.

Many comments about the show on Internet discussion boards crack me up. Here are two that hit the nail on the head:

Don't waste your time or money. Buy Terry Fator (ventriloquist/puppeteer) tickets instead. He makes his turtle levitate at half the cost.

And

One of his doves pooped on my friend's leg, and that about sums up the show.

CONSUMER TIPS Like all Cirque productions, *CRISS ANGEL Believe* makes use of the entire showroom. Consequently, sitting near the stage requires that you turn in your seat to see things going on overhead or behind you. The Luxor Theater is split into a front section and a rear section separated by a broad aisle. The best seats are in the first 10 rows of the rear section. Owing to the location of the showroom, it's just as convenient to park in Luxor's self-parking lot as to use valet.

Cirque du Soleil's KÀ ★★★★½

APPEAL BY AGE   UNDER 21 ★★★★   21-37 ★★★★★   38-50 ★★★★★   51+★★★★★

HOST CASINO AND SHOWROOM MGM Grand—*KÀ* Theater;
☎ 702-891-7777 or 866-774-7117; **mgmgrand.com/ka**

Type of show Fearsome ballet as epic journey. **Admission** Adults, $76–$165; children, $38–$83 (no tax or fees included). *Note:* Wheelchair-accessible seating available at all ticket levels. **Cast size** 80. **Night of lowest attendance** Wednesday. **Usual showtimes** Tuesday–Saturday, 7 and 9:30 p.m. **Dark** Sunday and Monday. **Topless** No. **Special comments** Guests age 12 and under permitted only if accompanied by an adult; no children under age 5. **Duration of presentation** 90 minutes.

DESCRIPTION AND COMMENTS *KÀ* is a departure for Cirque du Soleil in many ways. Most striking is the menacing atmosphere of the *KÀ* Theater. It has the look of an enchanted Asian foundry from space complete with 30-foot bursts of flame, performers hanging batlike from girders and scampering along catwalks, and industrial clangs reverberating as you find your seat. You are shown to your seat by one of many hair-raising Gatekeepers, who also serve as security during the show. (This reviewer would not advise breaking theater rules; it will be a Gatekeeper who sees to your punishment.) At the center of the theater, a gaping pit lurks where the stage would rightfully be. The overall effect, while chilling, isn't off-putting, but the proscription against very young children makes good sense.

KÀ is also unique in that it is the first Cirque production that attempts to tell a linear story that follows twins who have been separated and must each make a journey to meet their destiny. That journey is the focus of the show, and the twins travel through beaches, mountains, forests, and blizzards, face warriors and whimsical sea and forest creatures, and witness remarkable feats of strength and agility. All these, of course, completely overshadow the storytelling and relegate the story to something you're vaguely conscious of from time to time, but nothing more.

If there is a single star of *KÀ*, it is the gantry stage. From the pit emerges a large deck, supported by a boom, that is manipulated with computer precision to spin, tilt, raise, and lower throughout the show, all with surprising fluidity and speed. Not to knock the performers, who are as lithe and powerful as any cast of humans has a right to be, but the stage is an incredible industrial achievement. In one of the most breathtaking scenes, the stage tilts fully vertical as warriors loose arrows toward it and their intended victims scramble to find purchase. The arrows appear to stick in the stage, giving the "attacked" performers the handholds they need to dance and spin and flip their way up the vertical wall. As the performers ascend the wall, the "arrows" (which are actually 80 retractable pegs built into the stage) retract and the stage appears to shrug off the performers like so much detritus—an effect that is both unforgettable and disturbing.

In short, *KÀ* is a spectacle, and arguably the most technologically complex show in Las Vegas. The story line fails, but the production as a whole doesn't suffer from the loss. *KÀ* is a new breed of Cirque show, though it still contains the elements of all Cirque productions: elaborate costumes, haunting scores, physical prowess and beauty, and acrobatic feats. If you've already fallen hard for *Mystère*, KÀ may not be quite what you expect of a Cirque performance. While *KÀ* does display some of the whimsy of *Mystère,* the overall impression is shock, awe, and menacing power. If you are in a show-going mood, you can easily see both *KÀ* and *Mystère* in a single vacation without feeling over-Cirqued. In fact, we recommend it. *KÀ* is a fearsome production, and an elegant foil for the playful *Mystère.*

CONSUMER TIPS *KÀ* is a fine show—as virile and stirring as anything on the Strip—but the tariff is steep. Comparatively, though, the mid-priced seats are a better deal than similar seats at *"O,"* because *KÀ* Theater was thoughtfully designed without "limited-visibility" seats. *Note:* there are wheelchair-accessible seats in all three of the theater's ticketed sections.

If you do see *KÀ* and if you can manage to remember this tip with menacing creatures dangling overhead, arrows zipping at the performers, and a stage that's come shouldering to life in front of you, try to spot the three "performers" on stage who are actually technicians in costume.

Cirque du Soleil's *LOVE* ★★★★½

| APPEAL BY AGE | UNDER 21 ★★★ | 21–37 ★★★★ | 38–50 ★★★★ | 51+ ★★★★★ |

HOST CASINO AND SHOWROOM Mirage—*LOVE* Theater; ☎ 702-792-7777 or 800-963-9634; **mirage.com** or **cirquedusoleil.com/love**

Type of show Circus based on music of the Beatles. **Admission** $80–$180. **Cast size** 60. **Night of lowest attendance** Monday. **Usual showtimes** Thursday–Monday, 7 and 9:30 p.m. **Dark** Tuesday and Wednesday. **Topless** No. **Duration of presentation** 90 minutes.

DESCRIPTION AND COMMENTS *LOVE,* like most Cirque du Soleil shows, is nothing if not an overwhelming spectacle. But this latest Cirque extravaganza is a definite departure from what might be loosely called the norm. First, it's heavily multimedia, combining extensive video effects projected onto a variety of screens with dancers, acrobats, and aerialists in outlandish costumes and bizarre props, all driven by the most powerful soundtrack ever, perhaps, produced. And because music, especially familiar music, is the force behind the visuals and theatrics, *LOVE* is grounded in a reality that the audience shares, which renders this show unified and accessible in a way that *Mystère* approximates, but that *"O," Believe,* and even *KÀ* with its loose plot line, can never be.

That's not to imply, however, that *LOVE* doesn't have its extreme flights of fancy. The teaming of Cirque and the Beatles is, simply put, a marriage made in psychedelic heaven. Only Cirque could so effectively choreograph, costume, and showcase the characters, images, themes, humor, whimsicality, and all-around 1960s optimism, exuberance, and magic that the Beatles continue, 40 years later, to embody.

The show opens with a rousing rendition of "Get Back." Then it flashes back to begin a loose retrospective based on the Beatles' meteoric rise to become the most influential rock-and-roll band in history. "Eleanor Rigby" is set to theatrical scenes of the devastation that World War II wrought on the Beatles' Liverpool. "I Want to Hold Your Hand" introduces the collective planetary hysteria of Beatlemania. By now you know what you're in for. The stage, in pieces controlled by individual hydraulics, rises and falls as necessary. Visuals range from actual Beatles concerts and appearances to paisleys and spirals guaranteed to give (some of) you flashbacks. The music, which has been digitized and remixed by Sir George Martin (the fifth Beatle) and his son Giles, isn't exactly the same as on the LPs, as you might expect, and it's fun to listen for the little differences. The soundtrack consists of full songs, medleys, snippets of tunes down to a bar or two that disappear as soon as you recognize them, along with Beatles banter and fragments from recording sessions, plus suitably surreal transitions holding it all together. One thing's for sure: The acoustics are outstanding. More than 6,000 speakers surround you, with one installed in the backrest of every seat in the house.

Song after timeless song parades by. "Something in the Way She Moves" is accompanied by an aerial ballet; "Lucy in the Sky with Diamonds" is similar. The skit around "Blackbird" is hilarious, with spastic birds learning to fly. For "Strawberry Fields," big bubbles are blown from the top of a grand piano. "Octopus's Garden" has airborne squids and anemones. If you pay close attention, you'll catch new lyrics at the end of "While My Guitar Gently Weeps." Four skaters perform acrobatics on steep ramps to "Help," "Lady Madonna," "Here Comes the Sun," "Come Together," "Revolution Number Nine," "Back in the USSR," and "A Day in the Life"—ultimately, *LOVE* passes the true test of psychedelia: it doesn't matter if your eyes are open or closed.

For the finale, umbrellas spread confetti all over the room to "Hey Jude" and predictably, the show ends on "Sgt. Pepper's Lonely Hearts Club Band": "We hope you have enjoyed the show and we're sorry but it's time to go." The audience is sorry too. An encore of "All You Need Is Love" caps the evening.

CONSUMER TIPS *LOVE* plays in the space where Siegfried and Roy used to perform, but the new theater underwent a mere $120-million worth of renovations. There's not a bad seat in the new 2,000-seat theater-in-the-round, but the top $150 ticket might be too close. Since all the action occurs on the elevated stages and above, the eye-level mid-priced seats are better. You can't see *LOVE* anywhere else on the planet, folks, so be sure to buy your tickets by phone or online (**cirquedusoleil.com**) as far in advance as possible. The concession stand sells bottled water, beer, wine, and popcorn.

Cirque du Soleil's *Michael Jackson ONE* ★★★★★

APPEAL BY AGE   UNDER 21 ★★★★   21-37 ★★★★★ 38-50 ★★★★★ 51+ ★★★★★

HOST CASINO AND SHOWROOM Mandalay Bay—Michael Jackson ONE Theater; ☎ 702-632-7777 or 888-505-5211; **mandalaybay.com**

Type of show Cirque-style production show based on the music and dance of Michael Jackson. **Admission** $69–$180. **Cast size** 63. **Night of lowest attendance** Tuesday. **Usual showtimes** Friday–Tuesday, 7 and 9:30 p.m.; Sunday, 4:30 and 7 p.m. **Dark** Wednesday and Thursday. **Topless** No. **Duration of presentation** 90 minutes.

DESCRIPTION AND COMMENTS Michael Jackson moonwalked off this mortal coil more than half a decade ago, but the multifaceted idol's legacy as the King of Pop lives on in Cirque du Soleil's high-concept production, *Michael Jackson ONE*. Commemorating his vision and over-the-top talent, the dynamic staging combines the Cirque du Soleil and Michael Jackson brands in a spectacle of dance, gymnastic arts, and, of course, the time-less music. The cursory plot (which is relatively coherent by Cirque's stan-dards) involves a quartet of friends who gate-crash Neverland Ranch to liberate Michael's iconic talismans: shoes, hat, microphone, and bedazzled glove. Galvanized by MJ's magical musical objects, they replicate his agil-ity, courage, whimsical spirit, and love in their own lives. The protagonists are pursued throughout by trench coat–clad baddies representing the press and paparazzi. The paranoid demonization of the media, who sup-posedly "distorted and manipulated" Jackson's image, will raise eyebrows with anyone who gave credence to the many allegations made against the singer, but as a dramatic device it's effective in the context of the show.

The supple cast eerily recreates the Gloved One's idiosyncratic hip-hop and urban dance choreography (including the signature "Smooth Crimi-nal" 45-degree lean), while video clips and symbols race across huge screens. Production values are lavish, with the latest complex theatrical technologies allowing acrobats to soar over the audience's heads, and py-rotechnics to punctuate key climaxes. Each seat has three built-in speak-ers to enhance the clarity of lyrics and melody. The King of Pop's voice has been extracted from his recordings and is remixed with a live band, featur-ing a striking Lady Gaga–esque lead guitarist. Standouts include: "Billie Jean," with the performers in LED suits accompanied by Jackson in archi-val footage; ghouls interacting with the audience during the gothic "Thriller"; the Pilobolus-style oversized shadow puppets of "What About Us?"; and "The Way You Make Me Feel," spotlighting powerful females ig-noring the guys chasing them. Dancers perform wondrous tricks juggling hats, acrobats fly off slack lines and bungee from a Ferris wheel–like con-traption, and the focus of "Man in the Mirror" is an incomparable dancing hologram of MJ (created though the same Musion technology used in Uni-versal's Harry Potter attractions). Costumes reflect his glitzy taste, with an abundance of silver, gold, and crystal flash. The bold and strenuous athletic dance is interspersed with quietly conveyed messages of love, unity, and harmony during the few restrained segments. The show is vigorous, whim-sical, sentimental, and bittersweet.

CONSUMER TIPS *ONE* begins precisely at the scheduled time; late-comers will not be seated while acrobats perform among the audience. You'll miss the panorama if you sit too close to the stage. No one younger than age 5 is admitted, and those under age 18 must be accompanied by an adult. Though both shows were directed by choreographer Kenny Ortega (who also created the posthumous "This Is It" concert film), this is a completely different production than Cirque's *Michael Jackson Immortal* arena tour of recent years. That show was essentially a dance concert seasoned with some acrobatics, while *ONE* is a fully integrated Cirque experience with all-new acts and effects specifically designed for the show's permanent venue at Mandalay Bay.

Valet parking is available at the rear (west) entrance. Self-parking at Mandalay Bay is relatively convenient to the showroom. From the rear (west) entrance to the casino, bear left past several restaurants and then continue left, passing the sports book en route. Although there are rest-rooms just outside the theater and a bar in the theater lobby, you'll save time by using the restroom and bar facilities in the main casino. Hold on to your ticket stub, you'll need it to get back into the theater.

Cirque du Soleil's *Mystère* ★★★★★

APPEAL BY AGE   UNDER 21 ★★★★   21-37 ★★★★★   38-50 ★★★★★   51+ ★★★★½

HOST CASINO AND SHOWROOM TI—*Mystère* Theater; ☎ 702-894-7722 or 800-392-1999; **treasureisland.com**

Type of show Circus as theater. Admission $70–$120, limited seats. Cast size 72. Night of lowest attendance Tuesday. Usual showtimes Saturday–Wednesday, 7 and 9:30 p.m. Dark Thursday and Friday. Special comments No table service (no tables!). Topless No. Duration of presentation 90 minutes.

DESCRIPTION AND COMMENTS *Mystère* was the first permanent Cirque pro-duction in Las Vegas and the one that set the standard for all that fol-lowed. It is a far cry from a traditional circus but retains all of the fun and excitement. It is whimsical, mystical, and sophisticated, yet pleas-ing to all ages. The action takes place on an elaborate stage that incor-porates almost every part of the theater. The original musical score is exotic, like the show.

To categorize it as a circus does not begin to cover its depth, though its performers could perform with distinction in any circus on earth. Cirque du Soleil is much more than a circus. It combines elements of classic Greek theater, mime, the English morality play, Dalí surrealism, Fellini character-ization, and Chaplin comedy. *Mystère* is at once an odyssey, a symphony, and an exploration of human emotions. If this sounds overly intellectual, not to worry, Mystère is also the most fun show in the Cirque lineup. The show pivots on its humor, which is sometimes black, and engages the au-dience with its unforgettable characters. Though light and uplifting, it is also poignant and dark. Simple in its presentation, it is extraordinarily intri-cate, always operating on multiple levels of meaning. As you laugh and watch the amazingly talented cast, you become aware that your mind has entered a dimension seldom encountered in a waking state. The presenta-tion begins to register in your consciousness more as a seamless dream than as a stage production. You are moved, lulled, and soothed as well as excited and entertained. The sensitive, the imaginative, the literate, and those who love good theater and art will find no show in Las Vegas that compares with *Mystère* except Cirque's sister productions.

CONSUMER TIPS Be forewarned that the audience is an integral part of *Mystère* and that at almost any time you might be plucked from your seat to participate. Our advice is to loosen up and roll with it. If you are too rigid, repressed, hung over, or whatever to get involved, politely but firmly decline to be conscripted.

Because *Mystère* is presented in its own customized showroom, there are no tables and, consequently, no drink service. In keeping with the show's circus theme, however, spectators may purchase refreshments at nearby concession stands. Tickets for reserved seats can be purchased seven days in advance at the Cirque's box office or over the phone, using your credit card.

Cirque du Soleil's *"O"* ★★★★

APPEAL BY AGE UNDER 21 ★★★★ 21–37 ★★★★★ 38–50 ★★★★★ 51+★★★★½

HOST CASINO AND SHOWROOM Bellagio—"O" Theater; ☎ 702-693-7722 or 888-488-7111; **bellagio.com**

Type of show Circus and aquatic ballet as theater. Admission $99–$155 plus tax and $11 processing fee. Cast size 74. Night of lowest attendance Sunday. Usual showtimes Wednesday–Sunday, 7:30 and 10 p.m. Dark Monday and Tuesday. Topless No. Special comments Guests age 18 and under permitted only if accompanied by an adult. Duration of presentation 1 hour and 45 minutes.

DESCRIPTION AND COMMENTS The title *"O"* is a play on words derived from the concept of infinity, with 0 (zero) as its purest expression, and from the phonetic pronunciation of *eau,* the French word for water. Both symbols are appropriate, for the production (like all Cirque shows) creates a timeless dream state and (for the first time in a Cirque show) also incorporates an aquatic dimension that figuratively and literally evokes all of the meanings, from baptism to boat passage, that water holds for us. The foundation for the spectacle that is *"O"* resides in a set (more properly an aquatic theater) that is no less than a technological triumph. Before your eyes, in mere seconds, the hard, varnished surface of the stage transforms seamlessly into anything from a fountain to a puddle to a vast pool. Where only moments ago acrobats tumbled, now graceful water ballerinas surface and make way for divers somersaulting down from above. The combined effect of artists and environment is so complete and yet so transforming that it's almost impossible to focus on specific characters, details, or movements. Rather there is a global impact that envelops you and holds you suspended. In the end you have a definite sense that you *felt* what transpired rather than having merely seen it.

Though *"O"* is brilliant by any standard and pregnant with beauty and expression, it lacks just a bit of the humor, accessibility, and poignancy of Cirque's *Mystère* at TI. Where *"O"* crashes over you like a breaking wave, *Mystère* is more personal, like a lover's arrow to the heart. If you enjoyed *Mystère*, however, you will also like *"O,"* and vice versa. What's more, the productions, while sharing stylistic similarities, are quite different. Though you might not want (or be able to afford) to see them both on the same Las Vegas visit, you wouldn't feel like you saw the same show twice if you did.

CONSUMER TIPS If you've never seen any of the Las Vegas Cirque du Soleil productions, we recommend catching *Mystère* or *Zarkana* first. *Mystère* and *Zarkana* are more representative of Cirque du Soleil's hallmark presentation and tradition.

If you want to go, buy your tickets over the phone before you leave home. If you decide to see *"O"* at the spur of the moment, try the box office about 30 minutes before showtime. Sometimes seats reserved for comped gamblers will be released for sale.

Cirque du Soleil's *Zarkana* ★★★★

APPEAL BY AGE **UNDER 21** ★★★★ **21-37** ★★★★★ **38-50** ★★★★ **51+** ★★★★

HOST CASINO AND SHOWROOM Aria at CityCenter—*Zarkana* Theater; ☎ 702-590-7780 or 855-927-5262; **aria.com**

Type of show Circus as theater. **Admission** $69–$180. **Cast size** 68. **Night of lowest attendance** Monday. **Usual showtimes** Friday–Tuesday, 7 and 9:30 p.m. **Dark** Wednesday and Thursday. **Topless** No. **Duration of presentation** 90 minutes.

DESCRIPTION AND COMMENTS *Zarkana,* which has played to more than a million people in New York, Madrid, and Moscow, is permanently in residence at Aria. Like its title, the show borders on the arcane with a dose of the bizarre. Set in a long-abandoned Gothic theater, this acrobatic rock opera is dominated by an underground circus. Standout segments include acrobats cavorting perilously on a whirling Wheel of Death, a quartet of flag throwers who redefine flying colors, and a mesmerizing sand painter. Visually connecting with the audience are the supporting players, who include the crazed White Clowns, the seductive and scary mutant sirens, and a pack of eccentrics from a carnival sideshow who provide lots of front-curtain action while the sets are changed. The show achieves new dynamics in dazzling visual artistry and projections while adopting an edgier attitude than most of its local sister productions. The special effects reach a high threshold in 3-D and robotics; three LED panels, one a massive 40 by 90 feet, surround the performers with vibrant video. Sometimes it's impossible to discern the difference between what's projected on screen and what's happening on stage. The intense wall-to-wall rush of music is almost overwhelming. Lyrics are sung in the Cirque language of jabber chatter with a dash of English. It's all a high-tech pot au feu with the usual Cirque components of reimagined circus acts on steroids, daredevil acrobatics, and high-altitude feats while spooky spiders and snarky snakes slink above and below. The beguiling Snake Woman and Spider Lady are sensual nightmares. The show is a surreal Wow! from start to finish.

CONSUMER TIPS Cirque du Soleil goes back to its roots with *Zarkana,* reprising the humor, accessibility, and lovable characters that distinguish Las Vegas's oldest Cirque production, *Mystère*. Though not as warm and fuzzy as *Mystère*, *Zarkana* exhibits a technological fluency in its sets and effects that sometimes steal the show. Both *Zarkana* and *Mystère* are Cirque 101. If you've never seen a Cirque production, this is the place to start.

The custom-designed Zarkana Theater is a perfect venue with excellent sight lines from all but a few seats down close along the walls on the far sides. Almost all seats are plush theater seats with drink holders. Because the stage is very wide, you really need to be back about 20 rows or so to take it all in without a lot of head wagging. Aria's website has a seating chart with prices. There's a cash bar outside the showroom and convenient restrooms at both ends of the theater lobby.

CityCenter in general is a little confusing. If you want to valet park, use the Aria north valet rather than the front valet that serves the hotel reception area. Drive west on Harmon Avenue and follow the signs to Vdara and Aria. For self-parking turn onto CityCenter Place from the Strip and stay left to the garage. Once parked, take the escalator down to the south entrance of Aria. Inside Aria, turn left and continue until you see the escalators serving the buffet and Zarkana Theater. Signage is good throughout the casino and hotel, so you won't have any difficulty finding the showroom whichever Aria entrance you use.

Cirque du Soleil's *Zumanity* ★★★★

APPEAL BY AGE	UNDER 21—	21–37 ★★★★	38–50 ★★★★	51+ ★★★½

HOST CASINO AND SHOWROOM New York–New York—*Zumanity* Theatre;
☎ 702-740-6815 or 866-606-7111; **newyorknewyork.com** or **zumanity.com**

Type of show A risqué Cirque du Soleil. **Admission** $69–$142; duo sofas also available at $129 (sold in pairs). **Cast size** 50. **Night of lowest attendance** Monday. **Usual showtimes** Friday–Tuesday, 7 and 9:30 p.m. **Dark** Wednesday and Thursday. **Topless** Yes. **Special comments** For ages 18 and over due to adult themes and nudity. **Duration of presentation** 90 minutes.

DESCRIPTION AND COMMENTS *Zumanity* is about love, emotional and physical, in all its unrequited, sated, comedic, tender, and lunatic dimensions. It is also the first Cirque production to chart a decidedly adult course. As it turns out, Cirque does love and sex as well as it does everything else, and *Zumanity* is a hell of a ride.

Zumanity is zany, raucous, and decidedly outrageous. It is lovable in its humor and insightful in its understanding of sex. The visually rich production blends its challenging theme with Cirque du Soleil's signature music, color, acrobatics, and dance. *Zumanity* is sometimes very tender but at other moments hard-edged. It urges us to look at how we define human beauty and makes a plea for the acceptance of differences. *Zumanity* delivers a powerful message.

Like all Cirque productions, *Zumanity* is hauntingly dreamlike. But where other Cirque shows operate on multiple levels of meaning and interpretation, *Zumanity* tells us in unambiguous terms that sex is amazing, infinitely varied, and wonderful. As the production unfolds, you witness an artful sequence of sexual vignettes celebrating heterosexual sex, gay sex, masturbation, sex between obese lovers, sex with midgets, group sex, sadomasochistic sex, and sex enjoyed by the very old. As the name *Zumanity* implies, sex (and the varied emotions we bring to it) is a defining element of our humanity. Sex is happy, sex is sad, sex is of the moment, sex is transcendent, sex is funny, sex is bewildering. And as *Zumanity* so ably demonstrates, sex is a window into our essential being.

Now, after digesting the above, you might be thinking that's one window you're uncomfortable peering into, that you really don't need to know all that much about our essential being. But there's also this nagging impulse to take a little peek. You might even want to take a big peek, but aren't sure it's a good idea with your wife, mother, or father-in-law sitting beside you. That's the genius of *Zumanity:* it forces you to confront your own sexuality, including your hangups—all in the presence of your friends, family, and possibly your own lover (plus, of course, 1,200 strangers). For some it's very disquieting, even frightening. Tension is palpable. Some shift continuously in their seats. They laugh a bit too loud at the jokes, try to appear unaffected by the orgasmic groaning, pretend they're quite accustomed to leather and whips, and attempt to will themselves not to be aroused. Most people, however, will find *Zumanity* to be exhilarating, and more than a few find it absolutely liberating.

CONSUMER TIPS *Zumanity* is brilliant, but clearly not for everyone. Certainly, it's not for prudes, the sexually repressed, or the sexually phobic. Equally, it's not for the "gentlemen's club" set. *Zumanity* is altogether too complex, cerebral, and theatrical for their taste. Give some thought to who you see *Zumanity* with and make sure they know what they're getting into. Many readers have reported being so preoccupied with the reaction of their companion that they couldn't enjoy the show.

The production is staged in a 1,256-custom-seat, custom-designed showroom that facilitates a performer–audience intimacy remarkable for a theater so large and for a production of *Zumanity*'s scope. With the exception of some first-floor seats that make viewing aerial acts impossible, sight lines are excellent. The best seats are on the lower-floor center and about 12 rows or more back. As with all Cirque du Soleil shows, audience members are at risk of being hauled into the performance.

Country Superstars ★★★

APPEAL BY AGE	UNDER 21 ★★★	21-37 ★★★	38-50 ★★★½	51+ ★★★½

HOST CASINO AND SHOWROOM Bally's—Windows Showroom;
☎ 702-967-4567 or 800-237-SHOW; **ballyslasvegas.com**

Type of show Country music concert. **Admission** $60–$70. **Cast size** 12. **Night of lowest attendance** Wednesday. **Usual showtimes** Nightly, 8 p.m. **Dark** None. **Topless** No. **Duration of presentation** 75 minutes.

DESCRIPTION AND COMMENTS Formerly known as *Country Superstars Tribute,* the show was revamped to include a rotating cast of up-and-coming country music artists performing original songs alongside artists impersonating such country legends as Willie Nelson, Garth Brooks, Tim McGraw, Reba McEntire, Kenny Chesney, Keith Urban, George Strait, Brooks & Dunn, and Wynonna. The production is a feel-good toe-tapper that lets the music speak for itself.

CONSUMER TIPS The Windows Showroom is an intimate venue with west-facing floor-to-ceiling windows situated on the second floor near the front of the hotel. The Windows box office, however, is located on the main floor downstairs. Second only to the view of the Strip is the Windows sound system, with power and clarity that elevates any musical performance.

Crazy Girls ★★½

APPEAL BY AGE	UNDER 21 -	21-37 ★★★½	38-50 ★★★½	51+ ★★★½

HOST CASINO AND SHOWROOM Riviera—*Crazy Girls* Showroom;
☎ 702-794-9301 or 800-634-3420; **rivierahotel.com**

Type of show Erotic dance and adult comedy. **Admission** $45–$73. **Cast size** 8. **Nights of lowest attendance** Wednesday and Monday. **Usual showtimes** Wednesday–Monday, 9:30 p.m. **Dark** Tuesday. **Topless** Yes. **Duration of presentation** 75 minutes.

DESCRIPTION AND COMMENTS Celebrating its 28th anniversary in 2015, revamped *Crazy Girls* gets right to the point. This is a no-nonsense show for men who do not want to sit through jugglers, magicians, and half the score from *Oklahoma!* before they see naked women. The focus is on seven engaging, talented, and athletically built young ladies who bump and grind through more than an hour of exotic dance and comedy. The choreography is pretty creative, and the whole performance is highly charged and quickly paced, though most vocals are lip-synced. The dancers are supported by a stand-up comic/magician. Solo routines (which may be dancing or just sexy writhing) are shown in close-up on large video screens, but the videos are from previous performances, creating an odd disconnect when the video and the onstage performer get out of sync.

CONSUMER TIPS The show is not as risqué as the Riviera would lead you to believe, and the nudity does not go beyond topless and G-strings. While designed for men, there is not much of anything in the show that would make women or couples uncomfortable. Men looking for total nudity might try the Palomino Club in North Las Vegas.

Tickets may be reserved up to 21 days in advance at the Riviera box office or over the phone with a credit card up to 10 days in advance. Up-close VIP seating, available for old farts who forgot their glasses, includes a line pass.

David Copperfield ★★★★

APPEAL BY AGE	UNDER 21 ★★★★	21-37 ★★★★	38-50 ★★★★	51+ ★★★★

HOST CASINO AND SHOWROOM MGM Grand—Hollywood Theatre;
☎ 702 891-7777; **mgmgrand.com**

Type of show Illusion and magic. **Admission** $89 and $116 plus tax. **Cast size** 1. **Night of lowest attendance** Thursday. **Usual showtimes** Nightly, 7 and 9:30 p.m. plus 4 p.m. Saturday matinee. **Dark** None. **Topless** No. **Duration of presentation** 90 minutes.

DESCRIPTION AND COMMENTS David Copperfield has been the preeminent illusionist in Las Vegas for decades, including the Siegfried & Roy era. Lance Burton could give Copperfield a run for his money when it came to showmanship and sleight of hand, but Copperfield has always set the standard for originality and creativity. Magic and illusion shows in Las Vegas wrote the book on redundancy. Regardless whose name was on the marquee, one magic show was pretty much like the next. Production values varied wildly, ranging from Siegfried and Roy's extravaganzas to the modest Showgirls of Magic (whose show could fit on a 12-x-12-foot stage), but the content was largely the same. There were trends, of course, and for a while it was embarrassing to perform without a lion, tiger, leopard, or panther. Impaling devices were likewise all the rage for a time. We reviewed show after show and could barely keep them straight. That is, except for Copperfield.

Copperfield performs as a celebrity headliner, so he isn't in town all the time. Whenever we review him, however, we know we're seeing the illusions that the other magicians will try to emulate a year or two down the road. Like the other guys, Copperfield puts things in boxes or behind curtains and makes them disappear. But jaded reviewers aside, audiences still love that stuff, and even here Copperfield tops the competition. In one such illusion he selects 13 audience members at random and puts them in what looks like a suspended jury box and then makes them vanish. If you're wondering about animals that eat people, Copperfield eschews them in favor of a modest white duck.

Another Copperfield trademark is making use of his audience, as many as 40 of them in a given performance! Sometimes he selects them individually, and sometimes he tosses a number of large inflatable balls into the audience—if you catch one consider yourself conscripted. Illusions range from passing through a steel plate, to making a vintage auto appear, to sleight of hand only inches from an audience volunteer. Elaborate illusions, including walking through an industrial fan and guessing a lottery number, are punctuated with simpler, less prop-dependent illusions. Copperfield works alone (except for a crew who moves his heavy contraptions) and engages the audience in a nearly continuous repartee and chatter. The pace is measured and includes several illusions with lengthy (and sometimes schmaltzy) narratives, including the story of how a butterfly inspires a little girl imprisoned by the Nazis.

CONSUMER TIPS   Copperfield works hard cranking out a full 90-minute show, including encores. The Hollywood Theatre, located along the south wall of the main casino, is a perfect venue for Copperfield with good sight lines supplemented by large LED screens showing all the action. Except for cushy high-roller booths, seating is cramped at banquet tables and little round four-tops. Waitstaff take orders for an extensive and expensive selection of drinks before the show. The nearest restroom is in another zip code away and gone in the casino.

Defending the Caveman   ★★★½

APPEAL BY AGE   UNDER 21 ★★   21-37 ★★★★   38-50 ★★★★   51+ ★★★★

HOST CASINO AND SHOWROOM   Harrah's—The Improv Showroom;
☎ 702-369-5111; **harrahslasvegas.com**

Type of show Stand-up comedy. Admission $40–$66. Cast size 1. Night of lowest attendance Monday. Usual showtimes Nightly, 7 p.m. plus 4 p.m. Sunday and Monday. Dark None. Topless No. Duration of presentation 80 minutes.

DESCRIPTION AND COMMENTS   Veteran stand-up comic Chris Allen stars in this insightful and clever exploration of how men and women relate. Written by Rob Becker, *Defending the Caveman* was the longest-running solo play in the history of Broadway. In addition to the ongoing gig at Harrah's, eight other comics take the production on the road all across the country. Great material coupled with flawless timing and super delivery make for an excellent evening's entertainment. Dealing with sexuality, contemporary feminism, masculine sensitivity, and why women have more shoes than men, it's *Men Are from Mars, Women Are from Venus* on laughing gas.

CONSUMER TIPS   The show is a rare bargain among Las Vegas productions these days. Be forewarned that the show is pretty blue. If you're easily offended, you're better off with Donny and Marie. One detractor posted a comment on the Internet that "Cave Man is a one-man show and all he does is talk about relationships." Well, hello? We can't think of another topic that offers a comedian more grist for the mill. Also, you will discover that your gender-influenced behaviors are not unique to you and will be trotted out in all their embarrassing dimensions. Throughout the show you'll hear people whisper, "George, that's exactly what you do!" or "Sally, he absolutely has you nailed." The Improv showroom (which doubles as a comedy club) is at the top of the first escalator from the casino. The room is set up club style on a flat floor.

Donny & Marie   ★★★★

HOST CASINO AND SHOWROOM Flamingo—Flamingo Showroom;
☎ 702-733-3333 or 800-221-7299; **flamingolasvegas.com**

Type of show Celebrity headliner. **Admission** $105, $120, $137, and $260 plus tax. **Cast size** 19. **Night of lowest attendance** Wednesday. **Usual showtimes** Tuesday–Saturday, 7:30 p.m. **Dark** Sunday and Monday. **Topless** No. **Duration of presentation** 90 minutes.

DESCRIPTION AND COMMENTS Donny and Marie Osmond demonstrate the same chemistry that made them irresistible on TV in the 1970s and late 1990s—and both still have their chops. The production showcases their hits (mostly Donny's) like "Puppy Love," "Soldier of Love," and "Go Away, Little Girl," but also includes enough contemporary and Broadway tunes that you don't founder on Memory Lane. Marie provides the most surprises, strutting her stuff with torch songs and revealing her sensual side as she vamps around the stage. She even tosses in a little opera. There are lots of duets, but each also performs alone, and yes, they still do that brother-sister ribbing and arguing thing, and their fans still eat it up. They're backed by a nine-piece live band and eight very modestly attired dancers. Production values are high with compelling sets and a lot of nostalgic video footage.

CONSUMER TIPS The Flamingo Showroom is a good venue for this production, with good sight lines and the kind of intimacy desirable in a celebrity headliner show. The showroom has always had a hard time getting people in and seated expeditiously, so come prepared to wait in line to enter. As with Wayne Newton and other performers over the years, we've had readers recount being dragged to Donny and Marie by their spouse or friend and being blown away by the quality and energy of the performance. And, as you'd expect, Donny and Marie put on as squeaky clean a show as you'll find in Las Vegas, making it a great choice for the under-21 crowd.

Fantasy   ★★★

HOST CASINO AND SHOWROOM Luxor—Atrium Showroom;
☎ 702-262-4400 or 800-557-7428; **luxor.com**

Type of show Topless dance-and-comedy revue. **Admission** $39–$65. **Cast size** 12. **Night of lowest attendance** Tuesday. **Usual showtimes** Nightly, 10:30 p.m. **Dark** None. **Topless** Yes. **Special comments** Must be age 18 or older to attend. **Duration of presentation** 90 minutes.

DESCRIPTION AND COMMENTS Speculate on the anthropological reasons why the American appetite for female breasts is a cultural staple. *Fantasy,* possibly the Strip's most artistic topless show, satisfies this hunger in a tasteful, glamorous way in this smorgasbord of sexual scenarios. The cast consists of eight very adept dancers, power vocalist Jaime Lynch, and Sean Cooper, a comedian who very ably channels Tina Turner, Sammy Davis Jr., and James Brown. Rubber bondage, dominatrix office-politics, and light lesbianism are a few of the erotic offerings, none of which ever reach raunchy, which is perhaps why the audience includes many women. Breasts are indeed revealed early on in the show, but not every number is topless. The office scene, for example, is performed chiefly in men's business suits. The Vegas feeling of high production values with sets, lights, smoke, and bass-filled sound is certainly there to support the well-executed Bob Fosse–style choreography. While the sexually suggestive theme runs strongly throughout, most of the numbers could stand on their own without the topless element. It should be noted that some *Fantasy* cast members depicted in ads are no longer with the show.

CONSUMER TIPS Staged in the same fairly intimate room as Carrot Top's show, you can be pulled on stage if you are a man sitting in the first row or two. Row D offers the most leg room.

Frank Marino's *Divas Las Vegas* ★★★

APPEAL BY AGE	UNDER 21 ★★½	21-37 ★★★½	38-50 ★★★½	51+ ★★★

HOST CASINO AND SHOWROOM The LINQ Hotel & Casino—LINQ Theater; ☎ 702-777-2782; **caesars.com/thelinq**

Type of show Cross-dressing celebrity impersonator show. Admission $55 and up plus tax. Cast size 14. Night of lowest attendance Monday. Usual showtimes Saturday–Thursday, 9:30 p.m. Dark Friday. Topless No. Duration of presentation 75 minutes.

DESCRIPTION AND COMMENTS Frank Marino, who ages at the same rate as Tina Turner, has been heading boys-will-be-girls shows in Las Vegas for decades. Doing his signature impression of Joan Rivers (who's aged much more rapidly than he), Marino presides over a high-tempo revue where the guys impersonate such stars as Cher, Diana Ross, Beyoncé, Britney Spears, Madonna, and Dolly Parton. A crew of dancers, also men playing dress-up, give the presentation the feel of a quirky production show.

Some of the impersonators are convincing and pretty enough to fool just about anyone. Their costumes reveal slender, feminine arms and legs and hourglass figures. Others, however, look like who they are—men in drag. The cast performs with great self-effacement and gives the impression that nobody is expected to take things too seriously. As one impersonator quipped, "This is a hell of a way for a 40-year-old man to earn a living."

Divas is solid entertainment. It is also pretty popular and plays to appreciative straight audiences. If you're broad-minded and looking for something different, give it a try. If the idea of a bunch of guys traipsing around in fishnet stockings and feather boas gives you the willies, opt for something more conventional.

CONSUMER TIPS This is definitely a show where you want to pass on VIP seats—the illusion is much more effective if you are back a little. The theater is a little large for this type of production, but the big stage facilitates a more fully realized presentation. The showroom is at the top of the escalator behind the hotel check-in desk. Restrooms are adjacent.

Frankie Moreno ★★★★

APPEAL BY AGE	UNDER 21 ★★★	21-37 ★★★★	38-50 ★★★★½	51+ ★★★★

HOST CASINO AND SHOWROOM Stratosphere—Stratosphere Theater; ☎ 702-382-4446 or 800-998-6937; **stratospherehotel.com**

Type of show Celebrity headliner. Admission $43. Cast size 10. Night of lowest attendance Thursday. Usual showtimes Wednesday–Saturday, 8 p.m. Dark Sunday–Tuesday. Topless No. Special comments Minimum age 21. Duration of presentation 90 minutes.

DESCRIPTION AND COMMENTS Frankie Moreno wasn't on our show review schedule, nor for that matter on our radar. But that was before he began collecting kudos from top Las Vegas musicians and entertainers. We decided to work him in. Coming at us at bullet-train speed, the show blew us away. And Moreno? It felt like stumbling upon a talent that could easily be the phenom of the decade. Throughout Moreno's performance I kept thinking, where has this guy been hiding?

As it turns out he has been playing lounges for a decade or more, building a small cadre of fans, but lacking the exposure to fuel a breakout. Presumably that's what his gig at the Stratosphere is all about. Frankie Moreno is the Strat's big gamble, and it's doing all it can to get Frankie out from under the proverbial bushel basket.

Moreno is a skilled (and self-taught) pianist, an exceptional vocalist, a skilled showman, and, as one of our female reviewers volunteered when I was fishing for the perfect word, a hunk. He is backed by a string section consisting of violin, viola, and cello; a horn section of trumpet, sax, and trombone; as well as bass and lead guitars and drums. The playlist ranges from big band and pop to a good sampling of original compositions. Moreno easily establishes a playful rapport with his audience that is only too willing to play back.

While Moreno and his musicians are golden, a few elements of the show are disruptive and annoying. First, the sound volume is so amped up it gives you a migraine. This may be appropriate for Guns N' Roses playing Yankee Stadium but is molar-rattling overkill at the Stratosphere Theater. Also, I was excited to hear the string section, except they were routinely drowned out by the rest of the band. Then there's the pace, moving along smartly until Moreno tries to conjure up a little Rat Pack gestalt, stopping the show dead while band members each have a shot of Crown Royal. OK, kind of fun . . . the first time, but when Moreno repeats the shot thing another two times it torpedoes both pace and continuity.

CONSUMER TIPS At current prices, Frankie Moreno is one of the best show bargains in Las Vegas. Expect admission to go up, but even at twice the price it's a bargain. Don't spring for the VIP tickets—they only get you closer to the amplifiers. The showroom is set up club-style with cocktail tables. Sight lines are excellent. The restroom is conveniently situated just outside the showroom. Finally, don't get Frankie Moreno confused with female impersonator Frank Marino, who plays at The LINQ Hotel.

Gordie Brown ★★★½

APPEAL BY AGE   **UNDER 21** ★★★   **21–37** ★★★½   **38–50** ★★★½   **51+** ★★★½

HOST CASINO AND SHOWROOM Golden Nugget—The Showroom;
☎ 702-386-8100; **goldennugget.com**

Type of show Impressions with music and comedy. **Admission** $25, $30, $50, and $65. **Cast size** 8. **Night of lowest attendance** Wednesday. **Usual showtimes** Tues.–Sat. 7:30 p.m. **Dark** Sunday and Monday. **Topless** No. **Duration of presentation** 90 minutes.

DESCRIPTION AND COMMENTS Impressionists are almost as ubiquitous as showgirls in Las Vegas, so we weren't expecting anything special from Gordie Brown. *Wrong!* His is the sleeper show of Las Vegas. Brown sets the house on fire with his impressions, musicianship, and humor. Backed by a turbo-energized live band consisting of lead guitar, bass, two keyboard players, two drummers, and sax, Brown moves along at a gallop impersonating such artists as Travis Tritt, Roy Orbison, Willie Nelson, Paul Simon, Billy Joel, Henry Fonda, MC Hammer, and Frank Sinatra. Aside from nailing the voices and mannerisms of his celebrity subjects, Brown has an uncanny chameleon-like ability to change his countenance to actually look like them. Brown is at his best when he's moving quickly. Unfortunately, he has a pronounced tendency, particularly with his comedy, to drive a routine into the ground. As you would expect, trying to ride a horse that's been dead for 10 minutes isn't good for a show's momentum. Sooner or later though, Brown will plug the holes in his act.

CONSUMER TIPS Gordie Brown earned his stripes at the Golden Nugget and after gigs at the V Theater and The Venetian has come back. The Golden Nugget Showroom can be accessed via escalators located on the casino level just off the long pedestrian promenade that leads to the hotel lobby.

Hitzville The Show ★★★

APPEAL BY AGE	UNDER 21 ★★★	21-37 ★★★	38-50 ★★★½	51+ ★★★½

HOST CASINO AND SHOWROOM Miracle Mile Shops—V Theater;
☎ 866-932-1818; **vtheaterboxoffice.com/hitzville**

Type of show Motown music concert. **Admission** $50–$65. **Cast size** 14. **Night of lowest attendance** Tuesday. **Usual showtimes** Monday–Saturday, 5:30 p.m. **Dark** Sunday. **Topless** No. **Duration of presentation** 80 minutes.

DESCRIPTION AND COMMENTS This no-frills production offers a tight playlist of Motown hits competently performed by the four-man group Fair Play and a female group of four featuring Jin Jin Reeves. Reeves, the show's headliner, is equally at home with a ballad or blowing out the windows with a Gladys Knight or Tina Turner classic. A live five-piece band backs all of the vocalists. It's well paced, well executed, and overall a good night's entertainment. It may be overpriced for a show with such minimalist production values, but the music won't disappoint.

CONSUMER TIPS The V Theater is in the Miracle Mile Shops adjacent to Planet Hollywood. The box office is routinely undermanned, so arrive early if you're buying tickets or collecting them from will call. If driving, park in the Miracle Mile Shops self-parking garage as close to the door leading into the shops as possible. After entering the shopping complex, turn right to the V Theater.

Human Nature ★★★★

APPEAL BY AGE	UNDER 21 ★★★½	21-37 ★★★★	38-50 ★★★★	51+ ★★★★

HOST CASINO AND SHOWROOM The Venetian—Sands Showroom;
☎ 702-414-9000; **venetian.com**

Type of show Motown musical tribute. **Admission** $74–$118 plus tax. **Cast size** 10 including the band. **Night of lowest attendance** Monday. **Usual showtimes** Monday–Friday, 7 p.m. **Dark** Saturday and Sunday. **Topless** No. **Duration of presentation** 80 minutes.

DESCRIPTION AND COMMENTS *Human Nature* is an Australian vocal group, produced by Motown legend Smokey Robinson. Hugely popular down under, the group has racked up a number of multiplatinum albums and charted 17 Top-40 hits and 5 top-10 singles in wallaby land. Their first American album was released in 2009. Featuring the harmonies of Toby Allen, Phil Burton, Andrew Tierney, and Michael Tierney, *Human Nature* presents a high-energy musical field trip down Motown's Memory Lane. They nail the Motown sound as well as the smooth moves (their showmanship was honed opening for Celine Dion and Michael Jackson, respectively), a singular accomplishment for four white guys from Australia. They are backed by a live band.

CONSUMER TIPS The Sands Showroom is located on the main floor of the shopping plaza that connects The Venetian and The Palazzo. A perfect venue for *Human Nature,* the best seats can be found in the last four rows of the lower section. The showroom is convenient to Venetian self-parking, though finding your way from the garage to the theater can be challenging the first time.

Illusions ★★★½

APPEAL BY AGE	UNDER 21 ★★★½	21-37 ★★★½	38-50 ★★★½	51+ ★★★½

HOST CASINO AND SHOWROOM Riviera—Starlite Theater; ☎ 855-468-6748; **rivierahotel.com**

Type of show Magic and illusion. **Admission** $59-$99. **Cast size** 8. **Night of lowest attendance** Monday. **Usual showtimes** Saturday-Thursday, 7 p.m. **Dark** Friday. **Topless** No. **Duration of presentation** 80 minutes.

DESCRIPTION AND COMMENTS *Illusions* stars Jan Rouven, the latest challenger in the Las Vegas pantheon of magicians and illusionists. Graduated from the tiny showroom at the Clarion to the Starlite Theater at the Riviera, Rouven finally has a venue where he can realize the full potential of his craft. Rouven is young, speaks with an amusing German accent, and has a penchant for comical facial expressions. His illusions are little different from those in similar productions, though Rouven tends to perform them with unexpected creative twists. He's supported by several comely assistants and five dancers, the latter's primary role apparently is to keep things moving while the next illusion is being set up. A pounding music track drives the pace of the presentation.

CONSUMER TIPS We think Rouven has the skills and stage presence to eclipse the roster of gimmick-dependent illusionists in Las Vegas. He won't unseat David Copperfield any time soon, but the rest should keep an eye on him. He has a real breakout opportunity with his Starlite Theatre gig. Stay tuned.

JABBAWOCKEEZ *PRISM* ★★★★

APPEAL BY AGE	UNDER 21 ★★★★	21-37 ★★★★	38-50 ★★★½	51+ ★★½

HOST CASINO AND SHOWROOM Luxor—Jabbawockeez Theater; ☎ 702-262-4400; **luxor.com**

Type of show Ultra-hip-hop dance production. **Admission** $61-$91 plus tax. **Cast size** 12. **Night of lowest attendance** Thursday. **Usual showtimes** Sunday, Monday, and Thursday, 7 p.m.; Friday and Saturday, 7 and 9:30 p.m. **Dark** Tuesday and Wednesday. **Topless** No. **Duration of presentation** 75 minutes.

DESCRIPTION AND COMMENTS JABBAWOCKEEZ is an all-male modern-dance troupe disguised, or more correctly, rendered indistinguishable by white masks and loose-fitting clothes. The frenetic production features some of the best break and robotic dancing around. Sprinkle in some mime, humor, and a pulsing hip-hop score and you have one of the freshest and most energetic shows to hit Las Vegas in a long time.

The crew was introduced to a national audience on *America's Got Talent* and later won Season 1 of *America's Best Dance Crew*. The white masks create an overall homogeneous appearance, more or less forcing you to zero in on the choreography as a whole as opposed to being seduced by the looks and talents of any individual performer. The troupe's name is derived from the nonsense-verse poem "Jabberwocky" by Lewis Carroll. Interestingly, as per the JABBAWOCKEEZ name, if you don't understand the show, then by George, you've got it! That's the idea, as expressed by the Lewis Carroll character Alice (from *Through the Looking Glass*) after reading "Jabberwocky."

"'It seems very pretty,' she said when she had finished it, 'but it's rather hard to understand!' (You see she didn't like to confess, even to herself, that she couldn't make it out at all.) 'Somehow it seems to fill my head with ideas—only I don't exactly know what they are!'"

Bottom line, don't burn out your circuits trying to make sense of JABBAWOCKEEZ, just enjoy.

CONSUMER TIPS Anyone who enjoys modern dance will like JABBAWOCKEEZ. Beyond that, however, appreciation divides along chronological lines, with those under 40 wildly enthusiastic and those older than 40 pretty much mystified.

Jeff Civillico: Comedy in Action ★★★

APPEAL BY AGE	UNDER 21 ★★★★	21-37 ★★★	38-50 ★★★	51+ ★★★

HOST CASINO AND SHOWROOM The LINQ Hotel & Casino—LINQ Theater; ☎ 702-777-2782; **caesars.com/thelinq**

Type of show Comedy and juggling combo. **Admission** $33–$50 plus tax and fees. **Cast size** 1. **Day of lowest attendance** Monday. **Usual showtimes** Sunday, Monday, Wednesday, Thursday, and Saturday, 4 p.m. **Dark** Tuesday and Friday. **Topless** No. **Duration of presentation** 60 minutes.

DESCRIPTION AND COMMENTS Jeff Civillico is a world-class juggler with insane energy and a wit quicker than that of most stand-up comics. He performs at a blistering, almost manic, pace while bantering with the audience. The juggling part, which includes juggling clubs, balls (including bowling balls), sabres, rings, and most anything else that comes to hand, as well as balancing a 10-foot ladder on his chin and catching rings on his head, plays second fiddle to his warp-speed ad libs and ability to really connect with his audience. There's a lot of audience participation, and it might well include you unless you're in a dark corner. One memorable moment comes when two guys trying to help Civillico onto a very tall unicycle wind up with their faces planted in his crotch. Admittedly this isn't theater art in its highest form, but the way this unwanted intimacy develops is one of the funniest bits we've seen in more than 20 years of covering Las Vegas.

CONSUMER TIPS Jeff Civillico runs a family-friendly but not totally squeaky-clean show. Because afternoon shows rarely play to packed houses, you can be reasonably assured of getting a good seat without tipping. The

LINQ Theater is on the second floor at the top of the escalators on the left side of the casino. Restrooms are handy in the hall to the right of the showroom.

Jersey Boys ★★★★½

APPEAL BY AGE   UNDER 21 ★★★★   21-37 ★★★★½   38-50 ★★★★½   51+ ★★★★★

HOST CASINO AND SHOWROOM Paris—Le Theatre des Arts;
☎ 702-777-7776; **parislasvegas.com**

Type of show Broadway musical. **Admission** $60–$245. **Cast size** 20. **Night of lowest attendance** Wednesday. **Usual showtimes** Tuesday–Sunday, 7 and 9:30 p.m. **Dark** Monday. **Topless** No. **Duration of presentation** 2 hours and 10 minutes (including a 10-minute intermission).

DESCRIPTION AND COMMENTS Paris Las Vegas is the permanent home for the Las Vegas production of *Jersey Boys*, Tony Award winner of Best Musical in 2006. In addition to the Las Vegas show, *Jersey Boys* also plays on Broadway and in London, Melbourne, and Chicago.

Jersey Boys is the story of four blue-collar kids from Newark trying to escape the mean streets through their music. More in context, it's the compelling tale of Frankie Valli and the Four Seasons. If ever a musical group had an interesting history, it's this one: crazy managers, the mob, jail time, band and marriage make-ups and breakups—it's all there. And the music, well, as one audience member put it, "I can't believe one group had all those hits!" From the breakout "Sherry," through "Walk Like a Man," "Dawn," "Big Girls Don't Cry," "Let's Hang On," to "Oh What a Night," there are 30 songs and chances are you'll remember almost all of them. The arrangements and choreography are incredibly tight. The cast is so perfect that you can't imagine how they found enough talent to field five city-based productions plus a traveling road show. Likewise, the staging is some of the best we've seen in an entertainment scene that's known worldwide for pulling out all the stops.

CONSUMER TIPS *Jersey Boys* satisfies all age groups. If you weren't familiar with the music when you went in, you'll be a fan when you come out. The theater is huge, but the sight lines are all good. You'll be able to see fine if you go for the cheaper seats. A short 10-minute intermission is strictly enforced, so don't dally in the restroom or buying drinks at the cash bar.

Jubilee! ★★★★

APPEAL BY AGE   UNDER 21 –   21-37 ★★★   38-50 ★★★½   51+ ★★★★

HOST CASINO AND SHOWROOM Bally's—*Jubilee!* Theater; ☎ 702-967-4567 or 800-237-SHOW; **ballyslasvegas.com**

Type of show Grand-scale musical and variety production show. **Admission** $63–$123. **Cast size** 100. **Nights of lowest attendance** Sunday, Thursday. **Usual showtimes** Saturday–Thursday, 7 and 10 p.m. **Dark** Friday. **Topless** Yes. **Duration of presentation** 90 minutes.

DESCRIPTION AND COMMENTS *Jubilee!* is the quintessential, traditional Las Vegas production show, and with the closing of *Folies Bergère* in 2009, the last of its genre. Faithfully following a successful decades-old formula, *Jubilee!* has elaborate musical production numbers, extravagant sets, beautiful topless showgirls, and quality variety acts.

Ducking off the radar for a while, *Jubilee!* was reworked by Beyonce's choreographer, Frank Gatson Jr., who added a number of elements that attempt to "modernize" the production. Think contemporary jazz, Beach Boys, and such tunes as Beyonce's "Love on Top" and Justin Timberlake's "Take Back the Night." The new *Jubilee!* serves up a minimalist plot centering on the evolution of a lost showgirl named, you guessed it, Jubilee (who opens the show by sliding down a stripper pole). Big hats and feathers come later. Though she tries to tie things together, Jubilee mostly adds another layer of head scratching as you try to make a whole of the show's incongruous parts. It's hard to modernize something inspired by the 1907–1931 *Ziegfeld Follies* without mixing metaphors. In any event, don't plan on being riveted by either the story line or the character, or for that matter, gaining any insight into what you're watching. Take each act as a production unto itself rather than trying to make sense of the whole enchilada. You'll enjoy the show more and be saner for it.

With a cast of nearly 100, an enormous stage, and some of the most colossal and extraordinary sets found in theater anywhere, *Jubilee!* is supersized. Running 1 hour and 30 minutes each performance, the show is lavish, sexy, and well performed with strong vocals, Rockette-style tap dancing, and, of course, feathers and flamboyant headdresses. The finale remains true to tradition, with all 85 cast members passing in review down the historic mirrored staircase. Specialty acts, used in the old *Jubilee!* to keep the audience awake during set changes, have been replaced with "front of the curtain" dance numbers that accomplish the same thing. Have to say, though, that we kinda miss the crazy gauchos who could remove a cigarette from your mouth with a bullwhip. Not the easiest way to stop smoking, but effective nevertheless.

Two multiscene production extravaganzas top the list of *Jubilee!* highlights. The first is the sultry saga of Samson and Delilah, climaxing with Samson's destruction of the temple. Not exactly biblical, but certainly awe-inspiring. The second super-drama is the story of the *Titanic,* from launch to sinking. Once again, sets and special effects on a grand scale combine with nicely integrated music and choreography to provide an over-the-top spectacle.

CONSUMER TIPS The 1,035-seat Jubilee Theater, with its high, wide stage and multitiered auditorium, is one of the best-designed showrooms in town. It consists of seating at banquet tables at the foot of the stage (too close and cramped); a row of booths above the tables (more expensive but worth it); and 789 theater-style seats. The table and booth seats come with cocktail service; the theater-seat audience has to carry in their own drinks.

Lighting for the new *Jubilee!* is flat out weird, unnecessarily dark at times and like a car's high beams in your face at others.

Jubilee! is restricted to persons 18 years or older except for the 7 p.m. Saturday show, which is not topless. Ages 13 and older are welcome for this performance.

Jubilee! offers a backstage tour on Monday, Wednesday, and Saturday at 11 a.m. at a cost of $19.50 per person ($14.50 with a ticket). A *Jubilee!* dancer serves as tour guide and demonstrates how costumes, makeup, lighting, and elaborate sets combine to produce one of Las Vegas's most historic stage spectaculars. The tour is not physically challenging, but you must climb stairs. Call ☎ 702-967-4585 for additional information.

Le Rêve ★★★★

HOST CASINO AND SHOWROOM Wynn Las Vegas—Wynn Theater;
☎ 702-770-9966 or 888-320-7110; **wynnlasvegas.com**

Type of show Aquatic theater in the round. **Admission** $105–$195. **Cast size** 85.
Nights of lowest attendance Sunday and Monday. **Usual showtimes** Friday–Tuesday,
7 and 9:30 p.m. **Dark** Wednesday and Thursday. **Topless** No. **Special comments** No
seat is more than 42 feet from the stage. **Duration of presentation** 90 minutes.

DESCRIPTION AND COMMENTS Imagine a wet concoction of someone else's
dreams. The anchoring image is a nocturnal voyager in a red dress who
explores from her own bed of dreams. Her journey recalls images from
the swirling dark psychology of the fantastical movie *Brazil;* Busby
Berkeley's dance routines; swamp things with long tails; the rescuing
flights from *Angels in America;* "Baby Elephant Walk" from *Daktari;*
dancing flowers from *Fantasia;* the deft touch of Gene Kelly's *Singin' in
the Rain,* with a setting undercurrent of *Mad Max: Beyond Thunderdome.*
All this is a taste of the theatrical pastiche of Franco Dragone's specialty
production *Le Rêve* at Wynn Las Vegas.

  The collaboration of hands-on Steve Wynn and Belgian Dragone, who
logged 10 years with Cirque du Soleil, including designing their watery
world of "*O,*" was highly anticipated. *Le Rêve* (French for "the dream") requires a specially constructed amphitheater seating 2,100 where no seat is
more than 42 feet from the action (audience members in the front rows are
given water-protective clothing). Performed in the round, the cast of more
than 70 internationally assembled gymnasts, acrobats, synchronized swimmers, and dancers execute their impressive routines within an expansive,
mysterious tank of water. Mechanical lifts hoist various configurations of
the stage out of the seemingly bottomless reservoir. The set is heightened
by fire, smoke, and dripping skin. At times the performers are atop a rising
column, and at other times they appear to walk on water with the "beach"
platform, as they call it, just below the water's surface. Sometimes they are
hoisted straight up into the dome's opening. Sometimes they swing on tra-
pezes or they dangle in suspended contortions like a Michelangelo version
of hell. Yet none of these descriptions can do justice to the physical display
that arises everywhere before your eyes.

  Roman in its level of spectacle and operatic in its reach, *Le Rêve* is
indeed long on sensuality and short on narrative. Perhaps its only defense
of weak, illogical storytelling is its very title, for who can make true sense
of another's dream? Another criticism is that the water and Cirque-style elements have been seen before and arguably done better in "*O.*" As with
the comparable Cirque du Soleil shows, the concepts and especially the
physical feats invite a thinking person to reconsider the possibilities of what
it is to be human. While some may have a preference for "*O,*" *Le Rêve* is an
inspiring treat for the eye and ear.

CONSUMER TIPS Parking in Wynn's self-parking garage is more convenient
than using valet parking, if you drive. In our opinion, the first 15 rows are
too close and too low to take in the whole of this expansive production
that makes use of the entire theater.

Legends in Concert ★★★½

HOST CASINO AND SHOWROOM Flamingo—Flamingo Showroom;
☎ 702-733-3111; **flamingolasvegas.com**

Type of show Celebrity-impersonator and musical-production show. **Admission** $50 adult, $27 child. **Cast size** Approximately 20. **Night of lowest attendance** Tuesday. **Usual showtimes** Saturday–Thursday, 4, 7:30, and 9:30 p.m. **Dark** Friday. **Topless** No. **Duration of presentation** 90 minutes.

DESCRIPTION AND COMMENTS *Legends in Concert* is a musical-production show featuring a highly talented cast of impersonators who re-create the stage performances of such celebrities as Elvis, Cher, Jay Leno, Michael Jackson, and Aretha Franklin. Impersonators actually sing and/or play their own instruments, so there's no lip-syncing or faking. In addition to the impersonators, *Legends* features an unusually hot and creative company of dancers, much in the style of TV's *Solid Gold* dancers of yore. There are no variety acts.

   The impersonations are extremely effective, replicating the physical appearances, costumes, mannerisms, and voices of the celebrities with remarkable likeness. While each show features the work of about eight stars, with a roster that ensures something for patrons of every age, certain celebrities (most notably Elvis) are always included. Regardless of the stars impersonated, *Legends in Concert* is fun, happy, and upbeat. It's a show that establishes rapport with the audience.

CONSUMER TIPS In addition to the Las Vegas production, *Legends in Concert* also fields a road show. The second show makes possible a continuing exchange of performers between the productions, so that the shows are always changing. *Legends* is a good show for families.

The Mac King Comedy Magic Show ★★★★

HOST CASINO AND SHOWROOM Harrah's—Harrah's Theater;
☎ 702-369-5111; **harrahs.com** or **mackingshow.com**

Type of show Mostly comedy with some magic thrown in. **Admission** $33 plus tax and fees. **Cast size** 1. **Usual showtimes** Tuesday–Saturday, 1 and 3 p.m. **Dark** Sunday and Monday. **Appropriate for children** Yes. **Duration of presentation** 1 hour.

DESCRIPTION AND COMMENTS Our pick for the best afternoon show in town, Mac King uses magic and illusion as a platform for his unique brand of comedy. His humor pokes fun at Las Vegas, other Vegas magicians, and at himself. The show is fresh and imaginative, and the illusions are good. But it's King's ability to work an audience, coupled with his sheer insanity, that keeps audiences rolling. If it's really magic you crave (as opposed to comedy), then *Nathan Burton,* described on page 252, is a better choice.

CONSUMER TIPS Harrah's runs two-fer and discount specials on *Mac King,* but they come and go. Unique among afternoon shows, *Mac King* frequently sells out. So purchase tickets in advance if possible.

Marriage Can Be Murder ★★★½

HOST CASINO AND SHOWROOM The D—Showroom at The D;
☎ 702-388-2111; **thed.com**

Type of show Mystery dinner theater. **Admission** $72–$99 plus tax. **Cast size** 8.
Night of lowest attendance Monday. **Usual showtimes** Nightly, 6:15 p.m. **Dark** None.
Topless No. **Duration of presentation** 2 hours.

DESCRIPTION AND COMMENTS *Marriage Can Be Murder* is a well-paced, interactive murder mystery where you try to sniff out the real murderer from
among those present. Think of it as a dinner-party version of the board
game Clue. The brainchild of Jayne and Eric Post, who star, the production has improved immensely since its debut. Eric the cop grills audience
members while keeping up a constant banter with Jayne's character, a
hyper-ditzy blond named D. D. Other cast members pose as paying customers and intermingle with the real audience. It's all played for laughs,
with puns and one-liners flying throughout. There's naturally some corni-
ness, but the jokes have been sharpened to the point where you'll only
groan and roll your eyes occasionally. Oh, did we mention it's great fun?

CONSUMER TIPS Not the great bargain it once was, the production costs
upwards of $72 for general admission and includes dinner, non-alcoholic
beverage, tax, and tip. The two higher-priced VIP options also include
premium seating, a souvenir T-shirt, and either one or two alcoholic beverages. You can fully participate in the sleuthing regardless of which
admission you buy. Because you don't have to leave your seat, or mingle
with other guests (except at your dinner table), you can enjoy the show
even if you're a bit introverted. Plots change periodically throughout the
year. Children age 8 and older are welcome, provided they can distinguish reality from theater—it is about murder after all.

Menopause: The Musical ★★★★

APPEAL BY AGE	UNDER 21 ★★	21–37 ★★★	38–50 ★★★★★	51+ ★★★★★

HOST CASINO AND SHOWROOM Luxor—Atrium Showroom; ☎ 702-262-4000
or 800-557-7428; **luxor.com** or **menopausethemusical.com**

Type of show Off-Broadway musical comedy. **Admission** $55, $70. **Cast size** 4. **Night
of lowest attendance** Wednesday. **Usual showtimes** Wednesday–Monday, 5:30 p.m.;
Tuesday, 8 p.m. **Dark** None. **Topless** No. **Duration of presentation** 90 minutes.

DESCRIPTION AND COMMENTS This cabaret-style jewel was first launched in a
76-seat theater in Orlando in 2001. Only five years later it is a rollicking
frolic, packing in people in 15 major American cities, plus in Canada, Italy,
Korea, and Australia. Yes, it really is about "the change," and, yes, about
10% of the audience were unabashed men who were also having an
uproariously good time. But hands down and hot flashes up, this is a show
for anyone approaching, in, or past menopause.

Many of the heads in the audience are silver, but the punch of estrogen
is still palpable upon entering the theater. There was a preponderance of red
and purple clothing in the house, perhaps because members of the Red Hat
Society, the Red Hot Mamas, Heart Truth, and Minnie Pauz frequently attend
the show in groups. Creator Jeanie Linders summed up the crux of the production: "Four women meet at a Bloomingdale's lingerie sale with nothing
in common but a black lace bra, hot flashes, night sweats, memory loss,
chocolate binges, not enough sex, too much sex, and more." The soap star,

the earth mama, the power woman, and the Iowa housewife are each skillfully drawn and wonderfully executed. It would be hard to imagine how to improve upon the show we saw—the cast was perfect in physical style, comedic timing, and song-and-dance delivery.

The 90-minute production moves along by lyrically parodying 24 wonderful songs of the past, especially of the 1960s. For example, Aretha Franklin's "Chain of Fools" becomes "Change, Change, Change"; Irving Berlin's "Heat Wave" becomes "Tropical Hot Flash"; and "Looking for Love in All the Wrong Places" becomes "Looking for Food . . . ," with a chorus that begins "Now I'm packin' on pounds where I don't have spaces, / Looking for food in too many places . . . " You get the idea.

You must be 14 years of age to attend, for some of the content is deemed "mature." It's basically a clean, if anatomically forthright show, but if the idea of mechanical "Good Vibrations" paired with "What's Love Got to Do with It?" bothers you, maybe it's time to hit the nickel slots again instead. That would be something of a shame, however, because *Menopause: The Musical* is clever, tons of fun, and very self-affirming. The synergy cycling in the room between the cast and the audience is a jubilant intoxicant that you shouldn't miss imbibing.

Finally for men, this show is a total hoot, especially if you've been married or close to a menopausal woman.

CONSUMER TIPS Alcohol is not served in the theater. The theater is tiered, and seats (all with good sight lines) are preassigned.

Mike Hammer Comedy Magic Show   ★★★

APPEAL BY AGE	UNDER 21 ★★★½	21-37 ★★★	38-50 ★★★	51+ ★★★

HOST CASINO AND SHOWROOM Four Queens—Canyon Club Showroom; ☎ 800-634-6045; **fourqueens.com**

Type of show Comedy magic. **Admission** $23–$35 plus tax. **Cast size** 1. **Night of lowest attendance** Thursday. **Usual showtimes** Tuesday–Saturday, 7 p.m. **Dark** Sunday and Monday. **Topless** No. **Duration of presentation** 70 minutes.

DESCRIPTION AND COMMENTS Razor-sharp wit, a genial style, and competent close-up illusions distinguish this Downtown winner. Plus, it's a real bargain. Hammer warms up the crowd with videos of crashes and falls, such as you've seen on *America's Funniest Home Videos*. Then, recruiting "volunteers" for almost every trick, he launches a quickly paced 70-minute torrent of one-liners, asides, and exchanges with members of his audience. You've no doubt seen some of the illusions before, but not with the comic twist that is Hammer's signature. It's a minimalist production, devoid of contraptions, big cats, or comely assistants, but it exceeds expectations on both counts of comedy and magic.

CONSUMER TIPS The Canyon Club is located next to the hotel lobby in the back of the building. The room is set up club style, and though not tiered, it provides good sight lines. There's a bar (serving throughout the show) in the theater, as well as a restroom. Plan to arrive early and enjoy the videos.

Million Dollar Quartet   ★★★★

APPEAL BY AGE	UNDER 21 ★★★	21-37 ★★★★	38-50 ★★★★	51+ ★★★★★

HOST CASINO AND SHOWROOM Harrah's Main Showroom; ☎ 702-369-5111 or 800-745-3000; **harrahslasvegas.com**

Type of show Rock-and-roll biography. **Admission** $60–$117 plus tax. **Cast size** 8.
Night of lowest attendance Monday. **Usual showtimes** Tuesday, Wednesday, and Friday–
Sunday, 7 p.m.; Monday and Thursday, 5:30 and 8 p.m. **Dark** None. **Topless** No. **Special comments** Minimum age 5 years old. **Duration of presentation** 90 minutes.

DESCRIPTION AND COMMENTS Oh, to have been there for the real thing! The
show re-creates a historic night at the intimate Sun Records studio in
Memphis. Brought together for a recording session, Johnny Cash, Carl
Perkins, and Jerry Lee Lewis jam with Elvis Presley when he drops by on
December 4, 1956. Played with the youthful fire of their early careers, the
music was then and ever since a menu of terrific rockabilly, blues, and
rock and roll. There is no phantom playing to recorded music by the
actors; these four are the real deal, with each working their guitars and
piano in the same style as the characters they inhabit. The two back-up
musicians on bass and drums, one playing Perkins's brother, are intense
as well. As the evening progresses, personality nuances emerge as the
singers interact and compete. The narrator is Sam Phillips, owner of Sun
Records, who gave each performer his start and provides the backstory.
In addition to the 1950s music, the studio's props accurately reflect the
period, with vintage speakers, recording equipment, and drum kit. The
foursome slams through "Blue Suede Shoes," "Great Balls of Fire," "Ring
of Fire," "Hound Dog," "See You Later Alligator," and 18 other classics. On
the distaff side, Elvis's girlfriend-of-the-moment sizzles around "Fever"
and holds her own with the rambunctious guys. The blow-out finale
showcases the quartet as the rhinestoned icons they became.

CONSUMER TIPS The show is not a concert, a revue, or a tribute show; it is a
fast-moving fictionalized re-creation of a true event with lots of poetic
license, but that does not make it any less entertaining. The showroom
and box office are located near the front of the casino on the third floor.
From the casino, take the escalators opposite the elevator entrance to
Ruth's Chris steakhouse up two floors.

MO5AIC ★★★½

APPEAL BY AGE	UNDER 21 ★★★	21-37 ★★★★	38-50 ★★★★	51+ ★★★

HOST CASINO AND SHOWROOM Westgate Las Vegas—Shimmer Cabaret;
☎ 800-222-5361; **thelvh.com** or **westgateresorts.com**

Type of show Contemporary a cappella. **Admission** $39. **Cast size** 5. **Nights of lowest attendance** Tuesday and Wednesday. **Usual showtimes** Nightly, 8:30 p.m. (dates
vary). **Dark** Varies. **Topless** No. **Duration of presentation** 65 minutes.

DESCRIPTION AND COMMENTS *MO5AIC* is a cappella singing at its best and a
far cry from the traditional somber chorales usually associated with the
genre. Working their way through pop standards, rock, opera, and jazz,
with no accompanying instruments per the genre, five good-looking
dudes combine their excellent voices in perfect polyphony in an energetic turn through a too-short program of 11 songs, plus an encore of 3,
including a quick lean in to gangnam style. Highlights include the difficult "Bohemian Rhapsody" and the vocalese-infused "Take Five." Most of
the show is fast-paced, although a tedious time-filler is an indulgent
8-minute interlude as the beat box voice instructs the audience in the art
of oral onomatopoeia. The crowd cooperates, but it had also participated

in two previous sing-alongs. While the singers appeal to a variety of age groups and aptly demonstrate the versatility of the human voice, the majority of choices were safe selections. After the familiar aural fireworks of TV's *The Sing-Off* and *Glee, MO5AIC*'s live concert could be more edgy since the guys definitely have the chops.

CONSUMER TIPS Good family entertainment and great for kids aspiring to a singing career. The Shimmer Cabaret has a terrific sound system and excellent sight lines throughout the theater, so there are no bad seats. Better to sit back away from the stage, though, or you'll be recruited to sing a solo.

Nathan Burton Comedy Magic ★★★

APPEAL BY AGE	UNDER 21 ★★★½	21-37 ★★★	38-50 ★★★	51+ ★★★

HOST CASINO AND SHOWROOM Miracle Mile Shops—Saxe Theater; ☎ 866-932-1818 or 702-260-7200; **saxetheater.com** or **nathanburton.com**

Type of show Comedy magic (duh!). **Admission** $55, $66 (but check Burton's website for discounted tickets). **Cast size** 6. **Usual showtimes** Tuesday–Sunday, 4 p.m. **Dark** Monday. **Appropriate for children** Yes. **Duration of presentation** 1 hour.

DESCRIPTION AND COMMENTS The show begins with a collection of video clips on two large video screens flanking the stage (you may recognize Burton from his appearance on TV's *America's Got Talent,* which brought him a lot of attention). From there, he runs the magical gamut, from some baffling gimmick illusions to classic magic tricks. Burton doesn't break any new ground, but his illusions are current and represent the genre well. With a nod to magic's history, he performs Houdini's straitjacket escape with a modern twist—it's completely see through—and a levitation trick with what must be the world's largest hair dryer. High-energy (and very loud) music augments the upbeat pace of the show. Burton smiles his way through a production that is longer on magic than on comedy, but still, it all works well. If your primary interest is magic and illusion, Nathan Burton does a good job. If it's more comedy you crave, try Mac King at Harrah's.

CONSUMER TIPS The Saxe Theater in the Miracle Mile Shops is a perfect venue for Burton. From the Planet Hollywood casino, enter the Miracle Mile shops and turn right, walking in a counterclockwise direction. From the parking garage, turn left and proceed in a clockwise direction. The box office is often undermanned, and long queues form. If you are buying tickets, picking up tickets, or exchanging Tix4Tonight vouchers, arrive 35 minutes or more before showtime.

Panda! ★★★★

APPEAL BY AGE	UNDER 21 ★★★★★	21-37 ★★★★½	38-50 ★★★★	51+ ★★★½

HOST CASINO AND SHOWROOM The Palazzo—Palazzo Theater; ☎ 866-641-7469; **palazzo.com**

Type of show Kid-friendly kung fu panda pantomime. **Admission** $68–$158. **Cast size** Varies. **Night of lowest attendance** Monday. **Usual showtimes** Friday–Tuesday, 7:30 p.m. **Dark** Wednesday and Thursday. **Topless** No. **Duration of presentation** 80 minutes.

DESCRIPTION AND COMMENTS Combining family-friendly fantasy with a fascinating glimpse into Vegas's demographic future, *Panda!* is the first Chinese-produced show to sit down on the Strip, and presents that country's ancient culture as a colorful chop-sockey cartoon come to life. The show is produced by the same people who created the 2008 Beijing Olympics opening and closing ceremonies, and it features similarly spectacular displays of precision choreography and bleeding-edge technology. The pantomimed performance's only spoken dialogue comes in the brief English-language prologue, but any 5-year-old could probably follow the "Joseph Campbell's hero myth meets *Kung Fu Panda*" plot without assistance. Long Long, our portly panda protagonist, is about to marry his peacock princess paramour, when a jealous demon vulture swoops in and snatches the bear's bird. To reclaim his love, Long Long follows a magical map, which leads to the Monkey King (who demonstrates drunken boxing worthy of a Jackie Chan flick) and real-life board-breaking, spear-snapping Shaolin monks, including an astonishing preteen martial arts master who can flip and flail like an anime character.

The titular performing pandas aren't actual animals, of course, but amazingly athletic acrobats able to climb poles and flip from trampolines while wearing Disney-style furry costumes; their agility is especially amazing in light of the bulky bear suits. Age-old art-forms, such as traditional Chinese fan dancing and thunderous kettle drumming, are married with state-of-the-art effects, such as supersized sliding LED video walls, seamlessly building an aesthetic that feels futuristic yet timeless.

CONSUMER TIPS   Though obviously aimed at younger members of the audience, with physical humor that some adults may find cloyingly cringeworthy, *Panda!*'s brisk pacing and pulse-quickening stunts should make it a more-than-adequate alternative for adults who have already exhausted Cirque's repertory. It's also one of the best shows in town for non-English speakers; don't be surprised if more than half the audience is of Asian descent.

All seats in the 1,300-seat Palazzo Theater, except those on the extreme sides, should provide excellent sight lines, but only the patrons seated in the center orchestra will experience actors flying overhead. Don't sit too close, however, or the video screens may melt your eyeballs. The theatre is located off The Palazzo's ground-floor casino, which can be accessed via the Venetian. Arrive a little early to take photographs with panda performers in the lobby, because no pictures are allowed inside.

Penn & Teller   ★★★½

APPEAL BY AGE   UNDER 21 ★★★½   21–37 ★★★½   38–50 ★★★★   51+ ★★★★

HOST CASINO AND SHOWROOM   Rio—Penn & Teller Theater; ☎ 702-777-7776 or 888-746-7784; **riolasvegas.com** or **pennandteller.com**

Type of show Magic and comedy. **Admission** $75, $85, $95. **Cast size** 4. **Night of lowest attendance** Wednesday. **Usual showtimes** Saturday–Wednesday, 9 p.m. **Dark** Thursday and Friday. **Topless** No. **Special comments** Sometimes they reveal secrets to their tricks. **Duration of presentation** 90 minutes.

DESCRIPTION AND COMMENTS   OK, for starters, Penn is the big, loud one and Teller is the cute, passive little guy. They've been together for more than 30 years. The show is great fun, but long on talk (Penn's endless digressions tend to numb after 5 minutes or so), and short on magic. Well, not short actually. It's just that the setup for every illusion takes so much time that only a handful of tricks will fit in the allocated 90 minutes. But that's part of the show and provides the backdrop for Penn & Teller's playful tension and hallmark onstage chemistry. The illusions vary from the simple to the elaborate, with Penn & Teller sometimes sharing magician secrets of the trade along the way. Though most of the stuff, including Penn's occasionally blue monologues and the majority of the magic, is old hat to Penn & Teller followers, it works fine for the uninitiated. Plus, the duo always offer an illusion or two that you won't see in any of the other magic shows around town.

CONSUMER TIPS Strictly speaking, this show is about two parts comedy to one part magic. If you're hot primarily for magic, you'll be happier at one of the other magic productions in town. Penn & Teller don't perform any illusions on the order of Siegfried and Roy of old or Steve Wyrick, so sitting up front is fine. Be aware that Penn & Teller are the whole show. There are no showgirls, singing, dancing, or warm-up acts: just the big guy and the little guy.

Pin Up ★★★½

APPEAL BY AGE	UNDER 21 N/A	21-37 ★★★	38-50 ★★★½	51+ ★★★★

HOST CASINO AND SHOWROOM Stratosphere—Stratosphere Theater;
☎ 702-380-7777; **stratospherehotel.com**

Type of show Vintage-style variety burlesque. **Admission** $50–$60. **Cast size** 7 plus musicians. **Night of lowest attendance** Monday. **Usual showtimes** Thursday–Monday, 10:30 p.m. **Dark** Tuesday and Wednesday. **Topless** Yes. **Duration of presentation** 80 minutes.

DESCRIPTION AND COMMENTS *Pin Up* is a high-energy, highly entertaining slice of cheesecake that successfully seeks to revive the calendar-cutie tradition of the 1940s through early 1960s, back before Internet porn made nakedness nasty. Star Claire Sinclair was 2011's Playmate of the Year for *Playboy* (which is practically PG-13 compared to XXX Internet sites), so by modern standards her show seems as sweetly wholesome as the vintage girlie magazines stashed in your dad's garage. Each of the evening's dozen segments is inspired by a different month on the calendar, and pays tribute to all-American male-fantasy figures like airline stewardesses, bikini bunnies, or whip-cracking cowgirls.

Sinclair only appears sporadically in the production, usually at the tail end of the musical numbers, and her dancing and dialogue delivery are adorably amateurish. But she is endowed with a pair of enormous natural assets: a million-watt smile and an appealingly innocent personality (what were you thinking of?). Fortunately, she's ably supported by a clothed quartet of girl-next-door dancers (assuming Hugh Hefner is your neighbor) and one impressively acrobatic male. Music is provided by a cranking live band, including a hot horn trio, and terrific torch singer Lisa Marie, who delivers standards ("Come Fly with Me," "Sooner or Later") and latter-day tunes ("Jump, Jive, and Wail," Christina Aguilera's "Candy Man") with swingin' style.

CONSUMER TIPS This show is a strip tease in the truest sense—Claire conceals her crystal-covered pasties until nearly the 45-minute mark, and there's nary a nude nipple to be found—making it a topless revue you'll feel comfortable taking Grandma to. In fact, if it wasn't for a silly over-21-only restriction, it would be the perfect show to give your 14-year-old son a gentle push through puberty. Guests seated at the cocktail tables up front may be singled out for some audience interaction. The best views are from the first two rows of semicircular booths, but if you are a party of one or two you may be asked to share one with another couple.

Purple Reign ★★★½

HOST CASINO AND SHOWROOM The D—Showroom at The D;
☎ 702-388-2111; **thed.com** or **purplereign.net**

Type of show Prince tribute show. **Admission** $43–$81 plus tax. **Cast size** 8. **Night of lowest attendance** Sunday. **Usual showtimes** Thursday–Sunday, 10:30 p.m. **Dark** Monday–Wednesday. **Topless** No. **Special comments** Loud! **Duration of presentation** 90 minutes.

DESCRIPTION AND COMMENTS The 1990s are in the rearview mirror but not forgotten by avid fans of Prince. Jason Tenner, Prince look-alike and sound-alike, backed by a tight (and very loud) live band, shake the house in this driving tribute show. The name of the show and much of its content is inspired by Prince's performance in the 1984 film *Purple Rain*. Tenner's resemblance to Prince is uncanny, and it's not hard to pretend you're hearing the real thing. While many tribute shows lapse into redundancy, *Purple Reign* goes from electric to acoustic, up-tempo to ballad, serious to humorous, and manages to keep things fresh throughout. A major assist comes midway when impersonators of Morris Day and Jerome Benton hammer out a short set of Morris Day and The Time's hits, all while demonstrating the fanciest footwork in the production. Even if you're not a fan or familiar with Prince's music, *Purple Reign* is a great night's entertainment and is sure to exceed your expectations. Prince lovers will find it all but impossible to stay in their seats.

CONSUMER TIPS You can almost always find discounted tickets for *Purple Reign* at the half-price ticket outlets.

Raiding the Rock Vault ★★★★

HOST CASINO AND SHOWROOM Westgate Las Vegas—Westgate Theater;
☎ 800-222-5361; **raidingtherockvault.com**

Type of show Live rock music retrospective. **Admission** $ 49–$143 plus tax. **Cast size** 9 plus guest stars. **Night of lowest attendance** Monday. **Usual showtimes** Friday–Tuesday, 8 p.m. **Dark** Wednesday and Thursday. **Topless** No. **Special comments** Must be at least age 4 to attend. **Duration of presentation** 2 hours.

DESCRIPTION AND COMMENTS Veteran members of eight great rock groups, including Rock and Roll Hall of Fame member Howard Leese (Heart), Doug Aldrich (Whitesnake), Robin McAuley (Survivor), John Payne (Asia), Paul Shortino (Quiet Riot), Jay Schellen (Asia), Andrew Freeman (The Offspring), and Michael T. Ross (Lita Ford), team up to crank out anthems from the birth of rock and roll to 1989. Rotating female vocalists Carol-Lyn Liddle and Stephanie Calvert (Starship), along with occasional special-guest musicians, add to the mix. Bands covered include The Rolling Stones, The Who, The Doors, Led Zeppelin, Jimi Hendrix, The Eagles, Queen, AC/DC, Deep Purple, Van Halen, and Journey, among others.

To make this more than just a concert by the world's most overqualified cover band, a multilayered framing story has been added, with somewhat confusing results. First, there's an almost incomprehensible opening exposition about post-apocalyptic archaeologists in the year 2165 unearthing a Mayan temple containing a holographic history of 20th-century culture. That story line is swiftly abandoned and replaced by seriocomic skits between songs, tracing a baby boomer's journey from hippie stoner to Vietnam volunteer to yuppie salesman. The live music is also accompanied by historic news and concert footage, augmented by VH1 Pop-Up Video–style trivia subtitles. It's easy to see why this show is top-rated on Internet travel sites; every song is a solid-platinum crowd-pleaser, and performed with note-perfect precision (even the epic "Stairway to Heaven") and pulse-pounding enthusiasm.

CONSUMER TIPS The fact that *Raiding the Rock Vault* is staged in the showroom where Elvis Presley performed gives special meaning to this rock retrospective. The Westgate Theater is broad with good sight lines from every seat. The show is loud (but exceptionally well balanced), as you might expect, so seats more than 10 rows back are recommended. Discounted tickets are available to Nevada residents with photo ID.

The Rat Pack Is Back ★★★½

APPEAL BY AGE	UNDER 21 -	21-37 ★★★	38-50 ★★★½	51+ ★★★½

HOST CASINO AND SHOWROOM Rio—Crown Theatre; ☎ 702-777-2782 or 855-234-7469; **riolasvegas.com**

Type of show Celebrity impersonation. **Admission** $66–$134. **Cast size** 17, including 12-piece band. **Night of lowest attendance** Wednesday. **Usual showtimes** Nightly, 7 p.m. **Dark** None. **Topless** No. **Duration of presentation** 75 minutes.

DESCRIPTION AND COMMENTS The heart and soul of the original Rat Pack were crooners Frank Sinatra, Dean Martin, and Sammy Davis Jr., and comedian Joey Bishop. They all worked the Las Vegas showrooms of the 1960s, sometimes dropping in on each other's shows and sometimes working together. Their late-night antics at the old Sands, particularly, are among the richest of Las Vegas showroom legends.

The Rat Pack Is Back re-creates a night when the acerbic Bishop and hard-drinking Martin team up with Davis and Sinatra. Backed by piano, bass, drums, along with, get this, a nine-piece horn section, four talented impersonators take you back to a night at the Sands Copa Room in 1963. The impressionists are excellent: each impersonator captures his character's voice, singing style, and body language. The performers playing Bishop and Davis bear strong physical resemblances to the originals, and the Sinatra impressionist more or less squeaks by, but the Martin character looks more like an Elvis impersonator.

The casual interplay among the four effectively transports you back to the 1960s, and what you see is pretty much how it was. The humor was racist, sexist, and politically incorrect, the showroom packed and smoky, and the music, well . . . drop-dead brilliant.

CONSUMER TIPS There are usually discount coupons for *The Rat Pack Is Back* in the local tourists mags.

Recycled Percussion ★★★½

APPEAL BY AGE	UNDER 21 ★★★★	21-37 ★★★★	38-50 ★★★½	51+ ★★★½

HOST CASINO AND SHOWROOM The LINQ Hotel & Casino—LINQ Theater; ☎ 702-777-2782; **caesars.com/thelinq**

Type of show Loud. **Admission** $33 children 3–12, $66 adults. **Cast size 4. Night of lowest attendance** Monday. **Usual showtimes** Saturday–Thursday, 7 p.m. **Dark** Friday. **Topless** No. **Duration of presentation** 80 minutes.

DESCRIPTION AND COMMENTS *Recycled Percussion* is a long but continually inventive drum solo where a quartet of pounding, stick-juggling drummer boys stage a frontal assault on anything that makes a noise when hit with a drumstick. That would be pretty much anything in the theater except the audience. If you're thinking major headache, it's certainly possible, but more likely you'll be totally swept up in the complexity of the grooves and the remarkable stagecraft. It's physical comedic theater at its best, but laid on a foundation of extraordinary musicianship, surprising subtlety, and mind-blowing precision.

Recycled Percussion was a finalist on NBC's *America's Got Talent* and has been favorably described as a minimalist Blue Man Group. It's fast, relentless, powerful, and did we mention interactive? Each patron is issued a pair of drumsticks with which to play along or poke your neighbor. BIG fun.

CONSUMER TIPS The LINQ Theater, with its nightclub design, large stage, and strip-show runway, brings the drumming right into the audience. *Recycled Percussion* fills the space with beat rather than showgirls and is a good choice for the under-21 crowd.

Rita Rudner ★★★½

APPEAL BY AGE   **UNDER 21 ★★**   **21–37 ★★★★**   **38–50 ★★★★**   **51+ ★★★★**

HOST CASINO AND SHOWROOM The Venetian—Main Showroom;
☎ 702-414-9000 or 866-641-7469; **venetian.com**

Type of show Stand-up comedy. **Admission** $59–$109. **Cast size** 1. **Usual showtimes** Varies. **Topless** No. **Duration of presentation** 90 minutes.

DESCRIPTION AND COMMENTS After winding down her performance schedule in 2014, Rita Rudner joined *Lipschtick,* a stand-up comedy presentation featuring a rotating group of top female comics. Dates of Rudner's appearances can be found at **venetian.com.**

Rita Rudner walks onto the stage and holds forth for almost 90 minutes. No band, no singers or dancers, just Rita. And even if you've never heard of Rita Rudner, those 90 minutes will seem like 10. Her topics—male–female relationships, shopping, Las Vegas—are worn, but her perspective is fresh and her humor is sharp, very sharp. Like a good elementary-school teacher, she monitors her room, stopping to connect personally with a look, a smile, or even a question. In the end, we're all Miss Rudner's students and we find ourselves trying to file away some of her stories and zippy one-liners to repeat later to friends.

CONSUMER TIPS Rita Rudner has to be the cleanest stand-up comic working in Las Vegas. You forget it's possible to be uproarious in PG mode.

Rock of Ages ★★★★

APPEAL BY AGE   **UNDER 21 ★★★**   **21–37 ★★★★**   **38–50 ★★★★★**   **51+ ★★★★**

HOST CASINO AND SHOWROOM The Venetian—Rock of Ages Theater;
☎ 866-641-7469 or 702-414-9000; **venetian.com**

Type of show Rock musical. **Admission** $57–$167 plus tax. **Cast size** 17 plus 4-man back-up band. **Nights of lowest attendance** Tuesday and Wednesday. **Usual**

showtimes Tuesday–Friday and Sunday, 8 p.m., Saturday, 7 and 10 p.m. **Dark** Monday. **Topless** No. **Special comments** Adults must accompany those under age 14. **Duration of presentation** 100 minutes plus 10-minute intermission.

DESCRIPTION AND COMMENTS Do you remember the 80s? If you do, and even if you don't, *Rock of Ages* will transport you back to 1987 and LA's Sunset Strip scene to relive the era's over-the-top music, attire, culture, and hair. This show is bold, noisy, and fun. Instantly recognizable rock anthems and ballads link the girl-meets-boy rework of a small-town innocent who buses to LA to become an actress. She hooks up with a cute rocker, and the scenario plays out as the couple interacts with the denizens of Hollywood, including an egocentric rock star, musicians, strippers, groupies, and political activists who dance, drink, belt out songs, and connect. An incongruous couple enacts a hilarious pas de deux to "I Can't Fight This Feeling Anymore." Most of the action takes place in a gritty rock club or on the street. All the performers are exuberant, and the energetic backup band, Arsenal, is droll in its dislike of the rock star. But really, it's all about the music, a compilation of huge hits woven *ad migrainiam* into the slim plot: "Don't Stop Believin'," "Harden My Heart," "Hit Me with Your Best Shot," "I Love Rock 'n' Roll," and 23 more by Whitesnake, Styx, Poison, Journey, and other icons of the MTV era. Rock On!

CONSUMER TIPS The Rock of Ages Theater is located on the main floor of the shopping plaza that connects The Venetian and The Palazzo. No programs are distributed to the audience, a disservice to the fine actors and musicians. The show is raunchy; parents might want to gauge their tolerance for exposing their kids to no-holds-barred profanity and sexual situations. This *Rock of Ages* just slightly resembles the 2012 movie with Tom Cruise. Afterward, visit The Venetian's Bourbon Lounge, a re-creation of the show's nightclub, for more '80s music and memories.

Rod Stewart ★★★★

APPEAL BY AGE   **UNDER 21** ★★★   **21-37** ★★★   **38-50** ★★★★   **51+** ★★★★

HOST CASINO AND SHOWROOM Caesars Palace—Colosseum;
☎ 702-731-7333 or 800-745-3000; **caesarspalace.com, ticketmaster.com**

Type of show Celebrity headliner. **Admission** $49–$250. **Cast size** 1 plus 13-piece band. **Night of lowest attendance** Wednesday. **Usual showtimes** Sunday, Wednesday, and Saturday, 7:30 p.m. **Dark** Monday, Tuesday, Thursday, and Friday. **Topless** No. **Duration of presentation** 100 minutes.

DESCRIPTION AND COMMENTS Do ya think he's sexy? Even with a 50-year career behind him, Grammy winner and two-time Rock and Roll Hall of Famer Rod Stewart's still got it: sandpapery voice, spiky hair, and booty-shakin' moves in full view of sold-out audiences at Caesars Palace. Well paced with up-tempo hits and soulful ballads interspersed, Stewart moves through 19 of his bestselling pop hits—no traditional standards this time out. Early on, he invites audience members with an inclination to dance or take photos to mosh in a roped area in front of the stage. He's backed by three pink-sequined singers, a streamlined 10-piece band, which includes two ladies on brass and a third distaff utility player on violin, mandolin, and tambourine. Above the band is a five-section, high-def LED screen exhibiting geometric graphics and colors appropriate to the mood conveyed by the music and centered by footage of the performance as it plays out. During and after the "Hot Legs" number, the agile singer, a longtime fan of Glasgow's Celtics Football Club (that's soccer for the uninitiated), kicks innumerable soccer balls into the audience. Another crowd-pleaser occurs when the gregarious Stewart ventures into the aisles singing "High Heeled Sneakers" and high-fiving the audience as it crowds around him en masse. Two songs "Downtown Train" and "Love Train" reflect his passion for railroads. Throughout a patriotic segment, the screen shows footage of WWII, Vietnam, and Desert Storm soldiers while Stewart sings "Rhythm of My Heart" dedicated to all veterans. Sartorially insouciant, causal, engaging, and accessible, Rod's persona is that of a friendly "mate." The show is glossy, fun, and upbeat, celebrating a three-generation musical life.

CONSUMER TIPS Book early—Stewart is scheduled for about 25 shows a year through 2013, presenting 6 shows over several two-week periods. Arrive early—it takes a while to seat 4,298 fans per show, although the process moves quickly. Bring a camera for great photo ops.

Terry Fator ★★★★

APPEAL BY AGE   **UNDER 21** ★★★★   **21-37** ★★★★   **38-50** ★★★★   **51+** ★★★★

HOST CASINO AND SHOWROOM Mirage—Terry Fator Showroom;
☎ 702-792-7777; **mirage.com** and **terryfator.com**

Type of show Voice-impersonation ventriloquism. **Admission** $60, $80, $100, and $130 plus tax. **Cast size** 2 plus live band. **Night of lowest attendance** Wednesday. **Usual showtimes** Monday–Thursday, 7:30 p.m. **Dark** Friday–Sunday. **Topless** No. **Duration of presentation** 90 minutes.

DESCRIPTION AND COMMENTS As stated on Fator's website, it took him "32 years to become an overnight sensation." The catalyst was taking first place (and a million bucks) in the *America's Got Talent* television show. Though the talent-show win was long in coming, Fator's arrival in one of Las Vegas's most prestigious showrooms was near meteoric.

Terry Fator brings so many talents to the Mirage that his show is tough to categorize. He's a superb and versatile vocalist, a consummate comedian, a world-class ventriloquist, and an imaginative puppeteer. Fator can mimic virtually any voice, male or female, and during his ventriloquism routines, pulls it off with his mouth closed. His quirky puppet costars are what you might have expected from Jim Henson had he designed puppets for adults. Topping the list is Winston, the Impersonating Turtle, inspired by Henson's Kermit the Frog. Winston sings a duet of "Wonderful World" with Satchmo—one of the most magical moments in the show. Other puppet characters include Walter T. Airedale, a country singer; lovable and sassy Emma Taylor; Maynard Thomkins, an Elvis impersonator who doesn't know any Elvis songs; Julius, an African American soul singer who nails Marvin Gaye; Johnny Vegas, a lounge singer who impersonates the likes of Dean Martin and Tony Bennett; and Dougie Scott Walker, a hippy dippy heavy-metal dude. The latest addition is Vikki "The Cougar," a cut-up with a big mouth and plenty of attitude.

Ventriloquism isn't what usually comes to mind when you're shopping for a Las Vegas show, but ventriloquism is only the tip of Terry Fator's iceberg. Consider his ventriloquism and puppets as icing on some of the best voice impersonation and edgy humor you're likely to find. When he trots out a perfect duet between Garth Brooks and Michael Jackson, you won't believe what you're hearing. Never mind that he's belting it out with his mouth closed! Fator is backed by a seven-piece live band and a comely assistant. The show has great energy throughout and runs the gamut from zany to poignant. The puppets are a little hard to see from the seats in back, but large LED screens flanking the stage monitor the action. The main problem we'd like to see corrected is that of the band overwhelming the vocals.

CONSUMER TIPS Terry Fator's humor is definitely adult but not often blue, so the show is OK for those under 18, though they might not dig the music. Because of the location of the showroom, you're better off using Mirage self-parking rather than valet parking.

Thunder from Down Under   ★★★

APPEAL BY AGE	UNDER 21 ★★★	21-37 ★★★	38-50 ★★★	51+ ★★★

HOST CASINO AND SHOWROOM Excalibur—Thunder from Down Under Showroom; ☎ 702-597-7600; **excalibur.com** or **thunderfromdownunder.com**

Type of show Male revue. **Admission** $41–$70. **Cast size** 10. **Night of lowest attendance** Monday. **Usual showtimes** Sunday–Thursday, 9 p.m.; Friday and Saturday, 9 and 11 p.m. **Dark** None. **Special comments** Must be 18 or older to attend (guests ages 18–20 must be accompanied by an adult). **Topless** Yes (male). **Duration of presentation** 75 minutes.

DESCRIPTION AND COMMENTS Thunder from Down Under offers a naughty night of ladies' fun—a girls' night out that won't cause complete embarrassment for the conservative set. These Aussies are the guys next door—friendly and cute, but not the Chippendales dancers. Thunder is suggestive but not explicit, much tamer, in fact, than its American-based competitor. The scantily clad cast performs upbeat dance, acrobatics, and martial-arts routines, with a few comedy sketches tossed in (including one done in drag). Acts are performed to a varied soundtrack, resulting in a fast-paced, high-energy—but not always sexy—show.

There's lots of audience interaction as the Thundermen constantly pull girls out of the crowd and onto the stage. If you're shy and want to remain inconspicuous, try sitting in the back, where the lighting is also softer (our reviewer experienced light-blindness a few times from harsh overheads above her front-center seat in the 400-person showroom). After the show, cast members stick around to mingle with guests and offer photo opportunities.

Although there's lots of teasing and suggestion, the Thundermen never fully remove their G-strings (unlike the Chippendales guys). Thunder seemingly presumes that women can't appreciate blatantly risqué entertainment. Our female reviewer also got the distinct impression that the guys of Thunder would be more interested in each other than any of the hundreds of girls in the audience, which for some may diminish the show's sex appeal.

CONSUMER TIPS No smoking is allowed in the Thunder from Down Under Showroom, located on the "Medieval" level, above the casino. Conveniently, there's a restroom within the showroom. Drinks must be purchased directly from the bar (no at-the-table cocktail service).

Tony 'n' Tina's Wedding   ★★★½

APPEAL BY AGE	UNDER 21 ★	21-37 ★★★½	38-50 ★★★½	51+ ★★★

HOST CASINO AND SHOWROOM Bally's; ☎ 702-777-7776;
ballyslasvegas.com or **tonylovestina.com**

Type of show Interactive dinner theater. **Admission** $91–$135. **Cast size** 20. **Night of lowest attendance** Wednesday. **Usual showtimes** Monday, Wednesday, Friday, and Saturday, 6 p.m. **Dark** Sunday, Tuesday, and Thursday. **Topless** No. **Duration of presentation** 2 hours.

DESCRIPTION AND COMMENTS Have you ever been to a wedding or wedding reception where you really didn't know anyone? Well, that's the premise for *Tony 'n' Tina's Wedding.* You're a wedding guest, welcomed into a large banquet hall and seated at a dinner table with total strangers. There you sit befuddled and somewhat uncomfortable as members of the bride's family (actors) stop to say hello and reminisce about Tony and Tina. And this is just the beginning. If you thought you could sit passively and watch a show, you're quite mistaken. During the course of a panicky few minutes, you become acutely aware that you are being sucked into the cast of this strange piece of theater, or if you can suspend your disbelief, this wedding. First there's the ceremony, then obligatory toasts, then dancing, then dinner followed by more toasts, and the tossing of the bouquet and the garter. As it unfolds, you are taken back to all those weddings in your life where one of the bridesmaids gets drunk, where an uninvited guest makes a 5-minute toast, and where the best man wants to sing with the band. Inevitably it's you that the inebriated bridesmaid wants to spin around the dance floor, you who are pushed into the conga line, and you who are pulled into the throng to vie for the bouquet or garter.

There's a story line, of course, plus enough subplots to give Robert Ludlum a run for his money. The families don't get along well, and each in its own way tries to monopolize the reception. The strain is almost too much for the happy couple and for a while their minutes-old marriage hangs in the balance.

CONSUMER TIPS Is this fun? At the show we attended, we observed a pretty diverse range of audience reaction. Some really got into it, danced to every tune, and role-played right along with cast. Others kept as much as possible to themselves, refusing to the extent possible to be drawn in. With some difficulty, we warmed to the proceedings but nonetheless kept a wary lookout for the sloshed bridesmaid. It was impossible not to admire how exactly the production nailed every wedding cliché, and how, if you weren't familiar with the family members as individuals, you had met their characters at similar events dozens of times in real life. If it helps you make up your mind, we'll tell you that the dinner was passable, sort of a pasta buffet, and that you had one chance to go through the line and load up your plate. The only alcohol served was a splash of Champagne for one of the toasts, though there was a cash bar (where we spent a goodly sum trying to improve our attitude).

Tournament of Kings ★★★

APPEAL BY AGE **UNDER 21** ★★★★ **21–37** ★★★★ **38–50** ★★★★ **51+** ★★★★

HOST CASINO AND SHOWROOM Excalibur—King Arthur's Arena;
☎ 702-597-7600 or 877-750-5464; **excalibur.com**

Type of show Jousting and medieval pageant. **Admission** $45, $59 with dinner. **Cast size** 35 (with 38 horses). **Night of lowest attendance** Monday. **Usual showtimes**

Monday and Friday, 6 p.m.; Wednesday, Thursday, Saturday, and Sunday, 6 and 8:30 p.m. **Dark** Tuesday. **Topless** No. **Duration of presentation** 75 minutes.

DESCRIPTION AND COMMENTS *Tournament of Kings* is a retooled version of *King Arthur's Tournament*, which logged 6,000 performances. It's basically the same show, with a slightly different plot twist. If you saw one, the other will come as no surprise.

The idea is that Arthur summons the kings of eight European countries to a sporting competition in honor of his son Christopher. Guests view the arena from dinner tables divided into sections; a king is designated to represent each section in the competition. Ladies-in-waiting and various court attendants double as cheerleaders, doing their best to whip the audience into a frenzy of cheering for their section's king. The audience, which doesn't require much encouragement, responds by hooting, huzzahing, and pounding on the dinner tables. Watch your drinks—all the pounding can knock them over.

Soup is served to the strains of the opening march. The kings enter on horseback. Precisely when the King of Hungary is introduced, dinner arrives (big Cornish hen, small twice-baked potato, bush of broccoli, dinner roll, and dessert turnover). The kings engage in contests with flags, dummy heads, javelins, swords, and maces and shields and joust a while, too. The horse work, fighting, and especially the jousting are exciting, and the music (by a three-man band) and sound effects are well executed.

Right on cue, Mordred the Evil One crashes the party, accompanied by his Dragon Enforcers. Arthur is mortally slain and all the kings are knocked out, leaving Christopher to battle the forces of evil and emerge—surprise!—victorious in the end.

Except that . . . it's not over. The coronation is the culmination, after some acrobatics and human-tower stunts from a specialty act. Finally, the handsome new king goes out in a (literal) blaze of glory. It's a bit anticlimactic and bogged down, which helps hurry you out so the crew can quickly set up for the second show or clean up and go home.

CONSUMER TIPS One of the few Las Vegas shows suitable for the whole family, and one of the fewer dinner shows, *Tournament of Kings* enjoys great popularity and often plays to a full house. Reserved seats can be purchased with a credit card up to five days in advance by calling the number listed on page 261 (there's an extra $2 charge if you order by phone). Or you can show up at the Excalibur box office, which opens at 8 a.m., up to five days ahead.

No matter where you sit, you're close to the action—and the dust and stage smoke. The air-conditioning system is steroidal, so you might consider bringing a wrap. Seating is reserved, so you can walk in at the last minute and don't have to tip any greeters or seaters.

Dinner is served without utensils and eaten with the hands, so you might want to wash up beforehand. Eating a big meal is a bit awkward with the show going on and all the cheering duties, so you might consider bringing some aluminum foil and a bag to take out the leftover bird. Beverage is limited to soda with dinner, but the food server will bring you water, and a cocktail waitress will bring you anything else. Service is adequate; no one tips, so you'll be a hero if you do.

V: The Ultimate Variety Show ★★★★

HOST CASINO AND SHOWROOM Miracle Mile Shops—V Theater;
☎ 702-892-7790; **vtheshow.com**

Type of show A hodgepodge of variety acts. **Admission** $70–$90 plus tax and fees.
Cast size About 12 (varies). **Nights of lowest attendance** Monday and Wednesday.
Usual showtimes Nightly, 7 and 8:30 p.m. **Special comments** Some of Las Vegas's
quirkiest acts; great fun. **Topless** No. **Duration of presentation** 75 minutes.

DESCRIPTION AND COMMENTS In quite a few headlining Las Vegas shows, old
and new, intermissions are handled by variety acts—comics, jugglers,
acrobats, magicians, ventriloquists, and more. And in several of these
cases (particularly the older ones), these variety acts become more
entertaining than the headliners. The advantage of *V* is that the cast consists of a rotating stable of variety acts culled from Vegas and elsewhere.
This means that no act lasts longer than a few minutes; it's the show for
the short-attention-span set. Most of the acts are quite good. The emcee
is a hilariously flamboyant and aggressive comic-magician, and when we
visited, there was also an amusingly abusive juggler, a few species of
acrobats, and a bizarre ventriloquist who uses audience volunteers as his
"dummies," among others.

CONSUMER TIPS The V Theater is located in the Miracle Mile Shops at Planet
Hollywood. Self-parking at Planet Hollywood funnels you directly into
the Miracle Mile Shops not far from the theater. Because there are only a
couple of windows at the box office, arrive 35 minutes or more before
showtime if you are buying or picking up tickets, or redeeming ticket
vouchers. The split-level showroom has a bar on a mezzanine floor and
most seating on ground level. Because the V Theater is a multifunctional
facility, there's no vertical rise from front to back for the seating. If you
sit behind someone tall, in other words, your line of sight will be majorly
obstructed. Also be aware that the available restrooms are totally inadequate for the size of the audience.

Vegas! The Show ★★★★

HOST CASINO AND SHOWROOM Miracle Mile Shops—Saxe Theater;
☎ 866-932-1818 or 702-260-7200; **saxetheater.com**

Type of show Las Vegas production show. **Admission** $80–$100. **Cast size** 29.
Night of lowest attendance Monday. **Usual showtimes** Nightly, 7 and 9 p.m. **Topless**
No. **Duration of presentation** 90 minutes.

DESCRIPTION AND COMMENTS *Vegas!* is a quintessential Las Vegas production
show with feathered showgirls and lavish ensemble routines punctuated
by myriad specialty acts. Cleverly presented as a reminiscence of "old Las
Vegas," the show couples Las Vegas history with the evolution of the production show genre. Sets depict neon marquees of long-gone hotels such
as the Stardust, Dunes, Sands, and Desert Inn, while music and choreography capture the essence of classic Vegas productions such as *Lido
de Paris* and *Folies Bergère.* Though not topless, the statuesque
showgirls and dancers successfully recreate the feel of the extravagant

Ziegfeld-type shows. Add some great vocalists (Reva Rice and Josh Strickland) recalling iconic Vegas showroom personalities, and you have one hot and memorable show. Everything is live—no recorded tracks or lip-synching. Music is courtesy of a tight 11-piece band. Continuity is sustained by a film montage of Vegas past.

In the better production shows of old, specialty acts sometimes stole the show, transcending their utilitarian function of killing time while the next big number was being set up. So too with *Vegas!;* the specialty acts really grab you. Though acts change from performance to performance, the recent line-up has included Professor Wacko and his comedy trampoline, the roller skating duo of Bill and Yana, and former Cirque du Soleil gymnast Tamara Yeroffyeva.

CONSUMER TIPS Saxe Theater operations are a little different. The queue to enter the showroom starts on the ground level next to the bar, so neither the bar nor the queue functions efficiently. Compounding the congestion is the location of the restrooms next to the bar. Once you unscramble the folks in the queue from the barflies and the potty-goers, the queue winds up a staircase several stories and enters the theater at the top rear. From there an insufficient number of ushers help you find your seat. All seats are reserved, so you may as well relax at the bar until most of the queue has disappeared from the staircase (there's an elevator for non-ambulatory patrons).

Half-price tickets are usually available at the discount ticket outlets and sometimes coupons are available for *Vegas!* in the local visitor magazines. Discounted tickets are harder to score for the early show (which often sells out) than for the 9 p.m. performance. Park in the Miracle Mile Shops self-parking. Once you enter the mall proceed to the first intersection and turn left to the theater. The box office is routinely overwhelmed before the early show, so arrive 40 minutes or so in advance if you're buying tickets, exchanging vouchers, or picking up tickets at will call.

Vinnie Favorito ★★★

APPEAL BY AGE	UNDER 21 ★★★	21–37 ★★★½	38–50 ★★★½	51+ ★★½

HOST CASINO AND SHOWROOM Flamingo—Bugsy's Cabaret;
☎ 702-733-3333 or 800-221-7299; **flamingolasvegas.com**

Type of show Stand-up comedy. **Admission** $61–$110 plus tax. **Cast size** 1. **Nights of lowest attendance** Tuesday and Wednesday. **Usual showtimes** Nightly, 8 p.m. **Dark** None. **Topless** No. **Duration of presentation** 70 minutes.

DESCRIPTION AND COMMENTS Italian "shock"-comic Vinnie Favorito occupies Bugsy's Cabaret for the early show nightly at the Flamingo. Las Vegas has its fair share of blue comics, but this guy takes it to the next level. No ethnicity is safe as he works the room blasting every race with equal abandon. His humor is packed with stereotypes interrupted only by the occasional raunchy sex joke. The initial shock wanes as the audience realizes that everyone is picked on equally. His attempts at tempering the offensiveness with an occasional apology are transparent, but his real genius is his ability to build quips around the interactions with the audience. Eventually, it sinks in that he is getting laughs without prepared material. Before the set is through, he will have spoken to nearly a third of the audience, remembering each individual by name, occupation, and race. No small feat.

CONSUMER TIPS Vinnie Favorito is one offensive comic. If you have a gentle spirit or are easily offended, look elsewhere. Bugsy's Cabaret is an intimate venue with good sight lines, so you won't have any difficulty hearing or seeing. Favorito is likely to find and lampoon you no matter where you sit, though being up front makes you more of a target. Cocktails are served ($9 mixed drinks, $7 beer) before and during the show if your ruffled feathers need a little pain relief. You will hear as many groans as laughs—there are plenty of both. To enjoy Vinnie Favorito, try to go with the flow and recognize his point that we all sometimes take ourselves too seriously. Digital audio copies of the live show are made every night, and guests can wait outside the show to purchase a signed copy. Take it home and show ma and pa the new words you learned in Vegas.

X Burlesque ★★★

APPEAL BY AGE	UNDER 21 -	21-37 ★★	38-50 ★★½	51+ ★★½

HOST CASINO AND SHOWROOM Flamingo-X Showroom; ☎ 702-733-3333 or 800-221-7299; **flamingolasvegas.com**

Type of show Topless revue. **Admission** $62–$95 plus tax. **Cast size** 8. **Night of lowest attendance** Tuesday. **Usual showtimes** Nightly, 10 p.m. **Dark** None. **Topless** Yes. **Duration of presentation** 90 minutes.

DESCRIPTION AND COMMENTS Less erotic than athletic, *X Burlesque* features a half dozen skilled dancers performing highly choreographed routines to songs ranging from Broadway standards to techno. Some numbers feature all the dancers, while others involve only one or two. The dancers wear tops as often as not, and their bodies are lithe and toned rather than top-heavy, so guys looking for a hot and juicy T&A show may want to look elsewhere. Those seeking more subtle eroticism won't be disappointed. The audience sits at round tables, nightclub-style, and the comely dancers strut on and off the stage and through the tables, sometimes taking a swing on a pole near the back of the room. The variety of music, the lights and costumes, and the sensual images flashing on large screens at either side of the small stage give the show a charged energy that captures the crowd. Given the general tone of the show, the appearance of the stand-up comic constitutes a real interruption. In X's defense, however, it should be pointed out that a bit of stand-up comedy is pretty routine in topless revues as well as in many strip joints.

CONSUMER TIPS X Showroom is small, giving the production an appropriate intimacy, and most of the tables are set up near the stage on a flat floor. The music is loud, the images bright and quick, and the choreography often frenetic, so expect a full sensory experience. Pun intended.

X Rocks ★★★½

APPEAL BY AGE	UNDER 21 N/A	21-37 ★★★½	38-50 ★★★½	51+ ★★★½

HOST CASINO AND SHOWROOM Rio—Kings Room; ☎ 702-777-7776; **riolasvegas.com**

Type of show Topless revue. **Admission** $53–$81 plus tax. **Cast size** 6. **Night of**

lowest attendance Monday. **Usual showtimes** Nightly, 10 p.m. **Dark** None. **Topless** Yes. **Duration of presentation** 70 minutes.

DESCRIPTION AND COMMENTS Las Vegas topless revues rarely offer anything new or innovative. Thus, we were taken by surprise by *X Rocks*. First, the production features beautiful, skilled, and majorly athletic dancers, with choreography that makes the most of their talent. Second, the show is edgy and hot, the most sensual show of its kind save Cirque du Soleil's *Zumanity*. But what really grabbed us is the pace of the show—it comes at you in a blitz of 2- to 4-minute vignettes. Most topless shows can't get the dancers on and off stage in that amount of time. You literally don't have a chance to catch your breath between numbers. The staccato pace, all driven home by a backing track of classic rock, from Black Sabbath to the Beatles, leaves you wanting more of the act that just concluded and hyped in anticipation for the one to follow. It's high intensity all the way.

CONSUMER TIPS Bottom line, the show's great but the venue is crappy. *X Rocks* deserves better. Seating is on a non-tiered flat floor, and the stage is too low to see the performers if they're not standing. Acoustics are good, though, as is lighting. Just don't sit behind anyone taller than you.

A FEW COMMENTS
REGARDING SHOWS NOT PROFILED

THE FOLLOWING ARE SHOWS that you may have heard of or seen advertised. They were not profiled in the preceding section for various reasons, ranging from too few performances to unpredictable schedules to mediocrity or worse. Once again, the shows are listed alphabetically.

EVIL DEAD THE MUSICAL 4D **(MIRACLE MILE SHOPS)** Inspired by director Sam Raimi's three *Evil Dead* movies and Campbell's chainsaw-wielding hero, Ash, this odd production mixes equal portions of camp, raunch, and shock effect (ruptured intestines). As in *The Rocky Horror Picture Show,* the audience is as involved as the cast. Similar to Shamu Stadium at SeaWorld, *Evil Dead* has a "splash zone," except here you get splattered with fake blood instead of cold seawater. There's a plot, but it's mostly a blank check for unbridled insanity. At the end of the day, whether you like it is largely a matter of taste, or lack thereof. *Evil Dead The Musical* is licensed to theater companies all around the country, so you might be able to see it cheaper in your hometown.

MJ LIVE **(RIO)** A low-budget, minimalist tribute to Michael Jackson starring Michael Firestone, who does a good job with the moves and vocals. Supporting dancers likewise impress. Live guitar and drums augment the recorded tracks. A substitute for Cirque du Soleil's *Michael Jackson ONE?* Not hardly, and overpriced at $54–$90, especially for a short 60-minute show.

RIVIERA SHOWS In *Crazy Girls,* the Riviera has one of the oldest continuously running shows in Las Vegas. In the past decade, however, the entertainment mix has been chaotic and usually short-lived. In 2014, the Riv ran several new productions up the flagpole. In the casino-level Bistro Lounge are **Forever Doo Wop** and **Forever Motor City,** starring veterans of a Platters, Coasters, and Marvelettes reprise group that played for years in various Vegas showrooms. The names of the shows pretty much tell the story. Both are sung to track, and the same vocalists perform in each show. *Forever Doo Wop* has no direct competition, but *Forever Motor City* is pitted against Motown productions *Human Nature* at the Venetian and *Hitzville* at the V Theater at Planet Hollywood. The vocals are strong in all three Motown retrospectives, but *Human Nature* and *Hitzville* singers are backed by live bands and have superior showrooms to the Riviera's Bistro Lounge. *Forever Motor City* and *Hitzville* feature male and female talent. At *Human Nature*, it's all guys. *Hitzville* and *Human Nature* are reviewed in detail on pages 242–243. A third show at the Riv's upstairs Starlite Theater is a revised version of **Pawn Shop Live!**, a spoof of the *Pawn Stars* reality TV show, which is filmed in Las Vegas. Previously at the Golden Nugget, the latest iteration of *Pawn Shop Live!* is mildly amusing and rather sophomoric. You'd probably have more fun visiting Gold & Silver Pawn (**gspawn .com**), whose doings were chronicled in the TV series. And yes, the family featured in the show actually works there. For more information on all of the above, visit **rivierahotel.com.**

SHANIA TWAIN: STILL THE ONE (CAESARS PALACE) AND *TIM McGRAW AND FAITH HILL SOUL2SOUL* **(THE VENETIAN)** Country-music headliners Shania Twain at Caesars Palace and Tim McGraw and Faith Hill at The Venetian deliver the goods in productions we rate as four-star. In both shows you'll hear the singers' greatest hits and then some. McGraw and Hill's *Soul2Soul* is more intimate, with their husband–wife chemistry being the cornerstone of a very straightforward production. *Shania Twain: Still the One* is pure Vegas, an over-the-top, full-blown production show with elaborate sets and both special and natural effects (think horses). If you're not enamored of country music, you'll probably like Shania better for the spectacle, but the supporting musicians in each production are worth the price of admission even if the stars call in sick.

Both shows are hard on the wallet, with Shania tickets running $72–$278. Tim and Faith are even more expensive at $183–$304. Both shows are fine for under-21s.

LAS VEGAS NIGHTLIFE

AT FIRST BLUSH, LAS VEGAS'S NIGHTLIFE SCENE closely resembles the city's many buffets—amid the chaos, there's something for everybody. Today, Las Vegas makes billions as America's go-to city for dining, nightlife, and entertainment, not to mention its long history of gaming, but this was not always the case.

In the Rat Pack era, it was gaming that raked in the big bucks, with steakhouses and 99¢ breakfasts as loss-leaders, keeping you near the action at all times. Entertainment took the form of big-room shows with Elvis, Liberace, and Sinatra and the boys, and smoky lounges where the booze flowed endlessly. Disco wasn't even a twinkle in anyone's eye. Cut to 1988, when local bars Tramps and the Shark Club began—gasp—charging cover at the door. The 1990s brought the rise and subsequent fall of rave music and parties (much of which centered around Las Vegas's electronic-music trailblazers, Utopia nightclub and the Cande Factory), but by the Millennium the casinos themselves were creating nightlife worth getting off the couch for: Club Rio, Studio 54, C2K, Ra . . .

unofficial **TIP**
For a postclubbing dining experience that doesn't involve a grubby casino coffee shop, hit the nameless **"secret" pizzeria** on the third floor of The Cosmopolitan for floppy, New York–style slices and a strict no-ranch policy. (Just look for the hallway of album covers.) Or, if you're off the Strip or Downtown, head straight to **Herbs & Rye** (3713 W. Sahara Ave.; 702-982-8036; **herbsandrye.com**).

Today, creating fulfilling party opportunities for tourists, locals, and everyone in between is big business for the casinos. And it's only intensifying. New York, Chicago, Miami, and L.A. all have their flag planted somewhere on the Strip or just slightly off-Strip. Electronic dance music dominates the club scene, with Top 40 and hip-hop (often called "open-format") occupying what little balance remains. Celebrity nightclub appearances are waning as the dominant draw; today, it's the DJs who are the celebrities: Tiësto, Calvin Harris, Avicci, Nervo, and so on. Don't know who the heck these men and women are? You soon shall. And gone are the days of the DJ booth; DJs perform live on custom stages with confetti canons, light shows, and LED screens worthy of a stadium.

The annual spate of trendy new venues has slowed down since the arrival of The Cosmopolitan in 2010, with casinos favoring re-branding over new construction: **1 OAK** replaces Jet, **Hyde** supplants Fontana Lounge, **Lily** one-ups Caramel, and so on. But 2013 did see three high-profile openings: Angel Management Group's **Hakkasan** (for which the exterior of the MGM Grand was altered) and **Light** and **Daylight,** the nightclub and party pool duo by Light Group at Mandalay Bay. In 2014, we gained supper club **Rose. Rabbit. Lie.** at The Cosmopolitan, **Drai's Beach Club & Nightclub** at The Cromwell (the first freestanding boutique hotel on the Strip), and over at SLS, Labor Day weekend launched **Life** and **Foxtail,** both doing double duty as night- and dayclubs. Still, Las Vegas is a buyer's market, with more clubs than tourists to fill all of them. It would appear that the Great Recession is behind us—Vegas is back! Every visitor is ravenous for a piece of it, and every club wants to sell you something, anything to get you into *their* VIP booth rather than their neighbor's. Call it the upside. So keep your wits about you, and we'll show you how to reap the many benefits of the nightlife buffet.

Trend Alert! Sunday Brunch fever has utterly consumed Las Vegas: Hot people, cool music, bottomless drinks. Sounds like a nightclub, but it's brunch. Try **Bubbles & Brunch** at The Cosmopolitan, **Lavo Brunch** at The Palazzo (seasonal), and **Simon** at Palms Place for a party. For something truly out there, try the Italian dim sum brunch at

Giada in The Cromwell, or if you prefer something more traditional, Bouchon at The Venetian and La Cave and chef Carlos Guia's Jazz Brunch at the Wynn Country Club scratch that itch. Also consider heading to the pools—Marquee Dayclub, Drai's, Encore Beach Club, Liquid, Bare, Wet Republic, and Tao Beach all serve up exceptional poolside fare.

LAS VEGAS NIGHTLIFE BESTIARY

THE KEY TO UNLOCKING LAS VEGAS'S bewildering club scene is to do your homework *before* you arrive. You're already reading this handy guide, so that puts you light years beyond those who show up clueless, only to be preyed upon for being so unsavvy. But don't be discouraged if you de-plane at McCarran with little more of a clue than when you left home. Here's a quick-and-dirty rundown of just some of the categories of nightlife activity available to you.

CASINO BAR Casino bars, lobby bars, and center bars are generally open 24/7. These watering holes take their titles from whatever they are located nearest (hence, lobby bar) and generally have one thing in common: accessibility to a good drink. Some even count among the city's finest beverage programs. (Insert puns here about the proverbial bar having been raised.) Requirements for entry? A valid ID, a pulse, and a penchant for cocktails. One need never wander too far in Vegas sober.

Ones to try: Throw a rock and you'll hit one. Every casino has a bar, and most have several. But try Lobby Bar (formerly Galleria) in Caesars Palace; Fusion Mixology Bar and Laguna Champagne Bar (The Palazzo); Bond and Vesper (The Cosmopolitan); Aurora and Flight (Luxor); Rouge, Zuri, and Centrifuge (MGM Grand); Eyecandy (Mandalay Bay); Center Bar (Hard Rock); Social (The Palms); and Petrossian (Bellagio).

BARS AND PUBS Separated from the casino by actual walls, or perhaps even as freestanding structures, bars and pubs occupy the gap between the too-casual casino bar and the bottle-slinging lounges. Since they're less stringent about dress code than lounges and clubs, and often feature a bar menu and light entertainment, bars and pubs are a perfect place for large groups. Cover charges here are rare, and speed of entry is usually gauged by capacity.

Ones to try: Hussong's Cantina and Rí Rá Irish Pub (Mandalay Place); Public House (Luxor) and Public House (The Venetian; believe it or not, these two aren't related); Coyote Ugly and Nine Fine Irishmen (New York–New York); Book & Stage (The Cosmopolitan); Rhumbar (Mirage); Diablo's Cantina and The Pub (Monte Carlo); McFadden's (Town Square); Todd English P.U.B. (Crystals); and Yard House (Town Square, Red Rock, and the LINQ).

LOUNGE Whether Downtown, Center Strip, or off-Strip, lounges offer a heavy dose of class and ambience, forgoing the velvet rope dance in favor of getting you inside with a drink in your hand. Plush, open seating, elegant lighting, generous cocktails, and a possible bar menu are the calling cards of a proper lounge. The town being so spread out, Las Vegas locals are accustomed to having to come together in the middle; lounges being so plentiful and accessible, they are at the heart of the "meet market" singles scene. Locals love the happy hours (which usually last 2–4 hours), so expect an after-work crowd early and a pre-club party later. Ease of entry is generally dependent upon the day of the week, conventions, and holidays; sometimes, cover charges appear for special events. High-end restaurants also tend to have killer lounges for cocktails and small bites.

Ones to try: Fizz Champagne Bar (Caesars Palace); Mandarin Bar (Mandarin Oriental); Parasol Up and Down (Wynn); Eastside Lounge (Encore); Chandelier and Comme Ça (The Cosmopolitan); Downtown Cocktail Room, Scullery, and Wayfarer (Downtown); Blue Martini (Town Square); Lavo (The Palazzo); and Sage and Sirio (Aria).

ULTRALOUNGE This was a specious marketing term invented by Las Vegas promoters quite a few years back, but "ultralounge" serves as well as anything to describe high-end venues that charge dearly both at the door and at the bar. Such places are immaculately designed and furnished, staffed with gorgeous servers (and ogrelike security), and policed to ensure compliance with a snappy dress code. "Bottle service"—that is, paying hundreds of dollars for a bottle of booze—is typically the only way to reserve a table. Clientele tends toward the well-heeled and supercool, though if you don't mind standing, even the modestly loaded can pay the cover and drink à la carte. Space here is limited and therefore sold at a premium for cover charges rivaling those of full-scale nightclubs.

Ones to try: Revolution Lounge (Mirage); Ghostbar (The Palms); Lily (Bellagio); Lavo (The Palazzo); and Savile Row (Luxor).

BOUTIQUE/INTIMATE NIGHTCLUB Fed up with being pigeonholed as fashions trended toward smaller size, clubs for a time became "intimate" and "boutique" to differentiate themselves from ultralounges and megaclubs, taking advantage of hot hotel and travel buzzwords and thumbing their noses at the ever-swelling megaclub.

Ones to try: Surrender (Encore; well, the interior portion is small); Foxtail (SLS); The Bank (Bellagio); Ling Ling Lounge and Ling Ling Club inside Hakkasan (MGM Grand); and Hyde (Bellagio).

COUNTRY AND COUNTRY-CROSSOVER Line dancing to today's Top-40 hits? VIP bottle service and Stetsons? The latest trend to take root is the country-crossover nightclub, where you might find yourself two-stepping to the Black Eyed Peas, Kenny Chesney, and Justin Timberlake, then riding a mechanical bull to the sounds of crossover artists Taylor Swift, Keith Urban, and Carrie Underwood.

Ones to try: Revolver (Santa Fe Station), Stoney's Rockin' Country (Town Square), PBR Rock Bar (Miracle Mile Shops), Rockhouse (The Venetian), Coyote Ugly (New York–New York), Toby Keith's I Love This Bar & Grill (Harrah's) and Gilley's (TI).

NIGHTCLUB/MEGACLUB Resorts now customarily spend tens of millions on nightlife, so you can expect the best in everything from the attractive staff and the digs to the internationally renowned DJs and the celebrity contingent. These sprawling labyrinths may cover several floors and include dance room(s), side lounges, bars, a restaurant, uncountable VIP rooms, and possible access to a pool. They might even have multiple entrances. Count on long lines at every entrance regardless; more than anything else, the success of megaclubs have brought the era of door bribes to Vegas. Palm $20 at least (per person in your party) to the doorman, and you'll find your names appearing mysteriously (and invisibly) on his list; VIP host tips are now practically mandatory for the privilege of making a table reservation at the tonier spots. Otherwise, expect to wait an hour or more to get in, if ever. Inside, you'll find massive crowds of beautiful people, dressed to the nines and ready to party, plus a half dozen ways to entertain yourself—DJs, dance troupes, novelty performers, live "mannequins," you name it. The time and expense effectively kills the idea of club-hopping, but with all this on offer, you probably won't need anything else—unless it's a Red Bull at dawn. Promoters use every trick in the books to assemble the most attractive clientele in one place. Bottle service is king, and everyone else is there to merely fill in the spaces between the most valuable real estate. Check your ego at the door unless you intend to spend heavily to keep up with the wealthiest of the Joneses, and that means both once you are inside the ropes as well as just to make it through them—at the door, tip (or offer to tip) anything in a suit.

Ones to try: XS (Encore); Tryst (Wynn); Tao (The Venetian); Marquee (The Cosmopolitan); Body English (Hard Rock); House of Blues (Mandalay Bay); 1 OAK (Mirage); LAX (Luxor); Chateau (Paris); Hakkasan (MGM Grand); Light (Mandalay Bay); and newcomers Drai's (The Cromwell) and Life (SLS).

AFTERHOURS When the clubs close, the staff doesn't exactly rush home and go to bed, nor does the party crowd. Those wishing to test the limits of their endurance can do so at one of a few dedicated late-night joints offering after-hours parties. Doors open as early as midnight or as late as 4 a.m., but all keep the music and drinks flowing till dawn, and often well beyond that. Music usually tends toward house, trance, and electronica, but Drai's also offers a hip-hop room. While there is almost always a cover charge, lines are not so much a problem here as parking. But at 6 a.m., should you really be driving anyway?

Ones to try: Posh at The Playground and The Artisan (both West Side); After at 1923 Bourbon & Burlesque (Mandalay Bay); and Drai's, now back in its original home in the basement of the building that is now The Cromwell.

POOL PARTIES Incredible to think that only 11 years ago such an animal didn't exist. That is, until Rehab came on the scene turning day into nightlife. Six years ago, Wet Republic introduced the term "daylife" into the party lexicon. Just about every casino these days invests in the holy trinity of nightclub, ultra-lounge, and the hip

unofficial **TIP**
Pool parties don't just happen by day, and daylife doesn't necessarily happen by pools! Check out Sunday Nightswim at XS (Encore) and Eclipse Sunday nights and select holiday weekends at Daylight (Mandalay Bay). And in the off-season, GBDC (Ghostbar Dayclub; Palms) and Lavo Brunch (The Palazzo) keep partiers occupied.

dining experience loosely called "dining with a scene" or "vibe dining." All are run like battleships by a staff of pretty young things, the restaurants and lounges operating much the same as the nightclubs. But during the summer—roughly from March into October—adults-only party pools pop up, joining the trinity and boasting every amenity the clubs do, only without the roof: bottle service, VIP hosts, cocktail servers, DJ music. Just add water, cabanas, hot tubs, and, in some cases, European bathing (read: topless). Admittance to this kind of flesh parade is at the doorman's discretion and is very much determined by appearance and the maintenance of a healthy female-to-male ratio.

Ones to try: The Naked Pool (Artisan), Azure (The Palazzo), Bare (Mirage), Daydream (M Resort), Encore Beach Club (Encore), Liquid (Aria), Marquee Dayclub (The Cosmopolitan), Daylight (Mandalay Bay), Palms Pool & Bungalows (Palms), Rehab (Hard Rock), Tao Beach (The Venetian), Venus (Caesars Palace), Wet Republic (MGM Grand), and newcomers Drai's Beach Club (The Cromwell) and Life and Foxtail Pool Club (SLS).

What NOT to bring to a pool party:

- **Large backpacks:** Small purses and bags are OK but will likely be searched.

- **Valuables:** Unless you have a cabana with a safe (and many of the newer ones do), take only what you need.

- **Liquids:** All beverages must be purchased after going through security.

- **Medications:** Paramedics are almost always on hand, so leave all pills and potions behind. You can argue for inhalers, insulin syringes, and EpiPens, but be prepared for a fight.

- **Weapons** of any and all kinds.

- **Glass:** Duh.

CELEBRITIES

THEY'RE EVERYWHERE, and it isn't by happenstance. Celebrity sightings are rarely just common occurrences; more often than not, they are arranged in advance by ambitious nightclubs, promoters, and sponsors. Stars of film, music, and TV are regularly booked to tip their hat, make a toast, pose with their birthday cake, or belt out a tune or two. For a club to bill a star as a "guest performer" is to subject itself to a mandatory live-entertainment tax (LET) or casino-entertainment tax (CET). Many do this, but just as many do not, and prefer instead to keep a live mic on hand, you know, *just in case.* Often billed as a host or as making a special guest appearance, some of today's hottest artists can be seen performing a quick two- or three-song set. If you're fortunate enough to cross paths with actor-singer Jamie Foxx, clear your night—his visits are legendary.

INSIDER ADVICE

LAS VEGAS—NOT JUST FOR WEEKENDS ANYMORE Vegas was, is, and always will be a weekend destination—one that hits its stride at about 8 p.m. on Friday and doesn't slow down until early Monday morning.

It's a given that the town's bars, lounges, and clubs will be filled to the brim on Friday and Saturday nights. But what all locals (and few tourists) know is that Sunday–Thursday the clubs don't close their doors; they just refocus. The secret to midweek partying is finding out which night each club holds its local-industry night, thus avoiding the tourist traps that will take anyone off the street—Birkenstocks, shorts, and all. Expect gratuitous contests, costumes, gimmicky promotions, and hordes of locals and cognoscenti partying like it's Mardi Gras. While there, get on everyone's e-mail list, bring business cards, and if someone says they're a VIP host from another venue (as many will on industry nights), buy him a shot—he's your new best friend.

unofficial **TIP**

Mandalay Place—located between Luxor and Mandalay Bay—has about the fastest valet on the Strip and offers access to all the Luxor and Mandalay Bay clubs. Just tell them you're going shopping.

Ones to try: Industry Sundays at The Bank (Bellagio); Mondays at Marquee (The Cosmopolitan) and XS (Encore); Tuesdays at 1 OAK (Mirage) and Hyde (Bellagio); Wednesdays at LAX (Luxor), Surrender (Encore), and Chateau (Paris); Thursdays at Tao (The Venetian) and Tryst (Wynn).

GETTING IN Showing up is half the battle, so do so—nice and early. For any party size or gender mix other than two attractive young ladies by themselves, save yourself and your guests the agonizing, soul-crushing velvet-rope experience by doing some of the work ahead of time. At the rope, the uninitiated and uninformed can expect a long wait (30 minutes to upwards of 2 hours), a complete lack of eye contact, and even possible ridicule. Sometimes doormen employ intimidation and humiliation to pressure a group's point man into investing his life savings in bottle service or huge tips to pass through the pearly gates. Or worse, a doorman might keep you in line for an eternity only to finally grant you entry . . . into an empty club. The most notorious perps of ego-crushing entry experiences include The Bank, LAX, Tao, Surrender, XS, and Marquee. Hakkasan, Light, Drai's, and the clubs at SLS are the Strip's latest proving grounds, rivaling airport security lines. Consider yourself warned.

Your best bet for getting into your club of choice is to contact the club directly (consult **jackcolton.com** for the lead VIP hosts' direct e-mail address and cell numbers) or work with an independent VIP hosting company such as **VIP2Vegas.com.** For a small fee, these companies and individuals can walk you directly into the club of your choice or book you a table for bottle service. And yes, there is an app for that—hundreds of 'em actually. Try **partypetition.com** for starters.

TIME IS MONEY Ah yes, bottle service. If the dutifully paying customers who line the bars and walls of a club are the meat and potatoes of the industry, bottle-service patrons are the dessert. But nightclubs like to have dessert first, so you will see bottle-service patrons waiting far less time to get in. But remember that these patrons are paying a great deal more for that privilege. The bottom line is you will spend time or money. In other words, if you want to spend very little money, you can get in for just the cover charge, but you might wait a long time. Or, consider investing in bottle service (that is, buying a bottle—or, likely, multiple bottles—of liquor to get a VIP table or booth) to bypass the line entirely, thus spending very little time outside the club. Bottles can go up to the high hundreds, even into the thousands for rare Champagnes or Cognacs. The industry benchmark is Grey Goose vodka, a liter of which will cost you $250 at Downtown Cocktail Room, $425 at Tryst, $475 at Tao, and $575 at XS. But $100 bottles of newer, lesser-known vodkas are becoming more prevalent, too.

unofficial **TIP**
Look closely at that bill! If you're doing bottle service, inquire beforehand what taxes and gratuities will be added—it can reach as high as 40 percent! When the bill comes, make sure you're not adding an additional gratuity on top of the server's "auto-grat" (unless you mean to), and be careful not to put the total onto the sneaky extra line sometimes added below the customary server tip line for tipping your busser (unless you mean to).

While a liter of Goose is obtainable at any neighborhood liquor store for about $37, it's not what's inside the bottle you're paying for. It's the valuable real estate of having a private booth or table, the attention of an attractive cocktail server, a busser to clean up spills and refresh ice, and likely even a neighboring thug of a security guard to keep an eye on your prize. Bottle service is unique to each club: one table's price might be determined by location, while another's is by the number of people (usually three to four people per bottle). Be prepared for a possible shakedown; you might find yourself being walked to an undesirable table, past better ones, only to be told that those tables cost extra—cash preferably, payable right now to your host. If this happens, stand firm and ask to see other available tables within your price range. Once you have the table, take your time with your bottles and resist your server's offers to pour you shots, as you may find yourself required to order more bottles or else shove off to make room for another party. You will find this is more prevalent in clubs than lounges.

COMFORT ZONES A place for everyone, and everyone in their place. Vegas has it. Just as there are clubs, bars, and lounges where everyone can feel comfortable, there are some where not everyone would. The top clubs target a 21-to-35 age range, and though guests of any age (over 21) are welcome to try their luck at the rope or make a reservation, they may find that it's the other patrons who might make a club unfriendly to someone over that hump. Tight confines, loud music, inebriated neighbors, and little to no elbowroom might make for an uncomfortable evening.

But some venues make it easier for patrons of any age to enjoy themselves. The **Beatles Revolution Lounge** at the Mirage is situated just a stone's throw from Cirque du Soleil's show *LOVE*. It's Beatles-driven in design, though chic and young in music and live entertainment, making it a hot spot for any demographic early in the evening; as the hour grows late, it gives way to a younger, hipper crowd. Open seating helps too. The city's many dueling piano bars, such as Pete's at Town Square and Napoleon's at Paris, play everything from the best of the 1980s to today in a convivial environment that is inclusive rather than exclusive. **Downtown Cocktail Room** and **Wayfarer** will appeal to the sophisticated imbiber from any age bracket. Even from Light Group—who have Light and The Bank, two of Vegas's hottest clubs—**Lily** is small and approachable without giving up the Vegas excitement you came for. Just about every casino has something that will appeal to the 35-and-over set; they want to keep you on property and will do just about anything to satisfy, and that includes providing nightlife venues for every age group.

DRESS CODES Inside every club you will witness flagrant violations of dress code—hats, sneakers, T-shirts, ripped jeans, and more. Attempt to emulate this behavior and you may find yourself left on the wrong side of the ropes. The only people who can get away with this sort of rebellion are celebrities, well-known local socialites, and the DJ. Even if you think you are on close, personal terms with a doorman or VIP host, you might see him blanch and go cold when you show up in tennis shoes and a ball cap. Gentlemen, pack dress shoes, a nice pair of jeans, and remember that a sport coat (thrown over anything) cures most ills. Ladies, you pretty much have carte blanche, but think practical—comfiest heels, smallest purse.

TIPPING Keep plenty of small bills handy for tipping. Aside from the valet and the coat-check girl, tip anyone who goes out of their way for you. The doorman who looked the other way about your scuzzy loafers, the VIP host who walked you past the line, the bathroom attendant who got the cranberry juice out of your shirt . . . all are deserving of your monetary thanks. Bartenders and cocktail servers can usually be tipped on a bill if you're charging your round. Otherwise, cash tips are highly recommended lest you find yourself high and dry the rest of the night.

If your line situation is looking hopeless, you can try to encourage (read: tip, grease, bribe) a doorman or VIP host to expedite the process. A good rule of thumb is $20–$25 per head, but with so many trying the same thing, it's not so much the amount as the ease of his slipping you through that will help or hurt the situation. A doorman letting in 10 guys will get a stern look from his boss, while a doorman letting in six ladies and four guys might get a mere eyebrow raise. Gentlemen, pad your group heavily with women and keep the guy count low. Be discreet (don't wave money around), but make your presence and your willingness to play (pay) known.

THE DOWNTOWN RENAISSANCE Downtown Las Vegas is back in a big way! Fremont Street is the original Las Vegas Strip. It caps off the current or "New" Strip like a T, with a covered pedestrian entertainment zone called The Fremont Street Experience to the west of Las Vegas Boulevard and the Fremont East Entertainment District to the east. Tourists are generally drawn to the bright lights of "The Old Strip" like moths to the Luxor light, but savvy travelers are finally beginning to follow the locals' example and venture into Fremont East territory. There you will find the sophisticated and cocktail-centric **Downtown Cocktail Room,** the cavelike hipster haven **The Griffin, Atomic Liquors, Vanguard Lounge,** barcade **Insert Coin(s),** irreverent live music spot **Beauty Bar,** and piano bar **Don't Tell**

Mama, as well as newcomers **Scullery, Wayfarer, Park on Fremont,** and **Commonwealth,** with the speakeasy-esque **Laundry Room** within. For coffee, vinyl records, modern art, and even a beer (after 7 p.m.), visit **Emergency Arts** and **The Beat Coffeehouse** on East Fremont at 6th Street, and then venture just north of the Fremont Street Experience to find **Triple George Restaurant** and its satellite, **Mob Bar,** before letting your hair down and perhaps donating a bra to the impressive collection found at **Hogs & Heifers,** the iconic biker-friendly bar. In the nearby 18 blocks that make up Las Vegas's Arts District are **Bar + Bistro, Lady Silvia, Artifice,** and, most recently, **Mingo** and **Velveteen Rabbit.** If you can't find something to do every night in Las Vegas, you're just not trying that hard.

Note: All clubs profiled below can be found on the maps in Part 4, Dining and Restaurants, pages 377–387.

NIGHTCLUB PROFILES

1 OAK

New York's one-of-a-kind club is now two of a kind

The Mirage, 3400 Las Vegas Blvd. S.; ☎ 702-588-5656; **1oaklasvegas.com**
MID-STRIP AND ENVIRONS

Cover Friday and Saturday, $40 men, $30 ladies; Tuesday, $30 men, $20 ladies; locals free on Tuesday. **Mixed drinks** $10 and up. **Wine** $10 and up. **Beer** $6 and up. **Dress** Upscale chic. **Food available** None. **Hours** Tuesday, Friday and Saturday, 10:30 p.m.–4 a.m.

WHO GOES THERE Socialites in training, celebrity gawkers, and people still looking for Jet Nightclub, the space's previous incarnation.

WHAT GOES ON A raucous party focusing on the clubber as the main attraction, with occasional celebrity hosts (think Nicki Minaj, Ludacris, and Nick Cannon) and guest DJs spinning Top 40, hip-hop, and house. The Las Vegas outpost of the NYC club is a joint venture between the prolific Light Group and The Butter Group.

SETTING AND ATMOSPHERE A sexy yet unpredictable environment; visitors to the previous Jet Nightclub will be delighted to see the signature stripper poles and dance floor pit are still among the architectural features, but with updated design elements and a modern edge. Two rooms encompass 16,000 square feet.

IF YOU GO As with any Las Vegas hot spot, lines can be lengthy, so arrive early, perhaps even stopping by during the day to make friends with the lone promoter/promotrix stationed at the door on day duty. This might give you a chance to be put on his or her guest list for that night to possibly reduce your cover charge and bump you up to the shorter guest list line.

ALSO TRY Light in Mandalay Bay; ☎ 702-693-8300; **thelightvegas.com.**

Artisan Afterhours

The city's hottest underground afterhours

1501 West Sahara Ave.; ☎ 800-554-4092; **artisanhotel.com**
NORTH STRIP AND ENVIRONS

Cover Friday and Saturday, $10; locals and ladies always free. **Mixed drinks** $10 and up. **Wine** $10 and up. **Beer** $6 and up. **Dress** Stylish casual. **Food available** American cuisine served 5 p.m.–1 p.m. at Mood Restaurant. **Hours** Friday and Saturday, 5 p.m.–1 p.m.

WHO GOES THERE Vampires, party monsters, night crawlers, and off-duty industry members blowing off steam before (and even after) the next day dawns. Birthday boys and girls, ask about the free birthday bottle service.

WHAT GOES ON When the restaurants close and the clubs are already hitting their stride, the evening is just getting started at the Artisan. Early birds enjoy bottle specials, and those who simply can't call it a night at 4 a.m. enjoy the ultimate people-watching, plus friendly bartenders and special guest DJs bring true underground electronic music.

SETTING AND ATMOSPHERE Tucked away from the Strip less than a minute away, the Artisan Hotel features dark hues and classic masterpiece reproductions covering every inch of free space, including the ceilings. The Artisan Bar & Ultralounge off the main lobby, past the fountain, continues the unique decor with luxurious dark woods and leather couches.

IF YOU GO Go late. *Really* late. Why not? There are plenty of clubs that will help you see 4 a.m., maybe 5 a.m., but few can see you through till the dawn with such ease and little hassle at the door. The party is usually hopping inside until well after the sun is up.

ALSO TRY Drai's Afterhours in The Cromwell (☎ 702-737-0555, **draislv .com**) and Crazy Horse III (☎ 702-673-1700, **crazyhorse3.com**).

The Bank

Lavish jewel-box nightclub

Bellagio, 3600 Las Vegas Blvd. S.; ☎ 702-693-8300; **thebanklasvegas.com**
MID-STRIP AND ENVIRONS

Cover $40 men, $30 ladies; locals free on Thursdays and Sundays. **Mixed drinks** $9 and up. **Wine** $9 and up. **Beer** $6 and up. **Dress** Upscale chic; no hats, T-shirts, chains, excessive jewelry, athletic wear, shorts, baggy attire, sunglasses, sandals, or tennis shoes. **Specials** Ladies enjoy open bar till midnight on Thursdays; Sunday is industry night. **Food available** None. **Hours** Thursday–Sunday, 10:30 p.m.–4 a.m.

WHO GOES THERE Many will remember—and perhaps miss—the late, great Light Nightclub, which reigned in this space from 2001 to 2007. (Don't

Las Vegas Nightclubs

NAME OF CLUB	TYPE OF CLUB
1 OAK	New York's one-of-a-kind club is now two of a kind
Artisan Afterhours	The city's hottest underground afterhours
The Bank	Lavish jewel-box nightclub
Blue Martini Lounge	Casual, accessible, sprawling after-work date spot
Body English	Hard Rock Hotel's sexy, sophisticated nightclub returns
Chandelier Bar	Pre-post at the heart of the Strip's newest casino
Chateau Nightclub & Gardens	Indoor-outdoor rooftop nightlife
Commonwealth	Downtown's newest nightlife hub
Downtown Cocktail Room	Bohemian-chic speakeasy
Drai's Nightclub	The Strip's new rooftop megaclub and pool complex
Ghostbar	The Palms' enduring anchor lounge, post makeover
Hakkasan	60,000 square feet of party potential, plus celebrity DJs
House of Blues	Cover bands, live rock, and headliners in a casual scene
Hyde	Boutique-y L.A.-style club with an A-List view
Insert Coin(s)	Video game arcade, bar, and dance floor for adults
Lavo Lounge	The intimate, lounge side of Tao Group nightlife
LAX	Opulent, cavernous nightclub with a dramatic entryway
Light	Las Vegas's legendary hot spot is resurrected
Lily Bar & Lounge	Central gathering spot at the heart of Bellagio
Marquee	Glamorous megaclub and DJ magnet
Rí Rá	Authentic Irish music, food, drinks and *craic*
Rose. Rabbit. Lie.	Dine, drink, and dance at the city's newest supper club
Social	A high-energy whiskey-centric center bar
Stoney's Rockin' Country	Line dancing, two-stepping, and live country bands
Surrender	Party outside under the stars and inside with them
Tao	A labyrinthine restaurant, lounge, and megaclub
Tryst	Luxurious waterfall views from the dance floor
XS	Excessively beautiful, inside and out

mourn too long; Light is back and bigger than the original incarnation at Mandalay Bay.) Those who never bounced on Light's banquettes will still be impressed by the quality of the party Light Group continues to put on for longtime patrons, locals, and stars of sport and screen.

WHAT GOES ON Celebrities, sports figures, and foreign business magnates eagerly mix with tourists and locals to create a party that does not see its peak till at least 2 a.m.

SETTING AND ATMOSPHERE The intimate, elevated, square-shaped club welcomes you via twin escalators and through the Cristal Champagne–lined anteroom, to the main room, which unfolds down to the mezzanine and dance-floor levels. Understated 1950s-style and Atomic Era designs in gold stand out bravely against a backdrop of black dotted with pricey chandeliers and blessed with a booming sound system.

IF YOU GO Party with the professionals. Consider saving this one for a Sunday night, when the local nightlife set turns out in droves. Recent reviews have cooled off, especially since the arrival of 1 OAK and Light, the Group's newer focal points. Bottom line: This is a place best experienced from a VIP booth, so if that's not on your itinerary, plan to be separated from both your time and money, as well as from the bottle crowd.

ALSO TRY For something smaller, nearby Lily Lounge in Bellagio is an ideal spot in which to convene after dinner and before joining the fray; ☎ 702-693-8300; **lilylasvegas.com.**

Blue Martini Lounge

Casual, accessible, sprawling after-work date spot

6593 Las Vegas Blvd. S.; ☎ 702-949-2583; **bluemartinilounge.com**
SOUTH STRIP AND ENVIRONS

Cover Beginning at 11 p.m.: men $10 Wednesday–Saturday; ladies $5 Thursday–Saturday. **Mixed drinks** $12 and up. **Wine** $9 and up. **Beer** $7 and up. **Dress** Business casual; no caps or athletic wear; no flip-flops, sneakers other than Converse Chuck Taylor All Stars and Vans, or shorts for men after 8 p.m. **Specials** Happy hour daily, 4–8 p.m. **Food available** Large-portion tapas. **Hours** Wednesday–Saturday, 4 p.m.–3 a.m.; Sunday–Tuesday, 4 p.m.–2 a.m.

WHO GOES THERE Everyone. Locals and visitors with a car have no trouble journeying to the far south end of the Strip for this gem hidden within the Town Square Mall, above Yard House and just across from the AMC Town Square 18 movie theater.

WHAT GOES ON As a popular pre/post locale, Blue Martini catches all the after-work, post-movie, pre-party action and is also a destination unto itself. With live music nightly and four bars (three inside, one out), everyone seems to find their place, although the hottest action usually revolves around the outside bar.

SETTING AND ATMOSPHERE Surprisingly, the place is not overdone. In red, blue, and black, with generous additions of warm wood and subtle lighting, Blue Martini achieves its attractiveness without the use of props, themes, or much artwork. Unsurprisingly, the attractive staff is decoration enough.

IF YOU GO Flying solo, you might find it difficult to strike up a conversation here, as almost everyone comes with at least one friend. Bring a group of any size to create an instant party.

ALSO TRY Double Helix Wine & Whiskey Lounge and Yard House, both in Town Square Mall (**townsquarelasvegas.com**).

Body English

Hard Rock Hotel's sexy, sophisticated nightclub returns

Hard Rock Hotel, 4455 Paradise Rd.; ☎ 702-693-5555;
hardrockhotel.com   **EAST OF STRIP**

Cover $30 men, $20 ladies; locals receive $10 off on Friday and Saturday. **Mixed drinks** $10 and up. **Wine** $10 and up. **Beer** $8 and up. **Dress** Fashionable upscale. **Food available** None. **Hours** Thursday–Saturday (Sunday seasonally), 10 p.m. to close.

WHO GOES THERE Body English was instrumental in exposing Las Vegas to electronic dance music before the Strip's megaclubs turned DJs into the new celebrities and started bidding wars for their residencies. So nostalgia plays a role for many who return, elated to see that little has changed since her doors closed in 2010. The rest of the crowd is just excited to finally see the inside of a Las Vegas nightclub.

WHAT GOES ON Body English continues its history of introducing underground artists and trendsetting genres to the scene, showcasing indie, electronic, rock, and pop music.

SETTING AND ATMOSPHERE While the main entrance has moved to a more central location, guests still enter the masculine hideaway via the grand staircase. The space features two distinct rooms adorned with grommetted leather seating, vintage chandeliers, and rich dark woods, while the private Parlor plays host to even more intimate events.

IF YOU GO If you hit the club after a show at The Joint or Vinyl, many times you can find members of the band hanging out in Body English's VIP area.

ALSO TRY Without leaving the property, try the Hard Rock Hotel's other nightclub, Vanity (☎ 702-693-5555, **hardrockhotel.com**), which—attractive as she is—couldn't steal the thunder from her big sister, Body English. Or, venture over to Mandalay Bay to check out Light (☎ 702-693-8300, **thelight vegas.com**), the other club that was recently brought back from oblivion.

Chandelier Bar

Pre-post at the heart of the Strip's newest casino

The Cosmopolitan, 3708 Las Vegas Blvd. S.; ☎ 702-698-7000; **cosmopolitanlasvegas.com**   **MID-STRIP AND ENVIRONS**

Cover None. **Mixed drinks** $10 and up. **Wine** $10 and up. **Beer** $7 and up. **Dress** Casual. **Food available** None. **Hours** Level 1: 24/7; Level 1.5: 6 p.m.–4 a.m.; Level 2: 11 a.m.–11 p.m.

WHO GOES THERE 21–50; couples grabbing cocktails before or after dinner, groups fueling up before (or instead of) heading to the clubs.

WHAT GOES ON Whether for sheer convenience and location's sake, or because they heard there was a top-notch beverage program to be sampled, bodies pile up at the Chandelier Bar by evening time, when everyone kind of just joins together as one giant party.

SETTING AND ATMOSPHERE A thing of certain beauty: Multiple bar levels are stacked vertically within a massive three-story chandelier constructed of more than two million glass crystals, which dominates the center of the casino. Stairs and elevators connect Levels 1, 1.5, and 2, which cumulatively serve as a center bar, a stand-alone hot spot, and a central meeting point for Marquee Nightclub's VIP hosts and their would-be patrons.

IF YOU GO Find seats first, then either send emissaries to the bar or send up flares to attract the attention of a cocktail server. Off the menus, go for classics and award-winning cocktails on Level 1, flirty and feminine notions on Level 2, and avant-garde (read: experimental) mixology in between on Level 1.5.

ALSO TRY The Cosmopolitan's other fine jewels: Vesper just off the lobby, Bond by the Strip entrance, the Talon Club (The Cosmopolitan's highstakes gaming room, which offers bespoke cocktails and a self-serve whiskey bar to players), and Neapolitan, a poolside adult ice cream parlor offering spiked shakes and more treats for the over-21 crowd; **cosmopolitanlasvegas.com.**

Chateau Nightclub & Gardens

Indoor–outdoor rooftop nightlife

Paris Las Vegas, 3655 Las Vegas Blvd. S.; ☎ 702-776-7770; **chateaunightclublv.com** **MID-STRIP AND ENVIRONS**

Cover $30 men, $20 ladies; locals free on Wednesday, and local ladies always free. **Mixed drinks** $11 and up. **Wine** $12 and up. **Beer** $9 and up. **Dress** Fashionable; no sports jerseys, tank tops on men, tennis shoes, or athletic wear of any kind. **Specials** Get complimentary access to the club by starting early at the Beer Garden, Fridays and Saturdays at 6 p.m. **Food available** None, but the club sits directly above Sugar Factory American Brasserie, which serves 24/7. **Hours** Wednesday and Friday–Saturday, 10:30 p.m.–4 a.m.

WHO GOES THERE 21–45; tourists from all over, overjoyed to partake in the mass gawking at the usual suspects from this group's stable of celebrities, including the Kardashian clan, hot hip-hoppers, and young Hollywood.

WHAT GOES ON While there is a good party to be had inside the former Risqué Nightclub space, this new incarnation has more going for it outdoors. When the sun goes down, the beer garden joins up with the nightclub to become Chateau Terrace. Chateau Gardens, which is perched directly beneath the Eiffel Tower Restaurant, offers magnificent views of the Strip. For all its many bars, the best cocktails can be had in the Sugar Factory bar downstairs.

SETTING AND ATMOSPHERE Think *Alice in Wonderland,* assuming Wonderland was located in France. Here, nightlife coexists with its host casino in theme-y cooperation: oversized gilt and silver mirrors, exaggerated furniture, cocktail staff in French maid unis, one DJ booth atop a fireplace, another atop a bar, and so on. But implied Francophilia gives way to out-and-out luxury outside, where private VIP cabanas overlook the Strip and directly oppose the Bellagio fountains.

IF YOU GO Begin the evening downstairs with dinner at the Sugar Factory American Brasserie or, better yet, with chocolate fondue and paired wines in the Chocolate Lounge. Steal a quick look at the inside of the club but then make an immediate beeline straight for the outdoors.

ALSO TRY 1923 Bourbon & Burlesque by Holly Madison (Yes, *that* Holly Madison) in Mandalay Bay; ☎ 702-912-4001; **1923lv.com.**

Commonwealth

Downtown's newest nightlife hub

525 Fremont St.; ☎ 702-798-7000; **commonwealthlv.com** **DOWNTOWN**

Cover $5 Friday and Saturday. **Mixed drinks** $10 and up. **Wine** None. **Beer** $6 and up. **Dress** Fashionable. **Specials** Happy hour Wednesday–Friday, 6–9 p.m. **Food available** None. **Hours** Wednesday–Friday, 6 p.m.–2 a.m.; Saturday and Sunday, 8 p.m.–2 a.m.

WHO GOES THERE 21–40; hipsters, students, off-duty DJs, and diehard fashionistas. Don't be turned off by the velvet rope and tattooed doorman; Fremont Street is the epicenter of the Downtown Las Vegas revival, so there is still a rough element that occasionally needs bouncing.

WHAT GOES ON The owners cringe a little to hear it, but this antique-y, Boston-inspired bar and pub frequently becomes something of a nightclub. Fortunately, it's Downtown's hottest one. Wednesday nights, art, music, and fashion fuse together with rooftop music and playful signature cocktails. Thursday through Saturday, the emphasis is on live music, DJs, and special events. But it's almost never a dull scene at the bar.

SETTING AND ATMOSPHERE Awash in warm incandescent light, Commonwealth's downstairs bar is all dark, grainy wood and exposed brick. Artwork and photos are of the vintage and ironic variety. And, no, you're not hallucinating—that is indeed an albino peacock welcoming you to the bar. Crystal chandeliers are nicely juxtaposed against the worn, industrial ambience, much of it genuine, as this building was once the laundry facility for the nearby landmark El Cortez. Upstairs, one of Downtown's many rooftop bars offers 360-degree views of the area's burgeoning scene.

IF YOU GO Text your name, number in your party, and requested date and time to ☎ 702-701-1466 to inquire about getting a seat in the Laundry Room, the tiny speakeasy that used to be an alley behind the laundry facility; walk-ups are handled on a first-come, first-served basis. Inside, a lone mixologist stirs up classic and original cocktails to a soundtrack of Prohibition-era jazz and standards. The Laundry Room operates Wednesday–Sunday, 8 p.m.–late.

ALSO TRY Wayfarer Bar and the Roof bar in the Inspire Theater building at 107 Las Vegas Blvd. South (☎ 702-910-2390, **frglv.com**) and Park on Fremont at 506 Fremont St. (☎ 702-834-3160, **parkonfremont.com**).

Downtown Cocktail Room

Bohemian-chic speakeasy

111 Las Vegas Blvd. S.; ☎ 702-880-3696; **thedowntownlv.com DOWNTOWN**

Cover None. **Mixed drinks** $8 and up. **Wine** $5 and up. **Beer** $3 and up. **Dress** Casual and retro/vintage-friendly. **Specials** Happy hour Monday–Friday, 4–8 p.m. with reduced drinks. **Food available** Upscale bar hors d'oeuvres during happy hour. **Hours** Monday–Friday, 4 p.m.–2 a.m.; Saturday, 7 p.m.–2 a.m.

WHO GOES THERE 25–50; artists, musicians, writers, Zappos employees, and dilettantes.

WHAT GOES ON With the arrival of Downtown Cocktail Room, Las Vegas was made nearly whole. What has long been missing was an oasis to draw in the artists, writers, cognoscenti, and whiskey-bottle philosophers. Small-time filmmakers, big-time dreamers, and those who just like to be in a creative atmosphere flock to the corner of Las Vegas Boulevard and East Fremont Street (opposite the pedestrian-only, covered Fremont Street Experience).

SETTING AND ATMOSPHERE Showing up is half the battle, especially when faced with a puzzle at the door. The first hurdle here is locating the door. Inside, regulars chuckle as tourists and first-timers attempt to manipulate the glass panels to get in, completely ignoring the scuffed metal sheet that is the actual door; just push. Once inside, darkness pervades except for pin spotlights and flickering red candles. Partake of the open seating on chaises and leather-couch groupings, at the cement bar, or in the back room—called The Speakeasy—with its high-backed leather booths, tinkling chandeliers, and exposed pipes overhead.

IF YOU GO Keep an open mind. Classic cocktails and absinthe (once again legal in the United States) are a specialty, as is the seasonal cocktail list. Get your Red Bull–and–Jägermeister fixes elsewhere. Soak up the groovy vibes (music tends toward down-tempo, along with sexy vocal and instrumental house music), listen to a live singer-songwriter, or strike up a conversation with the bleary-eyed Hunter S. Thompson–looking fellow on the next barstool. He probably painted the art you were so admiring on the walls.

ALSO TRY Scullery at 150 Las Vegas Blvd. South, Suite 190 (☎ 702-910-2396, **scullerylv.com**); Herbs & Rye at 3713 W. Sahara Ave. (☎ 702-982-8036, **herbsandrye.com**); and Velveteen Rabbit at 1218 S. Main St. (☎ 702-685-9645, **facebook.com/velveteenrabbitlv**).

Drai's Nightclub

The Strip's new rooftop megaclub and pool complex

The Cromwell, 3595 Las Vegas Blvd. S.; ☎ 702-737-0555; **draislv.com**
MID-STRIP AND ENVIRONS

Cover $30 men ($40 Saturday), $20 ladies, local men $20 and local ladies complimentary before midnight on Thursday and Sunday. **Mixed drinks** $12 and up. **Wine** $12 and up. **Beer** $8 and up. **Dress** Upscale and fashionable attire—dress to impress. Collared shirts and dress shirts are encouraged. No baggy clothing, athletic wear, athletic sneakers, ball caps, men's shorts, men's sandals, or ripped pants. **Food available** Only at the pool club during the day. **Hours** Nightclub: Thursday–Sunday, 10 p.m.–4:30 a.m. Afterhours: Thursday–Sunday, 1 a.m.–8 a.m. Beach Club: Friday–Sunday, 11 a.m.–6 p.m.

WHO GOES THERE High net worth-y individuals with a taste for the finer things in life—or at the very least a desire to make other people think they have money and/or taste. Either way, when a true baller throws down for one of the insane bottle packages that come with a fireworks display, everyone wins.

WHAT GOES ON Contrary to what they might tell you, no nightclub has truly "reinvented" nightlife in Las Vegas since the days of the firsts: first club on the Strip, first club in a casino, first club in a casino on the Strip. . . . But with each successive major nightclub opening, the bar gets hoisted higher with regard to architecture, opulence, technology, vastness (or intimacy), DJ talent, and bottle service. And Drai's hits all the notes with pitch-perfection.

SETTING AND ATMOSPHERE Located atop the Strip's first freestanding boutique hotel, Drai's new spot—a beach club by day, nightclub thereafter—delivers on the promise of his reputation in Las Vegas and Los Angeles, and is replete with his signature touches (hey, the guy loves red) and a sexy indoor/outdoor French Riviera feel. Drai's Afterhours returns to it's original location in the resort's basement.

IF YOU GO Arrange your visit in advance. No, you don't have to throw down for the $737,000 package that includes a flight on a Boeing 737 and a fireworks display the entire Valley can enjoy, but you can book your table or buy tickets online. Unless you know someone (we suggest someone with the last name Drai), the city's newest hot spot is not the place to try out newly minted velvet rope swagger. The best time to arrive to the beach club is 11:30 a.m., nightclub 10:30 p.m., and afterhours 4 a.m. Download the Drai's mobile app to stay updated on events, earn loyalty points, and enter contests.

ALSO TRY Marquee Nightclub & Dayclub in The Cosmopolitan; ☎ 702-333-9000; **marqueelasvegas.com**.

Ghostbar

The Palms, 4321 W. Flamingo Rd., ☎ 702-942-6832; **palms.com**
MID-STRIP AND ENVIRONS

Cover Sunday–Thursday: $20 men, $10 ladies; Friday–Saturday: $25 men, $20 ladies. **Mixed drinks** $13 and up. **Wine** $13 and up. **Beer** $9 and up. **Dress** Chic nightclub attire. **Specials** Half off all drinks 8–10 p.m. nightly. **Food available** None. **Hours** Nightly from 8 p.m.

WHO GOES THERE Hotel guests, bachelorette parties, your parents. With Rain, The Playboy Club, and Moon all now closed, Ghostbar is the last remaining spot to party hearty at present. Everyone on property looking for a cold drink and a nice view (the skyline or someone attractive) eventually will find their way here.

WHAT GOES ON The Strip view only gets better each year from the 55 stories up. From 8 to 10 p.m., seating is open, the music is set to laid-back conversation levels, and cocktails are half off. Later in the night, Ghostbar becomes a busy boutique nightclub with VIP bottle service, attractive cocktail staff, DJ action in the booth, and nightclub volumes.

SETTING AND ATMOSPHERE Recently refreshed, Ghostbar features an elegant, feminine design in a palette of white, black, and fuchsia, and has a sensual, sophisticated vibe. Murano-style chandeliers, plush banquettes with ornately carved legs, and porcelain tile flooring appear alongside dramatic fairytale-style Brinton's carpet. The 14-foot floor-to-ceiling windows frame the lounge's unparalleled views.

IF YOU GO Go early to snag seats with a view of the mountains to the east reflecting the sunset light. Make your way through the all-rosé Champagne cocktail menu. Or, if you skipped dessert, try the Night Cap, featuring Smirnoff marshmallow vodka and cream, served in a stemmed cocktail glass rimmed with chocolate and graham cracker crust and topped off with roasted marshmallows.

ALSO TRY Scarlet cocktail bar and the bar at N9NE Steakhouse, also in The Palms (**palms.com**), and Mandarin Bar in Mandarin Oriental Las Vegas on the Strip (☎ 702-590-8888; **mandarinoriental.com/lasvegas**).

Hakkasan

MGM Grand, 3799 Las Vegas Blvd. S.; ☎ 702-891-3838; **hakkasanlv.com**
SOUTH STRIP AND ENVIRONS

Cover $50 men, $30 ladies. **Mixed drinks** $13 and up. **Wine** $16 and up. **Beer** $10 and up. **Dress** Upscale fashionable; collared shirts required for men; no hats, sandals, sneakers, hard-soled shoes or boots, ripped or oversize clothing, or athletic wear. **Food available** None in the club, but downstairs you'll find Hakkasan Restaurant, open till midnight on club nights. **Hours** Thursday–Sunday, 10 p.m.–close.

WHO GOES THERE As one of the newest nightclubs in town—not to mention the largest and most expensive—Hakkasan is a nightlife wonder that simply must be seen to be believed.

WHAT GOES ON The biggest electronic-dance-music DJs in the world call Hakkasan home. They're paid royally to do so, so expect lavish, spectacular sets with lighting and VJ teams giving the night's headliner the full festival treatment.

SETTING AND ATMOSPHERE A tangle of hallways, stairs, and elevators connects the first-floor restaurant to the second floor's private dining rooms. The next layer holds the open-format Ling Ling Club and the eclectic Ling Ling Lounge, a perfect respite for when the fourth-floor's spaceshiplike Main Room and Pavilion (straight outta *Kill Bill*) get to be too much. The fifth-floor mezzanine is the best way to experience the main room without going elbow-to-nose with everyone who came out to see Calvin Harris, Tiësto, or Steve Aoki and those floor-to-ceiling LED screens.

IF YOU GO Ladies, wear reasonably comfortable shoes (you might as well see the whole place!), and everyone should consider bringing earplugs; the better these sound systems are getting, the more efficient they are at wreaking havoc on your eardrums with nearly concussive bass.

ALSO TRY Light in Mandalay Bay; ☎ 702-693-8300; **thelightvegas.com.**

House of Blues

Cover bands, live rock, headliners

Mandalay Bay, 3950 Las Vegas Blvd. S.; ☎ 702-632-7605; **houseofblues.com/lasvegas** **SOUTH STRIP AND ENVIRONS**

Cover Cover for most shows; cost varies. **Mixed drinks** $8 and up. **Wine** $9 and up. **Beer** $6 and up. **Specials** Happy hour daily, 2–5 p.m. **Dress** Casual. **Food available** Southern-inspired Crossroads restaurant is open breakfast, lunch, and dinner Sunday–Thursday, 7 a.m.–10 p.m.; Friday and Saturday, 7 a.m.–11 p.m., plus Sunday Gospel Brunch at 10 a.m. and 1 p.m. **Hours** Daily, 5 p.m.–midnight or 1 a.m., depending on event.

WHO GOES THERE 21–65; locals, tourists, music lovers.

WHAT GOES ON House of Blues encompasses three venues: the 1,800-seat concert auditorium downstairs, the restaurant-bar upstairs (casino level), and the Foundation Room restaurant-lounge on the top floor (more on that later). In this review, we're talking about the live music that takes place in the restaurant nightly, when blues, rock, and R&B performers take the stage under lights that spell out "Have Mercy, Las Vegas." It's a cool, casual, and not-too-cacophonous scene, with an eclectic audience mix all grooving to some hot licks.

SETTING AND ATMOSPHERE House of Blues is one of the more evocative dining rooms in town, set to resemble an outdoor courtyard in the middle of a small bayou village, with a huge tree in the center and tables on a stone floor under and around it, as well as up on patio-style wooden decks. Wrought-iron railings, stone walls, etched and stained glass, and the facades of swamp shacks extend the theme, all under dim lighting. (They also account for the good acoustics.) The only incongruity is the collection of TV monitors on various walls throughout.

IF YOU GO Anything seems to go here during the music: big tables of beer-drinking college kids; couples (and singles) dancing all around the room; unreconstructed barefoot hippies in peasant blouses and patchouli perfume praising the Lord; lead singers or guitarists roaming the room wireless and interacting directly with the audience. It's best on nights when there's no concert downstairs and only those in the know are upstairs, enjoying some of the best bargain (free) entertainment in town.

ALSO TRY Foundation Room at House of Blues on the 63rd floor in Mandalay Bay, open nightly from 5 p.m., with dining from 6 p.m. and DJs from 10 p.m.; ☎ 702-632-7631.

Hyde

Boutique-y L.A.-style club with an A-List view

Bellagio, 3600 Las Vegas Blvd. S.; ☎ 702-693-8700; **hydebellagio.com**
MID-STRIP AND ENVIRONS

Cover $30 men, $20 ladies, locals free on Tuesdays. **Mixed drinks** $10 and up. **Wine** $12 and up. **Beer** $9 and up. **Dress** Trendy chic; no hats. **Food available** Gourmet small plates 5–9 p.m. **Hours** Lounge opens 5 p.m. nightly; club hours Tuesday, Friday, and Saturday, 10:30 p.m.–4 a.m.

WHO GOES THERE 25–45; tourists looking to start their night early, partiers looking for a gorgeous environment and unparalleled view of Bellagio's fountains rather than big-name DJs and celebs. Rub elbows with the industry crowd and snag a few business cards for future outings during Hyde's Lost Angels industry night.

WHAT GOES ON Hyde's once-monthly signature staple party, XIV Vegas Sessions, is the ultimate reason to stop by. With rotating themes and elaborate decor and costumes, it begins at 5 p.m. and goes strong till late one Sunday per month. The party goes on hiatus in summer.

SETTING AND ATMOSPHERE The first Las Vegas nightlife venture by LA-based SBE Entertainment, Hyde boasts a seamless indoor-outdoor patio jutting out into Bellagio's lake and floor-to-ceiling windows, plus multiple bars, 40 comfy VIP tables, and a diverse rotation of DJs nightly.

IF YOU GO Did we mention the view?

ALSO TRY SBE's three new nightlife darlings: Foxtail, Life, and Sayers Club at the new SLS Las Vegas in the former Sahara footprint; **slslasvegas.com.**

Insert Coin(s)

Video game arcade for adults

512 East Fremont St.; ☎ 702-477-2525; **insertcoinslv.com** **DOWNTOWN**

Cover Friday and Saturday: $10 after 10 p.m.; $5 locals; no cover Wednesday, Thursday, and Sunday. **Mixed drinks** $7 and up. **Wine** $6 and up. **Beer** $5 and up. **Dress** Casual. **Food available** None. **Hours** Wednesday–Sunday, 8 p.m.–4 a.m.

WHO GOES THERE 21–45; gamers, hipsters, and pop culture lovers.

WHAT GOES ON Resident and guest DJs spin eclectic sets, making Downtown the perfect alternative to the Strip. Bartenders craft fun, themed cocktails; there's a healthy craft-beer menu to boot. Video-game enthusiasts flock to the classic or modern console selections, while perfectly curated video loops of classic kung fu flicks and Japanese anime race across 40-plus plasma screens and a video wall above the DJ booth. Late night, a full-on dance party becomes the main draw.

SETTING AND ATMOSPHERE Graffiti-inspired art adorns the walls, as do rows of classics arcade consoles, but it's nearly impossible not to be lured like a moth to a flame by the expansive, glowing LED bar in the center of the room. Here, gamers' eyes are locked on the overhead TVs playing tournaments while the cool kids dance near the DJ booth in the back.

IF YOU GO Bring a pocket full of quarters for the machines, or at least cash to make change, while you sip on stiff drinks with a convenient beverage holder at the classic machines. Bottle service is available in the VIP booths equipped with modern consoles and a personal gaming host.

ALSO TRY Vanguard Lounge at 516 Fremont St.; ☎ 702-868-7800; **vanguardlv.com.**

Lavo Lounge

The intimate side of Tao Group nightlife

The Palazzo, 3325 Las Vegas Blvd. S.; ☎ 702-791-1818; **lavolv.com**
MID-STRIP AND ENVIRONS

Cover Only for special programming. **Mixed drinks** $14 and up. **Wine** $10 and up.
Beer $8 and up. **Dress** Stylish and trendy attire; collared shirts for men. **Specials** Buy
one, get one cocktails 6–8 p.m. Tuesday–Saturday; ladies drink free 11 p.m.–midnight
Friday. **Food available** Italian-inspired small-plates menu available from Lavo restaurant downstairs; full menu available by request. **Hours** Tuesday–Thursday, 6 p.m.–
1 a.m.; Friday and Saturday, 6 p.m.–2 a.m.

WHO GOES THERE Fans of Tao and Marquee looking for an intimate environment that's conducive to conversation with a unique mixology program.

WHAT GOES ON Since its metamorphosis from boutique nightclub to speakeasy-esque lounge, Lavo has been trying to figure out what it wants to
be and to whom. In the earlier hours, it's a little more laid back, with an
emphasis on cocktails and convos. But at 10 p.m. on Tuesdays, Fridays,
and Saturdays, a DJ takes over. Also, the Champagne Party Brunch held
in the restaurant every Saturday 2–6 p.m. October through March is a
highlight of the fall, winter, and spring seasons (while the party pools are
closed), complete with champagne showers and dancing on the tables.

SETTING AND ATMOSPHERE A nod to Italian and Mediterranean decor; accou-
terments hand-selected from around the globe lend to the opulence. The
upstairs lounge space is filled with creative works inspired by street artists with a warm intimate feel throughout.

IF YOU GO Dine first at the downstairs Lavo restaurant, then continue the
night with good company, conversation, and cocktails inspired by various moments in Las Vegas history.

ALSO TRY Marquee in the Cosmo (☎ 702-333-9000, **marqueelasvegas**
.com) and Tao in The Venetian (☎ 702-388-8588, **taolasvegas.com**).

LAX

Opulent, cavernous nightclub with a dramatic entryway

Luxor, 3799 Las Vegas Blvd. S.; ☎ 702-785-5555;
angelmanagementgroup.com **SOUTH STRIP AND ENVIRONS**

Cover $20 men, $10 ladies. **Mixed drinks** $10 and up. **Wine** $15 and up. **Beer** $9
and up. **Dress** Fashionable; no sports jerseys, tank tops on men, tennis shoes, or
athletic wear. **Specials** Wednesday is industry night. **Food available** None. **Hours**
Wednesday–Saturday, 10:30 p.m.–4 a.m.

WHO GOES THERE 21–45; spring breakers, wolf packs, bachelor/bachelorette
parties, homesick Los Angelenos, hip-hop royalty, and celebrities keen to
have a private VIP party on stage in front of thousands of people. The
place is at its busiest on Friday and Saturday nights at 11:30 p.m.

WHAT GOES ON LAX is best known for its industry Wednesdays, which features industry-focused events, such as local celebrity roasts. A rarity in
the new EDM Vegas, LAX still welcomes celebrities who couldn't spin a
top to host the night and just be their famous selves.

SETTING AND ATMOSPHERE It's hard to top the high you get from descending LAX's grand staircase, but this dramatic 26,000-square foot, two-story space awash in red and black does a pretty good job. Shimmering chandeliers create a modern, luxurious feel. The second story is home to seven lavishly appointed VIP lofts that overlook the main dance floor. You can see your house from here.

IF YOU GO Pop into Savile Row, the speakeasy-ish side room with a far more intimate hip-hop/Top-40 party going in a sweet little candlelit space, on Sunday and Monday.

ALSO TRY Light in Mandalay Bay; ☎ 702-693-8300; **thelightvegas.com.**

Light

Las Vegas's legendary hot spot is resurrected

Mandalay Bay, 3950 Las Vegas Blvd. S.; ☎ 702-693-8300; **thelightvegas.com SOUTH STRIP AND ENVIRONS**

Cover Starts at $30 men, $20 ladies, but goes up to $50 men, $30 ladies depending on the event. **Mixed drinks** $20 and up. **Wine** $12 and up. **Beer** $10 and up. **Dress** Upscale chic; no hats, T-shirts, chains, athletic wear, shorts, baggy attire, sunglasses, sandals, or tennis shoes. **Food available** None. **Hours** Wednesday, Friday, and Saturday, 10 p.m.–late.

WHO GOES THERE 21–40; Light Group devotees, herds of hotties, electronic-dance-music aficionados, staff of other nightclubs, and friends of the DJ.

WHAT GOES ON Light's raison d'être is its stable of resident DJs, joining the Heavy-Hitters Club that also includes Wynn Resorts (Surrender, Encore Beach Club, XS, and Tryst), Tao Group's Marquee Nightclub & Dayclub, Hakkasan Group's Hakkasan and Wet Republic, and newcomer Drai's Beach Club & Nightclub. Tops on that list of talent are Axwell, Sebastian Ingrosso, Zedd, Baauer, Nicky Romero, Skrillex, Alesso, Krewella, and more.

SETTING AND ATMOSPHERE Light may have reopened, but don't expect a faithful re-creation of the club that opened circa 2001 where The Bank is today. As the first-ever nightclub "turned on" by Cirque du Soleil, Light has huge shoes to fill, and does so by merging cutting-edge productions (that is, video mapping, lighting, sound, and special effects by experts, Moment Factory) with nightlife, as well as avant-garde costumes and unique choreography.

IF YOU GO Light has a large dance floor right in front of the DJ booth, so the DJ's fans can be front and center, even if they don't have a VIP table. Follow Light on its social media outlets to find out about upcoming contests and shows.

ALSO TRY Eclipse nighttime pool party at Daylight Beach Club, also in Mandalay Bay (☎ 702-693-8300, **daylightvegas.com**), and Hakkasan in MGM Grand (☎ 702-891-3838, **hakkasanlv.com**).

Lily Bar & Lounge

Central gathering spot at the heart of Bellagio

Bellagio, 3600 Las Vegas Blvd. S.; ☎ 702-693-8300; **lilylasvegas.com MID-STRIP AND ENVIRONS**

Cover None. **Mixed drinks** $11 and up. **Wine** $12 and up. **Beer** $8 and up. **Dress** Stylish nightlife attire. **Food available** none. **Hours** Daily, 5 p.m.–close.

WHO GOES THERE Nightclub pre-partiers and industry professionals touting their latest side project.

WHAT GOES ON Nightclub hosts rally the troops and wait for stragglers before heading over to The Bank, all while enjoying a cocktail.

SETTING AND ATMOSPHERE Located in the center of Bellagio, Lily offers a sophisticated atmosphere shielded from the bustling casino floor, including imported Spanish stone tabletops, antique-inspired mirrors, and plush leather couches.

IF YOU GO Pre-party for a price as the creations from Lily's bartenders will delight with more than a standard vodka Red Bull.

ALSO TRY Nearby Bellagio nightclubs include Hyde (☎ 702-693-8700, **sbe .com**) and The Bank (☎ 702-693-8300, **thebanklasvegas.com**).

Marquee Nightclub & Dayclub

Glamorous megaclub and DJ magnet

The Cosmopolitan, 3708 Las Vegas Blvd. S.; ☎ 702-333-9000; **marqueelasvegas.com** MID-STRIP AND ENVIRONS

Cover Monday: men $30, ladies $20, locals free; Thursday: $20, ladies free; Friday: men $40, ladies $20, local ladies free; Saturday: men $50, ladies $20, local ladies free. **Mixed drinks** $14 and up. **Wine** $10 and up. **Beer** $8 and up. **Dress** Stylish nightlife attire required; collared shirts for men. **Specials** Locals free on Marquee Mondays. **Food available** None. **Hours** Monday, 10 p.m.–4 a.m; Friday and Saturday, 10 p.m.–5 a.m; Thursday Boom Box Room only, 10 p.m.–4 a.m.

WHO GOES THERE Everyone. No, seriously—everyone.

WHAT GOES ON Thanks to Marquee's killer roster of today's top DJs—both residents and guests—the scene at the door is a cattle call of unthinkable proportions, the dance floor a sea of beautiful bodies, and the stairwells connecting the main room to the Boom Box Room and the Library surging arteries. So, why would you want to throw yourself into such a mix? Please refer back to "Who goes there" above. And check out Marquee's online calendar to see who will be manning the decks.

SETTING AND ATMOSPHERE Featuring similar attention to detail as big sister Tao (though without the Asian influence), Marquee makes luxury its theme. The circular main room is a well-appointed house-music amphitheater, perfectly arranged so that even someone in back can see the celebrity DJ jump up on his rig and feel the rush of wind as confetti cannons fire overhead. The Boom Box Room packs bodies in around the DJ and bar like a subway car, so New Yorkers should feel right at home. Upstairs in the Library, a fire roars, sexy librarians pop bottles, and a vintage pool table awaits your attention.

IF YOU GO Strategy is a must. Dine nearby at Holsteins or China Poblano. From there you can keep an eye on the velvet ropes. When the bodies begin to stack up, get the check and a to-go cocktail, and get in line. Among the first through the door that night, you will have the rare opportunity to see how beautiful the rooms are (and get to the bar) before all hell breaks loose. And don't miss out on Marquee Dayclub, open daily 11 a.m.–6 p.m. during season.

ALSO TRY Drai's Beach Club & Nightclub in The Cromwell; ☎ 702-737-0555; **draislv.com.**

Rí Rá Las Vegas

Authentic Irish music, food, drinks, and *craíc*

The Shoppes at Mandalay Place, 3930 Las Vegas Blvd. S.; ☎ 702-632-7771; **rira.com/las-vegas** SOUTH STRIP AND ENVIRONS

Cover None. **Mixed drinks** $5 and up. **Wine** $5 and up. **Beer** $5 and up. **Dress** Casual. **Food available** Authentic Irish cuisine with a hint of American flair; a wide selection of appetizers, sandwiches, and entrées 7 days a week. **Hours** Monday–Thursday, 8 a.m.– 3 a.m.; Friday, 8 a.m.–4 a.m.; Saturday, 9 a.m.–4 a.m.; Sunday, 9 a.m.–3 a.m.

WHO GOES THERE Eireophiles, Celtic music fans, and footy fiends.

WHAT GOES ON Deceiving from the outside, the seemingly endless interior of this lively, casual gastropub and bar is actually a buzzing hive of nearly constant activity. Bands Irish and beyond play for the exuberant crowd, those that are not entranced by a football game (that's soccer to the rest of us) showing on one of the infinitesimal flat-panel TVs that dot the space. The food is tasty and interesting, especially the generous fish-and-chips and the house-made soda bread; here, every Guinness is well poured.

SETTING AND ATMOSPHERE No expense was spared in bringing a whole lotta Ireland to Sin City. Professionals salvaged authentic 19th-century materials, millwork, and bric-a-brac from all over the Emerald Isle, including artifacts dating back to 1890 from the Olympia Theater in Dublin and a 500-pound carved statue of St. Patrick from 1850.

IF YOU GO Try not to be in a hurry; so much of pub life is about leaving the world out on the doorstep, or in this case, in the mall. Take time to experience and appreciate the individual personality of each room as well as the entertainment—this can mean the live music variety as well as the stars of sport and the friendly Irish staff.

ALSO TRY McMullan's Irish Pub (☎ 702-247-7000, **mcmullansirishpub .com**) and Nine Fine Irishmen in New York–New York (☎ 702-740-6463, **ninefineirishmen.com**).

Rose. Rabbit. Lie.

Dine, drink, and dance at the city's newest supper club

The Cosmopolitan, 3708 Las Vegas Blvd. S.; ☎ 877-667-0585; **roserabbitlie.com** MID-STRIP AND ENVIRONS

Cover None. **Mixed drinks** $14 and up. **Wine** $14 and up. **Beer** $9 and up. **Dress** Casual elegant; no athletic wear (flip flops, tennis shoes, shorts, hats, etc.), baggy jeans, or jeans with holes. **Food available** Modern small plates, as well as dramatic large-scale tableside offerings. **Hours** Wednesday–Saturday, 5:30 p.m. till late.

WHO GOES THERE 25 and up; tourists, hotel guests, and even locals happily queued up for Vegas Nocturn, a performance in three cantos that was once part of this venue. Producer Spiegelworld (see our review of *Absinthe* at Caesars Palace on page 216) has since pulled up stakes, but the mysterious and playful anything-could-happen atmosphere it created remains.

WHAT GOES ON At press time, this concept was in flux. After the show decamped, Rose. Rabbit. Lie. pledged to remain devoted to cocktails, cuisine, and live entertainment. It definitely has the first two down: The beverage program by mixologist Marshall Altier puts original cocktails alongside clever twists on classics; draft and bottled cocktails make it easy to get a drink or keep one handy. And chef Wesley Holton's menu of sharable plates focuses on caviar and re-imagined Continental classics. (For more on dining at Rose. Rabbit. Lie., see Part 4, page 408.) The live entertainment and late-night elements are what will have to be re-worked.

SETTING AND ATMOSPHERE Designed by AvroKO to optimize interaction, conversation, and curiosity, the mazelike space allows guests to mingle and drift in and out of a variety of entertainment events. The design is modeled on the idea of a 1920s-era mansion, though it is also infused with modern arts and technologies.

IF YOU GO Multiple bars and rooms mean that Rose. Rabbit. Lie. can be enjoyed in different ways, all on the same night. Start with cocktails in a handsomely appointed Study, then move on to the Library for dinner, and wind up in the Music Room for a nightcap and live entertainment.

ALSO TRY 1923 Bourbon & Burlesque by Holly Madison in Mandalay Bay (☎ 702-912-4001, **1923lv.com**); the Laundry Room in Commonwealth (☎ 702-798-7000, **commonwealthlv.com**); and Herbs & Rye at 3713 W. Sahara Ave. (☎ 702-982-8036, **herbsandrye.com**).

Social

A high-energy, whiskey-centric center bar

The Palms, 4321 W. Flamingo Rd.; ☎ 702-942-7777; **palms.com**
MID-STRIP AND ENVIRONS

Cover None. **Mixed drinks** $12 and up. **Wine** $10 and up. **Beer** $5 and up. **Dress** Casual. **Specials** Half-off drinks for industry members Tuesday and Friday after 5 p.m. **Food available** None. **Hours** Tuesday–Thursday, 11 a.m.–5 a.m.; Friday–Monday, 24/7.

WHO GOES THERE 21–50+; whiskey experts, whiskey fanciers, and those who just fancy themselves experts, plus locals and those who cannot make it from one end of the casino to the other without a cocktail.

WHAT GOES ON American whiskeys—especially bourbon and rye—fuel the fires at this convenient central gathering spot at the heart of the casino floor. Mini–bottle service (375 milliliters each) is manageable in both size and price, as there are nine options under $100. The barrel-aged whiskey cocktail is one of the best examples of this trend in town. Another is served in a souvenir flask. And the menu of Top 10 girls-night-out cocktails is as hilarious as its cumulative effect on a bachelorette party.

SETTING AND ATMOSPHERE There's nowhere to hide, as this social hub is completely open on all sides to the casino floor. Of course, this means that early birds get a front-row seat to watch all the action unfold on the casino floor. The scene here can get just as wild as a nightclub dance floor.

IF YOU GO Capitalize on the reasonable prices as a chance to try a number of whiskeys one at a time—there are more than 30 from which to choose—in a cocktail or in a flight. And while you're there, sign up for the Whiskey Social Club to receive invitations to exclusive tastings with visiting distillers and mixology lessons.

ALSO TRY Bourbon Room and Delmonico Steakhouse in The Venetian (☎ 702-414-1000, **venetian.com**), Tom Colicchio's Craftsteak in MGM Grand (☎ 702-891-7318, **mgmgrand.com**), and the Whisky Attic by UNLV (☎ 702-217-6794, **whiskyattic.com**).

Stoney's Rockin' Country

Line dancing, two-stepping, and live country bands

6611 Las Vegas Blvd. S., Suite 160; ☎ 702-435-2855;
stoneysrockincountry.com   SOUTH STRIP AND ENVIRONS

Cover $5 locals; $15 nonlocals. **Mixed drinks** $7 and up. **Wine** $7 and up. **Beer** $4 and up. **Dress** No beanies, bandannas, do-rags, jerseys, or cutoff sleeves. Think Levi's, 10-gallon hats, and truly massive belt buckles. **Specials** Visit the website for the events calendar. **Food available** None. **Hours** Nightly, 7 p.m.–4 a.m.

WHO GOES THERE 21–60+; country-music fans, cowboys, and ladies who like cowboys.

WHAT GOES ON Whether it's NASCAR, PBR, or just a Gretchen Wilson after-concert party, the dance floor at Stoney's new Town Square location is teeming on Saturday nights with two-stepping and boot-scootin' cowboys and cowgirls. Manners prevail as men still ask ladies to dance, let them pass, and take slooooow rides on the mechanical bull ahead of them. One for the bucket list is Thursday's ladies night, where fillies enjoy $1 drinks all night. Stoney's calls this "the biggest favor another man has ever done for you."

SETTING AND ATMOSPHERE Mechanical bull? Check. Custom, 2,000-square-foot, cushioned dance floor? Check. A VIP section, mile-long bars, beer tubs, and saloon girls housed within 20,000 square feet of pure country? Check. There's no mistaking owner Stoney Gray's intentions when he built his Rockin' Country nightclub, a follow-up to Gilley's at the since-imploded New Frontier Hotel (now reimagined at TI). A cowboy experience complete with pool tables and beer pong.

IF YOU GO Arrive early, not so much to beat the lines (and there definitely can be lines) but rather to avail yourself of the complimentary line-dancing lessons at 7:30 p.m. Check out Stoney's Facebook and Foursquare pages for front-of-line specials.

ALSO TRY Revolver in Santa Fe Station (☎ 702-658-4900, **nightlife station.com**) and Gilley's in TI (☎ 702-894-7111, **treasureisland.com**).

Surrender

Party outside under the stars and inside with them

Encore, 3131 Las Vegas Blvd. S.; ☎ 702-770-7300; **wynnsocial.com**
MID-STRIP AND ENVIRONS

Cover $40 men, $30 ladies. **Mixed drinks** $15 and up. **Wine** $15 and up. **Beer** $9 and up. **Dress** Resort casual and nightclub chic; no athletic gear or street clothes. **Food available** None, but dining at Andrea's—the hip Asian, dining-by-DJ joint next door—is highly encouraged. **Hours** Wednesday, Friday, and Saturday, 10:30 p.m.– 4 a.m.

WHO GOES THERE 21–45; local tastemakers, casino guests and tourists with the wherewithal to try anything Steve Wynn is backing.

WHAT GOES ON By day, Encore Beach Club offers 60,000 square feet of lush oasis with three tiered pools, daybeds, 26 cabanas, and a walk-up grill (daily, 11 a.m.–7 p.m.), but by night the smallish club (about 5,000 square feet) envelops the Beach Club into its embrace and offers a unique, climate-controlled combined 65,000 square feet of party acreage—Vegas's largest party spot at present. Fans of European-style electronic music and DJs will definitely want to make a pilgrimage, as Encore Beach

Club keeps an impressive stable of renowned resident DJs as well as fresh talent on tap, mostly in the electronic-dance-music genre.

SETTING AND ATMOSPHERE High ceilings, 20-foot-tall windows, wide-open spaces, and dramatic views of the pool deck create the "wow" factor. Playing on the theme of original sin, fabric and feature colors are eye-popping yellows, chrome is abundant, and the carpets leopard print—subtlety is for wusses.

IF YOU GO Consider stopping in at Encore Beach Club during the day and introducing yourself to some VIP host–looking fellows (they'll be the ones with furrowed brows, texting furiously on their smartphones) who will likely offer to help you out in returning that night.

ALSO TRY If you like the all-in-one club and pool complex, check out Foxtail Nightclub & Pool Club, Life Nightclub, and Beach Life rooftop pool in SLS; ☎ 702-737-2111; **slslasvegas.com.**

Tao

A labyrinthine restaurant, lounge and megaclub

The Venetian, 3377 Las Vegas Blvd. S.; ☎ 702-388-8588; **taolasvegas.com**
MID-STRIP AND ENVIRONS

Cover Thursday: $20 men, $10 ladies, locals free; Friday: $20, local ladies free; Saturday: $30 men, $20 ladies. **Mixed drinks** $14 and up. **Wine** $10 and up. **Beer** $8 and up. **Dress** Upscale casual; collared shirts or blazers for men. **Specials** Thursday is local/industry night. **Food available** Pan-Asian cuisine and sushi are available downstairs in the restaurant, Sunday–Thursday, 5 p.m.–midnight; Friday and Saturday, 5 p.m.–1 a.m. **Hours** Lounge: daily, 5 p.m.–close; nightclub: Thursday–Saturday, 10 p.m.–5 a.m.

WHO GOES THERE 21–45; Hard-core club crawlers, pretty people, young Hollywood, sexpots, the scantily clad, and hedonists.

WHAT GOES ON The Venetian finally hit the jackpot with Tao, after misfiring with several nightlife venues. A huge combination of restaurant, lounge, and nightclub, Tao offers highly sought-after dinner reservations, a cool lounge space, and a labyrinthine club that packs 'em in from the moment the velvet rope drops. Hordes of casino patrons and Strip-walkers swarm Tao. Entertainment is keyed to the hottest dance music and meant to move the most flesh as quickly as possible, en masse. It's meat-market central for the young, sweaty, and on the make.

SETTING AND ATMOSPHERE The pretty but minimally decorated lounge serves mainly as an air lock and chill-out space for the upstairs club space, which includes several bars, two levels of VIP cells, a recessed dance floor, several dancer showcase platforms, and a tiny bit of Strip-side balcony. Various Buddhas sit in nooks and crannies or in placid groups, while barely clad living models do the "human statue" thing in gauzy boudoirs. Vaguely exotic and certainly sexy, Tao's look and feel is downright aphrodisiacal when the crowd is right.

IF YOU GO Go early or go with your celebrity friends. The line will be long, but it does move, and everyone really does get a chance to get in eventually. Front-of-line passes available from various websites or other sources would come in handy here, and if you have (or are) a group of attractive females, your chances of skipping the line or portions thereof will be dramatically improved.

ALSO TRY Light in Mandalay Bay; ☎ 702-693-8300; **thelightvegas.com.**

Tryst

Luxurious waterfall views from the dance floor

Wynn, 3131 Las Vegas Blvd. S.; ☎ 702-770-3375; **wynnsocial.com**
MID-STRIP AND ENVIRONS

Cover $30 men, $20 ladies. **Mixed drinks** $12 and up. **Wine** $15 and up. **Beer** $11 and up. **Dress** Casual chic; no shorts or sandals on men. **Food available** Birthday cakes by request. **Hours** Thursday–Saturday, 10:30 p.m.–close.

WHO GOES THERE Tryst's hotter, taller, bustier younger sister XS gets all the attention, but Tryst's more subtle, sensual design still attracts nightlife aficionados, loyal locals, and high rollers. Just don't try to swim in the 90-foot waterfall's lagoon or you won't be going there. Ever. Again.

WHAT GOES ON Thursday is a huge draw, when Tryst hosts The Affair industry night. And instead of a different tabloid darling being hired to show up and pose for the camera, SKAM Artist Saturdays highlights a different DJ—usually someone really unique—each week.

SETTING AND ATMOSPHERE When it opened in 2005 as La Bete Nightclub, an indoor/outdoor dance floor was ahead of the curve. Today, the merging of the two is a standard component of many Las Vegas megaclub designs. Hollywood producer–turned–nightlife impresario Victor Drai came in and made the room even sexier with his signature red, opening the new space as Tryst. Although Drai is no longer involved, the room would still meet his exacting standards: VIP booths surround a sunken dance floor and overlook the lagoon and waterfall. The place even has its own red-light district, a red-lacquered library reminiscent of Drai's original subterranean afterhours club at The Cromwell. And, natch, a stripper pole that has seen more action than the casino floor.

IF YOU GO If you are so inclined (and financially equipped), here you can splurge on one of the city's most expensive cocktails. Costing a cool $3,000, the Ménage à Trois combines Cristal Rosé Champagne, Hennessy Ellipse Cognac, and 150-year-old Grand Marnier, and is served with 23-karat-gold flakes and liquid gold syrup, along with a gold-plated, diamond-accented straw to take home; always the showoff, XS has one for $10,000. Too pricey? "Ultra shots" are just $49–$995.

ALSO TRY If you're staying at Wynn or Encore, these are the party people in your neighborhood: XS (☎ 702-770-0097; **wynnsocial.com**) and Surrender (☎ 702-770-7300; **wynnsocial.com**).

XS

Excessively beautiful, inside and out

Encore, 3131 Las Vegas Blvd. S.; ☎ 702-770-0097; **wynnsocial.com**
MID-STRIP AND ENVIRONS

Cover $30 men, $20 women; $50 men on Saturday. **Mixed drinks** $15 and up. **Wine** $20 and up. **Beer** $10. **Dress** Casual chic; no hats, oversized jeans, or athletic wear. **Food available** None. **Hours** Friday–Monday, 10 p.m.–4 a.m.

WHO GOES THERE With 13,000 square feet of indoor space for bars, a dance floor, and VIP seating, and 27,000 square feet of exterior space for more bars, 95 additional VIP tables, an illuminated pool, a blackjack pit, and 30 poolside cabanas, XS is naturally a magnet for the well-heeled and wannabe-well-heeled.

WHAT GOES ON Supernatural beauty is rewarded by XS's cast of stunning servers and VIP hosts. Guests are encouraged to make use of the VIP table backs for elevated seating—all the better to view and be viewed— and to put the stripper poles to good use. XS enjoys the collaborative buying power of Wynn's nightlife contingent (which also includes Surrender, Encore Beach Club, and Tryst) to keep top DJs in its stable, from Avicii and David Guetta to Zedd and Steve Angello.

SETTING AND ATMOSPHERE Las Vegas's most beautiful nightclub was inspired by the sexy curves of the human body and boasts more than 10,000 individual light sources, including a disco chandelier and 16 stripper poles thinly disguised as lamps. Focal features include gold-leaf body forms, an illuminated outdoor pool (open summer Sunday nights for the XS Nightswim pool party), and a large circular dance floor surrounded by VIP tables.

IF YOU GO Bring your A-game and break out the good shoes. Long before you pass through XS's gilded gates, you will have to navigate a maze of admission lines (think Walt Disney World at its busiest) and pass through multiple sets of eyes critical of your attitude, dress, comportment, and entourage. A Darwinian process ensues, culling the herd down to the haves and the have-nots. Leave embarrassing in-laws, cousins, and friends in the casino, and expect to throw down a mortgage payment for a table and more bottles than your group could ever realistically consume.

ALSO TRY The other big kids on the Strip include Drai's Nightclub in The Cromwell (☎ 702-737-0555, **draislv.com**); Marquee Nightclub in The Cosmopolitan (☎ 702-333-9000, **marqueelasvegas.com**); and Hakkasan in MGM Grand (☎ 702-891-3838, **hakkasanlv.com**).

LAS VEGAS *below the* BELT

DON'T WORRY, BE HAPPY

IN MANY WAYS, LAS VEGAS is a bastion of hedonism. Simply being there contributes to a loosening of inhibitions and a partial discarding of the rules that apply at home. Las Vegas exults in its permissiveness and makes every effort to live up to its image and to bestow upon its visitors the freedom to have fun. Las Vegas has a steaminess, a cosmopolitan excitement born of superabundance, an aura of risk and reward, a sense of libertine excess. The rules are different here; it's all right to let go.

Behind the illusion, however, is a community, and more particularly, a police department that puts a lot of effort into making it safe for visitors to experience the liberation of Las Vegas. It is hard to imagine another city where travelers can carry such large sums of money so safely. A tourist can get robbed or worked over in Las Vegas, but it is comparatively rare, and more often than not is due to the visitor's own carelessness or naivete. The Strip and Downtown, especially, are well patrolled, and most hotels have very professional in-house security forces.

In general, a tourist who stays either on the Strip or Downtown will be very safe. Police patrol in cars, on foot, and, interestingly, on mountain bikes. The bikes allow the police to quickly catch pickpockets or purse snatchers attempting to make their escape down sidewalks or through parking lots. Cross-streets that connect the Strip with Paradise Road and the Las Vegas Convention Center are also lighted and safe. When tourists get robbed, they are commonly far from Downtown or the Strip and often in pursuit of drugs or sex.

ORGANIZED CRIME AND CHEATING

VERY FEW VISITORS WALK THROUGH a casino without wondering if the games are rigged or if the place is owned by the Mafia. During the early days of legalized gambling, few people outside of organized crime had any real experience in managing gaming operations. Hence, a fair number of characters fresh from eastern gangs and crime families came to work in Nevada. Since they constituted the resource pool for experienced gambling operators, the state suffered their presence as a necessary evil. In 1950, Tennessee senator Estes Kefauver initiated an attack on organized crime that led (indirectly) to the formation of the Nevada Gaming Commission and the State Gaming Control Board. These agencies, in conjunction with federal efforts, were ultimately able to purge organized crime from Las Vegas, or at least from the casinos. This ouster, coupled with the Nevada Corporate Gaming Acts of 1967 and 1969 (allowing publicly held corporations such as Hilton, Holiday Inn, and MGM to own casinos), at last brought a mantle of respectability to Las Vegas gambling.

Today the Gaming Control Board oversees the activities of all Nevada gaming establishments, maintaining tight control through frequent unannounced inspections of gambling personnel and equipment. If you ever have reason to doubt the activity or clout of the Gaming Control Board, try walking around the Strip or Downtown in a dark business suit and plain black shoes. You will attract more attention from the casino management than if you entered with a parrot on your head.

Ostensibly, cheating exists in Las Vegas gambling to a limited degree. But a case of a Nevada casino cheating customers hasn't been publicized for decades. "Gaffing" the games is seldom perpetrated by the house itself. In fact, most cheating is done at the expense of the house, though honest players at the cheater's table may also get burned. Sometimes a dealer, working alone or with an accomplice (posing as a player), will cheat, and there are always con artists, grab-and-run rip-off artists, and rail thieves ready to take advantage of the house and legitimate players.

SKIN GAMES—SEX IN LAS VEGAS

THOUGH NUDITY, PROSTITUTION, AND PORNOGRAPHY are regulated more tightly in Las Vegas than in many Bible Belt cities, the town exudes an air of sexual freedom and promiscuity. Las Vegas offers a near-perfect environment for marketing sex. More than 50% of all visitors are men, most ages 21–59. Some come to party, and many, particularly convention-goers, are alone and ready for action. Almost all have time and money on their hands.

Las Vegas evolved as a gambler's city, projecting the image of a trail town where a man could be comfortable and just about anything could be had for a price. It was not until strong competition developed for the gambling dollar that hotels sought to enlarge their market by targeting women and meetings. Today, though there is something for everyone in Las Vegas, its male orientation remains unusually strong.

STRIPPING ON THE STRIP Compared to the live adult entertainment in many cities, "girlie" (and "boy-ie") shows in Las Vegas, both Downtown and on the Las Vegas Strip, are fairly tame. In some of the larger showrooms, this is an accommodation to the ever-growing percentage of women in the audience. More often, however, it is a matter of economics rather than taste, the result of a curious City of Las Vegas law that stipulates that you can offer totally nude entertainment or you can serve alcoholic beverages, but not both.

MALE STRIPPERS Economics and the market have begun to redress (or undress) the inequality of women's erotic entertainment in Las Vegas. Spearheaded by the Rio, which features (*Chippendales*) male strippers for lengthy engagements, and empowered by the ever-growing number of professional women visiting Las Vegas for trade shows and conventions, the rules for sexual objectification are being rewritten. Today in Las Vegas, if watching a young stud flex his buns is a woman's idea of a good time, that experience is usually available. In addition to the Rio, male strippers perform at the Palomino Club (one of a handful of fully nude male revues in the United States). *Thunder from Down Under*, the Australian male revue, plays at the Excalibur, and *American Storm*, though touring periodically, plays at the Miracle Mile Shops.

Where the Girls Are

Below we describe a few of the better-known strip joints. If you want the whole scoop, check out Arnold Snyder's Topless Vegas at **toplessvegas online.com.** In a city where it's relatively easy to spend $400 at a topless club, Snyder's free site can save you a bundle. It tells you where the most beautiful dancers are and where they're not; how to have a great strip-club experience for $30 or less; topless-club etiquette (there's a lot more to this than you might imagine); lap dancing A–Z; and how to avoid taxi scams and scams at the clubs. There are detailed rankings and reviews of all-nude clubs and topless clubs, all topless shows playing at the casinos, and, for good measure, all of the city's topless pools. Straight talk is Snyder's trademark, so you can count on him to address just about any question you can think of, including those you'd be too embarrassed to ask. The site also encourages feedback, where visitors discuss such topics as the relative merits of fully nude versus topless clubs. One poster thought topless clubs superior because, as he put it, "I've never had anything contagious leap off a boobie at me." All righty, then.

Strip clubs are not the homogeneous experience you might expect. As a quick dichotomy, some clubs specialize in presentations where the focal point is one or several performing dancers on a central stage with the usual theatrical elements of music and lighting. The stage is the focal point, and seating is arrayed around it. In other clubs, the action is decentralized, and though there will be strippers performing somewhere (for example, in disco cages or on a bar top), there's no single stage at the center of the action. The breadwinning products of these clubs are lap dancing and shows in private or semiprivate rooms. Clubs can also be categorized as topless clubs or clubs offering full nudity. Concerning the latter, only the Palomino Club in North Las Vegas (see below) is licensed for total nudity and alcohol consumption. In case you're wondering, refreshments at the other all-nude clubs consist of froufrou (and outrageously expensive) fruit drinks.

Finally, if you're a nonlocal and arrive by cab, you'll be hit with a higher cover charge to pay a kickback to the driver. Taxi drivers get a kickback for delivering you to a particular gentlemen's club. Do not let a taxi driver talk you out of your chosen destination and take you someplace he recommends.

THE PALOMINO CLUB (☎ 702-327-7258; **palominolv.com**) At the Palomino Club, 10 minutes from Downtown, the customer can have it all. The Palomino Club is not inexpensive, but at least they're up front about what they're selling. As competition has heated up in the Las Vegas nude trade, Palomino's previously high prices have come down. Before 9 p.m. admission is free; after 9 it's $30. Things don't heat up till around 11 p.m., so you'll have to do a lot of sitting (and drinking) to beat the entrance fee. Still, though you have to be 21 to get in, dancers have to be only 18 to work there, so the scenery, if you're into youngish girls, is easy on the eyes.

An average of seven professionals dance nightly, performing in rotation and stripping nude. Most of the women are attractive and athletic. The Palomino delivers some of the best erotic dancing in town for about the same cost as a production show on the Strip.

LITTLE DARLINGS (☎ 702-366-1141, 1514 Western Ave., **dejavu .com**) If you can do without alcohol, Little Darlings is our pick for the best nude stage show in the state. Not only are the dancers stunningly gorgeous, but many of them are extremely athletic. Unlike many topless and nude shows where the performers pretty much clamber around the stage, Little Darlings' showgirls can dance. Beverage service is limited to non-alcoholic drinks. Cover is $30 for nonlocals, $10 for locals.

TOPLESS BARS The main difference between a topless bar and a totally nude nightclub (aside from the alcohol regulations) is a G-string. Unless you're a gynecology intern, you might be satisfied with a topless bar. If you have more than a few drinks, the topless bars aren't less expensive than the Palomino but are often more conveniently located. Downtown, on Fremont Street, is the **Girls of Glitter Gulch** (☎ 702-385-4774). There's no cover charge, but drinks average a stiff (no pun intended) $10 each, with a two-drink minimum. Clientele is almost all tourists, so the pressure to buy a lap dance and overpriced drinks is intense. There are exceptions, but by and large the dancers are a bit overweight and long in the tooth.

With two lower-level stages and an expansive L-shape runway stage on the second level, **Larry Flynt's Hustler Club** (6007 Dean Martin Dr.; ☎ 702-795-3131; **vegashustlerclub.com**) is our top-ranked topless club for stage shows. The upper level houses a roof-top bar with comfortable seating and great views of Las Vegas. The dancers are stunning, and the drink prices reasonable. Cover charge for nonlocals is $30; locals enter free.

The **Sapphire Club** (3025 Industrial Rd.; ☎ 702-796-6000; **sapphire lasvegas.com**) claims 6,000 women in its lineup of strippers (insiders say it's closer to 2,000, which is still plenty). By observation, the later you arrive in the evening, the better-looking the dancers. Though the club claims to be the largest of its kind in the world, much of the space is allocated to private rooms and VIP areas. For the average patron, Sapphire is upscale but doesn't seem all that big. The admission charge of $30, though, definitely does.

An equally upscale venue is **OG** (formerly Olympic Garden) at 1531 Las Vegas Blvd. S.; ☎ 702-385-8987; **ogvegas.com.** OG is the only strip club on the Strip (right across from Stratosphere). Given its location, it caters to out-of-town men, and its prices are a dead giveaway: a $33 cover charge and $380 for a half-hour in the VIP room.

Crazy Horse III (3525 W. Russell Rd.; ☎ 702-673-1700; **crazy horse3.com**) replaced The Penthouse Club in mid-2009 after a major overhaul. Admission is $30. The usual $9 beers and $20 lap dances are available. The venue is sprawling and swanky, and thanks to free-drink and other promotions, locals show up in droves, which attracts the hot dancers. They also have good deals on sushi (which is served all night), a hookah lounge, and Obsession afterhours club opening at 2 a.m.

EROTIC HERITAGE MUSEUM (☎ 702-794-4000; 3275 Industrial Rd.; **eroticheritagemuseumlasvegas.com**) Located just north of Desert Inn Road next door to the Déjà Vu all-nude club, this 17,000-square-foot museum exhibits a small part of the erotic art of two collectors who between them own whole warehouses full of the stuff. The permanent collection includes all the mid- to late-20th-century films that launched the sexual revolution; bondage paraphernalia from the famous bondage inventor Gord; arcade peep machines and other fetish equipment; a display devoted to Larry Flynt and the First Amendment; the work of urban sex artists (muralists, cartoonists, sculptors, photorealists, and the like); and much more. The boutique sells reproductions and posters of erotic art, classic erotic DVDs, books, T-shirts, and the like. Admission is a $15 donation, $10 for locals and students. The EHM is open daily, 11 a.m.–10 p.m.

PART THREE

GAMBLING

 The **WAY IT IS**

GAMBLING IS THE REASON LAS VEGAS (in its modern incarnation) exists. It is the industry that fuels the local economy, paves the roads, and gives the city its identity. To visitors and tourists, gambling may be a game. To those who derive their livelihood from gambling, however, it is serious business.

There is an extraordinary and interesting dichotomy in the ways gambling is perceived. To the tourist and the gambler, gambling is all about luck. To those in the business, gambling is about mathematics. To the visitor, gambling is a few hours a day, while to the casinos, gambling is 24 hours a day, every day. The gambler *hopes* to walk away with a fortune, but the casinos *know* that in the long run that fortune will belong to the house. To visitors, gambling is recreation combined with risk and chance. To the casinos, gambling is business combined with near-certainty.

The casino takes no risk in the games themselves. In almost all cases, in the long run the house will always win. The games, the odds, and the payoffs are all carefully designed to ensure this outcome. Yet the casino does take a chance and is at risk. The casino's bet is this: that it can entice enough people to play.

Imagine a casino costing hundreds of millions of dollars, with a staff numbering in the thousands. Before a nickel of profit can be set aside, all the bills must be paid, and the payroll must be met. Regardless of its overwhelming advantage at the tables, the house cannot stay in business unless a lot of people come to play. The larger the casino, the more gamblers are required. If the casino can fill the tables with players, the operation will succeed and be profitable, perhaps spectacularly so. On the other hand, if the tables sit empty, the casino will fail.

The gambling business is competition personified. All casinos sell the exact same product. Every owner knows how absolutely critical it is to get customers (gamblers) through the door. It is literally the *sine qua non:* no players, no profit. The casinos are aggressive and creative when it comes to luring customers, offering low-cost buffets, $2 shrimp cocktails, stage shows, lounge entertainment, free drinks, gambling tournaments, and players clubs.

The most common tactic for getting customers through the door is to package the casino as a tourist attraction in its own right. Take the Mirage. There are exploding volcanoes in the front yard, palm trees in the living room, and live sharks in the parlor. Who, after all, wants to sip their free drink in a dingy red-Naugahyde-upholstered catacomb when they can be luxuriating in such a resplendent tropical atrium?

THE SHORT RUN

ASK A MATHEMATICIAN OR A CASINO OWNER if you can win gambling in a casino, and the truthful answer is yes, but almost always only in the short run. Unless you're a professional player who only plays with the long-term edge on your side, the longer you play, the more certain it is that you will lose.

I (Bob here) learned about the short run (and the long run) on a road trip when I was in the fifth grade. My family lived in Kentucky, and every year we were fortunate enough to take a vacation to Florida. This particular year I was allowed to invite a schoolmate, Glenn, along.

As the long drive progressed, we became fidgety and bored. To pass the time, we began counting cars traveling in the opposite direction. Before many miles had passed, our counting evolved into a betting game. We each selected a color and counted the cars of that color. Whoever counted the most cars of his chosen color would win.

Glenn chose blue as his color. I was considering red (my favorite), when I recalled a conversation between my mother and a car sales-man. The salesman told my mother that white was by far the most popular color "these days." If this were true, I reasoned, there should be more white cars on the road than blue cars. I chose white.

As we rumbled through the hilly Kentucky countryside between Bowling Green and Elizabethtown, my friend edged ahead. This puz-zled me and I began to doubt the word of the car salesman. By the time we made it to Bowling Green, Glenn was ahead by seven cars. Because I was losing, I offered to call it quits and pay up (a nickel for each car he was ahead). Glenn, not unexpectedly, was having a high time and insisted we continue playing.

By the time we crossed the Tennessee line I had pulled even. Once again I suggested we quit. Glenn would have none of it. Gloating enormously, he regained a three-car lead halfway to Nashville. Slowly, however, I overtook him, and by Nashville I was ahead by four cars. Tired of the game, I tried once more to end it. Since he was behind, Glenn adamantly demanded that we play all the way to Atlanta. We did, and by the time we got there, Glenn owed me almost $4.

After a night in Atlanta and a great deal of sulking on Glenn's part, we resumed our travels. To my amazement, Glenn insisted—demanded, in fact—the opportunity to win back his previous day's losses. There would be one great "do-or-die battle, blues against whites," he said, all the way to our destination (St. Augustine, Florida). As we drove south, I went ahead by a couple of cars, and then Glenn regained the lead by a small margin. By the time we reached St. Augustine, however, Glenn owed me another $5.40.

Outraged (and broke), Glenn exercised the only option remaining—he complained to my parents. Shaking his head, my father said, "Give Glenn his money back. Everybody knows that there are more white cars than blue cars." Not so. Glenn didn't.

While Glenn's behavior is not particularly unusual for a preadolescent, you would assume that adults have better sense. Everybody knows there are more white cars than blue cars, remember? In Las Vegas, however, the casinos are full of Glenns, all over age 21, and all betting on blue cars.

I nailed Glenn on the cars because I knew something that he didn't. In casino games, patrons either do not understand what they are up against, or alternatively (and more intelligently), they do understand, but chalk up their losses as a fair price to pay for an evening's entertainment. Besides, in the short run, there's a chance they might actually win.

Glenn's actions on our trip mirrored almost exactly the behavior of many unfortunate casino gamblers:

1. He did not understand that the game was biased against him.
2. He did not take his winnings and quit when he was ahead in the short run.
3. On losing, he continued playing and redoubled his efforts to pull even or win, ultimately (in the long run) compounding his losses.

EAGLES AND ROBINS

IF ON OUR DRIVE I HAD SAID, "Let's count birds. You take eagles and I'll take robins," Glenn would have laughed in my face, instantly recognizing that the likelihood of spotting an eagle was insanely remote. While the casinos will not offer a fair game (like betting even money on the flip of a coin), they do offer something a bit more equitable than eagles and robins.

I had another friend growing up who was big for his age. Whenever I went to his house to play, he would beat me up. I was not a maso-chist, so I finally stopped going to his house. After a few days, however, he asked me to come back, offering me ice cream and other incentives. After righteously spurning his overtures for a time, I gave in and resumed playing at his house. True to his word, he gave me ice cream and generously shared his best toys, and from that time forward he beat me up only once a week.

This is exactly how the casinos operate, and why they give you a better deal than eagles versus robins. The casinos know that if they hammer you every time you come to play, sooner or later you will quit coming. Better to offer you little incentives and let you win every once in a while. Like with my big friend, they still get to beat you up, but not as often.

THE BATTLE AND THE WAR

IN CASINO GAMBLING, the short run is like a battle, and either player or casino can win. However, the casino almost always wins the war. The American Indians never had a chance against the continuing encroachment of white settlers. There were just too many settlers and too few Indians for the outcome ever to be in doubt. Losing the war, however, did not keep the Indians from winning a few big battles. So it goes in casino gambling. The player struggles in the face of overwhelming odds. If he keeps slugging it out, he is certain to lose. If, on the other hand, he hits and runs, he may come away a winner.

Gambling is like a commando raid: the gambler must get in, do some damage, and get out. Hanging around too long in the presence of superior forces can be fatal.

To say that this takes discipline is an understatement. It's hard to withdraw when you are winning, and maybe even harder to call it quits when you are losing. Glenn couldn't do either, and a lot of gamblers are just like Glenn.

THE HOUSE ADVANTAGE

IF CASINOS DID ENGAGE in fair bets, they would win about half the bets and lose about half the bets. In other words, the casino (and you), on average, would break even, or at least come close to breaking even. While this arrangement would be more equitable, it would not, as a rule, generate enough money for the casino to pay its mortgage, much less foot the bill for the dancing waters, lounge shows, $8 steaks, and free drinks.

HOUSE ADVANTAGES	
BACCARAT	1.17% on bank bets, 1.36% on player bets
BLACKJACK	0.5%-5.9% for most games
CRAPS	1.4% to almost 17%, depending on the bet
KENO	20%-35%
ROULETTE	5.26%-7.89%, depending on the bet
SLOTS	2%-25% (average 4%-14%)
VIDEO POKER	0.2%-12% (average 4%-8%)
WHEEL OF FORTUNE	11%-24%

To ensure sufficient income to meet their obligations and show a profit, casinos establish rules and payoffs for each game to give the house an advantage. While the house advantage is not strictly fair, it is what makes bargain rates on guest rooms, meals, and entertainment possible.

There are three basic ways in which the house establishes its advantage:

1. THE RULES OF THE GAME ARE TAILORED TO THE HOUSE'S ADVANTAGE In blackjack, for instance, the dealer by rule always plays his own hand last. If any player busts (attains a point total over 21), the dealer wins by default before having to play out his hand.

2. THE HOUSE PAYS OFF AT LESS THAN THE ACTUAL ODDS Imagine a carnival wheel with 10 numbers. When the wheel is spun, each number has an equal chance of coming up. If you bet a dollar on number 6, there is a 1-in-10 chance that you will win and a 9-in-10 chance that you will lose. Gamblers express odds by comparing the likelihood of losing to the likelihood of winning. In this case, 9 chances to lose and 1 to win, or 9–1. If the game paid off at the correct odds, you would get $9 every time you won (plus the dollar you bet). Each time you lost you would lose a dollar.

Let's say you start with $10 and do not win until your tenth try, betting your last dollar. If the game paid off at the correct odds, you would break even. Starting with $10, you would lose a dollar on each of your first nine attempts. In other words, you would be down $9. Betting your one remaining dollar, you win. At 9–1, you would receive $9 and get to keep the dollar you bet. You would have exactly the $10 you started with.

As we have seen, there is no way for a casino to play you even-up and still pay the bills. If, therefore, a casino owner decided to install a wheel with 10 numbers, he would decrease the payoff. Instead of paying at the correct odds (9–1), he might pay at 8–1. If you won on your last bet and got paid at 8–1 (instead of 9–1), you would have lost $1 overall. Starting with $10, you lose your first nine bets (so you are out $9) and on your last winning bet you receive $8 and get to keep the dollar you bet. Having played 10 times at the 8-to-1 payoff, you have $9 left, for a total loss of $1. Thus the house's advantage in this game is 10% (one-tenth).

The house advantage for actual casino games ranges from less than 1% for certain betting situations in blackjack to 35% on keno. Although 1% doesn't sound like much of an advantage, it will get you if you play long enough. Plus, for the house it adds up.

Because of variations in game rules, the house advantage for a particular game in one casino may be greater than the house advantage for the same game in another casino. In most Las Vegas casinos, for instance, the house has a 5.26% advantage in roulette. At European casinos, however, because of the elimination of 00 (double zero) on certain roulette wheels, the house advantage is pared down to about 2.7%.

The rule variations in blackjack swing the house advantage from almost zero in single-deck games (surrender, doubling on any number of cards, dealer stands on soft 17, etc.) to more than 6% in multiple-deck games with draconian rules, such as a recent wrinkle at blackjack, where a natural 21 pays off at 6–5 rather than the age-old 3–2. Quite a few mathematicians have taken a crack at computing the house's advantage in blackjack. Some suggest that the player can gain an advantage over the house by keeping track of cards played. Others claim that without counting cards, a player utilizing a decision guide known as "basic strategy" can play the house nearly even. The reality for 95% of all blackjack players, however, is a house advantage of between 0.5% and 5.9%, depending on rule variations and the number of decks used.

Getting to the meat of the matter: blackjack and some video poker played competently, baccarat, and certain bets in craps minimize the house advantage and give the player the best opportunity to win. Keno and wheel of fortune are outright sucker games. Slots, other video poker, and roulette are only marginally better.

How the house advantage works in practice causes much misunderstanding. In most roulette bets, for example, the house holds a 5.26% advantage. If you place a dollar on black each time the wheel is spun, the house advantage predicts that, on average, you will lose 5.26 cents per dollar bet. Now, in actual play you will either lose one whole dollar or win one whole dollar, so it's not like somebody is making small change or keeping track of fractional losses. The longer you play, however, the greater the likelihood that the percentage of your losses will approximate the house advantage. If you played for a couple of hours and bet $1,000, your expected loss would be about $53.

All right, you think, that doesn't sound too bad. Plus, you're thinking: I would never bet as much as $1,000. Oh, yeah? If you approach the table with $200 and make 20 consecutive $10 bets, it is not very likely that you will lose every bet. When you take money from your winning bets and wager it, you are adding to your original stake. This is known as "action" in gambling parlance, and it is very different from bankroll. Money that you win is just as much yours as the stake with which you began. When you choose to risk your winnings by making additional bets, you are giving the house a crack at a much larger amount than your original $200. If you start with $200, win some and lose some, and keep playing your winnings in addition to your original stake until you have lost everything, you will have given the house (on average) about $3,800 worth of action. You may want to believe you lost only $200, but every penny of that $3,800 was yours.

3. THE HOUSE TAKES A COMMISSION In all casino poker games and in certain betting situations in table games, the house will collect a commission on a player's winnings.

Sometimes the house combines its various advantages. In baccarat, for instance, rules favor the house; payoffs are less than the true odds; and in certain betting situations, the house collects a commission on the player's winnings.

GAMES OF CHANCE AND THE LAW OF AVERAGES

PEOPLE GET FUNNY IDEAS ABOUT the way gambling works. In casinos there are games of chance (roulette, craps, keno, bingo, slots, baccarat) and games of chance *and* skill (poker, blackjack, video poker).

A game of chance is like flipping a coin or spinning a wheel with 10 numbers. What happens is what happens. A player can guess what the outcome will be but cannot influence it. Games of chance operate according to the law of averages. If you have a fair coin and flip it 10 times, the law of averages leads you to expect that approximately half of the tosses will come up heads and the other half tails. If a roulette wheel has 38 slots, the law of averages suggests that the ball will fall into a particular slot one time in 38 spins.

The coin, the roulette ball, and the dice, however, have no memory. They just keep doing their thing. If you toss a coin and come up with heads nine times in a row, what are your chances of getting heads on the tenth toss? The answer is 50%, the same chance as getting heads on any toss. Each toss is completely independent of any other toss. When the coin goes up in the air that tenth time, it doesn't know that tails has not come up for a while, and certainly has no obligation to try to get the law of averages back into whack.

Though most gamblers are familiar with the law of averages, not all of them understand how it works. The operative word, as it turns out, is "averages," not "law." If you flip a coin a million times, there is nothing that says you will get 500,000 heads and 500,000 tails, no more than there is any assurance you will get five heads and five tails if you flip a coin 10 times. What the law of averages *does* say is that, *in percentage terms,* the more times you toss the coin, the closer you will come to approximating the predicted average.

If you tossed a coin 10 times, for example, you would not be surprised to get six tails and four heads. Six tails is only one flip off the five tails and five heads that the law of averages tells you is the probable outcome. By percentage, however, tails came up 60% (6 of 10) of the time, while heads came up only 40% (4 of 10) of the time. If you continued flipping the coin for a million tries, would you be surprised to get 503,750 tails and only 496,250 heads, a difference of 7,500 more tails than heads? The law of averages stipulates that the more we toss (and a million tosses are certainly a lot more than 10 tosses) the closer we should come to approximating the average, but here we are with a huge difference of 7,500 more tails. What went wrong?

Nothing went wrong. True, after 10 flips, we had only two more tails than heads, while after a million flips we had 7,500 more tails than heads. But in terms of percentage, 503,750 tails is 50.375% of one million, only about one-third of a measly percent from what the law of averages predicts. The law of averages is about percentages. Gambling is about dollars out of your pocket. If you had bet a dollar on heads each toss, you would have lost $2 after 10 flips. After a million flips you would have lost $7,500. The law of averages behaved just as mathematical theory predicted.

Games of Chance and Skill

Blackjack, poker, and video poker are games of chance and skill, meaning that the knowledge, experience, and skill of the player can have

The Intelligence Test

If you have been paying attention, here is what you should understand by now:

1. That all gambling games are designed to favor the house, and that in the long run the house will always win.

2. That it costs a lot to build, staff, and operate a casino, and that a casino must attract many players in order to pay the bills and still make a profit.

3. That casinos compete fiercely for available customers and offer incentives ranging from 99-cent hot dogs to free guest rooms to get the right customers to their gaming tables.

QUESTION: **Given the above, what kind of customer gets the best deal?**

Answer: The person who takes advantage of all the incentives without gambling.

QUESTION: **What kind of customer gets the next best deal?**

Answer: The customer who sees gambling as recreation, gambles knowledgeably, makes sensible bets, sets limits on the amount he or she is prepared to wager, and enjoys all of the perks and amenities, but stays in control.

QUESTION: **What kind of customer gets the worst deal?**

Answer: The person who thinks he or she can win. This person will foot the bill for everyone else.

some influence on the outcome. All avid poker players or bridge players can recall nights when they played for hours without being dealt a good hand. That's the chance part. In order to win, you need good cards. There is usually not much you can do if you are dealt a bad hand.

If you are dealt something to work with, however, you can bring your skill into play and try to make your good hand even better. In casino poker, players compete against each other in the same way they do at Uncle Bert's house back home. The only difference is that in the casino the house takes a small percentage of each winning pot as compensation for hosting the game (are you listening, Uncle Bert?). Although not every casino poker player is an expert, your chances of coming up against an expert in a particular game are good.

Our advice on casino poker: if you're not a tough fish, better not try to swim with the sharks.

Blackjack likewise combines chance and skill. In blackjack, however, players compete against the house (the dealer). Players have certain choices and options in blackjack, but the dealer's play is completely bound by rules. Much has been written about winning at blackjack. It's been said that by keeping track of cards played (and thereby knowing which cards remain undealt in the deck), a player can raise his or her bets when the deck contains a higher-than-usual percentage of aces, tens, and picture cards. In practice, however, the casino confounds efforts to count cards by combining several decks together, "burning" cards (removing undisclosed cards from play), and keeping the game moving at a fast pace. If an experienced gambler with extraordinary memory and power of concentration is able to overcome these obstacles, the casino will simply throw out this person.

In blackjack, as in every other casino game, it is ludicrous to suggest that the house is going to surrender its advantage. Incidentally, a super-gambler playing flawlessly and keeping track of every card will gain only a nominal and temporary advantage over the house. On top of playing perfectly and being dealt good cards, the super-gambler must also disguise his play and camouflage his betting so the house won't know what he's up to. It's not impossible, but very few players who try ever pull it off successfully.

Playing It Smart

Experienced, noncompulsive, recreational gamblers typically play in a disciplined and structured manner. Here's what they recommend:

1. **Never gamble when you are** tired, depressed, or sick. Also, watch the drinking. Alcohol impairs judgment (you play badly) and lowers inhibitions (you exceed prudent limits).

2. **Set a limit before you leave home** on the total amount you are willing to lose gambling. No matter what happens, do not exceed this limit.

3. **Decide which game(s) interest you and get the rules down before you play.** If you are a first-timer at craps or baccarat, take lessons (offered free at the casinos most days). If you are a virgin blackjack player, buy a good book and learn basic strategy. For all three games, spend an hour or two observing games in progress before buying in. Stay away from games like keno and wheel of fortune, in which the house advantage is overwhelming.

4. **Decide how long you want to play** and work out a gambling itinerary consistent with the funds you set aside for wagering. Let's say you plan to be in Las Vegas for two days and want to play about five hours each day. If you have $500 in gambling money available for the trip, that's $250 a day. Dividing the $250 a day by five hours, you come up with $50 an hour.

   Now, forget time. Think of your gambling in terms of playing individual sessions instead of hours. You are going to play five sessions a day with $50 available to wager at each session.

5. **Observe a strategy for winning and losing.** On buying in, place your session allocation by your left hand. Play your allotted session money only once during a given session. Anytime you win, return your original bet to the session-allocation stack (left hand), and place your winnings in a stack by your right hand. Never play any chips or coins you have won. When you have gone through your original allocation once, pick up the chips or coins in your winning stack (right hand) and quit. The difference between your original allocation and what you walk away with is your net win or loss for the session.

   During the session, bet consistently. If you have been making $1 bets and have lost $10, do not chase your losses by upping your bets to $10 in an effort to get even in a hurry.

   If you were fortunate and doubled your allocated stake during the session (in this case, walked away with $100 or more), take everything in excess of $100 and put it aside as winnings, not to be touched for the remainder of your trip. If you won, but did not double your money, or if you had a net loss (quit with less than $50 in your win stack), use this money in your next playing session.

6. **Take a break between sessions.** Relax for a while after each session. Grab a bite to eat, enjoy a nap, or go for a swim.

7. When you complete the number of sessions scheduled for the day, stop gambling. **Period.**

GAMING INSTRUCTION AND RESOURCES

MOST CASINO GAMES ARE ACTUALLY FAIRLY SIMPLE once you know what's going on. A great way to replace inexperience and awkwardness with knowledge and confidence is to take the free gaming lessons offered by the casinos. Going slowly and easily, the instructors take you step by step through the play and the betting without you actually wagering any money. Many casinos feature low-minimum-bet "live games" following the instruction. We also recommend the lessons to nonplaying companions of gamblers. For folks who usually spend a fair amount of time as spectators, casino games, like all other games, are more interesting if you know what is going on.

We highly recommend the free gaming lessons offered by casinos. They introduce you not only to the rules but also to the customs and etiquette of the respective games.

No matter how many books you have read, take a lesson in craps before you try to play in a casino. You don't need to know much to play baccarat, but *understanding* it is a different story. Once again, we strongly recommend lessons. Though you can learn to play blackjack by reading a book and practicing at home, lessons will make you feel more comfortable.

When "new games" are added to the traditional selection, casinos often offer instruction for a limited time. The latest rages are poker and a whole bunch of poker derivatives: Texas Hold 'Em, Let It Ride, Caribbean Stud, Three Card poker, Crazy 4 poker, 3-5-7 poker, along with Casino War, and, owing to the increasing number of Asian gamblers, Pai Gow and Pai Gow poker. Lessons are also available in traditional poker. A list of free gambling lessons currently offered in Las Vegas can be found at **lvahotels.com.** Click on "Gambling Advisor" at the top right of the page.

A great website for gambling odds, playing strategies, practice games, and general information is Michael Shackleford's **wizardofodds.com.**

WRITTEN REFERENCES AND THE GAMBLERS BOOK CLUB Most libraries and bookstores offer basic reference works on casino gambling. If you cannot find what you need at home, call the Gamblers Book Club at ☎ 800-522-1777 for a free catalog. If you would like to stop in and browse while in Las Vegas, the club's store is located at 800 S. Main St. (between Charleston and Fremont). The local phone is ☎ 702-382-7555, and visit online at **gamblersbookclub.com.** For those of you who visited the club at its Eastern Avenue location, it moved in 2013 to share space with the Gamblers General Store (☎ 702 382-9903, **gamblersgeneralstore. com**), the one-stop shop for all things gambling. Gamblers Book Shop, incidentally, sells single issues of the *Las Vegas Advisor,* quoted below.

WHERE TO PLAY

WE RECEIVE A LOT OF MAIL FROM READERS asking which

casino has the loosest slots, the most favorable rules for blackjack, and the best odds on craps. We directed the questions to veteran gambler and tournament player Anthony Curtis, publisher of the *Las Vegas Advisor*. Here's Anthony's reply:

> *Where's the best casino in Las Vegas to play blackjack, video poker, and the rest of the gambling games? It could be almost any place on any given day due to spot promotions and changing management philosophies. A few casinos, however, have established reliable track records in specific areas. Absent a special promotion or change in policy, I recommend the casinos in the chart on pages 312–313 as the best places for the games listed.*

Players Clubs

Most Las Vegas casinos now have frequent-player clubs, known as players clubs. The purpose of these clubs is to foster increased customer loyalty among gambling patrons by providing incentives. Even if you're not a gambler, or only gamble a little, you should sign up. This will get you on the casino's mailing/email lists identified as a gambler, and ensure that you receive lots of special offers and discounts on rooms, shows, dining, and more.

You can join a club by signing up at the casino or (at most casinos) by applying through the mail or online. There is neither a direct cost associated with joining nor any dues. You are given a plastic membership card that resembles a credit card. This card can be inserted into a special slot on any gambling machine in the casino. As long as your card is in the slot, you are credited for the amount of action you put through that machine. Programs at different casinos vary, but in general, you are awarded points based on how long you play and how much you wager. All clubs award points for slot play; some also use the card at the tables to input hours played and average bets into the player-tracking database. As in an airline frequent-flyer program, accumulated points can ultimately be redeemed for awards. Awards range from casino logo apparel to discounts and comps on meals, shows, and rooms.

Las Vegas is dominated by large casino companies such as Caesars Entertainment, MGM Resorts International, and local companies such as Boyd Gaming and Station Casinos. These major stakeholders respectively offer a players club card that can be used in any of their casinos. The following casinos' players club cards can be acquired online:

• Aria• Bally's • Bellagio • Caesars Palace • California
• The Cosmopolitan • The Cromwell • Downtown Grand • El Cortez
• Excalibur • Flamingo • Fremont • Gold Coast • Golden Gate
• Golden Nugget • Hard Rock • Harrah's • Hooters
• LINQ Hotel & Casino • Luxor • Main Street Station • Mandalay Bay
• MGM Grand • Mirage • New York–New York • The Orleans
• Palazzo • Palms• Paris • Planet Hollywood • Plaza • Rampart
• Rio • Riviera • Sam's Town • SLS • South Point • Suncoast • TI
• Tropicana • Venetian • Westgate LV• Wynn • Wynn Encore

Players clubs are evolving into loyalty programs where non-gambling spending on rooms, dining, entertainment, and shopping is tracked in addition to gambling action. As discussed in the introduction to this guide, gaming revenue has slipped into second place behind non-gaming revenue at many casinos, so this metamorphosis makes sense.

Most Strip casinos, except Circus Circus, Riviera, Stratosphere, Riviera, TI, Tropicana, and Wynn/Encore, track and reward all spending. At most off-Strip casinos, only spending on gaming is rewarded. Exceptions are the Hard Rock and the Rio.

One good thing about players clubs is that they provide a mechanism for slot players to obtain some of the comps, perks, and extras that have always been available to table players. The bad thing about a players club is that it confines your play. In other words, you must give most of your business to one or two casinos in order to accumulate enough points to reap rewards, though you will nonetheless receive the special offers mentioned earlier. If you are a footloose player and enjoy gambling all around town, you may never accrue enough points in any one casino to redeem a comp.

Join a players club so you can be identified as a gambler on the hotel-casino's mailing list. Just for joining, and without gambling that first quarter, you will be offered discounts on rooms and a variety of other special deals.

CHANGES IN ATTITUDE, CHANGES IN LATITUDE

MOST PEOPLE WHO LOVE TO GAMBLE are not motivated solely by greed. Usually it is the tension, excitement, and anticipation of the game that they enjoy. Misunderstanding this reality has led many naive and innocent people into the nightmare of addictive gambling.

Ed was attending a convention on his first visit to Las Vegas. One evening, he decided to try his luck at roulette. Approaching the table, Ed expected to lose ("I'm not stupid, after all"). His intentions were typical. He wanted to "try" gambling while in Nevada, and he was looking for an adventure, a new experience. What Ed never anticipated was the emotional impact gambling would have on him. It transcended winning and losing. In fact, it wasn't about winning or losing at all. It was the *playing* that mattered. The "action" made him feel alive, involved, and terribly sophisticated. It also made him crazy.

The "high" described by the compulsive gambler closely parallels the experience of drug and alcohol abusers. In fact, there is a tendency for chemical addiction and gambling compulsion to overlap. The compulsive gambler attempts to use "the action" as a cure for a variety of ills, in much the same way that people use alcohol and drugs to lift them out of depression, anxiety, or boredom, and make them feel more "in control."

Some people cannot handle gambling, just as some people cannot handle alcohol. The problem, unfortunately, is compounded by the

Anthony's Recommended Best Places to Play

BLACKJACK EL CORTEZ

El Cortez steadfastly continues to offer the 3-2 payoff for naturals on single-deck games, and at low ($5) stakes. Add in the good promotions here and you have the best place in town to play low-stakes blackjack.

QUARTER SLOTS RAMPART

Since you can't tell definitively whose slots pay best (they can't be analyzed like video-poker machines), picking a casino with strong player benefits and an overall policy of liberal gambling is as good a way to choose as any. Rampart fits that bill perfectly. And in addition to being one of the best gambling houses in Las Vegas, the Rampart also has excellent comp deals, so your players points from quarter slots will go farther here.

DOLLAR SLOTS PALMS

Evidence still points to the Palms as being another that's among the loosest for slots in general. Lots of promotions and a good slot club make it the pick at the dollar level (but video poker provides much better returns). Dollar slot players earn comps fast, and this is one of the best places in town to use them.

CRAPS MAIN STREET STATION

With last year's demise of 100X odds at Casino Royale, Main Street Station moves to the front of the craps pack with 20X odds. Since there's not much difference in the casino edge from one dice game to another, this odds multiple makes Main Street the best in town in this category.

QUARTER VIDEO POKER THE D

Finding 100%+ gambling isn't easy, but you can find it on the quarter games here. The good ones are on the second floor, including a bank with a sign that reads "Over 100% Payback." But the best machines are at the Vue Bar, where progressive-jackpot meters rise quickly to create frequent high-return situations.

DOLLAR VIDEO POKER SOUTH POINT

Hundreds of machines here pay at the 9/6 Jacks or Better level (99.54%) or better. Add the generous South Point slot club and other benefits and you're playing at a 100% theoretical return level 24/7. Plus, whereas many casinos now reduce players club benefits on machines with the best schedules, South Point pays full benefits on all machines.

ROULETTE MIRAGE

The best you can hope for with this game is a wheel with a single zero (as opposed to the standard two zeros). There are several in town, but almost all are in the high-limit rooms. Mirage is one of the few casinos with a single-zero game on the main floor.

BACCARAT PALACE STATION

Action around the clock at oversized mini baccarat tables. Minimums are low. If you get hungry, they'll deliver food to your table.

KENO EL CORTEZ

Better-than-average returns compared with keno norms and good promotions for players. The ever-improving El Cortez continues to maintain its homey lounge, even as the trend moves away from live to video keno.

BINGO SOUTH POINT

Several of the locals casinos have good bingo programs, and this is one of them. The tipping point, though, is free bingo. South Point calls 10 $100 games at the 9 a.m. session, Monday–Friday. It's hard to beat free!

POKER ARIA

Aria has emerged as the most consistently busy room in town by offering a good mix of games, lots of tournaments, and a strong comp structure where players earn $2 per hour at all game levels. There's also a good "poker rate" on rooms for players. On the high end, some of the biggest games in town run regularly out of the "Ivey Room."

Anthony's Recommended Best Places to Play

RACE AND SPORTS BETTING **ALIANTE**

This is one of Las Vegas's rare independent sports books, which means it makes its own lines. Consequently, you'll find numbers that vary from what's widely available around town, which is always a good thing. Aliante also runs the city's best NFL football contest, with a $25 entry fee and a buy-three-get-one-free deal. The book features lots of big screens and food and drink deals for bettors.

LET IT RIDE **FOUR QUEENS**

Not much separates one Let It Ride game from another, so a low-minimum-bet requirement is a good feature. The Four Queens usually has a game going with a $5 minimum. Show your players card—this casino's mailing list is a good one to be on.

CARIBBEAN STUD **THE VENETIAN**

Caribbean Stud is getting harder to find. Of the diminishing number of casinos that still deal it, the Venetian still has two tables, so it's a good bet you'll find one that's open.

PAI GOW POKER **GOLD COAST**

A favorite casino of local pai gow players, so there's constant action and low minimums.

attitude of our society. As we profess to admire the drinker who can "hold his liquor," we reinforce the gambler who beats the odds in Las Vegas. By glamorizing these behaviors we enable afflicted individuals to remain in denial about the destructive nature of their problem. The compulsive gambler blames circumstances and other people for the suffering occasioned by his or her affliction. One may hear excuses like: "I didn't get enough sleep; I couldn't concentrate with all the noise; I lost track of the time; I'm jinxed at this casino."

If this sounds like you or someone you love, get help. In Las Vegas there is a meeting of Gamblers Anonymous almost every Tuesday night. Call ☎ 855-222-5542 or check the web at **gamblersanonymous .org.** If, like Ed, you catch something in Las Vegas and take it home with you, Gamblers Anonymous is listed in your local *White Pages*.

RULES *of the* GAMES

SLOT MACHINES

SLOT MACHINES, INCLUDING VIDEO POKER, have long eclipsed table games in patron popularity. Few Las Vegas casinos remain that have not allocated half or more of their available floor space to various types of slot machines.

The popularity of slots is not difficult to understand. First, slots allow a person to enjoy casino gambling at low or high stakes. Except at the oldest and lowest-tier casinos, all slot machines are now multi-denominational, meaning you can play them for a penny, nickel, dime, quarter, dollar, and up. You don't need change to do so; slot machines no longer have slots. You load them up with bills, then play at your chosen denomination. Higher-stakes players can find machines that accept bets of $1 to $500 ($2,500 to load up a $500 video poker machine).

Second, many people like the slots because no human interaction is required. Absent in slot play is the adversarial atmosphere of the table games. Machines are less intimidating—at least more neutral—than dealers and pit bosses. A patron can sit at a machine for as long as his stamina and money last and never be bothered by a soul.

Finally, slot machines are simple, or at least ostensibly so. Although there are a number of things you should know before you play the slots, the only thing you have to know is how to put money (mostly bills) into the machine and press the spin button (it's the rare slot machine that still has a handle).

What You Need to Know before You Play Slot Machines

Starting at the beginning: All slot machines have a slot for inserting either coins, bills, or machine tickets, a button to push to activate the machine, a visual display where you can see the reels spin and stop or video symbols line up on each play, and a coin tray or machine-ticket dispenser out of which you hope some winnings will come. Today, almost all slot machines are essentially computers attached to a monitor. Gone are the mechanical reels, replaced by an electronic depiction of reels or other symbols illustrated on the monitor.

While slot machines used to have three mechanical reels, most today have been replaced by either three or four electronic reels or video screens with up to 12 depictions of reels. Each reel has some number of "stops," positions where the reel can come to rest. On each reel at each stop (or resting position) is a single slot symbol (a cherry, bar, themed symbol, etc.). What you hope will happen (when the video reels stop spinning) is that paying symbols will line up. If this happens, you win some number of coins or credits based on the bet and particular symbols. With the old slot machines things were pretty simple. There was one coin slot, one handle to pull, and a display with one pay line. Symbols either lined up or they didn't. The newer machines are much more complex. All modern machines accept more than one coin per play (usually three to five but up to 250). No matter how many coins the machine will take, it requires only one to play.

If you put in additional coins (bet more), you will buy one of the following benefits:

1. **Payoff schedules** On some slot machines, the payoff schedule is posted on the glass above the screen; on others, you have to press the See Pays button to determine the winning combinations. If you study these schedules you will notice that by playing extra coins you can increase your payoff should you win the grand jackpot. Usually there is a straightforward increase. If you play two coins, you will win twice as much as if you play one coin. If you play three coins, you will win three times as much as if you play one coin, and so on. Some machines, however, have a jackpot that will pay off only if you have played the maximum number of coins. If you line up the symbols for the

Slot-Machine Pay Lines

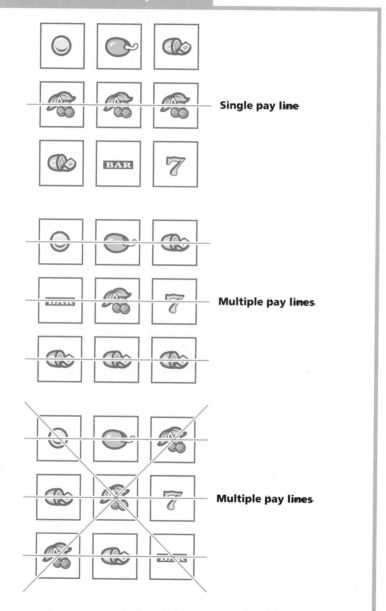

Single pay line

Multiple pay lines

Multiple pay lines

jackpot but have not played the maximum number of coins, you will not win the maximum amount possible. The machines with three or four reels, such as the venerable Red, White, and Blue; Double Diamonds; and Blazing Sevens, are easy to understand, with the payout schedules posted prominently on the glass screen above the reels. Video (also known as Australian) slots, on the other hand, which come in hundreds of different themes from oil wells to polar bears, are much more complicated. You can press the Help button at the bottom of the screen to bring up three or four additional screens that explain the machine. But most slot players don't bother, and it's not necessary to comprehend all the ins and outs. Just slip your money into the bill acceptor, press the button with the number of coins you want to play, and spin the reels; the machine does the rest.

Though most casino slot machines are kept in good working order, watch to make sure the machine credits you for every coin you play and for all the winnings due to you.

2. **Multiple pay lines** When you play your first coin, you buy the usual pay line, right in the center of the display. By playing more coins, you can buy additional pay lines.

Each pay line you purchase gives you another way of winning. Instead of being limited to the center line, the machine will pay off on the top, center, or bottom lines, and five-coin machines will pay winners on diagonal lines. Australian machines pay off on a dozen lines or more, criss-crossing symbols all over the screen. If you play machines with multiple pay lines, make sure that each pay line you buy is acknowledged by a light before you push the button.

An irritating feature of many multiple-line machines are "blanks" or "ghosts." A blank is nothing more than an empty stop on the reel—a place where you would expect a symbol to be but where there is nothing. As you probably know, you cannot hit a winner by lining up blanks.

NONPROGRESSIVE VS. PROGRESSIVE SLOT MACHINES Nonprogressive slot machines have fixed payoffs. You can read the payoff schedules posted on the machine and determine exactly how much you will get for each winning combination for any number of coins played.

A second type of machine, known as a progressive, has a top jackpot that grows and grows until it's hit. After the top prize has been won, the jackpot is reset and starts to grow. While individual machines can offer modest progressive jackpots, the really big jackpots (up to tens of millions of dollars) are possible only on machines linked in a system to other machines. Sometimes an "island," "carousel," or "bank" of machines in a given casino is hooked up to create a progressive system. The more these machines are played, the faster the progressive jackpot grows. The largest progressive jackpots come from huge multicasino systems that sometimes cover the entire state. Players have won more than $30 million by hitting these jackpots.

While nothing is certain in slot play, it is generally accepted that nonprogressives pay more small jackpots. Progressives, on the other hand, offer an opportunity to strike it really rich, but they give up fewer interim wins.

 The nonprogressive machine is for the player who likes plenty of action, who gets bored when credits aren't rising on the meter every four or five spins. The progressive machine is for the player who is willing to forgo frequent small payouts for the chance of hitting a really big one.

How Slot Machines Work

Almost all slot machines used in casinos today are controlled by microprocessors. This means the machines can be programmed and are more like computers than mechanical boxes composed of gears and wheels. During the evolution of the modern slot machine, manufacturers eliminated the traditional spinning reels in favor of a video display, and replaced the pull handle with a spin button. Inside the newer machines, there is a device that computer people call a "random number generator" and that we refer to as a "black box." What the black box does is spit out hundreds of numbers each second, selected randomly (that is, in no predetermined sequence). The black box has about four billion different numbers to choose from, so it's very unusual (but not impossible) for the same number to come up twice in a short time.

The numbers the black box selects are programmed to trigger a certain set of symbols on the display, determining where the reels stop. What most players don't realize, however, is that the black box pumps out numbers continuously, regardless of whether the machine is being played or not. If you are playing a machine, the black box will call up hundreds or thousands of numbers in the few seconds between plays while you sip your drink, put some money in the slot, and push the button.

Why is this important? Try this scenario: Mary has played the same quarter machine for hours, pumping an untold amount of money into it. She cashes out and gets up to stretch her legs for a few minutes, thinking she'll come back afterwards and keep playing. In the meantime, a man walks up to Mary's machine and hits the jackpot. Mary is livid. "That's my jackpot!" she screams. Not so. While Mary took her walk, thousands of numbers and possible symbol combinations were generated by the black box. The only way Mary could have hit the jackpot (even if the man had not come along) would have been to activate the machine at that same exact moment in time, right down to a fraction of a millisecond.

Another slot myth is that a machine is "overdue to hit." Each spin of the reels on a slot machine is an independent event, just like flipping a coin. The only way to hit a jackpot is to activate the machine at the exact moment that the black box randomly coughs up a winning number. If you play a slot machine as fast as you can, pushing the spin button like a maniac, the black box will still spew out more numbers (and possible jackpots) between each try than you will have spins in a whole day of playing.

CHERRY, CHERRY, ORANGE The house advantage is known for every casino game except slots. With slot machines, the house advantage is whatever the casino programs it to be. In Atlantic City the maximum legal house advantage is 17%. Nevada's limit for slot machines is a hold of 75%. This means that Nevada slot machines can have a house advantage of up to 25%. Interviews with ex–casino employees suggest, however, that the house advantage on casino slots in Las Vegas ranges from about 2.5% to 25%, with most machines giving the house an edge of between 4% and 14%.

Casinos advertise their slots in terms of payout or return rate. If a casino states that its slots return up to 97%, that's another way of saying that the house has a 3% advantage. Some casinos advertise machines that pay up to 98%, and on special-promotion occasions, a casino might advertise slots that pay more than 100%.

SLOT QUEST A slot machine that withholds only a small percentage of the money played is referred to as "loose," while a machine that retains closer to the maximum allowable percentage is called "tight." "Loose" and "tight" are figurative descriptions and have nothing to do with the condition of the machine. Because return rates vary from casino to casino, and because machines in a given casino are programmed to withhold vastly differing percentages of the money played, some slot players devote much time and energy to finding the best casinos and the loosest machines. Exactly how to go about this is the subject of much discussion.

In terms of choosing a casino, several theories have at least a marginal ring of truth. Competition among casinos is often a general indicator for finding loose slots. Some say that smaller casinos, which compete against large neighbors, must program their slots to provide a higher return. Alternatively, some folks will play slots only in casinos patronized predominantly by locals, such as Gold Coast, Sam's Town, and Arizona Charlie's, among others. The reasoning here is that these casinos vie for regular customers on a continuing basis and must therefore offer extremely competitive win rates. Downtown Las Vegas is likewise cast in the "we try harder" role, because smaller Downtown casinos must go head-to-head with the Strip to attract patrons.

Extending the logic, machines located in supermarkets, restaurants, convenience stores, airports, and lounges are purported to be very tight. In these places, some argue, there is little incentive for management to provide good returns, because the patrons will play regardless (out of boredom or compulsion or simply because the machine is there).

Veteran slot players have many theories when it comes to finding the loose machines in a particular casino. Some will tell you to play the machines by the door or in the waiting area outside the showroom. By placing the loose machines in these locations, the theory goes, the casino can demonstrate to passersby and show patrons that the house has loose slots. Perhaps the most accurate way to judge the relative looseness of reel slots is to monitor the payouts for video poker. As explained in the next section, knowledgeable players who know how to interpret video poker pay schedules can determine the payback percentage to thousandths of percentage points. It's safe to assume (as safe as it is to assume anything) that a casino with loose video poker machines will have loose slots as well.

I have had a slot manager admit to me that his quarter machines are looser than his nickel machines and that his dollar and five-dollar machines are the loosest of all. Tight or loose, however, all slots are programmed to give the casino a certain profit over the long run. It is very unlikely, in any event, that you will play a machine long enough to experience the theoretical payoff rate. What you are concerned about is the short run. In the short run anything can happen, including winning.

MAXIMIZING YOUR CHANCES OF WINNING ON THE SLOTS If you play less than the maximum number of coins on a progressive, you are simply contributing to a jackpot that you have no chance of winning. If you don't want to place a maximum bet, play a nonprogressive machine.

Slot-Machine Etiquette and Common Sense

Regardless of whether you are playing a slot machine, a video-poker machine, or any other type of electronic or mechanical gambling device, there are some things you need to know:

1. Realize that avid slot players sometimes play more than one machine at a time. Do not assume that a machine is not in use simply because nobody is standing or sitting in front of it. Slot players can be fanatically territorial.

2. Before you start to play, check out the people around you. Do you feel safe and comfortable among them?

3. Read the payout schedule of any machine you play; if you don't understand it completely, don't worry.

4. Almost all machines have credit meters; be sure to cash out your credits before you abandon the machine.

5. If the casino has a players club, join (this usually takes less than 5 minutes on-site, but can be accomplished through the mail or online prior to your trip). Use the club card whenever you play. When you quit, don't forget to take your club card with you.

6. Never play more machines than you can watch carefully. Be particularly vigilant when playing machines near exits and corridors. If you're asleep at the switch, you're vulnerable to victimization by thieves and scam

---

LAND OF THE LOOSE SLOTS

MOST RECREATIONAL SLOT PLAYERS play at the casino where they're staying, even if they know there are looser machines elsewhere. Those who are serious about finding the loosest slots, however, should check out *Casino Player Magazine*'s **casinocenter.com/loosest-slots.** According to its findings, the best machines, located at the Hard Rock, Palms, Orleans, and Silverton, return 94.64% of the money played. A tiny 1/4th of 1 percent behind are the Boulder Highway casinos, Boulder Station, Sam's Town, and Arizona Charlie's East. Strip casino slots are tight, and there's no data to rate Downtown, but its video poker schedules are superior to those of Strip casinos, so maybe their slots are better as well. Bear in mind, however, that a 94.64% return rate is just about the same house edge as double zero roulette. Not great.

artists, who have plenty of nefarious tricks up their sleeves to relieve you of your lucre. They even have ways of absconding with payout tickets issued from the machine while you're playing!

7. Keep your purse and your money in sight at all times. Never put your purse on the floor behind you or to the side.

8. If you line up a big winner and nothing happens, don't panic. Slot machines lock up when a jackpot exceeds the tax-reporting requirement. Any winning combination of more than $1,200 on a slot or video poker machine must be "hand paid" directly by a slot floorperson. If you're lucky and hit a big enough jackpot that tax paperwork needs to be filled out, the "candle" (light fixture) atop the machine will blink or some other indicator of a jackpot will manifest, summoning a slot attendant. Don't wander off to look for one; sit patiently and one will show up shortly.

9. If the appropriate payout sections or pay lines fail to illuminate when playing multiple coins, do not leave or activate the machine (push the button) until you have consulted an attendant.

The Future of Slot Machines

The bandits have always been stand-alone machines with individual controls, from mechanical cogs and gears in the early days to central-processing units in the electronic age. So in order to change a slot's games, denominations, or payback percentages, a slot technician has had to manipulate the circuitry of the machine itself. However, a new generation of slots, known as "server-based" machines, are all networked to a central back-office computer system; the machines on the floor essentially become dumb monitors dressed up in slot cabinets, into which (with the click of a back-room mouse) different games, denominations, payback percentages, bonuses, promotions, and so on can be downloaded.

From the casino's point of view, server-based slots allow managers, with a few keystrokes, to tailor their games to player preferences. Perhaps the casino needs more slots during the day and more video poker at night. Or maybe weekday crowds prefer penny games and free spins, while weekend players like quarter games and second-screen bonuses. Operators can also increase denominations, say from nickels to quarters and quarters to dollars, at prime time on Saturday nights. In short, casinos are able to adapt to changing conditions on the fly.

In addition, with the use of the player-tracking system, managers can record a player's preferred game, then offer those games on a machine as soon as a player inserts the card. The casino can also contact players right at the machine in real time. For example, a message that you've earned a free buffet or discounted show tickets could be sent to the display terminal on the machine.

From the player's perspective, server-based slots have to overcome a long-cherished myth: that casinos can change the payback of a machine at the flip of a switch, tightening games during busy times, then loosening them again when the crowds go home. Downloadable slots will certainly have that capability. Thus, the onus will be on the casinos and gaming regulators to make the process as transparent as possible, so that when a player suddenly goes from hot to cold, he won't suspect that a computer has just changed the payback percentage from 98% to 82%. For example, the machine's screen might display a "modification-in-progress" message, followed by, say, 5 minutes of down time.

Early adopters of server-based slots in Las Vegas include Aria and The Cosmopolitan. Stay tuned.

VIDEO POKER

NEVER IN THE HISTORY of casino gambling has a game become so popular so quickly. What's the allure of video poker? More people are familiar with poker than with any other casino game. The video version affords average folks an opportunity to play a game of chance and skill without going up against professional gamblers. Also, like slot machines, video poker is fast; you can play 300, 400, 500 hands per hour. And like blackjack, it's skilled, so you can study and become an expert player and gain an edge over the house. Finally, it's hypnotic; many people find it hard to get up from a video poker machine (if that's you, you might think twice about playing too much and becoming compulsive).

In video poker you play against a machine. The object is to make the best possible five-card-draw poker hand. In the most common rendition, you insert your money and push a button marked "deal." Your original five cards are displayed on the screen. Below the screen and under each of the cards pictured are "hold" buttons. After evaluating your hand and planning your strategy, designate the cards you want to keep by pressing the appropriate hold button(s). If you hit the wrong button or change your mind, simply "unhold" your choices by pushing the buttons again. If you do not want to draw any cards (you like your hand as dealt), press all five hold buttons. When you press the hold button for a particular card, the word "hold" will appear over that card on the display. Always double-check the screen to make certain the cards you intend to hold are marked before proceeding to the draw.

When you are ready, press the button marked "draw" (on many machines it is the same button as the deal button). Any cards you have not designated to be held will be replaced. As in live draw poker, the five cards in your possession after the draw are your final hand. If the hand is a winner (a pair of jacks or better on most non-wild-card machines), you will be credited the appropriate winnings on the credit meter on the video display. These are actual winnings that can be retrieved, mostly via a machine ticket, by pressing the "cash-out" button. If you choose to leave your winnings on the credit meter, you may use them to bet, eliminating the need to physically insert more money into the machine. When you are ready to quit, simply press the cash-out button and collect your coins from the tray or a ticket from the dispenser.

As with other slot machines, you can increase your payoffs and become eligible for bonus jackpots by playing the maximum number of coins. Note that some machines have jackpots listed in dollars, while others are specified in coins. Obviously, there is a big difference between $4,000 and 4,000 nickels.

Playing video poker is vastly different from playing live poker. There's no psychology involved. You can't bluff the machine. You can show all the emotion you want. In most games, you don't hold kickers. All you need to know to play is the hierarchy of winning poker hands (pair, two-pair, three-of-a-kind, straight, and so on). All the winning hands with their respective payoffs are enumerated on or above the video display.

But to play video poker well, you need two additional skills: selecting the right machine and playing the proper strategy. The first skill requires the ability to decipher the pay schedules posted prominently on the face-plates of every machine. Some machines have a high payback percentage, even higher than 100%, while others pay less. You're looking for the highest paying schedules within each variation of video poker—and there are dozens of variations, but you have to know only a few of them.

Two of these are Jacks or Better (JoB) and Double Bonus. The highest paying version of JoB is called 9/6, meaning it pays 9-for-1 per coin played when you hit a full house, and 6-for-1 when you hit a flush. When you check the payout schedule for a single coin played, it could read 8 for a full house and 5 for a flush, even 7 or 6 for a full house. But unless you're returned 9 for the full house and 6 for the flush, you might as well play any random slot machine. The payback percentage for 9/6 JoB is 99.5%, almost break-even.

The other schedule to look for is 10/7 Double Bonus. Again, this means 10-for-1 on a full house and 7-for-1 on a flush. You'll see lower paybacks, but it's only 10/7 that we play, which pays back 100.7%, a positive game.

Other payback schedules are also playable, such as Deuces Wild and Joker Wild. But you have to recognize the highest-paying versions, which you can learn easily and quickly. Read a few pages of a good gambling primer, such as *The Frugal Gambler, More Frugal Gambling, or Frugal Video Poker* by Jean Scott, and you'll be locating the beatable machines like a pro.

Learning the proper playing strategies requires a bit more work. Luckily, the tools are readily available, inexpensive, easy to use, and completely effective. In fact, the first tool, the computer tutorial, is also fun. These software programs, such as *Frugal Video Poker* and *Video Poker for Winners*, teach you "computer-perfect strategy" by alerting you to and correcting strategy mistakes as you play on your home or office computer. Programming yourself with the proper plays takes only four or five enjoyable hours; this is time extremely well spent for preparing to take on the casino with real money.

Problem is, you can't take the computer into the casino. That's where strategy cards come into play—the best video-poker aids of all. These $6.95 handy-dandy trifold pocket-size color-coded laminated cards use a sort of shorthand to list every decision by which you can possibly be confronted at a machine; they pay for themselves in one playing session with the saving gained by avoiding costly mistakes. And the best thing is, other than spending a few minutes deciphering the shorthand when you first receive them, you don't have to do anything with them, except remember to put them in your pocket and refer to them while you play.

The edge at video poker ranges from more than 10% on the worst schedules up to positive 1% (a player advantage) on the best.

 A computer tutorial and handy strategy cards will give you an edge in video poker.

An Example of Video-Poker Strategy

Each hand in a video-poker game is dealt from a fresh 52-card deck. Each hand consists of 10 cards, with a random number generator or "black box" selecting the cards dealt. When you hit the deal button, the first five cards are displayed face up on the screen. Cards 6–10 are held in reserve to be dealt as replacements for cards you discard when you draw. Each replacement card is dealt in order off the top of the electronic deck. The microprocessor "shuffles" the deck for each new game. Thus on the next play, you will be dealt five new and randomly selected initial cards, and five new and randomly selected draw cards to back them up. In other words, you will not be dealt any unused cards from the previous hand.

THE POWER OF THE ROYAL FLUSH In video poker, the biggest payout is usually for a royal flush. This fact influences strategy for playing the game. Simply put, you play differently than you would in a live poker game. If in Jacks or Better video poker you are dealt

A ♣   Q ♣   10 ♣   A ♠   J ♣,

you would discard the ace of spades (giving up a paying pair) to go for the royal flush. Likewise, if you are dealt

5 ♠   A ♠   K ♠   Q ♠   J ♠,

you would discard the 5 of spades (sacrificing a sure spade flush) in an attempt to make the royal by drawing the 10 of spades. If you are dealt

J ♥   Q ♥   K ♥   4 ♥   6 ♣,

draw two cards for the royal flush as opposed to one card for the flush.

The payoff for the royal flush is so great that it is worth risking a sure winning hand. The payoff for a straight flush, however, does not warrant risking a pat flush or straight.

OTHER SITUATIONS If you are dealt

Q ♦   A ♣   4 ♥   J ♠   4 ♣,

hold the small pair. But if you are dealt

K ♦   A ♣   4 ♥   J ♣   3 ♠,

hold the ace of clubs and the jack of clubs to give yourself a long shot at a royal flush. Similarly, if you are dealt

K ♣   A ♣   4 ♥   J ♣   3 ♠,

hold the ace of clubs, king of clubs, and jack of clubs.

DRAW POKER If you are playing draw poker (no wild cards), with a pair of jacks or better required to win, observe the following:

1. Hold a jacks-or-better pair, even if you pass up the chance of drawing to an open-end straight or to a flush. If you have

Q ♣   4 ♠   6 ♠   2 ♠   Q ♠

or

Q ♥   9 ♦   10 ♣   J ♠   Q ♣,

in each case keep the pair of queens and draw three cards.

2. Split a low pair to go for a flush. If you are dealt

2 ♦   4 ♣   4 ♦   8 ♦   10 ♦,

discard the 4 of clubs and draw one card to try and make the flush.

3. Hold a low pair rather than drawing to an inside or open-end straight.

4. A "kicker" is a face card or an ace you might be tempted to hang onto along with a high pair, low pair, or three-of-a-kind. If you are dealt, for example,

5 ♣   5 ♦   8 ♠   10 ♠   A ♥

or

2 ♣   2 ♣   2 ♥   8 ♠   A ♥,

hold the pair or the three-of-a-kind, but discard the kicker (the ace).

BLACKJACK

MANY BOOKS HAVE BEEN PUBLISHED about the game of blackjack. The serious gamblers who write these books will tell you that blackjack is a game of skill and chance in which a player's ability can actually turn the odds of winning in his favor. While that is true, we also know the casinos wouldn't keep the tables open if they were taking a beating.

The methods of playing blackjack skillfully involve being able to count all the cards played and flawlessly manage your own hand, while mentally blocking the bustle and distraction of the casino. The ability to master the prerequisite tactics and to play under casino conditions is so far beyond the average (never mind beginning) player that any attempt to track cards is, except for a talented and disciplined few, exhausting and futile.

This doesn't mean that you should not try blackjack. It is a fun, fast-paced game that is easy to understand, and you can play at low-minimum-wager tables without feeling intimidated by the level of play. Moreover, most people already have an understanding of the game from playing "21" at home. The casino version is largely the same, only with more bells and whistles.

In a game of blackjack, the number cards are worth their spots (a 2 of clubs is worth two). All face cards are worth 10. The ace, on the other hand, is worth either 1 point or 11, whichever you choose. In this manner, an ace and a 5 could be worth 6 (hard count) or 16 (soft count). The object of the game is to get as close to 21 as you

The Blackjack Table

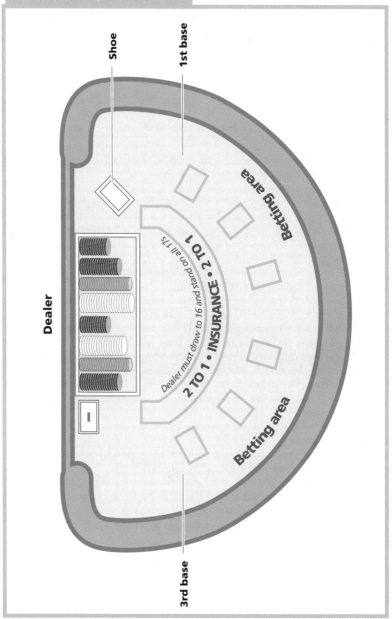

Shoe

1st base

Dealer

Betting area

Dealer must draw to 16 and stands on all 17s

2 TO 1 • INSURANCE • 2 TO 1

Betting area

3rd base

BASIC STRATEGY*

THE DEALER IS SHOWING:		2	3	4	5	6	7	8	9	10	Ace
YOUR TOTAL IS:	4-11	H	H	H	H	H	H	H	H	H	H
	12	H	H	S	S	S	H	H	H	H	H
	13	S	S	S	S	S	H	H	H	H	H
	14	S	S	S	S	S	H	H	H	H	H
	15	S	S	S	S	S	H	H	H	H	H
	16	S	S	S	S	S	H	H	H	H	H

S = STAND   H = HIT

*The correct term for the spots on playing cards is "pips."

can without going over (called "busting"). You play only against the dealer, and the hand closest to 21 wins the game.

The dealer will deal you a two-card hand, then give you the option of taking another card (called a "hit") or stopping with the two cards you have been dealt (called "standing"). For example, if your first two cards are a 10 and a 3, your total would be 13, and you would normally ask for another card to get closer to 21. If the next card dealt to you was a 7, you would have a total of 20 points and you would "stand" with 20 (that is, not ask for another card).

It makes no difference what the other players are dealt, or what they choose to do with their hands. Your hand will win or lose only in comparison to the hand that the dealer holds.

The dealer plays his hand last. This is his biggest advantage. All the players who go over 21 points, or bust, will immediately lose their cards and their bet before the dealer's turn to play. What this means in terms of casino advantage is that while the player has to play to win, the only thing the dealer has to do is not lose. Every time you bust, the casino wins. This sequence of play ensures a profit for the casino.

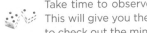 Take time to observe a few hands before you play blackjack. This will give you the opportunity to find a friendly dealer and to check out the minimum-bet signs posted at each table.

Be sure to check the minimum-bet signs posted at each table. They will say something like: "Minimum bet $2 to $500." This means the minimum wager is $2, and the maximum wager is $500. If you sit down at a blackjack table and begin to bet with insufficient cash or the wrong denomination chip, the dealer will inform you of the correct minimum wager, whereupon you may either conform or excuse yourself.

A blackjack table is shaped like a half-circle, with the dealer inside the circle and room for five to seven players around the outside. Facing the dealer, the chair on the far right is called "first base." The chair on the far left is called "third base." The dealer deals the cards from first base to third, and each player plays out his hand in the same order.

 If you can, try to sit at third base or as close to it as you can get. This gives you the advantage of watching the other players play out their hands before you play.

To buy in, find an empty seat at a table with an agreeable minimum wager and wait until the hand in progress is concluded. Though you can bet cash, most players prefer to convert their currency to chips. This is done by placing your money on the table *above* the bettor's box. Because blackjack is one of the many games in the casino in which the dealer is allowed to accept cash bets, he will assume that any money placed in the bettor's box is a wager.

Your dealer will take the cash, count out your chips, and push the money through a slot cut in the top of the table. Because he cannot give you change in cash, the total amount you place on the table will be converted to chips. You may at any time, however, redeem your chips for cash from the casino cashier. Once you have been given chips and have bet, you will be included in the next deal.

To confound a player attempting to count cards, many casinos deal blackjack with four to eight (two-hand held) decks shuffled together. This huge stack of cards is rendered manageable by dealing from a special container known as a shoe.

The dealer will shuffle the decks and may offer the cards to you to cut. The dealer offers you a plastic card stop. Place the card stop halfway or so into the deck, leaving the stop sticking out. The dealer will cut the deck at that point and put it into the shoe.

After he cuts a single deck, or puts the multiple deck into the shoe, the dealer will "burn" one or more cards by taking them off the top and putting them into the discard pile. This is yet another tactic to inhibit players from keeping track of cards dealt. Also to the advantage of the casino is the dealer's right to shuffle the cards whenever he pleases. Usually the dealer will deal from the shoe until he reaches the plastic stop card and then he will "break the deck," which means reshuffle and recut before dealing the next hand. In a single-deck game, the dealer will usually reshuffle about three-quarters through the deck.

Because the dealer always plays his hand last, you must develop your strategy by comparing your card count to what you assume (based on his visible card) the dealer has. The rule of thumb for most situations is to play your hand as if the dealer's down card has a value of 10. The principles governing when or when not to take a hit are known as "basic strategy" (see charts on pages 326, 329, and 330). If you elect to take a hit and go over 21 (bust), you lose. If you stand with your original two cards or take a number of hits without going over 21, you can relax for a few seconds while the dealer continues on around the table, repeating the same process with the other players. When the other players finish, the dealer exposes his "down" card and plays out his hand according to strict rules. He must take a hit on any total of 16 or less and must stand on any total of 17 or more. When he finishes his hand, the dealer goes from third base to first, paying off each winning player and collecting chips from the losers who didn't bust.

If you're closer to 21 than the dealer, you win. If he is closer (or if you busted), he wins. If there is a tie, neither hand wins. When you tie, the dealer will knock on the table above your bet to indicate that the hand is a tie, or a "push." You may leave your bet on the table for the next hand, or change it.

There is a way for you to win automatically, and that is to be dealt exactly 21 in the first two cards. This can be done with an ace and any 10-value card. Called a blackjack, or a natural, this hand is an automatic winner, and you should turn your cards face up immediately. The dealer will look to see if he ties you with a blackjack of his own; this is one of the only times a dealer will look at his cards before all the players have played. If the dealer does not have a blackjack, he will pay you immediately at 3-to-2 odds (or a punitive six-to-five payoff in most Strip single-deck or Super Fun 21 games), so your $5 bet pays off $7.50 and you keep your original wager. If the dealer has a blackjack too, then only you and any other players at the table with a natural will tie him. The rest lose their bets, and the next round will begin.

Nothing beats a natural. If the dealer has a 4 and a 6, then draws an ace, his 21 will not beat your blackjack. A blackjack wins over everything and pays the highest of any bet in the game. Just as you can win automatically, you may lose just as fast. When your count goes over 21 and you bust, you must turn your cards over. The dealer will collect your cards and your bet before moving on to the next player.

Hitting and Standing

When dealing, whether from the shoe or from a single deck in his hand, the dealer will give two cards to each player. Most casinos will deal both cards facedown, though some casinos, especially those that use large multiple decks, will deal both cards faceup. There is no advantage to either method. Most players are more comfortable with the secrecy of the facedown deal, but the outcome will not be affected either way. Starting with the player at first base, the dealer will give you cards to play out your hand. After the initial deal, you have two basic options: either stand or take a hit. If you are satisfied with your deal, then you elect to stand. If your cards were dealt facedown, slide them under the chips in the bettor's box with one hand, being careful not to touch your chips or conceal them from the dealer. If the cards were dealt faceup, wave your hand over the top, palm down, in a negative fashion, to signal the dealer not to give you another card.

Sometimes you will improve your hand by asking for another card. You signal for a hit by scratching the bottom of your cards toward you on the felt surface of the table. In a faceup game, scratch your fingers toward you in the same fashion. You may say, "Hit me," or "I'll take a hit," depending on the mood at your table, but use the hand gestures also. Because of noise and distractions, the dealer may misinterpret your verbal request.

The card you request will be dealt faceup, and you may take as many hits as you like. When you want to show that you do not want another card, use the signals for standing. If you bust, turn your cards faceup right away so the dealer can collect your cards and chips. He will then

SOFT-HAND STRATEGY*

THE DEALER IS SHOWING:		2	3	4	5	6	7	8	9	10	Ace
YOUR TOTAL IS:	Ace, 9	S	S	S	S	S	S	S	S	S	S, H
	Ace, 8	S	S	S	S	S	S	S	S	S	S
	Ace, 7	S	D	D	D	D	S	S	H	H	S
	Ace, 6	H	D	D	D	D	S	H	H	H	H
	Ace, 5	H	H	D	D	D	H	H	H	H	H
	Ace, 4	H	H	D	D	D	H	H	H	H	H
	Ace, 3	H	H	H	D	D	H	H	H	H	H
	Ace, 2	H	H	H	D	D	H	H	H	H	H

S = STAND   H = HIT   D = DOUBLE DOWN

*The charts reflect basic strategy for multiple-deck games. For single-deck games, a slightly different strategy prevails for doubling and splitting.

go to the next player. There are times when the dealer stands a good chance of busting. At these times, it is a good idea to stand on your first two cards even though your total count may seem very low. The accompanying basic strategy chart shows when to stand and when to take a hit. It is easy to follow and simple to memorize. The decision to stand or take a hit is made on the value of your hand and, once again, the dealer's up card, and is based on the probability of his busting. Although following basic strategy won't win every hand, it will improve your odds and take the guesswork out of some confusing situations.

Basic strategy is effective because the dealer is bound by the rules of the game. He must take a hit on 16 and stand on 17. These rules are printed right on the table so that there can be no misunderstanding. Even if you are the only player at the table and stand with a total of 14 points, the dealer with what would be a winning hand of 16 points *must* take another card.

There is one exception to the rule: Some casinos require a dealer to take a hit on a hand with an ace and a 6 (called a "soft 17"). Since the ace can become a 1, it is to the casino's advantage for the dealer to be allowed to hit a soft 17.

Bells and Whistles

Now that you understand the basic game, let's look at a few rules in the casino version of blackjack that are probably different from the way you play at home.

DOUBLING DOWN When you have received two cards and think that they will win with the addition of one and *only* one more card, then double your bet. This "doubling down" bet should be made if your two-card total is 11, since drawing the highest possible card, a 10, will not push your total over 21. In some casinos you may double down on 10, and some places will let you double down on any two-card hand.

To show the dealer that you want to double down, place your two cards touching each other faceup on the dealer's side of the betting box. Then place chips in the box that equal your original bet. Now, as at all other times, don't touch your chips once the bet is made.

DOUBLING DOWN											
THE DEALER IS SHOWING:		2	3	4	5	6	7	8	9	10	Ace
YOUR TOTAL IS:	11	D	D	D	D	D	D	D	D	D	H
	10	D	D	D	D	D	D	D	D	H	H
	9	H	D	D	D	D	H	H	H	H	H
H = HIT D = DOUBLE DOWN											

SPLITTING Any time you are dealt two cards of the same value, you may split the cards and start two separate hands. Even aces may be split, though when you play them, they will each be dealt only one additional card. If you happen to get a blackjack after splitting aces, it will be treated as 21; that is, paid off at one to one and not three to two or six to five.

SPLITTING STRATEGY											
THE DEALER IS SHOWING:		2	3	4	5	6	7	8	9	10	Ace
YOUR TOTAL IS:	2, 2	H	H	SP	SP	SP	SP	H	H	H	H
	3, 3	H	H	SP	SP	SP	SP	H	H	H	H
	4, 4	H	H	H	H	H	H	H	H	H	H
	5, 5	D	D	D	D	D	D	D	D	H	H
	6, 6	H	SP	SP	SP	SP	H	H	H	H	H
	7, 7	SP	SP	SP	SP	SP	SP	H	H	H	H
	8, 8	SP	SP	SP	SP	SP	SP	SP	SP	SP	SP
	9, 9	SP	SP	SP	SP	SP	S	SP	SP	S	S
	10, 10	S	S	S	S	S	S	S	S	S	S
	Ace, Ace	SP	SP	SP	SP	SP	SP	SP	SP	SP	SP
S = STAND H = HIT SP = SPLIT D = DOUBLE DOWN											

Any other pair is played exactly as you would if you were playing two consecutive hands, and all the rules will apply. Place the two cards *apart from each other* and above the betting box, so the dealer won't confuse this with doubling down. Then add a stack of chips equal to the original bet to cover the additional hand. Your two hands will be played out one at a time, cards dealt faceup.

You will be allowed to split a third card if it is the same as the first two, but not if it shows up as a later hit. Always split a pair of eights, since they total 16 points, the worst total. *Never* split two face cards or tens, since they total 20 and are probably a winning hand.

Some casinos will let you double down after splitting a hand, but if you're unsure, ask the dealer. Not all blackjack rules are posted, and they can vary from casino to casino, and even from table to table in the same casino.

INSURANCE When the dealer deals himself an ace as his second, faceup card, he will stop play and ask, "Insurance, anyone?" Don't be fooled.

You're not insuring anything. All he's asking for is a side bet that he has a natural. He must make the insurance bets before he can look at his cards, so he doesn't know if he has won or not when he asks for your insurance bets.

The insurance wager can be up to half the amount of your original bet. Place the chips in the large semicircle marked "insurance." As it says, it pays off two to one. If your original bet was $10 and you bet $5 that the dealer had a natural, you would be paid $10 if he actually did. Depending on your cards, you would probably lose your original $10 bet, but break even on the hand. If the dealer does not have a 10-value card, you lose your $5 insurance bet, but your $10 bet still can win.

This sounds deceptively easy, but you will lose this bet more often than you will win it, though the dealer may suggest it to you as a smart move. The dealer might also tell you to insure your own blackjack, though this should never be done. The odds are always against the insurance bet. When you insure your blackjack, you can be paid off for it at one to one, as if it were 21, instead of the three to two or six to five that you would normally be paid for the blackjack. Even though you may occasionally tie with the dealer, you will more than make up for it with the three-to-two or six-to-five payoffs on the blackjacks you don't insure.

 Insurance is a bad move for the basic-strategy player, because the odds are against the dealer actually having a natural.

Avoiding Common Pitfalls

1. Always check the minimum bets allowed at your table before you sit down. Flipping a $5 chip into a $25-minimum game can be humiliating. If you make this mistake, simply excuse yourself and leave. It happens all the time.

2. Keep your bet in a neat stack, with the largest value chips on the bottom and the smallest on top. A mess of chips can be confusing should you want to double down, and your dealer will get huffy if he has to ask you to stack your chips.

3. Never touch the chips once the bet is down. Cheaters do this, and your dealer may assume you're cheating. It's too easy for a player to secretly up his bet once he's seen his cards or lower it if the cards are bad. Do not stack a double-down bet or split bets on top of the original bet. Place them beside the original bet and then keep your hands away.

4. Along the same lines, don't touch a hand if the cards are dealt faceup. Use the hand signals to tell the dealer that you stand or that you want a hit. Never move your cards below the level of the table, where the dealer can't see them. When you brush your cards for a hit, do so lightly so that the dealer won't think that you are trying to mark them by bending them.

5. Take your time and count your cards correctly. The pace of the game in the casino can pick up to a speed that is difficult for a beginner. It's perfectly all right to take your time and recount after a hit. One hint: count aces as 1 first, then add 10 to your total. An ace and a 4 is equal to 5 or 15. Once you have this notion in your head, you won't make a mistake and refrain from hitting a soft hand. If you throw down an ace, a 10, and a 9 in disgust, for example, many dealers will simply pick up your cards and your bet, even though your 20 might have been a winning hand. If you are confused about your total, do not be embarrassed to ask for help.

6. Know the denomination of the chips that you are betting. Stack them according to denomination, and read the face value every play until you know for sure which chips are which color. Otherwise you might think you are betting $5 when you are actually throwing out a $25 chip on every hand.

7. Be obvious with your hand signals to the dealer. The casinos are loud and busy, and the dealer may be distracted with another player. Don't leave any room for misinterpretation. If some problem does arise, stop the game immediately; the dealer will summon a boss to mediate.

8. If cards fly off the table during the deal, pick them up slowly using two fingers. See number four, above.

9. Tip the dealer at your discretion if he or she has been friendly and helpful. One of the better ways to tip the dealer is to bet a chip for him on your next hand and say, "This one is for you." If you win, so does he. Never tip when a dealer has been rude or cost you money by being uncooperative. Then you should finish your hand and leave. Period.

CRAPS

OF ALL THE GAMES OFFERED IN CASINOS, craps is by far the fastest and, to many, the most exciting. It is a game in which large amounts of money can be won or lost in a short amount of time. The craps table is a circus of sound and movement. Yelling and screaming are allowed—even encouraged—here, and the frenetic betting is bewildering to the uninitiated. Don't be intimidated, however; the basic game of craps is easy to understand. The confusion and insanity of craps have more to do with the pace of the game and the amazing number of betting possibilities than with the complexity of the game itself.

The Basic Game

Because it is so easy to become confused at a crowded and noisy craps table, we highly recommend that beginning players study this section, read a more detailed book, and take advantage of the free lessons offered by most of the casinos. Once you understand the game, you will be able to make the most favorable bets and ignore the rest.

In craps, one player at a time controls the dice, but all players will eventually have an opportunity to roll or refuse the dice. Players take turns in a clockwise rotation. If you don't want the dice, shake your head, and the dealer will offer them to the next player.

All the players around the table are wagering either with or against the shooter, so the numbers he throws will determine the amount won or lost by every other player. The casino is covering all bets, and the players are not allowed to bet among themselves. Four casino employees run the craps table. The boxman in the middle is in charge of the game. His job is to oversee the other dealers, monitor the play, and examine the dice if they are thrown off the table.

The Craps Table

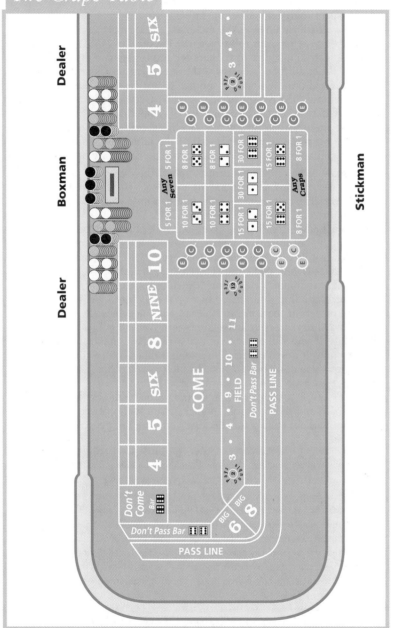

There are two dealers, one placed on each side of the boxman. They pay off the winners and collect the chips from the losers. Each dealer is in charge of half of the table.

The fourth employee is the stickman, so called because of a flexible stick he uses after each roll to retrieve the dice. His job, among other things, is to supply dice to the shooter and to regulate the pace of the game. When all bets are down, the stickman pushes several sets of dice toward the shooter. The shooter selects two dice, and the stickman removes the others from the table. Occasionally the stickman and boxman check the dice for signs of tampering.

The shooter then throws the dice hard enough to cause them to bounce off the wall at the far end of the table. This bounce ensures that each number on each die has an equal probability of coming up.

THE PLAY When it is your turn to throw the dice, pick out two and return the other to the stickman. After making a bet (required), you may throw the dice. You retain control of the dice until you throw a 7 ("seven out") or relinquish the dice voluntarily.

Your first roll, called the come-out roll, is the most important. If you roll a 7 or an 11 on your come-out roll, you are an immediate winner. In this case, you collect your winnings and retain possession of the dice. If your come-out roll is a 4, 5, 6, 8, 9, or 10, that number becomes "the point." A marker (called a puck or buck) is placed in the correspondingly numbered box on the layout to identify the point for all players at the table. In order to win the game, this number (the point) will have to be rolled again before you roll a 7.

Thus, if you roll a 5 on your first roll, the number five becomes your point. It doesn't matter how long it takes you to roll another 5, as long as you don't roll a 7 first. As soon as you roll a 7, you lose, and the dice are passed to another player.

Let's say 5 is your point, and your second roll is a 4, your third roll is a 9, and then you roll another 5. You win because you rolled a 5 again without rolling a 7. Because you have not yet rolled a 7, you

---

HOW NOT TO SHOOT CRAPS

ON A RECENT VISIT TO A DOWNTOWN CASINO, one *Unofficial Guide* researcher pleaded with a Las Vegas friend to teach her how to play craps. Our Vegas friend not only outlined the basics, he also rattled off descriptions of all the various side bets and offered advice on when each was appropriate. By the time the lady was handed the dice, she was so apprehensive about remembering the rules that she forgot to pay attention to her throw. She hurled the dice with all her might right into a stack of chips in front of the boxman, scattering the house chips all over the table. The boxman and dealers sighed in annoyance but didn't complain as they put the table back in order. The other players were not pleased, however. And it only got worse when the flustered lady threw again, this time so worried about the boxman that she overthrew the table entirely, striking another player in the chest with the dice. Shortly after that, it was decided that she'd best stick with slot machines.

retain possession of the dice, and after making a bet, you may initiate a new game.

Your next roll is, once again, a come-out roll. Just as 7 or 11 are immediate winners on a come-out roll, there are immediate losers, too. A roll of 2, 3, or 12 (all called "craps") will lose. You lose your chips, but you keep the dice because you have not yet rolled a 7.

If your first roll is 2, for example, it's craps, and you lose your bet. You place another bet and roll to come-out again. This time you roll a 5, so 5 becomes your point. Your second roll is a 4, your third is a 9, and then you roll a 7. The roll of 7 means that you lose and the dice will be passed to the next player.

This is the basic game of craps. The confounding blur of activity is nothing more than players placing various types of bets with or against the shooter, or betting that a certain number will or will not come up on the next roll of the dice.

THE BETTING Of the dozens of bets that can be made at a dice table, only two or three should even be considered by a novice crap player. Keeping your bets simple makes it easier to understand what's going on, while at the same time minimizing the house advantage. Exotic, long-shot bets, offering payoffs as high as 30–1, are sucker bets and should be avoided.

The line bets: pass and don't pass Pass and don't pass bets combine simplicity with one of the smallest house advantages of any casino game, about 1.4%. If you bet pass, you are betting that the first roll will be a 7 or 11 or a point number, and that the shooter will make the point again before he rolls a 7. If you bet don't pass, you are betting that the first roll will be a 2, 3, or 12, or, if a point is established, that the shooter will seven out and throw a 7 before he rolls his point number again. The 2 and 3 are immediate losers, and the casino will collect the chips of anyone betting pass. A roll of 12, however, is considered a standoff ("push") where the shooter "craps out" but no chips change hands for the "don't" bettor. Almost 90% of casino crap players confine their betting to the pass and don't-pass line.

Come and don't come Come and don't-come bets are just like pass and don't-pass bets, except that they are placed *after* the point has been established on the come-out roll. Pass and don't-pass bets must be placed before the first roll of the dice, but come and don't-come bets may be placed before any roll of the dice *except* come-out rolls. On his come-out roll, let's say, the shooter rolls a 9. Nine becomes the shooter's point. If at this time you place your chips in the come box on the table, the next roll of the dice will determine your "come number." If the shooter throws a 6, for example, your chips are placed in the box marked with the large 6. The dealer will move your chips and will keep track of your bet. If the shooter rolls another 6 before he rolls a 7, your bet pays off. If the shooter sevens out before he rolls a 6, then you lose. If the shooter makes his point (that is, rolls another 9), your come bet is retained on the layout.

ACTUAL-ODDS CHART

NUMBER	WAYS TO ROLL	ODDS AGAINST REPEAT
4	3	2-1
5	4	3-2
6	5	6-5
8	5	6-5
9	4	3-2
10	3	2-1

If you win a come bet, the dealer will place your chips from the numbered box back into the come space and set your winnings beside it. You may leave your chips there for the next roll or you may remove them entirely. If you fail to remove your winnings before the next roll, they may become a bet that you didn't want to make.

Don't-come bets are the opposite of come bets. A 7 or 11 loses, and a 2 or 3 wins. The 12 is again a push. The don't-come bettor puts his chips in the don't-come space on the table and waits for the next roll to determine his number. His chips are placed *above* the numbered box to differentiate it from a come bet. If the shooter rolls his point number before he rolls your number, your don't-come bet is retained on the layout. You are betting against the shooter; that is, that he will roll a 7 first. When he rolls 7, you win. If he rolls your don't-come number before he sevens out, you lose.

The come and don't-come bets have a house advantage of about 1.4% and are among the better bets in craps once you understand them.

Odds bets When you bet the pass/don't pass or the come/don't come, you may place an odds bet *in addition* to your original bet.

Once it is established that the come-out roll is not a 7 or 11, or craps, the bettor may place a bet that will be paid off according to the actual odds of a particular number being thrown.

Note that the Actual-Odds Chart shows the chances against a number made by two dice being thrown. For example, the odds of making a 9 are three to two. If you place an odds bet (in addition to your original bet) on a come number of 9, your original come bet will pay off at even money, but your odds bet will pay off at three to two.

Because this would make a $7.50 payoff for a $5 bet, and the tables don't carry 50-cent chips, you are allowed to place a $6 bet as an odds bet. This is a very good bet to make, and betting the extra dollar is to your advantage.

To place an odds bet on a line bet, bet the pass line. When (and if) the point is established, put your additional bet behind the pass line and say, "Odds."

To place an odds bet on a come bet, wait for the dealer to move your chips to the come number box, then hand him more chips and say, "Odds." He will set these chips half on and half off the other pile so that he can see at a glance that it's an odds bet.

Etiquette of Craps

When you arrive at a table, find an open space and put your cash down in front of you. When the dealer sees it, he will pick it up and hand it to the boxman. The boxman will count out the correct chips and give them to the dealer, who will pass them to you.

A craps table holds from 12 to 20 players and can get very crowded. Keep your place at the table. Your chips are in front of you, in the rail and on the table, and it is your responsibility to watch them.

After you place your bets, your hands must come off the table. It is bad form to leave your hands on the table when the dice are rolling.

Stick to the good bets listed here, and don't be tempted by bets that you don't understand. The box in the middle of the layout, for example, offers a number of sucker bets.

BACCARAT

ORIGINALLY AN ITALIAN CARD GAME, baccarat (bah-kah-rah) is the French pronunciation of the Italian word for "zero," which refers to the value of all the face cards in the game.

Because baccarat involves no player decisions, it is an easy game to play, yet a very difficult game to understand. Each player must decide to make a bet on either the bank or the player. That's it. There are no more decisions until the next hand is dealt. The rules of playing out the hands are ridiculously intricate, but beginning players need not concern themselves with them, because all plays are predetermined by the rules, and the dealer will tell you exactly what happened.

All cards, ace through 9, are worth their spots (the 3 of clubs is worth three). The 10, jack, queen, and king are worth zero. The easiest way to count at baccarat is to add all card totals in the hand, then take only the number in the ones column.

If you have been dealt a 6 and a 5, then your total is 11, and taking only the ones column, your hand is worth 1 point. If you hold a 10 and a king, your hand is worth zero. If you have an 8 and a 7, your point total is 15, and taking the ones column, your hand is worth 5. It doesn't get any simpler than this.

In baccarat, regardless of the number of bettors at the table, only two hands are dealt: one to the player and one to the bank. The object of the game is to be dealt or draw a hand closest to nine without going over. If the first two cards dealt equal nine (a 5 and a 4, for example), then you have a natural and an automatic winner. Two cards worth eight are the second best hand and will also be called a natural. If the other hand is not equal to or higher than eight, this hand wins automatically. Ties are pushes, and neither bank nor player wins, though a longshot bet on the tie (the third wager at baccarat) does.

If the hands equal any total except nine or eight, the rules are consulted. These rules are printed and available at the baccarat table. The hands will be played out by the dealer whether you understand the rules or not.

The Baccarat Table

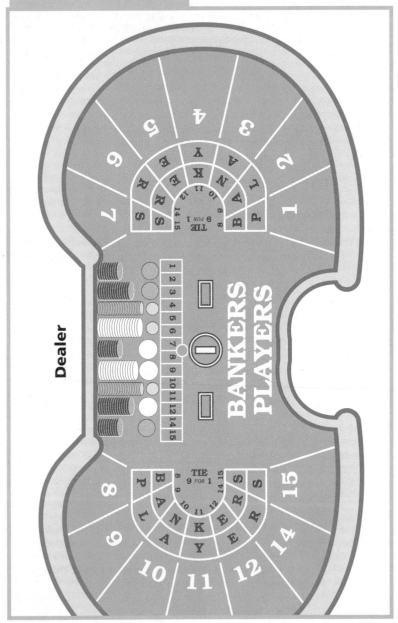

BACCARAT RULES

Player

When first two cards total		
1, 2, 3, 4, 5, or 10	player's third card is	
6 or 7	Stands	
8 or 9	A natural—stands	

Banker

Having	Draws when player's third card is	Does not draw when third card is
3	1, 2, 3, 4, 5, 6, 7, 9, 10	8
4	2, 3, 4, 5, 6, 7	1, 8, 9, 10
5	4, 5, 6, 7	1, 2, 3, 8, 9, 10
6	6, 7	1, 2, 3, 4, 5, 8, 9, 10
7	Stands	Stands
8 or 9	Stands	Stands

The rules for the player's hand are simple. If a natural is not dealt to either hand, and if the player holds 1, 2, 3, 4, 5, or 10 (zero), he will always draw a card. He will stand on a total of 6 or 7. A total of 8 or 9, of course, will be a natural.

The bank hand is more complicated and is partially determined by the third card drawn by the player's hand. Though the rules don't say so, the bank will always draw on zero, one, or two. When the hand is worth three or more, it is subject to the printed rules.

If you study a few hands, the method of play will be clear:

FIRST HAND The player's hand is worth three, and the bank's is worth four. The player always goes first. Looking at the rules for the player, we see that a hand worth three points draws a card. This time he draws a 9, for a new total of 12 points, which has a value of two. The bank, having four points, must stand when a player draws a 9. The bank wins four to two.

SECOND HAND The player's hand is worth six points, and the bank has two queens, for a total of zero. The player must stand with six points, while the bank must draw with zero. The bank gets another card, a 4. Player wins, six to four.

The Atmosphere

The casinos try to attract players by making baccarat seem sophisticated. The section is roped off from the main casino, and the dealers are often dressed in tuxedos instead of the usual dealer's uniforms. Don't be put off by glamorous airs; everyone is welcome to play.

Because the house wants baccarat to be appealing to what they consider to be their upper-crust clientele, the table minimums are usually very high in baccarat—usually $100 to $15,000. This means that the minimum bet is $100, and the maximum bet is $15,000.

Even the shuffle and deal of the deck is designed to perpetuate an exotic feeling. Elaborately cut and mixed by all three dealers, the cards are cut by one player and marked with the plastic card stop. The dealer will then separate the cards at the stop, turn the top card over, and discard, or burn, the number of cards equal to the face value of the upturned card. The cards are then placed in a large holder called the shoe.

THE PLAY If the game has just begun, the shoe will be passed to the player in seat number one, who is then called the bank. Thereafter, whenever the bank hand loses, the shoe is passed counterclockwise to the next player, until it reaches seat number 15, where it is passed to seat number one again.

When all bets are down, one of the three dealers will nod to the holder of the shoe, who will then deal out four cards in alternating fashion—two for the player and two for the bank.

The player's hand is passed (still facedown) to the bettor who has wagered the most money on the player's hand. He looks at the cards and passes them back to the dealer. The dealer then turns both hands faceup and plays out the game according to the rules.

THE BETTING In baccarat, you must back either the player or the bank. You do this by putting your chips in the box in front of you marked "player" or "bank." Once the bets are down, the deal will begin.

The house advantage on baccarat is quite low: 1.36% on player wagers and 1.17% on bank bets. Because the bank bet has such an obvious advantage, the house extracts a commission when you win a bank bet. This is not collected with each hand, but must be paid before you leave the table.

MINIBACCARAT Some casinos offer a version of baccarat in the main pit, usually near the blackjack games. The tables are smaller and lower than normal baccarat tables, with each table seating seven players. The dealers dress in the standard casino floor uniform and the table minimums (and maximums) are much lower than the more common high stakes version. It's the same game with the same house advantage, except that in minibaccarat, the shoe is never passed. In fact, the dealer places the cards right-side-up on the table and the players never touch them at all. Also, the dealer is always the banker.

All of the rules of baccarat apply to the mini version: eight decks are used; face cards and 10s count as zero and aces count as one; the casino collects a 5% commission on a winning banker hand (when the player is ready to leave). The minimum bet is $10, though sometimes you can find $5 minimums. However, since there's much less ritual and fewer players, the speed of the game is very fast, so often more is bet at a $10 minibaccarat table than a $25 baccarat table.

Some experts believe that because minibaccarat lacks the atmosphere of the big table, the game loses its charm and becomes redundant and boring. That could explain why minibaccarat is one of the least popular table games in the casino.

TEXAS HOLD 'EM

POKER HAS TAKEN THE GAMBLING WORLD by storm, and Texas Hold 'Em is the favorite game, both in ring games (a "live" poker game where actual money is in play) and tournaments (buy-ins for tournament chips). The combination of procedures, strategy and tactics, and psychology can take a lifetime to perfect, but the rules of the game can be learned from an hour of study and another hour of practice.

We recommend studying the game, then playing the free games online at poker sites such as **partypoker.com** and **ultimatebet.com.** You should also take a lesson offered by most casino poker rooms where you play with free chips. Then, when you're ready for a live game, look for one with the lowest betting limits, such as $1 to $2 and $2 to $4. As your skills improve, you can move up in denomination, all the way to no-limit hold 'em and $25,000 buy-in tournaments. If you're just playing for fun, you'll have little to worry about in low-limit games.

The following are the basic steps in a round of Texas Hold 'Em:

There are two types of bets: blinds and antes. Antes are rare in hold 'em ring games, but they're usually imposed in the later rounds of tournaments. Blinds, a forced bet that one or more players, typically to the left of the dealer, make before any cards are dealt are always used. This starts the action on the first round of betting.

The game starts when the two players to the left of the dealer make initial bets, also known as "posting the blinds." The player to the immediate left of the dealer is the small blind; he puts up a bet equal to half the minimum limit. The player two to the left of the dealer is the big blind; his bet is equal to the lower limit. If it's a $10–$20 game, the small blind bets $5 and the big blind bets $10.

Each player is dealt two cards facedown, known as hole (or pocket) cards. The first round of betting, "pre-flop," begins with the player to the left of the big blind. The betting structures can get a bit complicated, but to keep it simple, in our $10–$20 game, you'll bet $10 at a time pre-flop. You can bet four times *per betting round:* the initial bet can be "raised" by $10 three times. So if you initially bet $10, to stay in the pre-flop round, you might have to put up $30 more. "Checking" means you don't bet, but keep open your options of "calling" (betting an equal amount; not raising), raising, or folding later in the betting round. You can also "fold," which means throwing in your cards and ending your participation in the round.

At the end of the pre-flop betting rounds, the dealer "burns" (discards) the top card, then deals three cards face up on the table: "the flop." These three cards are combined with each player's two hole cards to form the initial five-card poker hand. Then there's another round of betting, starting with the player to the left of the dealer.

At the end of the post-flop betting, the dealer burns the top card, then deals one card face up on the table: "the turn." Players can now use this sixth card to improve their five-card poker hand. Another round of betting ensues. Often, this is where the betting limit doubles. So in our $10–$20 game, initial bets can be $20.

At the end of the turn betting, the dealer burns the top card, then deals one card face up on the table: "the river." Players can now combine any of the five community cards with his two pocket cards to make the best five-card hand. One more round of betting ensues, again beginning with the player to the left of the dealer.

Finally, the "showdown" occurs, when players reveal their hands. The player with the best hand wins the pot. The dealer rakes the house's cut (in a ring game), collects the cards, and another round begins.

It might sound simple, like a cousin of 7-Card Stud, but there's a lot of protocol and jargon to poker. Again, we highly recommend reading up on the game, then participating in the free tournaments at poker websites, before taking a lesson in a casino poker room. These steps can (and probably will) save you a certain amount of grief when you start playing for real money, even in the lowest-limit games.

KENO

KENO IS AN ANCIENT CHINESE GAME. It was used to raise money for national defense, including, some say, building the Great Wall. Keno was brought to America by the thousands of workers who came from the Far East to work on the railroads during the 1800s. It was once one of the most popular games in the Nevada casinos, though today it's very much on the wane.

This game has a house advantage between 15% and 35% or more, depending on the casino—higher than any other game in Las Vegas. Too high, in fact, for serious gamblers. If you're down to your last dollar and you have to bet to save the ranch, don't go to the keno lounge (if there is one).

While keno is similar to bingo, the betting options are reminiscent of exacta horse-race betting. It is like bingo in that a ticket, called a blank, is marked off and numbers are randomly selected to determine a winner. And it is similar to exacta betting because any number of fascinating betting combinations can be played in each game. The biggest difference between keno and bingo and exactas is that in the latter two, there's always a winner. In keno, hours can go by before anyone wins a substantial amount. The main excitement in keno lies in the possibility that large amounts of money can be won on a small bet.

Playing the Game

A keno lounge usually resembles a college lecture hall. The casino staff sit in front while players relax in chairs with writing tables built into the arms. It is not necessary to sit in the keno lounge to play. In fact, one of the best things about keno is that it can be played almost anywhere in the casino, including the bars and restaurants. As in bingo, it is acceptable to strike up a conversation with your neighbor during a game, and because the winning numbers are posted all over the place, keno also offers the opportunity to gamble while absent from the casino floor. Because keno numbers are posted in many locations, quite a few casinos no longer have a dedicated keno lounge, and more than a few don't offer keno at all.

Keno is one of the easiest games to understand. The keno blank can be picked up almost anywhere in any Nevada casino. On the blank are two large boxes containing 80 numbers: the top box with 1–40, and the bottom box with 41–80. Simply use one of the crayons provided with the blanks to mark between 1 and 15 (sometimes 20) numbers on the blank, decide how much you want to bet, and turn the blank in to a keno writer. The keno writer records your wager, keeping your original, and gives you a duplicate, which you are responsible for checking. The keno writer can be found at the front of the keno lounge. The keno runner is even easier to spot: she is usually a woman in a short skirt with a hand full of blanks and crayons. She will place your bets, cash in your blanks, and bring you your winnings. Of course, you are expected to tip her for this service.

The drawing of the winning numbers takes place in the keno lounge or is electronically generated. When the keno caller has determined that the bets are in for the current round, he will close the betting just like the steward does at the racetrack. Then the caller uses a machine similar to those employed by state lotteries: a blower with numbered Ping-Pong balls. Ten balls are blown into each of two tubes. These 20 balls bear the numbers that will be called for the current round. The numbers, as called out, are posted on electronic keno boards around the casino. If any of the lighted numbers are numbers that you marked on your card, you "caught" those numbers. Catching four or more numbers will usually win something, depending on how many numbers you marked on your card. The payoffs are complicated, but the more numbers you guess correctly and the more money you bet, the greater your jackpot. Suffice it to say, however, that you are not paid at anything even approaching true odds.

THE ODDS A "straight" or basic ticket is one where the player simply selects and marks a minimum of one number to a maximum of 8–15 numbers, depending on the casino. The ways to combine keno bets are endless and understandable only to astrophysicists. Any number can be played with any other number, making "combination" tickets. Groups of numbers can be combined with other groups of numbers, making "way" tickets. Individual numbers can be combined with groups of numbers, making "king" tickets. Then there is the "house" ticket, called different things at each casino, which offers a shot at the big jackpot for a smaller investment, though the odds won't be any better.

All of these options and the amounts that you are allowed to bet (usually from 70 cents up per ticket) are listed in the keno brochures, which are almost as ubiquitous as the blanks. The payoffs are listed for each type of bet and for the amount wagered. Keno runners and keno lounge personnel will show you how to mark your ticket if you are confused, but they cannot mark it for you.

If you want to play keno for fun (and that is the only rational reason to play), then understand that one bet is about as bad as another. Filling out a complicated combination ticket won't increase your chances of winning. If by some miracle you do win, accept the congratulations and the winnings, and then run, do not walk, to the nearest exit. The best strategy for winning at keno is to avoid it since the house has an unbeatable advantage.

ROULETTE

A QUIET GAME WHERE WINNERS MERELY SMILE over a big win and losers suffer in silence, roulette is very easy to understand. The dealer spins the wheel, drops the ball, and waits for it to fall into one of the numbered slots on the wheel. The numbers run from zero to 36, with a zero and double zero thrown in for good measure. You may bet on each individual number, on combinations of numbers, on all black numbers, all red numbers, and many more. All possible bets are laid out on the table (see illustration on next page).

ROULETTE BET AND PAYOFF CHART			
BET	PAYOFF	BET	PAYOFF
Single number	35-1	Six numbers	5-1
Two numbers	17-1	12 numbers (column)	2-1
Three numbers	11-1	1st 12, 2nd 12, 3rd 12	2-1
Four numbers	8-1	1-18 or 19-36	1-1
Five numbers	6-1	Odd or even	1-1
Six numbers	5-1	Red or black	1-1

Special chips are used for roulette, with each bettor at the table playing a different color. To buy in, convert cash or the casino's house chips to roulette chips. When you are ready to cash out, the dealer will convert your special roulette chips back to house chips. If you want cash, you must then take your house chips to a casino cashier.

To place a bet, put your chips inside a numbered square or choose one of the squares off to the side. A chip placed in "1st 12," for example, will pay off if the ball drops into any number from 1 to 12. The box marked "odd" is not for eccentrics—it pays when the ball drops into an odd-numbered slot.

Roulette is fun to play, but expect to pay! The house advantage on most bets is a whopping 5.26%, and on some wagers it can be 7%. Most American roulette wheels have both a zero and a double zero, while European wheels have a single zero, which cuts the house edge for red and black bets to 2.7%. Single zero wheels in Las Vegas are the exception, but there are always a couple to be found. For a list of casinos operating single zero wheels, see **lasvegasadvisor.com /inforoul.cfm.**

The Roulette Table

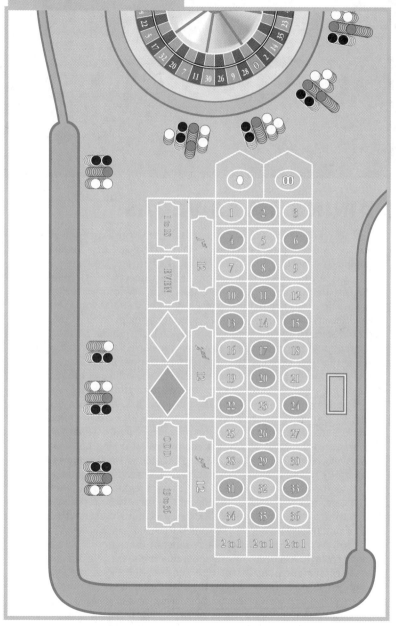

PART FOUR

DINING *and* RESTAURANTS

▌ DINING *in* LAS VEGAS

LAS VEGAS TOURISM continues to rebound, with expansion at a rate not seen since before the recession. Old players and new investors are pumping money into new ideas both on The Strip and Downtown, intent on providing tourists with new sights and experiences. Even frequent visitors are almost guaranteed to find something new on their next trip to town. There's no sign of the expansion slowing down anytime soon. The new Resorts World hotel-casino is currently being planned on the site of the old Stardust and the abandoned Echelon Place project. MGM Resorts International has announced plans for a massive City of Rock concert venue that will be home to a four-day US version of the Rock in Rio festival, as well as various other events over the course of the year. And the dining scene continues to keep pace with the growth.

The Downtown Las Vegas revival flourishes, thanks in no small part to Zappos founder Tony Hsieh and his **Downtown Project.** The group made a big splash with the opening of its **Container Park** outdoor recreation area, which is home to several dining hot spots. The reopening of the former Lady Luck, rechristened **The Downtown Grand,** has brought a slew of its own restaurants. On the independent scene, RM Seafood chef John Church has a new breakfast and lunch spot, **MTO Café,** and as of this writing, local celebrity chef Kerry Simon was preparing to open his first neighborhood venture, **Carson Kitchen.** For more on dining Downtown, see our sidebar on pages 358–361.

However, the Strip is still where most of the action is, and the big move recently has been toward spots that are accessible directly from the street without actually entering a casino. In the shadow of the new High Roller observation wheel, **The LINQ** has quickly become a favorite stroll, packed with places to shop, drink, and dine. Among its most popular restaurants, you'll find pizza at **Flour & Barley,** gourmet hotdogs at **Haute Doggery,** the eclectic Asian cuisine of **F.A.M.E,** and **Chayo Mexican.** LINQ guests looking for sweets on-the-go are flocking to the cupcake ATM at **Sprinkles.** But the center's biggest culinary draw is the combination bowling alley–concert venue–restaurant **Brooklyn Bowl,** which features food by New York's popular Blue Ribbon restaurant group.

Over at The LINQ Hotel & Casino (formerly known as the Imperial Palace, and briefly The Quad), TV superstar Guy Fieri is courting the walk-up crowd. **Guy Fieri's Kitchen** is neither a diner, a drive-in, nor a dive, but it does offer the type of burgers, wings, and tacos that you'd find on his hit show.

Mario Batali and Bobby Flay have also seized some sidewalk real estate—both for burger joints. Batali and his partner Joe Bastianich bring us yet another gourmet burger spot with **B&B Burger & Beer** at the Venetian. **Bobby's Burger Palace** at CityCenter, on the other hand, offers a more casual spin on the burger.

And to the south, the sidewalk in front of the Monte Carlo is now home to **Double Barrel Roadhouse, Yusho,** and the make-your-own pizza restaurant **800 Degrees** on one side of the casino entrance, and the dessert spot **BLVD Creamery Chills & Pops** on the other. More spots are being planned for the area between the Monte Carlo and New York–New York.

Some celebrity chefs are staying busy inside the casinos. Giada de Laurentiis has brought **GIADA** to the brand new Cromwell, which stands on the site of the old Bill's Gamblin' Hall/Barbary Coast. The Italian eatery is the first restaurant ever from the Food Network star.

Daniel Boulud has returned to Las Vegas. The chef operates eight restaurants in New York alone, but closed his **DB Brasserie** at Wynn Las Vegas in 2010. That restaurant has now reopened in The Venetian in the spot that once housed Valentino.

Michael Mina has made some changes to his Las Vegas empire. At the MGM Grand he has closed both SeaBlue and Nobhill Tavern and replaced the former with yet another gastropub called **Pub 1842.** The Nobhill space is now home to a small-plates concept by Michael Morton called **Crush.** And, as of this writing, plans are in the works to shutter **American Fish** in Aria and replace it with a new Mina concept called **Bardot Brasserie.**

Paris master Alain Ducasse is converting his top-floor restaurant Mix into a Las Vegas version of his St. Tropez outpost **Rivea,** as its host property THEhotel at Mandalay Bay transforms into Delano Las Vegas. The new restaurant will serve French and Italian cuisine.

Tom Colicchio has opened a new restaurant in the Mirage. **Heritage Steak,** his second Vegas steakhouse, is a more casual spot than his flagship **Craftsteak** in the MGM Grand.

In Caesars Palace, Elton John and his partner David Furnish have a new champagne lounge called **Fizz.** And Mary Sue Milliken and Susan Feniger are to open a second **Border Grill** in The Forum Shops.

Cake Boss star Buddy Valastro has put his name on two new spots in the Grand Canal Shoppes. The first is an Italian home-cooking restaurant called **Buddy V's Ristorante** inspired by his family's recipes. The

CELEBRITY CHEFS

CHEF	ORIGINAL RESTAURANT	LAS VEGAS RESTAURANT(S)
José Andrés	**Jaleo, Minibar, Café Atlántico** (Washington, D.C.)	**Jaleo** and **China Poblano** (The Cosmopolitan)
Paul Bartolotta	**Ristorante Bartolotta** (Milwaukee)	**Bartolotta Ristorante di Mare** (Wynn)
Mario Batali	**Po, Babbo Ristorante e Enoteca** (New York)	**B&B Ristorante** (Venetian) **Carnevino** (Palazzo) **Otto Pizzeria** (Venetian) **B&B Burger & Beer** (Venetian)
Daniel Boulud	**Daniel** (New York)	**DB Brasserie** (Venetian)
Tom Colicchio	**Craft** (New York)	**Craftsteak** (MGM Grand) **Heritage Steak** (Mirage)
Scott Conant	**Scarpetta** (New York)	**Scarpetta** and **D.O.C.G** (The Cosmopolitan)
Alain Ducasse	**Louis XV** (Monte Carlo, Paris)	**MIX in Las Vegas** (Mandalay Bay)
Todd English	**Olives** (Charlestown, MA)	**Olives** (Bellagio) **English P.U.B.** (Crystals)
Susan Feniger	**Border Grill** (Los Angeles)	**Border Grill** (Mandalay Bay)
Guy Fieri	**Johnny Garlic's** (Santa Rosa)	**Guy Fieri's Vegas Kitchen & Bar** (LINQ Hotel & Casino)
Bobby Flay	**Mesa Grill** (New York)	**Mesa Grill** (Caesars Palace) **Bobby's Burger Palace** (Crystals)
Pierre Gagnaire	**Pierre Gagnaire** (Paris)	**Twist** (Mandarin Oriental)
Hubert Keller	**Fleur de Lys** (San Francisco)	**Fleur, Burger Bar** (Mandalay Bay)
Thomas Keller	**French Laundry** (Yountville, CA) **Per Se** (New York)	**Bouchon** (Venetian)
Emeril Lagasse	**Emeril's** (New Orleans)	**Delmonico** (Venetian) **Emeril's New Orleans Fish House** (MGM Grand) **Table 10** (Palazzo)
Giada de Laurentiis	**N/A**	**GIADA** (The Cromwell)
Nobu Matsuhisa	**Matsuhisa** (Beverly Hills)	**Nobu** (Caesars & Hard Rock)
Shawn McClain	**Spring** (Chicago)	**Sage and Five50 Pizza** (Aria)

second, located just across the hall, is a local incarnation of his East Coast chain **Carlo's Bakery.**

Also on the Strip, preparations are still underway for the planned Labor Day opening of the SLS Las Vegas resort in the building that was once the Sahara. It will bring several popular restaurant brands to Las Vegas, including José Andrés's **Bazaar Meats** (an offshoot of Bazaar in L.A.), the Japanese concept **Katsuya,** L.A.'s Mediterranean-inspired **Cleo,** and the burger chain **Umami Burger.**

Heading out into the neighborhoods, Tivoli Village has lost Ogden's Hops & Harvest, which shuttered not long after opening.

CELEBRITY CHEFS

CHEF	ORIGINAL RESTAURANT	LAS VEGAS RESTAURANT(S)
Mary Sue Milliken	**Border Grill** (Los Angeles)	**Border Grill** (Mandalay Bay)
Michael Mina	**Aqua** (San Francisco)	**Michael Mina** (Bellagio) **Michael Mina PUB 1842** (MGM Grand) **Strip Steak** (Mandalay Bay)
Charlie Palmer	**Aureole** (New York)	**Aureole** (Mandalay Bay) **Charlie Palmer Steak** (Four Seasons)
Francois Payard	**Payard Patisserie & Bistro** (New York)	**Payard Patisserie & Bistro** (Caesars Palace)
Carla Pellegrino	**Baldoria** (New York)	**Bratalian Neapolitan Cantina** (Henderson)
Wolfgang Puck	**ORIGINAL RESTAURANT: Spago** (Los Angeles)	
	LAS VEGAS RESTAURANTS: CUT (Palazzo); **Spago** (Forum Shops); **Lupo** (Mandalay Bay); **Postrio** (Venetian); **Wolfgang Puck Bar & Grill** (MGM Grand); **Wolfgang Puck Pizzeria & Cucina** (Crystals at CityCenter)	
Gordon Ramsay	**Restaurant Gordon Ramsay** (London)	**Gordon Ramsay Steak** (Paris LV); **Gordon Ramsay BurGR** (Planet Hollywood); **Gordon Ramsay Pub & Grill** (Caesars)
Joël Robuchon	**Jamin, Joël Robuchon** (Paris)	**L'Atelier de Joël Robuchon,** **Joël Robuchon** (MGM Grand)
Guy Savoy	**Restaurant Guy Savoy** (Paris)	**Restaurant Guy Savoy** (Caesars Palace)
Julian Serrano	**Masa's** (San Francisco)	**Picasso** (Bellagio) **Julian Serrano** (Aria)
Kerry Simon	**Blue Star** (Miami)	**Simon at Palms Place** (Palms) **Carson Kitchen** (Downtown) **KGB** (Harrah's)
Joachim Splichal	**Patina, Pinot** (Los Angeles)	**Pinot Brasserie** (The Venetian)
Masa Takayama	**Masa** (New York City)	**barMASA** (Aria)
Jean-Georges Vongerichten	**JoJo** (New York)	**Prime** (Bellagio) **Jean-Georges Steakhouse** (Aria)
David Walzog	**Strip House** (New York)	**SW Steakhouse** (Wynn)
Roy Yamaguchi	**Roy's** (Hawaii)	**Roy's** (Flamingo Rd.)

But the Summerlin shopping complex has a new star on its hands with the butcher shop/steakhouse **Echo & Rigg.**

In Chinatown, the popular robata grill Raku has opened a sister restaurant in the same shopping center. **Sweets Raku** is a pastry shop specializing in a Japanese three-course dessert tasting.

Finally, the popular **Naked City Pizza** has expanded significantly. A second location has opened on Paradise Road near the Hard Rock. And the popular west side location has added a sister restaurant next door. That spot, **Desnudo Tacos,** is now among the town's top Mexican restaurants.

So while the Las Vegas restaurant scene is forever reinventing itself and in a constant state of flux, one thing is constant: This is an exciting city for dining, and a world-class destination for anyone who cares about food, wine, and a good time.

THE TOP 25

WE KNOW THAT NOT EVERYONE has the desire or can afford to drop $500 on a meal while visiting Las Vegas, so we present a broad range of restaurants for all tastes and price points. But we'd be remiss not to recognize the finest dining experiences and celebrity chefs who have restaurants here. On the facing page is a chart rating and ranking the top 25 restaurants in town, if price is no object.

BUFFETS

Buffet Speak	
ACTION FORMAT Cooking food to order in full view of patrons	
GLUTTONY A Las Vegas buffet tradition that carries no moral stigma	
GROANING BOARD A buffet table that "groans" beneath the weight of its bounty	
ISLAND Serving area for a particular cuisine or specialty—salads, desserts, Mexican, and the like)	
SHOVELIZER Diner who prefers quantity over quality	
FORK LIFT A device used to remove shovelizers	

TO SAY THE BUFFET HAS BEEN ELEVATED would be an understatement. What used to be considered a cost-effective and valuable way to feed guests looking more for a meal than a dining "experience," has evolved into an experience that satisfies both those who only look to food for sustenance and food aficionados alike. Some might say they're looking for quantity over quality when it comes to all-you-can-eat, but the Las Vegas buffet has willingly raised the quality so that even if you're there to simply eat all you can, you're also eating the best you can.

You could conceivably eat your three squares a day at the buffet at the same property where you rest your head (your hotel would love that). Caesars Entertainment has even created a 24-hour pass—**The Buffet of Buffets**—that allows you to dine at each of their properties, including Harrah's, Bally's, Rio, Paris, and, of course, Caesars Palace. But be warned: If you want to add the Bacchanal Buffet at Caesars or the Village Seafood Buffet at Rio, that will cost you an extra $15–$30, depending on which meal and which buffet you upgrade to.

When The Cosmopolitan opened in 2009, it raised the bar for the Vegas aesthetic, which included elevating the concept of the buffet. The $20-million **Wicked Spoon** was modeled after food courts in Asia, where food is portioned for individual servings rather than served from giant trays in steam tables behind sneeze glass. In a nutshell, Cosmo classed up the buffet, with grown-up dishes such as bone marrow, oysters Rockefeller, and short rib cavatelli. The single-serving

Top 25 Las Vegas Restaurants

	RESTAURANT NAME	CHEF	OVERALL RATING	PRICE RATING	HOST HOTEL	PROFILED
1.	JOËL ROBUCHON	Claude Le Tohic	★★★★★	Very Expensive	MGM Grand	Yes
2.	RESTAURANT GUY SAVOY	Guy Savoy	★★★★★	Very Expensive	Caesars Palace	Yes
3.	ESTIATORIO MILOS	Costas Spiliadis	★★★★★	Very Expensive	The Cosmopolitan	Yes
4.	TWIST	Pierre Gagnaire	★★★★★	Very Expensive	Mandarin Oriental	Yes
5.	barMASA	Masa Takayama	★★★★★	Very Expensive	Aria	Yes
6.	L'ATELIER de JOËL ROBUCHON	Steve Benjamin	★★★★★	Very Expensive	MGM Grand	Yes
7.	JALEO	José Andrés	★★★★½	Moderate	The Cosmopolitan	Yes
8.	PICASSO	Julian Serrano	★★★★½	Very Exp.	Bellagio	Yes
9.	SAGE	Shawn McClain	★★★★½	Very Exp.	Aria	Yes
10.	BARTOLOTTA RISTORANTE DI MARE	Paul Bartolotta	★★★★½	Very Expensive	Wynn Las Vegas	Yes
11.	AUREOLE	Vincent Poussel	★★★★½	Very Exp.	Mandalay Bay	No
12.	RX BOILER ROOM	Rick Moonen	★★★★	Expensive	Mandalay Bay	Yes
13.	RAKU	Mitsuo Endo	★★★★	Moderate	West of Strip	Yes
14.	GORDON RAMSAY STEAK	Gordon Ramsay	★★★★½	Very Expensive	Paris Las Vegas	Yes
15.	MICHAEL MINA	Michael Mina	★★★★	Very Expensive	Bellagio	No
16.	OSTERIA del CIRCO	Paul Lee	★★★★	Very Expensive	Bellagio	No
17.	CUT	Matthew Hurley	★★★★	Expensive	The Palazzo	No
18.	CRAFTSTEAK	Matt Seeber	★★★★	Expensive	MGM Grand	No
19.	NOBU CAESARS	Tommy Buckley	★★★★½	Very Expensive	Caesars Palace	Yes
20.	SCARPETTA	Scott Conant	★★★★	Expensive	The Cosmopolitan	Yes
21.	SENSI	Roy Ellamar	★★★½	Expensive	Bellagio	No
22.	MIX in LAS VEGAS	Bruno Riou	★★★½	Very Expensive	Mandalay Bay	No
23.	BOUCHON	Thomas Keller	★★★½	Moderate	The Venetian	Yes
24.	SPAGO	Eric Klein	★★★½	Moderate/ Expensive	Forum Shops, Caesars Palace	Yes
25.	B&B RISTORANTE	Mario Batali	★★★	Very Expensive	The Venetian	Yes

Las Vegas's Ten Best Buffets

RANK BUFFET	QUALITY RATING	LAST YEAR'S RATING
1. BACCHANAL BUFFET (Caesars)	99	2
2. WICKED SPOON (The Cosmopolitan)	99	1
3. THE BUFFET AT ARIA	98	8
4. BUFFET BELLAGIO	97	4
5. THE BUFFET AT WYNN	96	3
6. SPICE MARKET BUFFET (Planet Hollywood)	95	6
7. CRAVINGS (Mirage) / THE BUFFET AT TI	94	7/9
8. STUDIO B (M Resort)	93	5
9. FEAST BUFFET (Green Valley Ranch/Texas Station)	92	–
10. GARDEN COURT (Main Street Station)	90	–

pulled-pork eggs Benedicts are mandatory for breakfast, as are the chicken-apple sausages. At $33 for brunch and $38 for dinner, Wicked Spoon is reasonably priced for a dining experience of this caliber.

While Wicked Spoon may have been the rising tide that lifted all ships, **Bacchanal Buffet** at Caesars Palace has sailed ahead of the fleet. Bacchanal ascribes to both quality and quantity, with more than 500 items offered each day spread over three main dining rooms. Live-action stations include a smoked barbecue line, with sausages and meats hanging overhead, and a rotating *comal,* or tortilla griddle, for the Mexican cuisine. Like Wicked Spoon, Bacchanal offers dishes in individual portions, such as servings of fried chicken or sweet potato fries in mini, paper-lined wire baskets. Even more interesting are the ever-evolving specials—almost unheard of when you're cooking for volume. But the Bacchanal back of the house—which for buffet chefs, has a surprising number of toques that came from Michelin-starred kitchens—puts out around 15 daily, seasonal specials, such as chilled pea soup with crab or chicken marsala. Desserts are legendary, if tiny, so that you can eat many of them, including cookies, cake pops, tarts, and cupcakes, with a fun assortment of gelato, all made in-house. A true bacchanalia—festivals in honor of the Greek god Bacchus, god of wine—never comes cheap, and neither does this one: breakfast starts at $25, lunch at $35, weekend brunch at $44, and dinner will set you back $50–$53.

Bumped up the list this year is the only buffet at CityCenter. Thanks to a recent renovation that brightened up the decor and added some more ethnic options, **Buffet at Aria** is now one of the more diverse buffets. With one of the few tandoor ovens on the Strip, this is an unsung spot for Indian food, and you can watch as fresh naan bread is baked for you in the oven, along with kabobs and other Indian fare. Mediterranean cuisine goes beyond Greece, including bites from North Africa and the Middle East, while the humble pizza even sees multiple preparations: deep dish, New York style, and Stromboli. There's even variety during breakfast, with made-to-order classic, snow crab, or salmon eggs Benedicts. While the pricing at The Buffet at Aria—$19 for breakfast, $23 for lunch, and $34 for dinner ($40 on weekends)— might make it seem like a middle-of-the-road buffet, it excels in freshness and service, and delivers lots of bang for the buck.

The **Buffet at Bellagio** probably doesn't get as much credit as it should. As one of the first true luxury resorts in Las Vegas, it has always had a high standard for its buffet, with lots of seafood, unique salads, and fresh baked bread. Gourmet dinner service on Fridays and Saturdays breaks out the fish eggs, as in fine caviar with accoutrements, and fresh-rolled sushi and ahi tuna cones. And to keep itself relevant, Bellagio's all-you-can-eat has added a VIP experience that includes a chef's table. VIP guests bypass the (usually) long line and are seated at a private table with a menu, created especially for the party by a team of chefs, that might include charcuterie, caviar, and tableside preparations of fresh salads or carving of leg of lamb or prime rib. And yes, you still get to graze the buffet as well. Breakfast is easy at $18, with lunch and dinner setting you back $22 and $33, respectively; weekend brunch is $29, or $41 with bottomless champagne. If you're looking for more luxury on your plate, the gourmet dinner service is $39, while the chef's table is $53–$59 per person.

The **Buffet at Wynn** quietly chugs along, still offering really interesting bites to the high volume of discerning guests. Under the vaulted, airy ceilings, 15 live-action cooking stations produce gourmet dishes, such as waffle-battered fried chicken, Wagyu lasagna, and oven-roasted prime rib. Those who eschew animal products also flock here, thanks to the large selection of vegan items, including enchiladas and pastas, as well as desserts such as vegan ice cream. Cost is $20 for breakfast, $26 for lunch, and $39 for dinner ($40 Friday and Saturday).

Vegetarians have long made the trip to **Spice Market Buffet** at Planet Hollywood, thanks to its heavily Mediterranean-focused menu, even though it's a veritable crossroads of ethnic cuisines. Middle Eastern dishes, such as baba ghanoush, hummus, and stuffed grape leaves, are a big draw for non-meat-eaters, but the vegetarianism also expands to other fare, such as Thai eggplant and pesto penne. Carnivores don't have to worry, though, as Spice Market has them covered with marinated lamb kabobs, sausage and peppers, and chicken curry. Breakfast begins at $17, while dinner will run you $29, and you'll save a few bucks if you're a Total Rewards member. It would be safe to wrap up **Cravings** at the Mirage and **The Buffet at TI** along the same ranks as Spice Market Buffet, with maybe slightly less diverse cuisine, but both feature chefs cooking dishes to order at each station.

Farther south down Las Vegas Boulevard, The M Resort stands like a lighthouse, acting as a beacon for those driving in on I-15 to let them know they're close to the Strip. But if you're in the know, you won't drive past this lone property and miss one of the better off-Strip buffets. **Studio B** is the Vegas buffet in its purest form: nothing fancy, but high quality, free-flowing crab legs, prime rib, cocktail shrimp, oysters, and Asian specialties such as Korean kalbi and oxtail. There's also a live-action cooking studio, where chefs on display prepare dishes made to order. Top it off with a huge spread devoted to seafood on weekends and reasonable prices ($15 lunch, $23 dinner, $39 seafood buffet on weekends and Friday dinner) that include unlimited beer, wine, and champagne, and you've got a buffet worth the trek—from anywhere.

Among other off-Strip options, the **Feast Buffets** at the Station Casinos, which include Red Rock Resort, Sunset Station, and Fiesta, are a favorite among locals, not only because they're located in locals-friendly casinos but also because, even though they all share a name, there's something that makes each of them special. On seafood Fridays at the **Feast at Green Valley Ranch,** for example, people line up with a plate piled high with crab legs to have "Mama Sarah" treatment: crab legs are tossed onto the flat top; then coated with butter, herbs, and chilies; and slapped with a metal spatula to crack open the shells, allowing in more flavor (a preparation by beloved line cook "Mama" Sarah Jamerson). **Feast at Texas Station** is the only one with tacos al pastor made to order at their Mexican station, created from an 80-year-old family recipe of one of the cooks there.

Downtown's only buffet really worth mentioning is still Main Street Station's **Garden Court,** thanks to the dishes appealing to Hawaiian and Filipino clientele. You'll still get your standards, such as rotisserie chicken and prime rib, and T-Bone Tuesdays before Shrimp Scampi Thursdays. But what they do really well are island specialties, such as Portuguese sausage, oxtail stew, and kalua pork. An unofficial steal, breakfast at Garden Court is $6, lunch is $7, and dinner, depending on the nightly special, will run you $10–$21.

The highly anticipated SLS is set with its own modern buffet concept, cleverly named **The SLS Buffet.** The new space is designed in conjunction with consultant Philippe Starck to create what is referred to as a "cabin chic" feel (read: lots of wood and antler chandeliers). While the decor may be novel, SLS isn't reinventing the wheel with its buffet, which will include Mediterranean, Japanese, and wood-grilled offerings, but dishes will be prepared à la minute, or right as the guest orders it from the chefs manning the station. The cocktail program at The SLS Buffet is on point as well, designed to pair with the cuisine. The Fig Winner (Bulleit rye whiskey, Ancho Reyes liqueur, and fig and Dr. Pepper simple syrup), for example, is meant to hold up against dishes from the wood-fired grill.

Seafood Buffets

Several casinos feature these on certain days. The best of the bunch is the **Village Seafood Buffet** at Rio (daily). **The Orleans**'s seafood night is Friday, the **Fremont**'s are on Tuesday and Friday, **Main Street Station**'s is on Friday, and the **Golden Nugget**'s are on Friday, Saturday, and Sunday. The piscatory repasts at the **Cannery** (Thursday) and **Suncoast** (Friday) are worth trying as well.

Of the above, Rio's Village Seafood Buffet is the most expensive, at $45 plus tax, but the quality and variety are unbelievable, even for Las Vegas. Check it out: small lobster tails (dinner), peel-and-eat shrimp, Dungeness crab legs, Manila steamers, and oysters on the half-shell; seafood salads, chowders, and Mongolian grill; plus Italian, Mexican, and Chinese dishes, along with fried, grilled, broiled, breaded, blackened, beer-battered, and barbecued preparations. And if you have even a millimeter of stomach space left after the main courses, the dessert selection is outstanding.

Buffet-Line Strategy

Popular buffets develop long lines. The best way to avoid the crowds is to go Sunday–Thursday and get in line before 6 p.m. or after 9 p.m., but we recommend the early strategy, when the food is fresher. If you go to a buffet on a weekend, arrive extra-early or extra-late. If a large trade show or convention is in town, you'll be better off hitting the buffets of casinos that don't draw big convention business. Good choices among the highly ranked buffets include **Texas Station,** the two **Fiestas, Main Street Station, Boulder Station, Gold Coast, The Orleans, Suncoast,** and the **Fremont.**

BRUNCHES

UPSCALE, EXPENSIVE SPREADS with reserved tables, imported Champagne, sushi, and seafood have made an impact on the local brunch scene. Although there is a plethora of value-priced brunches, the big-ticket shindigs attract diners who are happy to pay a higher tab for fancy food and service at a place that takes reservations so they can avoid a wait. In general, the higher the price, the better the Champagne or other beverages served. **Bally's, Bellagio,** the **MGM Grand,** and **Wynn Las Vegas** serve decent French Champagne; California sparkling wine, mimosas, or Bloody Marys are the norm at the others. Reservations are accepted at all of the following:

- **COOKIN' WITH JAZZ BRUNCH** Country Club Grill, Wynn Las Vegas
  ☎ 702-770-7000; wynnlasvegas.com
  NEW ORLEANS NATIVE CARLOS GUIA, formerly with the sorely missed Vegas outpost of Commander's Palace, has taken over this steak joint overlooking the Wynn golf course. During the week, he sticks to a fairly standard steakhouse menu, but on weekends, the hotel allows him to riff on the dishes he grew up with—shrimp rémoulade, gumbo, various house-made sausages, grits, Southern soups, and bread pudding. Add a jazz trio, and the result is one of the most indulgent, enjoyable brunches in town. Adults, $65; children ages 5–12, $28. Sundays only, 10 a.m.–2 p.m.

- **GOSPEL BRUNCH** House of Blues, Mandalay Bay
  ☎ 702-632-7777 houseofblues.com/lasvegas
  PRAISE THE LORD AND PASS THE BISCUITS! This is the most raucous and joyous Sunday brunch in town. Grammy-winning gospel legend Kirk Franklin recently joined forces with the House of Blues to custom-tailor the joyous gospel performance in each city to suit its particular audience. The food is soulful as well: cornbread muffins and maple butter, Creole chicken and shrimp

jambalaya, chicken and waffles, carving stations, plus create-your-own Bloody Mary and mimosa bars. Purchase tickets at the House of Blues box office: adults, $50; children ages 3–11, $27.50. Seatings at 10 a.m. and 1 p.m.

- **FOUNTAINS BRUNCH AT JASMINE** Bellagio
  ☎ 866-259-7111; bellagio.com
  EXCEPT ON SUNDAYS, this space houses an elegant Chinese restaurant, notable for Cantonese cuisine and views of the Bellagio fountains. But on weekends, the room is transformed into Las Vegas's third most expensive brunch, with canapés, king crab, a seafood bar, and great desserts. There's dim sum from the Jasmine kitchen, too. Adults, $58, children ages 6–12, $25. Sundays, 11 a.m.–2:30 p.m.

- **SIMON BRUNCH** Palms Place; ☎ 702-944-3292; palms.com
  COME AS YOU ARE—pajamas included, if you dare—to celebrity chef Kerry Simon's imaginative take on the Sunday brunch. Buffet offerings include sushi, panini, peel-and-eat shrimp, smoothies, jars full of candy, and a junk-food dessert platter (think cotton candy and Rice Krispie treats); order eggs Benedict, pizza, and fried chicken off the accompanying menu. Adults, $40 (add $22 for make-your-own Bloody Marys or $22–$44 for Champagne); children age 11 and under, $12; fixed-price menu, $45. Available 10 a.m.–2:45 p.m.

- **STERLING BRUNCH** Bally's Steakhouse
  ☎ 702-967-7999; ballyslasvegas.com
  THIS PLACE PIONEERED THE VEGAS BRUNCH TREND. And it just got a much-needed makeover, as Bally's converted the old Bally's Steakhouse that housed it into the modernly redesigned BLT Steak. At $90 per person, plus tax (children ages 3–8, $30 plus tax; under age 3 free), it's still the big ticket, but there's no shortage of diners who love it. The lavish selection includes smoked salmon, freshly made sushi, real lobster salad, seafood, caviar, and French Champagne. Pheasant and rack of lamb appear regularly. The dessert selection is awesome. Entrée selections change weekly. Sundays, 9:30 a.m.–2:30 p.m.; reservations required.

Other good brunches can be found at **Aria, Caesars,** the **Mirage, Planet Hollywood,** and **Main Street Station** (the best bargain brunch, at $12).

MEAL DEALS

IN ADDITION TO BUFFETS, many casinos offer special dining deals, including New York strip, T-bone, and porterhouse steaks, prime rib, crab legs, lobster, and combinations of the foregoing, all at giveaway prices. There are also breakfast specials, burgers, hot dogs, and shrimp cocktails.

While the meal deals generally deliver what they promise in the way of an entrée, many of the extras that contribute to a high-quality dining experience are missing. With a couple of notable exceptions, the specials are served in big, bustling restaurants with all the atmosphere of a high-school cafeteria. When you're eating at closely packed Formica tables under lighting bright enough for brain surgery, it's difficult to pretend you're engaged in fine dining.

Our biggest complaint, however, concerns the lack of attention paid to the meal as a whole. We've had nice pieces of meat served with tired, droopy salads; stale bread; mealy microwaved potatoes; and tasteless canned vegetables. How can you get excited about your prime rib when it's surrounded by the ruins of Pompeii?

Deke Castleman, a contributor to this book and former editor of the *Las Vegas Advisor,* says discount dining actually isn't about food at all:

> A "quality dining experience" is not really what Las Vegas visitors are looking for, in my humble opinion, when they pursue an $8 steak, $12 prime rib, or $24 lobster. To me what they're after is twofold: (1) a very cheap steak, prime rib, or lobster—damn the salad, vegetable, and Formica; and (2) a cool story to take home about all the rock-bottom prices they paid for food.

Finally, it's hard to take advantage of many of the specials: They're offered only in the middle of the night, or you've got to wait an hour for a table, or you have to eat dinner at 3:30 in the afternoon. In restaurants all over town, in and out of the casinos, you'll find plenty of good food served in pleasant surroundings at extremely reasonable prices. In our opinion, saving $5 on a meal isn't worth the hassle.

Because Las Vegas meal deals often come and go, it's impossible to cover them adequately in a book that is revised annually. To stay abreast of them, your best bet is to subscribe to the *Las Vegas Advisor,* a monthly newsletter that provides independent, critical evaluations of meal deals, buffets, brunches, and drink specials. To order, call ☎ 800-244-2224 or visit **lvahotels.com.** If you're already in town and you want to pick up a copy, head to the **Gamblers Book Club** (5473 S. Eastern Ave.; ☎ 702-382-7555 or 800-522-1777; **gamblersbook.com**).

STEAK Though specials constantly change, a few have weathered the test of time. Our favorite is the 16-ounce porterhouse dinner at the **Redwood Bar & Grill** in the California (☎ 702-385-1222; **thecal.com /dine).** A complete meal, including soup or salad and steak with excellent accompanying sides, can be had for $24, excluding tax and tip. What's more, it's served in an attractive dining room. The porterhouse special, incidentally, isn't on the menu—you have to ask for it.

Ellis Island Casino (☎ 702-733-8901; **ellisislandcasino.com**), attached to the Super 8 motel on Koval Lane near East Flamingo Road, serves an excellent $8 New York strip dinner complete with salad, baked potato, green beans, and microbrewed beer or root beer. It's available 24 hours, but again, it's not on the menu. The **Hard Rock Hotel** (☎ 702-693-5000; **hardrockhotel.com**) has a steak-and-shrimp "Gambler's Special," served 24 hours a day in Mr. Lucky's coffee shop for about $8, also not on the menu. *Note:* Someone at the table must have a Hard Rock players club card to take advantage of this special.

Continued on page 361

Downtown Dining

THOUGH WE PROFILE only a couple of downtown restaurants in this guide, the restaurant scene there is both diverse and dynamic. You'll find a number of good steakhouses and seafood specialty restaurants, some of the city's better buffets, and a broad selection of ethnic cuisine, including Japanese, Hawaiian, Thai, Mexican, Chinese, and Italian. There are places that specialize in barbecue, hamburgers, shrimp cocktails, and chili dogs, among others. Restaurant settings range from luxurious to clubby to hole in the wall, with all concentrated in an area not much bigger than a large Strip hotel.

Most of the restaurants in the four blocks of Fremont Street from Main Street to 4th Street are in casinos. Moving east and north, however, the majority of eateries are freestanding. As the long-awaited revitalization of downtown Las Vegas finally becomes a reality, a number of new restaurants—many of them in the **Fremont East** entertainment district, which is, logically, along Fremont Street east of Las Vegas Boulevard and the Fremont Street Experience—are joining the roster of established spots, some of them of many years' duration.

One of the most exciting areas along Fremont East is **Downtown Container Park,** at Fremont and 7th Streets. As the name implies, the park is created of shipping-container modules, stacked in a multistory configuration around an interactive park for kids and a lawn and stage for the frequent live musical performances. While it's a family spot by day, no one younger than 21 is permitted after 9 p.m.

And, of course, the park is home to a number of restaurants—by necessity tiny restaurants—each of which have a few tables inside, but all of which share the many communal tables and chairs positioned around them outdoors. The startup-incubator nature of the park is perhaps most clearly personified by **Big Ern's BBQ,** serving St. Louis–style ribs, pulled pork, pulled chicken, creamy potato salad with a generous component of black olives, and cole slaw with a lovely crunch and vinegar tang, but perhaps most impressive is his brisket.

A much more established business is represented in Container Park by **Pinches Tacos,** whose subtext is "real Mexican food by real Mexicans." And then there's **Bin 702,** which serves charcuterie (much of it locally produced), cheeses, sandwiches, and snacks, all designed to go well with the 12 wines on tap. One sure bet is the turkey and Brie panini, another the chopped salad. One of the newest additions to Container Park is **Cheffini's Hot Dogs,** which began as a late-night hot dog cart. Try everything from traditional dogs with mustard and ketchup to creative versions with pineapple sauce and potato chips. For additional information on Container Park, visit **downtowncontainerpark.com.**

At 6th Street and Carson Avenue, one block south of Fremont, is **Carson Kitchen,** where you'll find traditional comfort food updated with contemporary flavors. The menu has an emphasis on shared plates, such as tempura green beans with pepper jelly and cream cheese, bacon jam with baked Brie and toasted baguette, and Devil's Eggs with crispy pancetta and caviar. The sandwich selection includes short-rib sliders and grilled cheese with apples and caramelized onion.

Just down the street from Carson Kitchen, at 7th Street and Carson Avenue, is **Eat** (see also page 388). This first restaurant from Strip veteran chef Natalie Young serves breakfast and lunch, including such dishes as shrimp and grits, free-range chicken, and the Killer Grilled Cheese, which truly lives up to its name. Another Young restaurant, **Wild,** in the Ogden residential building at Las Vegas Boulevard and Ogden Avenue, offers a completely gluten-free menu with numerous vegan offerings.

Across 6th Street from the Ogden is the venerable El Cortez, which extends from Ogden Avenue to Fremont Street and 6th to 7th Streets. The El Cortez dates to 1941 and was once run by the notorious Benjamin "Bugsy" Siegel. Its new **Siegel's 1941,** a 24-hour vintage-themed coffee shop, is a nod to the notorious mobster. Siegel's took over the Flame Steakhouse space, but it's expected to retain a few of the more popular menu items, such as the prime rib and seasonal stone crab.

Across Fremont Street from the El Cortez is **Le Thai,** which has a tiny dining room but an expansive walled patio, with pergola, heaters, and misters; its menu features such dishes as Three Color Curry and Short Rib Fried Rice. Around the corner is **La Comida,** which serves an updated urban Mexican menu, with such dishes as Mexican street corn and ahi tostadas, in a casual mix-and-match atmosphere reminiscent of a Baja beach bar.

Back on the main drag is **Park on Fremont,** which is pretty much whimsy from start to finish, from the picket fence–enclosed al fresco dining area out on the street to the herringbone-floored front entrance to the walled rear garden complete with seesaw. The gastropub menu includes such dishes as Mac & Cheese Balls, Fried Egg Burger, and Strawberry Summer Salad.

And Park on Fremont brings us back to **The Beat Coffeehouse** just a few doors down, a Fremont East pioneer that serves far more than coffee, with breakfast, salads, and sandwiches on the menu. The Caesar salad and croque monsieur may be somewhat conventional, but the same can't be said for the Slap & Tickle sandwich, which includes bacon, jalapeños, and peanut butter.

But back to classic steakhouses: When The D, which extends from Fremont to Carson Street and 3rd to 4th Streets, was renovated and updated, the Detroit-centric owners brought in **Andiamo Steakhouse** from Detroit restaurateur Joe Vicari, who has 10 restaurants in the Motor City. The Las Vegas Andiamo may be new, but it carries an Old World feel, with a brick-lined vaulted entrance, curtained booths, and attentive service augmenting a classic menu of steaks and chops and such steakhouse dishes as lobster bisque. The D is also home to Detroit favorite **American Coney Island,** serving chili dogs.

Continued on the next page

Downtown Dining *(continued)*

Just across 3rd Street from The D is the Four Queens, site of the landmark **Hugo's Cellar.** Hugo's really is in a sort of cellar (a rarity in Southern Nevada), brick-lined and below street level, and is a bastion of old-time elegance. Its hallmarks include a red rose for each female customer, a salad cart from which each customer chooses the items to customize his or her salad, old-school tableside preparations of Caesar salad, Bananas Foster, and Cherries Jubilee, and a menu heavy on dishes such as Chateaubriand and rack of lamb.

Continuing west on Fremont Street is the Golden Nugget, with **Vic & Anthony's,** an updated steakhouse, and such restaurants as the **Chart House** (complete with 75,000-gallon aquarium), **Lillie's Asian Cuisine,** and the **Grotto** for classic Italian. The Chart House, serving seafood, is a member of the chain, which is owned by the hotel-casino's owners.

Andiamo Steakhouse, Hugo's Cellar, and Vic & Anthony's are excellent choices if you either have a high budget or are looking for a blow-the-rent experience.

Skip north a block off the Fremont Street Experience and you'll encounter the Downtown Grand and its adjacent **Downtown 3rd** area. Downtown 3rd is perhaps best known for **Triple George Grill,** a knockoff of a classic San Francisco restaurant, known for excellent sourdough, fresh fish, steaks and chops, and comfort foods. Almost adjacent is **Pizza Rock,** from 11-time world pizza champion Tony Gemignani, which has pizza ovens heated to four different temperatures to properly prepare numerous styles of pizza. Just down the block is **The Commissary,** an updated Latin kitchen from chef Richard Sandoval. And inside the Downtown Grand is the **Red Mansion,** which serves Chinese food.

A few blocks west is Main Street Station, site of **Triple 7,** one of the city's most established brewpubs—and one that's known for excellent sushi (because of a large Hawaiian clientele), along with more beer-friendly foods like burgers and steaks. The Plaza, a few blocks south on Main Street, houses **Oscar's Steakhouse,** named in honor of former mayor Oscar Goodman. Oscar's is in an elevated circular structure at the mouth of Fremont Street and offers one of the best views of the Fremont Street Experience. Other dining options at the Plaza include the indoor-outdoor **Bier Garten, Hash House A Go Go,** and **Pop Up Pizza.**

Across the street from the Plaza is the Golden Gate, site of **Du-par's,** an outlet of the Los Angeles restaurant that dates to 1938 and is known for pancakes, pies, and other diner fare. It's also the home of the Golden Gate's legendary bargain shrimp cocktail (currently $2.99)—still a good deal.

Also off the Fremont Street Experience you'll find the California and the Fremont, both, like Main Street Station, owned by Boyd Gaming. The California, in particular, attracts a heavily Hawaiian clientele ("Aloha spoken here" is one of its slogans), and is home to **Aloha Specialties,** offering the flavors of the islands. The Cal's **Pasta Pirate** specializes in seafood, and its **Redwood Grill,** along with Hugo's Cellar and Binion's Steakhouse, is a quintessential old Las Vegas gourmet room, who's raison d'être was originally to provide top-quality intimate dining for high rollers. The porterhouse special is one of the best deals on the Sin City restaurant scene, but it's not on the menu, so you have to ask for it.

Good value also can be found at the Fremont's Pacific Rim–centric **Second Street Grill** and at Binion's next door, where the 24th-floor **Binion's Steakhouse** offers an epic view along with Old Vegas food and service.

One of the few stand-alone restaurants downtown is **Chicago Joe's,** in business since 1975 in a house built in the 30s at 820 S. 4th Street (Las Vegas Blvd. would be 5th, so this is one block to the west). Chicago Joe's serves old-school Italian and reportedly was a hangout for Oscar Goodman, back in his mob-attorney days, and such notorious clients as Tony Spilatro.

And, of course, the famous Las Vegas buffet reigns Downtown. The best one is at Main Street Station, but the Golden Nugget and the Fremont have good ones too.

Still not satisfied? Well, there's always the **Heart Attack Grill,** just east of the Fremont Street Experience. More of a gimmick than a restaurant, it offers food worthy of the name, and you eat for free if you weigh in at more than 350 pounds.

Note: All restaurants mentioned above in **boldface** in the "Downtown Dining" sidebar can be found on the map on page 387.

PRIME RIB One of the best prime-rib specials in a town full of prime-rib specials is available Downtown at the California's **Market Street Cafe** (☎ 702-385-1222; **thecal.com/dine**), where you can get a good cut of meat between 4 p.m. and 11 p.m. for $9.99; it comes with soup or salad, vegetable, starch of choice, and cherries jubilee for dessert.

Mr. Lucky's at the Hard Rock Hotel offers an exquisite all-you-can-eat prime rib special for $9.99. Served daily from 4 p.m. to 4 a.m., the cooked-to-order prime rib comes with soup or salad, baked potato, and veggies.

South Point, at the far south end of the Strip (☎ 702-796-7111; **southpointcasino.com/dining**), serves a big slab of prime rib prepared to order, with soup or salad, potato, rolls, and au jus, plus tear-inducing horseradish, if you ask. It's available from 11 a.m. to 11 p.m. in the Coronado Cafe for $12.95. For $5 more, you can enjoy the same dinner at the upscale **Primarily Prime Rib** restaurant on the second floor, where salads are mixed tableside and there's always a featured wine on sale for a bargain price. Primarily Prime Rib is open Wednesday–Sunday for dinner only. For reservations, call ☎ 702-797-8075.

LOBSTER AND CRAB LEGS Lobster-and-steak (surf-and-turf) combos and crab-leg deals no longer appear as regularly as they once did on casino marquees around Las Vegas. **Pasta Pirate** at the California (☎ 702-385-1222; **thecal.com/dine**) serves the best all-around shellfish specials. Unfortunately, they're on-again, off-again. When on, they alternately feature a steak-and-lobster combo, a lobster dinner, or a king crab dinner, all from $18 to $40, not including tax or tip. Entrées are served with soup or salad, pasta, veggies, garlic bread, and wine. The setting is relaxed and pleasant. Reservations are accepted.

unofficial **TIP**
Beware of lobster deals. You get what you pay for.

The best place for crab legs is at the gourmet buffets. **Aria, Bellagio, M Resort, Planet Hollywood,** and **Wynn Las Vegas,** serve all-you-can-eat cold king crab nightly; at Bellagio and Planet Hollywood, you can make a plate and ask a server to warm it for you in the kitchen.

SHRIMP COCKTAILS Peddled at nominal prices, these seafaring snacks are frequently used to lure gamblers into the casinos. The shrimp are the tiny bay variety, usually drowned in cocktail sauce. The best and cheapest shrimp cocktail can be found at the **Golden Gate** (☎ 702-385-1906; **goldengatecasino.com**), a small Downtown casino that's been serving this special for more than 50 years. The price: $2.99, raised a dollar in 2010 and 2012 after costing 99¢ for nearly 20 years. Other contenders are served at the **Four Queens** and **Palace Station** (coffee shop), as well as the **Skyline** on Boulder Highway.

PASTA AND PIZZA **Pasta Pirate** at the California offers some of the best designer pasta dishes in town. A good pizza play is to hit up satellite outlets—fast-food counters attached to the Italian restaurants—at **Boulder Station** and **Sunset Station** for a quickie slice. You can also get a good slice of New York–style pizza at the Rio's **Sports Deli. Metro Pizza** at Ellis Island wins local-media popularity contests. The Red Rock and Green Valley Ranch food courts have **Villa Pizza,** a local chain. The best pizza on the Strip is now found at the no-name hidden pizza place on the third floor of **The Cosmopolitan.**

BREAKFAST SPECIALS The best ham-and-eggs specials are found at the **Gold Coast, Arizona Charlie's Decatur,** and **Boulder Station.** All offer terrific prices, usually around $5. Arizona Charlie's Decatur also has decent steak and eggs for $4.49. Other worthwhile breakfast deals include the buffets at **Sam's Town, The Orleans,** and the **Rio.**

TASTING MENUS

DON'T LET THE PHRASE "tasting menu" be daunting—it's probably one of the most cost-effective ways to get to know a restaurant. When the economy tanked, restaurants turned to tasting, or *prix fixe,* menus to lure in guests to, well, taste their way through a restaurant's menu. For a set price, diners are guaranteed a certain number of courses (anywhere from a standard 3, such as lunch at Milos, to an exorbitant 16, as in the degustation at Joël Robuchon) that usually include signature dishes for which the restaurant is best known. Multiple courses usually mean smaller portions, but after six or seven, all those bites add up to a full belly, without breaking the bank.

- **SAGE** Aria THIS CONTEMPORARY AMERICAN restaurant by chef Shawn McClain at Aria offers two tasting menus: one early-bird special with three courses for $59, and the four-course signature tasting for $89 (with additional wine or beer pairing for $44). While the three-course menu is perfunctory, with options such as heirloom tomato salad or chilled sweet corn soup as a starter, and roasted chicken or flat iron steak as an entrée, the four-course menu can introduce you to the simple, clean flavors that McClain and his team do best. The signature menu presents the starter option of Kusshi oysters topped with Tabasco sorbet and tequila mignonette, or a crazy good Wagyu beef tartare adorned with a slow-poached egg and crispy chocolate. That follows up with grilled Spanish octopus, if you'd like, along with your choice of 48-hour braised beef belly or bacon-wrapped Iberico pork loin.

- **L'ATELIER DE JOËL ROBUCHON** MGM Grand ONE OF LAS VEGAS'S most formal temples of fine dining, Joël Robuchon at MGM Grand, with its 16-course degustation, will set you back $435 per person (and that's without wine). That can be a little hard to swallow, so the next best thing is heading to the more casual concept, L'Atelier de Joël Robuchon, next door, with its counter dining, where you can watch the chefs prepare your meal. While no less a fine-dining restaurant than its more regal neighbor, there's a more comfortable aspect to L'Atelier and an easier check average at $159 for the 10-course *Menu Decouverte de Saison* (that's their Seasonal Discovery Menu, if your French is a little rusty). And you shall discover the finest of Robuchon, from his elegant langoustines cooked in green curry and coconut milk, to his famous roasted quail stuffed with foie gras and legendary pommes puree, or mashed potatoes.

- **ESTIATORIO MILOS** The Cosmopolitan THERE ARE FEW PRIX-FIXE lunch menus on the Strip, but Milos gives new meaning to the term "power lunch." The midday meal consists of three courses for $22.14 (which will rise by a penny in 2015), and is considered one of the best deals in town. Begin your Greek journey with a selection of mezze, or dips such as *tarama* and *tzatziki* (salmon roe and cucumber and yogurt spreads), ripe tomato salad, or grilled, tender octopus. Your second course showcases what Milos is known for: fresh seafood, flown in straight from the Mediterranean daily. Choose from a whole *lavraki,* or grilled sea bass, dressed simply with good olive oil and lemon, or shrimp *saganaki,* or even a lamb chop, if you're feeling that Greek. Finish it off with true Greek yogurt or fresh fruit. It's such a simple elegant meal, but the price alone is enough to make you say "Opa!"

- **RESTAURANT GUY SAVOY** Caesars Palace AT $260 PER PERSON, the Guy Savoy Signature Menu is not cheap. But considering one of the first dishes, the Colors of Caviar, costs $90 à la carte, this nine-course menu might be considered a steal. Aside from the roe-laden starter, Savoy's famous artichoke and black truffle soup with black truffle mushroom brioche (a cool $70 on its own) makes an appearance, as does red mullet filet and the cute *tout petits pois,* or "peas all around."

Continued on page 366

Chinatown

LAS VEGAS HAS A RATHER EXTENSIVE CHINATOWN, but it's really a misnomer. Unlike other large cosmopolitan cities, like Los Angeles and New York, that have concentrated areas representing various Asian cultures (Chinatown, Koreatown, Little Saigon, Little Tokyo, or Japantown), it's all lumped in together in Las Vegas.

The traditional capital of Las Vegas's Chinatown is the **China Town Plaza** at 4215 Spring Mountain Road, between Valley View and Decatur Boulevards, a few blocks west of the Strip. China Town Plaza is the most visible symbol of the community, with a towering gateway and gilded statue, and it annually has one of the city's most colorful celebrations of the Chinese New Year, complete with Lion Dance. That can be quite a surprise to anyone who was just stopping by at 99 Ranch Market supermarket for some frozen banana leaves or fresh fish.

Despite the "China" in its name, the China Town Plaza is reflective of the melting-pot nature of the Asian community in Southern Nevada. Currently, it's home to restaurants serving Vietnamese (Mr. Sandwich and Pho Vietnam), Taiwanese (The Little Kitchen Cafe), Filipino (Kapit Bahay), Korean (Mother's Korean Grill), and Japanese (Yu-Yu Japanese Kushi Age Restaurant and Volcano Tea House) food, as well as general Chinese (Sam Woo BBQ Restaurant) and regional cuisines such as Mandarin (Da Sheng Restaurant), Mandarin and Szechwan (Emperor's Garden Restaurant), Cantonese (Harbor Palace Seafood), Yunnan (Spicy City), and southern China (Capital Seafood Restaurant).

How authentic are these restaurants? Many people think of this area as a tourist draw, but it's not the usual tourist; it's not unusual to see busloads of visitors from China parading into one of the plaza restaurants for a meal. Something else that's not unusual is to encounter a server who, faced with a table of Western customers, must go in the back for one who speaks English. And while the servers will, sometimes shame-facedly, slip a fork to a Westerner, most of the tables are set only with chopsticks.

Fifteen years ago, a motorist who saw the prominent CHINA TOWN exit sign along I-15, which runs along the Strip, might have been surprised to see things pretty much confined to the plaza, but the Asian district has grown greatly since then, with Asian businesses (some of them with signs only in their native languages) lining multiple blocks of Spring Mountain Road and the streets that lead off of it. On the far western extreme, at Rainbow Boulevard, is Koreatown Plaza, which has yet to establish its identity.

Chinese—and Japanese, and Korean, and Vietnamese, and on and on—restaurants are sprinkled throughout the Las Vegas Valley; don't assume that the best ones are confined to the Chinatown area. But here are a few noteworthy spots in that district.

ABRIYA RAKU OR JUST RAKU (5030 Spring Mountain Rd.) In its early days, this was a magnet for the area's chefs, drawn to its authentic Japanese specialties (including many that are grilled, but no sushi) and late-night hours so they could stop by after work. Today, those same chefs have a hard time getting into the tiny place. A specialty is house-made agedashi tofu. You never knew tofu could taste so good. (See profile on pages 406–407.)

CATHAY HOUSE (5300 Spring Mountain Rd.) Cathay House is one of the longest-standing restaurants in Chinatown (even though it's not in the China Town Plaza) and draws its share of tour buses, in part for its storied dim sum, with a focus on shrimp. There's an à la carte menu as well, though it doesn't attract much attention. What does is a surprisingly good view of the Strip.

CHINA MAMA (3420 S. Jones Blvd.) China Mama, which is in an old bank building, reached almost cult status early on for its impeccable execution of steamed juicy pork buns, dumpling-like shapes with broth and seasoned pork inside. But the green-onion pancake is excellent as well, as is the creamy chicken corn soup. (See profile on page 382.)

EMPEROR'S GARDEN (4215 Spring Mountain Rd.) Upstairs in the China Town Plaza, Emperor's Garden is so authentic that it draws Chinese tour groups, and you may well have to squeeze between a busload of them to make your way to a table. It also draws a large number of local regulars; on one visit, when a few buses had arrived and service started to slow down, we saw a woman march into the kitchen to help herself to more rice.

HONEY PIG (4725 Spring Mountain Rd.) This Korean barbecue is best known for its all-you-can-eat, including brisket, pork belly, and *bulgogi*, and the somewhat unusual round grills on which it's cooked.

HUE THAI (5115 Spring Mountain Rd.) Despite the "Thai" in its name, Hue Thai is most well known for its excellent execution of the Vietnamese *banh mi*, a layered sandwich on a crisp-crusted baguette that is a nod to the French influence in that country (think of it as a Saigon Sub). The house special is a winner, as is the charbroiled pork.

ICHIZA (4355 Spring Mountain Rd.) Ichiza is one of the Japanese restaurants in Las Vegas's Chinatown that's beloved by locals, especially for the Honey Toast, a dessert of crisp-edged sweet bread drizzled with honey and topped with vanilla ice cream. Remember to save room as you're partaking of the fried tofu and miso-based ramen. And remember to call ☎ 702-367-3151 to make reservations.

JOYFUL HOUSE (4601 Spring Mountain Rd.) Joyful House was founded in 1996, which makes it a landmark by Las Vegas standards. Located just west of the China Town Plaza, it's one of the city's most elegant Chinese restaurants, known for its live seafood and shark fin in various preparations, some of which must be ordered in advance.

KUNG FU PLAZA (3505 S. Valley View Blvd.) Tucked away at the east end of the China Town Plaza, Kung Fu is a venerable place dating to 1973,

Continued on the next page

Chinatown *(continued)*

which goes a long way toward explaining the name. Its proprietors are Thai, but they opened in Downtown Las Vegas before that cuisine became popular in the United States, so the emphasis has long been Chinese, and the mostly local, mostly Western clientele reflects all of the above. But they make a wonderful *pad thai,* and a nice crunchy *tom kha chicken.*

MONTA JAPANESE NOODLE HOUSE (5030 Spring Mountain Rd.) If your idea of ramen is limited to the cheap, salty packets you lived on in college, it's time for a welcome awakening. The ramen at Monta is limited to four basic styles—*tonkotsu* (pork), *shoyu* (chicken and vegetables), *tonkotsu-shoyu* (a combination of the two), and miso (nice and smoky). Get a bowl of *tonkotsu* and you'll be served a creamy, smoky, slightly buttery broth with lots of noodles and two slices of *chasu,* rolled and sliced pork that brings to mind nothing more than butter. And you can add vegetables, egg, whatever, if you feel a need to gild the lily. (See profile on page 401.)

MOTHER'S KOREAN GRILL (4215 Spring Mountain Rd.) Mother's is a classic Korean barbecue spot, downstairs in the China Town Plaza, with rectangular grills built into the tables. It's open 24 hours and attracts a large native clientele who like its authentic dishes, such as *dolsot bibimbap* and *bulgogi.* Of particular note are the *banchan* condiment/side dishes to the grilled meats, which include a truly stellar (and well balanced) *kimchi.*

PHO KIM LONG (4023 Spring Mountain Rd.) The racy name—racy, anyway, if you know how to pronounce "pho" correctly—might indicate a lack

- **ALIZÉ** Palms ANDRE ROCHAT WAS ONE OF THE FIRST established chefs in Las Vegas, and he has carried his legacy with him, and created some favorites along the way. The Sunset Prix Fixe at his restaurant at the Palms is ideal for the pretheater crowd, keeping things short and sweet with three courses for $75. Smoked Alaskan salmon with eggs mimosa, caviar, avocado, and potato crisp is an option for a signature starter, with heartier options, such as Chilean sea bass with prosciutto and lobster sausage, for the entrée. Add to this meal the spectacular view from the top of the Palms, and this is one of the most valuable packages overlooking the Strip.

The **RESTAURANTS**

OUR FAVORITE LAS VEGAS RESTAURANTS

WE'VE DEVELOPED DETAILED PROFILES for the best restaurants (in our opinion) in town. Each profile features an easily scanned heading that allows you, in just a second, to check out the restaurant's name, cuisine, overall rating, cost category, quality rating, and value rating.

of seriousness on the part of this restaurant, located in a strip center between the China Town Plaza and the Strip. But it's one of the best places in town to get a bowl of pho, the soup you build yourself from a basic meat broth and a veritable garden of fresh vegetables. Try the Rare Steak Noodle Soup or the Cantonese Roast Duck with Egg Noodle Soup.

PING PANG PONG (Gold Coast, 4000 W. Flamingo Rd.) Its Flamingo Road location technically removes Ping Pang Pong from the Chinatown area, but it's just a few blocks away down Valley View Blvd., and the Gold Coast has a huge proportion of Chinese guests—so many that they employ hosts who speak Mandarin and Cantonese. Ping Pang Pong is considered one of the best Chinese restaurants in town; a particular favorite is its dim sum, which draws a large contingent of expatriates. (See profile on pages 404–405.)

SWEETS RAKU (5040 Spring Mountain Rd.) When a place gets you started with an edible menu, you know there are lots of surprises in store, and that's true at this offshoot of Abriya Raku. Don't miss the Mount Fuji chestnut cream cake.

SAM WOO BBQ (4215 Spring Mountain Rd.) This is one of the longest-standing tenants of the China Town Plaza and, as the name indicates, is known for its *char siu,* or Chinese barbecued pork, which has levels of flavor that most American pitmasters can only dream about, including hints of star anise and fennel. But the egg drop soup also is one of the best in town.

VEGGIE HOUSE (5115 Spring Mountain Rd.) Whether you're a vegetarian or not, you'll probably find something to like at Veggie House, including a variety of faux-meat dishes.

OVERALL RATING This encompasses the entire dining experience: style, service, and ambience, in addition to taste, presentation, and food quality. Five stars is the highest rating possible and connotes the best of everything. Four-star restaurants are exceptional, three-star restaurants well above average, two-star restaurants good. One star indicates an average restaurant that demonstrates an unusual capability in some area of specialization—for example, an otherwise unmemorable place that serves great barbecued chicken.

COST Our expense description provides a comparative sense of how much a complete meal will cost. A complete meal for our purposes consists of an entrée with vegetable or side dish, and choice of soup or salad. Appetizers, desserts, drinks, and tips are excluded.

INEXPENSIVE	$14 or less per person
MODERATE	$15–$30 per person
EXPENSIVE	$31–$45 per person
VERY EXPENSIVE	$46 or more per person

QUALITY RATING Beneath each heading appear a quality rating and a value rating. The quality rating is based expressly on the taste, freshness of ingredients, preparation, presentation, and creativity of food served. Price is not a consideration. If you are a person who wants the best food available, and cost is not an issue, you need look no further than the quality rating. The quality ratings are defined as:

★★★★★ Exceptional quality
★★★★ Good quality
★★★ Fair quality
★★ Somewhat-subpar quality
★ Subpar quality

VALUE RATING If, on the other hand, you're looking for both quality and value, then you should check the value rating. Value ratings are a function of the overall rating, price rating, and quality rating:

★★★★★ Exceptional value; a real bargain
★★★★ Good value
★★★ Fair value; you get exactly what you pay for
★★ Somewhat overpriced
★ Significantly overpriced

LOCATION Beneath the value rating is an area designation. For ease of use, we divide Las Vegas into seven geographic areas:

• East of Strip • Downtown • Mid-Strip and Environs • North Strip and Environs
• South Strip and Environs • Southeast Las Vegas–Henderson • West of Strip

OUR PICKS OF THE BEST LAS VEGAS RESTAURANTS

BECAUSE RESTAURANTS OPEN AND CLOSE all the time in Las Vegas, we try to confine our list to those establishments with a proven track record over a fairly long period of time. Also, the list is highly selective. Exclusion of a particular place doesn't necessarily indicate that the restaurant is bad, only that we felt it wasn't among the best in its genre. Note that some restaurants appear in more than one category.

MORE RECOMMENDATIONS

The Best Bagels

• **Harrie's Bagelmania** 855 E. Twain Ave. (at Swenson)
☎ 702-369-3322. Baked on the premises. Locals' hangout.

The Best Bakeries

• **Bouchon Bakeries** 3355 Las Vegas Blvd. S. (The Venetian)
☎ 702-414-6203; **bouchonbakery.com**. Pastries, cookies, macaroons,

breads, and sandwiches at these three Venetian locations offer a taste of Thomas Keller's Bouchon without the formality of a sit-down meal.

- **Chocolate & Spice** 7293 W. Sahara Ave., Suite 8 and 9 ☎ 702-527-7772; **chocolatenspice.com.** Handmade chocolates, cookies, pastries, ice cream and sorbet, soups, salads, sandwiches, and more.
- **Great Buns Bakery** 3270 E. Tropicana Ave.; ☎ 702-898-0311; **greatbunsbakery.net.** Commercial and retail; fragrant rosemary bread, sticky buns, and apple loaf are good choices. More than 400 varieties of breads and pastries.
- **Retro Bakery** 7785 N. Durango Dr.; ☎ 702-586-3740; **retrobakerylv.com.** The best cupcakes in town in a family-run bakery.
- **Suzuya Pastries and Crepes** 7225 S. Durango Dr.; ☎ 702-432-1990; **suzuyapastriesandcrepes.com.** Sweet crepes, cakes, and truly original Japanese pastries in a small west-side setting.

The Best Brewpubs and Gastropubs

- **Gordon Biersch Brewery Restaurant** 3987 Paradise Rd. (Hughes Center); ☎ 702-312-5247; **gordonbiersch.com.** Upbeat brewpub with contemporary menu and surprisingly good food at reasonable prices.
- **Monte Carlo Pub** 3770 Las Vegas Blvd. S. (Monte Carlo) ☎ 702-730-7777; **montecarlo.com.** Adjacent to the pool area in a faux-warehouse setting, this brewpub offers over 300 different beers with more than 100 on tap, and affordable food options.
- **Pub 1842** 3799 Las Vegas Blvd. S. (MGM Grand); ☎ 702-891-3922; **michaelmina.net.** More than 50 beers, craft cocktails, and Michael Mina's take on casual pub fare.
- **Public House** 3355 Las Vegas Blvd. S. (The Venetian); ☎ 702-407-5310; **publichouselv.com.** Over 200 craft beers, including a rotating selection of cask beers, served alongside French, Canadian, and English cuisine.
- **Triple 7 Restaurant and Brewery** 200 N. Main St. (Main Street Station); ☎ 702-387-1896; **mainstreetcasino.com/dine.** Late-night happy hour with bargain beers and food specials.

The Best Burgers

- **Bobby's Burger Palace** 3750 Las Vegas Blvd. S.; ☎ 702-598-0191; **bobbysburgerpalace.com.** Bobby Flay offers the most casual celebrity chef burger place in town, with great toppings and amazing shakes.
- **Burger Bar** The Shoppes at Mandalay Bay Place, 3930 Las Vegas Blvd. S.; ☎ 702-632-9364; **mandalaybay.com.** Burgers of every description, some outrageous.
- **Champagnes Cafe** 3557 S. Maryland Pkwy.; ☎ 702-737-1699. Classic half-pounder with creative toppings.
- **KGB (Kerry's Gourmet Burgers)** 3475 Las Vegas Blvd. S. (Harrah's); ☎ 702-369-5065; **tinyurl.com/kgbvegas.** Creative burgers and sides from celebrity chef Kerry Simon.
- **Smash Burger** Multiple locations; **smashburger.com.** Made-to-order fast food burgers that outshine the competition.

The Best Delis

- **The Bagel Cafe** 301 N. Buffalo Dr., Summerlin; ☎ 702-255-3444; thebagelcafelv.com. They actually slice the lox by hand at this popular local deli. The pastry case is filled with traditional Jewish-bakery faves, such as black-and-white cookies and *hamantaschen*.

- **Carnegie Deli at Mirage** 3400 Las Vegas Blvd. S.; ☎ 702-791-7371; mirage.com. This outpost of the famous New York deli has the best pastrami and corned-beef sandwiches in town—so big you can barely pick them up with one hand.

- **Harrie's Bagelmania** 855 E. Twain Ave. (at Swenson) ☎ 702-369-3322. Breakfast and lunch only. Full-service bagel bakery and deli. The best bagels in the city are baked in this down-at-the-heels café—the only bagels in town with an actual crust. Tuesdays, buy bagels by the dozen at half-price.

- **Siena Deli** 9500 W. Sahara Ave.; ☎ 702-736-8424; sienaitalian.com. *Italiano* spoken here: everything is Italian and homemade. Excellent bread baked every morning; many of the area's Italian restaurants serve it. For the home cook, the selection of olive oils, tinned tomatoes, and balsamic vinegars is extensive and worthwhile.

- **Weiss Deli Restaurant Bakery** 2744 N. Green Valley Pkwy., Henderson; ☎ 702-454-0565. Home cooking by chef Michael Weiss is just like your Yiddish mama made, including terrific meatloaf, giant matzo balls, and rye bread baked on the premises.

The Best Espresso and Dessert

- **The Coffee Bean & Tea Leaf** 4550 S. Maryland Pkwy. ☎ 702-944-5029; coffeebeanlv.com. Many more locations around the city. California-based chain of specialty coffeehouses.

- **Coffee Pub** 2800 W. Sahara Ave., Suite 2A; ☎ 702-367-1913; coffeepublv .com. Great breakfast and lunch location with an imaginative menu.

- **Cypress Street Marketplace** 3570 Las Vegas Blvd. S. (Caesars Palace); ☎ 702-731-7110; caesarspalace.com. Caesars' bakers create pies, cakes, and cookies.

- **Palio** 3600 Las Vegas Blvd. S. (Bellagio); ☎ 702-693-8160; bellagio. com. Cafeteria-style coffeehouse with pastries and casual eats—quiche, salads, and sandwiches, plus ice creams by award-winning dessert chef Jean-Philippe Maury, who has other concessions here and at Aria.

- **Sambalatte Torrefazione** 3770 Las Vegas Blvd. S. (Monte Carlo), ☎ 702-730-7777; 750 Rampart Blvd., Summerlin, ☎ 702-272-2333; sambalatte.com. Many call this the best coffee in Vegas. Brazilian Luiz Oliveira sources all his coffee from plantations in Brazil and brews them in various ways: in Japanese siphon pots, in Chemex pots, and individually. His pastries and sandwiches are top-notch, too.

- **Spago** The Forum Shops at Caesars; 3500 Las Vegas Blvd. S.; ☎ 702-369-6300; wolfgangpuck.com. Wolfgang Puck's pastry chef crafts imaginative and sinful creations. Available all day in the café and at dinner in the dining room.

The Best Oyster and Clam Bars

- **Bouchon** 3355 Las Vegas Blvd. S. (The Venetian); ☎ 702-414-6200; bouchonbistro.com/lasvegas. French Laundry chef Thomas Keller sources the highest quality seafood possible.

- **Emeril's New Orleans Fish House** 3799 Las Vegas Blvd. S. (MGM Grand); ☎ 702-891-7374; mgmgrand.com. Check out the 2–6 p.m. happy hour, where oysters are just $1.50 apiece, and don't miss the banana cream pie after you've finished.

- **Morels Steakhouse** 3225 Las Vegas Blvd. S. (The Palazzo); ☎ 702-607-6333; morelslv.com. On any given day, you'll find at least six varieties of oysters at the iced seafood bar, as well as one of the town's best selections of gourmet cheese.

- **The Oyster Bar** 2411 W. Sahara Ave. (Palace Station); ☎ 702-367-2411; palacestation.sclv.com. Fans line up for hours for fresh oysters and clams, as well as gumbos, chowders, and pan roasts at this tiny, round-the-clock operation.

- **RM Seafood** 3950 Las Vegas Blvd. S. (Mandalay Bay) ☎ 702-632-9300; mandalaybay.com. A rotating selection of oysters from around the world from celebrity chef Rick Moonen.

The Best Pizza

- **Dom DeMarco's Pizzeria & Bar** 9875 W. Charleston Blvd. ☎ 702-570-7000; domdemarcos.com. This offshoot of Di Fara Pizza in Brooklyn has many devotees. The meatballs and sausage are made on-premises.

- **Due Forni Pizza & Wine** 3555 Town Center Dr.; ☎ 702-586-6500; dueforni.com. Carlos Buscaglia, former chef at Fiamma in the MGM Grand, cooks delicious pizzas in a pair of Cirigliano ovens imported from Naples (the pizzeria's name means "two ovens").

- **Metro Pizza** 1395 E. Tropicana Ave.; ☎ 702-736-1955; metropizza.com. Fast service and generous with the cheese. Try the Olde New York with thick-sliced mozzarella, plum tomatoes, and basil. Rich, hearty marinara.

- **Pizza Rock** 201 N. 3rd St.; ☎ 702-385-0838; pizzarocklasvegas.com. Nine different styles of pizza served in a nightclub environment. Look for a new location to open soon at Green Valley Ranch.

- **Pop Up Pizza** 1 S. Main St.; ☎ 702-366-0049; popuppizzalv.com. Creative signature pies and fresh ingredients in the newly remodeled Plaza Hotel.

- **Radio City Pizza** 508 E. Fremont St.; ☎ 702-982-5055; radiocitypizza .com. Try this Downtown spot for great specials, late-night weekend dining, and a wide assortment of specialty pizzas.

- **Settebello** 140 S. Green Valley Pkwy., Henderson; ☎ 702-222-3556; 9350 W. Sahara Ave., Suite 170; 702-901-4877; settebello.net. Real Neapolitan-style pizzas cooked in a wood-fired stone oven. Toppings are from Mario Batali's father's *salumeria* in Seattle. The city's best pizza, hands-down.

Continued on page 374

The Best Las Vegas Restaurants

CUISINE	OVERALL RATING	PRICE	QUALITY RATING	VALUE RATING
AMERICAN				
SAGE	★★★★½	Very Exp	★★★★½	★★★★
TOP OF THE WORLD	★★★★½	Expensive	★★★★½	★★★½
BOTERO	★★★★	Very Exp	★★★★½	★★★★
HONEY SALT	★★★★	Moderate	★★★★	★★★★
PUBLIC HOUSE	★★★★	Moderate	★★★★	★★★★
VINTNER GRILL	★★★★	Mod/Exp	★★★★	★★★★
SPAGO	★★★½	Expensive	★★★★½	★★½
WOLFGANG PUCK PIZZERIA & CUCINA	★★★½	Expensive	★★★★	★★★½
ENGLISH P.U.B.	★★★½	Expensive	★★★½	★★★★
EAT	★★★½	Inexpensive	★★★½	★★★½
TABLE 34	★★★½	Moderate	★★★½	★★★½
ASIAN/PACIFIC RIM				
ANDREA'S	★★★★½	Very Exp	★★★★½	★★★½
NOODLES	★★★	Moderate	★★★★	★★★½
BRAZILIAN				
FOGO DE CHÃO	★★★½	Mod/Exp	★★★★	★★★★
BURGERS				
GORDON RAMSAY BURGR	★★★½	Moderate	★★★★	★★★
CHINESE				
PEARL	★★★★	Expensive	★★★★	★★½
SHAANXI GOURMET	★★★½	Inexpensive	★★★½	★★★★
PING PANG PONG	★★★½	Moderate	★★★½	★★★½
CHINA MAMA	★★★	Inexpensive	★★★★	★★★★
CHINA POBLANO	★★★	Moderate	★★★★	★★★★
NOODLES	★★★	Moderate	★★★★	★★★½
CONTINENTAL/FRENCH				
TWIST	★★★★★	Very Exp	★★★★★	★★★★★
L'ATELIER DE JOËL ROBUCHON	★★★★★	Very Exp	★★★★★	★★★
JOËL ROBUCHON	★★★★★	Very Exp	★★★★★	★★★
RESTAURANT GUY SAVOY	★★★★★	Very Exp	★★★★★	★★★
PICASSO	★★★★½	Very Exp	★★★★	★★½
COMME ÇA	★★★★	Exp/V Exp	★★★★½	★★★★
MARCHÉ BACCHUS: FRENCH BISTRO AND WINE SHOP	★★★★	Moderate	★★★★	★★★★
BOUCHON	★★★½	Moderate	★★★★	★★★★
FLEUR	★★★½	Mod/V Exp	★★★★	★★★½
MON AMI GABI	★★★½	Mod/Exp	★★★★	★★★½
CENTRAL	★★★½	Mod/Exp	★★★★	★★★
CUBAN				
FLORIDA CAFÉ	★★★	Inexpensive	★★★½	★★★★½

The Best Las Vegas Restaurants

CUISINE	OVERALL RATING	PRICE	QUALITY RATING	VALUE RATING
GERMAN				
HOFBRÄUHAUS	★★★	Moderate	★★★½	★★★★½
GREEK				
ESTIATORIO MILOS	★★★★★	Very Exp	★★★★★	★★★★
EASTERN EUROPEAN				
FORTE	★★★	Moderate	★★★	★★★★
ECLECTIC				
ROSE. RABBIT. LIE.	★★★★	Exp/V Exp	★★★★½	★★½
POPPY DEN	★★★★	Moderate	★★★★	★★★★
RX BOILER ROOM	★★★★	Mod/Exp	★★★★	★★★½
ENGLISH				
ENGLISH P.U.B.	★★★½	Expensive	★★★½	★★★★
ITALIAN				
BARTOLOTTA RISTORANTE DI MARE	★★★★½	Very Exp	★★★★½	★★★★
FIAMMA TRATTORIA & BAR	★★★★	Mod/V Exp	★★★★	★★★½
SCARPETTA	★★★★	Expensive	★★★★	★★★½
DUE FORNI	★★★½	Moderate	★★★★	★★★★
B&B RISTORANTE	★★★	Very Exp	★★★★	★★★
RAO'S	★★★	Expensive	★★★★	★★
SINATRA	★★★	Expensive	★★★	★★
JAMAICAN/NEW MEXICAN				
DW BISTRO	★★★	Moderate	★★★½	★★★★
JAPANESE *(see also Sushi)*				
KABUTO	★★★★★	Very Exp	★★★★★	★★★★★
BARMASA	★★★★★	Very Exp	★★★★★	★★
NOBU	★★★★½	Very Exp	★★★★★	★★★½
MIZUMI	★★★★½	Very Exp	★★★★½	★★★
RAKU	★★★★	Moderate	★★★★	★★★★
KYARA	★★★½	Moderate	★★★★	★★★★★
TRATTORIA NAKAMURA-YA	★★★½	Moderate	★★★	★★★
NOODLES	★★★	Moderate	★★★★	★★★½
MONTA	★★½	Inexp	★★★★	★★★★★
MEXICAN				
DESNUDO TACOS	★★★½	Inexp	★★★★	★★★★★
CHINA POBLANO	★★★	Moderate	★★★★	★★★★
PIZZA				
SETTEBELLO	★★★½	Moderate	★★★★	★★★
SEAFOOD				
BARTOLOTTA RISTORANTE DI MARE	★★★★½	Very Exp	★★★★½	★★★★
JOE'S SEAFOOD, PRIME STEAK & STONE CRAB	★★★★½	Expensive	★★★★½	★★★½

The Best Las Vegas Restaurants

CUISINE	OVERALL RATING	PRICE	QUALITY RATING	VALUE RATING
SEAFOOD (continued)				
TODD'S UNIQUE DINING	★★★★	Mod/Exp	★★★★	★★★★
EMERIL'S NEW ORLEANS FISH HOUSE	★★★½	Expensive	★★★	★★★
SOUTH AMERICAN				
VIVA LAS AREPAS	★★★½	Inexp	★★★½	★★★★
SPANISH				
JALEO	★★★★½	Expensive	★★★★	★★★★
PICASSO	★★★★½	Very Exp	★★★★	★★½
JULIAN SERRANO	★★★★	Expensive	★★★★	★★★★
FORTE	★★★	Moderate	★★★	★★★★
STEAK				
GORDON RAMSAY STEAK	★★★★½	Very Exp	★★★★½	★★★½
JOE'S SEAFOOD, PRIME STEAK & STONE CRAB	★★★★½	Expensive	★★★★½	★★★½
OLD HOMESTEAD STEAKHOUSE	★★★★	Very Exp	★★★★½	★★★½
PRIME	★★★★	Very Exp	★★★★½	★★½
TODD'S UNIQUE DINING	★★★★	Mod/Exp	★★★★	★★★★
THE STEAK HOUSE	★★★½	Expensive	★★★½	★★★½
SUSHI (see also Japanese)				
KABUTO	★★★★★	Very Exp	★★★★★	★★★★★
BARMASA	★★★★★	Very Exp	★★★★★	★★
NOBU	★★★★½	Very Exp	★★★★★	★★★½
MIZUMI	★★★★½	Very Exp	★★★★½	★★★
SEN OF JAPAN	★★★★	Mod/Exp	★★★★	★★★½
THAI				
PENN'S THAI HOUSE	★★★★	Inexpensive	★★★★	★★★★★
CHADA THAI & WINE	★★★★	Inexp/Mod	★★★★	★★★★
LOTUS OF SIAM	★★★★	Moderate	★★★★	★★½
NOODLES	★★★	Moderate	★★★★	★★★½
VIETNAMESE				
NOODLES	★★★	Moderate	★★★★	★★★½
ROOMS WITH A VIEW				
TOP OF THE WORLD	★★★★	Expensive	★★★★	★★★½

Continued from page 371

- **Spago** The Forum Shops at Caesars, 3500 Las Vegas Blvd. S.
  ☎ 702-369-6300; **wolfgangpuck.com**. The duck-sausage and smoked-salmon-with-dill-cream pies are legendary.

Restaurants with a View

- **Alizé** 4321 W. Flamingo Rd. (Palms); ☎ 702-951-7000; **palms.com**. At the top of the Palms, Alizé has a panoramic view that takes in portions of the Strip.

- **Comme Ca** 3708 Las Vegas Blvd. S. (Cosmopolitan); ☎ 702-698-7910; **commecarestaurant.com/las-vegas.** David Myers' excellent French bistro has a third-floor patio with a great northward view of the Strip.
- **Eiffel Tower Restaurant** 3655 Las Vegas Blvd. S. (Paris Las Vegas); ☎ 702-948-6937; **parislasvegas.com.** Fancy French food in a drop-dead gorgeous setting that towers over the Strip. This is one spectacular view that encompasses the fountains at Bellagio.
- **Foundation Room** 3950 Las Vegas Blvd. S. (Mandalay Bay); ☎ 702-632-7631; **houseofblues.com/lasvegas/fr.** This private club and lounge run by the House of Blues has a public restaurant and patios with a great northward view of the Strip.
- **Marche Bacchus** 2620 Regatta Dr.; ☎ 702-804-8008; **marchebacchus .com.** French bistro and wine shop on a gorgeous man-made lake in the suburbs.
- **Picasso** 3600 Las Vegas Blvd. S. (Bellagio); ☎ 702-693-7223; **bellagio.com.** Highly original food and glorious original artwork by the master himself. As good as it gets . . . unless you eat at Le Grand Véfour in the Louvre.
- **Top of the World Restaurant** 2000 Las Vegas Blvd. S. (Stratosphere); ☎ 702-380-7711; **topoftheworldlv.com.** Revolving dining room with excellent food and the highest and best views of any of the other restaurants in this list.
- **VooDoo Steak & Lounge** 3700 W. Flamingo Rd. (Rio); ☎ 702-777-7800; **riolasvegas.com.** At the top of the Masquerade tower, VooDoo offers a complete view of the city, steaks and French-Creole dishes, and a late-night lounge.

RESTAURANT PROFILES

Andrea's ★★★★

PAN-ASIAN	VERY EXPENSIVE	QUALITY ★★★★	VALUE ★★★½

Wynn Encore Resort, 3131 Las Vegas Blvd. S.; ☎ 702-770-7000; tinyurl.com/andreaswynn   **Mid-Strip and Environs**

Customers Visitors, locals. **Reservations** Essential. **When to go** Anytime. **Entrée range** $18–$65. **Payment** All major credit cards. **Service rating** ★★★★½. **Friendliness rating** ★★★★½. **Parking** Valet, lot. **Bar** Full service. **Wine selection** Excellent. **Dress** Upscale casual. **Disabled access** Yes. **Hours** Daily, 6:40 p.m.–2 a.m.

SETTING AND ATMOSPHERE The sensuous, color-shifting eyes that flash over the bar at this Asian-fusion restaurant at Wynn Encore belong to Steve Wynn's wife, Andrea. The chic decor is by Todd-Avery Lenahan, an airy cream-and-gold space with windows that open to Surrender Night Club. The ceiling is studded with geometric rows of crystal teardrops. It's all quite impressive.

HOUSE SPECIALTIES Chef Joseph Elevado used to cook for Nobu, so don't be surprised to find sashimi, sushi, and loads of Japanese specialties on his menu. Many Asian bases are covered here, though. *Tom kha gai,* a creamy chicken soup with coconut and ginger, is distinctly Thai. One could argue that the chef's whole crispy fish in a tomato-and-egg broth is Filipino.

OTHER RECOMMENDATIONS Sixty-five bucks may seem a lot for a steak, but

Elevado does a Japanese Kobe rib cap worth the indulgence. Five-spice garlic lobster, served with long beans, is also great, in spite of another hefty price tag. For less-wallet-busting fare, shishito peppers and an excellent take on edamame (Japanese green soybeans) are a real bargain.

SUMMARY AND COMMENTS This restaurant may seem redundant, in the sense that the resort has three other Asian restaurants: Mizumi (see page 400), Wing Lei, and Wazuzu, a sushi-and-noodle house. But because Andrea's is targeting the nightclub crowd, it seems like a smart addition, as guests can slide effortlessly to Surrender next door.

L'Atelier de Joël Robuchon ★★★★★

FRENCH **VERY EXPENSIVE** **QUALITY ★★★★★** **VALUE ★★★**

MGM Grand, 3799 Las Vegas Blvd. S.; ☎ 702-891-7358; mgmgrand.com **South Strip and Environs**

Customers Visitors, locals. **Reservations** A must. **When to go** Anytime. **Entrée range** $70–$230. **Payment** All major credit cards. **Service rating ★★★★★**. **Friendliness rating ★★★**. **Parking** Valet, garage. **Bar** Full service. **Wine selection** Excellent. **Dress** Upscale casual. **Disabled access** Yes. **Hours** Daily, 5–11 p.m.

SETTING AND ATMOSPHERE Chef Joël Robuchon's casual concept offers guests a view into his culinary workshop, thanks to an open-air kitchen that dissolves the boundaries between kitchen and dining room. Chic and contemporary, with shades of black and red, L'Atelier is more laid-back than his fine-dining Joël Robuchon Restaurant next door (see page 396), and more interactive with the staff if you sit at the bar around the open kitchen.

HOUSE SPECIALTIES *Caille au foie gras:* tender roast quail stuffed with foie gras and served with Robuchon's famous mashed potatoes, equal parts butter and potato.

OTHER RECOMMENDATIONS To get the full experience, opt for the five-course tasting menu, which changes seasonally and offers L'Atelier's best dishes in a thoughtful progression. Those with theater tickets will find an early-bird menu featuring an appetizer and the roast of the day for $48.

SUMMARY AND COMMENTS L'Atelier is fun—a less buttoned-up way to enjoy fine dining. Dining aficionados will appreciate watching the silent orchestra of chefs and cooks in their element, and the care it takes to create one of Robuchon's masterly dishes.

B&B Ristorante ★★★

ITALIAN **VERY EXPENSIVE** **QUALITY ★★★★** **VALUE ★★★**

The Venetian, 3355 Las Vegas Blvd. S.; ☎ 702-266-9977; bandbristorante.com **Mid-Strip and Environs**

Customers Visitors, locals. **Reservations** Suggested. **When to go** Anytime. **Entrée range** $35–$60. **Payment** All major credit cards. **Service rating ★★★**. **Friendliness rating ★★★**. **Parking** Valet, garage. **Bar** Full service. **Wine selection** Comprehensive, with wines from every region in Italy. **Dress** Upscale casual. **Disabled access** Yes. **Hours** Daily, 5–11 p.m.; bar open until midnight.

SETTING AND ATMOSPHERE Dark woods and white tablecloths make this Italian restaurant feel like a classic supper club.

HOUSE SPECIALTIES Rustic Italian, of course. Cured meats are made in-house or from Salumi, the Seattle store of chef Mario Batali's father. Pastas are wonderful, such as *bucatini all'amatriciana* (hollow spaghetti-like pasta flavored

Dining and Nightlife on the South Strip

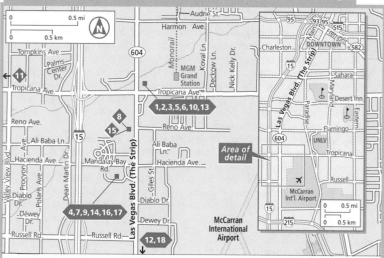

RESTAURANTS
1. L'Atelier de Joël Robuchon
2. Emeril's New Orleans Fish House
3. Fiamma Trattoria
4. Fleur
5. Jöel Robuchon
6. Pearl
7. Rx Boiler Room

Buffets:
8. Luxor's MORE Buffet
9. Mandalay Bay's Bayside Buffet
10. MGM Grand Buffet
11. Orleans French Market

NIGHTLIFE
12. Blue Martini Lounge
13. Hakkasan
14. House of Blues
15. LAX
16. Light
17. Rí Rá Las Vegas
18. Stoney's Rockin' Country

with cured *guanciale,* marbled hog jowl) or a seasonal offering like tiny ravioli stuffed with tomato confit and sauced with pork innards. That's just one example of how Batali loves to use organ meats in his cooking.

OTHER RECOMMENDATIONS Calamari Sicilian Lifeguard–Style, rings of delicate calamari with a subtly spicy tomato sauce, and an amazing beef *brasato.* A sumptuous five-course pasta tasting menu is available paired with wines, selected by Batali's partner, Joe Bastianich. (Hence B&B.)

SUMMARY AND COMMENTS For a more casual experience, check out the other Batali outpost within the Grand Canal Shoppes at The Venetian, Otto Enoteca & Pizzeria, which offers more of a wine-bar experience and great people-watching, plus that great *salumi* from Batali's father.

barMASA ★★★★★

| JAPANESE | VERY EXPENSIVE | QUALITY ★★★★★ | VALUE ★★ |

Aria at CityCenter, 3730 Las Vegas Blvd. S.; ☎ 702-590-7111; tinyurl.com/barmasavegas **Mid-Strip and Environs**

Customers Visitors. **Reservations** Essential. **When to go** Anytime. **Entrée range**

$18–$240; early-evening menu, $49. **Payment** All major credit cards. **Service rating** ★★★★★. **Friendliness rating** ★★★★★. **Parking** Valet, lot. **Bar** Sake, wine, beer. **Wine selection** Excellent. **Dress** Upscale. **Disabled access** Yes. **Hours** Thursday–Tuesday, 5–11 p.m.

SETTING AND ATMOSPHERE Unlike chef Masa Takayama's intimate bar at New York City's Time Warner Center, this is a huge, high-ceilinged room the size of an airplane hangar. The ultramodern design came from sketches done by the chef.

HOUSE SPECIALTIES There is much more than the exquisite *nigiri*-style sushi, made from fish flown in daily from Tokyo's Tsukiji Fish Market. Broiled skewers of Kobe beef and sizzling octopus salad are just a few of the nonsushi items gracing this eclectic menu. The *otoro,* fatty tuna belly said to be the world's best, is softer than butter.

OTHER RECOMMENDATIONS Tetsu, an amazing (and, yes, high-priced) teppanyaki bar, has been added alongside the dining room. The food is great, but don't expect any of the knife tricks you find at your local Benihana.

SUMMARY AND COMMENTS No one can deny the impeccable quality of the food, the wonderful service, or the stunning design. But this can be one of the most expensive restaurants in Vegas. If you want to sample the cuisine on a budget, dine between 5 and 7 p.m., when you can get a seven-course bento box for just $49, with a wine and sake pairing available for $24.

Bartolotta Ristorante Di Mare   ★★★★

ITALIAN/SEAFOOD	VERY EXPENSIVE	QUALITY ★★★★	VALUE ★★★★

Wynn Las Vegas, 3131 Las Vegas Blvd. S.; ☎ 702-770-7000; tinyurl.com/bartolottaristorante   **Mid-Strip and Environs**

Customers Visitors, locals. **Reservations** Recommended. **When to go** Anytime. **Entrée range** $24–$130. **Payment** All major credit cards. **Service rating** ★★★★½. **Friendliness rating** ★★★★★. **Parking** Valet, lot. **Bar** Full service. **Wine selection** Excellent. **Dress** Upscale. **Disabled access** Yes. **Hours** Daily, 5:30–10 p.m.

SETTING AND ATMOSPHERE Bartolotta is a bi-level restaurant done with elegant Italian appointments. The upstairs, just off a corridor of the Wynn shopping arcade, is slightly less ornate and well suited for business dinners. Downstairs are a pool with private tables by a cabana, perfect for a romantic tryst, and tables inside close to the action in the kitchen. The place recently received a makeover, but the overall feel hasn't changed.

HOUSE SPECIALTIES Chef Paul Bartolotta has fresh Mediterranean fish flown in from Italy several times a week. Spiny lobster, rockfish, bigeye, and sea bream are just a few of the selections. You can have them a variety of ways—grilled, encased in salt, or *alla palermitana* (Sicilian-style with capers, olives, and tomatoes). Try the *agnolotti del plin,* tiny stuffed pastas, for your appetizer.

SUMMARY AND COMMENTS This place can be quite expensive, but it's not Chef Bartolotta's fault. He must have the highest food costs in Vegas, thanks to Mr. Steve Wynn, who lets him travel and spend money as if it were going out of style. Nonetheless, it's an experience you can't get anywhere else in this country.

Botero   ★★★★

NEW AMERICAN	VERY EXPENSIVE	QUALITY ★★★★	VALUE ★★★★

Wynn Encore Resort, 3131 Las Vegas Blvd. S.; ☎ 702-770-7000; tinyurl.com/boterolv   **Mid-Strip and Environs**

Customers Visitors. **Reservations** Recommended. **When to go** Anytime. **Entrée range** $33–$115. **Payment** All major credit cards. **Service rating** ★★★★★.

Dining and Nightlife Mid-Strip

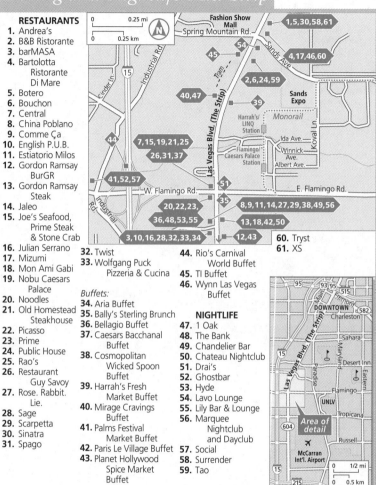

RESTAURANTS
1. Andrea's
2. B&B Ristorante
3. barMASA
4. Bartolotta Ristorante Di Mare
5. Botero
6. Bouchon
7. Central
8. China Poblano
9. Comme Ça
10. English P.U.B.
11. Estiatorio Milos
12. Gordon Ramsay BurGR
13. Gordon Ramsay Steak
14. Jaleo
15. Joe's Seafood, Prime Steak & Stone Crab
16. Julian Serrano
17. Mizumi
18. Mon Ami Gabi
19. Nobu Caesars Palace
20. Noodles
21. Old Homestead Steakhouse
22. Picasso
23. Prime
24. Public House
25. Rao's
26. Restaurant Guy Savoy
27. Rose. Rabbit. Lie.
28. Sage
29. Scarpetta
30. Sinatra
31. Spago
32. Twist
33. Wolfgang Puck Pizzeria & Cucina

Buffets:
34. Aria Buffet
35. Bally's Sterling Brunch
36. Bellagio Buffet
37. Caesars Bacchanal Buffet
38. Cosmopolitan Wicked Spoon Buffet
39. Harrah's Fresh Market Buffet
40. Mirage Cravings Buffet
41. Palms Festival Market Buffet
42. Paris Le Village Buffet
43. Planet Hollywood Spice Market Buffet
44. Rio's Carnival World Buffet
45. TI Buffet
46. Wynn Las Vegas Buffet

NIGHTLIFE
47. 1 Oak
48. The Bank
49. Chandelier Bar
50. Chateau Nightclub
51. Drai's
52. Ghostbar
53. Hyde
54. Lavo Lounge
55. Lily Bar & Lounge
56. Marquee Nightclub and Dayclub
57. Social
58. Surrender
59. Tao
60. Tryst
61. XS

Friendliness rating ★★★★★. **Parking** Valet, lot. **Bar** Full service. **Wine selection** Excellent. **Dress** Upscale. **Disabled access** Yes. **Hours** Sunday–Thursday, 5:30–10:30 p.m.; Friday and Saturday, 5:30–11 p.m.

SETTING AND ATMOSPHERE The restaurant is named for Fernando Botero, a Colombian sculptor who has a $2.3-million piece smack in the middle of the dining room. As if that weren't special enough, the best tables front the Wynn pool visible through panoramic floor-to-ceiling windows.

HOUSE SPECIALTIES Crispy frog legs and *hamachi* tartare are two of the appetizers on Mark LoRusso's menu. The chef is a Michael Mina product, which means he's adept at seafood, and his Mediterranean sea bass, olive oil-poached wild salmon, and crispy tai snapper are menu highlights.

Dining and Nightlife on the North Strip

◆ **RESTAURANTS**
1. Florida Café
2. THE Steak House
3. Top of the World

▰ **NIGHTLIFE**
4. Artisan Afterhours

OTHER RECOMMENDATIONS LoRusso, who is almost always in the kitchen, is a star with meats as well. Bone-in rib eye and filet mignon are accompanied by a choice of mouthwatering condiments such as *chimichurri* or pepper sauce. Kobe short rib and brioche-crusted Colorado lamb rack stand out as well. Botero also boasts one of the city's most accomplished vegan menus—dishes that will make you rethink eating meatless.

SUMMARY AND COMMENTS This is dining for grown-ups. Genteel and atmospheric, it's one of the best restaurants at Wynn Encore. The hotel has stocked the cellars with some of the best wines in town. Prices are commensurate.

Bouchon ★★★½

| FRENCH BISTRO | EXPENSIVE | QUALITY ★★★★ | VALUE ★★★★ |

The Venetian, 3355 Las Vegas Blvd. S.; ☎ 702-414-6200;
bouchonbistro.com/lasvegas   **Mid-Strip and Environs**

Customers Visitors, locals. **Reservations** A must on weekends. **When to go** Anytime. **Entrée range** $25–$45. **Payment** All major credit cards. **Service rating** ★★★★½. **Friendliness rating** ★★★★½. **Parking** Valet, garage. **Bar** Full service. **Wine selection** Very good. **Dress** Upscale casual. **Disabled access** Yes (elevator). **Hours** Daily, 7 a.m.–1 p.m. and 5–10 p.m.; Saturday and Sunday brunch, 8 a.m.–2 p.m.; Oyster Bar & Lounge, 3–10 p.m.

SETTING AND ATMOSPHERE Chef-owner Thomas Keller and renowned restaurant and hotel designer Adam Tihany have designed a Belle Époque room filled with ornate floor tiles and brass. You could easily be on a Paris boulevard.

HOUSE SPECIALTIES Fresh seafood *plateaus*—grand plates with an assortment of freshly shucked raw items and shrimp and lobster; superb oysters (selection changes with the season); country pâté served with cornichons and radishes; roast leg of lamb with flageolet beans in thyme jus.

OTHER RECOMMENDATIONS Salmon *rillettes* in a glass jar; steak *frites,* an herb-roasted flatiron steak or grilled New York strip with French fries; endive salad with Roquefort, apples, walnuts, and walnut vinaigrette; white sausage with potato puree and caramelized apples.

SUMMARY AND COMMENTS The most requested tables are on the outdoor terrace. They're difficult to get, but worth a try. Many à la carte options are available at a moderate cost.

Central ★★★½

| FRENCH/AMERICAN | MODERATE/EXPENSIVE | QUALITY ★★★★ | VALUE ★★★ |

Caesars Palace, 3570 Las Vegas Blvd. S., ☎ 702-731-7110;
tinyurl.com/centrallasvegas   **Mid-Strip and Environs**

Customers Locals. **Reservations** Not required. **When to go** Anytime. **Entrée range** $20–$65. **Payment** All major credit cards. **Service rating** ★★★. **Friendliness rating** ★★★. **Parking** Valet. **Bar** Yes. **Wine selection** Good. **Dress** Casual. **Disabled access** Yes. **Hours** Daily, 24 hours.

SETTING AND ATMOSPHERE Chef Michel Richard refers to his huge space as a bistro, handsome and extravagant though it is. The room is designed with a reflective silver-leaf ceiling, stacks of giant white plates, and bright, almost aggressive lighting. An intelligently placed lobby bar lets you see the action in Caesars Palace. Tables have laminated tops.

HOUSE SPECIALTIES The menu is pretty close to what you get in the original Central in Washington D.C.: sensational burgers, such as chicken and lemon with wafer-thin rounds of potato between meat and bun, along with a crab burger that would please a Marylander. Deviled eggs are exceptionally creamy yolks topped with a *boquerone,* or white anchovy from Spain. The fried chicken has a devoted following, too.

OTHER RECOMMENDATIONS Central has excellent breakfasts, from a finely minced corned-beef hash to one of Richard's signatures: French-toast crème brûlée, two pieces of brioche with pastry cream in the center. Pork loin with flageolet beans, sort of a poor man's cassoulet, is another must.

SUMMARY AND COMMENTS Richard began his career as a pastry chef, and he hasn't lost his touch; desserts here are among the best in the city. Save room for the Napoleon, layered with rich, deep yellow Bavarian cream. But Central isn't always as busy as it should be. It replaced a coffee shop, and a question remains: Will patrons pay uptown prices for what is essentially diner food?

Chada Thai & Wine ★★★★

THAI	INEXPENSIVE/MODERATE	QUALITY ★★★★	VALUE ★★★★

3400 S. Jones Blvd.; ☎ 702-641-1345; chadavegas.com   **West of Strip**

Customers Locals. **Reservations** Suggested. **When to go** Anytime. **Entrée range** $7–$23. **Payment** All major credit cards. **Service rating** ★★★½. **Friendliness rating** ★★★½. **Parking** Lot. **Bar** Beer and wine. **Wine selection** Excellent. **Dress** Casual. **Disabled access** None. **Hours** Daily, 5 p.m.–3 a.m.

SETTING AND ATMOSPHERE Former Lotus of Siam wine director Bank Atacharawan has done something truly original here, opening a wine-friendly small-plates Asian restaurant that features regional dishes from his native Thailand. Chada Thai & Wine is a narrow, minimalist space, with gray walls, black-leather banquettes, and a chandelier draped in faux red rubies that would look at home in a New Orleans cathouse.

HOUSE SPECIALTIES Chada's pad thai—*pad thai hor kai* on the menu—is mild and delicate, with a plain omelet wrapper like you'd get at a street stall in Bangkok. *Tod mun,* Thai fish cakes, are made with shrimp here; they're sweet, crisply fried, and delicious. *Nua dad diew,* which many call Thai beef jerky, is cut into small, manageable pieces, making it less chewy.

OTHER RECOMMENDATIONS *Eiw pung,* three bite-size clumps of sticky rice crowned with dry shrimp, barbecued pork, and crispy onion, reminds me of Chinese tamales. Panang curry, slow-cooked chunks of fall-apart-tender stewed beef in a rich coconut cream, works best spooned onto white rice.

SUMMARY AND COMMENTS The emphasis on wine adds to what is an outstanding concept. Spicier offerings go better with beer than with most wines, but some dishes, such as *peak kai nam peung* (superb grilled chicken wings with honey sauce) and *nuang buoy* (sea bass with piquant plum sauce), are amazing with one of Bank's off-dry Kabinett Rieslings.

China MaMa ★★★

CHINESE	INEXPENSIVE	QUALITY ★★★★	VALUE ★★★★

3420 S. Jones Blvd.; ☎ 702-873-1977   **West of Strip**

Customers Locals. **Reservations** Accepted. **When to go** Anytime. **Entrée range** $7–$12. **Payment** All major credit cards. **Service rating** ★★★. **Friendliness rating** ★★★★★. **Parking** Lot. **Bar** None. **Wine selection** None. **Dress** Casual. **Disabled access** Yes. **Hours** Daily, 11 a.m.–10 p.m.

SETTING AND ATMOSPHERE Just off the main drag of Las Vegas's Chinatown, China MaMa is bright and welcoming.

HOUSE SPECIALTIES Shanghai soup dumplings (called "juicy pork dumplings" on the menu) are dough-wrapped pockets of meat with steaming soup in the middle. Carefully bite off the top, slurp out the delicious, savory broth, and then add a bit of the Chinese black vinegar and ginger that accompanies the dish. Pot stickers are also done very well.

OTHER RECOMMENDATIONS The beef roll; fish filet poached in a fiery red chili oil and served in a giant clay pot—perfect with a bowl of rice.

SUMMARY AND COMMENTS Most dishes here have authentic flavors you won't find

Dining and Nightlife East of Strip

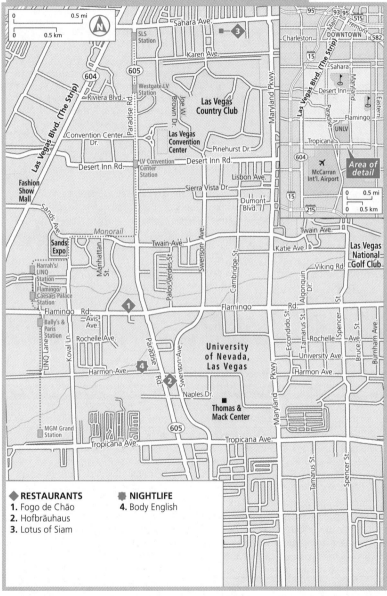

◆ RESTAURANTS
1. Fogo de Chão
2. Hofbräuhaus
3. Lotus of Siam

▪ NIGHTLIFE
4. Body English

in most other American Chinese restaurants. The Shanghai soup dumplings—ubiquitous in Asia—are finally done right here.

China Poblano ★★★

| CHINESE/MEXICAN | MODERATE | QUALITY ★★★★ | VALUE ★★★★ |

The Cosmopolitan, 3708 Las Vegas Blvd. S.; ☎ 702-698-7000; chinapoblano.com **Mid-Strip and Environs**

Customers Locals, hotel guests, conventioneers. **Reservations** Accepted. **When to go** Anytime. **Entrée range** $3.95–$20.95. **Payment** All major credit cards. **Service rating** ★★★★★. **Friendliness rating** ★★★★★. **Parking** Valet, garage. **Bar** Full service. **Wine selection** Fair. **Dress** Casual. **Disabled access** Yes. **Hours** Daily, 11:30 a.m.–11:30 p.m.

SETTING AND ATMOSPHERE Ultramodern, almost wacky decor features communal benches, conceptual art with Asian themes, and wall-mounted LCD panels streaming head shots of famous Asians. There are separate noodle and tortilla bars.

HOUSE SPECIALTIES Hand-rolled noodles with *dan dan* sauce; made-to-order dim sum; crispy quail; tacos such as the Cochinita (Yucatán-style barbecued pork) and the evocatively named Silencio (duck tongue with lychee); various rice plates; seaweed salad; conceptual desserts such as chocolate-enrobed statues representing the famed terra-cotta warriors of Xi'an, China, filled with peanut butter–chocolate mousse.

OTHER RECOMMENDATIONS The rolled pancakes with beef and onions are wonderful, as are a number of oddball China-meets-Mexico dishes that you'll have to see (and try) to understand.

SUMMARY AND COMMENTS This is a groundbreaking restaurant in terms of creativity—concept new to the planet. Chef José Andrés is a wonder, and so are these prices. This has to be the least expensive place to eat in the entire Cosmopolitan.

Comme Ça ★★★★

| CONTINENTAL/FRENCH | EXPENSIVE/VERY EXPENSIVE | QUALITY ★★★★½ | VALUE ★★★★ |

The Cosmopolitan, 3708 Las Vegas Blvd. S.; ☎ 702-698-7910; commecarestaurant.com/las-vegas **Mid-Strip and Environs**

Customers Visitors, locals. **Reservations** Recommended. **When to go** Anytime. **Entrée range** $24–$52. **Payment** All major credit cards. **Service rating** ★★★★½. **Friendliness rating** ★★★★. **Parking** Valet and garage. **Bar** Full service, with excellent cocktail program. **Wine selection** Excellent. **Dress** Upscale casual. **Disabled access** Yes. **Hours** Lunch: Friday–Sunday, noon–5 p.m. Dinner: daily, 5–11 p.m.

SETTING AND ATMOSPHERE Faux chalk drawings adorn the walls in this casual French bistro designed by Adam Tihany. The third-floor outdoor patio boasts one of the best views of the Strip in town; it's close enough to the street to feel the energy, but high enough to escape the madness.

HOUSE SPECIALTIES David Myers is concentrating on the classics these days, which means steak tartare, pan-roasted sweetbreads, onion soup, steak frites, steamed mussels, and boudin blanc, among others. The bar's 18A cocktail program (named after the 18th Amendment, which established prohibition) features expertly crafted prohibition-era libations.

OTHER RECOMMENDATIONS The daily Social Hour, which runs 5–8:30 p.m., offers some good deals, including $2 oysters.

Dining and Nightlife West of Strip

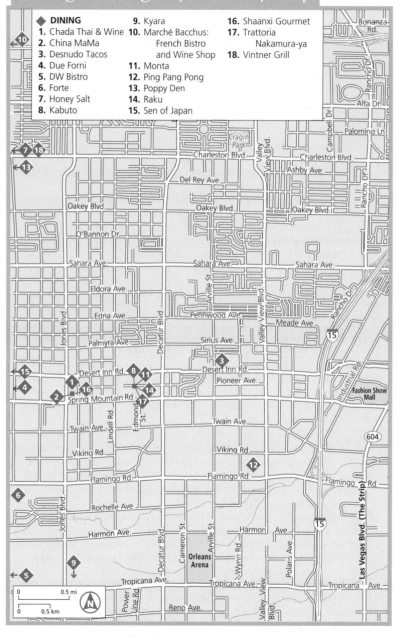

◆ **DINING**
1. Chada Thai & Wine
2. China MaMa
3. Desnudo Tacos
4. Due Forni
5. DW Bistro
6. Forte
7. Honey Salt
8. Kabuto
9. Kyara
10. Marché Bacchus:
    French Bistro
    and Wine Shop
11. Monta
12. Ping Pang Pong
13. Poppy Den
14. Raku
15. Sen of Japan
16. Shaanxi Gourmet
17. Trattoria
    Nakamura-ya
18. Vintner Grill

SUMMARY AND COMMENTS This is exactly what a bistro should be: casual, approachable, and perfectly executed. It's also one of the few places in the Cosmopolitan that's open for lunch.

Desnudo Tacos ★★★½

MEXICAN	INEXPENSIVE	QUALITY ★★★★	VALUE ★★★★★

3240 Arville St.; ☎ 702-243-6277; desnudotacos.com   **West of Strip**

Customers Locals, off-duty chefs. **Reservations** Not required. **When to go** Anytime. **Entrée range** $6–$10. **Payment** All major credit cards. **Service rating** ★★★. **Friendliness rating** ★★★★★. **Parking** Lot. **Bar** None, but full bar next door. **Dress** Casual. **Disabled access** Yes. **Hours** Monday–Thursday, 11 a.m.–10 p.m.; Friday and Saturday, 11 a.m.–11 p.m.; Sunday, 11 a.m.–8 p.m.

SETTING AND ATMOSPHERE Modern tattoo-style artwork honoring Día de los Muertos (Mexico's Day of the Dead) lines the walls. Fresh herbs grow on the counter for use in the dishes. And guests sit at communal picnic tables in this small, casual, hip restaurant.

HOUSE SPECIALTIES Owner Chris Palmeri once worked with the legendary Mexican chef Rick Bayless at the MGM Grand. The tacos here are almost identical to the ones his old boss taught him to prepare, at a fraction of the price.

OTHER RECOMMENDATIONS Don't ignore the rice, beans, or salsas, which Palmeri's ambitious head chef Christian Dolias changes daily.

SUMMARY AND COMMENTS Palmeri has already gotten national TV attention with the divey Naked City Pizza, located next door. At Desnudo (meaning "naked"), he's showing off his Mexican chops in a more upscale family-friendly setting.

Due Forni Pizza & Wine   ★★★½

ITALIAN	MODERATE	QUALITY ★★★★	VALUE ★★★★

3555 Town Center Dr., ☎ 702-586-6500; dueforni.com   **West of Strip**

Customers Locals. **Reservations** Essential. **When to go** Lunch or dinner. **Entrée range** $12–$23. **Payment** All major credit cards. **Service rating** ★★★. **Friendliness rating** ★★★★. **Parking** Lot. **Bar** Yes. **Wine selection** Excellent. **Dress** Casual. **Disabled access** Yes. **Hours** Sunday–Thursday, 11 a.m.–10 p.m.; Friday and Saturday, 11 a.m.–11 p.m.

SETTING AND ATMOSPHERE Due Forni ("two ovens") is dominated by a pair of stone ovens from Cirigliano of Naples, Italy, which take up most of the space in the restaurant's small but efficient open kitchen. Pizzas rotate while cooking, distributing heat evenly. Rows of Edison bulbs, glowing a faint amber, are suspended over the tables. One impressive extra is crockery from the French company Bernardaud, an elegant surprise.

HOUSE SPECIALTIES Pizza, of course. Due Forni serves two styles: an authentic Neapolitan crust (yeasty and medium-thick) and a style the menu calls Roman (cracker-thin and ultra-crisp). Either way, pizzas cook in 90 seconds at 900 degrees. These ovens are superhot, rather like the clay oven called a *tandoor,* used in Indian cooking.

OTHER RECOMMENDATIONS Chef Carlos Buscaglia, an Argentine who speaks fluent Italian, was formerly the chef at Fiamma at the MGM Grand and is an experienced Italian chef familiar with many cooking styles. Dishes such as *polpette* (Italian meatballs) and semolina gnocchi with Nueske's bacon, peas, and black truffle *crema* are wonderful. Salads are also a strong suit.

Dining and Nightlife Downtown

◆ RESTAURANTS
1. Aloha Specialties
2. American Coney Island
3. Andiamo Steakhouse
4. The Beat Coffeehouse
5. Bier Garten
6. Big Ern's BBQ
7. Bin 702
8. Binion's Steakhouse
9. Carson Kitchen
10. Chart House
11. Cheffini's Hot Dogs
12. Chicago Joe's
13. The Commissary
14. Du-par's
15. Eat
16. Grotto
17. Hash House A Go Go
18. Heart Attack Grill
19. Hugo's Cellar
20. La Comida
21. Le Thai
22. Lillie's Asian Cuisine
23. Oscar's Steakhouse
24. Park on Fremont
25. Pasta Pirate
26. Pinches Tacos
27. Pizza Rock
28. Pop Up Pizza
29. Red Mansion
30. Redwood Grill
31. Second Street Grill

32. Siegel's 1941
33. Triple 7
34. Triple George Grill
35. Vic & Anthony's
36. Viva Las Arepas
37. Wild

◼ NIGHTLIFE
38. Commonwealth
39. Downtown Cocktail Room
40. Insert Coin(s)

Fremont Street Experience

Pizza Due Forni, topped with San Marzano tomatoes, *mozzarella di bufala*, the chef's own sausage, Nueske's bacon, and piquillo peppers, is amazing.

SUMMARY AND COMMENTS Due Forni is a welcome addition to the Westside, and well worth the drive from the Strip for pizza-loving tourists. It's already one of the area's most popular places to socialize, and a great wine-by-the-glass program attracts a convivial oenophile crowd.

DW Bistro ★★★

JAMAICAN/NEW MEXICAN	MODERATE	QUALITY ★★★½	VALUE ★★★★

6115 S. Fort Apache Rd.; ☎ 702-527-5201; dwbistro.com   **West of Strip**

Customers Locals. **Reservations** Recommended for weekend brunch. **When to go** Anytime. **Entrée range** $14–$27. **Payment** All major credit cards. **Service rating** ★★★. **Friendliness rating** ★★★★★. **Parking** Lot. **Bar** Full service. **Wine selection** Average. **Disabled access** Yes. **Dress** Casual. **Hours** Tuesday–Thursday, 11 a.m.–9 p.m.; Friday, 11 a.m.–11 p.m.; Saturday, 10 a.m.–11 p.m.; Sunday, 10 a.m.–2 p.m.

SETTING AND ATMOSPHERE The front bar is decorated with starry chandeliers; more-intimate tables can be found in a white-brick alcove. Contemporary art fills the restaurant, which can best be described as cheery and comfortable.

HOUSE SPECIALTIES Two separate cuisines, those of Jamaica and New Mexico, are done expertly here, but it would be wrong to think of this as a fusion restaurant. A bowl of killer red New Mexican slow-cooked pork contrasts with a terrific Jamaican chicken-curry soup, which brims with chopped chicken.

OTHER RECOMMENDATIONS Come for weekend brunch; the jerk pork hash is one of the most compelling dishes in the city. From the more upscale dinner menu, try an irresistible plate of the jerk lamb chops.

SUMMARY AND COMMENTS This improbable place has already become a de facto social club for locals, who gather at the bar several times a week. Desserts, incidentally, such as a Jamaican carrot cake, are the bomb.

Eat ★★★½

AMERICAN	INEXPENSIVE	QUALITY ★★★½	VALUE ★★★½

707 Carson Ave.; ☎ 702-534-1515; eatdtlv.com **Downtown**

Customers Locals. **Reservations** Suggested. **When to go** Anytime. **Entrée range** $5–$13. **Payment** All major credit cards. **Service rating** ★★★. **Friendliness rating** ★★★★. **Parking** Street. **Bar** None. **Wine selection** None. **Dress** Casual. **Disabled access** None. **Hours** Monday–Friday, 8 a.m.–3 p.m.; Saturday and Sunday, 8 a.m.–2 p.m.

SETTING AND ATMOSPHERE Natalie Young's breakfast-and-lunch joint makes a big statement in a small space. Reclaimed furniture such as orange metal chairs and green banquettes blends well with a deconstructed duct ceiling and a dark cement floor. It can get noisy at lunch here, but somehow it manages to be relaxing.

HOUSE SPECIALTIES The ticket here is American comfort foods—anything from the best hot cakes in the city to the occasional fried-chicken special that Chef Nat, as her friends call her, serves from time to time. Young also makes lots of homey soups, salads, and sandwiches, but surprisingly, there is no burger. You'll dream about her mustard seed–driven potato salad, which is one of the best anywhere.

OTHER RECOMMENDATIONS Young makes terrific breakfasts, from shrimp and grits to golden-brown omelets. Her posole soup at lunch is a legend, and she makes a variety of terrific grilled-cheese sandwiches, to console those who come in looking for burgers.

SUMMARY AND COMMENTS Eat is a large part of the Downtown eating renaissance. Young had many fans when she cooked at P.J. Clarke's in The Forum Shops at Caesars, and she is clearly happy in her new digs, which have become a regular breakfast and lunch hangout for Downtown office workers, lawyers, and city officials. This is, to put it simply, down-home fare at its best.

Emeril's New Orleans FishHouse ★★★½

SEAFOOD/NEW ORLEANS	EXPENSIVE	QUALITY ★★★★★★0	VALUE ★★★

MGM Grand, 3799 Las Vegas Blvd. S.; ☎ 702-891-7374; tinyurl.com/emerilsfish **South Strip and Environs**

Customers Visitors, locals. **Reservations** Always. **When to go** Avoid convention times. **Entrée range** $26–$45. **Payment** All major credit cards. **Service rating** ★★★★½. **Friendliness rating** ★★★★½. **Parking** Valet, lot, garage. **Bar** Full service. **Wine selection** Excellent. **Dress** Upscale casual; no sleeveless shirts for men. **Disabled access** Yes, through casino. **Hours** Daily, 11:30 a.m.–2 p.m. and 5–10 p.m.; café and bar: daily, 11:30 a.m.–3 p.m. and 5–10 p.m.

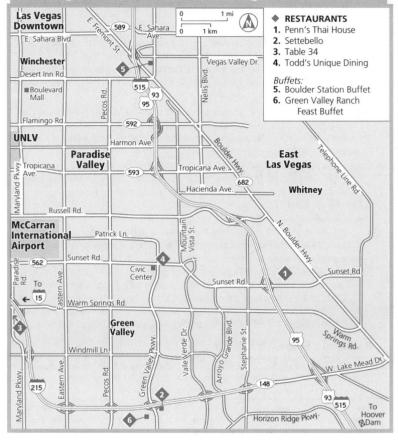

Dining in Southeast Las Vegas–Henderson

♦ RESTAURANTS
1. Penn's Thai House
2. Settebello
3. Table 34
4. Todd's Unique Dining

Buffets:
5. Boulder Station Buffet
6. Green Valley Ranch Feast Buffet

SETTING AND ATMOSPHERE "A bit of New Orleans" is how Emeril Lagasse describes his beautiful restaurant. The main room is comfortable and handsome, with fine appointments and accessories. A separate courtyard dining room is French Quarter pretty, with a faux balcony and louvered shutters. Real plants and a stone floor complete the illusion.

HOUSE SPECIALTIES The always-changing tasting dinners at the chef's table are a fine way to sample small portions of many dishes; some are special recipes being considered for the menu. Emeril's New Orleans–style barbecue shrimp is delicious. You can rely on the good gumbos, the fresh Gulf oysters, and the banana cream pie, which is the best anywhere. Emeril's homemade Worcestershire sauce is addictively good.

SUMMARY AND COMMENTS Emeril's trades heavily on the celebrity of the chef, but you have about a one-in-a-hundred chance of seeing Emeril. The faithful don't seem to care.

English P.U.B. (Public Urban Bar) ★★★½

ENGLISH/AMERICAN	EXPENSIVE	QUALITY ★★★½	VALUE ★★★★

Crystals at CityCenter, 3720 Las Vegas Blvd. S.; ☎ 702-489-8080;
toddenglishpub.com **Mid-Strip and Environs**

Customers Visitors, locals. **Reservations** Not required. **When to go** Avoid large conventions. **Entrée range** $12–$48. **Payment** All major credit cards. **Service rating** ★★★½. **Friendliness rating** ★★★★½. **Parking** Valet, garage. **Bar** Full service. **Wine selection** Good. **Dress** Casual. **Disabled access** Yes. **Hours** Monday–Friday, 11 a.m.–2 a.m.; Saturday and Sunday, 9:30 a.m.–2 a.m.

SETTING AND ATMOSPHERE P.U.B. is a cavernous space on the outskirts of the mall facing SHe, Eva Longoria's restaurant. Decor is traditional English pub, complete with dartboards, drinking games, a high ceiling, and an open kitchen with a huge rotisserie for carved meats.

HOUSE SPECIALTIES The Carvery features meats carved by the chefs, a wide variety of fare ranging from brisket and Long Island duck to roasted turkey breast and Greek-style leg of lamb. There are a number of sauces and breads to choose from as well.

OTHER RECOMMENDATIONS It would be a shame for anyone who likes beer to come here and not experience the super selection of microbrews, handcrafted ales, and imported beers from the major European countries. There are dozens of beers on draft. In addition, savory pub fare such as Welsh rarebit and shepherd's pie are also done well here.

SUMMARY AND COMMENTS This restaurant is a departure for celebrity chef Todd English, and it strikes almost everyone as a good idea. Keep in mind that things get a little rowdy during major sports weekends. Longtime local chef Jean Paul Labadie, an Emeril's alum, is cooking with gas at the rotisseries here.

Estiatorio Milos ★★★★★

GREEK	VERY EXPENSIVE	QUALITY ★★★★★	VALUE ★★★★

The Cosmopolitan, 3708 Las Vegas Blvd. S.; ☎ 702-698-7000;
milos.ca/restaurants/las-vegas **Mid-Strip and Environs**

Customers Visitors, locals. **Reservations** Always. **When to go** Avoid convention times. **Entrée range** $22–$75. **Payment** All major credit cards. **Service rating** ★★★★½. **Friendliness rating** ★★★★½. **Parking** Valet, lot, garage. **Bar** Full service. **Wine selection** Excellent. **Dress** Upscale casual. **Disabled access** Yes. **Hours** Sunday–Thursday, noon–11 p.m.; Friday and Saturday, noon–midnight.

SETTING AND ATMOSPHERE A dramatic, classically designed room filled with Greek urns and stonework. There is a classy bar area toward the front and a patio with Strip-facing views in the rear. Diners visit the fish market next to the open kitchen, where they choose the fresh live seafood they will eat for dinner.

HOUSE SPECIALTIES Milos is doing something few other American restaurants do at the moment: flying in fresh seafood daily from the Aegean, as do sibling Milos restaurants in New York City, Miami, and Montreal. Standouts include octopus, red mullet, Aegean sea bass, and a host of other fish. All are prepared simply and impeccably in the classic Greek manner.

OTHER RECOMMENDATIONS If you've never tasted a proper *avgolemono,* Greece's egg-lemon soup, Milos's is a must, made with jasmine rice, organic eggs, Meyer lemon, and capon broth. Meat dishes are also superb, such as lamb chops grilled with oregano and garlic. Desserts are simple but satisfying, such as the Greek yogurt with walnuts and thyme honey or the textbook baklava.

SUMMARY AND COMMENTS Milos has instantly rocketed to cult status in Vegas; it's the first high-end Greek restaurant in town, and one of the best in the country. Owner Costas Spiliadis is proud of his product, and rightly so. This is a not-to-be-missed experience, and the $22.14 three-course lunch, offered weekdays, is the best deal on the Strip.

Fiamma Trattoria & Bar ★★★★

ITALIAN	MODERATE/VERY EXPENSIVE	QUALITY ★★★★	VALUE ★★★½

MGM Grand, 3799 Las Vegas Blvd. S.; ☎ 702-891-7600; mgmgrand.com **South Strip and Environs**

Customers Visitors, locals. **Reservations** A must on weekends and holidays. **When to go** Avoid convention times. **Entrée range** $22–$55. **Payment** All major credit cards. **Service rating** ★★★½. **Friendliness rating** ★★★★½. **Parking** Valet, garage. **Bar** Full service. **Wine selection** Very good. **Dress** Upscale casual. **Disabled access** Main valet, garage. **Hours** Sunday and Monday, 5:30–10 p.m.; Tuesday–Thursday, 5:30–10:30 p.m.; Friday and Saturday, 5:30–11 p.m.

SETTING AND ATMOSPHERE This first Las Vegas venture for New York restaurateur Stephen Hanson is a casual version of Fiamma New York. A cheerful fireplace near the bar adds a comforting touch. Separate dining rooms that flow together make this sizable Italian restaurant more intimate.

HOUSE SPECIALTIES Sage-roasted chicken with roasted fingerling potatoes; braised short rib–filled ravioli with just enough meat and a drizzle of wine sauce; thin-sliced cured beef tenderloin with black truffle, arugula, and Parmesan cheese; wild king salmon with fava beans and bacon.

OTHER RECOMMENDATIONS Any of the creamy risottos that change each day; flan made with aged cheese; chanterelle-and-leek fondue; wonderful house-made pastas; irresistible pastries, especially the hot-from-the-fryer amaretti doughnuts served with dipping sauces.

SUMMARY AND COMMENTS Adventurers can order a multicourse tasting dinner. Pricey but wonderful.

Fleur ★★★½

TAPAS/FRENCH	MODERATE/VERY EXPENSIVE	QUALITY ★★★★	VALUE ★★★½

Mandalay Bay, 3950 Las Vegas Blvd. S.; ☎ 702-362-9400; mandalaybay.com/dining/fleur **South Strip and Environs**

Customers Tourists, conventioneers. **Reservations** Essential. **When to go** Anytime. **Entrée range** $9–$95. **Payment** All major credit cards. **Service rating** ★★★★★. **Friendliness rating** ★★★½. **Parking** Valet, lot, or garage. **Bar** Full service. **Wine selection** Excellent, eclectic list. **Dress** Casual. **Disabled access** Yes. **Hours** Daily, 11 a.m.–4 p.m.; Sunday–Thursday, 5–10 p.m.; Friday and Saturday, 5–10:30 p.m.

SETTING AND ATMOSPHERE Celebrity chef Hubert Keller has redone his formal dining room making it more casual. A large bar area with patio tables protrudes out onto the Mandalay Bay pedestrian walkway area. The sparse new design features lamps that look like sea anemones.

HOUSE SPECIALTIES Keller is a creative force. He's serving small plates, such as ahi tuna tacos, white onion soup veloutte, clams and white beans in a white wine reduction, and spicy Thai chicken wings, on a menu that features small plates from four countries, plus several full entrées and a nice selection of steaks.

OTHER RECOMMENDATIONS The bartenders like to use liquid nitrogen here to make frozen *treats. Be sure to check out some of them.*

SUMMARY AND COMMENTS Keller's through doing fancy-schmancy food in Vegas. This is the man who launched the burger craze with Burger Bar, and in spite of his classical French training, he remains terminally hip.

Florida Café Cuban Bar & Grill ★★★

CUBAN	INEXPENSIVE	QUALITY ★★★½	VALUE ★★★★

Howard Johnson Hotel, 1401 Las Vegas Blvd. S.; ☎ 702-385-3013; floridacafecuban.com **North Strip and Environs**

Customers Cuban community, locals, HoJo guests. **Reservations** Not necessary. **When to go** Anytime. **Entrée range** $6–$20. **Payment** All major credit cards. **Service rating** ★★★. **Friendliness rating** ★★★½. **Parking** Lot. **Bar** Wine and beer. **Wine selection** Small. **Dress** Casual. **Disabled access** Yes. **Hours** Daily, 7 a.m.–10 p.m.

SETTING AND ATMOSPHERE Colorful Cuban paintings adorn the walls, but it's still a coffee shop at heart.

HOUSE SPECIALTIES Cuban American food at value prices; Cuban breakfast eggs, stuffed potatoes, sweet plantains, and toast; croquettes; corn tamales; fresh seafood; real Cuban sandwiches, pressed thin on a special grill. All entrées include side dishes.

OTHER RECOMMENDATIONS *Arroz con pollo,* chicken with yellow rice; marinated leg of pork with burnt orange; *ropa vieja,* shredded beef with rice and beans; *tres leches* cake.

SUMMARY AND COMMENTS Little English is spoken here, but the staff is accommodating and menu descriptions are clear. Expect a crowd during the noon hour.

Fogo de Chão ★★★½

BRAZILIAN	MODERATE/EXPENSIVE	QUALITY ★★★★	VALUE ★★★★

360 E. Flamingo Rd., ☎ 702-431-4500; fogodechao.com **East of Strip**

Customers Visitors and locals. **Reservations** Essential. **When to go** Lunch or dinner. **Entrée range** $32.50 lunch, $51.50 dinner. **Payment** All major credit cards. **Service rating** ★★★. **Friendliness rating** ★★★★. **Parking** Lot. **Bar** Yes. **Wine selection** Excellent. **Dress** Casual. **Disabled access** Yes. **Hours** Monday–Thursday, 11:30 a.m.–2 p.m. and 5–10 p.m.; Friday, 11:30 a.m.–2 p.m. and 5–10:30 p.m.; Saturday, 4:30–10:30 p.m.; Sunday, 4–9 p.m.

SETTING AND ATMOSPHERE This is an enormous place, with plush booths, amber chandeliers, nine private dining rooms, and an abundance of wood. Walls are decorated with color-splashed murals. Wines are kept in a glass cellar visible from the floor of the dining room. The room's centerpiece is a giant salad bar stocked with everything from homemade chicken salad and fresh mozzarella to asparagus and sun-dried tomatoes.

HOUSE SPECIALTIES This is, in our opinion, the best place in Las Vegas to experience *churrasco,* or Brazilian-style barbecue—in this case, 15 cuts cooked on a fire and sliced tableside from skewers by a team of gauchos (their term for food servers). You'll also be plied with hot cheese rolls, sort-of mini-popovers that are insidiously seductive. Save room for the meat, though.

OTHER RECOMMENDATIONS We don't have room to describe all the meats, but each is well seasoned, and many are crusted with garlic, pepper, salt, and other spices. *Picanha,* Prime sirloin, is the real house specialty. *Costela de porco* are pork ribs, and the *frango,* or chicken, which comes in the form of moist leg meat or bacon-wrapped breasts, is amazing.

SUMMARY AND COMMENTS They want you to fill up on side dishes such as black beans, rice, and mashed potatoes, as well as *farofa,* the fried manioc flour that Brazilians religiously sprinkle on everything. Don't be sucked in. If you come at lunch, the feast is $19 less than dinner.

Forte ★★★

TAPAS/EASTERN EUROPEAN	MODERATE	QUALITY ★★★	VALUE ★★★★

4180 S. Rainbow Blvd.; ☎ 702-220-3876; barforte.com
West of Strip

Customers Visitors, locals. **Reservations** Not necessary. **When to go** Anytime. **Entrée range** $7–$10. **Payment** All major credit cards. **Service rating** ★★★½. **Friendliness rating** ★★★★. **Parking** Lot. **Bar** Full service. **Wine selection** Fair. **Dress** Casual. **Disabled access** Yes. **Hours** Sunday and Monday, 5–10 p.m.; Tuesday–Saturday, noon–10 p.m.

SETTING AND ATMOSPHERE A small neighborhood restaurant with moderate furnishings and funky paintings on the walls.

HOUSE SPECIALTIES While this restaurant bills itself as a tapas restaurant, and has a nice selection of Spanish small plates, what draws fans from across the valley is the Eastern European menu. Bulgarian charcuterie and egg come in a clay pot, and dumplings include the potato variety vareniki served with fried onions and Russia's beef palmeni sprinkled with fresh dill and sour cream.

OTHER RECOMMENDATIONS Don't miss the adjarski khachapurri: a traditional Georgian bread boat filled with two types of pickled cheese and a cracked egg. And check out the house-infused vodkas behind the bar.

SUMMARY AND COMMENTS Forte is a family-run operation unlike anything else in Las Vegas, which has made it a favorite of expatriates from Eastern Europe and a lot of other serious foodies.

Gordon Ramsay BurGR ★★★½

AMERICAN	MODERATE	QUALITY ★★★★	VALUE ★★★

Planet Hollywood, 3667 Las Vegas Blvd. S.; ☎ 702-785-5462; tinyurl.com/gordonramsayburgr **Mid-Strip and Environs**

Customers Visitors, locals. **Reservations** Essential. **When to go** Anytime. **Entrée range** $12–$18. **Payment** All major credit cards. **Service rating** ★★★★. **Friendliness rating** ★★★★½. **Parking** Valet, garage. **Bar** Full service. **Wine selection** Good. **Dress** Casual. **Disabled access** Yes. **Hours** Sunday–Thursday, 11 a.m.–12 a.m., until 2 a.m. Friday and Saturday.

SETTING AND ATMOSPHERE The third restaurant in Ramsay's trilogy is a vividly designed room highlighted by an undulating ceiling, a steel-and-concrete floor, a keg display, and an open kitchen. Servers are clad in designer uniforms. The ambience is both modern and stylish.

HOUSE SPECIALTIES Almost at once, Ramsay can lay claim to some of the best burgers on the Strip. All burgers are cooked over an open flame, basted with Devonshire butter for extra richness, and finished with creative toppings. His signature Hell's Kitchen Burger comes with asadero cheese, roasted jalapeño peppers, avocado, and oven-roasted tomato. The Chanterelle Burger gets lots of chanterelle mushrooms, arugula, and fig-onion jam.

OTHER RECOMMENDATIONS Nonburger items are equally good. Devil Dawgs are sumptuously adorned hot dogs that snap when you bite in. Potatoes are

Kennebec—lighter, less starchy, and crisp when fried. Pudding shakes are creamy handspun milkshakes with enough calories to fuel a large horse.

SUMMARY AND COMMENTS Ramsay has hit a home run with this concept. Yes, you'll pay a few dollars more for that burger, but it's worth it. The people-watching and close proximity to the Strip are one more draw. Finally, there are more than 30 craft beers to choose from, mostly American, and served frosty cold. A winner at every level.

Gordon Ramsay Steak ★★★★

STEAKHOUSE	VERY EXPENSIVE	QUALITY ★★★★	VALUE ★★★½

Paris Las Vegas, 3655 Las Vegas Blvd. S.; ☎ 702-944-4224; tinyurl.com/gordonramsaysteak   **Mid-Strip and Environs**

Customers Visitors, locals. **Reservations** Essential. **When to go** Anytime. **Entrée range** $32–$79. **Payment** All major credit cards. **Service rating** ★★★★½. **Friendliness rating** ★★★★½. **Parking** Valet, garage. **Bar** Full service. **Wine selection** Upscale. **Dress** Upscale. **Disabled access** Yes, valet or elevator. **Hours** Daily, 4:30–10:30 p.m.

SETTING AND ATMOSPHERE You enter this steakhouse through the "Chunnel," a makeshift replica of the tunnel under the English Channel, thus going from "France" to "England" (wink-wink, nudge-nudge). Stenciled on the ceiling, alongside the Union Jack, is a pop sculpture of the master's two hands, in motion. Seating is elegant, and there are private rooms in an upstairs mezzanine.

HOUSE SPECIALTIES The specialty here is beef: gaudy steaks presented on an eccentrically designed mirrored trolley. Pat LaFrieda, the legendary New York City butcher, is responsible for the excellent product, which doesn't come cheap. Expect to pay $48 for an 8-ounce American Kobe skirt steak, and upwards from there.

OTHER RECOMMENDATIONS Ramsay does a great beef Wellington, substituting a delicate mushroom duxelles for the out-of-favor foie gras, and lots more. His pricey fish-and-chips employs sea bass and is easily the best—and most expensive—version in the city. One of the best starters here is the English ale-and-cheese soup, the British answer to French onion soup. It's hard to go wrong on Ramsay's menu.

SUMMARY AND COMMENTS Ramsay's Vegas debut was indeed a splashy one. This has been one of the toughest tables on the Strip since opening day. The dining room is a bit noisy, and a few of the service gimmicks, such as an interactive iPad for ordering wines, seem gratuitous. But if you can afford it, this rivals Wolfgang Puck's CUT for the best all-around steakhouse on the Strip.

Hofbräuhaus ★★★

GERMAN	MODERATE	QUALITY ★★★½	VALUE ★★★★

4510 Paradise Rd.; ☎ 702-853-2337; hofbrauhauslasvegas.com
East of Strip

Customers Visitors, local German community, beer enthusiasts. **Reservations** Requested for main dining room. **When to go** Anytime. **Entrée range** $13–$20. **Payment** All major credit cards. **Service rating** ★★★½. **Friendliness rating** ★★★½. **Parking** Valet, large lot. **Bar** Limited. **Wine selection** Small. **Dress** Casual. **Disabled access** Ramp. **Hours** Sunday–Thursday, 11 a.m.–11 p.m.; Friday and Saturday, 11 a.m.–midnight; lunch specials served until 4 p.m. Monday–Friday.

SETTING AND ATMOSPHERE A mini-replica of Munich's Hofbräuhaus that required permission from the German government. The main dining room is where the action is. Communal tables and oompah bands flown in monthly put the din in dinner, yet the crowds love it. Comely *fräuleins* dressed in dirndls hoist as many as eight steins without a tray.

HOUSE SPECIALTIES Tennis ball–sized dumplings that accompany the pork stew and a few other braised dishes; sauerbraten that can be on the dry side (the beer makes it go down easier); roasted chicken and potato pancakes; pretzels baked throughout the day—the dough is shipped in containers from Germany, then shaped and baked in the kitchen.

OTHER RECOMMENDATIONS Perfect apple strudel—just delicious.

SUMMARY AND COMMENTS Hofbräuhaus serves the best beer in Las Vegas, and they've let go the notion that you shouldn't drink it cold. Take advantage of the discount coupons available in most hotels and taxis.

Honey Salt ★★★★

AMERICAN	MODERATE	QUALITY ★★★★	VALUE ★★★★

1031 S. Rampart Blvd.; ☎ 702-445-6100; honeysalt.com   **West of Strip**

Customers Locals. **Reservations** Essential. **When to go** Anytime. **Entrée range** $11–$32. **Payment** All major credit cards. **Service rating** ★★★★½. **Friendliness rating** ★★★★½. **Parking** Lot. **Bar** Full service. **Wine selection** Interesting selection of boutique American wines. **Dress** Casual. **Disabled access** Yes. **Hours** Sunday and Monday, 11:30 a.m.–9 p.m.; Tuesday–Thursday, 11:30 a.m.–10 p.m.; Friday and Saturday, 11:30 a.m.–10:30 p.m.

SETTING AND ATMOSPHERE Talented local decorator Randy Apel has converted the space that was formerly home to Nora's Wine Bar, using lime-green banquettes, funky mirrors, a chic bar, and an interior brick wall that provides hip, eccentric charm.

HOUSE SPECIALTIES The menu is as eclectic as the decor. You might find New England Fry, a lightly breaded combination of Ipswich clams and calamari from owner Elizabeth Blau's native Connecticut, alongside Nana's Tiffin Chicken Curry, reflective of the background of her husband and chef, Kim Canteenwalla, who has his roots on the Indian subcontinent.

OTHER RECOMMENDATIONS There are a host of delicious, approachable dishes here. Buttermilk fried chicken is one, roast swordfish with artichokes and sweet peppers is another. Almost everyone orders the turkey meatballs as well, one of the few dishes that Chef Kim held over from his tenure at the Society Café in the Wynn Las Vegas.

SUMMARY AND COMMENTS It's impossible to state the importance of this restaurant, which has been doing a brisk business with well-heeled locals since Day One. It brings fine dining at reasonable prices to the suburbs, and is well worth the trip from Strip casinos for anyone looking for an authentic local dining experience.

Jaleo ★★★★

SPANISH/TAPAS	EXPENSIVE	QUALITY ★★★★	VALUE ★★★★

The Cosmopolitan, 3708 Las Vegas Blvd. S.; ☎ 702-698-7000; jaleo.com/las-vegas   **Mid-Strip and Environs**

Customers Visitors, locals. **Reservations** A must. **When to go** Anytime. **Entrée range** $8–$45. **Payment** All major credit cards. **Service rating** ★★★. **Friendliness rating** ★★★.

Parking Valet, garage. **Bar** Full service. **Wine selection** Very good. **Dress** Informal. **Disabled access** Yes. **Hours** Daily, noon–midnight.

SETTING AND ATMOSPHERE Colorful, open restaurant filled with contemporary art from Spanish painters and sculptors. Seating is at small tables on one side of the room and at communal wooden tables that seat more than one party.

HOUSE SPECIALTIES Creative tapas from chef José Andrés, the man who imported this genre from his native Spain. Excellent chicken *croquetas.* Catalan sausage stew with braised onion and mushrooms is not to be missed. Excellent selection of Iberian hams and boutique cheeses. Imaginative desserts.

OTHER RECOMMENDATIONS Don't miss the paellas, cooked over olive and orange wood–burning fires in an open cooking area. The best choice is probably the *paella valenciana,* which features rabbit and chicken, but the seafood paella is also wonderful. Avant-garde Spanish cuisine is served in a small private room in the rear, but be sure to make reservations, as it's by prior arrangement only.

SUMMARY AND COMMENTS José Andrés once cooked with Ferran Adrià at elBulli in Roses, Spain, so he's comfortable with both traditional and cutting-edge Spanish cuisine. The *patatas bravas*—small, blistered potatoes served with a salt crust—come with a pair of exotic sauces from the Canary Islands. A most memorable experience.

Joël Robuchon Restaurant ★★★★★

FRENCH	VERY EXPENSIVE	QUALITY ★★★★★	VALUE ★★★

MGM Grand, 3799 Las Vegas Blvd. S.; ☎ 702-891-7925; mgmgrand.com
South Strip and Environs

Customers Visitors, locals. **Reservations** A must. **When to go** Special occasion. **Entrée range** Prix-fixe menus, $120–$240. **Payment** All major credit cards. **Service rating** ★★★★★. **Friendliness rating** ★★★. **Parking** Valet, garage. **Bar** Full service. **Wine selection** Excellent. **Dress** Formal. **Disabled access** Yes. **Hours** Sunday–Thursday, 5:30–10 p.m.; Friday and Saturday, 5:30–10:30 p.m.

SETTING AND ATMOSPHERE Small and intimate, this dining room whisks guests out of the Vegas experience and into a regal one. Adorned in hues of plush purple and gold, the room is elegant yet warm and inviting.

HOUSE SPECIALTIES Expect high-quality gourmet ingredients and treatments. *La langoustine truffée et cuite en ravioli* (truffled langoustine ravioli) is luxurious and divine. *La truffe noire* (shaved black truffles and potatoes topped with foie gras) has been known to make diners shed a tear from its pure decadence.

OTHER RECOMMENDATIONS For the full experience, opt for the 16-course tasting menu ($425 per person). There are also less-expensive and more-accessible abbreviated menus, starting at $120 per person.

SUMMARY AND COMMENTS Joël Robuchon is one of the most innovative chefs in the world (he was named "Chef of the Century" by *Gault Millau*), and a meal here is no small feat. It's the first and only three-star *Michelin Guide* winner in Las Vegas. Next door, L'Atelier de Joël Robuchon (see page 376) features a slightly more casual atmosphere where guests can watch chefs prepare their meals in an open-kitchen setting.

Joe's Seafood, Prime Steak & Stone Crab ★★★★

SEAFOOD/STEAK	EXPENSIVE	QUALITY ★★★★	VALUE ★★★½

The Forum Shops at Caesars, 3500 Las Vegas Blvd. S.;
☎ 702-792-9222; joes.net **Mid-Strip and Environs**

Customers Visitors and locals. **Reservations** A must for dinner. **When to go** Avoid conventions and holidays. **Entrée range** $15–$60. **Payment** All major credit cards. **Service rating** ★★★½. **Friendliness rating** ★★★★½. **Parking** Self, valet. **Bar** Bar and lounge. **Wine selection** Very good. **Dress** Business or upscale casual. **Disabled access** Yes (Forum Shops valet). **Hours** Sunday–Thursday, 11:30 a.m.–10 p.m.; Friday and Saturday, 11:30 a.m.–11 p.m.

SETTING AND ATMOSPHERE Handsome steakhouse decor that's a far cry from the original Miami Beach Joe's Stone Crab. The history of Joe's is chronicled in the artfully arranged photos that cover the dining-room walls. Joe's at The Forum Shops is fashioned after the Joe's in Chicago.

HOUSE SPECIALTIES Stone crab is available year-round. The-always-in-demand claws are shipped frozen when the season ends, yet are always wonderful. Jumbo lump-crabmeat cakes; chilled or warm seafood platters priced per person; glazed black cod; Prime steaks and chops.

OTHER RECOMMENDATIONS Signature bone-in steaks—the 22-ounce porterhouse is a terrific slab of beef. It's sliced in the kitchen and is perfect for sharing. Calf's liver with onions; superb hash-brown potatoes, crusty and golden brown with a creamy interior; outstanding side dishes—don't miss the fried green tomatoes or the signature grilled tomatoes with spinach and a cheddar-cheese topping.

SUMMARY AND COMMENTS Be prepared for noise—not overwhelming, but sometimes intrusive. Early dining is wise. Management prefers online reservations made well in advance. Walk-ins often have a wait at the bar.

Julian Serrano ★★★★

SPANISH/TAPAS	EXPENSIVE	QUALITY ★★★★	VALUE ★★★★

Aria at CityCenter, 3730 Las Vegas Blvd. S.; ☎ 702-590-7111; tinyurl.com/julianserrano **Mid-Strip and Environs**

Customers Visitors, locals. **Reservations** Recommended. **When to go** Anytime. **Entrée range** $8–$50. **Payment** All major credit cards. **Service rating** ★★★★★. **Friendliness rating** ★★★★★. **Parking** Valet, lot. **Bar** Full Service. **Wine selection** Excellent. **Dress** Casual. **Disabled access** Yes. **Hours** Sunday–Thursday, 11:30 a.m.–11 p.m.; Friday and Saturday, 11:30 a.m.–11:30 p.m.

SETTING AND ATMOSPHERE Contemporary Spanish décor with large open spaces and abundant pastel colors and earth tones. You may prefer to sit at the long tapas bar and watch the chefs putting together the small plates.

HOUSE SPECIALTIES Chicken croquettes; stuffed peppers; *albóndigas* (Spanish meatballs); *jamón ibérico* and *jamón serrano* (two types of Spanish ham); *paella valenciana; crema catalana*.

OTHER RECOMMENDATIONS Many of the small plates are irresistible, but the star dish is the paella, a rice casserole cooked in an iron pan. The Valenciana, with chorizo, chicken, and rabbit and redolent of saffron, is simply sensational.

SUMMARY AND COMMENTS Serrano is a native of Madrid, French-trained, and chef at Picasso in the neighboring Bellagio, but his native cuisine is his first love. Vegas has several tapas bars, but Serrano and Jaleo are really the Spanish restaurants the city has been waiting for.

Kabuto ★★★★★

JAPANESE/SUSHI	VERY EXPENSIVE	QUALITY ★★★★★	VALUE ★★★★★

5040 W. Spring Mountain Rd.; ☎ 702-676-1044; kabutolv.com **West of Strip**

Customers Locals, visitors. **Reservations** Strongly recommended. **When to go** Anytime. **Entrée range** Sashimi, $24; multicourse omakase dinners, $48–$120 **Payment** All major credit cards. **Service rating** ★★★★★. **Friendliness rating** ★★★★. **Parking** Lot. **Bar** Wine and sake. **Wine selection** Small. **Dress** Casual. **Disabled access** Yes. **Hours** Monday–Saturday, 6–11 p.m.

SETTING AND ATMOSPHERE A tiny sushi spot in the midst of a Chinatown shopping center that houses some of Las Vegas's top Japanese restaurants, Kabuto doesn't even have a sign on the door. Inside you'll find stark white walls, eight seats at the sushi bar, and two four-top tables. The bar seats are the most coveted, since they allow you to watch the chef's painstaking attention to detail on every piece of sushi.

HOUSE SPECIALTIES While other Japanese dishes are offered on the tasting menus, sushi is the star of the show. The menu changes daily and features fish imported from Japan that you'll only find at a handful of American restaurants.

SUMMARY AND COMMENTS This is some of the best sushi available in the United States, at a much more reasonable price than what you'll find at top Strip sushi restaurants.

Kyara ★★★½

JAPANESE	MODERATE	QUALITY ★★★★	VALUE ★★★★★

6555 S. Jones Blvd., ☎ 702-434-8856; kyaraizakaya.com   **West of Strip**

Customers Locals, chefs. **Reservations** Recommended. **When to go** Dinner or late night. **Entrée range** $9–$18. **Payment** All major credit cards. **Service rating** ★★★. **Friendliness rating** ★★★. **Parking** Lot. **Bar** Beer, wine, and a selection of sakes. **Wine selection** Good. **Dress** Casual. **Disabled access** Yes. **Hours** Monday–Friday, 11 a.m.–3 p.m.; daily, 5 p.m.–2 a.m.

SETTING AND ATMOSPHERE This is a small place, with a rabbit warren of semiprivate rooms that are fronted by white-birch slats. Tables are lacquered to a high gloss, and there are tiny white stones, *hashi-oki* in Japanese, on which your wooden chopsticks can rest, so as not to make contact with the table. There is also a counter at which to sit and watch the chefs ply their trade, but this is emphatically not a sushi bar.

HOUSE SPECIALTIES The idea is Japanese tapas: deep-fried, steamed, stir-fried, simmered, and skewered items. *Yamakake,* grated mountain potato served in a hot iron plate framed by a wooden platter, is astonishingly delicious. So is *agedashi* tofu, deep-fried tofu in Japanese broth; and *jidori tori kara,* a basket of delicately fried chicken.

OTHER RECOMMENDATIONS *Niku jaga,* a Japanese stew composed of sukiyaki beef, hunks of potato, and carrot, is a revelation. *Ayu,* a small fish in the trout family, salt-broiled, is wonderful when available on the blackboard. *Nankotsu* is soft shark's bone on thin slices of fresh cucumber. Skewers of charbroiled asparagus, chicken skin, beef tongue, and *tsukune* (soy-glazed chicken meatballs) are also a must.

SUMMARY AND COMMENTS Yasuo Komada, who owns Naked Fish, is the mastermind behind this place, which attracts many local chefs after their shifts. It's fun to watch the chefs turning skewers on the hibachis, shielded by a glass wall behind the counter. This place has become a veritable clubhouse for local foodies. As in Japan, beer, wine, and sake flow like a mountain stream.

Lotus of Siam ★★★★

THAI	MODERATE	QUALITY ★★★★	VALUE ★★½

Commercial Center, 953 E. Sahara Ave.; ☎ 702-735-3033;
saipinchutima.com **East of Strip**

Customers Locals, visitors. **Reservations** Recommended. **When to go** Anytime.
Entrée range $9–$21; lunch buffet, $10. **Payment** All major credit cards. **Service rating** ★★½. **Friendliness rating** ★★★★½. **Parking** Lot. **Bar** No. **Wine selection** Excellent. **Dress** Casually elegant. **Disabled access** Ground floor. **Hours** Monday–Friday, 11:30 a.m.–2:30 p.m. and 5:30–10 p.m.; Saturday and Sunday, 5:30–10 p.m.

SETTING AND ATMOSPHERE Attractive though modest decor; teak tables and comfortable chairs. Thai paintings and accessories.

HOUSE SPECIALTIES Beef jerky Isaan-style—crisp yet tender marinated beef served in a spicy sauce; *som tam,* green-papaya salad with salted crab; salmon panang—charbroiled fresh salmon, served Thai-style in a thick, creamy sauce laced with curry.

OTHER RECOMMENDATIONS Sticky rice steamed in a bamboo basket; crispy rice salad; sausages made in-house. Ask the staff to show you the Northern Thai menu, featuring specialties from the chef's hometown, Chiang Mai. *Khao soi,* Burmese-inspired noodles, and *nam prik noon,* a fiery green-chile dip, are just two of them.

SUMMARY AND COMMENTS The Isaan specialties come from the region of that name in the northeastern corner of Thailand, bordering Cambodia and Laos. These dishes are even hotter and more highly seasoned than most Thai food, but the chef-owner will temper the heat to suit your taste. Gentle, caring service and one of the best lists of Austrian and German wines in this country are bonuses.

Marché Bacchus: French Bistro and Wine Shop ★★★★

FRENCH BISTRO	MODERATE	QUALITY ★★★★	VALUE ★★★★

2620 Regatta Dr., Suite 106; ☎ 702-804-8008; marchebacchus.com
West of Strip

Customers Locals. **Reservations** Suggested weekends. **When to go** Anytime.
Entrée range $17–$40. **Payment** All major credit cards. **Service rating** ★★★★½. **Friendliness rating** ★★★★½. **Parking** Large lot. **Bar** Full service. **Wine selection** Extensive. **Dress** Casual. **Disabled access** On lower level. **Hours** Monday–Saturday, 11 a.m.–4 p.m.; Sunday–Thursday, 4–9:30 p.m.; Friday and Saturday, 4–10 p.m.; Sunday brunch, 10 a.m.–4 p.m.

SETTING AND ATMOSPHERE Walk through the wine shop to the adjacent bistro, or dine on the terrace with its gorgeous view of artificial Regatta Lake. Simply furnished, this neighborhood eatery is an escape from the cares of the day. After one visit, you're welcomed by owners Rhonda and Jeff Wyatt as if you're family.

HOUSE SPECIALTIES In addition to French-bistro classics, such as escargot in garlic butter and mussels in white wine, you'll find flavorful andouille-sausage gumbo.

OTHER RECOMMENDATIONS The adjoining wine shop is dazzling. Any wine can be purchased to enjoy with dinner for only $10 over retail. Executive chef David Middleton, a protégé of Alex Stratta (the bistro's culinary consultant), is a terrific talent, and the food here is better than ever.

SUMMARY AND COMMENTS Wines by the glass are terrific here, as is the charcuterie, made on premises. The terrace is favored by local sommeliers who bring visiting winemakers and chefs to relax here, making it a great place for networking.

Mizumi ★★★★

JAPANESE	VERY EXPENSIVE	QUALITY ★★★★	VALUE ★★★

Wynn Las Vegas, 3131 Las Vegas Blvd. S.; ☎ 702-770-7000;
tinyurl.com/mizumilv **Mid-Strip and Environs**

Customers Visitors, locals. **Reservations** Essential. **When to go** Anytime. **Entrée range** $18–$69. **Payment** All major credit cards. **Service rating** ★★★★★. **Friendliness rating** ★★★★. **Parking** Valet, garage. **Bar** Full service. **Wine selection** Excellent. **Dress** Upscale. **Disabled access** Yes. **Hours** Sunday–Thursday, 5:30–10 p.m.; Friday and Saturday, 5:30–10:30 p.m.

SETTING AND ATMOSPHERE Wynn chief architect Roger Thomas did this stunning redesign of the former Okada, a lavish extravaganza featuring dozens of Noh masks, walls of mock gold brick, a wall draped in antique Japanese sashes, and a private dining room affording direct views of Wynn Las Vegas's fabled waterfall.

HOUSE SPECIALTIES Creative Hawaiian-born chef Devin Hashimoto is one of the most talented cooks on the Strip. He excels at many genres, but you won't want to miss his *robata-yaki,* a method of cooking meats on wooden skewers over hot coals; seafood *bibimbap* rice bowl, inspired by his Korean-American wife; and wonderful fresh grilled seafood in season.

OTHER RECOMMENDATIONS Spicy king crab tacos and yellowtail sashimi with jalapeño gelée are both exemplary; so is a toothsome Wagyu-beef tartare, topped with a creamy quail egg.

SUMMARY AND COMMENTS Mizumi is a luxury experience on every level. Service commences with an elegant tea selection, and the sushi and sashimi are absolutely first-rate. If you've got the bucks, the restaurant's Floating Pagoda Table, the city's most elegant place to sit, will cost a few thousand to reserve.

Mon Ami Gabi ★★★½

CONTINENTAL/FRENCH	MODERATE/EXPENSIVE	QUALITY ★★★★	VALUE ★★★½

Paris Las Vegas, 3655 Las Vegas Blvd. S.; ☎ 702-944-4224;
monamigabi.com **Mid-Strip and Environs**

Customers Visitors, locals. **Reservations** Requested for dining room, not accepted for patio. **When to go** Anytime. **Entrée range** $13–40. **Payment** All major credit cards. **Service rating** ★★★½. **Friendliness rating** ★★★½. **Parking** Valet, garage. **Bar** Full service. **Wine selection** All French. **Dress** Upscale casual. **Disabled access** Yes. **Hours** *Brunch:* Saturday and Sunday, 11 a.m.–4 p.m.; *Breakfast:* daily, 7–11 a.m.; *Lunch:* Monday–Friday, 11:30 a.m.–4 p.m., Saturday and Sunday, 11 a.m.–4 p.m.; *Dinner:* Sunday–Thursday, 4–11 p.m., Friday and Saturday, 4 p.m.–midnight.

SETTING AND ATMOSPHERE Handsome brasserie with black-leather booths and tables. The main dining room leads to a wonderful, plant-filled patio and a marvelous sidewalk café with a view of the Strip.

HOUSE SPECIALTIES Steak *frites,* thin-sliced steak and French fries; an excellent selection of seafood and hors d'oeuvres; many hot seafood appetizers; the daily special listed on the blackboard; filet mignon and New York strip are among the regular steak selections.

OTHER RECOMMENDATIONS Crêpes; omelets and sandwiches at lunch; plates of seafood; mussels marinière.

SUMMARY AND COMMENTS Mon Ami Gabi is a charming dining place. Everyone wants to dine at the sidewalk café, but you'll have to come early to get a table (no reservations). The *frites* are actually curly fries, not steak fries, but they're crisp and good: so what if they're not authentic? Everything else is right on the mark. And for those whose dinner isn't complete without a good bottle of wine, there's a separate list of fine reserve wines.

Monta Japanese Noodle House ★★½

RAMEN	INEXPENSIVE	QUALITY ★★★★	VALUE ★★★★★

5030 W. Spring Mountain Rd., Suite 6; ☎ 702-367-4600; montaramen.com **West of Strip**

Customers Local Japanese. **Reservations** Not accepted. **When to go** Lunch or late dinner. **Entrée range** $7–$10. **Payment** Cash only. **Service rating** ★★★. **Friendliness rating** ★★. **Parking** Lot. **Bar** Beer and wine. **Dress** Casual. **Disabled access** None. **Hours** Daily, 11:30 a.m.–11 p.m.

SETTING AND ATMOSPHERE A rabbit warren–sized ramen bar where the chefs toil behind a counter. Seating is cramped, on wooden chairs, with tables crowded closely together. A mostly Japanese-speaking clientele predominates.

HOUSE SPECIALTIES The specialty here is ramen—long, wheat-based noodles slurped from giant bowls of broth. There are essentially two types: miso ramen, in a piquant broth made from fermented soybeans, and shoyu ramen, based on soy sauce. The flavorful broth is slow-cooked and tastes it, and the noodles are perfectly al dente.

OTHER RECOMMENDATIONS Toppings are to ramen as they are to pizza. Don't miss the melt-in-your-mouth, thinly sliced pork—slices so light they literally float up to the top of the broth. Corn, egg, and several other toppings enhance the ramen experience. There are also bowls of fried rice and several types of house-made Japanese pickles.

SUMMARY AND COMMENTS This place ain't fancy, but it's among the most authentic Japanese food in town, even more so than the so-called sushi palaces. Be prepared to wait in line—Monta is always in demand.

Nobu Caesars Palace ★★★★

JAPANESE/SUSHI	VERY EXPENSIVE	QUALITY ★★★★★	VALUE ★★★½

Nobu Hotel at Caesars Palace, 3570 Las Vegas Blvd. S.; ☎ 877-346-4642 (reservations); tinyurl.com/nobucaesars **Mid-Strip and Environs**

Customers Visitors, locals. **Reservations** Essential. **When to go** Anytime. **Entrée range** Sushi and sashimi, $12–$38; sushi dinners, $75 and $100; hot and cold dishes, $15–$50. **Payment** All major credit cards. **Service rating** ★★★★★. **Friendliness rating** ★★★½. **Parking** Lot, garage, valet. **Bar** Full service. **Wine selection** Excellent. **Dress** Upscale casual. **Disabled access** Yes. **Hours** Sunday–Thursday, 5–11 p.m.; Friday and Saturday, 5 p.m.–midnight.

SETTING AND ATMOSPHERE Architect David Rockwell has taken an enormous space—12,775 square feet—and somehow made it feel intimate. This is the largest of superstar chef Nobuyuki Matsuhisa's 27 Nobu restaurants worldwide, using semicircular banquettes, partially sequestered teppan tables, and an enormous sushi counter, where a team of up to 10 chefs makes magic while you watch.

HOUSE SPECIALTIES The menu is a reflection of Japanese technique and precision with South American ingredients and influence. Signature dishes include black cod with miso glaze and an exquisite chicken baked in a clay vessel, as well as *hamachi kama* (broiled yellowtail collar), which is one of the menu's best values.

OTHER RECOMMENDATIONS *Tiraditos,* South American takes on ceviche and sashimi, are top-drawer here, although you pay for them. Even more money, upwards of $150 per person, gets a delicious teppanyaki dinner—a prix-fixe affair that can soar to as high as $300 for the most luxe set menu offered.

SUMMARY AND COMMENTS Matsuhisa is the man who globalized the cuisine of his native Japan, with locations in such diverse ports-of-call as Budapest, Hungary; Cape Town, South Africa; Dubai; and Perth, Australia. There is still a second Vegas location at the Hard Rock, but for a few dollars more, you can eat at this more glamorous, more creative outpost—so why not?

Noodles ★★★

ASIAN	MODERATE	QUALITY ★★★★	VALUE ★★★½

Bellagio, 3600 Las Vegas Blvd. S.; ☎ 702-693-8131; bellagio.com/restaurants/noodles.aspx **Mid-Strip and Environs**

Customers Visitors, locals. **Reservations** No. **When to go** Anytime. **Entrée range** $12–$30, à la carte. **Payment** All major credit cards. **Service rating** ★★★½. **Friendliness rating** ★★★½. **Parking** Valet, lot. **Bar** Full service. **Wine selection** Good. **Dress** Casual. **Disabled access** Yes. **Hours** Daily, 11 a.m.–2 a.m.; dim sum served Friday–Sunday, 11 a.m.–3 p.m.

SETTING AND ATMOSPHERE Find Bellagio's baccarat bar and you'll find Noodles. Follow the marble floor, whose Chinese brass inlays represent bits of Asian wisdom, into this wonderful eatery. There's an open kitchen, a wall of artifacts, and the hustle and bustle of an authentic noodle place.

HOUSE SPECIALTIES Oodles of slurpy noodle dishes from China, Vietnam, Thailand, and Japan and authentic Hong Kong–style barbecue dishes. There's also a long list of appetizers and many different teas.

SUMMARY AND COMMENTS Noodles is small, so it's tough to get in at prime times, but it's open long hours, so you're bound to get in sometime. This is a favorite stop for Bellagio's Asian clientele.

Old Homestead Steakhouse ★★★★

AMERICAN/STEAK	VERY EXPENSIVE	QUALITY ★★★★	VALUE ★★★½

Caesars Palace, 3570 Las Vegas Blvd. S.; ☎ 877-346-4642 (reservations); tinyurl.com/oldhomesteadlv **Mid-Strip and Environs**

Customers Visitors, locals. **Reservations** Essential. **When to go** Anytime. **Entrée range** $28–$75. **Payment** All major credit cards. **Service rating** ★★★★★. **Friendliness rating** ★★★★★. **Parking** Valet, garage. **Bar** Full service. **Wine selection** Excellent. **Dress** Business casual. **Disabled access** Yes. **Hours** Sunday–Thursday, 4:45–10:30 p.m.; Friday and Saturday, 4:45–11 p.m.

SETTING AND ATMOSPHERE Just across Cleopatra's Way from Nobu (see page 401), this clubby, masculine room, filled with high-backed leather banquettes and black-and-white shots of bridge girders in Manhattan and Brooklyn, attempts to recall dining in the Big City.

HOUSE SPECIALTIES Meat is the ticket here. The good cuts come from Pat LaFrieda, a top butcher in New York's Meatpacking District who sells to more than 600 restaurants nationwide. Steaks here are dry-aged a minimum of 30 days, a number of them on the bone. It ain't cheap, of course: steaks start at $49 for an 8-ounce petite filet mignon.

OTHER RECOMMENDATIONS Appetizers, soups, and salads are done well here. The beefy, cheese-topped French onion soup is a hit, as are vine-ripened tomatoes with mozzarella and fresh basil. Don't miss the thick-cut applewood-smoked bacon, which feels like a bargain at about $5 a slice.

SUMMARY AND COMMENTS Most Strip steakhouses are similar in quality and price, lest they not skew the competition. Yet this place manages to stand out in the crowd. Tater Tots topped with "Fat Boy" sauce—stuff you'd pile on a baked potato—is the stuff dreams are made of, and the best dessert, a California-style carrot cake, will bring you back even if the meat doesn't.

Pearl ★★★★

CHINESE	EXPENSIVE	QUALITY ★★★★	VALUE ★★½

MGM Grand, 3799 Las Vegas Blvd. S.; ☎ 702-891-7380; tinyurl.com/pearlmgm   **South Strip and Environs**

Customers Visitors, locals. **Reservations** Recommended. **When to go** Anytime. **Entrée range** $22 and up. **Payment** All major credit cards. **Service rating** ★★★★½. **Friendliness rating** ★★★★½. **Parking** Valet, parking garage. **Bar** Full service. **Wine selection** Very good. **Dress** Business attire, casual chic. **Disabled access** Ramp. **Hours** Sunday, Monday, Thursday, 5:30–10 p.m.; Friday and Saturday, 5:30–10:30 p.m.

SETTING AND ATMOSPHERE Sleek and inviting, tall booths offer privacy and a view of the dining room. A private dining area next to the wine cellar is in great demand. Expert lighting and gorgeous appointments.

HOUSE SPECIALTIES The three-course tasting menu is worth it. Offerings include spider-prawn dumplings, minced tiger prawns and pine nuts in lettuce petals; deep-fried shiitake mushrooms glazed with spicy black vinegar; live-seafood selection; Dungeness crabmeat baked in the shell; Cantonese-style wok-fried filet of venison and asparagus.

OTHER RECOMMENDATIONS The signature Asian bouillabaisse; spiced king crab legs with chili and garlic; the steamed Maine and Australian lobster tasting; Maine lobster fried rice; braised Thai eggplant with chili-plum sauce; star-anise lamb chops with string beans; tableside tea service.

SUMMARY AND COMMENTS Dining at Pearl is relaxing and satisfying, elegant and inviting.

Penn's Thai House ★★★★

THAI	INEXPENSIVE	QUALITY ★★★★	VALUE ★★★★★

724 W. Sunset Rd., Henderson; ☎ 702-564-0162
Southeast Las Vegas–Henderson

Customers Locals. **Reservations** Not necessary. **When to go** Anytime. **Entrée range** $8–$15. **Payment** All major credit cards. **Service rating** ★★★½. **Friendliness rating** ★★★★★. **Parking** Lot. **Bar** Beer and wine. **Dress** Casual. **Disabled access** None. **Hours** Daily, 11 a.m.–9 p.m.

SETTING AND ATMOSPHERE Penn's Thai House is located in an obscure mini-mall across Boulder Highway on the city's far east side. The restaurant is small and modest to a fault. Seating is at down-at-the-heels booths, and the only decor to speak of comes from Thai objets d'art mounted on the walls.

HOUSE SPECIALTIES Chef-owner Penn Amarayapark makes everything from scratch, including red, green, and yellow curries, an incredible *tom yum* soup, and stuffed buns that she gives to favored customers. The Thai beef jerky here is exemplary, as are several cold and hot appetizers, such as Thai squid salad and homemade sausage.

OTHER RECOMMENDATIONS Noodles are a big part of any Thai menu. Penn's pad thai is never sweet and cloying, and *pad see ew*—flat rice noodles with black soy, bitter greens, and your choice of meats—is as delicious as the law allows. Penn also makes various types of *larb,* a ground-meat concoction with a wickedly spicy kick that you scoop up and eat inside a cabbage leaf.

SUMMARY AND COMMENTS Penn may be the most underrated chef in Las Vegas, undiscovered by the masses because of her far-flung location. If there is one restaurant in this city that is, to quote the *Michelin Guide,* "worth the journey," this is the place. The food is so honest and tasty here, it will make you rethink what you thought you knew about this seductive cuisine.

Picasso ★★★★

FRENCH/SPANISH	VERY EXPENSIVE	QUALITY ★★★★	VALUE ★★½

Bellagio, 3600 Las Vegas Blvd. S.; ☎ 702-693-7223; bellagio.com/restaurants/picasso.aspx **Mid-Strip and Environs**

Customers Visitors, locals. **Reservations** A must. **When to go** Anytime you can get a reservation. **Entrée range** Prix-fixe menus, $75–$125. **Payment** All major credit cards. **Service rating** ★★★★½. **Friendliness rating** ★★★★. **Parking** Valet, self. **Bar** Full service. **Wine selection** Excellent. **Dress** Casually elegant, jackets recommended. **Disabled access** Elevator. **Hours** Wednesday–Monday, 6–9:30 p.m.; pre-theatre seating at 5:30 p.m.

SETTING AND ATMOSPHERE Arguably the most beautiful dining room in Las Vegas, with original Picassos adorning the walls. The flower displays throughout the restaurant are exquisite. A wall of windows gives most tables a full view of Bellagio's dancing fountains.

HOUSE SPECIALTIES Selections on both the five-course degustation and the four-course prix-fixe menus change regularly according to the whim of the chef. The warm lobster salad, sautéed foie gras, sautéed medallions of swordfish, and aged-lamb *rôti* with truffle crust appear often. Chef Julian Serrano, formerly of Masa's in San Francisco, sometimes offers a sensational *amuse-bouche:* a tiny potato pancake topped with crème fraîche and osetra caviar.

SUMMARY AND COMMENTS This exceptional restaurant is grand yet unpretentious. Allow enough time to enjoy the experience. After dinner have a drink on the terrace. Where else but in Las Vegas can you have a view of Lake Como as well as one of the Eiffel Tower?

Ping Pang Pong ★★★½

CHINESE	MODERATE	QUALITY ★★★½	VALUE ★★★½

Gold Coast Casino, 4000 W. Flamingo Rd.; ☎ 702-367-7111; goldcoastcasino.com/dine/ping-pang-pong **West of Strip**

Customers Locals. **Reservations** Unnecessary. **When to go** Avoid Saturday and Sunday lunch hour. **Entrée range** $9–$29. **Payment** All major credit cards. **Service rating** ★★★. **Friendliness rating** ★★★★★. **Bar** Beer and wine. **Wine selection** Limited. **Dress** Casual. **Disabled access** Yes. **Hours** *Lunch,* featuring dim sum: daily, 10 a.m.–3 p.m.; *Dinner:* daily, 5 p.m.–3 a.m.

SETTING AND ATMOSPHERE A roomy, lightly themed space decorated with tables fronting slot machines on the casino floor. Servers hawk their wares from rolling carts that they push through the dining room, just as they do in Hong Kong or Canton.

HOUSE SPECIALTIES Dim sum are sweet and savory pastries, meats, and vegetable dishes that are consumed with tea, generally slowly, so Chinese people can socialize over them. Just a few to try are *chiu chow fun gor,* shrimp-and-pork dumplings; a shark-fin-soup dumpling; and crispy shrimp rolls.

OTHER RECOMMENDATIONS Night Market Fried Rice, a huge platter of spicy rice mixed with beef, onions, tomatoes, and hot chiles, will make you rethink take-out fried rice. There are also wonderful soups here, like hot-and-sour and a very Chinese West Lake Beef Soup.

SUMMARY AND COMMENTS Ping Pang Pong is owned by Karrie and Kevin Wu, who also run the very good Noodle Exchange just down the hall. The staff, mostly Chinese-speaking, will guide you through the experience. This is the only dim sum parlor in Vegas that can stand up to ones in L.A. or San Francisco.

Poppy Den ★★★★

ECLECTIC	MODERATE	QUALITY ★★★★	VALUE ★★★★

Tivoli Village, 440 S. Rampart Blvd., Suite 180; ☎ 702-802-2480; vegaspoppyden.com   **West of Strip**

Customers Locals. **Reservations** Suggested. **When to go** Lunch, dinner. **Entrée range** $14–$27. **Payment** All major credit cards. **Service rating** ★★★★½. **Friendliness rating** ★★★★. **Parking** Valet, lot. **Bar** Full service. **Wine selection** Very good. **Dress** Upscale casual. **Disabled access** Main entrance. **Hours** Sunday–Thursday, 4–10 p.m., until 11 p.m. Friday and Saturday.

SETTING AND ATMOSPHERE The main dining room here is a long, narrow space filled with cramped booths and tables done in black, polished to a mirror-like sheen. Upstairs, however, are a cozy Deco room and lounge; during the warmer months, a chic outdoor patio—invariably crowded with upscale locals from trendy Summerlin—is employed.

HOUSE SPECIALTIES Celebrity chef Angelo Sosa, who consults in Korea, has quite a vivid imagination in the kitchen. Sosa's food tends to be surprising spin-offs of dishes that you thought you were familiar with. Salmon is paired with shishito peppers. An appetizer called The General's Chicken Wings has powerful crunch, bionic size, and wicked spice.

OTHER RECOMMENDATIONS There are many dishes here that you've probably never imagined. A seemingly conventional burger is topped with Sriracha sauce and a fried egg. His Caesar salad surprises with smoked whitefish instead of the more usual anchovy dressing. *Tres leches* cake stands in for the usual dry biscuit in his original take on strawberry shortcake.

SUMMARY AND COMMENTS Although many dishes here seem contrived, they work like a charm, plus the prices are reasonable. Sosa, a major talent with super-model good looks, is already a star in New York City and on the East Coast. His presence at Tivoli Village has suffused Westside dining in Vegas with new energy. The bar scene here, even weekdays, is high-octane, too.

Prime Steakhouse ★★★★

STEAK	VERY EXPENSIVE	QUALITY ★★★★	VALUE ★★½

Bellagio, 3600 Las Vegas Blvd. S.; ☎ 702-693-7223; bellagio.com /restaurants/prime-steakhouse.aspx   **Mid-Strip and Environs**

Customers Visitors, locals. **Reservations** Requested. **When to go** Avoid convention times. **Entrée range** $25–$100. **Payment** All major credit cards. **Service rating** ★★★★½. **Friendliness rating** ★★★★½. **Parking** Valet, self. **Bar** Full service. **Wine selection** Excellent. **Dress** Casually elegant, jackets preferred. **Disabled access** Elevator. **Hours** Daily, 5–10 p.m.

SETTING AND ATMOSPHERE Dazzling powder-blue-and-chocolate carpets and wall hangings in a setting seldom seen for a steakhouse—it's gorgeous. In keeping with Bellagio's fine-arts policy, there's plenty of original art to view here. Have a drink at the elegant bar and take it all in.

HOUSE SPECIALTIES Prime aged steaks and seafood; lamb chops in balsamic syrup; filet mignon with tomatoes; veal chop in pineapple chutney. A choice of a variety of sauces and excellent side dishes.

SUMMARY AND COMMENTS Prime is on the lower level of the shopping corridor beside Picasso (see page 404), with which an outdoor patio is shared. Both restaurants get their share of lookers, but the staff keeps them from disturbing diners. Service here rarely misses a beat.

Public House ★★★★

AMERICAN	MODERATE	QUALITY ★★★★	VALUE ★★★★

The Venetian, 3355 Las Vegas Blvd. S.; ☎ 702-285-5544; publichouselv.com   **Mid-Strip and Environs**

Customers Locals, chefs. **Reservations** Essential. **When to go** Dinner or late night. **Entrée range** $12–$35. **Payment** All major credit cards. **Service rating** ★★★★. **Friendliness rating** ★★★★. **Parking** Valet and garage. **Bar** Beer and wine. **Wine selection** Extensive. **Dress** Casual. **Disabled access** Yes. **Hours** Daily, 11 a.m.–11 p.m.

SETTING AND ATMOSPHERE Local restaurant chain Block 16's entry at The Venetian is our first real example of a gastropub. The build-out is impressive: The space, formerly home to David Burke, is modern and spacious, thanks to a ceiling composed of giant wooden cubes, banquettes of tufted dark-brown leather, and a burnished-mahogany parquet floor.

HOUSE SPECIALTIES Chef Anthony Meidenbauer has created an impressive menu of snacks, savories, and large plates to go along with the pub's more than 200 brews and imaginative wine list. Meidenbauer's house-made charcuterie, Welsh rarebit, and house pickles are three items not to miss. The rarebit is an eccentric cheese toast with a bite—delicious. The pickles are wickedly sharp.

OTHER RECOMMENDATIONS Try the *poutine,* a French-Canadian dish composed of French fries, cheese curds, brown gravy, and, here, a rotating assortment of specialty ingredients, including duck confit. Potted farm egg comes in a casserole with lots of cheese sauce and a heap of sautéed mushrooms, the perfect complement to wedges of crusty house bread. Fried quail served on waffles and lamb pierogi shows off Chef Meidenbauer's awesome range.

SUMMARY AND COMMENTS Ask the restaurant's cicerone (beer sommelier), Michael Mateo, to turn you on to one of the two dozen brews he has on tap. The initial success of this place (opened in 2011) portends well for the Vegas food scene. The gastropub may just be here to stay.

Raku ★★★★

JAPANESE	MODERATE	QUALITY ★★★★	VALUE ★★★★

5030 Spring Mountain Rd.; ☎ 702-367-3511; raku-grill.com
West of Strip

Customers Visitors, locals. **Reservations** Recommended. **When to go** Anytime. **Entrée range** $15–$30. **Payment** All major credit cards. **Service rating** ★★★★★. **Friendliness rating** ★★★★★. **Parking** Lot. **Bar** Full service. **Wine selection** Fair. **Dress** Casual. **Disabled access** Yes. **Hours** Monday–Saturday, 6 p.m.–3 a.m.

SETTING AND ATMOSPHERE A small (seats 60), minimalist space decorated in dark woods with burgundy walls.

HOUSE SPECIALTIES Don't expect sushi at this Japanese restaurant; it's a *sakaba,* or sake bar, where small, salty dishes meant to encourage thirst are served. A Japanese lump charcoal–fired grill is the source of the wonderfully smoky flavor imparted to meats such as pork cheek, Kobe beef tendon, bacon-wrapped enoki mushrooms, and whole fish. House-made tofu is silky and creamy, especially when paired with fresh tomato and seaweed, a sort of Japanese take on a caprese salad.

OTHER RECOMMENDATIONS Check the nightly specials board for seasonal additions. Traditional Japanese flavors and techniques are the ticket. For dessert, walk a few doors down to sister restaurant Sweets Raku.

SUMMARY AND COMMENTS Raku is an off-Strip standout, garnering the attention of critics, locals, and, most importantly, other chefs in town. Chef Mitsuo Endo finds himself cooking for some of the biggest culinary names in Vegas after they get off work, so the restaurant is open late. A true Japanese *izakaya* (drinking–dining) experience, round after round of Raku's grilled small plates go well with beer, wine, or sake.

Rao's ★★★

ITALIAN	EXPENSIVE	QUALITY ★★★★	VALUE ★★

Caesars Palace, 3570 Las Vegas Blvd. S.; ☎ 877-346-4642 (reservations); tinyurl.com/raoscaesars **Mid-Strip and Environs**

Customers Visitors, locals. **Reservations** Suggested. **When to go** Anytime. **Entrée range** $25–$49. **Payment** All major credit cards. **Service rating** ★★★★★. **Friendliness rating** ★★★★★. **Parking** Valet, garage. **Bar** Full service. **Wine selection** Very good. **Dress** Casual. **Disabled access** Yes. **Hours** Daily, 5–10:30 p.m.

SETTING AND ATMOSPHERE The Las Vegas outpost of Rao's is nearly three times the size of the tiny New York original, but you can still feel the heart of this family-owned business. Christmas lights and decorations hang year-round, and the walls are adorned with framed photographs of Rao's customers old and new. Dark woods along the bar and dining room evoke a classic, traditional feel. Don't be surprised if you hear Italian-American classics such as "Volare" interspersed with covers by Michael Bublé from the jukebox; this restaurant is all about intermingling old and new traditions.

HOUSE SPECIALTIES Southern Italian red-sauce classics such as meatballs, gnocchi with Bolognese sauce, and Uncle Vincent's Lemon Chicken have been on the menu since the original restaurant opened in 1896. You'll also find some fresh seafood dishes and lighter pastas.

SUMMARY AND COMMENTS Rao's is a family-run joint—always has been and always will be. The restaurant in New York is notorious for being the hardest reservation to get, so when Rao's finally opened at Caesars Palace, those in the know rejoiced. Owner and partner Frank Pellegrino Jr. runs the front of the house, and chances are you'll find him there with guests, including the celebrities who frequent the place, on any given night.

Restaurant Guy Savoy ★★★★★

FRENCH	VERY EXPENSIVE	QUALITY ★★★★★	VALUE ★★★

Caesars Palace, 3570 Las Vegas Blvd. S.; ☎ 877-346-4642 (reservations); tinyurl.com/guysavoycaesars   **Mid-Strip and Environs**

Customers Visitors, locals. **Reservations** A must. **When to go** Special occasion. **Entrée range** À la carte, $80–$110; prix-fixe menus, $120–$300. **Payment** All major credit cards. **Service rating** ★★★★★. **Friendliness rating** ★★★★. **Parking** Valet, garage. **Bar** Full service. **Wine selection** Excellent. **Dress** Upscale. **Disabled access** Yes. **Hours** Wednesday–Sunday, 5:30–9:30 p.m.

SETTING AND ATMOSPHERE Clean lines and modern sophistication are the theme here. You'll find the same elegance and refinement you would expect from the original Paris restaurant. Top-notch French dining is alive and well in Las Vegas.

HOUSE SPECIALTIES The artichoke-and-black-truffle soup is one of Savoy's signature items all the way from his Paris restaurant. Served with toasted mushroom brioche and a little truffle butter, it's one of the most decadent dishes ever.

OTHER RECOMMENDATIONS As a starter, try Savoy's amazing "colors of caviar," his oysters ice gelée. And the recently added salmon Iceberg "cooked" on dry ice and served with warm consommé is truly jaw-dropping.

SUMMARY AND COMMENTS To get the full experience without breaking the bank, try either the four-course TGV prix-fixe menu or grab a seat in the Cognac Room for a rare spirit and one or two of Savoy's amazing appetizers.

Rose. Rabbit. Lie ★★★★

ECLECTIC	EXPENSIVE/VERY EXPENSIVE	QUALITY ★★★★½	VALUE ★★½

The Cosmopolitan, 3708 Las Vegas Blvd. S.; ☎ 877-677-0585; roserabbitlie.com
Mid-strip and environs

Customers Visitors, locals. **Reservations** Recommended. **When to go** When you're looking for an "experience." **Small plates range** $4–$36. **Payment** All major credit cards. **Service rating** ★★★. **Friendliness rating** ★★★★. **Parking** Valet, garage. **Bar** Full service. **Dress** Casual elegant. **Disabled access** Yes. **Hours** Wednesday–Saturday, 5:30 p.m.–late night.

SETTING AND ATMOSPHERE This adults-only bohemian take on a social club is part lounge and part restaurant. Unmarked doors and retractable walls separate the various components, and there are plenty of hidden surprises. The dining room, known as the library, is a large open room with a glass fireplace depicting Hieronymus Bosch's erotic masterpiece *The Garden of Earthly Delights* and musicians playing exotic instruments above certain tables. You can also grab light snacks in the study, which has a casual lounge feel.

HOUSE SPECIALTIES Small plates here are generally deconstructed and reinvented versions of American classics, such as crispy oysters Rockefeller, rabbit fricassee, and short rib stroganoff.

OTHER RECOMMENDATIONS If you want to splurge, check out the extensive caviar selection, with portions available from $55 to $5,000, or the $1,200 whole king crab stuffed with two types of lobster (it feeds an entire table).

SUMMARY AND COMMENTS Prices seem low, but the small plates add up quickly. It's worth it for an experience unlike anything in Las Vegas. For more on the nightlife vibe at Rose. Rabbit. Lie., see page 290.

RX Boiler Room ★★★★

ECLECTIC	MODERATE/EXPENSIVE	QUALITY ★★★★	VALUE ★★★½

Mandalay Place, 3960 Las Vegas Blvd. S.; ☎ 702-632-7200;
rxboilerroom.com   **South-Strip and Environs**

Customers Locals, visitors. **Reservations** Not necessary. **When to go** Anytime.
Entrée range $21–$34. **Payment** All major credit cards. **Service rating** ★★★★.
Friendliness rating ★★★★. **Parking** Valet, lot. **Bar** Full service; excellent cocktail
menu. **Wine selection** Limited. **Dress** Casual. **Disabled access** Yes. **Hours** Sunday–
Thursday, 5 p.m.–midnight; Friday and Saturday, 5 p.m.–2 a.m.

SETTING AND ATMOSPHERE The theme here is steampunk, so the decor is Victorian-
era sci-fi. It looks like a luxurious laboratory, and the waitresses dress in
corsets.

HOUSE SPECIALTIES Celebrity chef Rick Moonen branches out beyond the sustainable seafood he's known for, giving crazy tweaks to comfort food. Small
plates include bacon-wrapped bacon with quail egg, chicken pot pie nuggets, and inside-out French onion grilled cheese, while the entrée section of
the menu features squid-E-O's squid "pasta" with lamb meatballs and fried
game hen with waffles.

OTHER RECOMMENDATIONS Those bubbling and steaming potions behind the bar
aren't for show; the bartenders are using them to infuse original flavors into
their cocktails. Make sure to try a few.

SUMMARY AND COMMENTS This is one of the coolest, most original spots in town,
and worth a visit even if you've never heard of the phrase steampunk.

Sage ★★★★½

AMERICAN	VERY EXPENSIVE	QUALITY ★★★★½	VALUE ★★★★

Aria at CityCenter, 3730 Las Vegas Blvd. S.; ☎ 877-230-2742;
tinyurl.com/sagevegas   **Mid-Strip and Environs**

Customers Visitors. **Reservations** Essential. **When to go** Anytime. **Entrée range** À
la carte, $37–$54; prix-fixe menus, $59–$150. **Payment** All major credit cards. **Service
rating** ★★★★★. **Friendliness rating** ★★★★½. **Parking** Valet, lot. **Bar** Full service;
excellent cocktail menu. **Wine selection** Excellent. **Dress** Upscale. **Disabled access**
Yes. **Hours** Daily, 5–11 p.m.

SETTING AND ATMOSPHERE You enter through an elegant bar. The high-ceilinged
dining room is dark, clubby, and formal. Appointments, such as stemware
and table settings, are first-rate.

HOUSE SPECIALTIES Chicago's Shawn McClain (Spring) cooks smart American
fare with hints of almost everywhere on the planet. He refers to his cooking
as "refined American cuisine," and we're apt to agree. Kusshi oysters from
Vancouver Island are topped with Tabasco sorbet and aged tequila. Don't
miss the foie gras custard brûlée, the chef's signature.

OTHER RECOMMENDATIONS Don't miss the roasted loin of Ibérico pork, short ribs
braised in Belgian ale, and roast Sonoma chicken with a maitake-mushroom
persillade. The chef has added a small but imaginative vegetarian menu.
Slow-poached organic farm egg and Bellwether Farms sheep's-milk-ricotta
gnocchi are so good you would swear off meat to eat them.

SUMMARY AND COMMENTS Other than Bradley Ogden, Shawn McClain may be the
best example of a native American talent who sources the best American
products.

Scarpetta ★★★★

| ITALIAN | EXPENSIVE | QUALITY ★★★★ | VALUE ★★★½ |

The Cosmopolitan, 3708 Las Vegas Blvd. S.; ☎ 702-698-7000;
tinyurl.com/scarpettavegas **Mid-Strip and Environs**

Customers Locals, visitors. **Reservations** Essential. **When to go** On special occasions. **Entrée range** $23–$62. **Payment** All major credit cards. **Service rating** ★★★★★. **Friendliness rating** ★★★. **Parking** Valet, lot. **Bar** Full service. **Wine selection** Excellent. **Dress** Elegant. **Disabled access** None. **Hours** Daily, 5:30–11 p.m.

SETTING AND ATMOSPHERE Diners enter this elegant establishment through a long bar area. The dining room features unique yin–yang curving banquettes. Acoustics are intelligent, and the muted colors are relaxing. This is one of the few places at The Cosmo where you can have a conversation.

HOUSE SPECIALTIES Everyone is curious to try chef Scott Conant's $25 spaghetti, but there are many other dishes not to miss, such as the Sicilian-spiced duck breast and seared sea scallops.

OTHER RECOMMENDATIONS The real surprises are main dishes. Most Italian restaurants soar with starter courses and run out of steam. A black cod with crisp skin on one side and fennel and tomato is a must-try. Save room for the mouth-watering desserts.

SUMMARY AND COMMENTS Scarpetta is a mature restaurant owned by a mature chef. This is smart, tasty food that you want to eat. What's more, the service doesn't miss a beat.

Sen of Japan ★★★★

| SUSHI | MODERATE/EXPENSIVE | QUALITY ★★★★ | VALUE ★★★½ |

8480 W. Desert Inn Rd.; ☎ 702-871-7781; senofjapan.com **West of Strip**

Customers Locals. **Reservations** Recommended. **When to go** Anytime. **Entrée range** À la carte, $7–$48; omakase tasting menus, $55–$85. **Payment** All major cards. **Service rating** ★★★. **Friendliness rating** ★★★. **Parking** Lot. **Bar** Beer, wine, and sake. **Wine selection** Limited. **Dress** Casual. **Disabled access** None. **Hours** Monday–Saturday, 5 p.m.–1:30 a.m.; Sunday, 5–11:30 p.m.

SETTING AND ATMOSPHERE A pleasant but generic room in a mini-mall, the restaurant features a sushi bar and a comfortable dining area.

HOUSE SPECIALTIES *Omakase,* or chef's choice, is definitely the way to go here. Tell the server what you want to spend, and then let chef Hiro Nakano rock and roll. The salmon-skin salad is superb, and the quality of the chef's sushi rice, the *ne plus ultra* for a Japanese gourmet, is the best around.

OTHER RECOMMENDATIONS It doesn't just have to be sushi here. *Tsukune,* delicious meatballs of chicken with a soy glaze served on wooden skewers, and *shishito,* grilled Japanese green pepper, are wonderful, as is the tempura, served with a grated-radish dipping sauce.

SUMMARY AND COMMENTS This is some of Las Vegas's best sushi, and prices are about half what they would be in comparable sushi restaurants on or near the Strip, such as Nobu at the Hard Rock (where Nakano was previously head chef) or Yellowtail at Bellagio. If you're on the Westside and craving sushi, this place is a must.

Settebello ★★★½

| PIZZA | MODERATE | QUALITY ★★★★ | VALUE ★★★ |

140 Green Valley Pkwy.; ☎ 702-222-3556; settebello.net
Southeast Las Vegas–Henderson

Customers Visitors, locals. **Reservations** Recommended. **When to go** Anytime.
Entrée range $8–$15. **Payment** All major credit cards. **Service rating** ★★★.
Friendliness rating ★★★. **Parking** Lot. **Bar** Beer and wine. **Wine selection** Good.
Dress Casual. **Disabled access** Yes. **Hours** Daily, 11 a.m.–10 p.m.

SETTING AND ATMOSPHERE The restaurant has a decidedly neighborhood feel, but
those who've discovered the joys of Settebello's pizza find themselves trek-
king all the way to Green Valley for a slice.

HOUSE SPECIALTIES Settebello serves quite possibly the best pizza in Las Vegas,
made according to tenets of the Associazione Verace Pizza Napoletana, an
Italian organization dedicated to the preservation of true Napoli-style pizza.
The crust (which takes only about 45–60 seconds to cook in Settebello's
beautiful 950°F imported wood-fired oven) is crisp on the bottom from the
high heat, yet somewhat soft enough to tear. Toppings, such as the simplest
tomatoes, mozzarella, and olive oil, are mostly imported—pure ingredients
that taste fresh and wholesome.

SUMMARY AND COMMENTS Settebello has a cult following in Las Vegas. Chef Theo
Schoenegger of Sinatra (page 412) says it's his favorite pizza place. Owner
Brad Otton, who was trained as a *pizzaiolo* in Italy, oversees the place him-
self and greets regulars and newcomers on a daily basis.

Shaanxi Gourmet ★★★½

CHINESE	INEXPENSIVE	QUALITY ★★★½	VALUE ★★★★

3400 S. Jones Blvd.; ☎ 702-586-3311   **West of Strip**

Customers Locals. **Reservations** Not needed. **When to go** Anytime. **Entrée range**
$6–$13. **Payment** Visa/MasterCard. **Service rating** ★★★. **Friendliness rating**
★★★½. **Parking** Lot. **Bar** Beer and Wine. **Wine selection** House. **Dress** Casual.
Disabled access Yes. **Hours** Daily, 10 a.m.–10 p.m.

SETTING AND ATMOSPHERE The atmosphere here is pretty basic, but the lighting
is soft, which is a plus in any authentic Chinese restaurant, and booths are
reasonably comfy. It's also quiet, so conversation is possible, unlike at many
larger Cantonese restaurants.

HOUSE SPECIALTIES This is the first Vegas restaurant specializing in the spicy,
lamb-centric dishes of northwest China's Shaanxi Province, the most famous
place there being its oft-visited capital city of Xi'an. A branch of a successful
restaurant in Southern California, Shaanxi Gourmet brings a new dimension
to Las Vegas Chinese dining. Most of the best dishes here are based on lamb:
lamb noodle soup, lamb with cumin, and lamb skewers.

OTHER RECOMMENDATIONS You don't have to love lamb to find good things to eat
on this menu, which is very reasonably priced. Ox tongue in chili sauce and
knife-cut noodles with vegetables and tofu are both wonderful, and several
spicy chicken dishes use those *ma la* Chinese peppers to perfection.

SUMMARY AND COMMENTS Shaanxi Gourmet is for the adventurous—and patient—
diner. Service is cordial when you can communicate with the mostly mono-
lingual (in Mandarin Chinese) staff, but the food is so interesting, and the
prices so reasonable, that this is a must-visit for anyone seeking a different
kind of Asian-dining experience.

Sinatra ★★★

| ITALIAN | EXPENSIVE | QUALITY ★★★ | VALUE ★★ |

Wynn Encore Resort, 3131 Las Vegas Blvd. S.; ☎ 702-248-3463; wynnlasvegas.com **Mid-Strip and Environs**

Customers Visitors. **Reservations** Suggested. **When to go** Anytime. **Entrée range** $27–$58. **Payment** All major credit cards. **Service rating** ★★★★★. **Friendliness rating** ★★★. **Parking** Valet, garage. **Bar** Full service. **Wine selection** Very good. **Dress** Business casual. **Disabled access** Yes. **Hours** Sunday–Thursday, 5:30–10 p.m., until 10:30 p.m. Friday and Saturday

SETTING AND ATMOSPHERE Nothing says Las Vegas quite like Frank Sinatra, and Ol' Blue Eyes finally gets his restaurant at Encore. The room—more evocative of George Clooney's *Ocean's Eleven* than Sinatra's—is a blend of modern and midcentury, in natural hues of brown and green. Five custom-made olive-green chandeliers are composed of eco-friendly hemp rope and burlap. Frequent reminders of Sinatra's influence include his Oscar for *From Here to Eternity* and his Grammy for "Strangers in the Night," as well as gold albums and personal letters between him and his Rat Pack pals.

HOUSE SPECIALTIES The menu is a twist on Italian classics, some of which were Sinatra's favorites, along with some signature dishes such as *zuppa di fagioli* (made with borlotti beans); agnolotti with ricotta, herbs, and winter truffles; and Osso Bucco "My Way," with risotto Milanese and gremolata.

SUMMARY AND COMMENTS Michelin-starred chef Theo Schoenegger portrays his Italian roots in creative, modern ways for this menu. To be fair, we'd eat his food even if it didn't have an icon's name next to it.

Spago ★★★½

| AMERICAN | EXPENSIVE | QUALITY ★★★★ | VALUE ★★½ |

The Forum Shops at Caesars; 3500 Las Vegas Blvd. S.; ☎ 702-369-6300; tinyurl.com/spagolv **Mid-Strip and Environs**

Customers Visitors, locals. **Reservations** Recommended for dinner. **When to go** Anytime except during busy conventions. **Entrée range** $31–$50. **Payment** All major credit cards. **Service rating** ★★★½. **Friendliness rating** ★★★★½. **Parking** Valet, garage. **Bar** Full service. **Wine selection** Excellent. **Dress** Casual. **Disabled access** Yes. **Hours** *Café and bar:* Sunday–Thursday, 11:30 a.m.–11 p.m.; Friday and Saturday, 11:30 a.m.–midnight; *Restaurant:* daily, 5:30–10 p.m.

SETTING AND ATMOSPHERE There are two separate dining rooms. The casual café offers a bird's-eye view of The Forum Shops from the comfort of a European-style sidewalk setting. The restaurant inside is an eclectic mix of modern art, wrought iron, and contemporary tables, chairs, and booths. Each Sunday in the café from about 2:30–6:30 p.m., a jazz band entertains. A private banquet room is available for parties of up to 100. A small private room within the restaurant can seat up to 20.

HOUSE SPECIALTIES *Café:* Wolfgang Puck's signature pizzas; imaginative sandwiches; salads; pastas; and frequently, a supertasty meatloaf with port-wine sauce, grilled onions, and garlic-potato puree. *Restaurant:* exquisite appetizers; pastas; wiener schnitzel with potato salad and lemon-caper sauce; yellowfin tuna with jasmine rice, baby bok choy, and shiitakes; and striped bass with artichoke ravioli and garlic nage. Menus in the café and restaurant change daily. Signature dishes always available. New corporate pastry chef

Kamel Guechida brings an embarrassment of riches to the bread and dessert selections.

SUMMARY AND COMMENTS The bar is a busy centerpiece. Locals who've always considered Spago a favorite have their home parties catered by the restaurant. Puck surrounds himself with the best staff, the best ingredients, the best of everything. One caveat—on very busy nights, the dining room's noise level can make conversation difficult. But the people-watching is terrific.

THE Steak House ★★★½

STEAK	EXPENSIVE	QUALITY ★★★½	VALUE ★★★★

Circus Circus, 2880 Las Vegas Blvd. S.; ☎ 702-794-3767; circuscircus.com/dining/the_steakhouse.aspx   **North Strip and Environs**

Customers Visitors, locals. **Reservations** Required. **When to go** Anytime. **Entrée range** $30–$64, including choice of soup or salad, vegetable, and potato (add lobster, $55 or $75). **Payment** All major credit cards. **Service rating** ★★★½. **Friendliness rating** ★★★½. **Parking** Garage, lot, valet. **Bar** Full service. **Wine selection** Good. **Dress** Informal. **Disabled access** Ramps. **Hours** Sunday–Friday, 4–10 p.m.; Saturday, 4–11 p.m.

SETTING AND ATMOSPHERE Wood-paneled rooms. The small dining room is decorated like a manor-house library. A mesquite-fired broiler in the center of the main room creates a cozy atmosphere. The glass refrigerator case displays more than 3,000 pounds of meat.

HOUSE SPECIALTIES Thick steaks; black-bean soup; giant baked potato; shrimp, crab, and lobster cocktails; Caesar salad; grilled chicken.

SUMMARY AND COMMENTS Consistently high quality and service. Don't be fooled by the children running around the lobby. Inside THE Steak House, the atmosphere is adult, and the food is wonderful.

Table 34 ★★★½

CONTEMPORARY	AMERICAN	MODERATE	QUALITY ★★★½	VALUE ★★★½

600 E. Warm Springs Rd.; ☎ 702-263-0034; table34lasvegas.com
Southeast Las Vegas–Henderson

Customers Locals, visitors. **Reservations** Suggested on weekends. **When to go** Anytime. **Entrée range** $15–$35. **Payment** All major credit cards. **Service rating** ★★★★★. **Friendliness rating** ★★★★★. **Parking** Large lot. **Bar** Full service. **Wine selection** Good; many wines by the glass. **Dress** Casual. **Disabled access** Ground floor. **Hours** Monday–Friday, 11 a.m.–2:30 p.m.; Tuesday–Saturday, 5–9:30 p.m.

SETTING AND ATMOSPHERE A hip, appealing eatery with a freestanding bar and brilliant use of colors.

HOUSE SPECIALTIES Menu changes seasonally, but favorites such as chef Wes Kendrick's soups always remain. The cream of tomato with tarragon is a joy. Try house-smoked salmon on a crisp potato galette (pancake); grilled Maine sea scallops with braised greens and Dijon-barbecue sauce; or gratinéed macaroni and cheese with smoked ham and English peas. The all-beef meatloaf with mashed potatoes and onion gravy is like a taste of home.

OTHER RECOMMENDATIONS Grilled rack of pork with chipotle potatoes, asparagus, and hard-cider glaze; wild-mushroom pizza with fresh herbs; the signature Key lime pie. Note that menus change frequently; dishes listed here may not always be available.

SUMMARY AND COMMENTS Reasonable prices for fine bistro-style food.

Todd's Unique Dining ★★★★

STEAK/SEAFOOD   MODERATE/EXPENSIVE   QUALITY ★★★★   VALUE ★★★★

4350 E. Sunset Rd., Henderson; ☎ 702-259-8633; toddsunique.com
Southeast Las Vegas–Henderson

Customers Locals. **Reservations** Recommended. **When to go** Anytime. **Entrée range** $25–$38. **Payment** All major credit cards; gift cards available at website. **Service rating** ★★★. **Friendliness rating** ★★★★★. **Parking** Lot. **Bar** Full service. **Wine selection** Small. **Dress** Casual. **Disabled access** Yes. **Hours** Monday–Saturday, 5–9:30 p.m. (last seating).

SETTING AND ATMOSPHERE A small storefront among big-chain restaurants in Henderson, Todd's Unique Dining is homey, casual, and comfortable. A favorite with Green Valley residents, chef Todd Clore, a veteran of corporate Strip restaurants, makes his mark with this neighborhood restaurant.

HOUSE SPECIALTIES Mainly a seafood restaurant, Todd's Unique definitely has some Asian influence. Standards like the goat-cheese wontons are a surprising bite of pungent goat cheese balanced with an herby raspberry-and-basil sauce. Seared ahi tuna with wasabi and mashed leeks reveals a touch of East-meets-West, as does the Kobe skirt steak finished with black bean-and-chili sauce.

SUMMARY AND COMMENTS Clore has definitely elevated neighborhood dining for Green Valley, garnering local regulars night after night. It's solid, high-end cuisine without the prices, or pretensions, that plague many Strip restaurants.

Top of the World ★★★★½

AMERICAN   EXPENSIVE   QUALITY ★★★★½   VALUE ★★★½

Stratosphere Tower, 2000 Las Vegas Blvd. S.; ☎ 702-380-7711; topoftheworldlv.com   North Strip and Environs

Customers Visitors, locals. **Reservations** Required. **When to go** Anytime. **Entrée range** $40–$79; four-course tasting menu, $90. **Payment** All major credit cards. **Service rating** ★★★★½. **Friendliness rating** ★★★½. **Parking** Valet, garage, lot. **Bar** Full service. **Wine selection** Excellent. **Dress** Business casual. **Disabled access** Elevator. **Hours** Daily, 11 a.m.–11 p.m.

SETTING AND ATMOSPHERE Top of the World offers one of the most beautiful views of the city. The restaurant revolves as you dine, giving a panoramic spectacle of the surrounding mountains. One complete revolution takes an hour and 20 minutes. The dining room is elegant and sophisticated.

HOUSE SPECIALTIES Shrimp cocktail, four-course tasting menu, foie gras, Moroccan lamb, and many small plates from French chef Claude Gaty.

OTHER RECOMMENDATIONS Fresh Atlantic salmon encrusted with fresh sage and prosciutto di parma; lobster ravioli; the towering vacherin dessert; tiramisù or panna cotta.

SUMMARY AND COMMENTS The food is excellent but still takes a back seat to the view. You must check in at a podium, go through security, and ride an elevator to the top. Arrive before sunset for an unforgettably romantic experience. Tickets: $18 adults, $12 seniors and Nevada residents, $10 kids.

Trattoria Nakamura-ya ★★★½

JAPANESE   MODERATE   QUALITY ★★★   VALUE ★★★

5040 W. Spring Mountain Rd.; ☎ 702-251-0022   West of Strip

Customers Locals, chefs. **Reservations** Recommended. **When to go** Dinner. **Entrée range** $13–$24. **Payment** All major credit cards. **Service rating** ★★★. **Friendliness rating** ★★★. **Parking** Lot. **Bar** Beer, wine, and a variety of sakes. **Wine selection** Good. **Dress** Casual. **Disabled access** Yes. **Hours** Daily, 2 p.m.–midnight.

SETTING AND ATMOSPHERE Nakamura-ya is the first Vegas outpost of Italian-Japanese cuisine—classic Italian dishes like spaghetti carbonara, *fritto misto,* and pasta with creamy walnut sauce, each done in ways rarely seen outside Japan. Be prepared for a delightful experience in this dark, matchbox-sized room, where chef Kengo Nakamura does magic tricks in an open kitchen.

HOUSE SPECIALTIES Fritto misto—octopus, calamari, shrimp, and zucchini on wooden skewers—is accompanied by a pair of homemade dipping sauces. Manila clams, swimming in a rich broth with wine and enough garlic to end the *Twilight* franchise, is in reality the very Japanese dish called *asari sakamushi.*

OTHER RECOMMENDATIONS Fried Jidori chicken, the meat cut into bits only slightly larger than popcorn-chicken nuggets, is matchless and a tribute to the skill of the chef. Pasta and sea urchin in tomato cream sauce is a beautiful blend of Italian and Japanese cuisines. Miso carbonara is textbook, if you don't mind miso paste mixed into the eggs, bacon, and cheese blanketing the noodles.

SUMMARY AND COMMENTS The Japanese are obsessed with *itaria-ryori,* what they call Italian food. Tokyo has literally thousands of restaurants in which to eat this cuisine, characterized by light tomato sauce, scandalous amounts of garlic (a component conspicuously absent in Japanese cooking), and various riffs in the key of noodle, masquerading as pasta. This is the first such place we know of in Las Vegas.

Twist by Pierre Gagnaire ★★★★★

FRENCH	VERY EXPENSIVE	QUALITY ★★★★★	VALUE ★★★★★

Mandarin Oriental Las Vegas, 3752 Las Vegas Blvd. S.; ☎ 702-590-8888; tinyurl.com/twistvegas   **Mid-Strip and Environs**

Customers Visitors. **Reservations** Essential. **When to go** Dinner. **Entrée range** À la carte, $44–$182; prix-fixe menus, $95–$777. **Payment** All major credit cards. **Service rating** ★★★★★. **Friendliness rating** ★★★★★. **Parking** Valet. **Bar** Full service. **Wine selection** Reasonably priced list of upscale wines. **Dress** Upscale. **Disabled access** Yes. **Hours** Tuesday–Saturday, 6–10 p.m.

SETTING AND ATMOSPHERE On the 23rd and top floor of the chi-chi Mandarin Oriental Hotel; tables look out onto the Strip. The modern dining room is tastefully elegant and decorated with glass globes and decorative art.

HOUSE SPECIALTIES Colorful, creative canapés, such as gelée made from Guinness, are a calling card, as are the swank tasting menus. The food of Pierre Gagnaire is among the most creative of the world's chefs. It's food you not only haven't seen before, it's food that most have never even imagined. (Menus are seasonal, so dishes may differ from those mentioned here.)

OTHER RECOMMENDATIONS Langoustine five ways is a standout. The chef also does tricks with fish and game, incorporating flavors you don't expect, such as lavender or licorice, in combinations that work like magic. Save room for the wonderful desserts.

SUMMARY AND COMMENTS It's a feather in the proverbial cap to get this celebrated Parisian to open here, ably assisted by chef Ryuki Kawasaki. If you don't wish to order a tasting menu, just order an entrée à la carte and still experience all the bells and whistles, such as canapés and petit fours, without spending a fortune. However you dine, nothing here is for the unadventurous eater.

Vintner Grill ★★★★

AMERICAN	MODERATE/EXPENSIVE	QUALITY ★★★★	VALUE ★★★★

10100 W. Charleston Blvd.; ☎ 702-214-5590; vglasvegas.com
West of Strip

Customers Locals. **Reservations** Recommended. **When to go** Anytime. **Entrée range** $21–$39. **Payment** All major credit cards. **Service rating** ★★★★. **Friendliness rating** ★★★★★. **Parking** Lot, valet. **Bar** Full service. **Wine selection** Excellent. **Dress** Casual. **Disabled access** Yes. **Hours** Lunch: Monday–Friday, 11 a.m.–4 p.m. Dinner: Sunday–Thursday, 4–10 p.m.; Friday and Saturday, 4–11 p.m. Bar: Daily until midnight.

SETTING AND ATMOSPHERE Bathed in white with splashes of bright colors, this modern dining room is a favorite of Summerlin's powerbrokers. When the weather is nice, the tables on the outdoor patio with hanging lanterns are the most coveted. One surprise for a restaurant this nice is the presence of video poker machines at the bar.

HOUSE SPECIALTIES Chef Matt Silverman changes the menu frequently, but you'll always find great flatbreads, pastas and risottos, seafood, and wood-fired steaks.

OTHER RECOMMENDATIONS Be sure to get a meat and cheese plate. The selection is among the best in town, and includes house-cured meats and cheese Silverman makes himself from the milk of his own goats.

SUMMARY AND COMMENTS Vintner Grill was one of the first restaurants to bring this level of unpretentious-yet-sophisticated dining to this affluent neighborhood, and it continues to be one of its top spots.

Viva Las Arepas ★★★½

SOUTH AMERICAN	INEXPENSIVE	QUALITY ★★★½	VALUE ★★★★

1616 Las Vegas Blvd S., Suite 120; ☎ 702-366-9696; vivalasarepas.com
Downtown

Customers Locals. **Reservations** Not necessary. **When to go** Anytime. **Entrée range** $4–$14. **Payment** All major credit cards. **Service rating** ★★½. **Friendliness rating** ★★★½. **Parking** Limited lot, on street. **Bar** No alcohol served. **Dress** Casual. **Disabled access** Yes. **Hours** Sunday–Thursday, 9 a.m.–10 p.m.; Friday and Saturday, 9 a.m.–midnight.

SETTING AND ATMOSPHERE This unprepossessing, cafeteria-like room specializes in the *arepa,* a Venezuelan corn cake that is typically cut in half and stuffed with savory fillings. Eaten in a burger-style wrapper, one makes a satisfying meal; two constitute a trencherman's feast. Order from the counter and take your seat—you aren't here for the atmosphere.

HOUSE SPECIALTIES Arepas are what most people come for. The most popular one is *carne asada*—pounded, marinated rib eye finished on hickory and charcoal, as are all meats here. One of the more unusual choices is *reina pepiada,* its minced-chicken filling redolent of garlic and cilantro. *Arepa perico* is a South American Egg McMuffin, filled with ham, egg, and cheese. Garlic shrimp arepas are downright addictive. Owner Felix Arellano prepares some of the city's best barbecued meats, cooked on a wood grill as well.

OTHER RECOMMENDATIONS *Empanadas* and *pastelitos,* snack turnovers made from wheat or corn flour with savory fillings, are also a treat here. Arellano's mixed grill—sausages, pork ribs on the bone, amazing grilled chicken, and pounded steak—is one of the city's best values at under $15. If you fancy tropical beverages, try passion fruit, soursop (*guanabana* in Spanish), or other fruit drinks served over ice. The house rice-and-vegetable medley is another must.

SUMMARY AND COMMENTS Viva Las Arepas is the first Venezuelan restaurant in Vegas, and its authenticity is beyond reproach. It's already become a meeting place for locals from many South American countries, and the price point and wide variety of snacks and main dishes have made an indelible impression on Anglos—and greatly enhanced the Downtown dining scene.

Wolfgang Puck Pizzeria & Cucina ★★★½

AMERICAN	EXPENSIVE	QUALITY ★★★★	VALUE ★★★½

Crystals at CityCenter, 3720 Las Vegas Blvd. S.; ☎ 702-238-1000; tinyurl.com/puckpizzeriavegas **Mid-Strip and Environs**

Customers Visitors, locals. **Reservations** Suggested. **When to go** Anytime. **Entrée range** $21–$46. **Payment** All major credit cards. **Service rating** ★★★★★. **Friendliness rating** ★★★★★. **Parking** Valet. **Bar** Full service. **Wine selection** Very good. **Dress** Casual. **Disabled access** Yes. **Hours** Sunday–Thursday, 11:30 a.m.–10 p.m.; Friday and Saturday, 11:30 a.m.–11 p.m.

SETTING AND ATMOSPHERE This beautiful dining room sits on the mezzanine level of Crystals. The best tables overlook upscale shops such as Tom Ford and give diners a chance to watch the people shopping below.

HOUSE SPECIALTIES The menu is a compilation of Italian favorites. There is a delicious board of *salumi* (Italian cold cuts) and terrific fried calamari. Pizzas, such as the one with Italian sausage and rapini, come on thin crusts from a wood oven. Prime beef carpaccio, a fairly classic version of the dish, comes topped with celery hearts and shaved Parmesan.

OTHER RECOMMENDATIONS Main courses are usually a letdown at casual Italian restaurants, but here they come as a major surprise. The kitchen turns out a delicious osso buco and one of the best chicken piccatas in the city, slathered with a lemon-caper butter. Pastas are excellent as well, especially ricotta gnocchi with a sausage Bolognese.

SUMMARY AND COMMENTS Corporate chefs Lee Hefter and David Robins are masters, and the man in the kitchen, Dustin Lewandowski, who moved over from the Wolfgang Puck Bar & Grill in the MGM Grand, is talented. The original concept here, Brasserie Puck, didn't take. So Puck's management team has moved on, and now business is brisk.

PART FIVE

SHOPPING *and* SEEING *the* SIGHTS

SHOPPING *in* LAS VEGAS

THE MOST INTERESTING AND DIVERSIFIED specialty shopping in Las Vegas is centered on the Strip at the **Fashion Show Mall** (☎ 702-369-8382; **thefashionshow.com**), **The Forum and Appian Way Shops at Caesars Palace** (☎ 702-893-4800; **caesarspalace.com**), and the **Grand Canal Shoppes at The Venetian** (☎ 702-414-4500; **grandcanalshoppes.com**). These three venues, within walking distance of each other, collectively offer the most unusual, and arguably the most concentrated, aggregation of upscale retailers in the United States. It should be noted that The Forum Shops and the Grand Canal Shoppes are not your average shopping centers. In fact, both are attractions in their own right and should be on your must-see list even if you don't like to shop. Both feature designer shops, exclusive boutiques, and specialty retailers. Fashion Show Mall, by comparison, is plain white bread, with no discernible theme but a great lineup of big-name department stores.

At the intersection of Las Vegas Boulevard and Spring Mountain Road, the Fashion Show Mall is anchored by **Saks Fifth Avenue, Neiman Marcus, Macy's, Nordstrom, Forever 21,** and **Dillard's,** and contains more than 100 specialty shops, including three art galleries. There is no theme here—no Roman columns or canals with gondolas. At the Fashion Show Mall, shopping is king. And although there is no shortage of boutiques or designer shops, the presence of the big department stores defines the experience for most customers. The selection is immense, and most of the retailers are familiar and well known. To underscore its name, the mall stages free fashion shows most weekend afternoons.

unofficial **TIP**
The Fashion Show Mall is the place to go for that new sport coat, tie, blouse, or skirt at a reasonable price.

The Forum Shops is a *très chic (et très cher)* shopping complex situated between Caesars Palace and the Mirage. Connected to the Forum Casino in Caesars Palace, The Forum Shops offers a Roman market–themed shopping environment. Executed on a scale that is extraordinary even for Caesars, The Forum Shops replicates the grandeur of Rome at the height of its glory. More than 160 shops and restaurants line an ancient Roman street punctuated by plazas and fountains. Dozens of retailers and eateries populate the three-story, 175,000-square-foot Appian Way expansion. Though indoors, clouds, sky, and celestial bodies are projected on the vaulted ceilings to simulate the actual time of day outside. Statuary in The Forum is magnificent; some is even animatronic. Shops include the **Max Brenner** chocolate shop; clothing retailer **H&M; UGG,** featuring leathers, suedes, and sheepskin; **True Religion** for denim; and makeup retailer **Inglot.**

The Grand Canal Shoppes are similar to The Forum Shops in terms of the realistic theming, only this time the setting is the modern-day canals of Venice. More than 60 shops, boutiques, restaurants, and cafés are arrayed along a quarter-mile-long Venetian street flanking a canal. A 70-foot ceiling (more than six stories high) with simulated sky enhances the openness and provides perspective. Meanwhile, gondolas navigating the canal add a heightened sense of commerce and activity. The centerpiece of the Grand Canal Shoppes is a replica of St. Mark's Square, without the pigeons.

The Grand Canal Shoppes connect to **The Shoppes at The Palazzo** (☎ 702-414-4525; **theshoppesatthepalazzo.com**), at The Venetian's sister hotel. Anchored by **Barneys New York,** the two-story shopping arcade offers more than three dozen upscale retailers and restaurants. Unlike the Grand Canal Shoppes, The Shoppes at The Palazzo is essentially unthemed, or expressed differently, you should check your gondola at the door.

The CityCenter development situated between Bellagio and the Monte Carlo adds another mega-retail venue, **Crystals** (☎ 702-590-9299 and 866-754-2489; **crystalsatcitycenter.com**), to the Strip-shopping lineup. Because Crystals is located more or less across the street from the Miracle Mile Shops (described below), the two together offer the second-largest concentration of retailers on the Strip.

Crystals, a 500,000-square-foot high-end retail and entertainment center, is tightly wedged between Veer condominium towers and The Harmon boutique hotel (opening unknown). Conceived as an urban city park, exterior landscapes have moved inside. Tall deciduous trees line the walkways, and a sculpture of horizontal wooden slats at the midpoint looks like an avant-garde tree house. Displays throughout reflect and celebrate the four seasons. Crystals will eventually host 71 international luxury stores, including **Louis Vuitton, Tiffany & Co., Miki-moto, Prada, Christian Dior, Hermès, Versace, Gucci, Yves Saint Laurent, Stella McCartney,** and **Harry Winston** to drop a few well-recognized names. Several are two-level flagship stores. Don't expect coupons or deep discounts. Between the Mandarin Oriental and Aria is **Crystals Place,** a 4,200-square-foot annex and collection of several art galleries displaying the artwork, designs, and furniture of the CityCenter architects and artists. Seven restaurants, a 24,000-square-foot nightclub, and a bar and entertainment venues are also on-site. The hard-to-miss main

Las Vegas Strip Shopping and Attractions

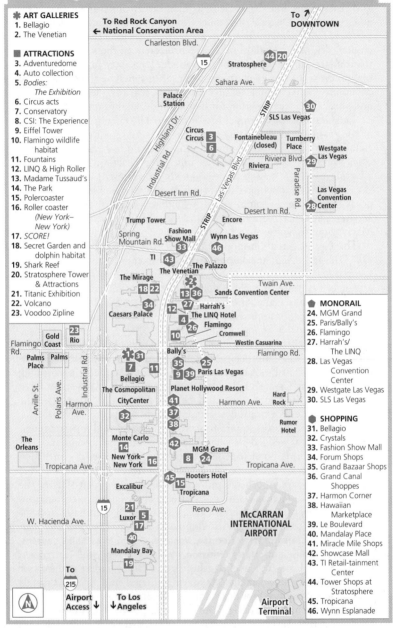

✻ ART GALLERIES
1. Bellagio
2. The Venetian

■ ATTRACTIONS
3. Adventuredome
4. Auto collection
5. *Bodies: The Exhibition*
6. Circus acts
7. Conservatory
8. CSI: The Experience
9. Eiffel Tower
10. Flamingo wildlife habitat
11. Fountains
12. LINQ & High Roller
13. Madame Tussaud's
14. The Park
15. Polercoaster
16. Roller coaster (New York–New York)
17. SCORE!
18. Secret Garden and dolphin habitat
19. Shark Reef
20. Stratosphere Tower & Attractions
21. Titanic Exhibition
22. Volcano
23. Voodoo Zipline

● MONORAIL
24. MGM Grand
25. Paris/Bally's
26. Flamingo
27. Harrah's/ The LINQ
28. Las Vegas Convention Center
29. Westgate Las Vegas
30. SLS Las Vegas

● SHOPPING
31. Bellagio
32. Crystals
33. Fashion Show Mall
34. Forum Shops
35. Grand Bazaar Shops
36. Grand Canal Shoppes
37. Harmon Corner
38. Hawaiian Marketplace
39. Le Boulevard
40. Mandalay Place
41. Miracle Mile Shops
42. Showcase Mall
43. TI Retail-tainment Center
44. Tower Shops at Stratosphere
45. Tropicana
46. Wynn Esplanade

To Red Rock Canyon ← National Conservation Area

To ↗ DOWNTOWN

Charleston Blvd.
Stratosphere
Sahara Ave.
Palace Station
SLS Las Vegas
Circus Circus
Fontainebleau (closed)
Turnberry Place
Westgate Las Vegas
Riviera Blvd.
Riviera
Las Vegas Convention Center
Desert Inn Rd.
Desert Inn Rd.
Trump Tower
Encore
Spring Mountain Rd.
Fashion Show Mall
Wynn Las Vegas
TI
The Palazzo
The Venetian
The Mirage
Twain Ave.
Sands Convention Center
Caesars Palace
Harrah's
The LINQ Hotel
Flamingo
Cromwell
Westin Casuarina
Gold Coast
Rio
Flamingo Rd.
Bally's
Flamingo Rd.
Palms Place
Palms
Paris Las Vegas
Bellagio
The Cosmopolitan
CityCenter
Planet Hollywood Resort
Harmon Ave.
Hard Rock
The Orleans
Monte Carlo
Rumor Hotel
New York–New York
MGM Grand
Tropicana Ave.
Tropicana Ave.
Excalibur
Hooters Hotel
Tropicana
W. Hacienda Ave.
Luxor
Reno Ave.
McCARRAN INTERNATIONAL AIRPORT
Mandalay Bay
To 215
Airport Access ↓
To Los ↓Angeles
Airport Terminal

Highland Dr.
Industrial Rd.
STRIP
Las Vegas Blvd.
Paradise Rd.
Industrial Rd.
Arville St.
Polaris Ave.
Harmon Ave.

entrance into Crystals is right on the Strip between Harmon Road and CityCenter Place. There is another entry inside CityCenter near Veer Towers and the tram station. Underground parking and valet service are available. Crystals is also the intermediate stop on the tram, which carries visitors between the Bellagio Spa Tower and the Monte Carlo.

A fifth major Strip shopping venue is **Miracle Mile Shops,** a 450,000-square-foot shopping and entertainment complex at Planet Hollywood (☎ 888-800-8284; **miraclemileshopslv.com**). The venue re-creates street scenes from a boutique shopping concourse and stretches around the periphery of the Axis Theater. The shop facades sit beneath an arched ceiling painted and lighted to simulate the evening sky. Overall, although the replication is effective, it is bland compared to The Forum Shops and the Grand Canal Shoppes. Like the Grand Canal Shoppes, Miracle Mile Shops offers primarily upscale boutique shopping, but more of it. A pedestrian bridge, situated mid-Strip from the north edge of CityCenter at The Cosmopolitan crossing into Planet Hollywood, makes the upgraded Miracle Mile Shops more accessible. Much of the affordable merchandise tends toward the flashy and glamorous—**Swarovski, Hervé Léger, Bettie Page,** and a **Victoria's Secret** prototype store. Spectators can enjoy the hourly indoor rainstorm and light shows at the central fountain. The complex houses three theaters. Several of the mall's 15 restaurants are open after midnight beyond retail hours.

Sun-drenched **Harmon Corner,** a triangular trilevel wedge at the key intersection of Harmon Avenue and the Strip, sits directly across from CityCenter and adjacent to Planet Hollywood and the Miracle Mile Shops. This New York Times Square–themed glass-and-steel complex is accessed via two elevated pedestrian walkways. Although the anchor is a two-story Walgreens, the 17 shops are primarily small mid-priced boutiques, and the mall includes three restaurants offering alfresco dining. Parking is limited since the mall caters to foot travelers.

At Paris is **Le Boulevard,** 31,000 square feet of upscale French boutique shopping. Modest in size by Las Vegas shopping standards, the Rue de la Paix re-creates a Paris street scene with cobblestone pavement and winding alleyways.

The Wynn Esplanade (**wynnlasvegas.com**) connecting Wynn Las Vegas and Wynn Encore is an insanely expensive array of upscale shops and boutiques, including **Brioni, Oscar de la Renta, Graff,** and **Manolo Blahnik.** Garnering the most attention is the **Penske-Wynn Ferrari Maserati** dealership, including a Ferrari merchandise store.

The **Tower Shops** at the Stratosphere (☎ 702-380-7777; **stratospherehotel.com**) are part midway and part strip mall. Extending along a narrow passageway on the hotel's second floor, the 35 establishments and kiosks are about 50-50 retail shops and fast-food purveyors. Merchants specialize in figurines, costume jewelry, leather, men and women's clothing, hats, tattoos, magic, Asian wear and gifts, and souvenirs. An oxygen bar and a daiquiri bar are next to each other by the fitness center.

Mandalay Place (**mandalaybay.com**), a mall with more than 25 boutiques and restaurants, also serves as the pedestrian connector linking Mandalay Bay and Luxor. The retailers seem more diverse and selectively chosen than at many other venues, making the shopping interesting even for those not hooked on shopping. There are nine upscale clothing and shoe retailers, a barber spa and retail shaving emporium for men, a candy store, and a Guinness store, among many others. Among the restaurants is the **Burger Bar,** featuring a $60 hamburger dressed with truffles. Fortunately, there are also less froufrou burgers at reasonable prices.

Another Strip shopping venue is the **Showcase,** adjacent to the MGM Grand. Although most of the 190,000-square-foot shopping and entertainment complex is devoted to theme restaurants, a Sega electronic games arcade, and an eight-plex movie theater, space remains for a number of retail specialty shops. Practically next door is the **Hawaiian Marketplace** (☎ 702-795-2247), an 80,000-square-foot mall. Though the theme is Polynesian, the mall's restaurants and retailers are an eclectic lot ranging from **Café Capri** to **Zingers.**

Just south of Mandalay Bay on Las Vegas Boulevard South is **Town Square** (☎ 702-269-5000; **mytownsquarelasvegas.com**). Town Square is designed as a multiblock village with streets, sidewalks, and even a park. The development is composed of almost 130 stores and businesses, large and small, including shops, restaurants, entertainment venues, beauty salons, and offices. Prominent retailers are **Abercrombie & Fitch, BCBG Max Azria, bebe, Whole Foods Market,** and **Sephora,** among others. Town Square is a dining destination that includes **California Pizza Kitchen, Claim Jumper, Tommy Bahama's Restaurant & Bar, Yard House, Texas de Brazil, Brio Tuscan Grille, Miller's Ale House, Blue Martini, Bonefish,** and **Kabuki Japanese Restaurant.** There is metered parking streetside (bring plenty of quarters) or free parking in large lots on the periphery.

unofficial **TIP**
For those without transportation, Las Vegas Citizen's Area Transit (CAT) operates a bus route that connects the various Strip and suburban shopping centers. Fare is $2 in residential areas and $6 on the Strip. Service is provided daily, 5:30 a.m.–1:30 a.m. For more information on CAT, call ☎ 702-228-7433.

Adjacent to Green Valley Ranch Resort & Spa, southeast of the Strip, **The District** (☎ 702-564-8595; **thedistrictatgvr.com**) offers 60 stores and restaurants. The shops line a long pedestrian plaza with two smaller plazas intersecting. Resembling a Georgetown, Washington, D.C., commercial and residential street, The District's shopping mix includes restaurants, apparel shops, and a couple dozen specialty stores, including **REI, Williams-Sonoma, and Pottery Barn.**

Tivoli Village at Queensridge, 13 miles west of the Las Vegas Strip via I-95 North and the Summerlin Parkway, features 33 retailers in an Italianate setting. The 370,000-square-foot open-air Mediterranean-style complex features eight restaurants plus shops, including **Charming Charlie, Kidville, Pandora,** and **Vasari.** At night, the mall's decorative cherry trees are lit with 5,000 LED bulbs, enveloping the complex in a cerise glow. Since Tivoli Village is located in a suburban neighborhood, there is plenty of above and below-ground parking. (☎ 702-570-7400; **tivolivillagelv.com.**)

Within the Village is **Market LV,** a separate two-level retail center featuring an eclectic mash of small and large boutiques and specialty foods. The urban *souk* offers 20-plus individual vendors of clothing, accessories, candy, desserts, cosmetics, flowers, pet supplies, home goods, and gifts in distinctive shops. There's also a wine bar, a piano bar, and a deli featuring pool and pinball.

Downtown is **Las Vegas Premium Outlets North** (☎ 702-474-7500; **premiumoutlets.com**), an $85-million, 150-store outlet mall. A clone of other Premium Outlet malls, featured brands include **AIX Armani Exchange, Dolce & Gabbana, Ann Taylor Factory Store, Kenneth Cole, Lacoste,** and **Coach.** The mall is just west of Downtown, between Downtown and Interstate 15. It's a bit far from Downtown to walk but is only a short cab ride away. From I-15, the mall entrance is off Charleston Boulevard.

The former Las Vegas Outlet Center has been expanded and fancified and now calls itself **Las Vegas Premium Outlets South** (☎ 702-896-5599; **premiumoutlets.com**) and is very similar to its sister mall Downtown. Located 5 miles south of Tropicana Avenue at 7400 Las Vegas Blvd. S., the remodeled discount shopping venue is near the Blue Diamond Road exit off I-15. The center added 70,000 square feet, more merchants, and a larger food court. Its inventory of 143 stores includes **Michael Kors, Coach Men's, Under Armour, Loft Outlet, and Toys "R" Us.** Promotional literature listing the individual shops is available in almost all hotel brochure racks. The easiest way to reach the outlets is to drive south on I-15 to Exit 33, Blue Diamond Road. Proceed east on Blue Diamond Road to the intersection with Las Vegas Boulevard. Turn left on Las Vegas Boulevard to the center.

About an hour southwest on I-15 in Primm, Nevada, is **Fashion Outlets of Las Vegas Mall** (☎ 702-874-1400; **fashionoutletlasvegas .com**), offering themed dining and 100 outlet stores. You'll find **American Eagle Outfitters, Williams-Sonoma, Fossil, Tommy Hilfiger, Kenneth Cole, DKNY, Kate Spade, Tommy Bahama,** and **Last Call from Neiman Marcus,** among others. The mall is adjacent to the Primm Valley Resort and Casino. For $15 round-trip, the Shoppers Shuttle runs consumers 40 miles to Primm from three locations: MGM Grand, Miracle Mile Shops, and the Fashion Show Mall. (☎ 888-424-6898.)

NEW LAS VEGAS SHOPPING VENUES

LAS VEGAS STRIP HOTELS that have heretofore offered minimal shopping are playing catch-up by undertaking major shopping developments. Those opening in 2015 and 2016 include venues at SLS, TI, New York–New York, Monte Carlo, Bally's, and the Tropicana. Shopping and restaurant initiatives at New York–New York and Monte Carlo are part of **The Park** project, a landscaped area connecting the two hotels.

More focused on aesthetics than retail, shopping is a relatively small part of the mix there. At Bally's, TI, and the Trop, however, shopping is the top banana.

GRAND BAZAAR SHOPS AT BALLY'S The zenith of alfresco merchandising is the new Grand Bazaar Shops (**grandbazaarshops.com**), situated Center Strip at Flamingo Avenue and Las Vegas Boulevard at the front entrance to Bally's. The two-acre lower plaza has been reconfigured to house 150 tony retail, food, and beverage enterprises. It's created to resemble an international outdoor marketplace, with mosaic patterns highlighting walkways and tent-like roofs. The centerpiece is a 14-foot-tall, 4,000-pound Swarovski crystal starburst resting on an 80-foot pole; it dazzles nightly with a midnight light show above the bazaar. Among the distinguished tenants are worldwide brands **Ralph Lauren, Swatch, Havaianas, Campo Marzio,** and **Superdry.**

THE SHOPS AT THE NEW TROPICANA Recognizing an opportunity to snare the thousands of visitors strolling daily across the quadrangle of bridges at Tropicana Avenue and the Strip, the Tropicana Resort is adding a two-level enclosed mall at the celebrated intersection. Retailers, bars, restaurants, and a food court will share space in the South Beach–flavored complex, scheduled to open in 2015. Part of the development is situated above the casino, with an entrance on the second level, so the graceful Tiffany stained glass ceiling is being repurposed elsewhere. With more than 20,000 hotel rooms encompassed in the four street corners, the potential market of shoppers is enormous.

TI RETAIL-TAINMENT CENTER The TI's flashy sirens-versus-pirates nightly encounter has bid adieu to fans and gawkers. The valuable Strip-front real estate sheltering the lagoon is being repurposed with a three-level shopping complex, also scheduled to open in 2015. Anchoring the center is a **CVS** pharmacy on the main floor, along with restaurants, shops, and bars on the upper two levels.

DOWNTOWN SUMMERLIN The affluent west side of Las Vegas is getting some new shopping of its own with **Downtown Summerlin** (☎ 702-832-1000; **shopsatsummerlin.com**). One hundred twenty-five stores and restaurants are concentrated on 26 acres at the corner of W. Sahara Avenue and the West 215 Beltway, just south of Red Rock Resort. The 30 single- and bi-level buildings are surrounded by hectares of free parking along the perimeter, as well as on-street parking in front of your favorite store. Anchors **Macy's, Dillard's,** and **Nordstrom Rack** share the promenades with **Sur La Table, American Eagle Outfitters, True Religion, Trader Joe's,** and many others. Several indoor-outdoor restaurants are centrally located overlooking the park. An eight-screen Regal theater completes the complex.

UNIQUE SHOPPING OPPORTUNITIES

ART Las Vegas is a great place to shop for contemporary and non-traditional art and sculpture, with galleries in the Fashion Show Mall,

The Forum Shops, the Grand Canal Shoppes, and elsewhere around town. Do not, however, expect any bargains.

If you're yearning to own artwork by Picasso, Dalí, Lichtenstein, Chagall, Miró, Murakami, Erté, or other popular 20th-century artists, visit the sophisticated **Martin Lawrence Gallery** in The Forum Shops. An immense vertical electric sign with the red letters *A R T* at the entrance lets you know what is for sale. Dealing in originals and limited-edition graphic prints, this sizable showcase presents fine art by the masters you know from art-history class and museum heists. Some pieces are surprisingly affordable . . . and some not so. There is an extensive rear area devoted to Andy Warhol's work. Browsers are welcome to stroll through the circuitous exhibits since today's gazer could be tomorrow's collector. Open daily, 10 a.m.–11 p.m.; ☎ 702-991-5990.

On the first Friday of every month from 5 to 11 p.m., the visual arts are celebrated in Las Vegas. In an eight-block area, generally bound on the north and south by Hoover and Wyoming Streets and on the west and east by Commerce and 3rd Streets, lies the Arts District. Eclectic and eccentric, the area is abundant with art galleries, restaurants and bars, gift emporiums, vintage couture, antiques shops, and malls of memorabilia; quality ranges from exceptional to godawful. With free parking at the Clark County Government Center, complimentary trollies transport arts lovers and the curious to this venerable commercial neighborhood. The lively First Friday festival (☎ 702-384-0092; **firstfridaylasvegas.com**) incorporates local bands, food, artist demonstrations, clairvoyants, and street performers. It's great for people-watching, and more than 60 businesses participate.

COSTUMES Halloween Experience (☎ 800-811-4877 or 702-740-4224; 6230 S. Decatur Blvd., Suite 101; **halloweenmart.com**) features thousands of costumes, masks, and accessories year-round. The showroom is open to the public Monday–Saturday (☎ 702-740-4224). For "sex-theme" apparel and costumes, try **Bare Essentials Fantasy Fashions** (☎ 702-247-4711; 4029 W. Sahara Ave.; **bareessentialsvegas.com**). You'll find everything from dresses to G-strings. There's even a selection of "bare essentials" for men. Some merchandise would be at home in suburbia, but some is strictly XXX. And XXX goes for sizes, too.

ETHNIC SHOPPING At the southwest corner of Spring Mountain and Wynn Roads is **Las Vegas Chinatown Plaza** with 22 outlets (☎ 702-221-8448; **lvchinatown.com**). This location offers Asian-theme shopping and Asian restaurants.

For Native American art, crafts, books, music, and attire, try the **Las Vegas Indian Center** at 2300 W. Bonanza Rd. (☎ 702-647-5842; **las vegasindiancenter.org**). And 25 minutes north of Las Vegas in Moapa, Nevada, you'll find the **Moapa Tribal Enterprises Casino and Gift Center** (☎ 702-864-2600). Take I-15 north to Exit 75.

GAMBLING STUFF As you would expect, Las Vegas is a shopping mecca when it comes to anything gambling related. If you are in the market for a roulette wheel, a blackjack table, or some personalized chips, try the **Gamblers General Store** at 800 S. Main St. (☎ 702-382-9903 or 800-322-CHIP outside Nevada; **gamblersgeneralstore.com**). For books and periodicals on gambling, we recommend the **Gamblers Book Shop,** now located inside the Gamblers General Store (☎ 702-382-7555 or 800-522-1777; **gamblersbook.com**).

GUNS Gun stores and firing ranges often come in the same package in Las Vegas, and it's debatable whether these establishments are retailers, attractions, or both. Want to fire a machine gun? There are a number of venues where anyone over 18 can blast away without a firearms license or any previous experience (God bless America!). All operate essentially the same way: you'll select a package (ranging from around $100 to $1,000 and up), including weapons rental, ammunition, paper targets, and safety equipment; then you'll receive basic handling instructions before stepping into the shooting range. Firearm brands typically include Uzi, Thompson, and Madsen; massive mini-guns, sniper rifles, and even cannons may be available.

Las Vegas's oldest established indoor shooting establishment is **The Gun Store** (☎ 702-454-1110; 2900 E. Tropicana Ave.; **thegunstorelasvegas.com**), founded by self-defense advocate Bob "Fired Up" Irwin, who furnished firearms for films like *Fear and Loathing in Las Vegas*. The staff focuses on customer service in a family-friendly environment, with accompanied minors as young as 5 permitted to shoot on a case-by-case basis.

Battlefield Vegas (☎ 702-566-1000; 2771 Industrial Rd.; **battlefieldvegas.com**), located just behind Circus Circus, has a parking lot full of decommissioned military vehicles to take photos with, including a Sherman tank and Vietnam-era helicopter. Call at least an hour ahead to reserve your shooting time, and they'll send a Humvee to pick you up at no extra charge.

The largest indoor facility in town is **The Range 702** (☎ 702-485-3232; 4699 Dean Martin Dr.; **therange702.com**), which features a café serving breakfast and lunch, and free carry concealed weapons (CCW) classes for Nevada and Florida residents.

For an upscale club-like experience, **MGV: Machine Gun Vegas** (☎ 800-75-SHOOT; 3501 Aldebaran Ave.; **machinegunsvegas.com**) ditches the drab warehouse look for hardwood floors and exposed brick. Their charming majority-female staff can arrange bachelor or bachelorette party packages, offering adventures with exotic dancers or exotic cars after your shoot-em-up experience. While you're in the neighborhood, stop by the **Zombie Apocalypse Store** (☎ 702-320-0703; 3420 Spring Mountain Rd.; **zombieapocalypsestore.com**) and stock up for the inevitable undead uprising. Along with authentic Army-Navy supplies, shelf-stable emergency rations, and a nice knife selection, you'll find a zombie shooting gallery and gory gag gifts.

HEAD RUGS The next time you go to a Las Vegas production show, pay attention to the showgirls' hair. You will notice that the same woman will have a different hairdo for every number. Having made this observation, you will not be surprised that the largest wig and hairpiece retailer in the United States is in Las Vegas. At 4515 W. Sahara Ave., **Serge's Wigs** inventories more than 7,000 hairpieces and wigs, made from both synthetic materials and human hair. In addition to serving the local showgirl population, Serge's Wigs also specializes in assisting chemotherapy patients. A catalog and additional information can be obtained at ☎ 702-207-7494 or **sergeswigs.com.**

SHOES If smoking stunted your growth, increase your height with custom-made platforms, boots, and high heels from **Red Shoes** at 4011 W. Sahara Ave., Unit 1 (☎ 702-889-4442). For a great selection of cowboy boots, try **Cowtown Boots** at 1080 E. Flamingo Rd. (☎ 702-737-8469; **cowtownboots.com**).

WESTERN WEAR **Sheplers,** the world's largest Western-wear retailer, can be found at Sam's Town on Boulder Highway (☎ 702-454-5266) and 4700 W. Sahara Ave. (☎ 702-258-2000); **sheplers.com.**

WINE AND LIQUOR Though not centrally located, **Lee's Discount Liquors** (☎ 702-269-2400; **leesliquorlv.com**) at 9110 Las Vegas Blvd. S., just south of Blue Diamond Road, offers the best selection of wine, liquor, and beer within easy access of the Strip. Unless your hotel is south of Tropicana, take I-15 to the Blue Diamond Road exit and then head south on Las Vegas Boulevard South. If your hotel is south of Tropicana you're just as well off taking Las Vegas Boulevard South the whole way. Though Lee's Discount Liquors has 10 locations around Las Vegas, the stores vary in size and selection. None are particularly convenient to the Strip or Downtown, but we can recommend the 3480 E. Flamingo Rd. and the 4230 S. Rainbow Blvd. locations in addition to the store mentioned above.

▌ **SEEING** *the* **SIGHTS**

RESIDENTS OF LAS VEGAS ARE JUSTIFIABLY PROUD of their city and are quick to point out that it has much to offer besides gambling. Quality theater, college and professional sports, dance, concerts, art shows, museums, and film festivals contribute to making Las Vegas a truly great place to live. In addition, there is a diverse and colorful natural and historical heritage. What Las Vegas residents sometimes have a difficult time understanding, however, is that the average business and leisure traveler doesn't really give a big hoot. Las Vegas differs from Orlando and Southern California in that it does not have any bona fide tourist attractions except Hoover Dam. Nobody drives all the way to Las Vegas to visit the Neon Museum, interesting as it is. While there have always been some great places to detox from a long trade show or too many hours at the casino, they are totally peripheral in the minds of visitors. Las Vegas needs a legitimate, nongaming tourist draw, but the strange aggregation of little museums, factory tours, and mini–theme parks is not it.

For two decades, Strip casinos, including the Mirage, Circus Circus, the Stratosphere, and New York–New York, opened new attractions.

They are, by and large, imaginative, visually appealing, and high-tech. Some would stand out as headliners in any theme park in the country. Others, while not up to Disney or Universal standards, represent a giant leap forward for Las Vegas.

BELLAGIO ATTRACTIONS

THE BIG DRAW AT THE BELLAGIO is the **Gallery of Fine Art,** which hosts temporary traveling exhibits. Tickets run about $16 for adults, $13 for seniors and Nevada residents, and $11 for children, teachers, and military; children age 12 and under are admitted free. For information, call ☎ 702-693-7871 or visit **bellagio.com.**

A very worthwhile and free attraction is the **Bellagio Conservatory and Botanical Gardens.** Located adjacent to the hotel lobby, the display features more than 10,000 blooming flowers, a diverse variety of plants, and even trees. The flora is changed periodically to reflect the season of the year or the theme of upcoming holidays.

Bellagio's free outdoor spectacle is a choreographed **water-fountain show** presented on the lake in front of the hotel (which stretches the length of three football fields). At the bottom of the eight-acre lake over 1,000 "water expressions"—think jets—and 4,000-plus individually programmable white lights are harnessed in choreography to "dance," if you will, to classical, popular, operatic, holiday, and sacred music. The waters are capable of reaching 240 feet into the air (approaching a football field's length), undulating in graceful S-curves, or cascading open like a gigantic surrendering lotus. Realized by WetDesigns, the entire vision, including the music selections, is Steve Wynn's, who is famous for his involvement with every detail of every aspect of the properties he designs. The magical waters of the Bellagio are for all to enjoy on the half-hour every Saturday, Sunday, and holidays from noon to 7 p.m. and every 15 minutes from 7 p.m. to midnight. Weekdays the schedule begins at 3 p.m. The view from the street is assuredly wonderful, but many of the rooms at Caesars and the Cosmopolitan can also offer a visual feast.

 Bellagio's dramatic three-story, glass-domed botanical garden provides a quiet oasis.

CIRCUS CIRCUS ATTRACTIONS

TO FURTHER APPEAL TO THE FAMILY MARKET, Circus Circus opened a small but innovative amusement park in August of 1993. Situated directly behind the main hotel and casino, the park now goes by the name of **Adventuredome.** Architecturally compelling, the entire park is built two stories high atop the casino's parking structure and is totally enclosed by a huge glass dome. From the outside, the dome surface is reflective, mirroring its surroundings in hot tropical pink. Inside, however, the dome is transparent, allowing guests in the park to see out. Composed of a multilayer glass-and-plastic sandwich, the dome allows light in but blocks ultraviolet rays. The entire park is air-conditioned and climate-controlled 365 days a year.

Adventuredome is a fun way to escape the heat of a Vegas summer day.

The park is designed to resemble a classic Western desert canyon. From top to bottom, hand-painted artificial rock is sculpted into caverns, pinnacles, steep cliffs, and buttes. Set among the rock structures are the attractions: two roller coasters, an array of spinning amusements, and some rides for small children. Embellishing the scene are a replica of Pueblo cliff dwellings, a rock-climbing wall, and a small stage featuring free magic and clown shows. Hidden in the center of the complex are a black-light laser tag arena and Batman-themed obstacle course. Finally, and inevitably, there is an electronic games arcade. As far as theme parks go, it can't compete with the world-class ones a few hours west in Anaheim, but it's a big improvement over your local bare-bones family entertainment center, and certainly offers enough to occupy a full afternoon of fun.

Adventuredome's premier attractions are the **Canyon Blaster,** the only indoor, double-loop, corkscrew roller coaster in the United States, which resembles a scaled-down sibling to Busch Gardens Williamsburg's classic Loch Ness Monster; and 2014's **El Loco,** an unconventional wild mouse-on-steroids steel coaster, with drops that exceed vertical and extended inversions that leave you hanging upside-down, secured only by a surprisingly comfortable lap-bar. Canyon Blaster and El Loco both wind in, around, and between the rocks and cliffs.

Other carnival-style thrill rides include **Sling Shot,** where you're shot vertically up a tower at 4 g's; **Inverter,** a pirate ship–style pendulum ride; **Chaos,** a vertical Tilt-A-Whirl that hauls riders randomly through three dimensions; and **Disk'O,** which has rocking motion and then spins you and about 20 other folks like a human discus. Adventuredome also features a *Happy Feet* simulator ride (with an aging ride vehicle shuddering along to blurry excepts from the CGI singing penguin movie) and a Special FX Theater showing Nickelodeon-inspired 4-D films (the *Spongebob Squarepants* one is witty enough to win over adults).

Guests can reach the theme park by proceeding through the rear of the main casino to the entrance and ticket plaza situated on the mezzanine level. Circus Circus has changed the admission policy so many times we have lost track. You can choose between paying for each attraction individually ($5–$10) or opting for an all-inclusive day pass ($29.95 adults; $16.95 juniors). For exact admission prices on the day of your visit, call ☎ 702-794-3939 or visit **adventuredome.com.**

DOWNTOWN ATTRACTIONS

DOWNTOWN LAS VEGAS is tied together under the canopy of the **Fremont Street Experience** (☎ 702-678-5777; **vegasexperience.com**), a high-tech, overhead sound-and-light show. The 12.5-million-light canopy extends from Main Street to Las Vegas Boulevard, covering the five-block pedestrian concourse where most Downtown casinos are situated. Canopy shows occur on the hour, with the first show at 8 p.m. and the last show at midnight (subject to seasonal change). The canopy show is free, as are nightly concerts on the **3rd Street Stage,** located outdoors between Four Queens and The D. Beer cans and glass containers are prohibited outdoors at the Fremont Street Experience. Across Las Vegas Boulevard beyond the canopied pedestrian plaza is the **Fremont East District,** a burgeoning nightlife and dining venue.

Replacing Flightlinez, the new **SLOTZILLA** higher-tech attraction at Fremont Street offers the intrepid and newly brave the thrill of flying under the 12.5 million LEDs of the Fremont Street Experience. Riders are strapped into a harness, take a flying leap, and whiz down a steel wire while controlling the momentum by tilting their bodies at various angles. There are two experience levels with four zip lines each. The lower zip launch is 75 feet above the pedestrian mall and extends 850 feet with riders in a seated position. The higher zoom launch begins as the reels spin on the 115-foot-high platform of world's largest slot machine; for this steeper run riders are horizontal and finish a third of a mile away. This hard-to-miss longer jaunt begins between Casino Center Boulevard and 3rd Street, soars over the traffic on 3rd, scoots through the LED canopy, and ends 4 blocks to the west in front of the Golden Gate Hotel. Speeds can reach 35 mph, and flyers can and do race. Open daily, noon–midnight (or later). Cost for the lower ride is $20 and the higher ride is $30; a package of both rides goes for $40.

Entertainment aside, Fremont Street's most renowned attraction is the flashing neon marquees of the Downtown casinos, the reason Fremont Street is called "Glitter Gulch." Augmenting the neon of the casinos are vintage Las Vegas neon signs dating back to the 1940s. The **Neon Museum,** located at 770 Las Vegas Boulevard N., is a visually opulent 2-acre outdoor collection of more than 150 vintage neon signs celebrating Las Vegas's small-town, bright-lights era. Signs are stacked along pathways winding through a maze of metal sculpture, huge panels of light bulbs, and yards of glass tubing. Among huge classic structures are Sassy Sally's facade of lights, Debbie Reynolds' autograph, the Barbary Coast's lavish "B," and the graceful green and yellow flowering plant designating the Yucca Motel. Each recalls the era when hotels and motels outdid each other with extravagant signage. The glory days of the now-departed Dunes, Moulin Rouge, Stardust, Sahara, and Desert Inn are also remembered by their signature marquees, which are prominently exhibited. Even the museum's name is spelled in capital letters from the famous hotels. The visitor center is vintage as well; the former lobby of the La Concha Motel, a midcentury-modern structure, was transported from its previous location next to the Riviera Hotel.

The guide's commentary about these treasures is intertwined with the colorful history of Las Vegas. Tours of the boneyard last 55 minutes and are conducted daily, every half-hour, from 10 a.m. until 5 p.m. After dusk, evening tours held between 7 and 8:30 p.m. show off the museum's four fully-restored neon signs, with the remainder of the collection illuminated by spotlights. The expanded tour schedule, combined with the new visitor center, transformed the experience from a junkyard stroll to an entertaining and educational retrospective of

Las Vegas history. Be sure to wear closed-toe shoes to avoid stepping on metal and glass and other detritus of disintegrating signs, though the gravel pathways are ADA compliant for wheelchair access. A still camera for personal use is the only photographic equipment allowed among the exhibits; no video or audio recording is allowed. Cost of the tour is $18 for general admission and $12 for seniors, students, active military and veterans, and Nevada residents; free for children age 6 and younger. Night tours cost $25 for general admission and $22 for the above-mentioned groups. Tours can be booked online, and those taking the daytime tour during warmer weather are advised to book for early in the day and wear a hat. For reservations or more information, call ☎ 702- 387-NEON (6366) or visit **neonmuseum.org.**

Icons such as the Horseshoe's H, the Hacienda's horse and rider, and the bow and arrow from its namesake property have been reconditioned and highlight the nearby median of Las Vegas Boulevard between Sahara Avenue and Washington Street, a National Scenic Byway. Additional historic signs were formerly positioned at the Fremont Street Experience, but were removed during the installation of the Slotzilla zip lines. However, you can still see a total of nine refurbished signs, including the Silver Slipper, the Lucky Cuss Motel, and the 5th Street liquor store, with the aid of a free map from the museum's website.

The **National Museum of Organized Crime and Law Enforcement,** or **The Mob Museum** (☎ 702-229-2734; **themobmuseum.org**), commemorates the extensive nationwide history of the La Cosa Nostra and its influence on Las Vegas. The interactive exhibits on three floors provide diverse viewpoints about the impact of organized crime and the feds who worked to crush the gangs. The museum is in the city's former federal courthouse (at 300 Stewart Ave.), the only Las Vegas building listed in the National Register of Historic Places. It houses the courtroom where the Kefauver Hearings on Organized Crime were conducted in 1950. Among the exhibits are the barber's chair where Albert Anastasia was shot and the bullet-strewn garage wall from Chicago's 1929 St. Valentine's Day Massacre. Admission is $14–$20 with discounts for seniors, locals, and groups.

LUXOR ATTRACTIONS

THE LUXOR OFFERS THREE continuously running gated (paid admission) attractions inside the pyramid on the level above the casino. *Bodies . . . The Exhibition* (☎ 702-262-4000; **bodiestheexhibition.com**) is an extraordinary introduction to human anatomy through authentic, preserved human bodies. Though somewhat grisly sounding, the exhibit is extremely tasteful and respectful. Arranged sequentially, Bodies takes you through every part of the human body, explaining its many systems. Though most of the exhibit deals with the anatomy of healthy people, there is some discussion of disease. One of the more arresting displays is that of a normal lung side-by-side with the lung of a smoker. A second

Luxor attraction is *Titanic: The Artifact Exhibition,* which takes guests on a chronological odyssey from the design and building of the ocean liner to life on board to its sinking (☎ 702-262-4400 or 800-557-7428; **luxor.com**). Allow a minimum of 2 hours to see *Bodies* and 90 minutes to take in *Titanic.* General admission for either exhibit is $32 adults, $24 children (ages 4–12). The third and newest attraction is *SCORE!,* a 10,000-square-foot interactive sports exhibit with eight galleries. Exhibits feature historic videos, photos, and memorabilia, including uniforms and equipment from the Naismith Memorial Basketball Hall of Fame, Pro Football Hall of Fame, Hockey Hall of Fame, Boxing Hall of Fame, and U.S. Soccer Federation. Also on display are pro-sports contracts, and sports agent–player correspondence. There is an interactive opportunity/challenge for most sports showcased. Open to all visitors, a couple of the challenges require a bit of athleticism, but most can be enjoyed by anyone. Our favorite was a peripheral vision reaction test, where your score is measured against that of NFL quarterbacks. If you're a sports fan, plan on about 2 hours, and make sure your companion is a fan as well, or you'll be rushed along. *SCORE!* is open daily, 10 a.m.–10 p.m. Admission, obtainable online or at the *Bodies/ Titanic* box office, runs $28 for adults and $15 for children under age 12. For additional information, see **scorelv.com** or call ☎ 702-262-4200. There's a gift shop, natch.

MANDALAY BAY ATTRACTION

THE BIG DRAW AT MANDALAY BAY is the **Shark Reef** aquarium featuring sharks, rays, sea turtles, venomous stonefish, and dozens of other denizens of the deep playing house in a 1.3-million-gallon tank. If you don't like fish, separate exhibits showcase rare pythons and golden crocodiles. In excess of 2,000 animals, covering 100 different species including 15 species of shark, are on display. The Shark Reef audio tour is open Sunday–Thursday 10 a.m.–8 p.m. and Friday and Saturday 10 a.m.–10 p.m. (last admission is 1 hour prior to close). Admission is about $18 for adults, $12 for children age 12 and under, and those age 4 and under are free. Additional information is available at ☎ 702-632-4555 or **sharkreef.com.**

MGM GRAND ATTRACTION

THE MGM GRAND sent its signature lion habitat packing, leaving the sprawling hotel with but one attraction: **CSI: The Experience (csithe experience.org).** Originally developed by the Fort Worth Museum of Science and History with a grant from The National Science Foundation (NSF), CSI: The Experience gives you the opportunity to play the role of a crime-scene investigator, learning scientific principles and real investigative techniques as you try to solve the case. Two state-of-the-art crime labs will help you piece together the evidence. Hands-on science combines with special effects to create an exciting, realistic, and educational experience. There are three different crime scenes to investigate (pick one), following which "new recruits" (yes, that would be you, Gladys) take their observations and hunches to the crime lab. With video input from investigators from the television show, you formulate a hypothesis, validate your findings, and then present your solution in a re-creation of the office of Gil Grissom—the enigmatic *CSI* head investigator. Of the three crime scenes to choose from, we thought the most interesting was Crime Scene 2: Who Got Served? It involves the discovery of a woman's body in an alley near a dumpster. Once you select your crime scene, you're issued a clipboard with an evidence form that has a diagram of the crime scene with space to record your observations. Each scene contains all sorts of evidence, from insects and latent fingerprints to vehicle tracks and various litter. Part of the challenge is discerning what at the crime scene is relevant and what is not. CSI: The Experience is self-guided and takes about an hour for most people.

The MGM Grand doesn't put much promotional oomph behind CSI, nor are there any signs in the casino to help you find it (follow the signs to the monorail). There's a box office next to CSI, but unfortunately it sells tickets to all MGM Grand shows. We waited a half-hour to buy our CSI admission behind folks picking out their seats for the *KÀ* show. CSI is open daily, 9 a.m.–9 p.m. Tickets are $28 for adults and $21 for children ages 4–11. From our observation, it's pretty much a waste of money to take children younger than 11.

MIRAGE ATTRACTIONS

THE VOLCANO AT THE MIRAGE goes off about every hour from 7 p.m. until 11 p.m., if the weather is good and winds are light. In winter, when it gets dark earlier, the volcano starts popping off at 6 p.m. With an exclusive soundtrack composed by Grateful Dead drummer and Rock and Roll Hall of Fame member Mickey Hart and Indian tabla virtuoso Zakir Hussain, the volcano fires massive fireballs more than 12 feet into the air, and eruptions of fiery "lava" flow down the mountain's fissures. Usually, because of the frequency of performances (eruptions?), getting a good railside vantage point is not too difficult. If you want to combine the volcano with a meal, grab a window table at the second-floor restaurant in the Casino Royale across the street.

The Mirage also has a nice dolphin exhibit, plus the **Secret Garden** next to the dolphin habitat, a small zoo with Siegfried and Roy's white and Bengal tigers, white lions, an Indian elephant, and more. Both are open weekdays 11 a.m.–6:30 p.m. and weekends and holidays 10 a.m.–6:30 p.m. The dolphin and Secret Garden exhibit cost $20 for adults and $15 for children. (Children age 3 and under get in free.) For more information, call ☎ 702-791-7111 or visit **mirage.com**.

PARIS LAS VEGAS ATTRACTION

THE BIG DRAW AT PARIS IS, of course, the 540-foot-tall replica of the **Eiffel Tower**. Requiring 10 million pounds of steel and more than two years to erect, the Las Vegas version is a little more than half the size of the original. Just below the top (at 460 feet) is an observation deck accessible via two 10-passenger glass elevators. It costs a stiff $11.50 to ride during the day, and the cost increases to $16.50 starting at 7:15 p.m. (express passes are available for $18.50–$24.50, depending on time of day), but that's just the beginning of the story. You must first line up to buy tickets. Your ticket will show a designated time to report to the escalator (that's right: *escalator*. You must take an escalator to reach the elevators). If you're late you'll be turned away, and there are no refunds. The escalator will deposit you in yet another line where you'll wait for the elevator. The elevators run from 9:30 a.m. until 12:30 a.m. (1 a.m. weekends), except when it's raining.

unofficial **TIP**
If accessing Paris's observation platform seems like too much work, take the separate elevator that serves the restaurant and bar on the 11th floor of the tower. You don't need reservations to patronize the bar, but you must be nicely dressed (absolutely no jeans, T-shirts, tank tops, or sandals). The bar is open 11:30 a.m.–midnight and serves lunch.

Though all this hopping from line to line is supposed to take 5–20 minutes, we found 40–60 minutes more the norm. Here's the rub: The observation deck holds fewer than 100 persons, and once people get up there, they can stay as long as they want. Hence, when the observation deck is at max capacity, nobody can go up unless someone comes down. Because the tower affords such a great view of the Bellagio across the street, gridlock ensues several times nightly while people squeeze on the observation deck overlong to watch Bellagio's dancing-waters show.

RIO ATTRACTION

JOINING THE LAS VEGAS ZIP LINE CRAZE, the Rio offers **VooDoo ZipLine,** an 845-foot zip line launched from the popular nightspot VooDoo Lounge, 490 feet in the air. Traveling at speeds of 33 mph, and accommodating two riders at a time, you descend to the roof of the Rio's Ipanema Tower before being hauled back to the starting point. The proximity of a fully-stocked bar and copious quantities of alcohol is not accidental. VooDoo ZipLine is open daily, noon–midnight. Cost is $25 for daytime rides and $37 from 5:30 p.m. until midnight.

STRATOSPHERE ATTRACTIONS

THE STRATOSPHERE TOWER STANDS 1,149 feet tall and offers an unparalleled view of Las Vegas. You can watch aircraft take off simultaneously from McCarran International Airport and Nellis Air Force Base. To the south, the entire Las Vegas Strip is visible. To the west, Red Rock Canyon seems practically within spitting distance. North of the Tower, Downtown glitters beneath the canopy of the Fremont Street Experience. By day, the rich geology of the Colorado Basin and Spring Mountains merge in an earth-tone and evergreen tapestry. At night, the dark desert circumscribes a blazing strand of twinkling neon.

A 12-level pod crowns the futuristic contours of three immense buttresses that form the Tower's base. Level 12, the highest level, serves as the boarding area for **X-Scream,** a dangle-daddy; **Insanity,** a sort of Tilt-A-Whirl in the sky; and the **Big Shot,** an acceleration–free-fall thrill ride. Latest to join the lineup is **SkyJump,** a parachute ride with an 855-foot "controlled" free-fall descent. Oh, did we forget to mention that there's no parachute? Instead you're hooked up to a zip line on the 108th floor of the tower where you heave yourself over the side of a platform. Happily, after reaching speeds of 40 miles per hour, you'll be slowed to a comfortable landing. The price to jump off a perfectly good building instead of taking the elevator is $110 and up. It's said the views on the descent are stupendous if you happen to open your eyes.

Levels 11 and 10 are not open to the public. An outdoor observation deck is Level 9, with an indoor observation deck directly beneath it on Level 8. Level 7 features a 220-seat lounge, and Level 6 houses an upscale revolving restaurant. Levels 4 and 3 contain meeting rooms, and the remaining levels—1, 2, and 5—are not open to the public.

 The view from the Tower is so magnificent that we recommend experiencing it at different times of the day and night. Sunset is particularly stunning, and a storm system rolling in over the mountains is a sight you won't quickly forget. Be sure to try both the indoor and outdoor observation decks.

The rides are a mixed bag. The Big Shot is cardiac arrest. Sixteen people at a time are seated at the base of the skyward-projecting needle that tops the pod. You are blasted 160 feet straight up in the air at 45 miles per hour and then allowed to partially free-fall back down. At the apex of the ascent, it feels as if your seat belt and restraint have mysteriously evaporated, leaving you momentarily hovering 100-plus stories up in the air. The ride lasts only about a half-minute, but unless you're accustomed to being shot from a cannon, that's more than enough.

If you're having difficulty forming a mental image of the Big Shot, picture the carnival game where macho guys swing a sledgehammer, propelling a metal sphere up a vertical shaft. At the top of the shaft is a bell. If the macho man drives the sphere high enough to ring the bell, he wins a prize. Got the picture? OK, on the Big Shot, you are the metal sphere.

In X-Scream, you ride in a large gondola attached to a huge steel arm. The arm dangles the gondola over the edge of the Tower, then releases it to slide forward a few feet as if the gondola is coming unglued from the arm. All and all, it's pretty dull.

The third ride, Insanity, is a little harder to describe. It consists of an arm that extends 64 feet over the edge of the Tower. Passengers are suspended from the arm in beefed-up swing seats and spun at up to three g's. As the ride spins faster and faster, the riders are propelled up to an angle of 70 degrees, at which point they're pretty much looking straight down. The Stratosphere touts the ride as providing "a great view of historic Downtown Las Vegas."

The elevators to the Tower are at the end of the shopping arcade on the second floor of the Stratosphere, above the casino. Get tickets for the Tower at the ticket center in the elevator lobby on the second floor or at various places in the casino. Tower tickets cost about $18 for adults and $10 for children. Packages including the Tower and the rides run $23–$34, depending on the number of rides included. You can purchase individual tickets for the rides at a cost of $15, in addition to your Tower admission.

Expect big crowds at the Tower on weekends. Once up top, the observation levels are congested, as are the lounge, snack bar, restrooms, and gift shops. If you want to try the rides, expect to wait an additional 20–40 minutes for each on weekends. When you've had your fill of the Tower and are ready to descend, you'll have another long wait before boarding the elevator. However, if you walk down to the restaurant (you'll take the emergency staircase; ask an attendant where to find it), you can catch the down elevator with virtually no wait at all.

Another way to see the Tower without a long wait is to make a reservation for the **Top of the World** restaurant. To be safe, make reservations at least two weeks in advance. When you arrive, inform the greeter in the elevator lobby that you have a dinner reservation and give him your confirmation number. You will be ushered immediately into an express elevator. The restaurant is pricey, but the food is good and the view is a knockout, and you do not have to pay the Tower admission. If you want to try the Big Shot or the High Roller, purchase ride tickets before taking the elevator to the restaurant. Finally, be aware that most folks dress up to eat at Top of the World.

unofficial **TIP**
If you must see the Tower on a weekend, go in the morning as soon as it opens.

On weekdays, it is much easier to visit the Stratosphere Tower. Monday through Thursday, except at sunset, the wait to ascend is usually short. Waits for the rides are also short. Tower hours are daily, 10 a.m.–1 a.m. For more information, call ☎ 702-380-7711 or visit **stratospherehotel.com.**

TROPICANA ATTRACTION

POLERCOASTER, THE WORLD'S TALLEST roller coaster, with a vertical rather than horizontal layout, is scheduled for completion next year. Topped by a circular observation tower and restaurant reached by two glass elevators, the cylindrical coaster begins with a spiral climb inside the tower's frame to an elevation of 650 feet, then nosedives along a steep grade on double helix tracks coiling around the structure's pillars. Pending FAA approval because the hotel is close to the airport, the vertical plunge raises the bar for adrenalin junkies.

VENETIAN ATTRACTIONS

LIKE NEW YORK–NEW YORK down the Strip, it can be argued that the entire Venetian is an attraction, and there's a lot to gawk at even if you limit your inspection to the streetside Italian icons and the Grand Canal Shoppes. But there's more. The Venetian is host to the first **Madame Tussauds Wax Museum** (☎ 702-862-7800; **madametussauds.com/las**

vegas) built in the United States. Covering two floors and 28,000 square feet, the museum is about half the size of the original London exhibit. More than 100 wax figures are displayed in themed settings. Some, like Frank Sinatra and Tom Jones, were central to the development of the entertainment scene in Las Vegas. Unlike at most wax museums, here you can touch and pose, and, in some cases, drape yourself over the statues; as a result, the figures aren't as pristine as those seen at other locations, with some showing significant wear. Wax figures rotate among other Madame Tussauds, but the collection here focuses on pop-culture celebrities to the general exclusion of historical figures.

The original "haunted dungeon" finale was replaced by a new 4-D Marvel Superheroes show, with in-theater effects (water spritzes, falling bubbles, leg ticklers, and the like) accompanying a computer-animated short film in which Spider-Man, Tony Stark, and their super-pals battle baddies Doctor Doom and Loki. It's all-ages appropriate, unlike the tour's old ending, but anyone who has experienced Universal Orlando's Marvel attractions, or seen *The Avengers* in IMAX 3-D, is unlikely to be impressed by the clunky script and chunky graphics. The museum opens daily at 10 a.m., and the self-guided tour takes about 50 minutes. Admission is $30 per adult and $20 per child, with $10-off coupons often available.

FREE STUFF

THE WATER-AND-LASER SHOW at Caesars' Forum Shops is also worthy of your consideration. Staged daily on the hour beginning at 11 a.m., the show combines animatronic statues as well as fire and laser effects. Outdoor productions at Bellagio, TI, and the Mirage (all described earlier) are also free.

STRIP ENTERTAINMENT DISTRICTS

The LINQ

At Center Strip, tucked into the corridor between the LINQ and Flamingo Hotels, is **The LINQ,** a conveniently walkable urban entertainment zone created by Caesars Entertainment. Low-rise buildings house 32 mostly causal food and beverage venues and on-trend retail shops. Stylish tenants include LA's **Kitson** boutique, **Goorin Bros.** headware, **Polaroid Fotobar, Chilli Beans** sunspecs, plus eateries **Flour & Barley** (pizza), **Chayo Cocina,** a cupcake ATM, **Haute Doggery,** and Asian fusion **FAME**. Nightlife includes **Purple Zebra, BLVD Cocktail, Stomping Grape Wine Bar,** and the one-off bowling-dining-concert mecca **Brooklyn Bowl**. Revelers will love the critical mass of outdoor restaurants, open-air drinking establishments, and late-night hot spots. Concerts are staged at the circular midpoint plaza, and a compact **O'Shea's Casino** rejoins the assemblage, preserving its prestige as beer pong central. All of this is overseen by an extraordinary attraction, the world's tallest observation wheel, appropriately named the **High Roller** (more on that below). Valet parking adjacent to the wheel is accessed going north on LINQ

Lane off Flamingo Avenue or west on Winnick Avenue from Koval Lane. The Venetian/Harrah's rear access road south of the Sands Expo also gets you there. Surface lots are behind (east of) The LINQ, along with neighboring parking garages, which are a quick trek from the Flamingo and LINQ Hotels. Signage is small, so drivers must pay attention or will end up where they don't want to be. A monorail station is being added at The LINQ Hotel. Targeted visitors are the 21–46 age groups of Gen X and Gen Y, but all generations will enjoy the mix.

Learn about the history of innovative Polaroid "instant" photography (precursor of the selfie), cameras, and film at the **Fotobar** flagship store in The LINQ. On the second level, the **Polaroid Museum** focuses on all facets of the groundbreaking cameras first sold in 1948. Product displays include the brand's polarizers, photos, vintage ads and art, rare photography equipment, and one of only five of the notable 20-by-24-inch large-format cameras, which weighs 230 pounds and is more than 6 feet high. Simultaneous rotating photo exhibits share space. The pervasive theme is pop culture and celebrities.

A FERRIS WHEEL . . . OR SOMETHING   Ask anybody having something to do with the **High Roller,** and you'll get, "It's NOT a Ferris wheel! It's an *observation wheel*!" OK, fine, it's an observation wheel (that bears a very close resemblance to every Ferris wheel you've ever seen). We'll go to our graves believing that the High Roller came from the same gene pool as the Ferris wheel, but here is the press-release difference: On a Ferris wheel you take a ride in the sense that you go around and around. On an observation wheel, you get on, slowly rotate one full circuit (which takes 30 minutes to an hour, giving you plenty of time to "observe"), and get off. No round and round. Also size counts—the average Ferris wheel would come up to an observation wheel's ankle.

The 550-foot **High Roller** is situated on the eastern end of The LINQ entertainment district. Each of the statuesque wheel's 28 transparent, spherical, climate-controlled globes can ferry 40 people aloft per 30-minute rotation. Once aboard, you'll inch your way up and then back down, never stopping. For about half the rotation you'll be high enough to enjoy uncluttered views all around.

The High Roller has its own ticket booth and is open noon–2 a.m. 365 days a year. A ride costs adults $25 from noon to 5:50, and $35 from 6 p.m. until closing. Children ages 13–18 pay $15 before 6 p.m. and $25 after. Ages 12 and under ride free. In addition to the ticket price, there's a hidden and aggravating $2 "service charge" per ticket. You can order tickets online at **caesars.com/thelinq** or buy them on-site from kiosks or the main ticket booth. You must ride within 30 minutes of purchasing your ticket. This holds equally for online purchasers who must designate a date and specific time of day in order to complete the transaction. To ride at a time of your own choosing, you'll have to pony up for a one- or three-day "flex ticket" at $45 and $55, respectively. At press time, local kids could ride free with a paying adult. The only other discount is $5 off for guests of the Flamingo or LINQ Hotels, and a slight discount for groups of 10 or more.

The boarding process is very Disneyesque. First, tickets are scanned before you're dispatched up an escalator. Next, each person or group is photographed in front of a green screen. In the final version your photo is digitally enhanced with scenes of the High Roller. Then, departing slightly from the Disney model, you are ushered into the bar (!!), where you can buy drinks to take on the ride. Drinks bought outside are also ok, provided they're in plastic cups. From the bar there are more escalators to the next room, where a half dozen or so cartoons and quirky videos play on a 270-degree screen. This is like Disney's "pre-show" rooms. Here, you'll also get some instruction from your "guide." Finally, it's on to the loading platform, where the wheel rotates continuously at about half normal walking speed. Getting on is no harder than stepping onto an escalator, except that if you screw it up you'll fall several feet off the loading platform into a convenient net. Wheelchairs and strollers are welcome, and the ride actually stops to position a ramp for wheelchairs. Stroller jockeys are on their own, and must board while the wheel is in motion like everyone else. If you think you might have issues, speak to a boarding/disembarking supervisor.

Once on board there are benches for about 16 riders (fewer if they are corpulent), but most people prefer to stand. The High Roller is built to withstand hurricane-force winds, plus it rotates so slowly that it's hard to tell you're moving. Motion sickness is not a factor here. There are views to the east and limited views to the west as soon as you board. Views north and south become visible approximately from clock positions 9 to 3. There's a recorded mix of witty and educational narration from your guide, plus some peppy tunes, but if the pod is more than half full, it will likely all be drowned out by conversation. The pods are temperature-controlled and are not the least claustrophobic. Sunsets are special, but with all the preboarding rigmarole, it's hard to time it just right. After sunset, the High Roller is illuminated by 2,000 LED lights.

You exit the ride into the gift shop, where you can check out your green-screen photos and select one of four backdrops. If you want to take a photo home, it's $25 for one print and $30 for two.

The Park

Not to be outdone, MGM Resorts International has created yet another entertainment district in the 63-acre canyon of open space on the Strip's west side between the Monte Carlo and New York–New York resorts. Christened **The Park,** this version spotlights an alfresco oasis slightly off-Strip and includes restaurant pavilions, nightclubs, shops, interactive attractions, performance stages, xeriscapes, and lush desert gardens with patio seating and water features. Whimsical 50-foot, tulip-shaped structures throughout provide daytime sun shelters and imaginative nighttime LED light shows. All merge into a leafy pedestrian avenue heading to a 20,000-seat indoor sports, concert, and events center behind the two hotels. The arena will be completed and ready to host world-class events by 2016.

The two bookend hotels have restructured their Strip-side façades with new-to-the-Strip dining sites on both arboreal plazas, and each has added cobblestone walks leading into The Park's streetscape. The innovative restaurants featured at New York–New York include **Shake Shack, Bruxie Waffles, Sake Rok, Cuba Libre, Dierks Bentley's Whiskey Row,** a **Robert Mondavi Jr. Wine Experience,** and an expanded **Nine Fine Irishmen** pub. Interspersed are merchandisers **Swatch, Stupidiotic** for offbeat items, and **I Love NYNY** souvenirs. The focal point is a bi-level **Hershey's Chocolate World,** with exterior sculptures of branded candies. Inside are models of the Statue of Liberty and Empire State Building fashioned from melted candy bars, a gluttony-inducing pastry counter, and a mini-kitchen where chocoholics can cook up personalized sweets. On the north side at the Monte Carlo, casual dining spots include **800 Degrees, Sambalatte, BLVD Creamery, Double Barrel Roadhouse,** and **Yusho** Japanese street food, along with the remodeled **Diablo Cantina.** From 3 p.m. until whenever, upbeat entertainment is featured.

A WORD ABOUT STRIP ROLLER COASTERS

THERE ARE CURRENTLY THREE ROLLER COASTERS on the Strip. After careful sampling, we have decided that, although shorter, the **Canyon Blaster** and **El Loco** at Adventuredome offer better rides than the more visually appealing **Roller Coaster** (formerly known as Manhattan Express) at **New York–New York.** The Canyon Blaster still provides a tight (if no longer oh-so-smooth) ride two decades after its construction, and El Loco redefines the concept of air-time with a truly twisted track design—thank goodness for the in-seat speakers blasting cheesy pop music to drown out your screams! The Roller Coaster at New York–New York, on the other hand, goes along in fits and starts, all of which are jerky and rough. Despite having been upgraded over the years with new trains and magnetic brakes by Premiere Rides, it remains one of the most painful rides defunct track manufacturer Togo ever created. It does, however, provide a great view of the Strip as it zips in and out of the various New York–New York buildings.

 El Loco at Adventuredome is the *Unofficial* team's favorite of the Vegas Strip coasters.

WATER PARKS

THE FORMER SPLASH CANYON water park is now **Wet 'n' Wild,** a family-friendly water park located 11 miles from the South Strip at 7055 S. Fort Apache Rd. Accessible seasonally Memorial Day weekend through September, the 41-acre park is a full-service hydro-adventure with sandy beaches, the 17,000-square-foot Red Rock Bay wave pond, the 1,000-foot Colorado Cooler lazy river, slides of various degrees and angles, a mat racer, the requisite altitudinal thrill experiences, and a lengthy, convoluted tube ride. Splash Island houses RainFortress, a four-story aquatic playground with a 500-gallon bucket that cascades water on all beneath and nearby. There's also a stage with a DJ spinning tunes. Private cabanas, free inner tubes, lounge chairs, lockers, and showers are available. Several refreshment stands are positioned throughout the complex. No coolers allowed. Admission is priced according to height: $39.99 plus tax for everyone 42 inches and taller, $29.99 for juniors under 42 inches, and free for children under age 2. Parking is $5. Wet 'n' Wild is open daily 10 a.m.–6 p.m. For more information and directions, call ☎ 702-979-1600 or visit **wetnwildlasvegas.com.**

An endless summer awaits at the 1960s surf-themed, 23-acre water park **Cowabunga Bay.** The new park salutes the many US beaches, from Atlantic City's Boardwalk to California's Surf Cities and across the Pacific to Hawaii's aloha sands. The park's focal point is Wild Surf, where four-rider rubber rafts are hurled from a height of 55 feet into huge waves thrusting them to and fro. You'll also find the six-story Cowabunga Splash, housing a net climb and a maze of tunnels, bridges, slides, platforms, and playful water devices; Surf-A-Rama, a 33,000-square-foot wave pool; and 25 more attractions, including body slides, two bucket dumps, a tube slide, kids' cove, and a vertical inner tube ride. Two restaurants and VIP cabanas with table service are also on site. Coolers are allowed in picnic areas outside the park. Located at Galleria Drive and Gibson Road in suburban Henderson, the park is a 25-minute drive from the South Strip. For more information, check out **cowabungabay.com.**

REALLY EXPENSIVE THRILLS

FOR $159 TO MORE THAN $3,000, you can fly a foot off the ground at the **Richard Petty Driving Experience.** Here you can get behind the wheel of a 600-horsepower NASCAR Winston Cup–style stock car. The Driving Experience is located at Las Vegas Motor Speedway. Call ☎ 702-643-4343 or visit **drivepetty.com** for additional information.

Also at Las Vegas Motor Speedway, you can drive a track-ready **Ferrari 430 GT** around a 1.1-mile track with nine low-, medium-, and high-speed corners. Cost is $600 for five laps plus 13 minutes of training in a 3-D simulator. For $200 you can ride two laps as a passenger with a professional driver. Race suit and helmet are included, as is round-trip transportation from Crystals. For additional information call ☎ 702-599-5199 or see **dreamracing.com.** Discounts are sometimes offered on the website.

GO-KARTS AND BUGGIES

DO YOU FEEL THE NEED FOR SCALED-DOWN SPEED? Vegas boasts a number of midget racetracks, where kids and adults alike can live out their Le Mans fantasies in souped-up go-karts.

Pole Position Raceway (4175 S. Arville St; ☎ 702-227-7223; **pole positionraceway.com/lasvegas**) houses a single snaking road-style track inside an air-conditioned warehouse, along with a small arcade and a snack bar serving alcohol (for after the race only, of course). Adults run a 10-minute, 12-lap race at speeds up to 45 mph; kids at least 6 years old and 4 feet tall can race at up to 25 mph. Group parties and free shuttles from the Strip are available, but you'll need an annual membership ($55 and up) or "temporary license" ($5.99 per week) before you can drive; after that, individual races cost $25.50 for adults ($22 for kids), including rental of mandatory full-face protective helmets.

If you can handle the heat, **Las Vegas Mini Grand Prix** (1401 N. Rainbow Blvd.; ☎ 702-259-7000; lvmgp.com) has four fun outdoor courses, including one reserved for little racers (38–54 inches), and another restricted to ages 16 and up that requires a real driver's license. The signature "Adult Grand Prix" course features vehicles that could hit an astonishing 80 mph with their automatic transmission engines, if not for all the hairpin turns. You'll also find a small arcade with redemption games; a food counter serving inexpensive sandwiches and pizza pies; and a few kiddie rides, such as a fun slide and Dragon mini-coaster. Each go-kart race requires a $7.50 ticket, or you can get a 1-hour wristband valid on all rides for $21.50.

If you're really looking to get off the beaten path, and are willing to get a little—ok, a lot—dusty, **Sunbuggy Fun Rentals** (6925 Speedway Blvd.; ☎ 866-728-4443; sunbuggy.com/lasvegas) will let you career over sand dunes in custom-built buggies that seat up to six. Driving instructions, safety helmets, and a trained guide are included in all packages, which start at $150 for a 30-minute "chase" through the desert; "insanely scary" nighttime trips are available for an extra charge. Round-trip transportation is offered, with the entire experience taking about 4 hours door-to-door from a Strip hotel.

QUIRKY TOURS

AMONG MANY GUIDED TOURS of various ilk available in Las Vegas are the **Vegas Mob Tour** and **Haunted Vegas Ghost Hunt.** The Mob Tour traces organized crime's history in Las Vegas and visits the sites of various murders, suicides, and celebrity deaths. The tour operates from the Tropicana and includes a pizza dinner. Cost is $106 for approximately 4 hours of Mob madness. The Haunted Vegas Ghost Hunt features haunted casinos, Elvis hauntings, and the antics of Bugsy Siegel's ghost, among other imponderables. The tour originates at The Royal Resort, located at 99 Convention Center drive just east of where Convention Center Drive intersects the Strip. The tour lasts about 2½ hours and costs $79.95 plus tax. For tickets and information call ☎ 866-218-4935 or visit vegasmobtour.com and hauntedvegastours.com. The minimum age is 13 for Haunted Vegas and 16 for the Vegas Mob Tour. Anyone under 18 must be accompanied by an adult. The tours, in addition to being great fun, serve up large doses of little-known Vegas history and are quite substantive. Look for discount coupons in *What's On* and other Las Vegas visitor magazines.

OTHER ATTRACTIONS

THERE ARE A GOODLY NUMBER of Las Vegas attractions that we don't have space to cover in the *Unofficial Guide*. All of them are listed and described at **vegas.com/attractions.** If you provide your name and address they'll mail you a free brochure. The site is sponsored by Museums and Attractions in Nevada (MAIN) in partnership with the Nevada Commission on Tourism.

▌ OTHER AREA ATTRACTIONS

THE LOCAL LAS VEGAS VISITOR GUIDES describe nearby attractions and sites pretty honestly. If you have children, try the **Discovery Children's Museum,** at 360 Promenade Pl., next to the Smith Center for the Performing Arts (☎ 702-382-5437; **discoverykidslv.org**), for a rewarding afternoon of exploration and enjoyable education. You can also check out the **Las Vegas Natural History Museum** (☎ 702-384-3466; **lvnhm.org**), about a mile away at 900 Las Vegas Blvd. N., near Heritage Park.

Near scenic Red Rock Canyon, a side trip just outside of Las Vegas is **Bonnie Springs Old Nevada.** This rustic re-creation of an Old West town features trinket stores, a saloon, two museums, a restaurant, a petting zoo, and guided horse rides. The hoot that goes with this holler is the low-budget melodrama. The kicker is the real, live Western hanging that takes place at noon, 2, and 4 p.m. "You can't hang me, sheriff!" "Why not?!" "Cause yer wife'll miss me!" Cost to get in—$20 per carload; ☎ 702-875-4191; **bonniesprings.com.** Real rope, real fun.

Adults who wax nostalgic over vintage automobiles should check out the **Auto Collection** at the LINQ Hotel & Casino, ☎ 702-794-3174, where more than 250 antique and historically significant vehicles are on display. The collection is well worth the admission price of $11.95, $8 for seniors and children under age 12, though discount coupons are readily available in the local visitor guides, and you can even print out a free admission pass at **autocollections.com.**

Unique to Las Vegas is the **Atomic Testing Museum,** which chronicles through exhibits and film the history of the Nevada Test Site, where atomic bombs were detonated only 65 miles from Las Vegas. A vital sense of place, artifacts, and good storytelling come together here to create a powerful museum experience. This museum is cerebral, instructive, and entertaining. Laden with artifacts, there is much to look at (and much to read for a full encounter). A good balance of videos and interactive stations can engage anyone with a passing interest in this seemingly and sadly ever-important topic. In one of two small theaters, the brief, overpowering experience of a nuclear test explosion is alone nearly worth the price of admission.

The museum is the first ever to feature a special exhibit, "Area 51: Myth or Reality," about that top-secret stretch of wasteland adjacent to the Mojave Desert range where atomic tests occurred in the 1950s. This interactive adventure takes you to the most classified place in America, long considered the domain of UFOs, extraterrestrials, and ancient visitors. Delineating the Extraterrestrial Highway, the Black Mailbox, and other enigmas of the last frontier and purposely ambiguous, film clips, photos, newspaper articles, and top-secret documents present the pros and cons of an aliens' universe. Eerie, suspenseful, and thought provoking, is it what you think it is or something else? Entrance fee is an additional $6.

If you are looking for some brain stimulation to escape the midway atmosphere of the casinos, you can't do better than the Atomic Testing Museum, created in association with the Smithsonian Institution. Furthermore, the museum store might be a good place to look for a stimulating present for that eggheaded child you left at home. Open daily, the museum is located at 755 E. Flamingo Rd. Admission is $14 adults and $12 children. Call ☎ 702-794-5161 for more information or see **atomictestingmuseum.org.**

Ever since you were a young boy (or girl) you've played the silver ball, but you ain't seen nothing like the **Pinball Hall of Fame** (1610 E. Tropicana Ave.; ☎ 702-597-2627; **pinballmuseum.org**). Whether you're an old-school Bally table king, or part of the post-Pong generation, you're sure to find a coin-operated time machine to transport you back to your youth inside this 10,000-square-foot all-ages arcade founded by Tim Arnold and operated by members of the Las Vegas Pinball Collectors Club. Housed in an unpretentious utilitarian warehouse, the Pinball Hall of Fame contains one of the world's largest pinball collections, all of which are available to play (as long as the staff can keep their flippers flipping), and many with informative handwritten histories. Machines range from the 1940s through the 1970s to the present, and include rare unreleased prototypes (a two-of-a-kind multilevel Pinball Circus), current pop-culture tie-ins (Star Trek, Transformers, The Dark Knight), and even a digital table that can emulate dozens of different models. Games cost between 25¢ and 75¢ for 5 balls, so bring cash for the quarter-changers; no tokens needed here.

Haven't had enough gaming? Check out **Gameworks** (**gameworks .com**), a 7,000-square-foot games arcade at Town Square specializing in classic video games and prize redemption games. It also features 80 personal computers for online gaming.

Only a half mile west of the Strip is **Dig This Heavy Equipment Playground** (3012 S. Rancho Dr.; ☎ 702-222-4344; **digthisvegas.com**), where you can play with real bulldozers and excavators. Following an orientation and a breathalyzer test—hey, it's Vegas—your personal instructor takes you out on the lot to move some dirt. Communicating with you over a headset, he actually teaches you to operate the earthmoving equipment (squishing the highway cones is considered bad form). Cabs are air-conditioned, so you'll be comfortable on hot days.

About 30 minutes southwest of Las Vegas, in the one-horse town of Goodsprings, Nevada, is the **Pioneer Saloon** (310 W. Spring St.; ☎ 702-874-9362; **pioneersaloon.info**). The saloon is pretty much the same as when it was built in 1913, with interior and exterior walls of stamped tin manufactured by Sears and Roebuck. Decorative accents include bullet holes from brawls dating back to 1915. The saloon became famous in 1941 when actress Carole Lombard's plane crashed not far away. Her husband, Clark Gable, sat at the bar chain-smoking for three days while awaiting word of Lombard's fate (all 22 aboard were killed). There's live rock or country music on Sunday afternoons if you're not nocturnal.

Also southwest of Las Vegas is **Sandy Valley Ranch** (1411 Kingston Rd., Sandy Valley, NV 80901; ☎ 702-242-0955; **sandyvalleyranch .com**), where you can get in touch with your inner bovine. Cut a steer from the herd, round up cattle and chase them into the corral, or trail-ride in the southern foothills of the Spring Mountains, all followed by a dinner featuring big wads o' meat and a near-conflagration of a campfire. No riding experience necessary—the horses are very smart and sweet (ask for old Gonad Stomper).

NATURAL ATTRACTIONS NEAR LAS VEGAS

IN THE MEXICAN PAVILION OF EPCOT at Walt Disney World, tourists rush obliviously past some of the rarest and most valuable artifacts of the Spanish Colonial period in order to take a short, uninspired boat ride. Many Las Vegas visitors, likewise, never look beyond the Strip. Like the Epcot tourists, they are missing something pretty special.

Las Vegas's geological and topographical diversity, in combination with its stellar outdoor resources, provides the best opportunities for worthwhile sightseeing. So different and varied are the flora, fauna, and geology at each distinct level of elevation that traveling from the banks of Lake Mead to the high, ponderosa pine forests of Mount Charleston encompasses (in 90 minutes) as much environmental change as driving from Mexico to Alaska.

Red Rock Canyon, the **Valley of Fire,** the **Mojave Desert,** and the **Black Canyon of the Colorado River** are world-class scenic attractions. In combination with the summits of the **Spring Mountains,** they compose one of the most dramatically diversified natural areas on the North American continent. So excuse us if we leave coverage of KISS Monster Mini Golf to the local visitors' guides.

Springs Preserve

If you like your outdoor experience with a healthy dose of history, Springs Preserve is the place for you. This 180-acre natural oasis, approximately 3 miles west of Downtown Las Vegas, is filled with museums, galleries, an interpretive trail system, botanical gardens, and plenty of wildlife. The **Origen Museum** is the preserve's focal point for history, geology, and wildlife and features three galleries with more than 75 exhibits. The preserve also features a 25-acre, re-created desert wetland with more than 35 species of wildlife and an 1,800-seat amphitheater. If you need a bite to eat after your hike, visit **Springs Cafe** for healthy American cuisine. The preserve is open daily, from 10 a.m. to 6 p.m. (trails close at dusk). Admission to museums and exhibits is $18.95 adults and $10.95 children (ages 5–17). Admission to trails is free. For more information, visit **springspreserve.org.**

Driving Tours

If you wish to sample the natural diversity of the Las Vegas area, we recommend the following driving tours. The trips begin and end in Las Vegas and take from 2 hours to all day, depending on the number of stops and side trips. The driving tours can conveniently be combined with picnicking, hiking, horseback riding, and sightseeing. If you have the bucks, we also recommend taking one of the air/ground tours of the Grand Canyon.

1. MOUNT CHARLESTON, KYLE CANYON, LEE CANYON, AND THE TOIYABE NATIONAL FOREST 4-6 hours If you have had more than enough desert, this is the drive for you. Head north out of Las Vegas on US 95 and turn left on NV 157. Leave the desert and head into the pine and fir forest of the Spring Mountains. Continue up Kyle Canyon to the Mount Charleston Inn (a good place for lunch) and from there to the end of the canyon. Backtracking a few miles, take NV 158 over Robbers Roost and into Lee Canyon. When you hit NV 156, turn left and proceed to

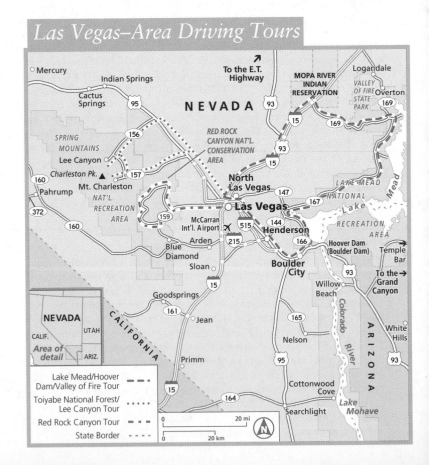

Las Vegas–Area Driving Tours

the Lee Canyon Ski Area. For the return trip, simply take NV 156 out of the mountains until it intersects US 95. Turn south (right) on US 95 to return to Las Vegas. If you start feeling your oats once you get into the mountains, there are some nice short hikes (less than a mile) to especially scenic overlooks. If you are so inclined, there is also horseback riding, and there are some great places for picnics.

2. RED ROCK CANYON SCENIC LOOP 1½–3 hours   Red Rock Canyon is a stunningly beautiful desert canyonland 20 minutes from Las Vegas. A scenic loop winds among imposing, rust-red Aztec sandstone towers. There is a visitor center, as well as hiking trails and picnic areas. With very little effort you can walk to popular rock-climbing sites and watch the action. From Las Vegas, head west on Charleston Boulevard (NV 159) directly to Red Rock Canyon. The scenic loop is 13 miles (one-way), with numerous places to stop and enjoy the rugged vistas. The loop road brings you back to NV 159. Turn left and return to town via Charleston Boulevard.

3. LAKE MEAD AND THE VALLEY OF FIRE 5–8 hours   This drive takes you to the Lake Mead National Recreation Area and Valley of Fire State Park. How long the drive takes depends on how many side trips you make. If you plan to visit Hoover Dam during your visit, it will be convenient to work it into this itinerary. The same is true if you wish to tour the Ethel M (as in Mars bars) Chocolate Factory and Cactus Garden.

Head south out of Las Vegas on US 95/93 (detour west on Sunset Road to visit the Chocolate Factory and Cactus Garden), continuing straight on US 93 to Boulder City. From Boulder City continue to the Hoover Dam on US 93 (if desired) or turn left on the Lakeshore Scenic Drive (NV 166) to continue the drive. Travel through the washes and canyons above the lake until you reach the Northshore Scenic Drive (NV 147 and NV 167). Turn right, continuing to the right on NV 167 when the routes split. If you wish, you can descend to the lake at Callville Bay, Echo Bay, or Overton Beach. If you are hungry, Callville Bay and Echo Bay have restaurants and lounges. Overton Beach has a snack bar, but Echo Bay has the best beach.

Near Overton Beach, turn left to NV 169 and follow signs for Valley of Fire State Park. Bear left on NV 169 away from Overton. Valley of Fire features exceptional desert canyon scenery, panoramic vistas, unusual and colorful sandstone formations, and Indian petroglyphs. A short 2-mile scenic loop makes it easy to see many of the valley's most interesting formations. If you have time, take the road past the visitor center and climb to the Rainbow Vista overlook. From here a new highway accesses some of the most extraordinary terrain in the American Southwest. After the loop (and any other detours that interest you), continue west on NV 169 until it intersects I-15. Head south to return to Las Vegas.

Eldorado Canyon

When you've covered Las Vegas for as long as we have it's really an event to bump into something totally new and different. Actually, to be precise, we stumbled onto something *old* and different. About a 40-minute drive from the Strip via US 95 and NV 165, is Eldorado Canyon, so named by the Spanish circa 1776 when gold and silver were discovered there.

Gold was rediscovered, along with nickel and lead, in 1859, leading to the establishment of the Techatticup Mine, which operated until 1945. A place of rough-and-tumble life with little order and much violence, the town of Nelson attracted a number of deserters from both the Union and Confederate armies during the Civil War. Lawlessness was so commonplace in the mine's heyday (the nearest sheriff was a one-week ride away on horseback) that a company of infantrymen was stationed nearby to discourage the killings and disputes among the miners themselves and with Native Americans.

At the bottom of the canyon was Nelson's Landing on the Colorado River, where the gold was loaded on riverboats to Yuma, Arizona, and sent downstream to California. The landing and a small village surrounding it were destroyed by a flash flood in 1974. By then, however, several dams had long since rendered the Colorado unusable for commercial purposes.

If you've ever wanted to drive from the canyon rim to the bottom of the Grand Canyon, the drive from the top of Eldorado Canyon to the Colorado River is a good facsimile. The road is good, and the vistas are glorious as you descend. At the bottom, there is a recreational area alongside the river, and the river itself, on a sunny day, is the darkest shade of blue imaginable. Be sure to top off your gas tank before leaving Las Vegas.

Eldorado Canyon is a recreational treasure trove. Mine tours, as well as guided kayak, mountain-biking, hiking, ATV, and horseback tours, are available. Outfitters for guided trips include **Awesome Adventures** (☎ 888-846-4747, **awesomeadventuretv.com**); **Adventure Las Vegas** (☎ 888-867-6259, **adventurelasvegas.com**); and **Desert Adventures** (☎ 702-293-5026, **desertadventureslv.com**). Of course, you can also do all of this on your own using your own or rented equipment. For mine tours, try **Eldorado Canyon Mine Tours** (☎ 702-291-0026, **eldoradocanyonminetours.com).**

Black Canyon Adventures (☎ 800-455-3490; **blackcanyonadventures.com**) offers a combo Eldorado Canyon tour and float trip on the Colorado River. Transportation is provided from the Las Vegas Strip to Eldorado Canyon and followed by 1 hour exploring the Techatticup Mine. Then you board a motorized raft at Nelson's Landing for a float to Willow Beach Marina. Guides discuss the geology, wildlife, history, and culture of the Colorado River, and lunch is served en route. After disembarking at Willow Beach, the tour stops at Hoover Dam before returning to the Strip. The tour takes about 5 hours, not counting transportation time to and from the Strip. If you meet the tour at the Hacienda Hotel near Boulder, the cost is $200 for adults, $194 for children ages 13–15, and $126 for children ages 5–12. Add $44 if you avail yourself of the transportation.

Pink Jeep Tours offers guided off-road experiences to Eldorado Canyon, Red Rock Canyon, and Valley of Fire in the Las Vegas area. Excursions farther afield include Death Valley, the Grand Canyon north, south, and west rims, and Zion National Park. Jeeps seat 10 persons and are pretty plushy. Guides are certified by the National Association for Interpretation. Lunch is included on most outings. For additional information and prices call ☎ 888-900-4480 or visit **pinkjeep.com/jeep-tours/lasvegas.**

Hoover Dam

Hoover Dam is definitely worth seeing. There is a film, a guided tour, and a theater presentation on the Colorado River drainage, as well as some static exhibits. Try to go on a Monday, Thursday, or Friday. Arrive no later than 9 a.m., when the visitor area opens, and do one of the tours first. You can choose between the guided, 30-minute **Power Plant Tour** that visits the power plant and visitor center ($15 adults, $12 children ages 4–16 and seniors) and the 1-hour **Hoover Dam Tour** that covers the dam passageways in addition to the visitor center and power plant. Admission for the Hoover Dam Tour is $30 (no children under 8 years of age allowed). Tickets for the Power Plant Tour can be purchased in advance through **usbr.gov/lc/hooverdam,** but you must purchase Hoover Dam Tour admissions in person on site. After 9:30 a.m. or so, long lines form for the tour, especially on Tuesday, Wednesday, Saturday, and Sunday. The dam is closed to visitors at 6 p.m. (tickets sold until 5:15 p.m.; 4:15 p.m. in winter). A ban on visitors inside the dam, initiated following 9/11, has been lifted, but there are security checkpoints on US 93 leading to the dam.

Other than chauffeured transportation, there is no advantage in going to Hoover Dam on a bus tour, although there is a $10 parking fee. You will still have to wait in line for the tour of the dam and to see the other presentations. If you are the sort of person who tours quickly, you probably will have a lot of time to kill waiting for the rest of the folks to return to the bus.

With the opening of the new bridge, those few miles of US Highway 93, which traverse the historic dam and pass by the visitors center, will no longer accommodate through traffic. Now the only access to the dam is from the Nevada side. An upgraded interchange on Highway 93 is under construction just east of the Hacienda Hotel and Casino on the outskirts of Boulder City. It is still possible to drive across the dam for a sweeping view of Lake Mead and the lower Colorado, but the existing road terminates on the Arizona side just above the last parking lot at the top of the hill. Keep an eye out for elusive desert bighorn sheep, as this is their primary migration route. For more information, call ☎ 702-494-2517.

HOOVER DAM BYPASS BRIDGE   The long-awaited and long-delayed $114-million Hoover Dam bypass bridge opened in 2010, saving travelers minutes to hours of driving time between Nevada and Arizona.

The old two-lane road, US Highway 93, which links the two states, incorporated hairpin turns and twisted down rocky canyons from both sides to cross the top of the dam. Traffic congestion mingled sightseers, commuters, truckers, and film crews, much to the frustration of all.

Officially named the Mike O'Callaghan–Pat Tillman Memorial Bridge after a former Nevada governor and an Arizona football player/US Army Ranger killed in Afghanistan, the structure features two enormous cable-less arches projecting from the sheer cliffs above the waterway to buttress the road. Intrepid visitors can walk across the one-third-mile, four-lane bypass rising 850 feet above the choppy Colorado River. A sidewalk begins on the Nevada side and stretches the length of the span. The view of the canyon, the river, and the bridge's remarkable engineering is stunning. It is the longest and highest arch concrete bridge in the Western hemisphere. An information plaza, hiking trail, and parking area are on the Nevada side.

The Canyons of the Southwest

Las Vegas tourist magazines claim **Bryce Canyon** (400 miles round-trip; ☎ 435-834-5322) and **Zion Canyon, Utah** (350 miles round-trip; ☎ 435-772-3256), as well as the **Grand Canyon, Arizona** (☎ 928-638-7888) as local attractions. We recommend all of the canyons if you are on an extended drive through the Southwest. If your time is limited, however, you might consider taking one of the air day-tours that visit the canyons from Las Vegas. Running roughly between $100 and $400 per passenger, the excursions follow one of two basic formats: air only, or air and ground combined. Some tour companies offer discounted fares for a second person if the first person pays full fare. Also, discount coupons are regularly available in *What's On* and *Today in Las Vegas*, distributed free of charge in most hotels.

Almost all canyon tours include a pass over **Lake Mead** and **Hoover Dam**. The trip involving the least commitment of time and money is a round-trip flyover of one or more of the canyons. A Grand Canyon flyover, for example, takeoff to touchdown, takes about 2 hours. While flying over any of the canyons is an exhilarating experience, air traffic restrictions concerning the Grand Canyon severely limit what air passengers can see. Flying over the other canyons is somewhat less restricted.

 If you want to get a real feel for the Grand Canyon particularly, go with one of the air/ground excursions. The Grand Canyon is much more impressive from the ground than from the air.

The air/ground trips fly over the Grand Canyon and then land. Passengers are transferred to a bus that motors them along the rim of the canyon, stopping en route for lunch. Excursions sometimes additionally include boat and helicopter rides. These multifaceted tours last 7–10 hours. Many flights offer multilingual translations of the tour narrative.

All of the aircraft used will feel very small to anyone accustomed to flying on big commercial jets. Most of the planes carry between 8 and

20 passengers. The captain often performs the duties of both flight attendant and pilot. Each passenger usually has a window, though some of the windows are pretty small. Cabin conditions for the most part are spartan, and there is usually no toilet on board.

Because small aircraft sometimes get bounced around and buffeted by air currents, we recommend taking an over-the-counter motion-sickness medication if you think you might be adversely affected. The other thing you want to do for sure is to relieve your bladder *immediately* before boarding.

Following are descriptions of the tours we consider the cream of the crop. Because they offer the most extensive introduction to the Grand Canyon, they rank among the most expensive (see the chart on page 453).

GRAND CANYON FUN TRIPS The **Grand Canyon West Rim Voyager** and **Grand Canyon 4 in 1 Best Adventures Airplane, Copter, and Boat Tours** from Grand Canyon Fun Trips are the best value. The only difference between the two tours is the transportation used to see Boulder City, Lake Mead, and the Hoover Dam, and to reach the Grand Canyon.

If you would prefer an aerial view of Boulder City, Lake Mead, and the Hoover Dam, then Grand Canyon 4 in 1 is your tour. All airplanes are high wing, and helicopters sport extra-large vista windows, allowing all passengers to have a spectacular view. If you wish for a more up-close and personal look at the attractions, and have an extra 3½ hours to allocate, the Grand Canyon West Rim Voyage tour incorporates the aforementioned sights into a 3-hour relaxing motorcoach ride en route to the Canyon.

The tours are identical once you reach the Grand Canyon. You take a chopper to the Canyon floor (15 minutes) and shuffle onto a pontoon boat for a 25-minute ride down a flatwater section of the Colorado River. After the ride, you are airlifted back up to the West Canyon Rim to enjoy a barbecue lunch. Following lunch, you reboard the coach or plane and head back to Vegas.

HELI USA Grand Canyon Explorer is the best package we reviewed for those wanting to combine a lengthy helicopter tour with other activities. Leaving from Las Vegas, the tour consists of a 45-minute helicopter flight with views of the Hoover Dam and Lake Mead, and flying through the Canyon at 1,500 feet below the rim.

Upon arrival at the Grand Canyon West Ranch, about 12 miles from the West Rim, you are shuttled in about 10 minutes from the landing pad to the ranch in a horse-drawn wagon. At the ranch, horseback riding is available for an additional charge of $49 for a half hour. A Western-style dinner along with songs and stories around a campfire complete the ranch experience. Alcohol is available at an additional charge, and the ranch buildings are air-conditioned. The return bus trip to Las Vegas takes about 2½ hours.

SUNDANCE HELICOPTERS If all you seek is a helicopter ride without the added bells and whistles of additional activities, then go with the

Sundance Grand Canyon Picnic Tour. You will arrive at the launch pad in style by a ride in the complimentary limousine.

The helicopter tour is a round-trip 1½ hours spent in the air, viewing the Hoover Dam, Lake Mead, extinct volcanoes, lava formations, and the West Rim of the Grand Canyon. A maximum number of six people can fit in the helicopter. However, if a guest weighs over 275 pounds, he or she will have to purchase two seats. All guests have unobstructed views.

The helicopter lands on a plateau between the river and the ridge. A box lunch and Champagne are provided, and there is time to do a little exploring on foot before jumping back in the helicopter for the ride back to the Strip. Reserve the flight through **looktours.com** and save well over $100 per person as opposed to reserving through the Sundance company directly.

IF YOU GO Grand Canyon tours are a perfect respite from the glitz and frenetic activity of the Strip. Whether you're looking for a flyby, great photo ops, or a cowboy ranch experience, it can be found with one of the tours we describe.

All tours described here are geared toward families and people of all ages. The tours involving a boat ride use craft that guests of all ages can easily board, and the gentle, scenic section of the river featured contains no rapids.

SKYWALK Located 121 miles from Las Vegas over some primitive roads, Skywalk is a horseshoe-shaped observation platform projecting from the remote western edge of the Grand Canyon on the Hualapai reservation. The ends of the horseshoe are anchored to the rim of the canyon while the rounded section, the observation platform, cantilevers into space 4,000 feet above the canyon floor. Both the sides and the floor of the platform are transparent. Although the flexible Skywalk is designed to withstand 100-mile-per-hour winds and 8.0-magnitude earthquakes and to support 71 million pounds—it wobbles and vibrates a little. The sensation is a bit like walking on a cruise ship—not unpleasant at sea but disconcerting when you're hanging over the Grand Canyon. Add the fact that the walls are only about mid–chest high and Skywalk begins to seem as much a thrill ride as a spectacular viewing spot.

Speaking of the view, it's magnificent. From Skywalk you can see standing waves on the Colorado River to the left (they look like tiny ripples from this height) and Eagle Point to the right, where the configuration of the canyon looks like the outstretched wings of a bird.

To walk on Skywalk you must purchase a Legacy Gold package, which also includes a visit to the Hualapai Ranch, Guano Point, and Eagle Point, a Native American cultural performance, and an all-you-can-eat meal among other things (see **grandcanyonwest.com** or call ☎ 888-868-9378). The package runs $86 (including taxes and fees) for adults and $72 for children ages 4–11. A wheelchair ramp is available. There's no limit to the time you can spend on Skywalk and no maximum weight for visitors. You are not allowed to bring

Grand Canyon Tours

GRAND CANYON WEST RIM VOYAGER ☎ 702-851-8436; grandcanyonfuntrips.com

- **Transportation** Bus, boat , helicopter • **Cost** $234 if you book online
- **Sightseeing** Boulder City, Hoover Dam, Lake Mead, West Rim, Colorado River
- **Length** 11 hours *(including hotel pickups and drop-offs.)*

GRAND CANYON 4 IN 1 BEST ADVENTURES ☎ 702-851-8436; grandcanyonfuntrips.com

- **Transportation** Airplane, helicopter, boat • **Cost** $364 if you book online
- **Sightseeing** Boulder City, Hoover Dam, Lake Mead, West Rim, Colorado River
- **Length** 7½ hours

GRAND CANYON EXPLORER ☎ 800-359-8727; heliusa.com

- **Transportation** helicopter, wagon, bus, horseback • **Cost** $439
- **Sightseeing** Hoover Dam, Lake Mead, Canyon West Rim, Ranch
- **Length** 9 hours *(including hotel pickups and drop-offs.)*

GRAND CANYON PICNIC ☎ 800-653-1881; sundancehelicopters.com

- **Transportation** helicopter, wagon, bus, horseback *(additional charge)*
- **Sightseeing** Hoover Dam, Lake Mead, extinct volcanoes, lava flows, Canyon West Rim
- **Length** 3½ hours (including hotel pickups and drop-offs.)
- **Cost** $449 (discounts at looktours.com)

cameras or any personal belongings onto Skywalk. For additional information see **grandcanyonskywalk.com.**

If you drive from Las Vegas but don't want to drive the final 14-mile graded but unpaved road to the reservation, make a reservation to use the Park & Ride service by calling ☎ 702-260-6506. The service costs $15 per person. Because the drive is a little more than 3 hours one-way from Las Vegas, you'll have to leave early to take advantage of all the elements of the tour package. If you want to drive over prior to your tour, you can spend the night at the Hualapai Lodge in the hardscrabble town of Peach Springs (49 miles away), the center of the Hualapai Tribe; call ☎ 928-769-2230 or visit **hualapaitourism .com** for reservations.

If you don't want to drive, these companies will fly you there:

VISION HOLIDAYS **visionholidays.com** | ☎ 800-256-8767

MAVERICK HELICOPTERS **maverickhelicopter.com** | ☎ 888-261-4414

SUNDANCE HELICOPTERS **sundancehelicopters.com** | ☎ 800-653-1881

Fares range from $250 to more than $500 round-trip, although sometimes a discount can be found on the Internet.

PART SIX

EXERCISE *and* RECREATION

WORKING OUT

MOST OF THE FOLKS ON OUR *UNOFFICIAL GUIDE* research team work out routinely. Some bike; some run; some lift weights or do yoga. Staying in hotels on the Strip and Downtown, they realized that working out in Las Vegas presents its own peculiar challenges.

The best time of year for outdoor exercise is October–April. The rest of the year it is extremely hot, though mornings and evenings are generally pleasant in September and May. During the scorching summer, particularly for visitors, we recommend working out indoors or, for bikers and runners, very early in the morning.

 If you do anything strenuous outside, at any time of year, drink plenty of water. Dehydration and heat exhaustion can overtake you quickly in Las Vegas's desert climate. For outdoor workouts in Las Vegas comparable to what you are used to at home, you will deplete your body's water at 2–3 times the usual rate.

WALKING

PRIMARILY FLAT, LAS VEGAS IS MADE FOR WALKING and great people-watching. Security is very good both Downtown and on the Strip, making for a safe walking environment at practically all hours of the day and night. Downtown, everything is concentrated in such a small area that you might be inclined to venture away from the casino center. While this is no more perilous than walking in any other city, the areas surrounding Downtown are not particularly interesting or aesthetically compelling. If the Downtown casino center is not large enough to accommodate your exercise needs, you are better off busing or cabbing to the Strip and doing your walking there.

If you are walking the Strip, it is about 4 miles from Mandalay Bay on the south end to the Stratosphere on the north end. Because the topography is so flat, however, it does not look that far. We met a

Las Vegas Strip Walking Map

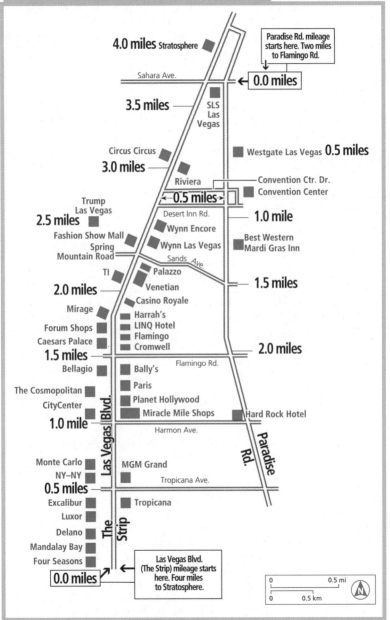

4.0 miles Stratosphere

Paradise Rd. mileage starts here. Two miles to Flamingo Rd. → 0.0 miles

Sahara Ave.

3.5 miles — SLS Las Vegas

Circus Circus
3.0 miles

Westgate Las Vegas 0.5 miles

Riviera

Convention Ctr. Dr.
Convention Center

← 0.5 miles →

Trump Las Vegas
2.5 miles

Desert Inn Rd. — 1.0 mile

Fashion Show Mall
Spring Mountain Road —

Wynn Encore

Wynn Las Vegas

Best Western Mardi Gras Inn

Sands Ave.

TI
2.0 miles —

Palazzo

Venetian — 1.5 miles

Mirage

Casino Royale

Forum Shops
Caesars Palace

Harrah's
LINQ Hotel
Flamingo
Cromwell — 2.0 miles

1.5 miles —

Bellagio

Bally's

Flamingo Rd.

The Cosmopolitan

Paris

CityCenter

Planet Hollywood

1.0 mile —

Miracle Mile Shops

Hard Rock Hotel

Harmon Ave.

Las Vegas Blvd.

Monte Carlo
NY–NY
0.5 miles

MGM Grand

Paradise Rd.

Tropicana Ave.

Excalibur
Luxor

Tropicana

The Strip

Delano
Mandalay Bay
Four Seasons
0.0 miles

Las Vegas Blvd. (The Strip) mileage starts here. Four miles to Stratosphere.

0   0.5 mi
0   0.5 km

N

number of people who set out on foot along the Strip and managed to overextend themselves. Check out our Strip walking-distances map on the previous page before you go, and bear in mind that even without hills, marching in the arid desert climate will take a lot out of you.

 When walking the Strip, carry enough money to buy refreshments en route and to take a cab or bus back to your hotel if you poop out or develop a blister.

RUNNING

IF YOU STAY ON THE STRIP, you will have more options than if you stay Downtown. Those of us who are used to running on pavement ran on the broad sidewalks of Las Vegas Boulevard South. These runs are great for people-watching also, but are frequently interrupted by long minutes of jogging in place at intersections, waiting for traffic lights to change. Our early risers would often run before 7:30 a.m. on a golf course. This was the best (and safest) running in town, with good footing, beautiful scenery, and no traffic. However, course managers were less than overjoyed to see a small platoon of travel writers trotting off the 18th fairway. If you run on a golf course, stay off the greens and try to complete your run by 7:30 a.m. In addition to area golf courses, the Westgate Las Vegas and Mandalay Bay each have a jogging circuit.

If you stay Downtown, you must either run on the sidewalks or drive to a more suitable venue. Sidewalks Downtown are more congested than those on the Strip, and there are more intersections and traffic lights with which to contend. If you want to run Downtown, particularly on Fremont Street, try to exercise before 10 a.m.

For those who dislike pounding the blacktop, sneaking onto golf courses, or exercising early in the morning, a convenient option is to run on the track at the University of Nevada, Las Vegas. Located about 2 miles east of the Strip on Harmon Avenue, **UNLV** offers both a regulation track and some large, grassy athletic fields. Park in the dirt lot near the tennis courts if you do not have a university parking sticker. For more information, call ☎ 702-895-4729.

If you have a car and a little time, two of the better off-road runs in the area are at **Red Rock Canyon,** out Charleston Boulevard, 35 minutes west of town. Red Rock Canyon Conservation Area, managed by the U.S. Bureau of Land Management, is Western desert and canyon scenery at its best. Spectacular geology combined with the unique desert flora and fauna make Red Rock Canyon a truly memorable place. Maps and information can be obtained at the visitor center, on-site.

A 2-mile round-trip, **Moenkopi Loop,** begins and ends at the visitor center. A 3-mile circuit, **Willow Springs Trail,** begins at Willow Springs Picnic Area and circles around to Lost Creek Canyon. Both routes are moderately hilly, with pretty good footing. Moenkopi Loop is characterized by open desert and expansive vistas, while the Willow Springs Trail ventures into the canyons. The Willow Springs Trail is also distinguished by numerous Indian petroglyphs and other artifacts. Both trails, of course, are great for hiking as well as for running.

Finally, if you want to hook up with local runners, join the Las Vegas Track Club for a weekly run to **Tule Springs** (north of Downtown on US 95) or many other area locations. For a current schedule or additional information, call the Village Runner at ☎ 702-898-7866 or visit **villagerunner.com.**

SWIMMING AND SUNBATHING

SWIMMING, DURING WARM-WEATHER MONTHS, is the most dependable and generally accessible form of exercise in Las Vegas. Most of the Strip hotels and a couple of the Downtown hotels have nice pools. Sometimes the pools are too congested for swimming laps, but usually it is possible to stake out a lane.

If the pool at your hotel is a funny shape or too crowded for a workout, there are pools more conducive to serious swimming at the **Las Vegas Athletic Club** on Flamingo Road and in the **McDermott Physical Education Complex** of UNLV.

For those who want to work on their tans in style, the **Mirage, Cosmopolitan, Tropicana, Wynn Las Vegas, Wynn Encore, M Resort, Mandalay Bay, Venetian, Palazzo, Aria, Paris, Monte Carlo, MGM Grand, TI, Caesars Palace, Rio, Westgate Las Vegas, Flamingo, Palms, Green Valley Ranch, Hard Rock Hotel, Bellagio, Planet Hollywood,** and **JW Marriott Las Vegas,** among others, have particularly elegant facilities.

Be forewarned that sunbathing in Las Vegas can be dangerous. The climate is so arid that you will not feel yourself perspiring: perspiration evaporates as soon as it surfaces on your skin. If there is a breeze, particularly on a pleasant fall or spring day, you may never feel hot, sticky, or in any way uncomfortable until you come out of the sun and discover that you have been fried.

You can get sunburned quickly if you do not protect yourself properly. Even those with a tan should be careful. Use a broad-spectrum sunscreen with an SPF of 15 or higher, and reapply it often. There is no such thing as waterproof sunscreen.

HEALTH CLUBS

IF YOU CAN GET BY WITH A LIFECYCLE, a StairMaster, or a rowing machine, the fitness rooms of most major hotels should serve your needs. Fortunately, local health clubs welcome visitors for a daily ($15–$20) or weekly ($30–$50) fee. All of the clubs described here are coed.

The **Las Vegas Athletic Clubs,** with six locations, offer racquetball, tennis, basketball, exercise equipment, and aerobics, though not all features are provided at each location. These clubs depend more on local patronage than on visitors; their facilities are commodious but not luxurious, and fees are at the lower end of the range. While reasonably convenient to the Strip, only the West Sahara club is within walking distance. For rates and additional info visit **lvac.com** or call:

- 5200 W. Sahara Ave. ☎ 702-364-5822
- 1725 N. Rainbow Blvd. ☎ 702-835-5822
- 2655 S. Maryland Pkwy. ☎ 702-734-5822
- 3830 E. Flamingo Rd. ☎ 702-898-5822
- 9065 S. Eastern Ave. ☎ 702-853-5822
- 9615 W. Flamingo Rd. ☎ 702-798-5822

The **24 Hour Fitness** centers, with two locations, run an excellent aerobics program and have an extensive weight and exercise facility. While the facilities are good and the use fees midrange, locations are a little remote for most visitors staying on the Strip or Downtown.

• S. Eastern near Sahara ☎ 702-641-2222 • Cheyenne and Rainbow ☎ 702-656-7777

FREE WEIGHTS AND MACHINES

ALMOST ALL OF THE MAJOR HOTELS have a spa or fitness room with weight-lifting equipment. Some properties have a single Universal machine, while others offer a wide range of free-weight and Nautilus/Cybex equipment. Hotels with above-average facilities for pumping iron are the **Westgate Las Vegas, Bellagio, The Venetian, Caesars Palace, Cosmopolitan, Aria, Golden Nugget, Mirage, Paris, Wynn Las Vegas, Wynn Encore, M Resort, Mandalay Bay, Monte Carlo, MGM Grand, Luxor,** and **TI.**

For hard-core power lifters and bodybuilders, try **Gold's Gym.** Gold's is coed and offers daily and monthly rates ($20 and $70, respectively) for use of its weight machines and free weights. Contact them at any one of their five locations: South, ☎ 702-914-5885; Southeast, ☎ 702-269-0828; Summerlin, ☎ 702-360-8205; Centennial, ☎ 702-657-0171; and Aliante, ☎ 702-396-0800.

GOLF

PEAK SEASON FOR GOLF in Las Vegas is October through May. The other four months are considered prohibitively warm for most golfers, but greens fees are reduced substantially at most courses during summer. While Las Vegas tourism has recovered from the sharp drop that accompanied the economic downturn four years ago in terms of visitor numbers, people are still spending less, and golf nationwide is suffering, so golf in Vegas has not bounced back. As a result, deals abound more than ever. One profound shift is that today, in almost every case, you can get the best rates through individual course websites, where all sorts of Internet specials can be found daily. Most courses also have reduced rates for locals, and many offer discounts for guests staying at partner hotels or discounted stay-and-play packages combining lodging and greens fees. These discounts are also online, so make sure you check the course's website before booking.

Also, almost all Las Vegas–area courses offer discounted twilight rates, which, depending on time of year, start as early as noon. In general, morning tee times are more desirable and difficult to arrange than afternoons. Call the pro shop at least one day before you wish to play. Same-day phone calls are discouraged. In summer most courses and driving ranges stay open until at least 7:30 p.m.

Another way to save is with **GolfNow,** a company that offers last-minute unsold tee times from about 40 courses in Las Vegas, plus more in Laughlin and Mesquite as well, from same day to a week in advance at discounts of 40–80%. These include most of the area's best courses, and recently they even added the exclusive Wynn Golf Club. For more information, visit **golfnow.com/lasvegas.**

In winter and early spring, temperatures drop rapidly near sundown, so always bring a sweater or jacket. It can also be very windy. Las Vegas has an elevation of 2,000 feet and is considered high desert. Take this into account when making club selections.

IMPORTANT NOTES Several top Las Vegas courses are private clubs that do not allow outside access, and thus are not listed. Additionally, during its boom years, Las Vegas created a unique sort of "almost private" golf course. This started with **Shadow Creek Country Club,** which was built specifically for the highest of high rollers and originally had neither members nor allowed paying guests. Now privately owned by MGM Resorts International, the course is open to guests of all its many hotels, but on a very limited basis. Only a handful of public tee times are available each day (Monday through Thursday only) and always at a cost of $500 per person. Two other courses run by MGM competitors took the same tact, requiring lodging and charging $500, but both have opened the doors to the public and rolled back prices, while only top-rated Shadow Creek stands firm. Cascata, owned by Caesars, was the latest to embrace economic reality, allowing outside play from $250—plus additional discounts for guests of Caesars Palace and affiliated hotels. Wynn likewise dropped the overnight stay requirement at its Wynn Country Club course and dropped prices to $300–$350, added a $200 replay option, and occasionally discounts rates even more. Neither of these are exactly cheap, but they are compared to their $500 prices. Not quite so extravagant is **The Tournament Players Club,** which has been open to the general public for the past few years, while guests of JW Marriott Las Vegas at Summerlin receive preferred tee times and personalized service. This is where Tiger Woods won his very first PGA Tour event back in 1996. The Summerlin course was designed by architect Bobby Weed with assistance from player-consultant Fuzzy Zoeller and has been rated by both *Golf Digest* and *Golfweek* magazines as the second-best course in Nevada, behind Shadow Creek. The opulent Wynn course once fell into the almost-private category, but feeling the pressure of Vegas's economic downturn has now opened its course to fully public outside play.

Despite the number of golf courses in the Las Vegas area, for serious golf travel fans there are only three choices that could accurately be called golf resorts—and that is still a bit of a stretch. **Lake Las Vegas,** about half an hour from the Strip, was once one of the top self-contained golf resorts in the nation. However, it has been an economic victim of over-leveraging, losing both its resort courses and the Ritz-Carlton and Loews hotels. The now-defunct flagship layout, Reflection Bay, was arguably the best course in town. The good news is that the hotels reopened, with Hilton reviving the Ritz property and Westin taking over the Loews. There is also an Aston hotel in the resort's pedestrian village. With both resort courses shuttered, the hotels have partnered with the struggling private, resident-only country club course at Lake Las Vegas, the Jack Nicklaus–designed South Shore Golf Club. Only hotel guests can play South Shore, a very good course. Raintree, an investment firm for New York hedge fund manager John Paulson, brought renewed hope for the Reflection Bay course when it acquired both defunct golf courses in 2013. Partnering with the Henderson Development Association in 2014, Raintree committed to restoring Reflection Bay in return for being allowed to build houses on the acreage previously occupied by The Falls course. An agreement has been signed with Arnold Palmer Golf Management to operate Reflection Bay. The 18-hole Jack Nicklaus Signature course is scheduled to reopen by the end of 2014—we'll see. . . . In **Summerlin,** about 25 minutes from the Strip, the JW Marriott is surrounded by six courses within 10 minutes and is about 20 minutes from the trio at the Paiute Golf Club. The resort offers preferred tee times and free shuttles to several of them, making it a true destination golf resort, and is partnered with the top-tier TPC Las Vegas, offering attractive stay-and-play packages year-round. In the city, the **Wynn** is the only hotel with an on-site course, making it an urban golf resort of sorts, though a very pricey one. All three properties have lavish spas, pools, activities, multiple restaurants, bars, and casinos.

Bali High is the only championship course located directly on the Las Vegas Strip. The Schmidt/Curley–designed course is highlighted by 7 acres of water features, a spectacular island green, and more than 4,000 trees, including 2,500 stands of towering palms and 100,000 tropical plants and flowers. Amazing views of the Strip can be found from fairways and tee boxes throughout the course. The other course on the Strip is Wynn Golf Club, but it's scheduled to be plowed under for new construction at some point. There have been no new courses of note in greater Las Vegas in the past several years, and the area's last acclaimed new full-size course was in Mesquite, NV, about 80 miles away. Conestoga was named one of the nation's best new courses in 2011 by *LINKS* and *Golfweek* magazines.

The one big new addition to the Vegas golf scene is the recent opening of the **TaylorMade Golf Experience** (**taylormadegolfexperience.com**) along Las Vegas Boulevard just south of Mandalay Bay. A division of Adidas, leading equipment manufacturer TaylorMade has for years been the number one driver of choice for PGA Tour players. Recently, the company has been busy rolling out high-tech custom fitting centers, where the public can strap on sensors and use the same proprietary computerized MAT-T system (Motion Analysis Technology by TaylorMade) that sponsored pros, such as Justin Rose and Sergio Garcia, use to tweak their shafts and clubs. But the Las Vegas campus is the first that adds a golf course to the MAT-T center. The new 9-hole, par three course features holes playing 110–185 yards, plus there's a bi-level, 113-bay driving range; a short game practice area; a bar and grill; and full retail and club demo facilities.

GOLF COURSE RATINGS	
QUALITY RATING	**VALUE RATING**
★★★ Championship, challenging	**1** A good bargain
★★ Playable, suitable for all caliber golfers	**2** A fair price
★ Preferred by beginners and casual golfers	**3** Not a good bargain

Angel Park Golf Club

ESTABLISHED 1989 | STATUS MUNICIPAL | QUALITY ★★ | VALUE ★★

100 S. Rampart Blvd., Las Vegas, NV 89145; ☎ 702-254-4653; angelpark.com

TEES

PALM COURSE
- Professional: 6,500 yards, par 70, USGA 70.3, slope 124
- Championship: 5,857 yards, par 70, USGA 67.1, slope 115
- Forward: 4,578 yards, par 70, USGA 66.8, slope 110

MOUNTAIN COURSE
- Professional: 6,722 yards, par 71, USGA 71.1, slope 130
- Championship: 6,223 yards, par 71, USGA 68.8, slope 125
- Forward: 5,150 yards, par 71, USGA 69.1, slope 114

FEES Nonresidents: $79–$135; Residents: $40–$49

FACILITIES Pro shop, night-lit driving range, 12-hole par-3 course and 9-hole putting course, putting green, restaurant, snack bar, bar, tennis courts, golf club and shoe rentals.

COMMENTS Angel Park, a good, functional golf complex, is rapidly becoming one of the most successful public golf facilities in the United States. Its courses are well designed—by Arnold Palmer, no less—and the sophisticated 18-hole putting course is a popular attraction even for nongolfers. Its Cloud Nine short course is unique and great for golfers needing a quick fix, with reproductions of 12 famous par-3 holes from around the world, 9 of which are lit for night play. There is also a lighted natural-grass putting course— think fancy mini-golf. Both courses are crowded year-round, as the facility is close to the Strip and popular with locals.

Bali Hai

ESTABLISHED 2000 | STATUS PUBLIC | QUALITY ★★ | VALUE ★★

5160 S. Las Vegas Blvd., Las Vegas, NV 89119; ☎ 888-427-6678; balihaigolfclub.com

TEES
- Black: 7,002 yards, par 71, USGA 73.0, slope 130
- Gold: 6,601 yards, par 72, USGA 70.2, slope 125
- Silver: 6,156 yards, par 72, USGA 68.6, slope 113
- Bronze: 5,511 yards, par 72, USGA 71.5, slope 122

FEES $199–$349, depending on time of day and year; see website for details. The course also offers some discounted lodging-and-golf packages. Club rentals, $55–$100.

FACILITIES Pro shop, driving range, putting green, snack bar, restaurant, full locker facilities, caddies, fore-caddies, club and shoe rentals.

COMMENTS In real estate, location is everything, and the only reason Bali Hai commands these outrageous greens fees is its location on the Strip next to

Mandalay Bay. It is the only course, besides the Wynn Golf Club, located so close to the major casinos. Designed in a tropical theme, Bali Hai features water everywhere, with an island green, endless tropical flora, and vast expanses of black "coral" and white sand. Bali Hai is undeniably beautiful, but that does not make it a great course. Better golf can be had for less, even with taxi fares.

Bear's Best

ESTABLISHED 2002 | STATUS PUBLIC | QUALITY ★★★ | VALUE ★★

11111 W. Flamingo Rd., Las Vegas, NV 89135; ☎ 702-804-8500; clubcorp.com

TEES

- Gold: 7,194 yards, par 72, USGA 74.0, slope 147
- Blue: 6,628 yards, par 72, USGA 71.3, slope 130
- White: 6,043 yards, par 72, USGA 68.3, slope 122
- Red: 5,043 yards, par 72, USGA 68.7, slope 116

FEES $89–$250, depending on time of day; see website for details. Club rentals, $65.

FACILITIES Pro shop, driving range, putting green, restaurant, full locker facilities, golf academy, caddies, fore-caddies, club and shoe rentals.

COMMENTS One of only two Bear's Best courses (the other is in Atlanta), this is a tribute by Jack Nicklaus, aka the Golden Bear, to himself. Here Nicklaus has re-created holes from his favorite original designs, but unlike most tribute or replica courses, including Vegas's Royal Links, the holes were specifically chosen to fit the desert setting. As a result, this is one of the best of these gimmicky layouts in the world. Fans have the opportunity to play holes from Nicklaus's most acclaimed public courses, such as Cabo del Sol, Palmilla, and Castle Pines, along with very private ones from Desert Mountain, Desert Highlands, and PGA West. Since opening it has been ranked among the city's best courses. Since the demise of Reflection Bay, this is the best public course in the Vegas area other than the barely public Shadow Creek. The facility is now home to the Paul Wilson Golf School.

Black Mountain Golf and Country Club

ESTABLISHED 1959 | STATUS SEMIPRIVATE | QUALITY ★ | VALUE ★

500 Greenway Rd., Henderson, NV 89015; ☎ 702-565-7933; golfblackmountain.com

TEES

- Championship: 6,556–6,613 yards, par 72, USGA 70.6–71.1, slope 124–129
- Men's: 6,148–6,279 yards, par 72, USGA 69.0–69.6, slope 121–128
- Ladies': 5,148–5,319 yards, par 72, USGA 69.4–70.2, slope 111–114

FEES Nonresidents: high season, $80 (carts included on weekends only); low season, $60. Residents: high season, $70; low season, $60. Club rentals $20–$45.

FACILITIES Pro shop, clubhouse, driving range, putting green, restaurant, club rentals, snack bar, bar.

COMMENTS 27-hole Black Mountain is set amidst the Henderson hills, 20 minutes from the Strip. Many who prefer walking to riding play here, as it's one of the few area courses that doesn't require electric carts during the week. Many bunkers and unimproved areas off fairways make for tough recovery shots. A good course for beginning and intermediate golfers and juniors—and a good value year-round. The course wrapped up a $2-million renovation in late 2008 and is uniquely semi-public, fully owned by members but wide-open and welcoming to visitors.

Cascata

ESTABLISHED 2000 | STATUS PUBLIC | QUALITY ★★★ | VALUE ★★★

1 Cascata Dr., Boulder City, NV 89142; ☎ 702-294-2005; cascatagolf.com

TEES
- Black: 7,137 yards, par 72, USGA 74.6, slope 143
- Blue: 6,664 yards, par 72, USGA 71.7, slope 138
- Gold: 6,206 yards, par 72, USGA 69.9, slope 135
- Red: 5,591 yards, par 72, USGA 67.2, slope 117

FEES $250–$395. Fees do not include transportation or caddy (caddy required, fee $25, plus recommended tip of $25 per person). Discounted golf and lodging packages are available with Caesars properties.

FACILITIES Pro shop, driving range, putting green, restaurant, full locker facilities, caddies.

COMMENTS After the runaway success of Shadow Creek, another casino group built the even more expensive Cascata, said to have the highest golf course construction price tag ever, for its high rollers. Now owned by Caesars Entertainment, it is a truly unique design in golf. Acclaimed designer Rees Jones blasted the course out of a rocky mountain. The holes are built in a series of narrow, parallel finger canyons radiating from the summit and running up and down the rocky slopes. Sitting in the canyons, the lush green fairways are completely isolated from one another by sloped canyon walls. The par-3s are especially dramatic, often backed by amphitheater cliffs and waterfalls. Because its name is Italian for "waterfall," Jones built one 40 stories high that pours through the center of the marble Italian palazzo–style clubhouse. Among the three $500 Vegas courses, Cascata was the first to blink in the recession and has been offering public rates of "only" $250–$395, and prime tee times 7 days a week. The $250 rate is now standard all day, every day, all summer long.

Coyote Springs Golf Club

ESTABLISHED 2008 | STATUS SEMIPRIVATE | QUALITY ★★★ | VALUE ★★

3100 State Route 168, Coyote Springs, NV 89037; ☎ 702-422-1400; coyotesprings.com

TEES
- Black: 7,471 yards, par 72, USGA 75.8, slope 141
- Blue: 6,807 yards, par 72, USGA 72, slope 137
- White: 6,215 yards, par 72, USGA 69.3, slope 132
- Red: 5,288 yards, par 72, USGA 70.5, slope 127

FEES Peak: daily, $139 ($99 after 11 a.m.); off-peak (after June 1): daily, $75 ($60 after 11 a.m.).

FACILITIES Pro shop, driving range, putting green, snack bar, restaurant, full locker **FACILITIES**.

COMMENTS Originally called The Chase at Coyote Springs, the course has been renamed simply Coyote Springs, and PGA was also dropped from the name, implying a cutback from the once grand residential and multicourse development vision. Developed by the PGA of America, the course opened in May 2008 to rave reviews—named "Best New U.S. Public Course" in 2009 by *Links* and in the top 10 new courses by *Golf Magazine* and *Golf Digest*. It is the first of several Jack Nicklaus Signature courses planned for the community, with the same designer who has had so much success locally with Reflection Bay and Bear's Best. Coyote Springs is reminiscent of Reflection Bay, with elaborate rock-lined water features—11 lakes in all—but has more dramatic fairways and pronounced undulations, and the desert hazards are sandier and more landscaped, less wild, than many area courses. Nicklaus is famed for his dramatic waterfront finishes, and this course is no exception, with the last four holes curving around lakes. Prices are in line with the more expensive Vegas-area courses, but the quality is better than most. However, it's not as good a value as the equally far-flung courses of Primm and Mesquite, Nevada. In an interesting homage to the setting, each hole is named for Vegas slang, such as On Tilt and Shooter. In summer, free replay is offered daily.

Desert Pines Golf Club

ESTABLISHED 1997 | STATUS PUBLIC | QUALITY ★ | VALUE ★★

3415 E. Bonanza Rd., Las Vegas, NV 89101; ☎ 702-450-8170; desertpinesgolfclub.com

TEES
- Championship: 6,810 yards, par 71, USGA 70.6, slope 125
- Men's: 6,494 yards, par 71, USGA 67.9, slope 118
- Ladies': 5,873 yards, par 71, USGA 69.4, slope 116

FEES Peak Season: $169 Sunday–Thursday, $200 Friday–Sunday ($99 twilight). Rates vary widely by time, even in peak season. Walters Golf's website (**waltersgolf.com**) offers a low-rate guarantee and up-to-date deals for same- and next-day bookings. Golf and lodging packages with major Strip hotels now offered.

FACILITIES Pro shop, driving range, putting green, snack bar, restaurant.

COMMENTS Desert Pines is a 6,810-yard course on Bonanza Road between Mojave and Pecos roads. Inspired by the Pinehurst courses in North Carolina, its fairways and greens are flanked by trees, some already as tall as 40 feet. Instead of rough, developer Bill Walters laid down 45,000 bales of red-pine needles imported from South Carolina, making it hard to lose a ball here. Its very low off-season rates make it one of the best hot-weather choices in the region. The course recently renovated its fairways and putting surfaces and is in its best shape in years. Owner Walters Golf has partnered with MGM Grand, Aria, and Hard Rock hotel-casinos and now offers some excellent stay-and-play packages.

Highland Falls Golf Club

ESTABLISHED 1992 | STATUS SEMIPRIVATE | QUALITY ★★★ | VALUE ★★

10201 Sun City Blvd., Las Vegas, NV 89134; ☎ 702-254-7010; golfsummerlin.com

TEES
- Championship: 6,512 yards, par 72, USGA 70.1, slope 119
- Men's: 6,017 yards, par 72, USGA 68.1, slope 118

- Gold: 5,579 yards, par 72, USGA 71.4, slope 122
- Ladies': 5,099 yards, par 72, USGA 68.4, slope 112

FEES Nonresidents: $80 daily; $60 twilight. Residents: $60 daily; $50 twilight.

FACILITIES Pro shop, driving range, putting green, restaurant, luncheon area, patio for outside dining, bar.

COMMENTS In a local shocker, readers of the *Review-Journal* voted this the best golf in Las Vegas for 2011. It's hard to fathom, but the course is good, a testing layout designed by Hall of Famer Billy Casper's company, Casper-Nash Associates. The unique design sits in the mountains at over 3,000 feet, and the cooler weather allows it to use superior quality bentgrass greens, unusual in this climate, and Bermuda fairways to combine the best of both worlds. More undulations than most desert courses, with several demanding holes. No one broke par for the first six months after opening. The course now offers specials to its Twitter and e-club followers.

Lake Las Vegas

ESTABLISHED 1998 | STATUS RESORT, PUBLIC | QUALITY ★★★ | VALUE ★★

101 Montelago Blvd., Henderson, NV 89011; ☎ 702-567-6000

TEES

- Black: 6,917 yards, par 72, USGA 72.6, slope 135
- White: 6,524 yards, par 71, USGA 70.7, slope 130
- Blue: 6,254 yards, par 71, USGA 70.4, slope 130
- Gold: 6,204 yards, par 71, USGA 66.5, slope 123
- Red: 4,852 yards, par 71, USGA 67.9, slope 115

FEES Weekday $190, weekend $210, resort guests only. Lodging and golf packages available from $299 per night.

FACILITIES Pro shop, driving range, putting green, snack bar, restaurant, full locker facilities.

COMMENTS Expensive but worth it. Replacing the shuttered Reflection Bay and The Falls courses is access to the private South Shore Golf Club—but only for guests of the Hilton, Westin, and Aston hotels. With sweeping views of Lake Las Vegas, the waterfront signature design by Jack Nicklaus was named one of the "Top 10 Private Golf Courses in America" by *Golf Digest* when it opened in 1996 and has hosted the Wendy's 3-Tour Championship. The course is both beautiful and challenging, with numerous forced carries over canyons and water and substantial elevation changes, plus high-quality bentgrass greens.

Las Vegas Golf Club

ESTABLISHED 1949 | STATUS PUBLIC | QUALITY ★ | VALUE ★★

4300 W. Washington Ave., Las Vegas, NV 89107; ☎ 702-646-3003; lasvegasgc.com

TEES

- Championship: 6,290 yards, par 72, USGA 69.8, slope 121
- Men's: 5,917 yards, par 72, USGA 68.2, slope 116
- Ladies': 5,260 yards, par 72, USGA 69.9, slope 113

FEES Nonresidents: weekdays $65, $49 twilight; weekends $75.

FACILITIES Pro shop, night-lit driving range, putting green, restaurant, snack bar, bar, and beverage-cart girls who patrol the course.

COMMENTS The past several years have seen $5 million in renovations and improvements pumped into the first and oldest golf course in Las Vegas, laid out by the legendary William Bell in 1938, including a new clubhouse. It has remained a popular public course and a site of many local amateur tournaments. Formerly owned and managed by Senior PGA star Jim Colbert, then American Golf, it again changed hands and is now operated by well-regarded OB Sports. A good choice for recreational golfers, with fairly wide-open fairways and little trouble, so play should move briskly.

Las Vegas National

ESTABLISHED 1961 | STATUS PUBLIC *(PRIVATELY OWNED)* | QUALITY ★★ | VALUE ★★

1911 E. Desert Inn Rd., Las Vegas NV 89169; ☎ 888-695-1961 or 702-734-1796 (tee-time service and other reservations); lasvegasnational.com

TEES
- Championship: 6,773 yards, par 72, USGA 73.5, slope 137
- Men's: 6,260 yards, par 71, USGA 71.6, slope 133
- Ladies': 5,640 yards, par 72, USGA 68.8, slope 130

FEES Monday–Thursday, 6–8 a.m. and 11:30 a.m.–close, $79; 9–11:20 a.m., $99. Friday–Sunday, 6–8 a.m. and 11:30 a.m.–close, $89; 9–11:20 a.m., $89.

FACILITIES Pro shop, night-lit driving range, putting green, restaurant, bar.

COMMENTS Lower rates, almost always less than $99, with $45 fees after 2:30 p.m. nearly year-round, make this one of the best and most convenient buys in town. A championship course that has at one time cohosted the Tournament of Champions, the Sahara Invitational, and the Ladies' Sahara Classic. Tiger Woods is a past champion here (he shot 70 to win his very first PGA Tour event). The course is convenient to the Strip ($10 cab ride) and offers an excellent variety of holes, with good bunkering and elevation changes uncharacteristic of a desert course. Better for intermediate and advanced golfers. Take in the local history with a post-round cocktail in the Rat Pack Bar & Grill.

Las Vegas Paiute Resort

ESTABLISHED 1995 | STATUS PUBLIC | QUALITY ★★ *(Snow/Sun)* ★★★ *(Wolf)* VALUE ★★ *(Snow/Sun/Wolf)*

10325 Nu-Wav Kaiv Blvd., Las Vegas, NV 89124 (US 95 between Kyle Canyon and Lee Canyon turn-off to Mount Charleston); ☎ 702-658-1400 or 800-711-2833; lvpaiutegolf.com

TEES

SNOW MOUNTAIN
- Tournament: 7,146 yards, par 72, USGA 73.3, slope 125
- Championship: 6,645 yards, par 72, USGA 71.2, slope 120
- Regular: 6,035 yards, par 72, USGA 68.6, slope 112
- Forward: 5,341 yards, par 72, USGA 70.4, slope 117

SUN MOUNTAIN
- Tournament: 7,112 yards, par 72, USGA 73.3, slope 130
- Championship: 6,631 yards, par 72, USGA 70.9, slope 124
- Regular: 6,074 yards, par 72, USGA 68.8, slope 116
- Forward: 5,465 yards, par 72, USGA 71.0, slope 123

WOLF
- Tournament: 7,604 yards, par 72, USGA 76.3, slope 149
- Black: 7,009 yards, par 72, USGA 73.5, slope 134

- Yellow: 6,483 yards, par 72, USGA 71.4, slope 130
- White: 5,910 yards, par 72, USGA 76.5, slope 125
- Red: 5,130 yards, par 72, USGA 68.5, slope 116

FEES Prices are $39–$229 and depend on day of week and time of day. There is always a $10–$20 surcharge to play the Wolf course. They offer a wide array of discounts for multiday play, for military, plus Internet specials.

FACILITIES Pro shop, driving range, 2 putting greens, restaurant, snack bar, bar with gaming.

COMMENTS The region's only 54-hole resort golf complex, all three courses are Pete Dye designs. The original two layouts, Snow and Sun Mountain, are comfortable desert courses, beauty without brawn, and have remained among the public favorites in the region since opening. Not so for the newer Wolf, which is one of, if not the most, difficult courses in Las Vegas. From the tips it is 500 yards longer than any course most golfers have played, and strewn with hazards of the wet and dry variety. Still, it is as well conditioned and thought out as its tamer siblings and has a near re-creation of Dye's famous island hole par-3 he pioneered at the TPC Sawgrass. Despite its stiff challenge, it has quickly become the most demanded course here and is accordingly priced slightly higher. In keeping with Las Vegas's recent aggressive discounting, the Paiute Resort offers a staggering five different price times daily, from early bird to super-twilight, plus heavily discounted same-day replays and full-day Golfapalooza packages, which include lunch, 50% off rentals, and two same-day rounds on different courses from just $135.

Legacy Golf Club

ESTABLISHED 1989 | STATUS PUBLIC *(PRIVATELY OWNED)* **| QUALITY ★★ | VALUE ★★**

130 Par Excellence Dr., Henderson, NV 89074; ☎ 888-629-3930; thelegacygc.com

TEES

- Championship: 7,233 yards, par 72, USGA 74.5, slope 137
- Men's: 6,744 yards, par 72, USGA 71.5, slope 128
- Ladies': 5,340 yards, par 72, USGA 71.5, slope 128
- Resort: 6,211 yards, par 72, USGA 69.3, slope 119

FEES Weekdays, $109; weekends and holidays, $119. All greens fees include mandatory carts. Club rentals, $60 ($35 twilight).

FACILITIES Clubhouse, pro shop, driving range, chipping facility, putting green, restaurant, snack bar, bar.

COMMENTS A long course by Arthur Hills, the Legacy is a mixture of rolling fairways and target golf. It is also one of the most photographed courses in Vegas because its tees are shaped like playing card suits. Championship tees require a long carry on the tee-ball to clear desert mounding. One big plus for visiting golfers without rental cars is that the Legacy added a free golf shuttle with pick-up from most major casinos.

Painted Desert

ESTABLISHED 1987 | STATUS PUBLIC | QUALITY ★★ | VALUE ★★

5555 Painted Mirage Dr., Las Vegas, NV 89149; ☎ 702-645-2570; painteddesertgc.com

TEES

- Championship: 6,781 yards, par 72, USGA 71.8, slope 129

- Men's: 6,269 yards, par 72, USGA 69.9, slope 125
- Ladies': 5,647 yards, par 72, USGA 72.2, slope 126

FEES Peak season: Monday–Thursday, $99; twilight rate, $69; Friday–Sunday, $109; twilight rate, $79. Off-peak: Monday–Thursday, $69; Friday–Sunday, $79. Club rentals, $45 (includes 2 sleeves of golf balls).

FACILITIES Pro shop, driving range, putting green, restaurant, bar.

COMMENTS Target course designed by renowned architect Jay Morrish, Tom Weiskopf's partner. Lush fairway landing pads and well-manicured greens, but make certain you're on target. The rough is pure waste-area. Now operated by nationally renowned management company OB Sports, the course offers numerous discounts seasonally, and for 2013 added online dynamic, demand-based pricing, similar to airline tickets, fluctuating in real time based on sales and availability.

The Revere at Anthem

ESTABLISHED 1999 | STATUS PUBLIC | QUALITY ★★ | VALUE ★★

2600 Hampton Rd., Henderson, NV 89052; ☎ 702-259-4653 or 877-273-8373; reveregolf.com

TEES
LEXINGTON
- Black: 7,143 yards, par 72, USGA 73.5, slope 138
- Gold: 6,590 yards, par 72, USGA 70.8, slope 131
- Silver (Ladies'): 5,941 yards, par 72, USGA 73.3, slope 127
- Bronze (Ladies'): 5,216 yards, par 72, USGA 69.9, slope 118

CONCORD
- Black: 7,034 yards, par 72, USGA 72.8, slope 126
- Gold: 6,546 yards, par 72, USGA 69.8, slope 121
- Silver: 6,094 yards, par 72, USGA 67.6, slope 119
- Bronze (Ladies'): 5,171 yards, par 72, USGA 69.7, slope 118

FEES $55–$199; rates are seasonal—visit their website for the most current information. Club rentals, $65.

FACILITIES Fully stocked clubhouse and snack bar, golf shop, restaurant.

COMMENTS This 36-hole facility was named the nation's best facility operated by Troon Golf. Both courses were designed by Billy Casper and Greg Nash, and the club is consistently rated among the city's top 10. About 20 minutes from the Strip in the southeast Las Vegas Valley, Revere is built in a natural canyon, with a feel that is secluded and intimate. Lexington is the longer and more challenging layout, with numerous risk-reward opportunities, while the slightly shorter and newer Concord features wider fairways and larger greens. Much of the year, 36-hole specials are offered for playing both courses in the same day. They also offer specials that allow visitors to mix and match benefits such as free transportation, breakfast or lunch, rental clubs, or a second round within 7 days.

Rio Secco Golf Club

ESTABLISHED 1997 | STATUS RESORT, PUBLIC | QUALITY ★★ | VALUE ★★★

2851 Grand Hills Dr., Henderson, NV 89052; ☎ 888-867-3226 or 702-777-2400; riosecco.net

TEES
- Championship: 7,313 yards, par 72, USGA 75.0, slope 153
- Blue: 6,927 yards, par 72, USGA 73.0, slope 149
- Middle: 6,375 yards, par 72, USGA 70.7, slope 136
- Forward: 5,758 yards, par 72, USGA 70.7, slope 127

FEES $79–$219; rates vary—visit their website for the most current information. Club rentals, $55 (includes 2 sleeves of balls).

FACILITIES Pro shop, driving range, putting green, snack bar, restaurant, full locker facilities, Butch Harmon Golf School.

COMMENTS The best and closest of Las Vegas's pure desert-style courses, Rio Secco is set amid 240 acres of dramatic canyons just 12 minutes from the Strip. Variety, beauty, and strategic design highlighted by 88 bunkers make this a challenging but beautiful course. However, its perimeter is heavily lined with homes, negating some of the desert feel. It is also one of the more expensive rounds in the area, not really reflecting the recent drop in Vegas golf prices. Rio Secco is also golf-school headquarters for celebrity instructor Butch Harmon, whose former pupil, Tiger Woods, holds the course record with a stunning 63. Like Cascata, the course is owned by Caesars and recently added a T-Mates program, a combination of Las Vegas showgirls with (scantily clad) forecaddies.

Royal Links

ESTABLISHED 1999 | STATUS PUBLIC | QUALITY ★★ | VALUE ★★★

5995 E. Vegas Valley Rd., Las Vegas, NV 89142; ☎ 888-427-6678; royallinksgolfclub.com

TEES
- Royal: 7,029 yards, par 72, USGA 73.7, slope 135
- Gold: 6,602 yards, par 72, USGA 71.2, slope 131
- Ruby: 5,864 yards, par 72, USGA 68.4, slope 125
- Emerald: 5,142 yards, par 72, USGA 69.8, slope 115

FEES September–April: weekdays $219, weekends $249. Summer rates: weekdays $129, weekends $159. Club rentals (includes golf shoes), $75, lower in summer. Walters Golf's website (**waltersgolf.com**) offers a low-rate guarantee and up-to-date deals for same- and next-day bookings.

FACILITIES Pro shop, driving range, putting green, restaurant, English pub, full locker facilities, fore-caddies.

COMMENTS Royal Links sets out to emulate 18 holes from British Open venues in England and Scotland. In many ways the course succeeds, with excellent representations of links bunkering, exposure to fierce winds, and authentic rough and gorse. But nearly every course represented is on the ocean, something that cannot be replicated in the desert, and the re-creations are far from exact. As a result, the course is more fun the less you know about the real thing. Once very expensive among Vegas courses, the layout is now middle-of-the-pack and worth playing, especially as a novelty if you've never been to the British courses. Royal Links now has stay-and-play packages with a number of top resorts such as Aria, and may be the first golf resort in Las Vegas to ever offer "mancation" packages that include a visit to a gentleman's club. In this vein, they offer the Parmates program—a female caddy staff of beautiful women hired to sex up the golf experience.

Shadow Creek Golf Club

ESTABLISHED 1990 | STATUS RESORT | QUALITY ★★ | VALUE ★★★

3 Shadow Creek Dr., Las Vegas, NV 89030; ☎ 866-260-0069; shadowcreek.com

TEES

- Championship: 7,560 yards, par 72, USGA 71.0, slope 115
- Regular: 7,102 yards, par 72, USGA 68.9, slope 113

FEES Monday–Thursday $500, includes caddy and round-trip limo transportation; must be a guest of an MGM Resorts International hotel to play, but weekends it's invited guests only.

FACILITIES Pro shop, driving range, putting green, restaurant, full locker facilities, caddies.

COMMENTS Shadow Creek is widely rated as not just the best course in Las Vegas, but among the best in the country. It is ranked 57th in the nation, including privates, by *Golf Magazine,* and in the top 10 among public courses, deservedly. Shadow Creek is better considered barely near public, with the nation's highest greens fees, and those allowed only Monday through Thursday, with weekends reserved for VIPs and high-rolling gamblers. Nonetheless, when the required lodging and dining are thrown in, Shadow Creek falls in the same price range as Pebble Beach and Pinehurst Number Two and offers a far more luxurious experience than either. The course is always empty and meticulously maintained, the caddies are excellent, and the layout is both gorgeous and fun to play. Despite the high level of conditioning, Shadow Creek closed for nearly seven months in 2008 for extensive improvements, including all new tees and greens and the addition of a comprehensive short-game practice area to further enhance the already royal treatment—it is now better than ever. An engineering marvel that transported a classic, heavily wooded Carolina-style parkland layout to the desert, it is rumored to be one of the most expensive courses ever built, having cost about $38 million in the 1980s. The finishing three holes are as memorable and dramatic a close as you will find in the golf world.

Siena Golf Club

ESTABLISHED 2000 | STATUS SEMIPRIVATE | QUALITY ★★ | VALUE ★

10575 Siena Monte Ave., Las Vegas, NV 89135; ☎ 888-689-6469; golf shop, ☎ 702-341-9200; sienagolfclub.com

TEES

- Gold: 6,843 yards, par 72, USGA 71.7, slope 131
- Black: 6,538 yards, par 72, USGA 70.4, slope 129
- Blue: 6,146 yards, par 72, USGA 68.6, slope 125
- White: 5,639 yards, par 72, USGA 66.4, slope 114
- Green: 4,978 yards, par 72, USGA 68.0, slope 112

FEES $99–$189; rates are seasonal—visit their website for the most current information; special twilight rates available.

FACILITIES Pro shop, driving range, putting green, snack bar, restaurant, full locker facilities.

COMMENTS A sleeper course in the Summerlin residential community, Siena welcomes outside play and is one of the region's best buys. The bargain replay option is a good deal, and other special promotions are occasionally offered.

The course showcases extensive rock outcroppings and water features, including cascading waterfalls around the 18th green. All four par-3s are unique and notable, including sunken treasure, a gorgeous island green. Well-separated tees offer the right challenge for every player.

TPC Las Vegas

ESTABLISHED 1996 | STATUS PUBLIC | QUALITY ★★★ | VALUE ★★★

9851 Canyon Run Dr., Las Vegas, NV 89144; ☎ 702-256-2000; tpc.com

TEES
- TPC: 7,081 yards, par 71, USGA 73.4, slope 136
- Blue: 6,769 yards, par 71, USGA 71.0, slope 128
- White: 6,047 yards, par 71, USGA 68.0, slope 127
- Red: 4,963 yards, par 71, USGA 67.8, slope 117

FEES $80–$250; rates are seasonal—visit their website for the most current information.

FACILITIES Pro shop, driving range, putting green, snack bar, restaurant, full locker facilities.

COMMENTS Long known as TPC Canyons, this course by any name is one of the few public offerings among the Tournament Players Clubs, or the TPC network, so-called "stadium courses," designed specifically to host and showcase tournaments and owned by the PGA Tour. Designed by Bobby Weed and Ray Floyd, it hosts the Las Vegas Invitational and has hosted the Michelob Championship. This is a tough desert course, with plenty of opportunities to lose balls in the dry wash and cacti, but is well designed and appealing to the better player. The facilities are first-rate, but they should be at this price. The course has packages with the adjacent JW Marriott Summerlin and Red Rock Casino resorts.

Wynn Golf Club

ESTABLISHED 2005 | STATUS PRIVATE | QUALITY ★★ | VALUE ★★★

3131 Las Vegas Blvd. S., Las Vegas, NV 89109; ☎ 702-770-4653; wynnlasvegas.com

TEES
- Back: 7,042 yards, par 70, USGA 73.9, slope 124
- Black: 6,464 yards, par 70, USGA 72.5, slope 120

FEES $500 ($300–$375 in summer). Fees include caddy.

FACILITIES Pro shop, driving net, putting green, restaurant, full locker facilities, caddies.

COMMENTS Steve Wynn collaborated with Tom Fazio, widely considered one of the top golf architects in the world, to build Shadow Creek when Wynn owned Mirage Resorts. The duo got together again for this course on the former site of the Desert Inn Country Club. Nothing of the old layout is recognizable, as Fazio moved 800,000 cubic yards of earth and changed the flat course to one with rolling elevation changes, boulder-strewn creeks, a huge four-story waterfall you drive carts behind, and endless flowerbeds. The fairways and greens are immaculate, and the devotion to maintenance and aesthetics are obvious, making Wynn GC a very attractive and playable course, but frankly it is not on par with its high-priced Vegas brethren,

Cascata and Shadow Creek, as once-in-a-lifetime experiences. Anywhere else this course would be lucky to command $200, but as the old real estate adage goes, location is everything, and this is the only hotel course on the Strip where guests can walk to the first tee rather than face daunting cab rides. Still, the location comes at a cost: the Las Vegas Monorail runs along the perimeter, and instead of majestic trees, skyline views are of the Eiffel Tower, Stratosphere, and myriad condo high-rises. Lack of space explains the par-70 design, and even at that length it remains a bit crowded. In a big change of direction, Wynn GC opened to the public two years ago, and you no longer need to stay here to play.

OUTDOOR RECREATION

LAS VEGAS AND THE SURROUNDING AREA offer a host of outdoor and adventure activities. The following section provides information on the activities available.

BICYCLING

ASK ANY CYCLIST IN LAS VEGAS about the on- and off-road riding nearby and you'll probably hear two kinds of comments. First, why pedaling in the desert is such a treat: excellent surface conditions; the option of pancake-flat or hilly riding; starkly beautiful scenery any time of year, and cactus blossoms in March and April; the possibility of spying raptors or jack rabbits or wild burros as you pedal; the unbelievably colorful limestone and sandstone formations.

Unfortunately, newcomers to desert and high-elevation biking often recall only these comments and not the "Be sure to carry . . ." warnings, which fellow riders usually provide after getting you all revved up. So read the following and remember that bikers are subject to those same conditions—heat and aridity—that make the desert so breathtaking.

Biking Essentials

1. TIME OF DAY Desert biking in late spring, summer, and early fall is best done early or late in the day. Know your seasons, listen to weather reports, and don't overestimate your speed and ability.

2. CLOTHING Ever see someone perched on a camel? What was he wearing? Right, it wasn't a tank top and Lycra shorts. The point is protection—from the sun during the day, from the cold in the morning and evening. And if you don't use a helmet (and you should), wear a hat.

3. SUNSCREEN In the desert, even well-tanned riders need this stuff.

4. SUNGLASSES The glare will blind you without them.

5. WATER The first time we rode in the desert, we carried as much water as we would have used on a ride of comparable distance in the eastern United States. Big mistake. Our need for water was at least twice what it normally would be in New York or Atlanta. We were thirsty the entire trip and might have gotten into serious trouble had we not cut our ride short.

You already know that you will need extra water, but how much? Well, a human working hard in 90°F temperature requires 10 quarts of fluid replenishment every day. Ten *quarts*. That's two and a half gallons—12 large water bottles, or 16 small ones. And with water weighing in at 8 pounds per gallon, a one-day supply comes to a whopping 20 pounds.

 Pack along two or three bottles even for the shortest rides. For longer rides, we carry a large Camelbak water carrier along with two bottles of water on the bike frame and a third stuffed inside the mesh of the Camelbak.

In the desert, the heat is dry, and you do not notice much perspiration because your sweat evaporates as quickly as it surfaces. Combine the dry heat with a little wind, and you can become extremely dehydrated before realizing it. Folks from the East (like us) tend to regard sweating as a barometer of our level of exertion (if you are not sweating much, in other words, you must not be exercising very hard). In the desert, it doesn't work that way. You may never notice that you are sweating. In the desert you need to stay ahead of dehydration by drinking more frequently and more regularly and by consuming much more than the same amount of exercise would warrant in other climates. Desert days literally suck the water right out of you, even during the cooler times of the year.

6. TOOLS Each rider has a personal "absolute minimum list," which usually includes most of the following:

• tire levers	• spoke wrench
• chain rivet tool	• allen wrenches (3, 4, 5, and 6 mm)
• spare tube and patch kit	• 6-inch crescent (adjustable-end) wrench
• spare chain link	• small flat-blade screwdriver
• air pump or CO2 cartridges	

7. FIRST-AID KIT This, too, is a personal matter, usually including those items a rider has needed due to past mishaps. So, with the desert in mind, add a pair of tweezers (for close encounters of the cactus kind).

Road Biking

Road biking on the Strip, Downtown, or in any of Las Vegas's high-traffic areas is suicidal. Each year an astoundingly high number of bikers are injured or killed playing Russian roulette with Las Vegas motorists. If you want to bike, either confine yourself to sleepy subdivisions or get way out of town on a road with wide shoulders and little traffic.

There are a number of superb rides within a 30- to 40-minute drive from Downtown or the Strip. The best is the **Red Rock Canyon Scenic Loop ride,** due west of town, which carves a 15.4-mile circuit through the canyon's massive, russet-colored, sandstone cliffs. The route is arduous, with a 1,000-foot elevation gain in the first 6 miles, followed by 8 miles of downhill and flats with one more steep hill. One-way traffic on the scenic loop applies to cyclists and motorists alike. Although there is a fair amount of traffic on weekends, the road is wide and the speed limit is a conservative 35 miles per hour. If you park your car at the Red Rock Canyon Visitor Center, take careful note of when the area closes. If you are delayed on your ride and get back late, your car might be trapped behind locked gates.

A second ride in the same area follows NV 159 from the town of Blue Diamond to the entrance of Red Rock Canyon Scenic Loop Drive and back again, approximately 15.5 miles. From Blue Diamond the highway traverses undulating hills, with a net elevation gain of 193 feet on the outbound leg. In general, the ride offers gentle, long grades alternating with relatively flat stretches. Cliff walls and desert flora provide stunning vistas throughout. Traffic on NV 159 is a little heavy on weekends, but the road is plenty wide, with a good surface and wide shoulders. In the village of Blue Diamond there is a bike shop and a small store.

Another good out-and-back begins at Overton Beach on Lake Mead, northeast of Las Vegas, and ascends 867 feet in 8 miles to the visitor center at the Valley of Fire State Park. (You can, of course, begin your round-trip at the visitor center, but we always prefer to tackle the uphill leg first.) Geology in the park is spectacular, with the same red sandstone found in the cliffs and formations of the Grand Canyon. There are no shoulders, but traffic is light and the road surface is good. Since the route runs pretty much east–west, we like to schedule our ride in the afternoon so that we will have the setting sun at our back as we coast down to the lake on the return leg. Another good option is an early-morning ride with the sun at your back as you ascend and high in the sky as you return.

Dressing for a bike ride in the canyons and high country around Las Vegas is a challenge. In early December, when we rode the Red Rock loop, it was about 62°F in town and about 10°F cooler in the canyon. We started out in Lycra bike shorts and polypro long-sleeve windbreakers. By the time we completed the 6-mile uphill, we were about to die of heat prostration. On the long, fast downhill, we froze. Our recommendation is to layer on cooler days so that you can add or shuck clothing as conditions warrant. On warm days, try to bike early in the morning or late in the afternoon and wear light clothing. Always wear a helmet and always, always carry lots of water.

Except for the bike shop in Blue Diamond, there is no place on any of these routes to get help with a broken bike. You should bring extra tubes and a pump or CO_2 cartridges and know how to fix flats and make other necessary repairs. Water is available at Blue Diamond and at the Red Rock and Valley of Fire visitor centers, but almost no place else. Always replenish when you have the opportunity.

If you have a car, there are plenty of places to rent bikes, including four shops on the west side of town close to the rides described above. The shop in Blue Diamond also rents. For any of the five, just park, rent, and go. If you want to ride farther afield, some stores rent bike racks for your car. For a list of the shops, Google "bike rentals Las Vegas."

Mountain Biking

Las Vegas, most unexpectedly, has become a mountain-biking destination. Southwest of Las Vegas on NV 160 is Cottonwood Valley, with more than 200 miles of singletrack and doubletrack for all skill levels. There are five named loop trails, two named out-and-backs, and miles of unnamed trails and unpaved roads. Trail surface is mostly packed sand (good traction) with loose rock and a little soft sand. Trails on the north side of NV 160 are mellower in general, though there's some advanced riding below the east face of Wilson Cliffs. If it's your first time in the area, start with the figure-eight Mustang Trail. Almost all singletrack on good surface, this trail over rolling high desert offers moderate climbs, gradual descents, and great views of the Red Rock cliffs and valleys. A number of trails branch off Mustang if you want to lengthen your ride or opt for more advanced terrain.

On the south side of NV 160, the rides require more climbing. The showcase trail is the Dead Horse Loop, 14 miles of intermediate to advanced singletrack. Site of NORBA races, the route climbs to an overlook, with a stunning view of Las Vegas in the distance, and then drops off the mountain in a blue-cruiser known locally as the 3-mile smile. Out-and-backs and additional loops connecting to Dead Horse serve up more technical climbs and descents.

There are two ways to reach Cottonwood Valley. The fastest is to go south on I-15, exit onto NV 160, and head west 16 miles to the Mustang Trailhead parking lot (on the right) or 17 miles to the Cottonwood Valley Trailhead on the left. You can also go west out of town on Charleston Boulevard, which becomes NV 159. Take NV 159 until it intersects NV 160 south of Blue Diamond. Turn right on NV 160 for 5–6 miles to the parking lots.

 Try riding Cottonwood Valley first. If Cottonwood doesn't offer enough challenge, try Bootleg Canyon.

Southeast of Las Vegas near Boulder City, Hoover Dam, and Lake Mead is Bootleg Canyon, primarily an advanced-skill-level mountain-bike park, though it does offer something for all skill levels on its 36 miles of trails. While mostly known for its full-body-armor downhills and jumps, the park also serves up some technical cross-country, great views of Boulder City, and, on the backside, Lake Mead. Though hard to get really lost, the layout, with lots of crisscrossing trails, is confusing to many bikers riding there for the first time. A lot, if not most, of the riding is hard core, as are the riders who hang here. Surface is packed dirt or sand and a lot of rock, much of it loose. Trails, carved into the side of the hill, are frequently off-camber. To get there from Las Vegas, take NV 93 to Boulder City. Turn left at the light onto Buchanan Boulevard, and then left onto Canyon Road. Continue beyond where the pavement gives way to dirt to the Bootleg Canyon parking lot situated between two hills. Usually there are freebie maps of the park in a box at the parking lot, but if possible, team up with locals who know the area and terrain.

If you're not used to riding in the high desert, you won't believe how much water you consume. We recommend a full Camelbak plus as many water bottles as you can carry on the frame. If you can jam an extra water bottle into the deep pouch on your Camelbak, or carry extra water in a day pack, you'll be glad you did. Wind, almost always howling out of the west, is a factor at both biking destinations, so much so that trails are generally laid out on a north–south axis with as little east–west as possible. Even so, tackling a tough climb into a headwind will probably be part of your Nevada biking baptism. Finally, almost all of the riding is exposed. If you want shade, bring an umbrella—seriously.

Other area rides include the Bristlecone Pine Trail in Lee Canyon on Mount Charleston, about an hour northwest of Las Vegas. Though just under 6 miles in length, this loop trail is at altitude (above 7,500 feet) with a 700-foot rise and fall in elevation. Take US 95 north and then follow NV 157 for 17 miles up into the mountains until you see a dirt road where you can turn off and park.

Bicycles are available for rent at **Escape Adventures,** 10575 Discovery Dr. (☎ 702-596-2953 or **escapeadventures.com**). Helmets, bike racks, water bottles, Cottonwood Valley trail maps, and other gear are likewise available for rent or for sale. Escape also offers guided mountain-bike tours daily, with trails chosen based on the skill level of the group. If you book a tour, Escape will pick you up at your hotel or one close by.

Another option is to rent a bike from **McGhie's Bike Outpost** (☎ 702-875-4820 or **mcghies.com**), in the little desert town of Blue Diamond. Blue Diamond is off NV 159 about 3 miles north of the intersection with NV 160. Located on the east end of Cottonwood Valley, you can actually get on the trail outside the back door of the shop. That said, you have to bike quite a way uphill and west to access the popular loop trails.

In addition to the foregoing, many mountain bikers ride the paved scenic loop at Red Rock Canyon (described under "Road Biking," pages 473–474). Visit **redrockcanyonlv.org** for more information.

HIKING AND BACKPACKING

HIKING OR BACKPACKING IN THE DESERT can be a very enjoyable experience. It can also be a hazardous adventure if you travel unprepared. Lake Mead ranger Debbie Savage suggests the following:

The best months for hiking are the cooler months of November through March. Hiking is not recommended in the summer, when temperatures reach 120°F in the shade. Never hike alone and always tell someone where you are going and when you plan to return. Carry plenty of water (at least a half-gallon per person) and drink often.

Know your limits. Hiking the canyons and washes in the desert often means traveling over rough, steep terrain with frequent elevation changes. Try to pick a route that best suits your abilities. Distances in the desert are often deceiving. Be sure to check the weather forecast before departure. Sudden storms can cause flash flooding. Seek higher ground if thunderstorms threaten.

Essential equipment includes sturdy walking shoes and proper clothing. Long pants are suggested for protection from rocks and cacti. A hat, sunscreen, and sunglasses are also recommended. Carry a small daypack to hold items such as a first-aid kit, lunch, water, a light jacket, and a flashlight.

Canyons and washes often contain an impressive diversity of plant life, most easily observed during the spring wildflower season. Desert springs are located in some of the canyons and support a unique community of plants and animals. They are often the only source of water for many miles around. Take care not to contaminate them with trash or other human wastes. Along similar lines, understand that desert soils are often very fragile and take a long time to recover if disturbed. These surfaces are recognizable by their comparatively darker appearance and should be avoided whenever possible.

Poisonous animals such as snakes, spiders, and scorpions are most active after dark and are not often seen during daylight hours by hikers. Speckled rattlesnakes are common but are not aggressive. Scorpion stings are no more harmful than a bee sting, unless you are allergic. Black widow spiders are shy and secretive and are most often found around man-made structures. Watch where you place your hands and feet, and don't disturb obvious hiding places.

The Las Vegas area offers quite a diversity of hiking options. Trips that include a choice of canyons, lakes, desert, mountains, or ponderosa pine forest can be found within an hour's drive of Las Vegas. There are two great guidebooks to hiking the Las Vegas–southern Nevada area: *Hiking Las Vegas: The All-in-One Guide to Exploring Red Rock Canyon, Mt. Charleston, and Lake Mead,* by Branch Whitney (Huntington Press, 392 pages, $24.95) and *Afoot and Afield Las Vegas and Southern Nevada: A Comprehensive Hiking Guide,* by Brian Beffort (Wilderness Press, 312 pages, $18.95). You really can't go wrong with either guide.

The Lake Mead National Recreation Area, an hour southeast of Las Vegas, offers a variety of hiking experiences, although there are few designated trails. Included within the NRA are Lakes Mead and Mohave, and part of the Mojave Desert. Ranger-led hikes are offered February–April. Outings cover 6–8 miles and are moderate to strenuous in difficulty. If you prefer to explore on your own, detailed maps and instructions to the most popular areas are available at the visitor centers. An admission fee of $10 per vehicle ($5 on foot or bike) is good for seven days. For information, call ☎ 702-293-8990 or visit **nps.gov/lame.**

The Red Rock Canyon National Conservation Area contains some of the most rugged rock formations in the West. Only 40 minutes from Las Vegas, Red Rock Canyon offers loop as well as out-and-back trails of varying lengths (see map on page 479). The short Moenkopi Loop originates at the visitor center, and it takes about 90 minutes to walk over undulating terrain in a broad desert valley. Other popular short hikes include out-and-backs to Lost Creek (0.3 mile, one-way), Icebox Canyon (1.3 miles, one-way), and Pine Creek Canyon (1.5

miles, one-way), leading to the ruins of a historic homestead near a running creek surrounded by large ponderosa pine trees. Our favorite trail, and certainly one of the most scenic, is the out-and-back Calico Tanks Trail (2.5 miles, round-trip), which winds up through a narrow canyon to a *tinaja*—a circular canyon, or "tank," that forms a natural lake. The hike is a stunner, even in hot dry months when there's little or no water in the tank, and ends at the top of the canyon with a knockout view of Las Vegas on the distant valley floor. However, the trek does involve a lot of boulder scrambling.

Altogether there are 19 trails: 4 rated easy, 5 rated easy to moderate, 9 rated moderate, and 1 classified as difficult. Distances range from 0.75 mile to 6 miles. We should emphasize that Red Rock trail ratings are astonishingly understated. Many of the trails rated "moderate" would be rated "difficult" by hikers not used to a steady diet of boulders. Most trails are poorly marked and require a great deal of boulder scrambling. Often a trail dead-ends at a boulder canyon. You intuit that the trail picks up again beyond the boulders, but there's not a hint regarding which boulders to climb to get you there. Hiking poles are great on the trail but just get in the way when you're bouldering. Hiking time for the easier trails is 1–2½ hours, and up to 4½ hours for the more difficult ones. Hiking guidebooks for the area generally use the Recreation Area's ratings, so be sure to read all of the detail relating to the hike you're contemplating. Most of the easy and easy-to-moderate trails are pretty level. Elevation gain for moderate and difficult trails is 300–1,700 feet. Maps and hiking information are available free when you pay your entrance fee and for sale in the visitor center. For more information about Red Rock trails, see **sunsetcities.com/redrock.html**. If you'd like to spend a few days here and camp, Red Rock offers a campground (see profile below). For more information, call ☎ 702-515-5350, or check out **desertusa.com/redrock**.

Red Rock Canyon Campground

RV ★★★   TENT ★★   BEAUTY ★★★   SITE PRIVACY ★   SPACIOUSNESS ★★½
QUIET ★★★½   SECURITY ★★   CLEANLINESS ★★★   INSECT CONTROL ★★★

Red Rock Canyon National Conservation Area, HCR 33, Box 5500, Las Vegas, NV 89124; ☎ 702-515-5350; nv.blm.gov/redrockcanyon

FACILITIES Acres 60. **Number of RV sites** 5. **Number of tent-only sites** 71. **Number of multipurpose sites** 52. **Site to acreage ratio** 1:0.8. **Hookups** None. **Each site** Table, fire pit. **Dump station** No. **Laundry** No. **Pay phone** No. **Restrooms and showers** Restrooms, no showers. **Fuel** No. **Propane** No. **Internal roads** Dirt. **RV service** No. **Market** No. **Restaurant** No. **General store** No. **Vending** No. **Swimming** No. **Playground** No. **Nearby attractions** Red Rock Canyon National Conservation Area.

KEY INFORMATION **Operated by** Bureau of Land Management. **Open** September–May. **Site assignment** First come, first served. **Registration** At ranger station. **Fee** $15 per day per site. **Parking** Maximum 2 vehicles per site.

Red Rock Canyon

White Rock 🚶🚶

Willow Springs
🌲 ⬆ 🚶🚶

🚶 Icebox Canyon

Red Rock
Canyon Visitor Ctr.
⬆ 🚰 🕐 🚶🚶 👓

Pine Creek
Canyon 🚶🚶

Oak Creek
Canyon
⛺ 🚶🚶

🚶 First Creek Canyon

Spring Mtn.
Ranch State Park
⬆ 🚰 🌲 🏛 🕐 👓

La Madre Mtn.
7000'
6000'

White Rock Hills

6000'

Turtlehead
▲ Mtn.

5000'

Sandstone
Quarry
⬆ 🚶🚶

Calico
Hills 🚶🚶

Moenkopi
Trail 🚶🚶

North
Peak ▲

Bridge ▲
Mtn.

Red Rock

Red Rock Wash

4000'

7000'

Wilson

Rainbow ▲
Mtn.

Cliffs

5000'

Mt. ▲
Wilson

Indecision ▲
Peak

Sandstone Mtn. ▲

Black Velvet
Peak ▲

▲ Windy Peak

5000'

SPRING MOUNTAINS

7000'

Loop
Entrance

159

To
Las
Vegas →

Loop Exit

4000'

Bonnie Springs/
Old Nevada
⬆ 🚰 🕐 🍽 🐎

Blue
Diamond
🔋 🍶

159

6000'

4000'

4000'

6000'

Mountain Springs ◉

To →
15

Cottonwood Valley

160

Lovell Canyon Rd.

Red Rock Canyon

0 _____ 2 mi
0 _____ 2 km

Ⓝ

Primary roads
Secondary roads
4WD roads
• • • • • Hiking trails

Rest rooms .... ⬆	Telephone .... 🕐	Groceries .... 🍶
Drinking water .... 🚰	Gasoline .... 🔋	Primitive camping .... ⛺
Picnic area .... 🌲	Restaurant .... 🍽	Hiking/photography ..... 🚶🚶
Group facilities ... 🏛	Riding stables ..... 🐎	Natural history .... 👓

RESTRICTIONS **Pets** On leash only. **Fires** Allowed; sites have fire pits, and firewood is available for purchase from campground hosts September 1–May 31. **Alcoholic beverages** Not allowed. **Vehicle maximum length** 16 feet.

TO GET THERE From Las Vegas, drive west on Charleston Boulevard/NV 159 for 6 miles. Just 2 miles before the Red Rock Canyon scenic drive, turn left on Moenkopi Drive. Pass the fire station on the right, the group campground on the left, then drive down the hill to the campground.

DESCRIPTION It's the desert, and nothing but. Set in a low hollow just below the Calico Hills, Red Rock Canyon Campground offers the bare minimum: a place to pitch your tent. The campground's compact main loop is bisected by two spoke roads, with sites feathering off at regular angles. Pit toilets are set at the corners. There's no foliage to screen your site from neighbors, who are not that far off in any case. A small RV loop and a similar-sized walk-in tent-only loop dangle off to the south, near the campground host. Five large group sites are set out near the entrance. The low setting makes views of the hills problematic, but it's extremely serene and quiet—and even with the lights of the Strip a few miles away, the clear night sky makes for great stargazing.

The Humboldt-Toiyabe National Forest, high in the mountains 40 minutes northwest of Las Vegas, provides a totally different outdoor experience. The air is cool, and the trails run among stately forests of ponderosa pine, quaking aspen, white fir, and mountain mahogany. Hikes range in distance from 0.1 mile to 21 miles, and in difficulty from easy to very difficult. Most popular are the Cathedral Rock Trail (2 miles round-trip), which climbs 900 feet to a stark summit overlooking Kyle Canyon, and Bristlecone, a 5-mile loop that traverses the ridges above the Lee Canyon Ski Area. Though the distances of these loops are not great, the terrain is exceedingly rugged, and the hikes are not recommended for one-day outings unless you begin very early in the morning and are used to strenuous exercise at high elevations. For more information, call ☎ 775-331-6444.

The Valley of Fire State Park, 45 minutes northeast of Las Vegas, rounds out the hiking picture. This park features rock formations similar to those found in the Grand Canyon, as well as a number of Indian petroglyphs. The *Las Vegas Advisor* compares hiking the Valley of Fire with being "beamed" onto another planet. Trails traverse desert terrain and vary from 0.5 mile to 7 miles in length. Visitors should check in at the visitor center before they begin hiking. The park fee is $12 ($10 for locals); for more information, call ☎ 702-397-2088 or visit **parks.nv.gov/parks/valley-of-fire-state-park.**

Guided Hikes and Tours

Rocky Trails (☎ 888-892-5380; **rockytrails.com**) offers guided tours to the natural sites described above as well as to Death Valley, the Grand Canyon, Bryce Canyon, and Zion National Park. Guests are picked up at their hotel and transported in Suburbans or vans. Lunch or dinner is included. Expeditions to the Valley of Fire, Red Rock Canyon, Death Valley, and the Grand Canyon last 6–10 hours and cost $99–$539.

ROCK CLIMBING AND BOULDERING

THE RED ROCK CANYON National Conservation Area is one of the top rock-climbing resources in the United States. With more than 1,000 routes, abundant holds, and approaches ranging from roadside to remote wilderness, the area rivals Yosemite in scope and variety for climbers. Offering amazing diversity for every skill level amid desert canyon scenery second to none, the area is less than a 40-minute drive from Las Vegas.

Though there is some granite and limestone, almost all of the climbing is done on sandstone. Overall, the rock is pretty solid, although there are some places where the sandstone gets a little crumbly, especially after a rain. Bolting is allowed but discouraged (local climbers have been systematically replacing bolts on some of the older routes with more modern bolts that blend with the rock). There are some great spots for bouldering, some of the best top-roping in the United States, a lifetime supply of big walls, and even some bivouac routes. Climbs range in difficulty from nonbelayed scrambles to 5.13 big-wall overhangs. You can climb year-round at Red Rock. Wind can be a problem, as can most of the other conditions that make a desert environment challenging. Having enough water can be a logistical nightmare on a long climb.

The Red Rocks of Southern Nevada by Joanne Urioste describes a number of the older routes. Newer route descriptions can be obtained from **Desert Rock Sports** in Las Vegas (☎ 702-254-1143; **desert rocksportslv.com**). Desert Rock Sports can also help you find camping and showers and tell you where the loose rock is. Offering climbing-shoe rentals, the store is at 8221 West Charleston, conveniently on the way to the canyon from Las Vegas. The **Red Rock Climbing Center** (☎ 702-254-5604; **redrockclimbingcenter.com**) is next to Desert Rock Sports and offers excellent indoor climbing and showers. Guides and/or instruction are available from Desert Rock Sports.

RIVER RUNNING

THE BLACK CANYON of the Colorado River can be run year-round below Hoover Dam. The most popular trip is from the tailwaters of the dam to Willow Beach. In this 9.5-mile section, canyon walls rise almost vertically from the water's edge, with scenery and wildlife very similar to that of the Colorado River in the Grand Canyon above Lake Mead. There are numerous warm springs and waterfalls on feeder streams, presenting the opportunity for good side-trip hikes. Small beaches provide good rest and lunch sites. Bighorn sheep roam the bluffs, and wild burros can often be seen up the canyons. The water in the river, about 53°F year-round, is drawn from the bottom of Lake Mead and released downstream through the Hoover Dam hydroelectric generators.

Under normal conditions, the Black Canyon is a nice flatwater float trip with a steady current to help you along. There are places along the river, such as Ringbolt Rapids and the Chute, that are named for falls and rapids long since covered up and flattened out by the voluminous discharge of water from the dam. There is nothing remaining on the run in the way of paddling challenges beyond a few swells and ripples. The Black Canyon is suitable for canoes, kayaks, and rafts. Motorized craft cannot be launched below the dam but can come upstream to the dam from Willow Beach or from other marinas farther downstream. The trip takes about 6 hours, including side trips and lunch, for a canoe or kayak, and about 3½ hours for a commercial motorized raft.

There are several ways you can get into serious trouble. The put-in below the dam is rocky and slippery. More than a few boaters have accidentally launched their boat before they climbed aboard, while others have managed to arrive in the river ahead of their boat. Once you're under way, it's important to keep your group close together. With the water temperature at 53°F, you want to pluck people out of the river posthaste in the event of a capsize. When you go ashore to explore, pull your boat way up out of the water and tie it to something sturdy. If at the dam they happen to crank up an extra generator or two while you're off hiking in a side canyon, it's possible for the river to rise several feet, sweeping any unsecured boats and equipment downstream.

 If the weather service predicts headwinds in excess of 12 miles an hour, cancel your paddling trip, even if it means losing your permit fee.

For the most part, the 9.5-mile run from the dam to Willow Beach does not require any prior paddling experience. On most days, you could practically float to the takeout, with breaks for lunch and exploring, in 5 hours. The exception, and it's a big one, is when headwinds blow up the canyon from the west. Though headwinds of less than 10 miles an hour won't affect the paddling situation much, winds of 10 miles an hour or higher require more experience and advanced boat-handling skills. When the wind is high, it can blow you upstream, making forward progress grueling or impossible, and can whip up crosscurrents as well as waves up to 3 feet high. Chances of capsizing grow exponentially with wind speed, and rescue efforts become correspondingly more difficult.

Private parties must obtain a launch permit from **Black Canyon/Willow Beach River Adventures** (☎ 800-455-3490, **blackcanyonadventures .com**); **Desert River Outfitters** (☎ 888-KAYAK-33, **desertriveroutfitters .com**); or, **Boulder City River Riders** (☎ 800-RIVER-02, **bouldercityriver riders.com**). The permits are sold as part of a launch/shuttle package and are not available except from licensed outfitters. The outfitter of your choice, along with dam security officers, will take you into the dam's secure area to put in below the dam.

Only 30 boats are allowed to launch from below the dam each day, so weekends sell out well in advance. On weekdays, it's sometimes possible to get a permit on short notice. Permits can be obtained on a first-come, first-serve basis six months in advance. The permits and fees apply to a specific date and are nonrefundable, though if there's space available, the permitting authority will try to assign you an alternate date in the event of bad weather, high winds, or other mitigating circumstances.

The best time to run the Canyon is in the fall through December. The spring is prettiest, with new green foliage seen on the beaches and in the side canyons. The spring, along with January and February, tend to be the windiest times of year, however. Summers are hot, and the canyons tend to hold the heat. The water, however, provides some natural cooling. Canoeists and kayakers can make the run in one day or alternatively camp overnight in the canyon en route. Commercial raft trips are one-day affairs.

If you don't have your own equipment, you can rent one- and two-person kayaks (including shuttle and permit) from Boulder City River Riders and Desert River Outfitters referenced above. The kayaks are open-cockpit and usually rented without spray skirts. This essentially means that 53°F water drips off the paddle into your lap every time you take a paddle stroke. If spray skirts are available, we recommend you use them. In addition to providing equipment, the outfitters also transport you and your boat to the river. At the end of the run, they pick you up at Willow Beach and drive you back to your car. If you have your own boat, the same shuttle service is available for $50 *per person.*

Boulder City River Riders also offers guided one- and two-person kayak tours from the bottom of Hoover Dam to Willow Beach. Trips include lunch, transportation to and from the river, and paddling instruction if necessary. Trip cost is $210 with a minimum group size of 2 and is offered year-round except Thanksgiving and Christmas.

In addition to granting launch permits, Black Canyon/Willow Beach River Adventures also operates guided, motorized raft trips, with guest transportation provided from the Strip and Downtown. No permit is required for these trips.

The raft outing is unlike most commercial river trips. First, the rafts are huge, accommodating more than two dozen guests. Second, the trip is entirely passive—no paddling or anything else required. The rafts motor up from Willow Beach in the morning and pick up their passengers at the put-in below the dam. From there, it's a scenic, narrated 3-hour-or-so float back to Willow Beach, where guests are loaded up and transported back to their cars or delivered to their Las Vegas hotel. The trips run $88 for adults, $83 for children ages 13–15, and $54 for children ages 5–12. For transportation from your Las Vegas hotel, add $44.

 There is little protection from the sun in the Black Canyon, and temperatures can surpass 110°F in the warmer months. Long-sleeve shirts, long pants, tennis shoes, and a hat are recommended minimum attire year-round. Be sure to take sunscreen and lots of drinking water.

SNOW SKIING

THE LAS VEGAS SKI AND SNOWBOARD RESORT at Lee Canyon is a 45-minute drive from Las Vegas. Situated in a granite canyon in the Spring Mountain range, the resort provides one quad, one triple, one double chairlift, and a surface lift servicing 30 runs. Though the mountain is small and the runs short by Western standards, the skiing is solid intermediate. Of the 30 named runs, 14 are blue, 15 are black (mostly short), and there is one short green. Base elevation of 8,510 feet notwithstanding, snow conditions are usually dependable only during January, though snow-making covers 43% of the lifts. Because of its southerly location and the proximity of the hot, arid desert, there is a lot of thawing and refreezing in Lee Canyon, and hence, frequently icy skiing conditions. If the snow is good, a day at Lee Canyon is a great outing. If the mountain is icy, do something else.

Snowmaking equipment allows the resort to operate from Thanksgiving to Easter. There is no lodging on site and only a modest restaurant and bar. Parking is quite a hike from the base facility. From Las Vegas, take US 95 north approximately 30 miles to NV 156, Lee Canyon. Follow NV 156 for 17 miles to where it dead-ends at the resort. Flash floods, which recently devastated neighboring Kyle Canyon, have not affected Lee Canyon or the ski resort.

Skis can be rented at the ski area. For information on lift tickets or snow conditions, call the ski-area office at ☎ 702-385-2754 or see **skilasvegas.com.** For summer events, check the resort's website.

HORSEBACK RIDING

THE CLOSEST HORSEBACK-RIDING OUTFITTERS are in the Red Rock Canyon area half an hour west of Las Vegas. Riding is allowed on only a couple of trails in the Red Rock National Conservation Area, but there's a lot of riding to be found just outside the Conservation Area. **Bonnie Springs** (☎ 702-875-4191; **bonniesprings.com**) and **Cowboy Trail Rides** (☎ 702-387-2457; **cowboytrailrides.com**) are both located within a 4- to 10-minute drive from Red Rock Canyon.

FISHING

THE LAKE MEAD NATIONAL RECREATION AREA offers some of the best fishing in the United States. Lake Mead is the largest lake, with Lake Mohave, downstream on the Colorado River, offering the most diverse fishery. Largemouth bass, striped bass, channel catfish, crappie, and bluegill are found in both lakes. Rainbow and cutthroat trout are present only in Lake Mohave. Remote and beautiful in its upmost reaches, Lake Mohave is farther from Las Vegas but provides truly exceptional fishing. Bass and trout often run 3 pounds, and some trout weigh 10 pounds or more. Willow Beach, near where the Colorado River enters the pool waters of Lake Mohave, is where many of the larger trout are taken.

Lake Mead, broader, more open, and much closer to Las Vegas, has become famous for its stripers, with an occasional catch weighing in at over 40 pounds. Bass fishing is consistently good throughout Lake Mead. The Overton Arm (accessed from Echo Bay or Overton Beach) offers the best panfish and catfish action.

Because Lakes Mead and Mohave form the Arizona–Nevada state line, fishing license regulations are a little strange. If you are bank fishing, all you need is a license from the state you are in. If you fish from a boat, however, you need a fishing license from one state and a special-use stamp from the other. All required stamps and licenses can be obtained from marinas and local bait and tackle shops in either state.

Nonresidents have the option of purchasing 1- to 10-day fishing permits in lieu of a license. Permits are $18 for one day (with a $7 charge per additional consecutive days) and $69 for annual, and apply to the entire state of Nevada. In addition to the permit, a special-use stamp costing $3 is required for those fishing from a boat. Plus, a $10 trout stamp is necessary to take trout if you buy the annual permit; the trout stamp is included in the price of the daily permit. In addition, a $10 stamp is available for fishing with two rods. Youngsters age 12 years and under in the company of a properly licensed, permitted, and stamped adult can fish without any sort of documentation.

Seventeen-foot aluminum fishing boats (that seat five) can be rented on both lakes by the hour (about $40 with a 2-hour minimum), by the half-day (4–5 hours for about $50), or by the day (about $90–$215). Bass boats, houseboats, and pontoon craft are also available. Rods and reels rent for about $5 for 4 hours or less and about $12 a day.

LAKE MEAD BAIT AND TACKLE, BOAT RENTAL, FUEL, AND SUPPLIES
CALLVILLE BAY RESORT ☎ 702-565-8958; callvillebay.com
COTTONWOOD COVE RESORT ☎ 702-297-1464; cottonwoodcoveresort.com
LAKE MOHAVE RESORT (AZ) ☎ 928-754-3245; sevencrown.com
TEMPLE BAR RESORT (AZ) ☎ 928-767-3211; templebarlakemead.com

PLEASURE BOATING, SAILING, WATER SKIING, AND JET SKIING

LAKE MEAD AND LAKE MOHAVE are both excellent sites for pleasure boating, water skiing, and other activities. Both lakes are so large that it is easy to find a secluded spot for your favorite boating or swimming activity. Rock formations on the lakes are spectacular, and boaters can visit scenic canyons and coves that are inaccessible to those traveling by car. Boats, for example, can travel into the narrow, steep-walled gorge of Iceberg Canyon in Lake Mead or upstream into the Black Canyon from Lake Mohave.

First-timers, particularly on Lake Mead, frequently underestimate its vast size. It is not difficult to get lost on the open waters of Lake Mead or to get caught in bad weather. Winds can be severe on the lake, and waves of six feet sometimes arise during storms. In general, there is no shade on the lakes, and the steep rock formations along the shore do not make very hospitable emergency landing sites. When you boat on either lake, take plenty of water, dress properly, be quipped, and be sure to tell someone where you are going and when you expect to return.

Most of the resorts listed under "Fishing" rent various types of pleasure craft and water-skiing equipment, and the Callville Bay Resort also rents personal watercraft. In addition, at Callville Bay on Lake Mead and Cottonwood Cove on Lake Mohave, luxury houseboats are available for rental. The boats sleep up to 12 adults and have fully equipped galleys and heads. For rates and other information concerning houseboats, call ☎ 800-255-5561 or visit **callvillebay.com** or **cottonwoodcoveresort.com**.

SPA 101

GETTING THE INSIDE TRACK ON SPA KNOW-HOW

LET'S FACE IT. Most people spend more time and money on preventive maintenance for their cars than on themselves. After all, changing the oil and checking tire pressure go a long way in extending the life of a car, let alone ensuring a smoother ride along the way. Believe it or not, this analogy fits for why we should participate in spa experiences. Call it preventative or maintenance medicine of your chassis, and a whole lot more.

SPA LINGO

ACUPRESSURE AND ACUPUNCTURE Acupressure, or fingertip massage, is said to free the body's energy channels, or "meridians," for a relaxing and energizing treatment. Acupuncture uses ultrafine needles for more specific and chronic ailments.

AROMATHERAPY A full-body massage using scented essential oils and light, smoothing movements. Different oils are used for different therapeutic benefits.

AYURVEDA The ancient system of traditional Indian medicine and science that incorporates nutrition, herbal medicine, aromatherapy, massage, and meditation.

BODY SCRUB A light massage and exfoliation that stimulates blood circulation and prepares the skin for mineralization and moisturizing.

BODY WRAP Cotton sheets or strips of cloth, steeped in a variety of aromatic herbs and/or sea enzymes, are wrapped around the body, which is then covered with blankets or towels to prevent the moist heat from escaping. Body wrap is a relaxing treatment to soothe soreness and soften skin.

HOT-STONE MASSAGE This type of massage—also known as La Stone

Therapy—uses smooth, dark, heated stones to relieve stiffness and soreness and to restore energy.

HYDROTHERAPY This relaxing therapy includes underwater jet massage, showers, jet sprays, and mineral baths.

MASSAGE THERAPY Massaging skin, muscles, and joints relieves muscle spasms and tension, and improves flexibility and circulation. Various types of massage range from gentle aromatherapy to a sports massage directed at specific muscles used in athletic activities to deep-tissue Swedish massage, which kneads and separates muscle groups while stretching connective tissue to help realign the body.

MINERAL WATERS Originating from natural springs and wells, these waters contain high concentrations of rare or biologically active elements that are claimed to improve circulation, detoxify the body, and ease ailments such as rheumatism and arthritis.

REFLEXOLOGY A Chinese-based massage of the feet and hands that includes pressure points to areas said to correspond with organs and tissues throughout the body. Treats a wide range of ailments.

SALT GLOW A mixture of salt, oils, and water is used to scrub the body to remove dead skin, clean pores, and stimulate circulation.

SHIATSU A Japanese massage therapy during which practitioners apply rhythmic finger pressure at specific points on the body in order to relieve pain, and release and balance blocked energy.

THAI MASSAGE In this form of massage a therapist manipulates the body using passive, yogalike stretching and applies gentle pressure with his or her hands and feet along "energy lines" in the body.

THALASSOTHERAPY A full-body exfoliation and detoxification treatment that uses nutrient-rich marine elements along with other skin-conditioning agents.

VICHY SHOWER MASSAGE This relaxing massage is performed under sprinklers to improve the body's circulation; water is heated to body temperature.

THE 21ST-CENTURY SPA

TODAY, SPAS HAVE REINVENTED THEMSELVES into exotic environments, where professional practitioners trained in a variety of traditional and alternative approaches to wellness offer pampered luxury. Look beyond everyone's favorite, the relaxation massage, and you're likely to find more spa-treatment options than there are flavors of Baskin-Robbins ice cream.

The competition for your spa dollar is so fierce that resort spas in particular are constantly upping the ante for your spa experience. More than ever, with basic spa treatments, resorts are including value-added services such as the complimentary use of mineral pools, waterfall massages, and detoxifying steam rooms and saunas—amenities that can turn a manicure or facial into an all-out getaway.

GETTING DOWN TO SPA BASICS

A GOOD SPA is defined by the purity of experience it provides and how it makes you feel the moment you enter it. A spa needs to engage and soothe all five senses and provide an ambience that removes you from the outside world. Often you can't put into words the nurturing wave of care that envelops you, yet the feeling is instant and palpable.

Five things to watch for in a spa:

- The hair salon should be well separated from the spa—the noise of dryers and smell of perm solution fly in the face of serenity and jasmine-scented air.

- The gym should be considered a part of the spa in name only; sharing locker space with treadmill enthusiasts isn't conducive to the spa ethos.

- Retail sales should be physically a part of the reception and transaction area rather than any transition zone.

- There should be RMTs (registered massage therapists) on staff, in addition to body-care workers.

- Skin-care products should be eco-friendly and free from animal testing.

SPA NEOPHYTE: THE NAKED TRUTH

ALL SPAS CATER TO THE FIRST-TIME VISITOR—and ease anxiety about those nagging questions regarding nudity and massage. Don't worry. Treatments are usually explained to you prior to the start of any session, and therapists use professional draping techniques to ensure privacy; there's no need to mentally race ahead of the treatment process with niggling doubts as to what's coming next. For example, when you're having a full-body massage and are asked to turn over, your therapist will raise the covering sheet so high that no one gets a boo at your privates, and the sheet will be settled over your body only when the therapist notes that your feet are facing in the right direction. Always let the spa know if you have a preference for either a male or female therapist.

Most people strip to the buff for full-body massages and wraps, but if modesty is a concern, disrobe to your level of comfort, keep your undies on, or ask the spa if they have disposable panties. If you and your teen are venturing into a side-by-side massage, spas usually ask that your child wear a swimsuit so that they (and you) have a sense of comfort about being touched. If you are having any form of body treatment or men's facial, don't shave for at least 4 hours before your service. And let the spa know in advance of any special conditions such as pregnancy, high blood pressure, heart ailments, or any condition where certain heat therapies, massage, or skin care might not be appropriate. If waxing services are on your agenda, a pre-steam or sauna is not recommended, and, please, don't eat a full meal just before any spa visit. Lastly, remove your contact lenses before heading into a eucalyptus steam as its astringent qualities may cause your eyes to sting.

During your treatment, your therapist will take their lead from you and be as silent or as talkative as you wish. Some will talk you through the process, especially during a facial, so that you know what sensations to expect as the therapist cleanses, tones, steams, and applies a mask. The choice is always yours.

THE "SHOULDS" TO NOTE

THERAPISTS SHOULD ALWAYS check in on your comfort with and preference for lighting (too bright?), music (too loud or not loud enough?), warmth (we love spas with heated bed pads), and pressure of massage touch.

On the latter, be aware that an RMT is highly skilled at finding those stubborn knots, and kneading their release might cause minor discomfort; that's why you warm muscles up in a steam or sauna first. Still, RMTs are not there to hurt you. Breathe, moan, whimper, exhale dramatically—these are all great ways to help your therapist help you relieve tension.

Don't think you have to buy into the spa silence, although if your treatment involves a shower, please don't practice your operatic arias, however good you feel.

And don't think you have to buy into product sales pitches. Estheticians are well versed to share the benefits of the products they use, and experienced practitioners should share comparisons between these and others you might know. Conversation should be informational only.

THE "SHOULD NOTS" TO NOTE

YOUR THERAPIST SHOULD NOT leave the room without informing you. After all, when you're cocooned in a cellophane wrap, you feel pretty helpless. And if you're having a sensitive beauty or refinement service like an eyelash tint, sudden light, sound, and chatter can cause your eyelids to flicker involuntarily; tint in your eyes is no fun.

During your treatment, therapists should not move around the room in search of products, water, and equipment. Everything should have been preset for easy access. For full-body work, they should have warmed their hands before contact, "tuned" into your space by noting the rhythm of your breathing, and never should they lose contact with you for more than a split second. An unexpected touch, however gentle, can awaken the senses very abruptly. At the conclusion of your session, therapists shouldn't flick on the lights or slap you on the backside and say "Go, bucko, go." Bedside manner is everything.

SPA BELLS AND WHISTLES

UNLESS YOU'RE VISITING A SMALL DAY SPA where space limits facilities, here are some complimentary amenities you can expect.

- Same-sex changing rooms with personal lockers, spa sandals, robes, and towels.
- Some spas will have either same-sex (swimsuit-optional) steam rooms, saunas, and mineral pools, or will provide direct access to similar coed facilities (swimsuit mandatory).
- A grooming bar with hairstyling products, moisturizers, and sundry items.

- Easy or direct access to either a same-sex or coed relaxation area for pre- and posttreatment "integration" time. This is an opportunity to snooze, bask in your newly acquired mellow mood, and read. Popular magazines and inspirational texts are usually on hand.
- The relaxation area should also provide healthy grazing foods like nuts and fresh fruit as well as tea infusions and other refreshments. Don't expect coffee.
- When you have a body scrub, it is customary for the spa staff to offer you the loofah brush or mitten to take home.
- When you receive a manicure or pedicure, some spas provide mini-bottles of polish for touch-ups, as well as the emery board used during the treatment.
- When you enjoy a facial, ask for free samples (see A Word about Retail below) of the products used or recommended. That way you'll always have a travel-sized supply at hand for that overnight getaway.
- Spas that are really on the ball will offer value-added services to every treatment, at no additional cost. Examples include a hand, foot, or scalp massage with every facial and a paraffin-wax treatment with every manicure. The idea is to engage as many of the five senses as possible with every treatment.

TO TIP OR NOT TO TIP?

GRATUITIES ARE USUALLY left to a guest's discretion and are similar to that given for hair-salon services, that is, 15–20% of the price of the service provided. At all-inclusive resorts, verify the spa's tipping policy upon arrival. Unlike a hair salon where you sometimes have to track down your stylist and slip a little gratitude into their pocket, spas operate with gratuity envelopes, which are administered by the reception staff. Tips can also be charged to your debit or credit card.

BE THERE OR BE SQUARE

TREATMENTS ARE BLOCKED BY TIME, and synchronized with Swiss efficiency so that rooms can be quickly flipped. As a courtesy, arrive early (especially if you want to take advantage of a spa's amenities) and leave your treatment room promptly. You can take all the "zone-out" time you wish in the relaxation lounge. Be aware that if you arrive late, your treatment will still end at the appointed time since there's another client scheduled right behind you. Be sure to check the spa's cancellation policy when you make your reservation; no-shows are generally charged at least 50% of the full treatment fee. Remember to silence your cell phone before entering the spa.

A WORD ABOUT RETAIL

SPA-INDUSTRY EXPERTS CLAIM that retail sales should make up some 30% of a spa's revenues, but most spas generate about half that figure, largely because, inexplicably, they haven't caught up with the very world they have created in terms of maximizing retail opportunities. Consequently, there's pressure on staff to sell, and estheticians especially walk a fine line of wanting to be genuinely helpful and needing to meet commission quotas. There is absolutely no obligation to buy, however nicely the product is presented (often in a basket at the end of your treatment alongside a customized treatment regimen for you to take home).

However, if you honestly like a product and feel its results, then why not buy it? Ask for travel samples as well. After all, you have just spent good money for an excellent treatment, and manufacturer's samples cost the spa nothing but goodwill.

If the product is indigenous to the region (for example, seaweed from Vancouver Island or Tahitian balm from Polynesia), consider it an indulgence in the same way as you would a specialty soap or hand-crafted wine. Treat a spa's own signature line in the same vein; items are usually just repackaged versions of a well-to-do product line that could well be sitting on the same shelf.

Lastly, if the product you like is widely available, it might be less expensive at home, or even cheaper on eBay.

UNOFFICIAL OVERVIEW OF SIN CITY SPAS

IN A CITY THAT REINVENTS ITSELF at least every decade, it comes as no surprise that its spas do the same. With more than 45 luxury resort spas, Las Vegas spas have transformed themselves from being simply sidekicks that offer guests beauty amenities to lucrative mind-body-soul profit centers of Disneyesque proportions.

In the competition to entertain an increasingly aware spa crowd, destinations are constantly trying to out-spa one another in design, therapies, products, and promises. Like everything in Las Vegas, most spas present larger-than-life experiences within vast expanses of square footage with lots of service add-ons such as steam rooms and saunas, thus turning a simple pedicure into an all-day retreat. However, the trip from changing room to treatment area can be a hike unto itself, and although the walk is usually more like a shuffle in disposable slippers, without an escort or a trail of bread crumbs, you could be hard-pressed to find your way from one area to the next.

Surprisingly, in spite of the spa scene's meteoric growth, the overall quality and professionalism of practitioners are high. The desire to be a part of "the next big idea" sees therapists move from one spa to the next. Consequently, many of them not only maintain a hyper, Red-Bull enthusiasm (sometimes rather counterintuitive to the spa experience) but also a diverse knowledge of different products and competitive brands. If products are your thing, then therapists are a resource worth plumbing. Most staff members are equally polished at delivering pampering services with efficiency. Sometimes that's noticeable, but when you're able to languish laconically, the concept of time simply dissolves and all is forgiven.

Our advice is to take full advantage of a spa's facilities. Get a day pass so you can pop back in later for a relaxing steam—trust us, the moisture will feel delicious after traipsing around in the desert heat. Ask the spa if they'll spring for a pass for your partner; it only costs

Las Vegas Health Spas

SPAS OPEN TO THE PUBLIC

- **Aria** The Spa at Aria ☎ 702-590-9600
- **Bellagio** Spa Bellagio ☎ 702-693-7472
- **Caesars Palace** Qua Baths and Spa ☎ 866-782-0655
- **The Cosmopolitan** Sahra Spa & Hammam ☎ 702-698-7000
- **Excalibur** The Spa at Excalibur ☎ 702-597-7772
- **Flamingo** The Spa at Flamingo ☎ 702-733-3535
- **Four Seasons** The Spa at Four Seasons ☎ 702-632-5302
- **Golden Nugget** The Spa at Golden Nugget ☎ 702-386-8186
- **Green Valley Ranch Resort and Spa** The Spa at Green Valley Ranch ☎ 702-617-7570
- **Hard Rock Hotel** Reliquary Spa & Salon ☎ 702-693-5520
- **Harrah's** The Spa at Harrah's ☎ 702-369-5126
- **Luxor** Nurture Spa ☎ 702-730-5721
- **MGM Grand** MGM Grand Spa ☎ 702-891-3077
- **Mirage** The Spa at the Mirage ☎ 702-791-7472
- **Monte Carlo** The Spa at Monte Carlo ☎ 702-730-7590
- **New York–New York** The Spa at New York–New York ☎ 702-740-6955
- **Paris Las Vegas** Spa by Mandara ☎ 702-946-4366
- **Planet Hollywood** Mandara Spa ☎ 702-785-5772
- **Red Rock Resort** The Spa at Red Rock (Mon.–Fri.) ☎ 702-797-7878
- **Rio** Rio Spa ☎ 702-777-7779
- **Riviera** Zeba Beauty Salon ☎ 702-735-2475
- **TI** Oleksandra Spa & Salon ☎ 702-894-7472
- **The Venetian** Canyon Ranch SpaClub ☎ 702-414-3600
- **Westgate Las Vegas** The Spa at Westgate ☎ 702-732-5648
- **Westin Lake Las Vegas** Spa Moulay ☎ 702-567-6049 (Thurs.–Mon.)
- **Wynn Encore** The Spa at Wynn Encore ☎ 702-770-8000 (Sun.–Thurs.)

SPAS FOR HOTEL GUESTS ONLY

- **Mandalay Bay** Spa Mandalay ☎ 702-632-7220
- **Wynn Las Vegas** Spa at Wynn Las Vegas ☎ 702-770-8000

them laundry pennies to extend this privilege. Be aware, though, that their answer may depend on whether your service is a multisensory package or just a quick polish change. If you're a hotel guest, however, negotiate a pass for the hotel's on-site spa regardless. Tough times have humbled Vegas, and spa inducements are proving a valuable marketing tool to boost hotel occupancies.

Las Vegas's keep-up-with-the-Joneses climate means that spas are constantly catching, or creating, the newest wave. In recent years

Caesars Palace, Mandalay Bay, Bellagio, and **The Venetian** have all undergone multimillion-dollar expansions for an updated look and service standard, while the **Wynn** and **Trump** (owned by the two most competitive egos in town) hotels have countered the city's penchant for splashy with more intimate spa surroundings. Meanwhile, traditionalists like the **Four Seasons** hotel have stayed the course with pricey, elegant refinement.

The spa scene in Las Vegas can be large-scale, confusing, and generic, but the individual Strip spas are opulent, accessible, diverse, and pay-through-the-nose fun. Spa snobs need to chill out and enjoy. For *Unofficial* purposes, we're staying on the Strip (Trump is the exception) with what we consider the spas that best epitomize Las Vegas's sizzle and audacity.

Bathhouse ★ ★ ★ ★

Delano 3950 Las Vegas Blvd. S.; ☎ 877-632-9636; mandalaybay.com

Customer service ★★★★. **Facilities** ★★★★. **Amenities** ★★★★. **Sales pressure** Low. **Price range** $65–$265, spa services; $45–$130, nail and refinement services. **Spa amenities** Complimentary with spa services for hotel guests; complimentary for non-hotel guests with spa services over $60; spa pass $30 per day for hotel guests only.

SUMMARY AND COMMENTS The Bathhouse pioneered communal spa-ing on the Strip. With its granite and suede-covered walls, stylish fixtures, and brightly colored furniture, including orange-fur benches, it retains a quasi-nightclub atmosphere, only rock and rhythm is replaced with sounds of trickling water at every turn. This is in-your-face, modern-bat-cave relaxation with soaring, monolithic black-slate walls and floors inset with a narrow, softly lit soaking pool. With only 12 treatment rooms, this spa is small by Las Vegas standards, but because every room has a private shower, they feel like mini-suites. A hybrid massage of hot stones, aromatherapy, and Swedish techniques is excellent. Add an express facial with an oxygen spray for a "wow" youthful glow.

RECOMMEND The Bathhouse Sampler combines a customized Scents-of-You bath, a Swedish massage, a refresher facial, and classic pedicure.

LOVE The contrasting exotica (no, not erotica) environment of Mandalay Spa. Its traditional Zen environment is a sigh of relief to the Bathhouse.

THE ULTIMATE It may be an illusion, but the Mocha Java Sculpting Wrap really does seem to dissolve some of those cellulite dimples, at least for a while.

DISLIKE A private cabana is nice, but Mandalay would do well to have a spa-only area on the Beach to keep moods mellow.

TIP Organize a spa treatment for every day of your stay to enjoy free daily access to the spa and fitness amenities; includes muffins at the spa bar.

Canyon Ranch SpaClub ★ ★ ★ ½

The Venetian/Palazzo 3355 Las Vegas Blvd. S.;
☎ 702-414-3600; canyonranch.com/lasvegas

Customer service ★★. **Facilities** ★★★★★. **Amenities** ★★★★★. **Sales pressure** Medium. **Price range** $150–$355, spa services; $25–$155, nail and refinement services. **Spa and fitness center amenities** $25 with the purchase of any service; $40 per day without spa services; SpaClub Day Passport includes access to fitness center.

SUMMARY AND COMMENTS Covering a staggering 134,000 square feet of treatment areas, this is the mother of all spas, complete with a separate gym. There's even a climbing wall that rises 40 feet in the middle of the cavernous reception area. If you enter from the Palazzo side, bring along a GPS. It's a long walk down faceless corridors through expansion space that the economic downturn has halted mid-plan. Don't be dissuaded, though. This is a top-notch spa that exemplifies the venerable and much-heralded Canyon Ranch ethos of promoting lifestyle wellness. It's also the spa that forced the other casino resorts to get serious about their facials. The rather aloof front desk staff doesn't always convey the care you'll receive once you're in the spa's inner sanctum. Canyon Ranch is often described as an upmarket (read: celebrity) spa, and because there are no easy-to-buy packages, spa-ing here can add up to a chunk of change when stringing together different services, which include everything from 18-karat facials and Abhyanga massage from India to vibrational therapy. If money's tight, buy a SpaClub Day Passport that lets you into the fitness center and all its classes and wellness presentations, as well as enjoy the spa's extensive amenities that are nothing short of fabulous. Coed environments (bring your swimsuit) include a salt grotto and a multisensory wave room that simulates the look and feel of breaking waves under a domed canopy.

RECOMMEND Rasul Ceremony. Slather your skin, or your partner's, with purifying mud and relax for 50 minutes in a gently warmed, tiled chair in a private, ornately tiled steam chamber.

LOVE Canyon Ranch's skin-care products—Pro-NAD—which deliver time-released vitamin-B complex, as well as Goji juice, one of nature's most powerful antioxidants derived from the wolfberry.

THE ULTIMATE Canyon Ranch has the most "shared-experience" spa space on the Strip, so share this spa with your honey.

DISLIKE Services such as a jet-lag-relief scalp massage that come as add-on expenses rather than easy-to-incorporate value-added inclusions.

TIP Pretreatment, mix your oils, scrubs, and body butters at the spa's Living Essentials boutique.

Qua Baths and Spa ★★★★½

Caesars Palace 3570 Las Vegas Blvd. S.; ☎ 866-782-0655; caesarspalace.com

Customer service ★★★★. **Facilities** ★★★★★. **Amenities** ★★★★★. **Sales pressure** Medium. **Price range** $90–$325, with specialty treatments up to $1,200; $45–$150, nail and refinement services. **Spa amenities** Complimentary with all spa treatments; $25-per-day pass ($20 Mon.–Thurs.) without services or $45 with Qua baths.

SUMMARY AND COMMENTS Qua Baths and Spa is top-class branding and Las Vegas showmanship—a 21st-century Roman-inspired pleasure that has set the standard for "gathering-space" spas. Innovation makes this a must-try spa, especially since prices are comparatively reasonable. The Roman baths consist of three distinct pools of varying temperatures: the Tepidarium, a warm mineral-enriched bath; the hotter Caldarium; and the much cooler Frigidarium. You can also languish in the coed, circular Laconium sauna, where the climate is kept at a constant 140°F and 35% humidity—the optimum conditions for relaxation. The Laconium is also quite the hot spot for get-togethers. The Arctic room is a real treat. The floor and benches are heated even though the room temperature is a crisp 55°F—cold enough to have snow fall from the ceiling and melt on your hot skin. Qua's menu of services runs the gamut of wet rooms with Vichy showers to a crystal–body–art room where a body scrub and massage are combined with a style of Swarovski body art. It might sound somewhat anomalous, but if you're serious about energy-related treatments, Qua has some of the better ones available.

RECOMMEND Chakra Balancing Treatment—a combination of energy and massage that balances your energy centers.

LOVE The in-house tea sommelier who pairs various teas with spa treatments. The dream-interpretation coach runs a close second.

THE ULTIMATE The personal hydrotherapy tub with its changing pulsating rhythms and colored lights.

DISLIKE Shopaholics might think this is a real bonus, but Qua has retail down to an art; a plethora of spa stuff bombards you coming and going.

TIP Remember your swimsuit.

Sahra Spa & Hammam ★★★½

The Cosmopolitan of Las Vegas 3708 Las Vegas Blvd. S.; ☎ 702-698-7000; cosmopolitanlasvegas.com

Customer service ★★★★. Facilities ★★★★. Amenities ★★★. Sales pressure Low. **Price range** $80–$380 spa services; $15–$165 for most nail and salon services. **Spa amenities** Complimentary with treatment; spa and fitness center pass $30 a day without treatment; $20 for fitness center only.

SUMMARY AND COMMENTS Sahra Spa & Hammam provides a serene oasis amid the natural grandeur of the desert. Breathtaking sculptural walls mirror poetic canyons. Veining of silver throughout the facility reflects the naturally occurring metallic element of the region. Soothing artesian wells quench the mind, body, and soul. At the heart of Sahra's 45,000-square-foot, bi-level sanctuary is the stone hammam, a ritual space that pays modern homage to a sensual, centuries-old practice of purification. Steady heat provides detoxification and renewal, conducted amid the heated stone slab and separate alcoves for steam and cool-water plunge pools. Sahra Spa & Hammam features a full menu of services to achieve total relaxation and balance. Separate men's and women's lounges include steam rooms, saunas, vitality pools with experiential monsoon rain showers, cold mist rooms, and wet lounges with meditation loungers. The Bridge Lounge is a comfortable co-ed area where couples can meet between treatments. Sahra also boasts a full-service salon and a state-of-the-art fitness center. Unique to the center is the boxing ring, where guests can take one-on-one classes for the ultimate workout. The fitness center also boasts two tennis courts, a rare find in today's Las Vegas resorts.

RECOMMEND Take in the view of the magnificent Bellagio fountains while working out in the fitness center. Schedule a one-on-one training prior to the spa treatment for the ultimate wellness experience.

LOVE The Space Between is a virtual transport, surrounded by towering sculptural sandstone walls. The traditional Turkish hammam is one of two in the city, and the boxing facility is distinctively unique to the spa.

THE ULTIMATE The well-appointed Sahra Suite offers exclusive pampering with closest friends. Arrive via the private VIP elevator to a relaxing and comfortably plush living and entertaining area. The suite is complete with a wet bar, flat-panel television, semi-private treatment area, side-by-side whirlpool tubs, steam room, shower, and changing and vanity area.

DISLIKE The waiting areas, while intimate, fall a bit short in offering and showcasing all the nutritious edibles that you would expect in a resort spa. Furthermore, the drinks are lost behind a solid refrigerator door.

TIP Try the cool mist shower for an invigorating experience after a hot soak in the warm vitality pool. The spa's rugged and masculine atmosphere makes it a great option for men.

The Spa at Aria ★ ★ ★ ★

Aria 3730 Las Vegas Blvd. S.; ☎ 702-590-9600; arialasvegas.com

---

Customer service ★★★★. Facilities ★★★★. Amenities ★★★★. Sales pressure Low. **Price range** $90–$540 spa services; $13–$195 nail and refinement services. **Spa amenities** Complimentary with treatment; spa and fitness center pass $30 a day without treatment.

SUMMARY AND COMMENTS The Spa at Aria synchronizes beauty and progressive luxury with a conscious respect and preservation of nature's elements. Natural stone, wood, and metal mingle like a melodic dance inside the 80,000-square-foot, bi-level total wellness sanctuary. Inspired by the East, from the freestanding petrified wood from Thailand that greets salon customers to Japanese water gardens adorned with sacred Aji stones, the spa is distinctively warm and tranquil. The Spa at Aria features a full complement of services to promote peace and harmony, with such offerings as Ashiatsu, couples' massage, Thai massage, hydrotherapy, and Vichy. The Japanese Ganbanyoku stone-bed relaxation area—the only one in the country—provides guests with heated black mineral stone beds that emit negative ions, helping to improve circulation and increase metabolism. Two steps away is the Shio Salt Room lined entirely with illuminated amber-colored salt blocks, providing dewy, marine-rich salt-infused air. The Spa at Aria also boasts a full-service salon, which includes one barber station for gents. An advanced fitness center showcases top-of-the-line equipment, a semiprivate stretch area, one-on-one training sessions, and movement classes. Finally, for those who enjoy a unique hiking experience, the spa offers the Indoor Hike. While carrying a stretch mat on their backs, guests are guided through the most scenic areas of the resort and challenged with an exhilarating and heart-pumping workout that focuses on the whole body. The Spa at Aria is a complete wellness center that elevates guests to a meditative state for introspection, relaxation, and inspiration.

RECOMMEND The Thai Poultice Massage, a signature service, is based on a century-old healing practice that soothes away tension with a set of warm poultices infused with lemongrass, ginger, and prai extract.

LOVE The Spa is loaded with coed spaces, such as the fitness center, the Ganbanyoku heated-stone beds, Shio Salt Room, an outdoor balcony, a therapy pool, and a fire lounge.

THE ULTIMATE A "spa within a spa" private suite comes complete with a personal spa attendant and amenities such as a three-person hydrotherapy tub, relaxation area, and flat-panel television.

DISLIKE The spa offers far too many "add-on" services, when in fact some of them should be included in their signature offerings.

TIP Don't forget your swimsuit to experience the outdoor infinity-edge therapy pool. Take in the view and experience the social vibe.

The Spa at Bellagio ★ ★ ★

Bellagio 3600 Las Vegas Blvd. S.; ☎ 702-693-7111; bellagio.com

Customer service ★★★★. Facilities ★★★. Amenities ★★★. Sales pressure Low. **Price range** $130–$285, spa services; $25–$100, nail and refinement services. **Spa amenities** Complimentary with any spa service over $50; spa pass $29 per day without services; $70 3-day and $100 5-day passes also available.

SUMMARY AND COMMENTS While the bright and airy entrance of this 56-room classic spa bespeaks "spa," the rest of the decor misses the mark. Because it doesn't have the techno-wizardry of some of its competitors, it would have done well to employ some of Dale Chihuly's glass art that has made the Bellagio lobby such a landmark; instead, the long corridors are nondescript and dimly lit, so the water wall and illuminated aqua-colored glass features lose their impact. But overall, this is a classy spa with an exceptionally high standard of treatments, especially in skin care. In-the-know spa-goers would choose nowhere else for their facials. And Bellagio does a better job than most in delivering world treatments—therapies from different continents that appeal to Bellagio's international guest set. Attention to detail and value-added extras make every treatment here a five-sensory affair.

RECOMMEND Bellagio's signature Watsu Massage, an aquatic experience in which you float, cradled in the arms of a therapist who combines gentle Shiatsu stretches with movements in, out, under, and over the 94°F warm water. The sensations are almost sensual.

LOVE Hot Toe Bliss, a warm-stone tootsies massage (with elements of reflexology) that truly works wonders after walking the Strip.

THE ULTIMATE Ultimate HydraFacial. Unlike its competitors, Bellagio includes all five specialty-treatment steps in the service, including a crystal-free microdermabrasion. It's pricey but it works.

DISLIKE Decor doesn't reflect the elegance of the Bellagio name.

TIP This place has a great range of product samples.

The Spa at Trump ★ ★ ★ ★

Trump International Hotel 2000 Fashion Show Dr.; ☎ 702-476-8000; trumplasvegashotel.com

Customer service ★★★★★. Facilities ★★★★. Amenities ★★★. Sales pressure Low. **Price range** $40–$275, spa services; $35–$125, nail and refinement services. **Spa amenities** Complimentary with any spa service over $95; $12 hotel guests; pass includes access to fitness center.

SUMMARY AND COMMENTS With only nine treatment rooms, this refreshingly small spa emanates a modern elegance with quiet finesse. *New York*

magazine voted it the best hotel spa in Las Vegas, and it's already made *Condé Nast*'s hot list. Spa treatments embrace the philosophy described in the best-selling *The Secret*—each blends your personal intention with oils and lotions that are mixed to embody balance, healing, revitalization, calm, and purity. Rooms are named for the healing intentions of various gemstones, as are many oils. Choose Ruby to fire enthusiasm and detoxify the body, blood, and lymph systems. Opt for Emerald to overcome misfortunes, or go for rebalancing Diamond.

RECOMMEND Royal Lulur Ritual involves a body scrub, bath, and moisturizing massage with jasmine- and frangipani-infused products.

LOVE The Morning After Eye Cure, a 30-minute makeover for tired eyes.

THE ULTIMATE Trump Luxury, a 7-hour package for $955.

DISLIKE Twenty-percent service charge that's automatically charged to your bill, even though it's a discretionary gratuity.

TIP Spa-goers have direct access to the hotel's sun deck and outdoor pool. Have your personal spa attaché organize lunch in a shaded cabana.

The Spas at Wynn ★ ★ ★ ½

3131 Las Vegas Blvd. S.; ☎ 702-770-8000; wynnlasvegas.com

Customer service ★★★★. Facilities ★★★★. Amenities ★★★★. Sales pressure Medium. **Price range** $135–$370, spa services; $35–$120, nail and refinement services. **Spa amenities** Complimentary with treatment of $75 and above; spa and fitness center pass $40 per day without treatment; $15 for fitness pass only.

SUMMARY AND COMMENTS Wynn is all about over-the-top indulgence, so the spas at Wynn and Encore radiate lavish elegance that appeals to the heavy-wallet brigade and honeymooners. The full spa experience is as much about anticipation as it is delivery, and on this, in both spas, Wynn scores top marks. Encore's spa, however, raises the bar even higher with an opulent Zen-inspired lush tropical environment. The staff is excellent. Not only have they been drilled in customer service, but also spa practitioners are knowledgeable, professional, and top of their form. Wynn has a good number of male estheticians, so be sure to specify if you have a gender preference. In terms of services, the menus may appear different in treatment descriptions between the two spas, but, in reality, a number of therapies are quite similar. If you have the time, enjoy a treatment in both. If not, go for Encore. It has an atmosphere of tranquil glitz, which is an oxymoron only possible in a place like Las Vegas.

RECOMMEND The signature Good Luck Ritual Massage is based on the five elements of feng shui: health, wealth, prosperity, happiness, and harmony. It's a yummy head-to-toe event.

LOVE A massage in a private poolside cabana, or even in-room.

THE ULTIMATE A couple's stone massage in one of the four oversized couples suites—the nicest on the Strip.

DISLIKE Like most casino resorts, getting to anywhere is a marathon through a maze of slot machines (in Encore especially); directional signs need improvement.

TIP Spa is exclusive to hotel guests Friday and Saturday.

INDEX

If you'd like to express your opinion in writing about Las Vegas or this guidebook, complete the following survey and mail it to:

Unofficial Guide Reader Survey
P.O. Box 43673
Birmingham, AL 35243

Inclusive dates of your visit: _____

Members of your party:	Person 1	Person 2	Person 3	Person 4	Person 5	Person 6
Gender:	M F	M F	M F	M F	M F	M F
Age:	_____	_____	_____	_____	_____	_____

How many times have you been to Las Vegas?_____

LODGING On your most recent trip, where did you stay?

Concerning your accommodations On a scale of 100 as best and 0 as worst, how would you rate:

- The quality of your room? _____ • The quietness of your room _____
- Shuttle service to the airport? _____ • The value of your room?_____
- Check-in/check-out efficiency? _____ • Swimming pool facilities?_____

CAR RENTALS Did you rent a car? If so, from what company?_____

Concerning your rental car, on a scale of 100 being best and 0 worst, how would you rate:

Pickup-processing efficiency?_____   Cleanliness of the car? _____

Return-processing efficiency?_____   Airport-shuttle efficiency? _____

Condition of the car? _____

DINING Concerning your dining experiences, estimate your meals in restaurants per day?

_____

Approximately how much did your party spend on meals per day? _____

Favorite restaurants in Las Vegas:_____

Did you buy this guide before leaving?_____   While on your trip?_____

How did you hear about this guide? (check all that apply)

❏ Radio or TV   ❏ Library   ❏ Internet   ❏ Newspaper or magazine

❏ Bookstore salesperson   ❏ Chose it on my own   ❏ Loaned or recommended by a friend

What other guidebooks did you use on this trip?
Please rate them on a scale of 100 as best and 0 as worst. _____

_____

_____

_____

Using the same scale, how would you rate the *Unofficial Guides*(s)? _____

Are *Unofficial Guides* readily available at bookstores in your area? _____

Which other *Unofficial Guides* have you used? _____

_____

_____

If you like, on a separate sheet include comments about your Las Vegas trip or the *Unofficial Guides*(s).